THE INUIT WORLD

The Inuit World is a robust and holistic reference source to contemporary Inuit life from the intimate world of the household to the global stage. Organized around the themes of physical worlds, moral, spiritual and intellectual worlds, intimate and everyday worlds, and social and political worlds, this book includes ethnographically rich contributions from a range of scholars, including Inuit and other Indigenous authors. The book considers regional, social, and cultural differences as well as the shared histories and common cultural practices that allow us to recognize Inuit as a single, distinct Indigenous people. The chapters demonstrate both the historical continuity of Inuit culture and the dynamic ways that Inuit people have responded to changing social, environmental, political, and economic conditions. Chapter topics include ancestral landscapes, tourism and archaeology, resource extraction and climate change, environmental activism, and women's leadership.

This book is an invaluable resource for students and researchers in anthropology, Indigenous studies, and Arctic studies and those in related fields including geography, history, sociology, political science, and education.

Pamela Stern is Associate Professor of Anthropology at Simon Fraser University, Canada.

THE ROUTLEDGE WORLDS

THE MODERNIST WORLD
Edited by Allana Lindgren and Stephen Ross

THE EARLY CHRISTIAN WORLD, SECOND EDITION
Edited by Philip F. Esler

THE ETRUSCAN WORLD
Edited by Jean MacIntosh Turfa

THE SWAHILI WORLD
Edited by Stephanie Wynne-Jones and Adria LaViolette

THE MEDIEVAL WORLD, SECOND EDITION
Edited by Peter Linehan, Janet L. Nelson, and Marios Costambeys

THE ELAMITE WORLD
Edited by Javier Álvarez-Mon, Gian Pietro Basello and Yasmina Wicks

THE FIN-DE-SIÈCLE WORLD
Edited by Michael Saler

THE GNOSTIC WORLD
Edited by Garry W. Trompf, Gunner B. Mikkelsen and Jay Johnston

THE ANDEAN WORLD
Edited by Linda J. Seligmann and Kathleen Fine-Dare

THE SYRIAC WORLD
Edited by Daniel King

THE FAIRY TALE WORLD
Edited by Andrew Teverson

THE MELANESIAN WORLD
Edited by Eric Hirsch and Will Rollason

THE MING WORLD
Edited by Kenneth M. Swope

THE GOTHIC WORLD
Edited by Glennis Byron and Dale Townshend

THE IBERIAN WORLD
Edited by Fernando Bouza, Pedro Cardim, and Antonio Feros

THE MAYA WORLD
Edited by Scott Hutson and Traci Ardren

THE WORLD OF THE OXUS CIVILIZATION
Edited by Bertille Lyonnet and Nadezhda Dubova

THE GRAECO-BACTRIAN AND INDO-GREEK WORLD
Edited by Rachel Mairs

THE UMAYYAD WORLD
Edited by Andrew Marsham

THE ASANTE WORLD
Edited by Edmund Abaka and Kwame Osei Kwarteng

THE SAFAVID WORLD
Edited by Rudi Matthee

THE BIBLICAL WORLD, SECOND EDITION
Edited by Katharine J. Dell

THE TOKUGAWA WORLD
Edited by Gary P. Leupp and De-min Tao

THE INUIT WORLD
Edited by Pamela Stern

https://www.routledge.com/Routledge-Worlds/book-series/WORLDS

THE INUIT WORLD

Edited by

Pamela Stern

Routledge
Taylor & Francis Group

LONDON AND NEW YORK

First published 2022
by Routledge
2 Park Square, Milton Park, Abingdon, Oxon OX14 4RN

and by Routledge
605 Third Avenue, New York, NY 10158

Routledge is an imprint of the Taylor & Francis Group, an informa business

© 2022 selection and editorial matter, Pamela Stern; individual chapters, the contributors

The right of Pamela Stern to be identified as the author of the editorial material, and of the authors for their individual chapters, has been asserted in accordance with sections 77 and 78 of the Copyright, Designs and Patents Act 1988.

All rights reserved. No part of this book may be reprinted or reproduced or utilised in any form or by any electronic, mechanical, or other means, now known or hereafter invented, including photocopying and recording, or in any information storage or retrieval system, without permission in writing from the publishers.

Trademark notice: Product or corporate names may be trademarks or registered trademarks, and are used only for identification and explanation without intent to infringe.

British Library Cataloguing-in-Publication Data
A catalogue record for this book is available from the British Library

Library of Congress Cataloging-in-Publication Data
A catalog record has been requested for this book

ISBN: 978-0-367-22539-1 (hbk)
ISBN: 978-1-032-10692-2 (pbk)
ISBN: 978-0-429-27547-0 (ebk)

DOI: 10.4324/9780429275470

Typeset in Sabon
by Deanta Global Publishing Services, Chennai, India

CONTENTS

Acknowledgments viii
List of illustrations ix
List of contributors xii

Inuit worlds: An introduction 1
Pamela Stern

PART I: PLACING INUIT WORLDS 15

1 Ancestral landscapes: Archaeology and long-term Inuit history 17
  Max Friesen

2 Enduring social communities of the Inuvialuit: From the Yukon North
  Slope to the circumpolar stage 34
  Natasha Lyons, Lisa Hodgetts, Mervin Joe, Ashley Piskor,
  Renie Arey, David Stewart, Jason Lau, Rebecca Goodwin,
  Walter Bennett, Cassidy Lennie-Ipana, Mataya Gillis,
  Hayven Elanik, Angelina Joe, and Starr Elanik

3 Tourism and archaeology in Nunatsiavut 52
  Lisa Rankin, Laura Kelvin, Marjorie Flowers, and Charlotte Wolfrey

4 Nipivut and the restorying of Inuit life in Montreal 70
  Mark K. Watson, Christopher Fletcher,
  Donna Patrick, and Sara Breitkreutz

5 Urban Inuit in Canada: A case study of Ottawa 87
  Donna Patrick, Marika Morris, and Qauyisaq Etitiq

— Contents —

6 Building booms and shipping container housing: Geographies of urbanization and homelessness in Nuuk, Greenland 105
Julia Christensen and Steven Arnfjord

PART II: MORAL, SPIRITUAL, AND INTELLECTUAL WORLDS 121

7 Resource exploration and extraordinary happenings in Greenland's coastal northwest 123
Mark Nuttall

8 Changing times for people and polar bears 137
Nina H.S. Lund

9 Speaking the Inuit language in the 2020s 150
Louis-Jacques Dorais

10 Inuit bilingual education 166
Shelley Tulloch

11 Literacy and Christianity in Greenland 187
Flemming A.J. Nielsen

12 Everyday intersections of Inuit health and biomedical knowledge 207
Christopher Fletcher

PART III: INTIMATE AND EVERYDAY WORLDS 223

13 "Real Northern Men": Performing masculinity and culture in Ulukhaktok, Canada 225
Peter Collings

14 Keeping busy in Savissivik: Women and work in Northwest Greenland 242
Janne Flora, Kirsten Hastrup, and Astrid Oberborbeck Andersen

15 "I don't even sew for myself anymore": The role of sewing in a northern Inuit economy 257
Tristan D. Pearce and Kristin Emanuelsen

16 "We are starving for our food": Country food (in)security in Inuvik, Northwest Territories 270
Cahley Tod-Tims and Pamela Stern

17 Social relations among Inuit: Tuqłuraqtuq and Ilagiit 288
Christopher G. Trott

— Contents —

PART IV: SOCIAL AND POLITICAL WORLDS 305

18 Indigenous Westphalian sovereignty?: Decolonization, secession, and Indigenous rights in Greenland — 307
    Rauna Kuokkanen

19 Inuit Nunangat: The development of a common Inuit territorial and policy space in Canada — 321
    Nadine C. Fabbi and Gary N. Wilson

20 Energy extraction, resistance, and political change in Inuit Nunangat — 340
    Warren Bernauer and Jonathan Peyton

21 *Atsunai* ("be strong"): Inuit women's leadership in Labrador — 359
    Andrea Procter, Peggy Andersen, Beverly Hunter, and Tracy Ann Evans-Rice

22 Challenges for Greenland's social policies: How we meet the call for social and political awareness — 375
    Steven Arnfjord

23 Re-claiming Inuit governance and revitalizing autonomy in NunatuKavut — 395
    Amy Hudson

24 The predicament of sustainability: Solutions in Greenland — 414
    Frank Sejersen

Afterword: Inuit worlds in a global Arctic — 433
Peter Schweitzer
Index — 439

ACKNOWLEDGMENTS

I first traveled to the Arctic in 1982. I went to the Inuvialuit and Innuinait community of Ulukhaktok (at the time called Holman) to assist Rick Condon with an ethnographic study of Inuit adolescence. I was 23 years old and did not have a clue how to be an ethnographer. I still recoil in horror when looking at references to the "work" I did in Condon's book *Inuit Youth* (Rutgers Press, 1987). But something about the community stuck with me. I tell anthropology students that it is important to like the food in your field site, and I did, but more importantly, I liked being among Ulukhaktokmiut. I liked being able to spend time with people who were gracious and welcoming and tolerant of me and my naivety. And I liked that it was perfectly appropriate – correct, in fact – to sit quietly together and not feel the need to talk. I've been to other Inuit communities in Alaska, Canada, and Greenland, but Ulukhaktok remains a special place for me.

This volume has largely come together during the COVID-19 pandemic – I'm not sure whether that was a help or a hindrance. Being stuck at home gave me the time to focus my efforts on writing and editing, but it was also easy to lose that focus when the days blended together. A two-month-long visit from my grandson, Micah (and his parents), helped break the monotony. I am also grateful to SFU graduate students Ece Arslan, Cheyanne Connell, Sam Lee, Marina Mikhaylova-Kadriu, Madelyn Prevost, Chantelle Spicer, and Cahley Tod-Tims for our regular Friday afternoon virtual seminars. I learn much more from them than they do from me. I could not have managed to get this manuscript into a coherent form without the editorial assistance of the amazing Jelena Golubović.

I thank Katherine Ong at Routledge Press for the confidence she expressed in me when she invited me to edit this book. And I thank all of the authors for their diverse and interesting scholarship. It's been a pleasure to work with all of you. I look forward to a time when we can gather in person.

Finally, my partner, Peter Hall, is always in my corner and is always available to discuss ideas and to cast a critical (in the best sense) eye over all my work.

ILLUSTRATIONS

FIGURES

0.1	Blanket toss in the Iñupiat town of Barrow (Utqiaġvik), Alaska, c. 1986	3
0.2	Arctic char drying at a camp near Ulukhaktok, 1999	3
0.3	Streetscape Nuuk	7
0.4	Produce aisle in a Nuuk supermarket	10
1.1	A cultural landscape on southern Victoria Island, Nunavut	18
1.2	Map of Chukotka and the North American Arctic	19
1.3	Decorated Old Bering Sea artifacts from Chukotka	22
1.4	Excavation of a very large Inuvialuit house	27
2.1	Map of Yukon coast and Mackenzie Delta region	35
2.2	Starr Elanik learning to use a gimbal	41
2.3	Culture camp participants hiking in the British Mountains	42
2.4	Hayven Elanik, Renie Arey, and Starr Elanik in the girls' great-great-grandmother Sarah Kalinek's cabin at Niaqulik	43
2.5	Cover of Nipaturuq magazine	44
2.6	Preparing magazine layout	45
3.1	Map of Nunatsiavut	53
3.2	"Iceberg in the Atlantic Ocean, off the Coast of Labrador" by photographer William H. Pierce, 1864	56
3.3	Community gathering at the Netloft	62
3.4	Expedition cruise visitors touring Hopedale	63
4.1	*Qulliq* (traditional oil lamp) and radio equipment	72
4.2	Banner for the CKUT90.3FM Homelessness Marathon event	78
5.1	Aigah Atigutsiak outside St. Margaret's Anglican Church in Ottawa	91
5.2	Jessie Kangok and Janet Evic, 2019	99
5.3	COVID-19 infographic from Inuit Tapiriit Kanatami	101
6.1	Construction cranes for new housing, Nuuk, summer 2018	106
6.2	Blok Q apartment housing in Nuuk	111
7.1	Melville Bay, northwest Greenland	124

7.2	Kangersuatsiaq, Upernavik district	130
8.1	Polar bear patrol at Ittoqqortoormiit garbage dump	140
8.2	Polar bear and sled dogs, Ittoqqortoormiit	145
9.1	National Library and Ilisimatusarfik Institute in Nuuk	158
9.2	Inuit culture class, Nunavut Arctic College	159
9.3	Bilingual street signs in Iqaluit, Nunavut, 2010	160
10.1	Inuktut calendar, Nain, Nunatsiavut (Labrador) classroom	170
10.2	Inuktut language curriculum materials	177
10.3	2009 Inuit master's of education graduates, University of Prince Edward Island	178
11.1	Text of a Greenlandic song recorded by Hans Egede	191
11.2	Illustration of Pooq and Qiperoq in Copenhagen	198
11.3	Front page of the first issue of *Atuagagdliutit*, 1861	199
12.1	Hunting canoes and with CMS Amunsden, 2018	211
12.2	Canadian Cancer Society Relay for Life, Puvirnituq, Nunavik, 2017	212
13.1	Ulukhaktok Elder Jimmy Memogana at Fish Lake, 1997	233
13.2	Jimmy Memogana and grandson Buddy Allikamek drumming, 2000	234
13.3	Inuvialuit style drummers and dancers, Ulukahktok, 2019	234
14.1	Map of Avanersuaq region and Savissivik	243
14.2	Village of Savissivik, 2014	245
14.3	Scraping the blubber from a sealskin	252
15.1	An Ulukhaktomuit needleworker cutting a pattern from a tanned seal skin	261
15.2	Skin of a bearded seal bleaching in the sun	263
15.3	Modern *kamiks*	266
16.1	Freezer with country food for sale in Inuvik, February 2020	277
16.2	Elders' lunch of country food, Inuvik, 2020	281
17.1	Kinship diagram showing naming practices	292
17.2	Group of North Baffin Inuit at Uluksan, at the mouth of Arctic Bay, 1926	299
18.1	Protest against uranium mining, Narsaq, Greenland	312
19.1	Inuit Tapiriit Kanatami map of the four Inuit land claims settlement regions in Canada	328
19.2	Prime Minister Justin Trudeau and Inuit Tapiriit Kanatami President Natan Obed sign the Inuit-Crown Partnership Declaration, Iqaluit, 9 February 2017	333
21.1	Kitora Boase, Hopedale	363
21.2	Miriam Brown, Nain	367
22.1	Change in the number of welfare recipients in Greenland, 2015–2018. Greenland Statistics	377
22.2	Change in the number of unemployed in Greenland, 2015–2018	378
22.3	Older apartment housing in Nuuk	379
22.4	Unemployment rate for Nuuk, Ilulissat, Nanortalik, and Taasiilaq, 2015–2018	382
23.1	Map of NunatuKavut	398
23.2	NunatuKavut youth in a sewing class	405
23.3	NunatuKavut youth on the land	406

24.1	Maniitsoq, Greenland	419
24.2	Harbor in Nuuk	425
24.3	Greenland fishing fleet	427

TABLES

9.1	Geographic distribution of first language Inuktut speakers in Canada	161
15.1	Demographic characteristics of interview participants, Ulukhaktok	258
15.2	Prices for selected sewing materials at the Northern Store in Ulukhaktok	265
16.1	Household consumption of country food in Inuvik, 2018	273
22.1	Median annual income in Greenland, 2014–2018	381

CONTRIBUTORS

Astrid Oberborbeck Andersen is associate professor at the Department of Culture and Learning, Aalborg University. Her research centers on human–environment relations, and she has carried out fieldwork about water politics and climate change in Peru and the uses and management of wildlife and ecosystems in Greenland. While trained in anthropology, she specializes in work across disciplines and experiments with formats for ethnographic knowledge production.

Peggy Andersen was born and raised in Makkovik, Nunatsiavut, and now lives in Nain with her family. She is the former executive director of Torngat Arts and Crafts and is well-known for her skill in sewing sealskin. Peggy is passionate about her Inuit culture, history, language, and way of life.

Renie Arey is an InuvialuK Elder from Aklavik. As a young person, she worked to establish the Inuvialuit land claim, serving as chair of the Hunter's Committee and as a researcher for the Committee for Original People's Entitlement (COPE). Having lost her language in residential school, she regained it with the help of Elders and went on to teach the Inuvialuktun language at Moose Kerr School, write books for children in the language, and worked as a producer at Inuvialuit Communications Society.

Steven Arnfjord is head of Social Sciences at Ilisimatusaffik/University of Greenland. His research concerns the history of Greenlandic social welfare policies, housing and homelessness, the professionalization of social work, and disability.

Walter Bennett was an Elder from Akalvik, and grew up on the land with his grandparents. He has family ties to Alaska and Yukon. Walter spoke his language growing up but lost a lot of his ability to speak it while away at residential school. Walter spent many years working in the oil and gas industry. The Inuvialuit Living History Project team is grateful for having had the opportunity to learn from Walter out on the land at the culture camp and for the stories, experiences, and laughter he shared.

Warren Bernauer is postdoctoral fellow at the University of Manitoba. His research focuses on the political economy of extraction and conservation in northern Canada.

— Contributors —

Along with Inuit Elder Joan Scottie and social science researcher Jack Hicks, he is co-author of *I Will Live for Both of Us: Colonialism, Uranium Mining, and Inuit Resistance in Nunavut* (forthcoming).

Sara Breitkreutz is a doctoral candidate in social and cultural analysis in the Department of Sociology and Anthropology at Concordia University in Montreal. Her research interests include anti-colonial approaches to Indigenous community-based research and the role of new digital media in shaping contemporary practices of storytelling, community-building, and self-representation.

Pete Collings is associate professor of anthropology at the University of Florida. He has conducted research in Ulukhaktok, Canada, since 1992. In addition to his work on Inuit masculinity, his projects address aging and the life course, change and continuity in food sharing practices, and the economics of contemporary subsistence. His current research addresses the relationships between stress, food insecurity, and health and well-being.

Julia Christensen is a social and cultural geographer who writes on housing, home, health, and urbanization in the Canadian North and Greenland. She is associate professor in the Department of Geography and the Canada Research Chair in Northern Governance and Public Policy at Memorial University.

Louis-Jacques Dorais holds degrees in anthropology (Université de Montréal) and linguistics (Université de Paris-III). He is professor emeritus at Université Laval, where he taught in the Department of Anthropology between 1972 and 2011. He has authored several articles and books on Inuit language and culture, including *The Language of the Inuit. Syntax, Semantics, and Society in the Arctic* (2010) and *Words of the Inuit. A Semantic Stroll through a Northern Culture* (2020).

Hayven Elanik is a young Inuvialuk from Aklavik. She recently graduated from Moose Kerr School and hopes to pursue college in Whitehorse. One day she wants to work in early childhood education so she can teach the next generation of Inuvialuit.

Starr Elanik is an Inuvialuk teen raised in Aklavik. She is learning to sew and embroider as a way of connecting with her Inuvialuit heritage. She loves being out on the land because of the beautiful landscapes and hopes to spend more time outdoors in the future.

Kristin Emanuelsen earned an MA in geography and continues to write about her thesis research on the role and importance of sewing to Inuit women in Ulukhaktok, Canada.

Qauyisaq Etitiq currently manages the Inuit Impact Benefit Agreement for Baffinland, but has also worked for Inuit organizations, and as a consultant providing cultural competency training and Inuit awareness workshops to governments, non-profit organizations, and private companies. As education policy advisor for Tungasuvvingat Inuit in Ottawa, Qauyisaq led community engagement efforts with Inuit across Ontario. Qauyisaq has a BA in sociology with a minor in Aboriginal studies from Carleton University in Ottawa.

Tracy Ann Evans-Rice is an Inuk woman who has worked as the Status of Women Coordinator for the Nunatsiavut Government for 13 years. She currently works as

Assistant Director, Employment and Training with the Education division of the Nunatsiavut Government in her hometown of Makkovik, Nunatsiavut, where she resides with her family.

Nadine C. Fabbi is managing director of the Canadian Studies Center in the Henry M. Jackson School of International Studies at the University of Washington. She is co-founder and lead of the Arctic and International Relations initiative in the Jackson School. Nadine sits on the editorial board of the *American Review for Canadian Studies* and is part of the University of the Arctic's Academic Leadership Team. Her research interests include how we understand the Arctic as a unique region in the field of area studies and international studies; how Arctic Indigenous internationalism is influencing international relations; and how policy and spatial activism are reshaping how we think about international relations and social justice. Recent publications include "Makippugut (We Are Standing Up): Public Policy and Self-Determination in Nunavik," *American Review of Canadian Studies* 47(2), 2017.

Christopher Fletcher is a medical anthropologist whose research focuses on collaborative projects exploring cultural perspectives on health in Indigenous communities. He is professor in the Department of Social and Preventative Medicine at Université Laval, and a researcher at the Population Health and Optimal Practices in Health Research Unit, CHU de Québec.

Janne Flora is associate professor in the Department of Anthropology, Aarhus University. She has carried out ethnographic and interdisciplinary fieldwork in regions throughout Greenland, exploring issues ranging from kinship and suicide to hunting and landscape. Janne is the author of the monograph *Wandering Spirits: Loneliness and Longing in Greenland* (2019) and is currently the principal investigator of the project: "Muskox Pathways," which elucidates the long-term relations between humans and muskoxen in Greenland.

Marjorie Flowers is an advocate for men, women, and children who need a little extra help. She trained in nursing, but her passion is the Moravian Church where she has spent the last 29 years as a lay pastor. She was the first female chairperson elected to the Provincial Moravian Church Board in 500 years. Marjorie also served as councillor and mayor (AngujakKâk) in her hometown of Makkovik before moving to Hopedale to work for the then Labrador Inuit Health Commission and later for the Nunatsiavut Department of Health and Social Development. She spent two terms as councillor for the town of Hopedale and was elected AngujakKâk in 2015.

Max Friesen is an archaeologist in the Department of Anthropology at the University of Toronto. He has worked collaboratively with northern organizations in several regions of Inuit Nunangat, with an emphasis on Victoria Island and the Mackenzie Delta Region. He is co-editor of the *Oxford Handbook of the Prehistoric Arctic* (2016) and co-author of *Out of the Cold: Archaeology on the Arctic Rim of North America* (2017).

Mataya Gillis A recent high school graduate, Mataya has been heavily involved in youth and student leadership in and around Inuvik. She is passionate about sharing Inuvialuit culture and traditions with youth around the world. She has also traveled across the country to participate in conferences such as the National Inuit Studies

Conference at Ottawa in 2019. As editor-in-chief, she runs a popular youth magazine, Nipatuȓuq, leading the full production process from brainstorming to publishing.

Rebecca Goodwin is a doctoral candidate at the University of Western Ontario. She has been an arctic archaeologist for over a decade, living and working in the North. She is a team member on the Inuvialuit Living History Project, contributing to social media and running community outreach events. Rebecca's current research is focused on gender in the Inuvialuit past, and she is privileged to learn from Inuvialuit Knowledge Holders. She strives to be community-focused and decolonial in her work.

Kirsten Hastrup is professor emeritus in the Department of Anthropology, University of Copenhagen. Her main ethnographic fields have been Iceland and Northwest Greenland. In both fields, she has studied both historical and contemporary issues, with a focus on the entwinement of nature and social life. She has headed a number of collaborative research projects, and has published widely, including monographs, edited volumes, and numerous articles.

Lisa Hodgetts is associate professor in the Department of Anthropology at University of Western, Ontario. She has conducted archaeological research throughout the circumpolar north for over two decades, most of it community-based. She co-directs the Inuvialuit Living History Project with Natasha Lyons and is currently president of the Canadian Archaeological Association. Her publications span ethical archaeological practice, community archaeology, zooarchaeology, geophysical techniques, and landscape archaeology.

Amy Hudson earned a PhD in interdisciplinary studies from Memorial University, an MA in Sociology from the University of Victoria, and a BA from Memorial University. She is from Black Tickle, a remote Labrador coastal community in NunatuKavut, a traditional homeland of Inuit. Amy's doctoral research was in the area of Inuit governance and sustainability planning. She currently works as a negotiator and Governance and Strategic Planning Lead with NunatuKavut Community Council (NCC).

Beverly Hunter is an Inuk woman from Hopedale, Nunatsiavut. She is a former counselor for the Trauma and Addictions Mobile Treatment team with the Nunatsiavut Government and currently works as an Elder's Coordinator.

Angelina Joe is an Inuvialuk teen from Aklavik. She loves going out on the land because it makes her feel more connected to her culture and her past. She especially appreciates being able to learn from her Elders about how they used to live. When she graduates, Angelina hopes to work out on the land and become a wildlife monitor to serve her community.

Mervin Joe is resource conservation officer with Parks Canada Inuvik. He began his career with the Western Arctic Field Unit in 1993 and has had experience working on numerous archaeological projects, including excavation, monitoring, site documentation and preservation, and interpreting Inuvialuit cultural heritage to visitors. He has been a part of the Inuvialuit Living History Project for over a decade.

Laura Kelvin is assistant professor in the Department of Anthropology at the University of Manitoba. She has been working on community-based archaeology projects with northern communities for the past ten years.

— Contributors —

Rauna Kuokkanen (Sámi) is research professor of Arctic Indigenous Studies at the University of Lapland, and adjunct professor of Indigenous Studies at the University of Toronto. She is the author of *Reshaping the University: Responsibility, Indigenous Epistemes and the Logic of the Gift* (2007), *Boaris dego eana: Eamiálbmogiid diehtu, filosofiijat ja dutkan* (in Sámi, translated title: *As Old as the Earth. Indigenous Knowledge, Philosophies and Research*, 2009), and the award-winning *Restructuring Relations: Indigenous Self-Determination, Governance and Gender* (2019).

Jason Lau is an award-winning designer for whom human-centered design and art-making are at the foundation of everything he does. His search for meaning led him to anthropology, the study of human stories. He specializes in multifaceted creative projects which help other individuals tell their own stories. Jason's work draws from his commitment and passion for understanding people, communities, and cultural contexts. His work can be found at www.lauj.ca.

Cassidy Lennie-Ipana is an Inuvialuk youth born and raised in Inuvik. She enjoys going out on the land with her family. Family and community play an important part in her life. Schooling is also very important to her, and she is pursuing a Bachelor's of Commerce degree at the University of Calgary. In her participation in the Inuvialuit Living Histories project, she co-founded with Mataya Gillis the magazine Nipatuȓuq, which in a platform for Inuvialuit youth and means to have a loud voice in Inuvialuktun.

Nina H.S. Lund is an anthropologist, trained at Aarhus University and the University of Southern Denmark. Her research investigates human and non-human relationships in the context of climate change. She is interested in the dynamic interactions that occur among people, resources, and management systems, especially in Arctic regions.

Natasha Lyons is a founding partner of Ursus Heritage Consulting and adjunct faculty member in the Department of Archaeology at Simon Fraser University. She has over 20 years of experience conducting collaborative, community-based research with Indigenous communities throughout western Canada and the Arctic and co-directs the Inuvialuit Living History Project with Lisa Hodgetts. Natasha practices and publishes widely on critical community archaeology, ethical research practice, digital representation, and palaeoethnobotany.

Marika Morris is a research, evaluation, and training consultant in Ottawa who has worked with Tungasuvvingat Inuit, Pauktuutit Inuit Women of Canada, and Nunavut Tunngavik Inc. She is also adjunct research professor in the School of Indigenous and Canadian Studies at Carleton University, Canada.

Flemming A.J. Nielsen earned his PhD at the University of Copenhagen in 2000 and is associate professor of Theology at Ilisimatusarfik/University of Greenland. His research interests include the Inuit encounter with Christianity, Inuit culture and religion in Greenland from the 18th century, and the development of theological tradition, literary language, and literacy in Greenland.

Mark Nuttall is professor and Henry Marshall Tory Chair of Anthropology at the University of Alberta and Fellow of the Royal Society of Canada. He is also adjunct professor in the Department of Social Science at Ilisimatusarfik/University of Greenland and the Greenland Climate Research Centre. His research focuses on climate change, energy and resource development, conservation, environmental politics, and political geology. He is the author of *Climate, Society and Subsurface Politics in Greenland: Under the Great Ice* (2017), co-author of *The Scramble for the Poles: the geopolitics of the Arctic and Antarctic* (2016), and *The Arctic: What Everyone Needs to Know* (2019), and co-editor of *Anthropology and Climate Change: From Actions to Transformations* (2016) and *The Routledge Handbook of the Polar Regions* (2018).

Donna Patrick is professor in the Department of Sociology and Anthropology at Carleton University in Ottawa. She has worked with Inuit and Inuit languages for over 30 years and since 2003 has worked with urban Inuit on a number of participatory research projects in Ottawa and Montreal.

Tristan D. Pearce is associate professor in the Global and International Studies Program and Tier II Canada Research Chair in the Cumulative Impacts of Environmental Change at the University of Northern British Columbia. His research and teaching interests focus on climate change vulnerability and adaptation with a strong focus on traditional knowledge systems.

Jonathan Peyton teaches environmental geography at the University of Manitoba. His research is on the social and environmental effects of resource development and extractive economies in the Canadian North and is currently focused on the early history of oil and gas in the offshore Arctic. He is the author of *Unbuilt Environments: Tracing Postwar Development in Northwest British Columbia* (2017).

Ashley Piskor joined the Inuvialuit Living History team in 2018 in her role as a Parks Canada Cultural Resource Management Advisor. She has since moved on to pursue a PhD in anthropology at the University of Western University Ontario, where she will focus on collaborative, community-based archaeology and heritage management. Ashley is passionate about working with communities and helping to connect people to cultural knowledge and materials.

Andrea Procter was born in Toronto and now lives in St. John's, Newfoundland and Labrador with her family. She is an anthropologist with 20 years of experience in working with Indigenous communities in Labrador and was the co-ordinator of the Daughters of Mikak project. She earned a PhD from Memorial University.

Lisa Rankin is professor and Memorial University research chair in the Department of Archaeology at Memorial University. Since 2001 she has conducted research in Labrador in collaboration with Inuit communities.

Peter Schweitzer is currently professor of anthropology at the Department of Social and Cultural Anthropology of the University of Vienna. He is a founding member of the Austrian Polar Research Institute and served as its director from 2016 to 2020. He is one of two Austrian representatives to the Social and Human Working Group (SHWG) of the International Arctic Science Committee (IASC) and was the first chair of the SHWG from 2011 to 2015. Peter served as president of the International Arctic Social Science Association (IASSA) from 2001 to 2005 and is professor emeritus at the University of Alaska-Fairbanks. His theoretical interests range from kinship and

Contributors

identity politics to human–environmental interactions, including the social lives of infrastructure and the community effects of global climate change; his regional focus areas include the circumpolar north and the former Soviet Union. He has published widely on all of these issues.

Frank Sejersen is an anthropologist at the University of Copenhagen. His research concerns environmental use and its importance for the negotiation of identities and societal development. He addresses historical as well as contemporary debates and issues in Greenland, in particular. Questions of hunting, environmental management, urbanization, climate change, indigenous rights, and mining are approached as cross-cultural fields of negotiation and analyzed from a perspective of post-colonialism and political ecology.

Pamela Stern is a sociocultural anthropologist. Her research examines the ways that people as members of social groups interact with the institutions of the state. Her current project examines ways that social scientists, especially anthropologists, and Canadian government officials collaborated to create knowledge about Canadian Inuit in the decades immediately following World War II.

David Stewart is a filmmaker and senior producer at the Inuvialuit Communications Society (ICS) who has lived in Inuvik for 14 years. David enjoys traveling in the Inuvialuit Settlement Region helping Inuvialuit to tell their stories and preserve and share their language and culture. You can see all of David's work including every program produced by ICS on the Inuvialuit Communications YouTube page and Facebook accounts as well as on APTN.

Cahley Tod-Tims earned both her BA and MA in anthropology from Simon Fraser University. She conducted her MA thesis research on the exchange of and access to country foods in Inuvik during the winter of 2020. Her interests lie in the connection between arctic Indigenous identity and food as well as the circulation of traditional foods in the market economy. She was the recipient of a Social Science and Humanities Research Council of Canada scholarship for her master's degree studies.

Christopher G. Trott began working with Inuit on Baffin Island in 1979 on issues surrounding social organization. Out of that experience, he has also conducted work on the history of Christian missions among Inuit, gender, and symbolic organization. He earned his PhD from the University of Toronto in 1989 and since 1998 has taught in the Native Studies Department at the University of Manitoba. He is a Retired Fellow at St. John's College, Winnipeg.

Shelley Tulloch is professor and chair of Anthropology at the University of Winnipeg. She has conducted community-partnered research in Inuit communities for 20 years, with a focus on language revitalization, youth, leadership, and bilingual education. She holds a PhD in Linguistics from Université Laval.

Mark K. Watson is a participatory researcher who has partnered on different projects with Inuit organizations in Montreal since 2010. His research interests include the history and practice of collaborative and action-based research in anthropology, and he is associate professor in the Department of Sociology and Anthropology, Concordia University, Canada.

— *Contributors* —

Gary N. Wilson is professor in the Department of Political Science and Coordinator of the Northern Studies Program at the University of Northern British Columbia. His research examines politics and governance in the Canadian and circumpolar north, with a particular focus on Inuit self-government in the Canadian Arctic. He has published scholarly articles in a number of journals, including the *Canadian Journal of Political Science*, *American Review of Canadian Studies*, and *Regional and Federal Studies*. His most recent book *Nested Federalism and Inuit Governance in the Canadian Arctic* (co-authored with Christopher Alcantara and Thierry Rodon) was published in 2020. He is currently serving as president of the Association of Canadian Universities for Northern Studies (ACUNS) and is a member of the Council of the International Arctic Social Sciences Association (IASSA).

Charlotte Wolfrey has served on regional, provincial, national, and international committees, including Pauktuutit Inuit Women of Canada and the Provincial Advisory Council on the Status of Women in Newfoundland and Labrador. She served for many years on the Rigolet Inuit Community Government and the Labrador Inuit Association and is currently the AngajukKâk (mayor) for Rigolet.

INUIT WORLDS
An introduction

Pamela Stern

There is no single Inuit world. Rather, Inuit share many worlds. These worlds extend from the eastern edges of Chukotka, along the west and north coasts of Alaska, through the Canadian Archipelago and Arctic coast, Labrador, and Greenland. Inuit worlds also include places not always thought of as Inuit – the cities of Anchorage, Fairbanks, Seattle, San Francisco, Toronto, Ottawa, Montreal, Winnipeg, St. Johns, Paris, London, Copenhagen, Aberdeen, and elsewhere. In short, as Mark Watson and his colleagues observe in their chapter in this volume, "an 'Inuit world' is anywhere Inuit choose to be, and where they see themselves as Inuk."

"Inuit" is a modern ethnonym for the descendants of peoples who archaeologists say lived in and around the Bering Strait some 2,000 years ago. Current evidence indicates that descendants of those ancient Inuit migrated throughout northern coastal regions of North America and Greenland in the 13th century absorbing or more likely replacing earlier occupants. The ancestors of contemporary Inuit were well established in their contemporary homelands, now referred to as Inuit Nunangat in Canada and Inuit Nunaat in Greenland, before the European age of exploration and before the subsequent colonization of the Americas reached the Arctic. Colonization during the 19th century and incorporation into nation-states – Denmark, Canada, United States, and Russia/Soviet Union – in the 20th, shaped the social, cultural, and political worlds of contemporary Inuit that comprise the chapters in this volume.

Historically, Inuit societies consisted of small groups of a few dozen to usually no more than a few hundred people associated with an area of land and water (ice). Each group was identified with a primary place and called themselves after that place, adding the suffix -miut, meaning "the people of." The different groups were not so dissimilar as to constitute distinct cultures, and indeed, they had common cultural practices and beliefs and spoke dialects of a single language, Inuktut. According to Dorais (this volume), aside from regional differences in pronunciation, the Inuktut vocabulary is remarkably similar across dialects.

The word Inuit is a plural meaning "people" in Inuktut. (The word for a single individual is Inuk.) Following colonization, the meaning of the term Inuit came to encompass an additional meaning, one that defined speakers of Inuktut and their descendants as a single people. While Inuit is an appropriate general term and is widely used in Canada, other ethnonyms may be more appropriate in certain circumstances.

For example, Inuit in Greenland refer to themselves as Kalaallit (singular, Kalaaleq). Inuit from north and northwest Alaska are known as Iñupiat (singular, Iñupiaq), while Inuvialuit (singular, Inuvialuk) is the name for Inuit from the Mackenzie Delta region of western Canada.

The Inuit worlds we know today began to take shape in the 19th century. Then and still today, history, geography, and language are important sites of social and cultural differentiation between Inuit communities. To the European explorers, and later the missionaries, traders, and government officials who encountered them, Inuit may have seemed quite distant and insulated from global events. After all, those people were far from their homes. But Inuit were not isolated peoples before Europeans arrived in their lands. The westernmost part of the prehistoric Inuit world, especially, "was a complex melting pot of people with diverse identities, interacting in complex networks of trade, alliance, and conflict" (Friesen and Arnold 2008, 534). Like Inuit today, the ancestors of contemporary Inuit participated in global exchanges, engaging with neighbors as well as with members of more distant societies.

PAST AND PRESENT INUIT WORLDS

The film *One Day in the Life of Noah Piugattuk* (Kunuk 2019) tells the story of a 1961 meeting on the ocean ice between a group of North Baffin Inuit and a Canadian government official. The encounter re-enacted for the screen is based on an actual event in the life of the title character, though similar encounters must have played out across Inuit Nunangat. The official had been tasked with moving the last families from their self-organized camps to Igloolik, a government-administered town, and enrolling the children in school. What is most notable about the extended encounter is the calm, but implacable manner in which Noah refuses to accept the official's entreaties to move into Igloolik where the government can "help" him. For Noah Piugattuk and others in his party, their camp and the surrounding land and sea is their home. He tells the official, "I am born here. It is perfect ... I have everything I need here." Further, he sees no purpose in sending his children to school. "You say ... we [will] learn your ways. What will our children do if they move there? If they move there, there is nothing to do."

Noah Piugattuk and his campmates were among the last Inuit families to move from seasonally shifting camps to modern government-administered towns and villages. Permanent settlement occurred many decades earlier in Greenland and Alaska. But Canadian officials, in contrast to their Danish and American counterparts, initially sought to stop Inuit from settling around trading posts and government and military installations. If Inuit were to live among white people, those officials imagined, they would become dependent on government support (Marcus 1995) and they would lose their Inuit culture. But by the late 1950s, at least some Canadian officials believed fervently that, regardless of the social costs, all Inuit needed to be brought under the protection and surveillance of the state. They mistakenly assumed that if this occurred Inuit would readily take up the lifestyles, goals, and values of non-Indigenous southern Canadians. Canadians did not act in isolation. Across the North, the provision of social services has been a tool employed to bring Inuit "into the administration and culture of the [colonial] state" (Christensen and Arnfjord, this volume).

Figure 0.1 Blanket toss in the Iñupiat town of Utqiaġvik (Barrow), Alaska, c. 1986. Photo: Richard Condon.

Figure 0.2 Arctic char drying at a camp near Ulukhaktok, 1999. Many Ulukhaktokmiut families set up camps close to town which they use in the summer. The proximity to town allows them to spend time on the land while also attending to their jobs. Photo: Pamela Stern.

If the establishment of modern arctic towns in Canada, Greenland, and North Alaska was meant to serve the colonial administration of Inuit and their lands, what has become clear is that decades, even centuries later in the case of Greenland, these urban settlements remain Inuit cultural spaces. Friesen, in this volume, observes that "people living in modern towns have direct connections to places on the landscape where their parents, grandparents, or great-grandparents camped." These connections are more than physical and material. They include intangible practices like naming, childrearing, and knowledge sharing (Stevenson 2006; Trott, this volume). Inuit cultural values continue to inform intimate social relations as well as local, national, and international policy work (Dahl 2012; Fabbi and Wilson, this volume; Hicks and White 2015; Kuokkanen, this volume). The worlds that contemporary Inuit create are different from the worlds their ancestors knew in the 13th century, different than the worlds of the 19th century, and different than the worlds of the 1950s. We must also bear in mind that the worlds of contemporary Danes, Canadians, and Americans are equally different from those of their ancestors.

KNOWLEDGE, ENVIRONMENT, AND SOVEREIGNTY

In their chapter in this volume Natasha Lyons and her co-authors observe that key concerns for Inuit today include (re)asserting sovereignty over their lands and communities, diplomatic engagement with national and international bodies, and well-being in terms of health, economic, and cultural security. None of these exist in separate domains, but rather are tightly bound together as fields of experience and sites of action for contemporary Inuit.

One place where this complex field becomes apparent is climate change. Warming in the Arctic is occurring at approximately twice the rate of the Earth as a whole, causing physical changes to every aspect of the Arctic ecosystem. Less well known are the effects that a warming Arctic has on the social life and security of the people who live there. For example, melting permafrost threatens modern infrastructure including houses, airport runways, and public buildings. The absence of landfast ocean ice causes land to wash into the sea during winter storms. Coastal erosion has reached a crisis point for several Iñupiaq towns in northwest Alaska. Climate change also threatens Inuit communities indirectly when it makes travel on the land or sea ice difficult or dangerous. The land and sea remain vitally important to Inuit as a source of food, but also as places of inherent social value. Former president of the Inuit Circumpolar Council, Sheila Watt-Cloutier has argued that the observational skills, environmental knowledge, and patience that previous generations of Inuit developed traveling, spending time, and hunting on the land and sea enabled them to develop ways of problem-solving that was useful in meeting other challenges (2018; also Briggs 1998). Thus, Watt-Cloutier says, the greatest risk to Inuit from climate change is not food insecurity, but rather the threat to the resilience of youth who may be forced to go without the mental training acquired through travel on the land. Reaching a similar conclusion, Natasha Lyons and her co-authors describe "the inherent pragmatism of land-based life and teachings" as the basis of Inuit social systems.

Not all Inuit view the warming Arctic as a problem. For some, mostly evangelical Christians, the appearance of plants, insects, and animals, recent migrants from the sub-Arctic, is evidence of God's blessing (Johnson 2012). More commonly, however, those who regard the warming Arctic as positive are excited by the potential melting glaciers and ice-free water hold for mineral extraction and transportation. Whether and how to permit the development of non-renewable resources such as oil and gas, precious and non-precious metals, and rare-earth minerals is a vexing challenge facing Inuit governments and organizations (Kuokkanen, this volume; McGee 2021; Nuttall 2017). With the development of non-renewable resources, some Inuit see an existential threat to their lands and communities. Others believe that development, which they would control, will secure Inuit futures and break their economic dependence on non-Inuit governments. For Inuit, climate change has crucial implications for health, environmental protection, sovereignty and decolonization, and international relations.

The experience of colonization is another field that is implicated in all aspects of the Inuit world. During the 20th century widely dispersed groups of Inuit within and across national borders began to engage in world-making projects that positioned them to act as a singular Arctic Indigenous people, or as an imagined community as Benedict Anderson (1983) would have put it. One of these projects, the Inuit Circumpolar Council (ICC), established in 1977, represents Inuit and Yupik peoples from Greenland, Canada, Alaska, and Chukotka in international fora. ICC and its national member bodies use their presence in these forums to advocate for Indigenous peoples all over the world and on matters specific to Inuit and other arctic peoples. Inuit participation in global bodies has proven quite effective in dealing with national governments, as well. For example, ICC-Greenland used international "discourse on the rights of indigenous peoples to put pressure on the Danish government when they compiled their demands for increased self-government" (Dahl 2012, 223).

Through participation in national and international meetings and establishing multiple regional and national organizations, Inuit from different places discovered that they had common experiences with colonization, including paternalism, residential schooling, language loss, hunting restrictions, forced relocations, and lack of consultation about resource development. Greenlanders sought remedies to colonial rule by pushing for autonomy through Home Rule, with the eventual goal of full independence. In Canada and Alaska sovereign states are not contemplated. Instead, Inuit have sought to enforce their Aboriginal rights through the courts and land claims. Iñupiat along with other Alaska Native peoples are participants in the 1971 Alaska Native Claims Settlement Act. In Canada, Inuit in four regions – Inuvialuit, Nunavut, Nunavik, and Nunatsiavut – have settled land claims. While there are differences in the various land claims agreements, they all involve the extinguishment of Aboriginal title in exchange for certain ownership of a portion of their traditional lands, cash, and authority over some areas of policy such as education, health, and land management (see Bernauer and Peyton, this volume).

The arts are another forum in which Inuit unite in new forms of collective action. Inuit lives are quite different today than in previous eras. However, Inuit and other Indigenous peoples are constantly called upon to demonstrate that they remain tied to the traditions and practices of their ancestors. In other words, unlike non-Indigenous peoples, Inuit are expected to prove their authenticity. Creative arts including film, music, literature, and visual arts are a vibrant arena in which Inuit are able to express both the continuity of their traditions and their engagements with global modernity. But creative arts are not just, or even primarily for external consumption. Mark Nuttall points out that in

> the late 1960s, an ethnic political awareness rippled through Greenland. Along with artists, musicians, writers and others concerned with spreading Inuit activism and ideas about autonomy, young political leaders (many of whom were being educated in Denmark) and their nascent parties nurtured feelings of *kalaaliussuseq* (identity as a Greenlander).
>
> (2017, 11)

In Canada, the Avataq Cultural Institute and the Kitikmeot Heritage Society collect, curate, and share Inuit materials. The Interviewing Elders project of Nunavut Arctic College in Iqaluit is a model of how to engage Elders and youth in knowledge creation projects. And IsumaTV provides a platform for sharing commercial quality feature films made by Inuit and other Indigenous peoples. These well-established programs and many others constitute collective statements about the importance Inuit place on collecting, curating, and sharing their historical and cultural knowledge.

While external events were the immediate catalysts for pan-regional and transnational organizing, it is a mistake to think of these developments as merely driven by resistance to colonial pressures. All national identities are constituted in ways that highlight the contrasts with other peoples. In other words, they result from a group of people recognizing themselves as sharing a common history and culture that is distinct from other peoples, other nations. Inuit are no different.

ORGANIZATION OF THIS VOLUME

Many of the chapters that follow were written by university-based researchers, including Indigenous university-based scholars. Also included are chapters produced through collaboration by university and non-academic Inuit researchers. Together, the chapters present a diversity of past and present Inuit worlds. They are organized in four parts dealing respectively with the physical, intellectual, interpersonal, and socio-political worlds created and lived by people who identify as Inuit. This was a conscious choice to move away from a more commonly used national-regional or temporal organizing logic, and instead to highlight just some of the dynamic, emplaced, and heterogeneous dimensions of these worlds. That said, readers should not feel bound to read the chapters in any particular order.

Placing Inuit worlds

The six chapters in this first part focus on the presence of Inuit, past and present, on their traditional lands, at academic conferences, and in urban centers. The opening chapter by archaeologist Max Friesen describes the origins and depth of Inuit social, cultural, and economic life in North America and Greenland. The chapter by Natasha Lyons and her colleagues as well as the one by Lisa Rankin and hers speak to the different ways that Inuvialuit in western Canada and Inuit from Nunatsiavut (northern Labrador) are reasserting the authority of their histories and knowledges while also nurturing traditional knowledge and practices. Both the Inuvialuit culture camp project and the Nunatsiavut tourism program reflect a kind of historical consciousness that is a characteristic of modernity (Graburn 1998; 2006).

If the preceding chapters are concerned with Inuit lives in traditional places, the next three offer evidence that Inuit lifeworlds are also part of urban landscapes. Cities are, according to Mark K. Watson and his co-authors, "an important and, now, permanent extension of Inuit geography and social life." Both Watson et al. and Donna Patrick et al. identify the multiple ways that Inuit residents of Montreal and Ottawa, citizens of Canada, enact a right to the city (Lefevbre 1968) through place-making activities. Just as with other migrant groups, some Inuit who have taken up the opportunities of urban life experience poverty, homelessness, and racism, but that is not necessarily the norm. As Patrick and her co-authors argue, the city is also home to "happy Inuit families."

It is perhaps necessary to state that Inuit living in northern towns and cities may also suffer from homelessness and overcrowded housing, modern problems that have not been solved by Inuit-led governments (Tester and The Harvest Society 2006). In their chapter about housing provision in Nuuk, Julia Christensen and Steven Arnfjord show how the urbanization and marketization strategies of Greenland's Self Rule government have resulted in growing economic disparity within a nominally social democratic system (see also Arnfjord on social policy, this volume). While new high-quality housing is available for well-educated professionals, little attention is paid to the housing needs of recent rural immigrants.

Figure 0.3   In some ways Nuuk is like many North American or European cities.
Photo: Pamela Stern.

Moral, spiritual, and intellectual worlds

In the 1930s, Danish anthropologist Knud Rasmussen published several volumes describing the "intellectual culture" of the Inuit groups he and other members of the Fifth Thule Expedition (1921–1924) visited on their dogsled journey from Greenland to the Bering Sea. The intellectual culture Rasmussen recorded included stories, songs, religious beliefs and practices, shamanist language, divination, and healing. Inuit today, like the people Rasmussen encountered, have a rich intellectual culture expressed in domains as diverse as knowledge of child development (Briggs 1998; Stern 1999), formal statements about appropriate conduct such as *Inuit Qaujimajatuqangit* (Arnakak 2002; Laugrand and Oosten 2009) and *Iñupiaq Ilitquisiat* (Hensley 2009; McNabb 1991), and, of course, art, literature, and filmmaking (Igloliorte 2017; Langgård 2011; Martin 2012; McKenzie and Stenport 2014).

The breadth of contemporary Inuit intellectual culture is large and beyond the scope of any single volume. The chapters in this second part are limited to a few topics, namely relations between humans and the non-human world, language and literacy, and Inuit perspectives on health and well-being. Intellectual culture concerns the world of thought. How people think and what they think about affects how they live in the world and the actions that they take. Writing about Inuit and non-Inuit approaches to health, Christopher Fletcher observes: "How people think about and know health also has broad repercussions for the institutional and practical worlds of governance, health systems, and the work of people who make them run." Similar statements could be made about legal systems, environmental regulation, education, and every other domain of human life. Fletcher's chapter lays out the complex connections between ideas about health, institutional health systems, and seemingly mundane aspects of daily life.

Similarly, relations between human and non-human worlds are integral to the ways that Inuit think about and interpret theirs and others' roles and responsibilities in a changing physical and social environment. The sources of environmental change include not only well-publicized climate change, but also multinational mining corporations, non-governmental organizations, and multilateral governmental agencies and agreements. While outsiders have long regarded the Arctic as a repository of resources – renewable and non-renewable – current debates about resource extraction are questions about more than development versus environmentalism. Active and proposed mineral extraction in Greenland has, according to Mark Nuttall, awakened interest and concern among both humans and other-than-human beings. He writes: "Along the world's surface, the subterranean, the ocean depths, and the atmospheric are enmeshed with the lives of humans, animals, and more-than-human beings and entities." Where Nuttall considers the effects of human activity on non-human persons, the chapter by Danish anthropologist Nina H.S. Lund considers a shift in the social relationship between humans and polar bears. Lund tells how the residents of the tiny East Greenland village of Ittoqqortoomiit interpret the intentions and respond to the actions of the polar bears that now interfere with humans' everyday life and sense of safety.

Chapters by Louis-Jacques Dorais, Shelley Tulloch, and Flemming A.J. Nielsen tackle matters related to language and literacy. Inuktut (called Kalaallisut in

Greenland) is still widely spoken in Greenland and substantial portions of the Canadian North. Dorais credits the polysynthetic structure of Inuktut for keeping foreign loan words out of the Inuit language: "Inuit speakers coined hundreds of neologisms: words denoting the objects, habits, and concepts newly introduced by *qallunaat*."[1] Instead of adding foreign terms to their vocabulary, Inuit mostly created new terms based on the function or appearance of the new thing or idea, allowing "Inuit to express in their own language the near totality of new situations brought about through contact and, more generally, modernity."

Nonetheless, external institutions such as schools, the Church, television, and radio have eroded the intergenerational transmission of the Inuit language, imposing, as Tulloch points out, a form of "cognitive imperialism." Schooling has produced perhaps the most serious challenge to the retention of the Inuit language as an everyday vernacular. It has proved very difficult for Inuit to create educational institutions that are truly based on Inuit values and ways of sharing knowledge. In Greenland, Kalaallisut is the primary medium of instruction, but this not the situation elsewhere. Despite formal policies to favor instruction in Inuktut, in most cases, Inuit language instruction is an add-on to an otherwise non-Inuit curriculum.

One of the keys to the survival of Indigenous languages in the contemporary era is both literacy in those languages and the existence of a literature. Nielsen presents a case for crediting early Christian missionaries with establishing the basis for today's vibrant Kalaallisut literary scene. While the missionaries' primary goal was to allow Inuit to read the Gospels in their own language, Inuit throughout the North quickly found that literacy in their own language suited many everyday purposes, including letter-writing (Tester et al. 2001); recording significant events (Graburn 1998); creating grammars and dictionaries (Qumaq 1990); and recording Inuit histories (Hendrik 2014 [1887]; Lutz 2005; Nuligak 1966; Qumaq 2020; Pitseolak and Eber 1993). With few exceptions, however, aside from Greenlanders, most Inuit contemporary fiction and essay writers publish in English.

Intimate and everyday worlds

The third set of chapters concerns everyday matters of work and family in northern Inuit communities. The local communities vary in size from around 60 people in tiny Savissivik, Greenland, to around 3,000 people in the administrative center of Inuvik in the Inuvialuit Settlement Region of Canada. As should be expected, daily life in a remote village is very different than it is in a multi-ethnic town. And yet, read together, it becomes clear that Inuit across the North approach day-to-day concerns in similar ways that draw on shared cultural values and expectations.

Anthropologists have long observed a gendered division of social and work life in Inuit communities. On this topic, the academic literature has been overwhelmingly materialist, often concerned with subsistence work to the exclusion of other types of gendered expression. Scholars and the general public often mistakenly assume that the quest for food and shelter precluded other social and cultural activities. In his discussion of the lives of young Ulukhaktokmiut, Peter Collings, considers how generational differences in men's life experiences produce tensions and disparities in knowledge as well as in tangible resources like money and hunting equipment.

Collings describes how some young men, cut off from traditional masculine labors, perform masculinity (cf. Butler 1990), literally, by drum dancing.

Janna Flora and her co-authors are also concerned with the performance of gender, in this case by women married to successful hunters. "Being busy ... is not merely something hunters' wives are – it is something they *perform* as they go about their work in the everyday." Tristan D. Pearce and Kristin Emanuelsen also raise the matter of busyness; the needleworkers that they discuss distinguish between the sewing they do for paying customers and the sewing they do for their families, finding the former both less interesting and more demanding than when they sew for their loved ones. All three chapters speak of the social value Inuit place on being active, being busy (cf. Guemple 1986).

Historically, Inuit life was organized primarily around kinship, which, to an extent, has been disrupted by population concentration in larger towns (Nuttall 2017, 10). Certainly, food-sharing largely occurred through kinship networks, and still does in small communities. In larger towns, however, sharing remains an important value but is now organized through institutions or commercial markets (see Patrick et al., this volume). In their chapter, Cahley Tod-Tims and Pamela Stern consider ways that Inuvialuit have organized to address local food insecurity and reflect on some of the limitations of current programs.

This part concludes with a chapter prepared by Christopher G. Trott describing the ways that naming connects people across generations and forges intimacy within and across families. Together, the five chapters in this part concern the production and maintenance of Inuit selves and social bonds. These include the social

Figure 0.4 As this produce aisle in a Nuuk supermarket shows, Greenlanders are part of global networks. Photo: Pamela Stern.

connections formed by working alongside and for the benefit of intimate others. As Flora et al., show for Inuit in Savissivik, everyday activities "bind people together in a way that is steeped in knowledge and tradition." Equally important are the ways that the social connections are made by sharing, whether country food, drum songs, knowledge, advice, or names.

Social and political worlds

Chapters in the final part of this volume focus on Inuit engagement in local, national, and international politics. Attention is on the different avenues available to contemporary Inuit to exercise their agency as an Indigenous people, as Inuit, and as citizens of different nations. Topics range from women's roles in public life, to sovereignty and self-governance, to the practical and political debates around wildlife management, resource development, and public services.

Sámi scholar Rauna Kuokkanen considers the uneasy relationship between sovereignty and indigeneity in the context of Greenlanders' aspirations for a fully independent nation-state. She notes that the United Nations Declaration on the Rights of Indigenous Peoples (UNDRIP) anticipates Indigenous self-determination within existing nation-states rather than independent Indigenous states, but as a former overseas colony of Denmark, international law regards Greenland differently than Indigenous nations within settler states like Canada and the United States. "If Inuit Greenlanders will indeed one day be sovereign in the Westphalian sense of the term, it is not because of their indigeneity but because of the country's history and demographics."

Inuit in Canada have taken a distinctly different approach to self-determination than Kuokkanen describes for Greenland, one that asserts their identity and citizenship as both Canadians and a First People. In their chapter, Nadine C. Fabbi and Gary N. Wilson trace the development of Inuit Tapiriit Kanatami (ITK) from its origins at the 1970 Coppermine Conference, to the main advocate for Inuit land claims in Canada, to, now, the political voice of Canadian Inuit. In the 1990s, Inuit Tapirisat of Canada (ITC) as ITK was known prior to 2001, was a key voice for the creation of the multilateral Arctic Council.

Rather than the independence sought by Greenlanders, Inuit in Canada and Alaska have pursued the settlement of land claims, along with regional control of some institutions and co-management of wildlife and non-renewable resources. Focusing on the Canadian cases, Warren Bernauer and Jonathan Peyton review the process by which energy projects – both proposed and completed – drove the settlement of land claims in each of the four Inuit settlement regions and were critical to Inuit political development. Now, with the possibility of resource royalties and other benefits from energy extraction, Inuit political bodies in Canada, Alaska, and Greenland face dilemmas about which projects to support and which to oppose.

The approximately 6,000 Inuit of NunatuKavut (southern Labrador) do not have a settled land claim, and until recently were recognized as people with mixed European and Inuit heritage rather than as a distinct group of Inuit. The matter of land claims for NunatuKavut is complicated by historical territorial overlap with Innu and others. Inuk scholar Amy Hudson writes: "NunatuKavut Inuit [seek] to live in freedom, safety, health, and happiness upon the lands of their ancestors, according to their own vision for the future, and rooted in their traditional way of life."

With land claims blocked at present, the Inuit of NunatuKavut are instead pursuing a formal process for self-determination that will, they anticipate, allow them to enact social policies that are compatible with their Indigenous values.

As Inuit lives and lands fell under the administration of colonial authorities, government agents as well as traders and Christian missionaries who acted as government surrogates worked to transform Inuit forms of leadership and authority. Almost everywhere, these external agents took the unequal gender roles in their own societies as natural and correct. Where they permitted Inuit to hold formal leadership positions, these were positions for men, ignoring or denying the leadership of Inuit women. Andrea Procter and her co-authors report on a video project they undertook in Nunatsiavut (northern Labrador) to identify and recognize ways in which women have led and continue to enact leadership. The leadership qualities their participants identified – modesty, patience generosity, an even disposition – are widely documented Inuit values. In making an explicit link to leadership, Procter and her colleagues extend our knowledge of Inuit moral worlds:

> These women embody physical and mental strength in their perseverance, courage, and ability to remain composed, patient, and humble in the face of challenges. They also create strength in others by binding people together, helping those in need, and inspiring others to follow their lead.

The Self Rule that Greenlanders secured in 2009 gives them control over almost all governmental functions. For the most part, however, self-government has not led to a Greenlandization of social policy. Instead, as Steven Arnfjord and Frank Sejersen each discuss in very different policy arenas, Greenland is taking a globalist route. As described by Arnfjord, Greenland provides social welfare benefits and social services comparable to those in Denmark and other Scandinavian countries. Nonetheless, Greenland has not succeeded in eliminating the social problems that the benefits and services are meant to alleviate, and in some cases, economic and social disparities have become greater.

The issue considered by Sejersen is wildlife management, and the question Greenlanders confront is whether efforts to manage wildlife sustainability by techno-scientific standards should override the emplaced and practical knowledge of hunters and fishers. Where hunters and fishers assert that regulated wildlife is a local resource essential to their livelihoods and ways of life, Greenlandic regulators recognize the animals as "national population[s] to be cared for" and protected. Thus, management of wildlife is entangled in Greenlanders' state-building apparatus. In the case of Greenland halibut, a commercial catch, "the value of the fish [to the nation] is not the fish itself (quality, price, and quantity), but rather what the Greenlandic society as a whole can generate on the basis of catches." In Greenland today, sustainability, scientifically measured, thus, serves as currency in international arenas.

The chapters in this volume present many Inuit worlds, but it is not comprehensive. In part, this is because there is no single, easily delineated Inuit world. Keavy Martin, who studies Inuit literature, observes that Inuit Elders are reluctant to describe events they have not experienced, and they are reluctant to claim hearsay as fact. "The critical discourse of Inuit elders is geared toward the telling of individual truths, rather than the discovery of Truths, as the latter will—ironically—almost always be too general to be accurate" (Martin 2012, 109). The same must be said about Inuit worlds – any effort to condense Inuit history and lifeways into a single Inuit world is too general, too flat to be accurate. There are shared experiences among the widely dispersed Inuit communities, and some practices transcend geography and time, but in depicting Inuit worlds social, political, and historical contexts matter. Like all peoples, Inuit have frequently been caught up in worlds that are not of their making. At the same time, we must remember that Inuit are themselves engaged in many projects of world-making. The chapters in this book offer a window into those worlds.

NOTE

1 The Inuktitut term *qallunaat* is used in Canada to refer to white people/white culture.

REFERENCES

Anderson, Benedict R. O'G. 1983. *Imagined Communities: Reflections on the Origin and Spread of Nationalism*. London: Verso.

Arnakak, Jay. 2002. "Incorporation of Inuit Qaujimanituqangit, or Inuit Traditional Knowledge, into the Government of Nunavut." *Journal of Aboriginal Economic Development* 3(1): 33–39.

Briggs, Jean L. 1998. *Inuit Morality Play: The Emotional Education of a Three-Year-Old*. New Haven, CT: Yale University Press.

Butler, Judith. 1990. *Gender Trouble: Feminism and the Subversion of Identity*. New York: Routledge.

Dahl, Jens. 2012. *Indigenous Space and Marginalized Peoples in the United Nations*. New York: Palgrave Macmillan.

Friesen, T. Max and Arnold, Charles D. 2008. "The Timing of the Thule Migration: New Dates from the Western Canadian Arctic." *American Antiquity* 73 (3): 527–538.

Graburn, Nelson. 1998. "Weirs in the River of Time: Development of Historical Consciousness among Canadian Inuit." *Études/Inuit/Studies* 22 (1): 18–32. https://doi.org/10.1525/mua._1998.22.1.18.

———. 2006. "Culture as Narrative." In *Critical Inuit Studies: An Anthology of Contemporary Arctic Ethnography*, edited by Pamela Stern and Lisa Stevenson, 139–154. Lincoln, NE: University of Nebraska Press.

Guemple, Lee. 1986. "Men and Women, Husbands and Wives: The Role of Gender in Traditional Inuit Society." *Études/Inuit/Studies* 10 (1–2): 9–24. https://www.jstor.org/stable/42869538.

Hendrik, Hans [Suersaq]. 2014 [1887]. *Memoirs of Hans Hendrik the Arctic Traveller*, translated by Henry Rink, edited by George Stephens. Cambridge: Cambridge University Press.

Hensley, William L. Iggiagruk. 2009. *Fifty Miles from Tomorrow: A Memoir of Alaska and the Real People*. New York: Farrar, Straus & Giroux.

Hicks, Jack and Graham White. 2015. *Made in Nunavut: An Experiment in Decentralized Government*. Vancouver, BC: UBC Press.

Igloliorte, Heather. 2017. "Curating Inuit Qaujimajatuqangit: Inuit Knowledge in the Qallunaat Art Museum." *Art Journal* 76(2): 100–113. https://doi.org/10.1080/00043249.2017.1367196

Johnson, Noor. 2012. "'Healing the Land' in the Canadian Arctic: Evangelism, Knowledge, and Environmental Change." *Journal for the Study of Religion, Nature, and Culture* 6 (3): 300–318. https://doi.org/10.1558/jsrnc.v6i3.300

Kunuk, Zacharias. 2019. *One Day in the Life of Noah Piugattuk*. Igloolik, NU: Kingulliit, video download from http://www.isuma.tv/movies

Langgård, Karen. 2011. "Greenlandic Literature from Colonial Times to Self-Government." In *From Oral Tradition to Rap: Literatures of the Polar North*, edited by Karen Langgård and Kirsten Thisted, 119–187, Nuuk: Ilisimatusarfik/Atuagkat.

Laugrand, Frédéric and Jarich Oosten. 2009. "Transfer of *Inuit Qaujimajatuqangit* in Modern Inuit Society." *Études/Inuit/Studies* 33(1–2): 115–131. https://doi.org/10.7202/044963ar

Lefevbre, Henri. 1968. *Le droit à la ville*. Paris: Anthropos.

Lutz, Hartmut. 2005. *The Diary of Abraham Ulrikab: Text and Context*. Ottawa, ON: University of Ottawa Press.

MacKenzie, Scott and Anna Westerståhl Stenport. 2014. *Films on Ice: Cinemas of the Arctic*. Edinburgh: Edinburgh University Press.

Marcus, Alan. 1995. *Relocating Eden: The Image and Politics of Inuit Exile in the Canadian Arctic*. Hanover and London: University Press of New England.

Martin, Keavy. 2012. *Stories in a New Skin: Approaches to Inuit Literature*. Winnipeg, MB: University of Manitoba Press.

McGee, Niall. 2021. "Indigenous Opposition to Arctic Mine Expansion Could Halt Development." *The Globe and Mail*, 31 January, www.theglobeandmail.com, accessed 6 Feb 2021.

McNabb, Steven. 1991. "Elders, Iñupiat Ilitqusiat, and Culture Goals in Northwest Alaska." *Arctic Anthropology* 28(2): 63–76.

Nuligak. 1966. *I, Nuligak*, edited and translated by Maurice Metayer, Toronto, ON: Peter Martin and Associates.

Nuttall, Mark. 2017. *Under the Great Ice: Climate, Society, and Subsurface Politics in Greenland*. New York: Routledge.

Pitseolak, Peter and Dorothy Harley Eber. 1993. *People from Our Side: A Life Story with Photographs*. Montreal, QC: McGill-Queens University Press.

Qumaq, Taamusi. 1990. *Inuit uqausillaringit [The Real Inuit Words]*. Montreal and Quebec City, QC: Avataq Cultural Institute and Association Inuksiutiit Katimajiit.

———. 2020. *Je veux que les Inuit soient libres de nouveau [I Want Inuit to Be Free Again]*. Quebec City, QC: Presses de l'Université de Québec.

Stern, Pamela. 1999. "Learning to Be Smart: An Exploration of the Culture of Intelligence in a Canadian Inuit Community." *American Anthropologist* 101 (3): 502–514.

Stevenson, Lisa. 2006. "The Ethical Injunction to Remember." In *Critical Inuit Studies: An Anthology of Contemporary Arctic Ethnography*, edited by Pamela Stern and Lisa Stevenson, 168–183. Lincoln, NE: University of Nebraska Press.

Tester, Frank James and Paule McNichol. 2001. "Writing for Our Lives: The Language of Homesickness, Self-Esteem, and the Inuit TB 'Epidemic'." *Études/Inuit/Studies* 25 (1–2): 121–140.

Tester, Frank James and The Harvest Society. 2006. *Iglutaq (In My Room): The Implications of Homelessness for Inuit*. Kinngait, NU: The Harvest Society. Accessed 30 January 2021 from http://www.tunngavik.com/documents/publications/2006-04-00-Iglutaq-The-Implications-of-Homelessness-for-Inuit.pdf

Watt-Cloutier, Sheila. 2018. *The Right to Be Cold: One Woman's Fight to Protect the Arctic and Save the Planet from Climate Change*. Minneapolis, MN: University of Minnesota Press.

PART I
PLACING INUIT WORLDS

CHAPTER 1

ANCESTRAL LANDSCAPES
Archaeology and long-term Inuit history

Max Friesen

Walking on the Arctic tundra, even an outsider new to the North will be struck by the omnipresent human history written on the landscape. Coasts and riverbanks are frequently covered with stone-built features such as storage caches and tent rings. These often display varying amounts of lichen, implying complex and long-term histories – bare rock is a sign of recent activity, while heavy lichen indicates older structures. Meanwhile, animal bones spilling out of the eroding edges of ancient sites tell the story of hunting and fishing in the past. In many areas there are no real boundaries to what archaeologists elsewhere might call "sites"; instead, the landscape holds a continuous array of the remnants of past human activities (Figure 1.1).

To contemporary Inuit[1] the landscape is immeasurably richer than for outsiders. These visible traces of the past mesh with place names, travel routes, multi-sensory memories of personal experiences, and historical knowledge passed through generations, to form an entangled present directly connected to the past. The connection from modern life back to ancient settlement is not abrupt – it is gradual; people living in modern towns have direct connections to places on the landscape where their parents, grandparents, or great-grandparents camped. These same places usually hold somewhat earlier structures that are similar to the recent ones and, in addition, there are often layers of older remains – obviously different, and perhaps even foreign-looking, but connected through similarities such as the bones of game animals indicating that some aspects of those ancient peoples' lives were similar to their own.

In this chapter, I outline what we know about Inuit society over the past 2,000 years. This is an important part of global history, representing one of the most widely distributed cultural and linguistic groups on Earth. The chapter is based mainly on the cultural landscape, as approached through archaeology, and is intended to provide context for the more recent periods that comprise the remainder of the book.

PROLOGUE: THE INUIT WORLD IN THE 19TH CENTURY

As an entry point to long-term history, it is useful to understand what the Inuit world looked like in the recent past, before settlement in modern more permanent towns. While all Inuit societies were dynamic and developed at different paces depending on a host of variables, a good place to start is the situation of the 19th century

Figure 1.1   A cultural landscape on southern Victoria Island, Nunavut. A Thule Inuit site in the foreground is part of a continuous distribution of cultural features that includes the modern hamlet of Cambridge Bay in the background. Photo: Max Friesen.

(Figure 1.2). This is a period to which contemporary Elders are closely connected, when the impacts of external forces were not yet overwhelming, and for which ethnohistoric information collected by Europeans had become more frequent than in the previous century. While Inuit societies of this era should never be considered as isolated and unchanging, they were living a lifeway that was in most cases very similar to that of earlier centuries, before intensive European contact.

Inuit societies during this period had much in common with each other, but also demonstrated a great range of variability. In terms of language, the greatest split was between Yupik languages of Chukotka and southwestern Alaska, and Inuit-Iñupiaq languages of northern Alaska, Inuit Nunangat (Arctic Canada), and Greenland (Woodbury 1984). Within each of these areas, adjacent dialects were generally very similar, though they became less mutually intelligible as physical distance increased. All other aspects of society were also variable, including population density, level of mobility (how often and how far people traveled over the course of a year), economic organization (level of reliance on different resources), and social organization (leadership roles, gender roles, kinship). All Inuit groups had highly specialized technologies; particularly noteworthy were their elaborate skin clothing, transportation consisting of sleds and two types of skin boat, sophisticated and variable dwellings, and complex hunting and fishing equipment. However, the exact nature of this technology varied across the Inuit world due to constant innovation and refinement on the part of each regional group. This variability in all aspects of culture was the result

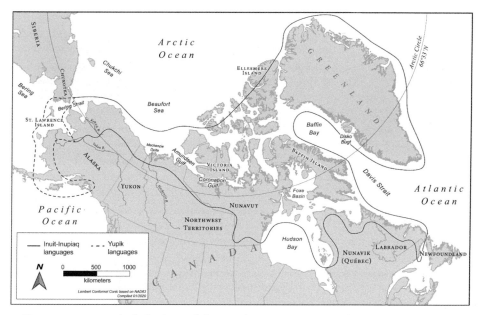

Figure 1.2 Map of Chukotka and the North American Arctic, showing the maximum extent of Inuit settlement in the 19th century and earlier. The two major language groups are indicated by solid lines (Inuit-Iñupiaq) and dashed lines (Yupik). Map drafted by Taylor Thornton.

of many influences, ranging from local environmental factors such as the density of subsistence resources, to levels of interaction with neighboring Inuit societies, interior First Nations, and Europeans.

Some idea of the range of variability can be indicated by describing two quite different groups: Inuinnait of the Coronation Gulf region (known in earlier anthropological literature as Copper Inuit) and Inuvialuit of the Mackenzie Delta region (sometimes known as Mackenzie Inuit). Despite occupying adjacent regions, these two societies were far apart in many aspects of their lifeways.

The Inuinnait lifeway is well known from modern Elders' knowledge (e.g., Kitikmeot Heritage Society 2019) and comprehensive early ethnographic work (e.g., Jenness 1922; 1946; Rasmussen 1932; Stefansson 1919) – it was, in many ways, similar to that of their eastern neighbors, the Netsilik Inuit, made famous in the films of Asen Balikci (1970). Their years were divided into two roughly equal halves. The warm season was spent on land with movements closely attuned to the locations of caribou, fish (especially Arctic char), and migratory waterfowl. Small groups, at times consisting only of individual families, lived in skin tents with driftwood frames, moving frequently. In the fall, larger groups congregated at coastal locations, where preparations were made for winter, including the sewing of winter skin clothing. The other half of the year was very different; it was spent living in snow houses on the sea ice and hunting almost exclusively for seals at their breathing holes. In many cases, the largest aggregations of the year occurred in these winter sea-ice villages, which would often include at least one very large communal structure for drum dances and other social activities in which all participated. Snow house villages were abandoned, with their inhabitants moving to new ones, several times over the winter whenever local seal populations were hunted out. Inuinnait social organization was relatively fluid, characterized by frequent fluctuations in group size, bilateral kinship ties, a variety of partnerships linking kin and non-kin, and a lack of elaborate leadership roles.

The ancestors of today's Inuvialuit of the Mackenzie Delta lived very different lives, according to modern Elders' knowledge (e.g., Hart 2011; Nuligak 1966) as well as an incomplete ethnographic record (e.g., Petitot 1876; 1887; Stefansson 1919). The region between the Alaska-Yukon border and Amundsen Gulf was home to about eight named regional groups, each of which had well-defined borders and was centered on a particularly large and permanent winter village. Subsistence varied across the region, with each regional group depending on a different mix of resources including seals, caribou, moose, waterfowl, many species of fish, bowhead whales, and beluga whales. However, the two largest and most populous groups, centered on the East Channel of the Mackenzie River near modern-day Tuktoyaktuk, were focused on the summer hunt of the thousands of beluga whales that congregated there each year. Winters were spent in large, driftwood-framed, semi-subterranean houses with sunken entrance tunnels, with some groups occupying very large three-alcove houses that could accommodate up to 30 people. During fall and spring, people often dispersed in smaller groups to travel and pursue seasonal resources; summer was highly variable, though on the East Channel this season saw particularly large aggregations of hundreds of people pursuing beluga whales. Their social organization was relatively complex, as seen in formalized leadership positions, large summer *kajigis* (communal structures), widespread trade in exotic materials, and a wide variety of ornamental objects such as earrings and labrets (lip plugs).

These two groups, while very different from each other, illustrate just part of the range of variability. Some Alaskan and Siberian groups – both Yupik and Iñupiat – lived in even larger and more permanent villages than Inuvialuit, where local conditions led to particularly dense and reliable resource concentrations. In some cases, organized warfare occurred, and trade systems were extremely elaborate (Burch 2005), though it can be difficult to reconstruct the degree to which these 19th-century patterns were impacted by the advent of Russian trade. To the east, some Inuit groups were even smaller in scale and more mobile than the Inuinnait. For example, inland Inuit west of Hudson Bay (often known as Caribou Inuit) were highly mobile as they pursued the very large caribou herds of the region (Birket-Smith 1929), and Inughuit of northwest Greenland consisted at times of only about 200 people, separated from their nearest neighbors by hundreds of kilometers of unoccupied territory (LeMoine and Darwent 2016).

This situation represents the end-point of a long and complex history that began in the Bering Strait region around 2,000 years ago. The remainder of this chapter is about the long-term processes that led to the Inuit worlds of the 19th century.

INUIT ORIGINS IN THE BERING STRAIT REGION

Inuit cultures have flourished in the Arctic for millennia, however, their full modern distribution was only established within the last 800 years. While not covered in this chapter, it is important to note that in all Arctic regions, other, more ancient people lived before Inuit arrived (Mason and Friesen 2017).

The earliest societies that are clearly and directly ancestral to Inuit emerged around 2,000 years ago (dating is very uncertain) in the Bering Strait region, especially on St. Lawrence Island and on the coasts of the easternmost extension of Siberia's Chukotka Peninsula. Here, the Old Bering Sea (OBS) culture appears in a remarkable fluorescence of new technology and living patterns (Bronshtein et al. 2016; Mason 2016a). OBS people were accomplished hunters of sea mammals, particularly walrus and several seal species; they also likely obtained gray and bowhead whales in some regions, especially in Chukotka (Mason 2017). In the winter, they lived in settlements consisting of semi-subterranean pit houses of varying sizes. However, they are best known for their spectacular artistic achievements in the form of engraved designs on a wide variety of objects, mainly on walrus ivory (Figure 1.3).

Where did OBS come from? Its sudden appearance in the archaeological record may result in part from the difficulty in finding early sites, or their destruction through erosion. However, many of the earliest OBS sites were the first in their locations, sitting directly on sterile soil, indicating a lack of earlier settlement (Mason 2017). Thus, OBS must ultimately represent a migration from elsewhere. Some attributes of stone tools can be tentatively traced either to the west (northeast Asia) or east (Alaska) of the main OBS homeland (Mason 2017); however, there is no agreement on a single "ideal" antecedent culture. A recent development in this regard is the study of ancient and modern DNA, which is beginning to narrow down where OBS may have originated (Flegontov et al. 2019). The leading possibility is that its ultimate origin is mainly in southwest Alaska, around 2000 BC, though the path from there to OBS 2,000 years later remains mysterious; it might include some interaction with Norton Tradition cultures in coastal Alaska.

Over time, many aspects of OBS culture changed, leading to several later named cultures including Punuk, represented mainly on St. Lawrence Island and the Bering Strait coasts; and Birnirk on the coasts of northern Chukotka and northern Alaska (Mason 2017). These societies developed in the later centuries of the first millennium AD, and despite their common origin, several differences are apparent. Punuk was quite closely connected to Asian trade and military networks, as seen in an apparent increase in iron use, as well as the adoption of slat armor and evidence for intergroup conflict (Bandi 1995). Punuk people maintained many aspects of the earlier OBS economic system, but may have been particularly adept at whaling. Birnirk people, on the northern coasts, lived in elaborate multi-roomed dwellings; they were able to exploit the full range of resources available in the region, including bowhead whales (Mason 2016b).

Around AD 1000, subtle shifts led to the emergence of a new culture known to us as Thule, the name based on the Danish scientific "Fifth Thule Expedition," which was in turn named after an ancient Greek term for a mythical northern land. Thule culture developed from Birnirk in northern Alaska, in the context of an interaction network that included Birnirk, Punuk, and other regional societies across northern coastal regions of Alaska and Chukotka. Most classes of Thule technology are very similar to those in Punuk and especially Birnirk sites; differences are mainly subtle and stylistic. The elaborate and specialized material culture of Thule sites is clearly recognizable as Inuit; it is in most cases virtually identical to the clothing, tools, hunting weapons, and dwellings used by Inuit across the Arctic in the 19th century.

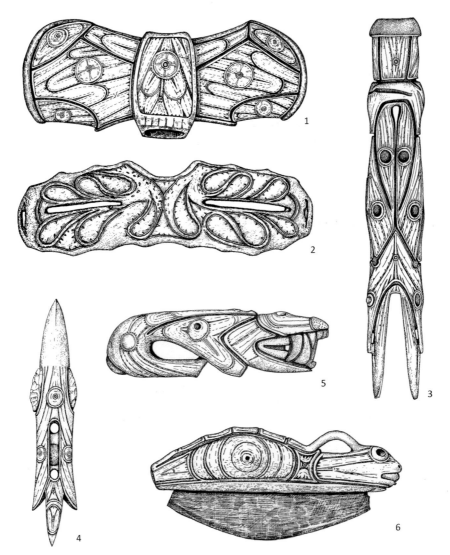

Figure 1.3 Decorated Old Bering Sea artifacts from Chukotka (scale varies). (1) Harpoon counterweight, ivory, 19.0 cm; (2) snow goggles, ivory, 12.5 cm; (3) harpoon socket piece, ivory, 25.9 cm; (4) harpoon head, ivory with stone side blades, 15.1 cm; (5) animal figure, ivory, 13.2 cm; (6) *ulu*, ivory with a stone blade, 11.5 cm. Drawings by Nina Survillo, originally published by Mikhail M. Bronshtein, Kirill A. Dneprovsky, and Arkady B. Savinetsky (2016). Courtesy of the authors and the State Museum of Oriental Art (Moscow).

Because the Thule period represents the common cultural background of all Inuit across the Arctic, it is worth describing this lifeway in some detail. Thule (and later Inuit) were probably the most technologically complex hunter-gatherer society ever to have existed. The combined stresses of cold temperatures, long distances traveled, regional variability in major subsistence resources, and extreme seasonal changes meant that generalized and simple tools were not sufficient for a successful lifeway. Instead, specialization was the key, with, for example, multiple distinctive categories within each general technological class (such as harpoons) rather than a single multipurpose tool (Maxwell 1985). Due to often extraordinary preservation in permafrost (permanently frozen soil), we know that Thule skin clothing, probably the most important of all technological classes for life in the Arctic, was also elaborate and specialized, comparable to the remarkably finely tailored clothing of the 19th century (e.g., McCullough 1989). Manufacturing technology was likewise highly specialized, with many needles, awls, scrapers, and knives for skin work, and bow drills, engraving tools, wedges, and knives for working in harder materials like bone, antler, ivory, and wood. For transport, Thule used sleds (often dog-hauled, but likely also pulled by people [Savelle and Dyke 2014]), kayaks (single-person covered skin boats, used more for hunting than long-distance travel [Walls et al. 2016]), and *umiaks* (large, open skin boats capable of transporting many people and loads of up to several tons [Anichtchenko 2016]). Winter housing consisted of semi-subterranean dwellings with deep cold-trap entrances, constructed of stone, wood, or whalebone (depending on locally available resources), and covered with sod for insulation (Lee and Reinhardt 2003). In the summer, skin tents with driftwood frames were used; fall and spring sometimes saw intermediate forms heavier than skin tents, but lighter than full semi-subterranean houses. Large sites usually contained *kajigis* (communal structures) (Friesen and Norman 2016).

In terms of social organization, based on site size (McGhee 1984) and structure (Whitridge 1999), it is often assumed that the basis of society was the "compound family" as defined by Burch (2006) for 19th century northern Alaska, usually consisting of several related families occupying separate dwellings. Extrapolation from ethnographic analogy can be used to infer that these families were probably led by *umialiks* (literally "boat owner") and their wives; in some regions, especially where bowhead whales could be reliably hunted, these positions may have been associated with high status and a significant level of authority (Whitridge 2002). Trade in exotic goods such as copper, iron, and soapstone indicate frequent interaction between regional groups (Cooper 2016; Rasic 2016). One of the most noteworthy aspects of the Thule archaeological record relates to the interpretation of gender. Because the record of 19th century Inuit indicates a strong level of differentiation of tasks and their associated tools for women and men, it is reasonable to extend this interpretation to the past, for example with tools relating to skin clothing production generally associated with women, and those relating to the manufacture of bone or antler tools generally with men. Of course, exceptions exist: where flexibility demanded, women or men could perform each other's tasks, and gender was not always manifested in terms of binaries (Guemple 1986; Walley 2018). However, on a general level, we can talk about tools and tasks as usually relating to a particular gender.

THE SPREAD OF INUIT CULTURE ACROSS NORTH AMERICA

One of the most dramatic series of events in world history happened early in the Thule period. At this time, Thule culture expanded in several directions in a series of waves, including inland within Alaska as seen most notably on the Kobuk River (Giddings 1952). Changes also occurred down the coast of Alaska as far as the Cook

Inlet region in areas currently occupied by Yupik speakers (see Figure 1.2). However, this latter spread does not necessarily represent actual migration as opposed to the adoption of material culture traits by neighboring peoples (Mason 2017). Most remarkably, though, during the 13th century AD, Thule families migrated thousands of kilometers from Alaska eastward across the entire North American Arctic, eventually settling all but the most remote coastal regions of Inuit Nunangat and Greenland, as far south as southern Labrador, as well as some interior regions (Friesen 2016; Morrison 1999).

This migration deserves a significant level of attention, since it is so central to the "big picture" of Inuit history. By the time of the migration, Thule had reached a peak of technological elaboration, environmental knowledge, and social organization that allowed them the flexibility to live successfully in almost any Arctic environment. Thus, when moving east they could take advantage of the full range of resources in each new region encountered, including caribou, muskox, fish, migratory birds, ringed, bearded, and harp seals, walrus, beluga whales, and bowhead whales. However, the largest sites from the early Thule period tend to be concentrated in areas that gave access to bowhead whales and walrus. Whaling sites are often associated with large numbers of bowhead bones, and the age profiles of the individual whales indicate selective hunting, where possible, of relatively small (nine-meter-long) yearlings (Savelle and McCartney 1994).

Why did Thule Inuit move east? A number of causal factors have been suggested, each of which is difficult to address fully with archaeological data. For decades, the leading explanation was related to the well-documented climate change that occurred across northern regions in the past. Based on radiocarbon dates that have since been questioned (Friesen and Arnold 2008; McGhee 2000), the migration was originally thought to have occurred around AD 1000. This would have placed it in the middle of the "Medieval Warm Period," a period of generally warmer temperatures. This in turn was interpreted to indicate that warmer temperatures and reduced levels of sea ice led to the expansion of bowhead whale populations – a key Thule resource – which drew Thule to the Eastern Arctic (McGhee 1969/70). Warmer temperatures might also have aided the migration by making transportation in umiaks easier due to longer open-water periods.

A second set of factors that has been suggested relates to a desire for metal, and particularly iron (Gulløv and McGhee 2006; McGhee 2009). In Alaska, Thule Inuit and their ancestors had had access to iron and other metals from Asian trade for centuries, and it was likely highly desired not only for its technological advantages but also as a source of increased social status. Several potential sources of metal exist in the Eastern Arctic, including pure copper nodules in the Coronation Gulf area and meteoritic iron in northwest Greenland (Cooper 2016); as well as iron or bronze trade goods from Norse who had arrived in southern Greenland by about AD 980–990 (Frei et al. 2015). Thus, it has been suggested that if Thule in northwest Alaska had somehow learned of these metal sources, this could have motivated the migration.

Finally, a quite different set of factors might have existed within the Alaskan homeland itself to spur the migration. Rather than being drawn east by the availability of particular resources such as whales or metal, some Thule groups may have been forced to leave home to escape local social difficulties or economic hard times

(Mason 2009). Alaska at this time may have had many aspects in common with its 19th-century situation, with high levels of conflict and competition between individuals, families, and regional groups. This may in turn have led ambitious individuals or families to explore new areas to make a better living; or forced families to leave in order to escape economically unstable or socially risky, even potentially violent, situations. Under such circumstances, new lands to the east may have appeared ripe for exploration (Friesen 2016).

Recent developments in our understanding of radiocarbon dates and the paleoclimatic record have furthered our understanding of the reasons for this large-scale population movement. For example, now that the migration has been re-dated to the 13th century AD (rather than the 11th century as previously thought), it no longer coincides with the generally warm Medieval Climatic Anomaly. In fact, recent reconstructions show cooling in many areas beginning by around AD 1200 (Friesen et al. 2019). Thus, the migration was not spurred by warm temperatures, expanded open water, and increased bowhead whale populations (though early migrants may still have pursued bowheads). Furthermore, we currently have no evidence that Alaskan Thule could have learned of metal sources, particularly those in northwest Greenland, prior to initiating the migration. Thus, the likeliest scenario for the initiation of the migration would see complex social and political factors in Alaska, possibly amplified by the effects of cooling temperatures, leading extended family groups to move. While these movements fanned out in several directions, the way east apparently proved particularly attractive, with groups from several Alaskan regions rapidly moving thousands of kilometers, making it as far as northwest Greenland within only a few decades (Friesen 2016).

A final aspect of the Thule migration that must be addressed is the question of relations with other peoples in areas to which Thule expanded. In much of coastal northern Alaska, Thule seems to have developed in place from preceding Birnirk peoples. Likewise, in the Bering Strait region and to its south on the Alaskan coast, there is a relatively direct development from Old Bering Sea and Punuk to more recent Yupik populations. However, the migration to the east represented expansion into areas that were already occupied by very different Paleo-Inuit peoples known as Late Dorset. While there is some uncertainty about the size of the Late Dorset population and its distribution in the 13th century, they probably occupied several regions including Victoria Island, northwest Greenland, Foxe Basin/Baffin Island, and Nunavik (northern Québec) (Friesen 2020). In fact, Inuit oral historical accounts from several regions refer to meetings with "Tuniit," an earlier group often portrayed as strong and shy, who initially interacted briefly with Inuit, but eventually fled after some conflict (Bennett and Rowley 2004). We know from recent studies of ancient DNA that there is little or no trace of genetic contact between Dorset and Inuit in most regions (Raghavan et al. 2014; cf. Zhou et al. 2019), and very few sites show possible interaction in the form of trade or exchange of ideas. Thus, all evidence points to rapid displacement by Inuit, who simply outcompeted Dorset in each new region encountered. The Thule Inuit ability to hunt bowhead whales, possession of bow and arrow (which Dorset did not have), use of more advanced transportation technology including dog sleds and umiaks, and social structures which made them well suited to inter-group conflict, all led to a relatively brief overlap of the two peoples in the Eastern Arctic (Friesen 2000).

REGIONALIZATION AND INTERACTION

By about AD 1400, Thule Inuit had settled a vast region in the Eastern Arctic, including most of the Canadian Arctic Archipelago and the adjacent mainland, and large areas of Greenland. Thus, Inuit occupied almost the full range they do today, including both sides of the Bering Strait in Chukotka and Alaska. In the following centuries, Inuit societies continued to change in a dynamic fashion, as a result of factors that affect all cultures (including modern global society): interactions between groups, environmental change, and political and social dynamics internal to each regional group.

Two factors stand out as particularly relevant to the last 600 years of Inuit history. The first is climate change. Much of the period after AD 1400 coincides with a particularly widespread (though regionally variable) cooling episode known as the Little Ice Age (Finkelstein 2016). Cooling temperatures and their impacts on sea ice location and extent, terrestrial vegetation, and annual weather patterns could potentially have had major impacts on interannual variability in the location and abundance of major resources ranging from bowhead whales and seals to caribou.

The second major set of factors relates to interactions between Inuit and Europeans. These interactions often had devastating negative consequences, particularly in relation to the spread of epidemic diseases that often resulted from meetings (Fortuine 1992). However, in many instances, European explorers, whalers, traders, and settlers represented a highly desirable source of useful materials. The early Thule occupations of the eastern Arctic Archipelago and northwest Greenland correspond with the final two centuries of the Norse occupation of Greenland, which lasted until around AD 1450 (Gulløv 2008). Early Thule occupations in northwest Greenland and Ellesmere Island have yielded a range of Norse items including a wooden carpenter's plane, woolen cloth, and a variety of metal items including chain mail, rivets, and knife blades – it is unclear whether these resulted from direct trade or some other source, such as the salvage of a Norse shipwreck (McCullough 1989; Schledermann 1996). Of much greater impact were the ever-increasing interactions with Europeans in the 16th century and later, initially at the margins of the Arctic but gradually working their way to its center. In the western regions, Inuit societies of Alaska and Chukotka had been at the outer periphery of northeast Asian trade networks for over 1,000 years. However, Russian exploration, particularly in the 18th century and later, led to ever-increasing trade; Russian iron eventually reached as far as the Coronation Gulf region in the Central Arctic via Inuvialuit intermediaries (Black 2004; Morrison 1991). In the east, European exploration and resource extraction started in Labrador in the 16th century and expanded over time until, by the mid-19th century, most areas of the Arctic had seen at least brief direct interaction between Inuit and Europeans (Neatby 1984).

This period saw rapid change across the Arctic, leading to the regional diversity seen in the 19th century. In Alaska, interaction networks expanded during this period, characterized by territorial regional groups, intensive trade, intergroup conflict, and elaborate feasts and ceremonies (Burch 2005). Many regional groups developed new dwelling forms, for example extremely large semi-subterranean houses were introduced in Labrador, Greenland, and the Mackenzie Delta (Figure 1.4) (Lee and Reinhardt 2003). In the Eastern Arctic, many regions were

Figure 1.4 Excavation of a very large Inuvialuit house at the Kuukpak site in the Mackenzie Delta. These houses had three sleeping platforms and held up to 30 people. Photo: Max Friesen.

subject to radical change in settlement patterns, as seen most clearly in the abandonment of semi-subterranean winter houses on land, in exchange for winter snow houses on the sea ice (Savelle 1987). Snow houses offered greater mobility (they could be relatively rapidly constructed wherever appropriate snow was found) and gave direct access to seal breathing holes, since snow house villages could be constructed in the middle of the ocean on the ice. Some areas of the northern Arctic Archipelago were abandoned, particularly those where bowheads had been hunted earlier in the Thule period. At the same time, Inuit occupations expanded down the coasts of Labrador and Hudson Bay, as well as inland in the region west of Hudson Bay. These population movements appear to have initially been a reaction to the Little Ice Age, whose cooling temperatures led to increasing sea ice, which in turn potentially impacted a number of species including bowhead whales (Friesen et al. 2019).

However, much of the change that occurred must have resulted from a desire on the part of Inuit for increased access to European trade (e.g., Friesen 2013; Hall and Fullerton 1990; Walls 2009). Though much of this trade was initially triggered by European activities, Inuit were autonomous and independent agents in the process, choosing whether and how to interact. Many trade items offered enormous technical advantages, as in the case of metal needles, blades, files, and saws, and eventually firearms. Others allowed a greater degree of self-expression or status, such as glass beads and items of fabric clothing. Still others provided novel and desirable flavors, such as tea, sugar, and flour. These were important enough that Inuit were often willing to alter their annual cycles of subsistence activities to incorporate trade opportunities at trading posts or other areas, such as stretches of coastline where whalers or fishers were known to appear annually (Rankin and Crompton 2016). In some instances, trade also spurred long-distance movements, for example down the western coast of Hudson Bay (Burch 1978; Dawson 2016) and the coast of Labrador (Kaplan 1985; Fitzhugh 2016), toward sources of desirable materials. It must, in some cases, have also fed into other changes internal to Inuit societies; in the Labrador case, there is a suggestion that trade was dominated by a set of important men whose extended families gained prestige through the organization of trade (Kaplan and Woollett 2016).

Archaeological sites from this period portray Inuit society as highly dynamic. Inuit lifeways were still in most ways "traditional," but at the same time, people were actively and selectively incorporating trade goods and ideas from outside that they considered useful. This is seen in many ways, but particularly in artifacts that show active experimentation with new materials. For example, glass beads become quite common, often sewn onto traditional skin clothing; and iron blades replace earlier ground slate blades in locally manufactured knife handles or harpoon heads.

CONCLUSION

Archaeology has been practiced in the North for over 100 years, during which it has cycled through several phases of interaction between Inuit and archaeologists (Lyons 2016). Over the past several decades, it has become more common for these two groups to work collaboratively on projects that bring together Elders, northern and southern researchers, and often youth. The advantages of these collaborations for archaeologists are obvious – otherwise mysterious stone features and artifacts are often easily interpreted by Inuit colleagues and can immeasurably add to the depth and breadth of the interpretation of the region's history. On the other hand, heritage sites are often excellent contexts to record Elders' knowledge; being on the land amidst the physical remains of past campsites provides a jump start for the flow of memories. In some cases, this direct connection between archaeology and modern life is also being used for broader cultural programs, and as a device to engage young people with local heritage and language.

Ultimately, all of these strands are coming together to form a robust history of the region. The long-term historical patterns outlined in this chapter form the social, political, and cultural framework within which modern Inuit society continues to develop. Modern Elders in every northern community hold particularly detailed historical knowledge of their region, which extends back for generations and eventually joins with the far less precise information that can be obtained from archaeology for earlier periods. Under the right circumstances, these two sources of knowledge can overlap seamlessly on the still-evolving cultural landscape.

ACKNOWLEDGMENTS

I wish to thank my northern collaborators for their insight, support, and fellowship through the years – in particular everyone associated with the Pitquhirnikkut Ilihautiniq/Kitikmeot Heritage Society and the Inuvialuit Cultural Centre.

NOTE

1 In this chapter, the term "Inuit" is used to refer, broadly, to the related group of mainly coastal northern peoples who refer to themselves by a variety of names including Inuit, Inuvialuit, Iñupiat, and Yupik. While it is imperfect, and more locally relevant terms should be used where possible, it is the best general term currently available.

REFERENCES

Anichtchenko, Evguenia V. 2016. *Open Passage: Ethno-Archaeology of Skin Boats and Indigenous Maritime Mobility of North American Arctic*. PhD dissertation, University of Southampton.

Balikci, Asen. 1970. *The Netsilik Eskimo*. Garden City, NY: Natural History Press.

Bandi, Hans G. 1995. "Siberian Eskimos as Whalers and Warriors." In *Hunting the Largest Animals: Native Whaling in the Western Arctic and Subarctic*, edited by Allen P. McCartney, 165–184. Studies in Whaling No. 3, Occasional Paper 36. Edmonton, AB: Canadian Circumpolar Institute.

Bennett, John, and Susan Rowley. 2004. *Uqalurait: An Oral History of Nunavut*. Montreal, QC: McGill-Queen's University Press.

Birket-Smith, Kaj. 1929. *The Caribou Eskimos: Material and Social Life and Their Cultural Position, I and II. Report of the Fifth Thule Expedition 1921–24, Vol. 5*. Copenhagen: Gyldendalske Boghandel Nordisk Forlag.

Black, Lydia. 2004. *Russians in Alaska, 1732–1867*. Fairbanks, AK: University of Alaska Press.

Bronshtein, Mikhail M., Kirill A. Dneprovsky, and Arkady B. Savinestky. 2016. "Ancient Eskimo Cultures of Chukotka." In *The Oxford Handbook of Prehistoric Arctic Archaeology*, edited by T. Max Friesen and Owen K. Mason, 469–488. New York: Oxford University Press.

Burch, Ernest S. 1978. "Caribou Eskimo Origins: An Old Problem Reconsidered." *Arctic Anthropology* 15 (1): 1–35.

———. 2005. *Alliance and Conflict: The World System of the Iñupiaq Eskimos*. Lincoln, NE: University of Nebraska Press.

———. 2006. *Social Life in Northwest Alaska: The Structure of Iñupiaq Eskimo Nations*. Fairbanks, AK: University of Alaska Press.

Cooper, H. Kory. 2016. "Arctic Archaeometallurgy." In *The Oxford Handbook of Prehistoric Arctic Archaeology*, edited by T. Max Friesen and Owen K. Mason, 175–196. New York: Oxford University Press.

Dawson, Peter. 2016. "The Thule-Inuit Succession in the Central Arctic." In *The Oxford Handbook of the Prehistoric Arctic*, edited by T. Max Friesen and Owen K. Mason, 915–936. New York: Oxford University Press.

Finkelstein, Sarah A. 2016. "Reconstructing Middle and Late Holocene Paleoclimates of the Eastern Arctic and Greenland." In *The Oxford Handbook of the Prehistoric Arctic*, edited by T. Max Friesen and Owen K. Mason, 653–672. New York: Oxford University Press.

Fitzhugh, William W. 2016. "Archaeology of the Inuit of Southern Labrador and the Quebec Lower North Shore." In *The Oxford Handbook of the Prehistoric Arctic*, edited by T. Max Friesen and Owen K. Mason, 937–960. New York: Oxford University Press.

Flegontov, Pavel, N. Ezgi Altınışık, Piya Changmai, Nadin Rohland, Swapan Mallick, Nicole Adamski, Deborah A. Bolnick, Nasreen Broomandkhoshbacht, Francesca Candilio, Brendan J. Culleton, Olga Flegontova, T. Max Friesen, Choongwon Jeong, Thomas K. Harper, Denise Keating, Douglas J. Kennett, Alexander M. Kim, Thiseas C. Lamnidis, Ann

Marie Lawson, Iñigo Olalde, Jonas Oppenheimer, Ben A. Potter, Jennifer Raff, Robert A. Sattler, Pontus Skoglund, Kristin Stewardson, Edward J. Vajda, Sergey Vasilyev, Elizaveta Veselovskaya, M. Geoffrey Hayes, Dennis H. O'Rourke, Johannes Krause, Ron Pinhasi, David Reich, and Stephan Schiffels. 2019. "Palaeo-Eskimo Genetic Ancestry and the Peopling of Chukotka and North America." *Nature* 570: 236–240. https://doi.org/10.1038/s41586-019-1251-y.

Fortuine, Robert. 1992. *Chills and Fever: Health and Disease in the Early History of Alaska*. Fairbanks, AK: University of Alaska Press.

Frei, Karin M., Ashley N. Coutu, Konrad Smiarowski, Ramona Harrison, Christian K. Madsen, Jette Arneborg, Robert Frei, Gardar Guðmundsson, Søren M. Sindbæk, James Woollett, Steven Hartman, Megan Hicks, and Thomas H. McGovern. 2015. "Was It for Walrus? Viking Age Settlement and Medieval Walrus Ivory Trade in Iceland and Greenland." *World Archaeology* 47 (5): 439–466. https://doi.org/10.1080/00438243.2015.1025912.

Friesen, T. Max. 2000. "The Role of Social Factors in Dorset-Thule Interaction." In *Identities and Cultural Contacts in the Arctic*, edited by Martin Appelt, Joel Berglund, and Hans Christian Gulløv, 206–220. Copenhagen: National Museum of Denmark and Danish Polar Center.

———. 2013. *When Worlds Collide: Hunter-Gatherer World-System Change in the 19th Century Canadian Arctic*. Tuscon, AZ: University of Arizona Press.

———. 2016. "Pan-Arctic Population Movements: The Early Paleo-Inuit and Thule Inuit Migrations." In *The Oxford Handbook of the Prehistoric Arctic*, edited by T. Max Friesen and Owen K. Mason, 673–692. New York: Oxford University Press.

———. 2020. "Radiocarbon Evidence for Fourteenth-Century Dorset Occupation in the Eastern North American Arctic." *American Antiquity* 85 (2): 222–240.

Friesen, T. Max, and Charles D. Arnold. 2008. "The Timing of the Thule Migration: New Dates from the Western Canadian Arctic." *American Antiquity* 73: 527–538. www.jstor.org/stable/25470503.

Friesen, T. Max, Sarah A. Finkelstein, and Andrew W. Medeiros. 2019. "Climate Variability of the Common Era (AD 1–2000) in the Eastern North American Arctic: Impacts on Human Migrations." *Quaternary International*. https://doi.org/10.1016/j.quaint.2019.06.002.

Friesen, T. Max, and Lauren E. Y. Norman. 2016. "The Pembroke Site: Thule Inuit Migrants on Southern Victoria Island." *Arctic* 69 (1): 1–18. https://doi.org/10.14430/arctic4545.

Giddings, J. Louis. 1952. *Arctic Woodland Culture of the Kobuk River*. Philadelphia, PA: University Museum and University of Pennsylvania.

Guemple, Lee. 1986. "Men and Women, Husbands and Wives: The Role of Gender in Traditional Inuit Society." *Études / Inuit / Studies* 10: 9–24. https://www.jstor.org/stable/42869538.

Gulløv, Hans Christian. 2008. "The Nature of Contact between Native Greenlanders and Norse." *Journal of the North Atlantic* 1: 16–24. https://doi.org/10.3721/070425.

Gulløv, Hans Christian, and Robert McGhee. 2006. "Did Bering Strait People Initiate the Thule Migration?" *Alaska Journal of Archaeology* 4 (1–2): 54–63.

Hall, Edwin S., and Lynne Fullerton, eds. 1990. *The Utqiaġvik Excavations*, 3 volumes. Barrow, AK: North Slope Borough Commission on Iñupiat History, Language, and Culture.

Hart, Elisa J. 2011. *Nuna Aliannaittuq – Beautiful Land: Learning about Traditional Place Names and the Land from Tuktoyaktuk Elders*. Inuvik: Inuvialuit Cultural Resource Centre.

Jenness, Diamond. 1922. *The Life of the Copper Eskimos*. Report of the Canadian Arctic Expedition, 1913–1918, vol. 12. Ottawa, ON: King's Printer.

———. 1946. *Material Culture of the Copper Eskimo*. Report of the Canadian Arctic Expedition, 1913–1918, vol. 16. Ottawa, ON: King's Printer.

Kaplan, Susan A. 1985. "European Goods and Socio-Economic Change in Early Labrador Inuit Society." In *Cultures in Contact: The European Impact on Native Cultural Institutions in Eastern North America, A.D. 1000–1800*, edited by William W. Fitzhugh, 45–70. Washington, DC: Smithsonian Institution.

Kaplan, Susan A., and James M. Woollett. 2016. "Labrador Inuit: Thriving on the Periphery of the Inuit World." In *The Oxford Handbook of the Prehistoric Arctic*, edited by T. Max Friesen and Owen K. Mason, 851–872. New York: Oxford University Press.

Kitikmeot Heritage Society. 2019. https://www.kitikmeotheritage.ca/. Accessed November 14, 2019.

Lee, Molly, and Gregory A. Reinhardt. 2003. *Eskimo Architecture: Dwelling and Structure in the Early Historic Period*. Fairbanks, AK: University of Alaska Press.

LeMoine, Genevieve M., and Christyann M. Darwent. 2016. "Development of Polar Inughuit Culture in the Smith Sound Region." In *The Oxford Handbook of the Prehistoric Arctic*, edited by T. Max Friesen and Owen K. Mason, 873–896. New York: Oxford University Press.

Mason, Owen K. 2009. "Flight from the Bering Strait: Did Siberian Punuk/Thule Military Cadres Conquer Northwest Alaska?" In *The Northern World AD 900–1400*, edited by Herbert Maschner, Owen Mason, and Robert McGhee, 76–128. Salt Lake City: University of Utah Press.

———. 2016a. "The Old Bering Sea Florescence about Bering Strait." In *The Oxford Handbook of the Prehistoric Arctic*, edited by T. Max Friesen and Owen K. Mason, 417–442. New York: Oxford University Press.

———. 2016b. "Thule Origins in the Old Bering Sea Culture: The Interrelationship of Punuk and Birnirk Cultures." In *The Oxford Handbook of the Prehistoric Arctic*, edited by T. Max Friesen and Owen K. Mason, 489–512. New York: Oxford University Press.

———. 2017. "Archaeology of the Western Arctic." In *Out of the Cold: Archaeology on the Arctic Rim of North America*, edited by Owen K. Mason and T. Max Friesen, 11–131. Washington, DC: Society for American Archaeology Press.

Mason, Owen K., and T. Max Friesen. 2017. *Out of the Cold: Archaeology on the Arctic Rim of North America*. Washington, DC: Society for American Archaeology Press.

Maxwell, Moreau S. 1985. *Prehistory of the Eastern Arctic*. Orlando, FL: Academic Press.

McCullough, Karen M. 1989. *The Ruin Islanders: Early Thule Culture Pioneers in the Eastern High Arctic*. Archaeological Survey of Canada, Mercury Series 141. Gatineau, QC: Canadian Museum of Civilization.

McGhee, Robert. 1969/70. "Speculations on Climate Change and Thule Culture Development." *Folk* 11–12: 172–184.

———. 1984. *The Thule Village at Brooman Point, High Arctic Canada*. National Museum of Man Mercury Series No. 125. Ottawa, ON: National Museums of Canada.

———. 2000. "Radiocarbon Dating and the Timing of the Thule Migration." In *Identities and Cultural Contacts in the Arctic*, edited by Martin Appelt, Joel Berglund, and Hans Christian Gulløv, 181–191. Copenhagen: National Museum of Denmark and Danish Polar Center.

———. 2009. "When and Why Did the Inuit Move to the Eastern Arctic?" In *The Northern World AD 900–1400*, edited by Herbert Maschner, Owen Mason, and Robert McGhee, 155–163. Salt Lake City, UT: University of Utah Press.

Morrison, David. 1991. "The Copper Inuit Soapstone Trade." *Arctic* 44 (3): 177–265. https://doi.org/10.14430/arctic1544.

———. 1999. "The Earliest Thule Migration." *Canadian Journal of Archaeology* 22: 139–156.

Neatby, L. H. 1984. "Exploration and History of the Canadian Arctic." In *Arctic*, edited by David Damas, 377–390. *Handbook of North American Indians*, Vol. 5. Washington, DC: Smithsonian Institution.

Nuligak. 1966. *I Nuligak*. Edited and translated by Maurice Métayer. Toronto, ON: Peter Martin Associates.

Petitot, Émile. 1876. *Monographie des Esquimaux Tchiglit du MacKenzie et de l'Anderson*. Paris: E. Leroux.

———. 1887. *Les Grands Esquimaux*. Paris: E. Plon, Nourrit. Translated by E. Höhn as *Among the Chiglit Eskimos*, 1981. Edmonton, AB: Boreal Institute for Northern Studies, University of Alberta.

Rankin, Lisa K., and Amanda Crompton. 2016. "Meeting in the Straits: Intersecting Inuit and European Trajectories in Southern Labrador." In *Contacts in the 16th Century: Networks among Fishers, Foragers and Farmers*, edited by Brad Loewen and Claude Chapdelaine, 11–29. Mercury Series Archaeology Paper No. 176. Ottawa, ON: Canadian Museum of History.

Raghavan, Maanasa, Michael DeGiorgio, Anders Albrechtsen, Ida Moltke, Pontus Skoglund, Thorfinn S. Korneliussen, Bjarne Grønnow, Martin Appelt, Hans Christian Gulløv, T. Max Friesen, William Fitzhugh, Helena Malmström, Simon Rasmussen, Jesper Olsen, Linea Melchior, Benjamin T. Fuller, Simon M. Fahrni, Thomas Stafford, Vaughan Grimes, M. A. Priscilla Renouf, Jerome Cybulski, Niels Lynnerup, Marta Mirazon Lahr, Kate Britton, Rick Knecht, Jette Arneborg, Mait Metspalu, Omar E. Cornejo, Anna-Sapfo Malaspinas, Yong Wang, Morten Rasmussen, Vibha Raghavan, Thomas V. O. Hansen, Elza Khusnutdinova, Tracey Pierre, Kirill Dneprovsky, Claus Andreasen, Hans Lange, M. Geoffrey Hayes, Joan Coltrain, Victor A. Spitsyn, Anders Götherström, Ludovic Orlando, Toomas Kivisild, Richard Villems, Michael H. Crawford, Finn C. Nielsen, Jørgen Dissing, Jan Heinemeier, Morten Meldgaard, Carlos Bustamante, Dennis H. O'Rourke, Mattias Jakobsson, M. Thomas P. Gilbert, Rasmus Nielsen, and Eske Willerslev. 2014. "The Genetic Prehistory of the New World Arctic." *Science* 345 (6200). https://doi.org/10.1126/science.1255832.

Rasic, Jeffrey. 2016. "Archaeological Evidence for Transport, Trade, and Exchange in the North American Arctic." In *The Oxford Handbook of Prehistoric Arctic Archaeology*, edited by T. Max Friesen and Owen K. Mason, 131–152. New York: Oxford University Press.

Rasmussen, Knud. 1932. *Intellectual Culture of the Copper Eskimos. Report of the Fifth Thule Expedition 1921–24*, Vol. 9. Copenhagen: Gyldendalske Boghandel Nordisk Forlag.

Savelle, James M. 1987. *Collectors and Foragers: Subsistence-Settlement Systems in the Central Canadian Arctic, AD 1000–1960*. BAR International Series 358. Oxford: Archaeopress.

Savelle, James M., and Arthur S. Dyke. 2014. "Prehistoric Neoeskimo Komatiks, Victoria Island, Arctic Canada." *Arctic* 67 (2): 135–142. https://doi.org/10.14430/arctic4383.

Savelle, James M., and Allen P. McCartney. 1994. "Thule Inuit Bowhead Whaling: A Biometrical Analysis." In *Threads of Arctic Prehistory: Papers in Honour of William E. Taylor, Jr.*, edited by David Morrison and Jean-Luc Pilon, 281–310. Archaeological Survey of Canada, Mercury Series 149. Gatineau, QC: Canadian Museum of Civilization.

Schledermann, Peter. 1996. *Voices in Stone: A Personal Journey into the Arctic Past*. Komatik Series No. 5. Calgary, AB: Arctic Institute of North America.

Stefansson, Vilhjalmur. 1919. *The Stefansson-Anderson Arctic Expedition of the American Museum: Preliminary Ethnological Report*. Anthropological Papers of the American Museum of Natural History, Vol. 14, Part 1. New York: American Museum of Natural History.

Walley, Meghan. 2018. "Exploring Potential Archaeological Expressions of Nonbinary Gender in Pre-Contact Inuit Contexts." *Études / Inuit / Studies* 42 (1): 269–289. https://doi.org/10.7202/1064504ar.

Walls, Matthew. 2009. *Caribou Inuit Traders of the Kivalliq, Nunavut, Canada*. BAR International Series No. 1895. Oxford: Archaeopress.

Walls, Matthew, Pauline Knudsen, and Frederik Larsen. 2016. "The Morris Bay Kayak: Analysis and Implications for Inughuit Subsistence in the Pikialarsorsuaq Region." *Arctic Anthropology* 52 (1): 1–21. https://doi.org/10.3368/aa.53.1.1.

Whitridge, Peter. 1999. *The Construction of Social Difference in a Prehistoric Inuit Whaling Community*. PhD dissertation, Arizona State University.

———. 2002. Gender, Households, and the Material Construction of Social Difference: Metal Consumption at a Classic Thule Whaling Village. In *Many Faces of Gender: Roles and Relationships Through Time in Indigenous Northern Communities*, edited by Lisa Frink, Rita S. Shepard, and Gregory A. Reinhardt, 165–192. Boulder, CO: University Press of Colorado.

Woodbury, Anthony C. 1984. "Eskimo and Aleut Languages." In *Handbook of North American Indians*, vol. 5, *Arctic*, edited by David Damas, 49–63. Washington, DC: Smithsonian Institution Press.

Zhou, Sirui, Pingxing Xie, Amélie Quoibion, Amirthagowri Ambalavanan, Alexandre Dionne-Laporte, Dan Spiegelman, Cynthia V. Bourassa, Lan Xiong, Patrick A. Dion, and Guy A. Rouleau. 2019. "Genetic Architecture and Adaptations of Nunavik Inuit." *Proceedings of the National Academy of Sciences* 116 (32): 16012–16017. https://doi.org/10.1073/pnas.1810388116.

CHAPTER 2

ENDURING SOCIAL COMMUNITIES OF THE INUVIALUIT

From the Yukon North Slope to the circumpolar stage

Natasha Lyons, Lisa Hodgetts, Mervin Joe, Ashley Piskor, Renie Arey, David Stewart, Jason Lau, Rebecca Goodwin, Walter Bennett, Cassidy Lennie-Ipana, Mataya Gillis, Hayven Elanik, Angelina Joe, and Starr Elanik

INTRODUCTION

Sharing is central to Inuvialuit life. The practice of sharing stories, laughter, space, and time with family on the land is as old as the culture itself and forms the basis for futures envisioned by youth and Elders alike. This chapter looks at the enduring importance of Inuvialuit social communities on the Yukon North Slope and the connections forged by contemporary Inuvialuit to both memories of traditional places on this coastal landscape and the material remnants left behind by their remembered residents. It also explores how Inuvialuit youth are forging connections with other Inuit youth who share similar experiences and are drawing from their Elders to help shape their futures.

At the center of this story is the Imniarvik culture camp held in Ivvavik National Park in the summer of 2019. The week-long camp was co-hosted by the Inuvialuit Living History (ILH) project and Parks Canada with input and support from the Inuvialuit Cultural Resource Centre and the Northwest Territories' Prince of Wales Northern Heritage Centre. The camp brought three generations of interrelated Inuvialuit, along with anthropologists and videographers, together in a land-based setting to learn and practice traditional Inuvialuit activities and skills, share time and knowledge, and have youth document their real-time experiences using digital and analog tools of their choosing. Several of these participants would later travel to the Inuit Studies Conference in Montreal to present their Imniarvik experiences and engage with Inuit issues on a much larger stage.

The Inuvialuit are the Inuit of the Canadian Western Arctic. Having historically consisted of a distinct set of local groups speaking different dialects of Inuvialuktun,[1] they joined together in the 1960s and 1970s to lobby for a collective land claim, settled as the Inuvialuit Final Agreement in 1984 (IFA 1984; Lyons 2009). The social and geographic focus of this chapter is the western extent of Inuvialuit territory

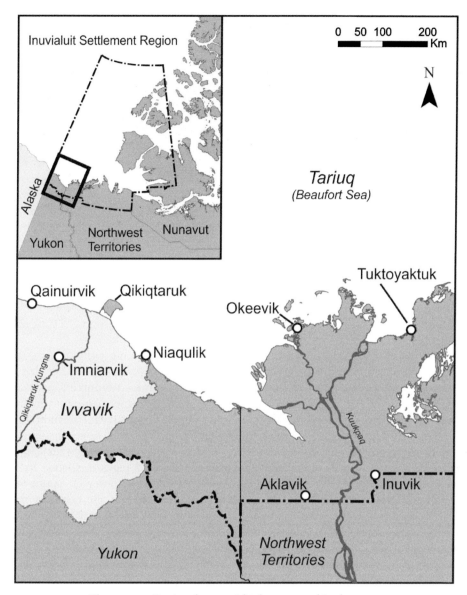

Figure 2.1   Regional map with places named in the text.

(Figure 2.1). Renie Arey, who was a signatory to the land claim, noted that their negotiating team was intent upon the inclusion of the Yukon North Slope within the Inuvialuit Settlement Region because of its ancestral and ongoing significance to Uummarmiutun speakers who continue to have strong family connections in Alaska. Uummarmiut, meaning "people of the evergreens and willows," are those who came to the Mackenzie Delta from the Alaskan North Slope, Anaktuvuk Pass, and Old Crow regions in a series of migrations from the 1870s through the 1940s (Nagy 1994, 1–2; Stefansson 1919). Sallirmiutun speakers, traditionally from the lower

Mackenzie Delta region, also frequented this area historically, and the two groups commonly intermarried. Thule ancestors of all Inuvialuit inhabited this area from at least the 13th century AD (Friesen and Arnold 2008), giving present-day communities an extraordinary legacy of continuity and resilience.

Genealogy and family history, and how both map onto the landscape, are central to Inuvialuit social memory (Lyons 2010; see also Davies 2020). Inuvialuit identify each other and establish connections through their family lines. Traditionally, of course, family histories were recited in stories in the winter sodhouse (Alunik et al. 2003). Many Inuvialuit in the post-contact era, like Old Irish Kiuruya who ran the Hudson's Bay post at Qainuirvik (Clarence Lagoon), taught themselves to read and write even before the residential schools arrived circa the 1920s (Lyons 2007, 99–100). The maternal great-great-grandfather of Mataya Gillis, one of our youth campers, wrote the first and much celebrated Inuvialuit autobiography about his life in the whaling era, *I Nuligak* (Nuligak 1966). Inuvialuk scholar Ishmael Alunik, born in Old Crow, Yukon, in 1922 and raised on the North Slope, wrote the book *Call Me Ishmael*, recounting his family's history and stories of life on the land (Alunik 1998), as well as a collaborative history of the Inuvialuit called *Across Time and Tundra: The Inuvialuit of the Western Arctic* (Alunik et al. 2003). A ground-breaking oral history of the Yukon North Slope funded by the Inuvialuit Social Development Program was conducted and published in the 1990s by Murielle Nagy (1994) with Inuvialuit researchers and interpreters Renie Arey and Agnes White.

The desire of Inuvialuit to record and share family and community histories has evolved into a robust publishing tradition (Lyons 2013, 39–47) complemented by an equally strong film industry. Both the Inuvialuit Cultural Resource Centre and Inuvialuit Communications Society (ICS) were founded with the signing of the land claim and have mandates to document, foster, produce, and share Inuvialuit culture. *Tusaayaksat*, the glossy magazine produced by ICS, is a popular quarterly in the Western Arctic that focuses on different facets of the lives of contemporary Inuvialuit. The explosion of multi-media technologies and platforms, such as the iPhone, and their relative accessibility compared to video technologies of the past, has only increased the opportunities for Inuvialuit to document and celebrate their cultural traditions. Across Inuit Nunangat, the Inuit homeland in Canada, the use of new media technologies for documenting and asserting Inuit knowledge works to keep this knowledge part of living traditions (Graburn 1998), at the same time "'push[ing]' Inuit culture out into the world and 'pull[ing]' at the national power centre that continues to ignore Northerners' policy needs" (Alexander et al. 2009, 220). We also see the power of new media to bring Inuvialuit together to articulate their perspectives, sometimes in ways that challenge the southern norm.

In this chapter, we set the scene by describing the people, places, and activities of the Imniarvik culture camp. We recount the social histories of two traditional sites we visited, Niaqulik (Head Point) and Qikiqtaruk (Herschel Island), and then showcase the digital products and written reflections created by five Inuvialuit youth to document their Imniarvik experience. We combine dialogue, memory, and material and digital engagement with Inuvialuit culture experienced as part of the camp, journeying with the youth as they learn aspects of their family histories on the North Slope through the stories and teachings of their Elders.

The transmission of Inuvialuit social values and knowledge exhibited in traditional and land-based settings provide a prism to view how northern Indigenous communities are facing the larger issues that confront them on the global stage (Lyons 2014). Inuit across the circumpolar north are dealing with massive change wrought by shifting climate and the ethnocentric agendas of sovereign nation-states (Hodgetts 2013). In discussion, we describe the experiences of youth and adult members of our Imniarvik camp at the Inuit Studies Conference held in Montreal in October 2019, as youth presented at an international gathering for the first time, and we all listened to and engaged with Inuit leaders who discussed critical northern issues related to sovereignty, diplomacy, wellbeing, and environment. We consider the enduring value of Arctic social communities in visioning and asserting desired futures in the face of profound change, and how these connect to the inherent pragmatism of land-based life and teachings.

THE IMNIARVIK CULTURE CAMP

The Inuvialuit Living History Project, initiated in 2009, is a partnership between the Inuvialuit Cultural Resource Centre, Inuvialuit Communications Society, Simon Fraser University, University of Western Ontario, Ursus Heritage Consulting, Parks Canada, Prince of Wales Northern Heritage Centre, and the Smithsonian Institution, that focuses on documenting and celebrating Inuvialuit culture and traditions. In 2012, our project team launched *Inuvialuit Pitqusiit Inuuniarutait*, the Inuvialuit Living History website: www.inuvialuitlivinghistory.ca (Hennessy et al. 2013; Lyons 2013; Lyons et al. 2012). As current directors of the project, Natasha Lyons and Lisa Hodgetts conceived the Imniarvik culture camp with our project team as a way to facilitate knowledge exchange and transmission between Elders and youth, and have our participants together generate content about living Inuvialuit traditions for the website.

Imniarvik (Sheep Creek), a remote base camp in the heart of Ivvavik National Park, provided us with the conditions to fulfill this mandate and many options for visiting cultural sites, exploring different ecosystems with abundant animal and plant life, reading the weather, and fishing. Our camp built on the close relationship that Parks Canada shares with Aklavik – the closest Inuvialuit community to Ivvavik, whose residents have long used this region – to offer a variety of land-based opportunities for community members. Having hosted a large cultural gathering focused on storytelling, games, and crafts in Inuvik in 2018, our project team chose to hold the camp in this remote setting in order to practice and share Inuvialuit activities and pastimes in a more traditional context away from the distractions of town. While this choice limited the number of participants in this rich experience, the materials created during the camp and other project events are being transformed for presentation on our website, allowing others to view and experience the knowledges, skills, and activities that transpired in these many intergenerational exchanges.

The rise in land-based culture camps developed and hosted by Indigenous communities reflects the physical and emotional connections these venues create for community members to places, practices, stories, and songs. Cultural landscapes are places where the ancestors live, where their belongings reside, where they can be visited and remembered, and their deeds, knowledges, and ways of life recognized.

The immersive experience is a way to enhance Indigenous languages through side-by-side learning of skills such as fishing, crafting, trapping, and plant lore, which, in the North, are central to Arctic survival, and becoming more so with the need and desire to increase food security (Tod-Tims 2020). Being on the land also unites tangible and intangible sources of cultural knowledge and fosters intergenerational sharing and cultural continuity for youth (Fienup-Riordan and Rearden 2003; Schaepe et al. 2020). Tangible land-based practices, in turn, have been shown to build cultural resilience and well-being in youth (Big-Canoe and Richmond 2014).

The Imniarvik camp participants included Inuvialuit youth and Elders and southern-based ILH team members. Three teenage girls from Aklavik (Angelina Joe and sisters Hayven and Starr Elanik) and two from Inuvik (Mataya Gillis and Cassidy Lennie-Ipana) were chosen through an application process that involved writing a paragraph about their interest and involvement in cultural and land-based activities and using selection criteria co-developed with the relevant community corporations and school administrators. Two Inuvialuit Elders, Renie Arey and Walter Bennett, and a cook, Arlene Kogiak, from Aklavik were selected with the assistance of the Aklavik Community Corporation. Mervin Joe, an Inuvialuit Parks Canada Resource Management Officer and core ILH team member with extensive knowledge of the land and cultural sites, served as our primary wildlife monitor. Mervin is commonly known throughout the Inuvialuit community as the "mayor" of Imniarvik! In addition to Natasha and Lisa, non-Inuvialuit team members included Ashley Piskor, previously the Cultural Resource Management advisor for Parks Canada's Western Arctic Parks and now an ILH graduate student along with Rebecca Goodwin and Jason Lau at the University of Western Ontario; and David Stewart, our camp videographer, representing Inuvialuit Communications Society.

All the Inuvialuit at the Imniarvik culture camp have family connections to the coastal communities that once existed, and most are descended from Uummarmuitun speakers in Aklavik and Inuvik. Both Walter Bennett and Renie Arey were born in 1944 in Aklavik. They attended residential school and spent the summers of their youth traveling with their families on their grandfathers' schooners. Renie's mother died when she was a young girl and she was raised by her father and paternal grandparents. Renie has worked through the course of her life at the Aklavik fur shop, on the land claim, as a researcher and interpreter, and in media. Renie is Mervin's dad's cousin and the two have a close and lifelong relationship; he calls her Auntie. Both have connections to Niaqulik and are related to Angelina, Starr, and Hayven. Walter's Daduk (grandfather), Bennett Ningasuk, and his parents were Iñupiat from Alaska. Walter took care of the dogs for his Daduk, and like Cassidy's Daduk, Roy Ipana, went beluga whaling in and around Okeevik (Kendall Island; Figure 2.1). Later he worked on the oil rigs across Tariuq (the Beaufort Sea). Among our camp participants, Renie, Walter, and Mervin have spent considerable time on the Yukon North Slope. Two of our youth participants, Mataya and Angelina, have family connections to Qikiqtaruk and have visited there with their families. None of the girls had ever been to Niaqulik.

SOCIAL HISTORIES OF THE YUKON NORTH SLOPE

Archaeological remains from the Yukon North Slope show some 11 millennia of use by Inuvialuit and their cultural predecessors (Adams 1995). Ancestral Inuvialuit emerged from their Thule forebears circa AD 1300–1400, when they began to develop signature skills such as net fishing and community beluga hunting (Alunik et al. 2003, 10). In the ensuing centuries, Inuvialuit enjoyed consistent commerce and social interaction with their Alaskan Iñupiat relations, and the North Slope saw lively use for subsistence, travel, and trade. Lifestyles changed irrevocably between 1890 and 1910 – the intense and short-lived period of the EuroAmerican bowhead whaling industry centered at Qikiqtaruk – when written documentation becomes far more prominent. Foreign whalers primarily focused on oil and baleen production, wasting meat, *muktuk*, and other whale products traditionally used by Inuvialuit and other Inuit (Peter Thrasher in Nagy 1994, 33–34). The primary role of Inuvialuit in this trade was as provisioners of fresh game (the whalers preferred terrestrial to marine sources), winter clothing made by Inuvialuit seamstresses, and knowledge to prevent scurvy and avoid environmental hazards (Jacobson in Nagy 1994, 36). By 1910, overhunting of bowheads and caribou had wrought devastation on both these populations (Bockstoce 1986; Usher 1971a).

The trapping industry arose in the wake of the whalers' exodus from the Beaufort Sea region. The European market for pelts to adorn clothing soared between the 1910s and 1930s, during which time many Inuvialuit trappers became cash and commodity rich, allowing them to buy schooners for summer travel and other goods (Ishmael Alunik and Sarah Meyook in Nagy 1994, 82-82). Fox and wolverine were trapped on the Arctic coastline, mink and muskrat in the Mackenzie Delta. Walter Bennett remembers:

> I stayed with my grandparents, that's where I learned most of the land – where I learned my language ... Long ago, my grandfather had a schooner [called the Shamrock], and it can fit two to three families, as long as he had his schooner he took people out. To grab their winter provisions – we did hunting in summer to survive the winter ... My dad was a trapper all his life; my grandpa looked after his boat. My grandfather was the founder of that place [Paulatuk], Old Bennett. The only reason they moved down east was there was a lot of foxes. It's how they bought their schooners; a lot of people moved from the Delta, to Banks Island [to trap].

Qikiqtaruk had a substantial Hudson's Bay post, in addition to an Anglican mission and Northwest Mounted Police post, yet many traditional aspects of the culture persisted. For instance, the famed *angatkuq* (shaman) Kublualuk – who was jailed for unknowingly contravening the new hunting laws, and repeatedly escaped by turning into a bird or a feather, until the police decided to employ rather than contain him (Alunik et al. 2003, 101–102) – still lived in a sod house at Qikiqtaruk in the 1920s, next door to a young Jimmy Jacobson (in Nagy 1994, 32). The growing town of Aklavik, on the West Channel of Kuukpaq (Mackenzie River), rose to have dozens of fur trade posts by 1920 (Usher 1971b), while coastal locales such as Qainuirvik (Clarence Lagoon) and Tapqaq (Shingle Point) had subsidiary ones, and Captain Pedersen ran a floating post based out of Qikiqtaruk to provision these smaller posts (Figure 2.1; Alunik et al. 2003; Nagy 1994, 51; Nuligak 1966).

Both Ishmael Alunik and Sarah Meyook (in Nagy 1994, 83) remembered Niaqulik as one of several places to camp while checking traps after freeze-up. The Kurugak,

Inglangasuk (Joe), Irigagtuak (Archie), and Alunik families inhabited Niaqulik variously from the early 1920s to as late as 1940 (Kathleen Hanson, Nagy interviews 1991, tape 1B). In winter, they lived in sod and wood-frame houses, and in summer, in canvas wall tents or traditional caribou skin tents (Kathleen Hansen, Nagy interviews 1991, tape 1B). Fred Inglangasuk, Mervin Joe's uncle, remembered picking *aqpik* (cloudberries, *Rubus chamaemorus*) with Renie's mother Martha as children (Nagy interviews 1991, tape 18a). Summer activities included fishing and making dryfish, stocking and preparing the ice house. In the early 20th century, caribou migrated through this site, as Fred told Renie in a 1991 interview: "Long ago the caribou used to come right by there. And they still have trails. Sometimes here, they go right to the houses, they go right to us! They [the adults] just go out and kill the caribou."

The fur trade came to an abrupt end in the 1930s with the Depression in Europe and North America. Fred Inglangasuk, Sarah Meyook, and Dora Malegana told Renie in interviews how difficult it was to find food, especially large game, on the coast in the 1940s, even to the extent of their much-loved dogs dying (in Nagy 1994, 86–88). Through the 1930s and 1940s, most Inuvialuit from the Yukon North Slope, and another wave of Iñupiat, moved from Alaska into towns in the Mackenzie Delta, primarily Aklavik and secondarily Tuktoyaktuk, well before Inuvik was built in the mid-1950s (Figure 2.1).

Inuvialuit continue to visit and use the North Slope sites for seasonal hunting, beluga whaling, fishing, and berry-picking, though traditional places closer to the delta see more intensive use. Inuvialuit, particularly from Aklavik, continue to travel this coastal corridor by boat and skidoo to visit Iñupiat relations. Qikiqtaruk is a Yukon territorial park, managed by rangers, and forming an important summer destination for Inuvialuit and a center for international, community-supported research on Arctic environments, Inuvialuit archaeology, and climate change (see Burn 2012; Friesen 2009; 2013; Fritz et al. 2017; Lantuit et al. 2012; Myers-Smith et al. 2019).

LEARNING AND SHARING CULTURE IN DIGITAL AND REAL-TIME AT THE IMNIARVIK CAMP

In the lead-up to camp, Jason spent time with our youth participants in Aklavik and Inuvik. He described the parameters of the camp and the campers' prospective projects. Together, they produced "principles of community" for our time in camp, a co-developed document that articulates how a group aspires to work together, treat one another, make decisions, and share outcomes (Lau et al. n.d.; Lyons et al. 2019). As part of this process, they discussed their creative interests, artworks, and literature that inspired them, the stories and topics they were interested in pursuing as projects, the types of media that might accomplish these, and questions they would like to ask the Elders in camp. This work helped create an emotional connection between participants which was fostered in camp by daily check-ins among participants and particularly between adults and youth.

On the first day of camp, we arrived at Imniarvik on consecutive twin otter flights from Inuvik and Aklavik, set in the striking landscape of the British Mountains in Ivvavik National Park. Mervin oriented us to the camp and we got settled in. We visited an old gold-panning site and swam in one of Sheep Creek's eddies. On the second morning of camp, we introduced youth participants to different media tools, provided them with journals and craft supplies, and taught them some basic documentary techniques (Figure 2.2). The girls started to formulate both digital and analog media projects of their choosing to document their camp experiences with help from the Elders as knowledge holders, and support from other project team members. The Elders are very accustomed to new media technologies – Renie worked for many years with David Stewart at Inuvialuit Communications Society and was herself using an iPad to document her time in camp. Mervin commended the new technologies for documentation with Elders because they are small and unobtrusive, facilitating spontaneous recording.

The following morning, the girls participated in a short workshop on interviewing and came up with a series of questions for their Elders. They conducted a group interview with Renie, Walter, and Mervin which they recorded using various devices. Although this was clearly a learning process for the girls, the Elders were encouraging and supportive. Our next few days were alternately taken up with developing ideas for the girls' projects, starting to execute them, and participating in activities in and around Imniarvik, including fishing in Qikiqtaruk Kungna (Firth River), hiking (Figure 2.3), picking berries, and harvesting spruce gum to make medicine. We did a morning workshop with Inuvialuit artifacts from the North Slope loaned by the Prince of Wales Northern Heritage Centre, and spent time at a couple of archaeological sites drawing and imagining what once happened there. Craft projects and games took up the long Arctic evenings. Walter watched the weather and scouted for game.

On days four, five, and six of camp, we had helicopter time funded by the Polar Continental Shelf Program and the fortune of great weather. Our Niaqulik visit was

Figure 2.2 Starr Elanik learning to use a gimbal. Photo: Rebecca Goodwin.

Figure 2.3 Camp participants Cassidy, Starr, Jason, Ashley, and Angelina hike in the mountains near Imniarvik. Photo: Lisa Hodgetts.

an emotional one. This is the place where Renie's mother Martha was born and raised by Charlie Kurugaq and Rebecca Alunik, and where Martha married Owen Allen. Mervin's Dad, Andrew Joe, and his siblings were born to Mervin's Daduk, Laughing Joe Inglangasuk, and Nanuk, Annie Kurugaq. Angelina discovered that these were also her great-great-grandparents on her father's side. Hayven and Starr's great-great-grandmother, Sarah Kurugaq, was also born and raised here. She married Isaac Alunik and they had several children including Maggie, the girls' great-grandmother. After Isaac's death in an accident, Sarah married Tommy Kalinek. Several of the houses that these relations lived in at Niaqulik, including both sod and frame structures, are still in existence (Adams 2004). We visited and filmed Renie telling the girls about their ancestry and showing them how the houses were arranged inside (Figure 2.4). Cassidy and Mataya filmed, photographed, and interviewed Inuvialuit camp participants about their lives and experiences. Lisa and Becky worked with the girls on making 360-degree photospheres of the historic buildings on site. In the bright and blowing conditions of the Tariuq coastline, we had a char cookout on the beach with fish caught the previous day by Mervin and Mataya.

Our Qikiqtaruk day was a great adventure. As a Yukon territorial park, Qikiqtaruk is staffed by Inuvialuit rangers who oversee the small settlement and manage the busy summer traffic, when the island is frequented by Inuvialuit visitors and cultural programs as well as research personnel from around the world. Mataya's and Angelina's maternal grandmothers, Topsy Cockney and Ester Elanik, were both born here. Park rangers Samuel and Edward McLeod from Aklavik took us on a tour of the whaler's buildings, and we learned about ongoing projects from Scottish, Canadian, and German researchers. The highlights of the day were definitely spending time in the island's sauna, swimming in Pauline Cove, and digitally documenting our play on the sandy foreshore.

Figure 2.4 Hayven Elanik, Renie Arey, and Starr Elanik in the girls' great-great-grandmother Sarah Kalinek's cabin at Niaqulik. Photo: Lisa Hodgetts.

The students presented their projects on the penultimate evening of camp. Angelina Joe showed the sketches she had produced of Inuvialuit traditional seasonal activities and screened her 20-minute interview with Renie and Walter. Of her camp experience, Ange wrote: "Being on the land, I feel free, and I feel like I'm at home. Learning from the Elders feels different because I'm learning the language more and I'm actually gonna speak it." Starr Elanik shared the embroidery she was learning from Becky, drawing on wildflowers of the area that she had photographed all week. Sewing and embroidery are skills that Starr missed out on learning from her female relatives but she now has a basis to build on. Her older sister Hayven presented a poster about Inuvialuit traditional teachings and activities. All week she had worked on a detailed family history using Renie as a primary source. In her presentation, Hayven talked about what she learned at Niaqulik from Renie. Renie told the girls:

> You are all connected onto this land here in some way. I'm very proud of you coming out to learn more about your background. Be proud of who you are, even when you fall down, get up and try it again. Move forward like your great-great grandparents did. They didn't live on social services, they didn't have family allowance or anything. They went out there on the land and got what they needed.

Mataya and Cassidy produced a digital magazine (Figures 2.5 and 2.6) called Nipatuȓuq which means "having a loud voice" in Uummarmiutun. They envision the magazine as a forum for bringing youth and Elders together to learn from one another, and as a "place where everyone's opinions are heard, where Inuvialuit can

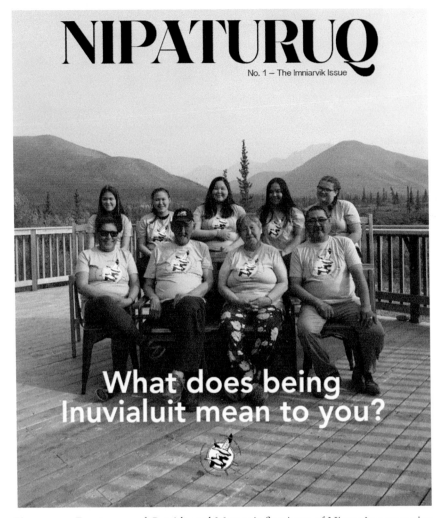

Figure 2.5 Front cover of Cassidy and Mataya's first issue of Nipaturuq magazine.

express and share their culture." Cassidy conducted and recorded audio interviews with each Inuvialuk in camp using a digital voice recorder, focusing on the question "What does it mean to be Inuvialuit?" Mataya took portraits of each interviewee. The girls transcribed part of their audio, and with Jason's assistance, developed the magazine using Adobe InDesign software. Reflecting on this experience, Mataya wrote:

> To me, being Inuvialuit just means that ... I have a big support system. Having the Inuvialuit community is just super strong. It's like we're one giant team and they've always got your back and they're always pushing you to do better and supporting you no matter what. It just makes me feel ... like a giant family. It's awesome.

Figure 2.6   Jason (Centre) helps Mataya (L) and Cassidy (R) with magazine layout while Renie (far R) looks on. Photo: Rebecca Goodwin.

Cassidy wrote:

> Being Inuvialuit is ... being able to do sewing projects, or to learn the language or even just spending time with Elders and listening to all the stories, which I think is really important, and on the way to keep up the tradition, as most of our stories were told orally. And we gotta keep it up too, so it doesn't die out. Being Inuvialuit, it's not turning your back. It's everyone together. Even if you're not related, you're always told to share your stuff and just be kind overall. Being Inuvialuit means that we connect for a bigger purpose, so we're not just about our own selves but the whole community.

DISCUSSION: PLACING INUVIALUIT SOCIAL VALUES ON THE CIRCUMPOLAR STAGE

Despite centuries of colonial impacts and profound historical change, Inuvialuit social values continue to revolve around sharing and land-based living. Inuvialuit Elders work hard to instill a strong work ethic in their children and grandchildren, exhort them in their quiet but insistent ways to learn by watching and listening, to tell the truth, to be kind, and to share what they have (Lyons 2010; 2013). In a camp setting, Inuvialuit of all ages set to a job – gutting fish, flensing a whale, or picking spruce gum for medicine – until it is done. Many Inuvialuit Elders, including Renie Arey and Walter Bennett, recall how hard they worked on the land in their youth, how much they learned, and how much they enjoyed it. Life has changed for northern youth, with technology and foreign methods of schooling as well as the need for advanced (Western) educations, which Elders accept. At the same time, they urge youth to keep their traditional values and language, and their special way of seeing and being in the world.

In this chapter, we have explored enduring social communities of Inuvialuit on the Yukon North Slope by sharing the time we spent at the Imniarvik camp and the journey five youth took to learn more about their culture and personal (her)stories. The girls planned and executed projects in digital and real-time that focused on learning specific skills, reflecting on traditional activities and values. They worked with Uumaarmiutun through naming and song, and documented the places we went, the things we did, and the conversations we had, particularly with their Elders. Mataya Gillis wrote of this experience:

> The most important thing I learned this week is that I can be someone powerful and that I can make a change. Renie taught me that and I hope one day I will be as amazing and loving and hold as much knowledge as her.

Sisters Starr and Hayven Elanik told us that discovering more about their Mom's ancestry was a major milestone in their young lives. Angelina Joe expressed how keen she is to use the language she is learning from both her grandmothers more.

The pragmatism that derives from a land-based livelihood is the cornerstone of Inuit teachings. Paatlirmiut Elder Donald Uluadluak (2017) observes that Inuit pedagogies teach right to the heart of the child. At the hand of a good teacher, children learn skills, fail, are encouraged, and try again; they learn kindness, responsibility, and empathy, at the same time as discovering what they are good at. Elders give youth the confidence and footing to move forward in the world and to ascertain and assert their individual and collective needs. At its best, Inuit pedagogy toggles between the highly localized practice of traditional activities and much larger social, economic, and political arenas. It is in this way that Inuvialuit leaders like Nellie Cournoyea, Gerry Kisoun, Renie Arey, Duane Smith, and the many role models that went before them, represent the Inuvialuit community at the negotiating table and on national and territorial governing bodies, and yet are equally at home cutting *muktuk* and brewing smoked tea on the ice during spring jamboree. And it is in this way that Inuvialuit and other Indigenous youth take the resilience, grounding, and knowledge from land-based skills with them when they engage with the world beyond their cultural and geographic borders.

How, then, do sharing and learning in a camp setting transfer to wider social experiences in the Inuit world? Several participants from the Imniarvik camp attended the 21st Inuit Studies Conference in Montreal together in October 2019. Mataya and Cassidy, with Mataya's Mom Melinda Gillis as chaperone, were funded through the Inuvialuit Regional Corporation, Mervin by Parks Canada, and Becky, Lisa, and Natasha through the Inuvialuit Living History project. We gave a presentation about the Imniarvik camp in a lively, youth-focused session, and met many friends and colleagues from across the North, including those whom the girls knew through their sports, school, and extra-curricular activities.

We attended keynote addresses by notable and highly inspirational Inuit scholars, leaders, and activists who spoke about representation, diplomacy, sovereignty, hunting, and other topics central to the health and well-being of circumpolar communities.

Dr. Dalee Sambo Dorough (2019), Chair of the Inuit Circumpolar Council, discussed Inuit rights in relation to threats and interests of both Arctic and non-Arctic nation-states. She put climate change, food security, access to education, and the right to self-determination at the top of her list of critical issues, positioning them as both rights and responsibilities that Inuit must demand in their pursuit of sustainable development in their communities. Her message was that development – sustainable and equitable or otherwise – cannot be imposed from outside but must come from the free and prior consent of Inuit. She effectively challenged the ongoing structural colonialism asserted by federal states and international bodies, and provided Inuit leaders and communities with tools to undermine it by pointing explicitly to language in the United Nations Declaration on the Rights of Indigenous People, which Canada endorsed in 2010 and has supported without qualification since 2016.

In her keynote address, Alethea Arnaquq-Baril (2019) discussed her choices as a filmmaker, activist, and artist to empower community voices, un-shame traditional practices, and institute Inuit protocols on film sets. She recently produced *The Grizzlies*, a film about a lacrosse team in Kugluktuk that helped to stem the tide of youth suicides in that community. Mataya and Cassidy listened particularly raptly as Ruth Kaviok (2019), the outgoing President of the National Inuit Youth Council, and a panel of Inuit youth leaders, discussed issues that are vital to their growth and entry into the adult world. The girls had the opportunity to meet Hannah Tooktoo from Kuujjuaq, whom they had closely followed on social media throughout her 2019 cycling journey across Canada to raise awareness of Inuit youth suicide. They came away from this conversation star-struck *and* full of vigour and enthusiasm about engaging with Inuit social issues. Each of the keynote presentations was followed by a long and impassioned audience engagement session, predominantly among speakers and Inuit conference participants.

Inuit across the circumpolar north were among the first Indigenous communities to recognize the power of new media to express their unique perspectives and to assert the connection and application between ancient knowledge systems and present-day challenges (Alexander et al. 2009). With their input, each of the girls' projects from the Imniarvik camp will be incorporated into the Inuvialuit Living History website using different media – graphic design, photography, digital audio, and video. Their contributions have each been featured on the project's Facebook page. In this way, the experiences of the girls and the knowledge exchanged during camp will be widely accessible and the camp's impact will extend well beyond the circle of participants as a resource and inspiration for others. Each of the girls is also moving towards new horizons of experience and knowledge. Cassidy and Mataya have secured funding to produce more issues of Nipaturuq magazine and distribute it along with the Inuvialuit magazine Tusaayaksat. Angelina is interested in pursuing a land-based career in her future as a basis to learn from and about her ancestors. Starr Elanik is continuing to develop her sewing skills, and Hayven is hoping to pursue post-secondary studies, perhaps with a focus on early childhood education. Each of them expressed the importance of their families and communities to their ability to move forward – they may move away geographically but not emotionally.

There are lessons in the way that Inuvialuit and other Indigenous communities take their land-based teachings and values out into the wider world, in both digital and analog fashion. These are lessons in humility and finding your sense of place

(Hoffmann 2020), in working for the common good (Karetak and Tester 2017), in learning "good talking and good listening" (Fienup-Riordan and Rearden 2003,102), and in choosing your obligations and priorities wisely (Hodgetts and Kelvin 2020). In the Anthropocene era of unprecedented impacts on the environment, when climate change at the poles is occurring at twice the global rate, Inuit across Inuit Nunangat have much to teach us about sovereignty, communal thinking, appreciation for the plants and animals that feed us, and the long-term well-being of these resources and their environments (see Hodgetts 2013; Karetak et al. 2017).

Time and again, Inuvialuit and other communities throughout the circumpolar north demonstrate that facing change is imperative, but not at the expense of culture, land, and desired futures. How have Inuvialuit (and other Inuit) endured as social communities for such great lengths of time? The answer is that they have always embraced incoming knowledges and technologies as tools that help them understand present circumstances and chart their ways forward. In the political and economic realms, Inuit are asserting their needs within the rights-based discourse of international legal statutes. In the arts realm, they are producing daring and original cinema and music that expresses who they are with uncompromising clarity. In the research realm, they are stating what is good for their communities and assessing what partnerships are most useful, productive, and mutualistic for the questions they want answered (ITK 2018). And despite the often ethnocentric attitudes of settlers involved in these transactions, Inuit have consistently welcomed outsiders as they were taught to do, and shared knowledge about themselves and their northern homelands. Sharing is the value at the core of all these actions and is vital to circumpolar security of all kinds – food security, border security, community security – rather than the fear-based thinking that often emanates from nation-states and media around northern issues (Shea 2019). Sharing is instrumental to a vision of the enduring and emerging north and its profoundly important cultural and geopolitical place in our world.

ACKNOWLEDGMENTS

We dedicate this paper to Walter Bennett, who passed on in the spring of 2020 and is greatly missed. We gratefully acknowledge project partners Ethel-Jean Gruben, Beverly Amos, and Lena Kotakak at Inuvialuit Cultural Resource Centre; Chuck Arnold, and Sarah Carr-Locke, Susan Irving, Rosalie Scott, and Ryan Silke at Prince of Wales Northern Heritage Centre. We thank many folks for helping to make our culture camp such a great success: Shauna Charlie and the Aklavik Community Corporation; Vivian Wirth at Moose Kerr School in Aklavik; Gene Jenks at East 3 Secondary School in Inuvik; Qikiqtaruk rangers Sam and Edward McLeod; and, helicopter pilot Connor Gould. We thank Ed Eastaugh for producing Figure 2.1 and Gerry Kisoun for providing Inuvialuktun place names. We also acknowledge the excellent body of archaeology and oral history work conducted on the North Slope by Gary Adams, Sharon Thomson, and Murielle Nagy. Melinda Gillis, Elizabeth Linn, and Bernard Monnin made our trip to the Inuit Studies conference a real delight. We thank Pamela Stern, Lisa Rankin, and an anonymous reviewer for their careful and insightful comments which improved the final character of this chapter. Finally, we acknowledge our funders: Indigenous Skills and Education Training initiative at the

Inuvialuit Regional Corporation, Social Sciences and Humanities Research Council of Canada, and Polar Continental Shelf Project, with much appreciated logistical support from Parks Canada, Inuvialuit Communications Society, and Inuvialuit Cultural Resource Centre.

NOTE

1 There are three dialects of Inuvialuktun: Kangiryuarmiutun, Sallirmiutun (formerly Siglitun), and Uummarmiutun. Kangiryuarmiutun is spoken in the Inuvialuit community of Ulukhaktok on Victoria Island and by some community members in Sachs Harbour. Kangiryuarmiut means "people of the large bay." It is a dialect of Inuinnaqtun, the language of the Kitikmeot region in Nunavut. Sallirmiutun is spoken by people in the coastal communities of Tuktoyaktok, Paulatuk, and Sachs Harbour. It is also spoken in Inuvik, where many coastal people now live. Sallirmiut means "people located closest to the shore." Uummarmiutun is spoken in the inland communities of Aklavik and Inuvik. It has its origins in the Alaskan Iñupiaq language.

REFERENCES

Adams, Gary. 1995. *Cultural History along the Firth River*. Winnipeg, MB: Parks Canada, Western Canada Service Centre, and Cultural Resource Services.

———. 2004. *Niaqulik: A Chapter in Inuvialuit Lifestyles*. Winnipeg, MB: Parks Canada Western Canada Service Centre, and Cultural Resource Services.

Alexander, Cynthia, Agar Adamson, Graham Daborn, John Houston, and Victor Tootoo. 2009. "Inuit Cyberspace: The Struggle for Access to Inuit Qaujimajatuq." *Journal of Canadian Studies/Revue d'études canadiennes* 43 (2): 220–249. https://doi.org/10.3138/jcs.43.2.220.

Alunik, Ishmael. 1998. *Call Me Ishmael: Memories of an Inuvialuk Elder*. Inuvik: Kolausok Ublaaq Enterprises.

Alunik, Ishmael, Eddie Kolausok, and David Morrison. 2003. *Across Time and Tundra: The Inuvialuit of the Western Arctic*. Vancouver, BC/Seattle, WA/Gatineau, QC: Raincoast Books/University of Washington Press/The Canadian Museum of Civilization.

Arnaquq-Baril, Alathea. 2019. "Keynote Address." Presented at the Inuit Studies Conference, 5 October, Montreal, QC.

Big-Canoe, Katie and Chantelle A. M. Richmond. 2014. "Anishinabe Youth Perceptions about Community Health: Toward Environmental Repossession." *Health and Place* 26: 127–135. https://doi.org/10.1016/j.healthplace.2013.12.013.

Bockstoce, John. 1986. *Whales, Ice, and Men: The History of Whaling in the Western Arctic*. Seattle, WA: University of Washington Press, in association with New Bedford Whaling Museum.

Burn, Christopher. 2012. *Herschel Island Qikiqtarjuk: A Natural and Cultural History of Yukon's Arctic Island*. Calgary, AB: University of Calgary Press.

Davies, Michelle Tari. 2020. "Unsettled Archaeology with a Resettled Community: Practicing Memory, Identity and Archaeology in Hebron." *Canadian Journal of Archaeology* 44: 66–82.

Dorough, Dalee Sambo. 2019. "Keynote Address." Presented at the Inuit Studies Conference, 4 October, Montreal, QC.

Fienup-Riordan, Ann, and Alice Rearden. 2003. "'Kenekngamceci Qanrutamceci (We Talk to You Because We Love You)': Yup'ik Culturalism at the Umkumiut Culture Camp." *Arctic Anthropology* 40 (2): 100–106.

Friesen, T. Max. 2009. "Event or Conjuncture? Searching for the Material Record of Inuvialuit–Euro-American Whaler Interaction on Herschel Island, Northern Yukon." *Alaska Journal of Anthropology* 7 (2): 45–61.

———. 2013. *When Worlds Collide: Hunter-Gatherer World-System Change in the 19th Century Canadian Arctic*. Tucson, AZ: Arizona University Press.

Friesen, T. Max, and Charles D. Arnold. 2008. "The Timing of the Thule Migration: New Dates from the Western Canadian Arctic." *American Antiquity* 73 (3): 527–538. https://doi-org.proxy.lib.sfu.ca/10.1017/S0002731600046850.

Fritz, Michael, Jorien Vonk, and Hugues Lantuit. 2017. "Collapsing Arctic Coastlines." *Nature Climate Change* 7: 6–7. https://doi.org/10.1038/nclimate3188.

Graburn, Nelson. 1998. "Weirs in the River of Time: Development of Historical Consciousness among Canadian Inuit." *Etudes/Inuit/Studies* 22 (1): 18–32. https://doi.org/10.1525/mua.1998.22.1.18.

Hennessy, Kate, Natasha Lyons, Stephen Loring, Charles Arnold, Mervin Joe, Albert Elias, and James Pokiak. 2013. "The Inuvialuit Living History Project: Digital Return as the Forging of Relationships between Institutions, People, and Data." *Museum Anthropology Review* 7 (1–2): 44–73.

Hodgetts, Lisa. 2013. "The Rediscovery of HMS Investigator: Archaeology, Sovereignty and the Colonial Legacy in Canada's Arctic." *Journal of Social Archaeology* 13 (1): 80–100. https://doi.org/10.1177/1469605312458735

Hodgetts, Lisa, and Laura Kelvin. 2020. "At the Heart of the Ikaahuk Archaeology Project." In *Archaeologies of the Heart*, edited by Kisha Supernant, Jane Eva Baxter, Natasha Lyons, and Sonya Atalay, 97–115. New York: Springer.

Hoffmann, Tanja. 2020. "'We Ask Only that You Come to Us with an Open Heart and an Open Mind': The Transformative Power of a Humble Archaeology of Heart." In *Archaeologies of the Heart*, edited by Kisha Supernant, Jane Eva Baxter, Natasha Lyons, and Sonya Atalay, 59–68. New York: Springer.

Inuit Tapiriit Kanatami. 2018. *National Inuit Strategy on Research*. https://www.itk.ca/national-strategy-on-research/

Karetak, Joe, Frank Tester, and Shirley Tagalik, eds. 2017. *Inuit Qaujimajatuqangit: What Inuit Have Always Known to Be True*. Blackpoint, NS: Fernwood Publishing.

Karetak, Joe, and Frank Tester. 2017. "Introduction: *Inuit Qaujimajatuqangit*, Truth and Reconciliation." In *Inuit Qaujimajatuqangit: What Inuit Have Always Known to Be True*, edited by Joe Karetak, Frank Tester and Shirley Tagalik, 1–17. Blackpoint, NS: Fernwood Publishing.

Kaviok, Ruth. 2019. "Keynote Address." Presented at the Inuit Studies Conference, 5 October, Montreal, QC.

Lantuit, Hugues, Pier Paul Overduin, Nicole Couture, Sebastian Wetterich, Felix Aré, David Atkinson, Jerry Brown, Georgy Cherkashov, Dmitry Drozdov, Donald Lawrence Forbes, Allison Graves-Gaylord, Mikhail Grigoriev, Hans-Wolfgang Hubberten, James Jordan, Torre Jorgenson, Rune Strand Ødegård, Stanislav Ogorodov, Wayne H. Pollard, Volker Rachold, Sergey Sedenko, Steve Solomon, Frits Steenhuisen, Irina Streletskaya, and Alexander Vasiliev. 2012. "The Arctic Coastal Dynamics Database: A New Classification Scheme and Statistics on Arctic Permafrost Coastlines." *Estuaries and Coasts* 35: 383–400. https://doi.org/10.1007/s12237-010-9362-6.

Lau, Jason, Cassidy Lennie-Ipana, Hayven Elanik, Mataya Gillis, and Starr Elanik. n.d. *Imniarvik Creative Project Brainstorm*. Document produced June-July 2019 in preparation for the Imniarvik Culture Camp.

Lyons, Natasha. 2007. *Quliaq tohongniaq tuunga* (Making Histories): *Towards a Critical Inuvialuit Archaeology in the Canadian Western Arctic*. PhD dissertation, University of Calgary.

———. 2009. "Inuvialuit Rising: The Evolution of Inuvialuit Identities in the Mackenzie Delta." *Alaska Journal of Anthropology* 7 (2): 63–79.

———. 2010. "The Wisdom of Elders: Inuvialuit Social Memories of Continuity and Change in the 20th Century." *Arctic Anthropology* 47 (1): 22–38. http://doi.org/10.1353/arc.0.0034.

———. 2013. *Where the Wind Blows Us: Practicing Critical Community Archaeology in the Canadian North*. Tuscon, AZ: University of Arizona Press.

———. 2014. "Localized Critical Theory as an Expression of Community Archaeology Practice: With an Example from Inuvialuit Elders of the Canadian Western Arctic." *American Antiquity* 79 (2): 183–203.

Lyons, Natasha, Kate Hennessy, Mervin Joe, Charles Arnold, Albert Elias, Stephen Loring, and James Pokiak. 2012. "The Inuvialuit Living History Project." *The SAA Archaeological Record* 12 (4): 39–42.

Lyons, Natasha, Kisha Supernant, and John R. Welch. 2019. "What Are the Prospects for an Archaeology of Heart?" *The SAA Archaeological Record* 19 (2): 6–9.

Myers-Smith, Isla, Meagan Grabowski, Haydn Thomas, Sandra Angers-Blondin, Gergana Daskalova, Anne Bjorkman, Andrew Cunliffe, Jacob Assmann, Joseph Boyle, Edward McLeod, Samuel McLeod, Ricky Joe, Paden Lennie, Deon Arey, Richard Gordon, and Cameron Eckert. 2019. "Eighteen Years of Ecological Monitoring Reveals Multiple Lines of Evidence for Tundra Vegetation Change." *Ecological Monographs* 89 (2): e01351. http://doi.org/10.1002/ecm.1351

Nagy, Murielle. 1991. *Yukon North Slope Cultural Resources Survey Transcripts*. Inuvik: Inuvialuit Social Development Program.

———. 1994. *Yukon North Slope Inuvialuit Oral History*. Occasional Papers in Yukon History No. 1. Whitehorse, YT: Yukon Tourism Heritage Branch.

Nuligak. 1966. *I, Nuligak*. Translated by Maurice Metayer. New York: Pocket Books.

Schaepe, David, Natasha Lyons, Adrienne Chan, Andy Phillips, and Kate Hennessy. 2020. "The Sq'éwlets Youth Origins Experience: Providing Tangible and Intangible Experiences of Ancestral Places and Belongings in Supporting Wellness among Indigenous Youth and Community." In *Material Connections: Exploring the Role of Objects in Learning and Wellbeing*, edited by Thomas Kador and Helen Chatterjee, 79–104. New York: Routledge.

Shea, Neil. 2019. "A Thawing Arctic is Heating Up a New Cold War." *National Geographic*, September 2019: 50–73.

Stefansson, Vijlhalmur. 1919. "Stefansson-Anderson Arctic Expedition." *Anthropological Papers of the American Museum of Natural History XIV*. New York: Trustees of American Museum of Natural History.

Tod-Tims, Cahley. 2020. "'Hungry All the Time': Contemporary Experiences of and Perspectives on Traditional Food Access in Inuvik." Unpublished MA thesis, Simon Fraser University.

Uluadluak, Donald. 2017. "Pamiqsainirmik: Training Children." In *Inuit Qaujimajatuqangit: What Inuit Have Always Known to Be True*, edited by Joe Karetak, Frank Tester and Shirley Tagalik, 147–173. Blackpoint, NS: Fernwood Publishing,

Usher, Peter. 1971a. "The Canadian Western Arctic: A Century of Change." *Anthropologica* 13: 169–183. http://doi.org/10.2307/25604848.

———. 1971b. *Fur Trade Posts of the Northwest Territories, 1870–1970*. Ottawa, ON: Northern Science Research Group, Department of Indian Affairs and Northern Development.

CHAPTER 3

TOURISM AND ARCHAEOLOGY IN NUNATSIAVUT

Lisa Rankin, Laura Kelvin, Marjorie Flowers, and Charlotte Wolfrey

INTRODUCTION

Inuit Nunangat has long captured the imagination of southern travelers eager to experience the ice-covered landscapes, iconic wildlife, European colonial history, and Indigenous people (Hall and Saarinen 2010). As northern sea ice declines, cruise ships have easier access to routes and isolated Inuit communities, resulting in a tourism boom in northern Canada. This boom is partially fueled by "extinction tourism," or "last chance tourism," where tourists are drawn to see and experience landscapes, Indigenous cultures, and species threatened by climate change before they are gone (Fugmann 2012; Stephen 2018). These tourism tropes, developed by southern marketers without input from Inuit, create social, cultural, and environmental concerns for destination communities in northern Canada (Stephen 2018) because they limit the ways Inuit can present their history, identity, and homeland to visitors. Without the power to control representation, Inuit culture is exoticized and subject to negative stereotypes. Any economic benefits "last chance" tourism brings to communities has limited potential to counter this marginalization. However, tourism is capable of empowering Inuit communities when it is Inuit-led. Sustainable Indigenous tourism prioritizes locally conceived, culturally driven tourist experiences which allow communities to control their representation and explain their culture and history to tourists in their own voices (Bunten and Graburn 2018, 3, 21; Tate-Libby 2013, 192). Used this way, tourism can be a powerful tool for building cultural understanding between host communities and visitors (Bunten and Graburn 2018, 3), while developing local economies. This emergent tourism movement can also support long-term cultural goals by sustaining traditional knowledge, promoting local priorities, and "honour[ing] the past while investing in the future" (Bunten and Graburn 2018, 21; Hamilton 2013). Indigenous tourism movements are now taking hold in Inuit Nunangat and formed part of the ambitious tourism strategy 2014–2020 planning document developed by the Nunatsiavut Government, an Inuit self-government within Newfoundland and Labrador, Canada.

The Nunatsiavut Government, established in 2005, was the result of the most comprehensive Indigenous land claim achieved to date in Canada. The Inuit government maintains authority over health, education, culture, language, justice, and community matters with the power to enact its own policies and laws. Since its formation, this autonomous government has made significant investment in community-based tourism development (Fugmann 2012; Nunatsiavut Government 2017). Rather than develop a blanket tourism strategy for the territory, the Nunatsiavut Government recognized that the five towns within Nunatsiavut (Rigolet, Postville, Makkovik, Hopedale, and Nain) have unique histories and local cultures (Figure 3.1). Therefore, when developing their 2014–2020 tourism strategy, each community was able to develop goals specific to local context and focus on developing a local visitor economy that promoted "everything that makes a place special, distinctive, and capable of

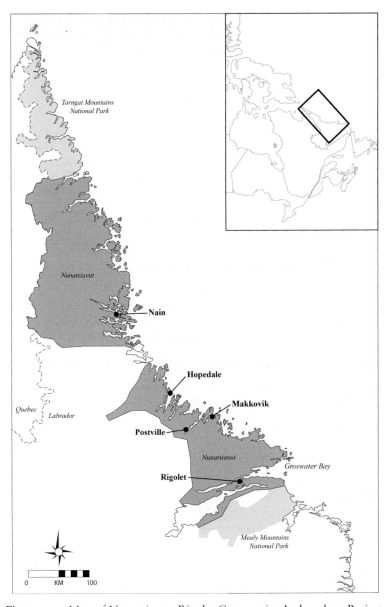

Figure 3.1 Map of Nunatsiavut. Rigolet Community Archaeology Project.

engendering pride and interest in a place worth visiting" (Nunatsiavut Government 2017, 2). At its core, the strategy prioritizes the celebration of Labrador Inuit culture and history.

Two communities, Rigolet and Hopedale, identified the development of local archaeological sites as essential to their tourism plans, citing an interest in archaeology and cultural history among the expedition cruise passengers who were beginning to arrive in their communities each summer, as well as other tourists making short community visits en route to or from the two national parks (Torngat Mountains National Park [Torngait KakKasuangita SilakKijapvinga] in the north and Mealy Mountains National Park [Akami–Uapishk^U–KakKasuak] in the south) abutting Nunatsiavut lands (Nunatsiavut Government 2008; 2014) (see Figure 3.1). These two communities developed their archaeological projects with the assistance of a formal research partnership between Memorial University of Newfoundland and Labrador and the Nunatsiavut Government, known as Tradition and Transition Among the Labrador Inuit.[1] In this chapter, we present two cases drawn from our experience in Rigolet and Hopedale to explore how community-based archaeology can support local tourism objectives. These are the excavation of the Double Mer Point site near Rigolet, and the search for vestiges of the Agvituk site located in Hopedale. We highlight the need for flexible research methodologies and goals that respect local community interests and needs as well as their distinct histories.

THE RISE OF INDIGENOUS TOURISM

Since the early 19th century, the rugged landscape, animals, and Inuit communities of northern Labrador have attracted visitors from across the world. In Labrador, as elsewhere, the earliest "tourists" were engaged in colonial exploration. Thus, right from the beginning, tourism in Labrador was a colonial enterprise, embodying "an institutionalized web of power relationships" (Bresner 2010, 10). This emergent tourism allowed some Labrador Inuit to assert their agency and benefit from encounters with visitors by working as guides and by selling locally made goods. However, as a whole, Inuit had no substantial control of early tourism in Labrador, so it did not benefit Inuit communities, and in many instances has had lasting negative effects. Published travel accounts written by these early tourists created and perpetuated stereotypes of the Inuit. Furthermore, the collecting of Inuit material culture and human remains as souvenirs without Inuit consent desecrated graves and separated Inuit from parts of their history.

Early tourism in Labrador was both different from, and similar to, the formalized tourism industry we know today. The earliest "tourists" were often part of scientific expeditions, medical and religious missions, or those engaged in economic pursuits such as trade and resource extraction. Visitors were mainly educated, white men, who visited mission communities and local historic (archaeological) sites, collected souvenirs, and engaged in hunting and fishing. Over time, excursions to Labrador became more formalized, particularly after a push from the Newfoundland Government during the late 1800s to diversify the colonial economy by focusing on tourism (Higgins 2015). Cities in that era were loud, crowded, and polluted, and feelings of alienation and depression were common among city dwellers. Many middle-class, educated businessmen and professionals believed that reconnecting with nature would help alleviate these feelings (Higgins, 2015). This "back to nature" movement brought tourists to Newfoundland and Labrador from other parts of North America and from Europe to experience the region's wilderness. Americans were particularly interested in Labrador because it represented the wildness they saw disappearing from their own frontier (O'Flaherty 1979). Inuit culture and history were also of interest to early tourists. The notion of the "vanishing Indian" that predicted the inevitable and rapid extinction of Indigenous cultures in North America was widespread, and well-heeled tourists rushed to see Indigenous peoples before they disappeared (Bresner 2010; Plane, 2010; Raibmon 2005). Many visitors to Labrador wrote about their encounters with local Inuit communities. Some traded for or purchased Inuit-made crafts, and some stole material culture or even human remains from archaeological sites as keepsakes, souvenirs, or scientific specimens.

Although journals, travelogues, and scientific publications included information about Inuit lives and cultures, many of the writers' mentalities were shaped by colonial ideologies. Most visitors left Labrador with the same romanticized or racist attitudes and ill-informed understandings of Inuit culture that they had when they arrived. In turn, their views shaped the portrayal of Inuit culture to the rest of the world. American landscape painter William Bradford offers an apt example. During the 1860s, Bradford organized a voyage to Labrador to photograph and paint icebergs (Figure 3.2). To fund his expedition, he invited 12 paying passengers, who mainly took part in hunting and fishing activities during the voyage. David Atwood Wasson was a passenger whose role was to generate publicity for Bradford's work. He published a series of articles, "Icebergs and Esquimaux," depicting the voyage, where he described the Inuit he encountered as an evolutionary dead end. These publications reached influential national and international audiences and contributed to the rise of Social Darwinism (Little 2016). The misinformation and stereotypes spread by early tourists like Wasson continue to negatively impact the way Inuit are portrayed in mainstream media today (Bresner 2010; Steckley 2009).

Many early visitors took part in collecting Inuit material culture as personal souvenirs or scientific specimens to donate to museum collections, as a way to preserve remnants of what they perceived to be the dying Inuit culture (Bird 1945; MacGregor 1910, 99). This collecting often involved purchasing or trading for Inuit handmade goods, but it also involved collecting cultural objects from archaeological contexts, and sometimes even human remains or objects from burials. In most cases, collecting was a side interest for people traveling through Labrador. For example, Eliot Curwen came to the coast of Labrador in 1893 to work as a medical missionary and collected Inuit material culture which he donated to the British Museum in London (Rompkey 1996), and William MacGregor (MacGregor 1910), the colonial governor of Newfoundland from 1904–1909, conducted a scientific research trip in Labrador in 1905 and collected an abundance of Inuit material culture from old village sites and burials, which he later donated to the Marischal Museum in Aberdeen, Scotland (Reid 1912). However, there is at least one man who traveled to Labrador to specifically take part in what can be considered archaeological tourism. American archaeologist Junius Bird came to the coast of Labrador in 1934 with his wife Peggy for their honeymoon. During this trip, they carried out extensive archaeological research along the northern coast of Labrador, including the excavation of nine of the 20 sod house ruins at Agvituk (Bird 1945). The artifacts from these

Figure 3.2 "Iceberg in the Atlantic Ocean, off the Coast of Labrador" by photographer William H. Pierce, 1864. Bradford hired Pierce to work as a photographer for his voyage to paint icebergs along the coast of Labrador during the 1860s. Library of Congress item 2012645577.

excavations are now housed at the American Museum of Natural History in New York. In each of these cases, collecting was motivated by a desire to secure evidence of "pure Eskimo culture" (Bird 1945), which they believed was being destroyed by contact with Europeans.

Early tourism in Labrador was induced by colonial expansion and flourished on colonial rhetoric. "Extinction tourism" compelled white, wealthy, educated visitors like Wasson, Curwen, MacGregor, and Bird to come to Labrador to witness a dying culture, and collect information about and relics of "an evolutionary dead end" for southern consumption. Their publications based on their travels perpetuated these false concepts among people in the south, and their archaeological collecting desecrated graves, removed Inuit material culture without community consent, and effectively separated Inuit from parts of their history.

Today, tourists are attracted to Labrador for many of the same reasons as the colonial explorers and scientists. Key tourist activities in Nunatsiavut still include outdoor exploring and cultural/Indigenous interactions. According to the 2011 Labrador Travel Survey, 76 percent of non-resident tourists had a university or post-graduate degree, and many had household incomes of $100,000 or more (MQO Research 2012). As in the past, many contemporary tourists are taking part in a form of "extinction tourism," only now they are drawn to see northern landscapes, animals, and cultures that are being impacted by climate change before they disappear (Stephen 2018). Despite these similarities, the experiences that tourists have and the long-term outcomes of tourism in Nunatsiavut are drastically different, in large part because the Inuit residents are choosing how and where they want to present their history and their culture.

Indigenous tourism has been broadly defined as tourism that involves Indigenous people "in the provision of the attraction, either through control and/or by having their culture serve as the essence of the attraction" (Hinch and Butler 1996, 9). But Indigenous tourism can be so much more than that. As Indigenous communities take back control of their lands, they are also indigenizing the tourist industry, seeing it as one way to empower their communities. By developing their own tourism strategies, they are able to capitalize economically, socially, and culturally, while also protecting their environment and resources (Colton 2005). Indigenous tourism has the potential to nurture economic independence, which then helps to advance self-determination (Hinch and Butler 1996). Tourism can foster economic diversification through the creation of new jobs. For example, it can support land-based economies such as guiding, and solidify traditional activities such as sewing, story-telling, and singing through craft sales and performance (Notzke 1999), thereby preserving traditional knowledge and strengthening Indigenous cultures (Hinch 1995). Indigenous-led tourism can also help protect Indigenous lands, resources, and culturally important sites including archaeological sites, by managing the types of interactions tourists have with them. Indigenous-led tourism in which communities are able to control their own history and representation is also a tool for generating cross-cultural understanding that can advance reconciliation between Indigenous and non-Indigenous communities (Maureira and Stenbacka 2015).

Indigenous tourism is not perfect and the commodification of culture for outsiders presents abundant challenges. Small Indigenous communities may be overwhelmed by the arrival of large numbers of tourists, like those visiting Inuit villages from cruise ships, and may feel objectified by the incessant picture-taking and voyeuristic exploration of their houses and businesses (Graburn 2018). Indigenous communities may also feel pressure to provide visitors with activities that support tourist expectations for encounters with ancient, authentic cultures, indirectly reinforcing pre-existing stereotypes that portray their cultures as static (Beck et al. 2005, 238; Bunten 2018). Nevertheless, Nunatsiavummiut have decided that the opportunities provided by tourism to nurture traditional knowledge and practices, increase well-being and pride in their communities, and stimulate local economies, outweigh the risks. To that end, the Nunatsiavut Government has engaged in multi-year planning strategies to develop Indigenous tourism and take ownership of their representation to visitors.

THE NUNATSIAVUT TOURISM STRATEGY

Following the settlement of their land claim, the Nunatsiavut Government was quick to prioritize tourism, establishing the Department of Culture, Recreation, and Tourism as one of its original government ministries. By 2008, this department released its first tourism strategy which was used to identify tourist markets, create an inventory of extant visitor resources and experiences throughout Nunatsiavut, and identify ways to market and measure the impact of the tourism industry locally (Nunatsiavut Government 2008). Unlike earlier forms of tourism which disenfranchised Inuit from economic benefits, as well as their history, identity, and way of life, the Nunatsiavut Government strategy put Nunatsiavummiut-led tourism front and center to benefit the people and economy of the region (Nunatsiavut Government 2008, 3). Two of the most successful outcomes of this strategy include the development of culturally immersive tourism programming alongside Inuit youth and Elders at the Torngat Mountain National Park basecamp, and the Inuit care-taker program established at the Hebron National Historic site which allows Hebron-descended families to reconnect with the homeland while welcoming and interacting with visitors, and caring for abandoned community buildings (Fugmann 2012, 20; Nunatsiavut Government 2008, 8–28).

In 2014 a new strategic plan, the 2014–2020 tourism strategy, *Sharing Our Story, Our People, Our Land*, outlined new goals and values and called on each of the five Nunatsiavut communities to develop plans to expand tourism based on their unique histories (Nunatsiavut Government 2014). The strategy articulated five values: (1) to respect and honor the Inuit, their stories, knowledge, language, history, and heritage; (2) to share stories with children, grandchildren, and visitors so that they may learn the ways of the past as a foundation for building the future; (3) to foster meaningful connections with Inuit and special places through engaging visitors in authentic, memorable experiences that touch the hearts and minds; (4) to innovate, co-create, and collaborate in building a responsible, sustainable tourism industry through profitable partnerships with those who share our interests and values; and, (5) to earn trust through honest, transparent communication with visitors, hosts, host communities and partners (Nunatsiavut Government 2014, 1). This document makes it clear that tourism should both educate visitors on the Inuit way of life and celebrate Inuit culture by providing mechanisms for both economic development and cultural sustainability. Nunatsiavummiut would therefore be empowered to tell the stories they wanted both Inuit and visitors to learn.[2]

The communities of Rigolet and Hopedale each identified archaeological sites as foundational tourism projects (Nunatsiavut Government 2014, 16), believing that archaeology had the potential to educate tourists about their lengthy history while simultaneously celebrating the traditional Inuit knowledge still part of contemporary Inuit life. Each community established community-based archaeological programs in partnership with Memorial University designed to help them meet their archaeo-tourism goals.

COMMUNITY-BASED ARCHAEOLOGY

Archaeology is the study of the past drawn from the remains of structures, and the discarded material and organic detritus of daily life. It is also a western science with its own colonial history which often alienated Indigenous people by neglecting to consult with them prior to excavation, by removing Indigenous material culture and human remains without Indigenous permission, and by overlooking the contributions

Indigenous knowledge can make to interpreting and understanding the past (Freisen, this volume; Rowley 2002; Weetaluktuk 1978). This is changing as more archaeologists adopt community-based approaches to research. Community-based archaeologists explicitly acknowledge their authoritative and ethnocentric biases and work to build strong collaborative relationships with Indigenous communities with the goals of making archaeological research inclusive, engaged, ethical, and socially responsible to local communities. Importantly, this approach requires that space is created within the discipline for Indigenous voices that were previously marginalized, embracing Inuit agency to interpret and narrate their own history. In contrast to archaeology, Inuit make sense of their past through traditional oral histories, through memory, and through experiential connections to traditional places and activities that permeate daily lives such as sewing, fishing, and hunting (Kelvin 2017). Community archaeology seeks to blend these traditional ways of knowing and understanding history with archaeological accounts to create a much more coherent narrative of the past that is more recognizable and personal to those whose history is being told.

Tourism provides a significant opportunity for Inuit communities and archaeologists to work together. The inclusion of archaeological research brings technical and interpretive skills to culture-tourism programming, helping Inuit to educate visitors about their lengthy and dynamic history by providing observable connections between contemporary Inuit culture and its ancient history, and promoting the intimate relationship between Inuit and the land they inhabit. These benefits might also extend to local Inuit audiences, helping them to expand and preserve traditional knowledge for future generations, by recording and archiving data. Archaeologists also bring the potential for providing local jobs and training depending on what the community has requested. The involvement and requirements of different communities can be understood as a spectrum, where the degree of participation depends on the desires and capacity of the community with whom archaeologists are collaborating (Atalay 2012; Colwell-Chanthaphonh and Ferguson 2008). Furthermore, there is no standard set of guidelines for undertaking this type of research as every community is unique and will have its own goals for partnerships and for the tourist programming it envisions (Atalay 2008; Colwell-Chanthaphon et al. 2010). However, all community-based research partnerships aim to respect and apply Indigenous experience and epistemologies to their working practices and interpretive frameworks, and to prioritize community goals above traditional archaeological research pursuits (Atalay 2008).

The success of any community-based project, whether linked to tourism or not, is dependent on developing equitable partnerships to co-create research agendas that are either mutually acceptable or driven directly by the concerns and requests of the community. To build these partnerships it is essential that archaeologists and Indigenous communities learn about one another. The Nunatsiavut communities of Rigolet and Hopedale, for example, were in need of archaeological research skills to help develop their emergent tourist economy, but initially had limited understanding of archaeological practice. Conversely, the archaeologists approached to do this work had not previously worked in these communities and were, therefore, unfamiliar with their needs, politics, and local culture. As will be discussed below, during the process of relationship-building the focus of the work which was initially requested may shift.

Our mutual starting point was the Tradition and Transition Among the Labrador Inuit research partnership between Memorial University and the Nunatsiavut Government. The partnership was created to respond to Nunatsiavummiut requests for research and to enable them to implement a number of Inuit-driven policies such as the Nunatsiavut Government's 2014–2020 tourism strategy and to develop in-house legislation governing archaeological sites. The Nunatsiavut Government identified academic assistance with research skills, training for youth and middle generations, as well as creating a system of research-data archiving as priorities. In turn, students and faculty from Memorial University would be allowed to reinvigorate social sciences and humanities research in northern Labrador, by publishing extant data, creating new academic content, and training a new generation of community-minded scholars. Two key archaeological projects were initiated by communities of Rigolet and Hopedale to help implement the goals of the Nunatsiavut Tourism Strategy: the Double Mer Point excavations and the Agvituk Archaeology Project. To meet community needs, these projects required much more than simply excavating archaeological sites. Taking a community-based approach to archaeology, the aim for these projects was to assist these communities to undertake research they considered particularly significant and beneficial to their communities, while helping to build their fledgling tourism industry. These initiatives were shaped by the unique history of each community and resulted in two very distinct projects, shaped by similar goals.

DEVELOPING THE DOUBLE MER POINT SITE FOR TOURISM

In 2013 Lisa Rankin and her students were invited into the community of Rigolet by Charlotte Wolfrey, the *AngajukKâk* of the Rigolet Inuit Community Government, which serves a village of approximately 250 people. Ms. Wolfrey asked if Rankin's archaeology team had any interest in excavating the Double Mer Point site, a late 18th-century Inuit winter village, located on the outskirts of Rigolet that had been selected by the community for reconstruction and interpretation and was part of a small suite of activities being developed for tourists (Nunatsiavut Government 2014). Tourism was forecast to increase in the Rigolet area, particularly among day-trippers. Already, the coastal ferry, which connects all Nunatsiavut villages during the summer months, stopped in Rigolet for several hours en route north or south from Goose Bay, bringing local, national, and international travelers into the community for brief visits. Rigolet's tourism strategy was designed to entice this population with nearby activities. Furthermore, expedition cruise ships were increasing their activity along the Labrador coast, and the development of Mealy Mountains National Park was about to be announced. The national park was particularly significant to Rigolet's tourism development as it would be co-managed by Nunatsiavut, the Innu Nation, and NunatuKavut, and it was expected that Rigolet would become a gateway community for tourists accessing the park's backcountry. Rigolet's tourism plan anticipated an increase in short-stay visitors – people spending a few hours waiting for a ferry to depart, while on anchor during a cruise, or perhaps staying overnight while waiting to embark on a wilderness adventure. They hoped to develop tourist activities to both celebrate Inuit culture and contribute to the local economy.

The tourism development began with the construction of a nine-kilometer coastal boardwalk terminating at the Double Mer Point archaeological site. Tourists could easily pass several hours along the boardwalk, learning about regional Inuit history and culture. In order to reconstruct the archaeological site for public consumption, the Nunatsiavut Government's archaeology office required that the site undergo full remediation so as not to lose any significant historical data in the process of development – a costly scenario if the town were to hire a private company. Instead, they turned to the Tradition and Transition research partnership for assistance. The partnership between the Nunatsiavut Government and Memorial University pairs academic researchers with specific skills, like archaeology, with communities in need of assistance to accomplish their goals. The partnership grant was also able to cover the costs of excavation – although the process would take several years longer than private industry. During five summers between 2014 and 2019, the Rigolet Inuit Community Government worked in partnership with Rankin and her students, using the excavation to bring as many benefits to Rigolet and its developing tourism industry as possible. Almost immediately, the excavation became a destination for tourists. The Rigolet Inuit Community Government and local heritage committee allowed the excavations to form the basis of several graduate student theses so that the site was well-studied, but this information was fed directly back into the community through multiple meetings to help develop locally-driven interpretive narratives about the daily lives of site occupants. For example, residents aided in the interpretation of archaeological objects, defining their use and ongoing connection to local Inuit culture. They also outlined their ongoing use of the Double Mer area for fishing and sealing. These details were then developed for tourism purposes through the manufacture of interpretive panels to be placed along the boardwalk. Further panels are currently planned for other important sites in the area. This information was also accessible to locals to be used in community education programming, as well as providing a conduit for knowledge exchanges between Elders and youth.

Local Inuit students worked alongside university students, providing the former with income, training, and the skills to interpret the site to visitors. Additionally, a two-part Aboriginal Peoples Television Network series called "Wild Archaeology" highlighted not only the site, but the role the excavations played in the community. The broadcast brought many inquiries about the community from across Canada and was much enjoyed in Rigolet as well. Perhaps the most significant, if unexpected, outcome, was the way that the excavation brought the community together. The vast majority of lab work associated with the excavation took place at the town's museum, known as the Netloft, run by the Rigolet Heritage Society. Initially, the lab, which is located by the ferry dock, was opened daily in order to provide visitors to the community with a destination. But the archaeology lab quickly became a hub of activity for community members of all ages who stopped by each day to review new finds, help the archaeologists understand how artifacts were used, and tell stories about life on the land (Figure 3.3). The archaeological materials themselves, therefore, became a conduit for knowledge exchange between archaeologists and Inuit and among generations of Rigolet Inuit.

Not everything has worked perfectly. The primary disappointment concerned the removal of artifacts from the community at the end of each season which was done for conservation and long-term, climate-controlled storage, the specifics of which are mandated by the Nunatsiavut Government. Since there was no appropriate long-term storage facility in Nunatsiavut, the artifacts had to be taken to St. John's, removing

Figure 3.3   Community gathering at the Netloft. Photo: Rigolet Community Archaelogy Project.

them from the context in which they best served the community. As a necessary stop-gap, a program of 3D-printed replica artifacts selected by the community for exhibit in the Netloft museum has been initiated, as well as significant social media outreach, largely through the Facebook page, "Rigolet Community Archaeology," which documents not only the excavations, laboratory, and conservation work, but also creates a digital archive of finds until the material can be returned to a repository in Nunatsiavut. These are not the best solutions, but they are fulfilling an important role until artifacts can be stored in Nunatsiavut.

The lengthy archaeological process has allowed Rigolet to evaluate its tourism strategy, reflect on its success, and concentrate on other components of its tourism strategy such as the daily opening of a craft shop located beside the Netloft museum, where local craftspeople often gather to work. The inclusion of contemporary cultural practices as part of its tourism strategy is incredibly important as it adds balance to the narrative provided by the archaeological work. By experiencing both the archaeological and contemporary Inuit culture side by side, tourists are educated about the long-term connections of Inuit people to the region. Without the inclusion of contemporary culture, tourists may be left feeling that Inuit culture is something that happened in the past, rather than something that is very much alive and vibrant today.

DEVELOPING AGVITUK FOR TOURISM

In 2017, based on the success of the Double Mer Point Project, the Inuit Community Government of Hopedale decided to develop an archaeology program in its community – also in association with its tourism strategy. Marjorie Flowers, the *AngajukKâk* of the Hopedale Inuit Community Government, invited Rankin and Kelvin to undertake the work. Hopedale's approach to its tourism strategy was distinct from Rigolet's. Hopedale was already well-known for the beautiful historic structures associated with the Moravian mission station, originally constructed in the late 18th century (Figure 3.4). In fact, it was the Hopedale Mission National Historic Site, which already drew tourists each year, that was initially identified as an archaeological priority in the Nunatsiavut Tourism Strategy. To that end, some archaeological work had been undertaken by Parks Canada at the Provisions House, the oldest standing building at the Moravian Mission Station, but by 2017, Hopedalimiut made the decision to expand on this initial priority and include archaeological research concerning the pre-Moravian Inuit history of their community. The ultimate goal was to gather information required for the community to be considered for a World Heritage designation from UNESCO. Having learned about the archaeological work underway in Rigolet, Hopedale residents decided it was important to engage local youth with archaeology in ways that would facilitate knowledge exchange with Elders. The community of Hopedale, therefore, initiated the Agvituk Archaeology Project to generate tourism activity, but also to ensure the transfer of traditional knowledge and strengthen connections between generations.

The UNESCO Heritage Site application focuses on the three periods of Hopedale's history. The first is the initial Inuit occupation, known as Agvituk, starting from the 16th century; the second is the Moravian mission era and associated Inuit village; and the third is the contemporary role of Hopedale as the legislative capital of Nunatsiavut. Agvituk, the focus of the archaeology project, was a large Inuit whaling site that was important in the Inuit-European coastal trade network during the 16th to 18th centuries (Arendt 2013; Bird 1945). The site is located within the current boundaries of the Hamlet of Hopedale and remains culturally important to the

Figure 3.4 Expedition cruise visitors touring Hopedale. Photo: Agvituk Archaeology Project.

community. However, modern homes, road construction, and water and sewer work have all impacted Agvituk, and much of the site has unfortunately been destroyed. The original goal was to identify areas within the present community that contain intact remnants of the site in order to study and protect them, and to build tourism activities in these locations.

The archaeological search for Agvituk has not been straightforward. Since the late 19th century, Agvituk has been subject to many archaeological investigations, most notably the excavation of nine of the 20 house ruins led by Junius Bird in the 1930s. Although several intact midden areas have been located by Memorial University's archaeological team, structural remains have been elusive. However, by comparing Junius Bird's original site map and excavation photos, with recent Google Earth images of modern Hopedale the archaeologists believe that they have located three large relatively unexcavated sod houses, currently under rubble that was laid down during road construction. The town has agreed to remove the rubble, but as a small community with many pressing projects on the go, they have been unable to do so yet. The archaeology team will excavate these houses only when the town is ready. In the meantime, the archaeologists have developed a strategy that devotes more time to recording and interpreting the many smaller Inuit settlements surrounding Hopedale in order to demonstrate the significance of the entire bay as an Inuit whaling center for UNESCO purposes. We have also focused on documenting artifacts recovered from Agvituk and surrounding sites that are now housed in museums in the south, and elsewhere in the world, and preparing a digital archive to be kept in the community that can be used as a resource to inform tourism programing and support the application to UNESCO.

During the research in Hopedale, archaeologists put out invitations for community members to visit the excavations and the lab in hopes of facilitating community engagement and knowledge exchange. Although there were some community visitors, the archaeological work did not attract the same level of engagement seen in Rigolet. This may stem from the fact that Hopedale is significantly larger than Rigolet, but it may also reflect the location of the lab in the historic Moravian buildings, which are considered to be haunted by many locals. To enhance community participation, and to bridge the community-perceived knowledge gap between Elders and youth, the project turned instead to social media, film, and interviews. To this end, the archaeologists have been working with Hopedale youth to interview community Elders about Agvituk, other nearby sites, and traditional knowledges. Hopedalimiut continued to prioritize youth involvement in their tourism planning even as the Agvituk Archaeology Project shifted focus, hoping the experience would help connect youth to their culture. Ensuring cultural continuity and the well-being of the youth who may feel physically, emotionally, and socially disconnected from their heritage (Kelvin et al. 2020), continues to be an essential component of Hopedale's tourism development.

Archaeologists helped the Hopedale youth develop interview skills and turn aspects of their interviews into short films about different elements of cultural life, archaeology, and the history of Hopedale and the surrounding area. The videos are available on our YouTube channel (https://www.youtube.com/channel/UCE7rjhJFWhVb nHqXC7ueqbA), shared on our Facebook page (Agvituk Archaeology Project), and are now accessible on the new Nunatsiavut Stories website (http://nunatsiavutstories

.ca/stories/avertok-archaeology-project/) developed by the Nunatsiavut Department of Culture, Recreation and Tourism. The videos have been well received by both the community and the students who worked on them. Various community members stated that they were not only happy to learn something from the videos, but also happy to have a chance to be taught by the students and see what the archaeologists have been working on. Many of the students who worked on the videos have stated that they were surprised to learn that the community members they interviewed knew so much, and they now felt more comfortable going to them in the future if they had a question about their culture or past. This much-loved series of videos facilitated knowledge exchange between youth and Elders, celebrated tradition, and provided a solid base for ongoing archaeological exploration.

The Agvituk Archaeology Project highlights the holistic approach of Indigenous tourism. The project not only helps to generate tourism programming that could lead to economic benefits for the community, but it also works to promote knowledge transmission between Elders and youth to help ensure cultural continuity and community well-being. The flexible nature of community-based approaches to archaeology helped the project adapt and evolve to the changing needs of the Hopedale community.

DISCUSSION/CONCLUSIONS

Self-governance has enabled the people of Nunatsiavut to take control of their own tourism industry. In developing an Inuit-centered Indigenous tourism strategy, Nunatsiavummiut seek to replace colonial models of tourism with self-determined visitor engagement that focuses on their vibrant culture and substantial history. In this manner, traditional knowledge acts as a foundation for building an economically and culturally sustainable future for their communities, and can be used as a tool for building cross-cultural understandings that can help move us towards creating strong, positive relationships between Nunatsiavummiut and the rest of the world.

The Nunatsiavut communities of Rigolet and Hopedale chose to use local archaeological histories to tell stories that they wanted to share with tourists. With limited resources, a federally awarded partnership grant provided a means for these communities to collaborate with researchers with shared interests and values to achieve their goals. Given the colonial history of archaeology, it was important to pursue this partnership in respectful and culturally appropriate ways. The result was two distinct community-based archaeology projects. The Rigolet project was the first to be developed. This tiny community requested excavation of a specific site that could be used to interpret the Inuit past to tourists. The community engagement and training components were not part of the initial request, but followed organically from the increasing local interest in the Double Mer Point site and the developing pride that was enabled by daily gatherings at the community lab. Hopedale initially envisioned a similar project, but local conditions obscured the archaeological remains, and ambiguous feelings about the Moravian mission meant that the Rigolet project could not be directly replicated. Furthermore, Hopedale placed a much greater initial emphasis on using the project for knowledge transfer between youth and Elders. While ultimately successful, the approach taken relied much more on diversifying our approach to archaeological research by looking beyond survey and excavation to fully engage community members and satisfy community requests. This project was also dependent on building trust with community youth, which required learning about their social context and why it was so important to the community that the project helped foster their connections with Elders (Inuit Tapiriit Kanatami 2016). To help empower youth, we worked to incorporate strength-based approaches that encompassed education, employment, and healing (Kelvin et al. 2020).

Thus, the process of developing a community-based research agenda revolved around building personal relationships between archaeologists and community members, and researchers needed to be flexible and prepared for changes as they developed the trust of the community. This is an ongoing process meant to be sustained over the long term, and capable of responding to new community needs over time. But above all, these projects were about creating respectful and helpful relationships to enable communities to reach their tourism goals. It should be pointed out here that diversity also exists within each community, and community members have different understandings of the past and opinions of archaeology and how objects from the past should be approached and cared for. Part of undertaking this research necessitated that we be knowledgeable and respectful of other understandings and opinions.

Finally, it is important to note that the incorporation of archaeo-tourism initiatives into the Rigolet and Hopedale Indigenous tourism strategy was ultimately successful because it linked the past and the present. The work undertaken provided opportunities for knowledge exchange between generations, and for celebrating the long-term continuity of Inuit culture, but it also attempted to replicate this experience for tourists who visit both the archaeological sites and contemporary communities. It is important that the tourist experience does not stop with the archaeological site, in order to disabuse visitors of the belief that Inuit culture is vanishing. Nunatsiavummiut-led tourism can show visitors there is long-term cultural continuity between the past and the present, that Inuit culture has flourished because of its ability to adapt to challenges, and that Inuit have adapted their culture to navigate and thrive in a modern world. However, it is unfair and unrealistic to expect Inuit communities to take on the burden of educating visitors alone. Tourists continue to be influenced by colonial narratives that mediate their experiences as consumers. Combating colonial rhetoric is exhausting and can be harmful to Indigenous people working in the tourism industry (Bresner 2010, 10). Through collaborative projects that support Indigenous tourism, others can help take on some of this burden and assist in dismantling colonial constructs.

ACKNOWLEDGMENTS

The authors would like to acknowledge the invaluable participation of students from Rigolet, Hopedale, and Memorial University whose work has helped to make these projects a success, as well as the community members whose interest and logistical support has sustained the archaeological work over several seasons – especially late Elders Andrea Flowers, Sandra Flowers, and Richard Rich without whom these projects would not have been possible. The Inuit community governments of Rigolet and Hopedale, the Rigolet Heritage Society, and Agvituk Sivumuak in Hopedale have all provided invaluable support to the community archaeology teams. Thanks must also be given to SSHRC, NSTP, the JR Smallwood Foundation, ISER, Newfoundland

and Labrador Provincial Archaeology Office, Nunatsiavut Government Language, Culture, and Tourism Department, Inuit Pathways, and Young Canada Works in Heritage for the financial support that enabled these projects.

NOTES

1. Tradition and Transition Among the Labrador Inuit/PiusituKaujuit Asianguvalliajuilla is a federally funded SSHRC Partnership (2015–2022) between the Nunatsiavut Government and Memorial University (MUN). Lisa Rankin is the principal investigator representing MUN and director of the archaeological research in the communities of Rigolet (the Rigolet Community Archaeology Project) and Hopedale (the Agvituk Archaeology Project). Laura Kelvin was a SSHRC post-doctoral fellow affiliated with the T&T Research Partnership and leader of the Agvituk Digital Archive Project in Hopedale which uses archaeology to support knowledge transfer between youth and Elders. Marjorie Flowers is the *AngajukKâk* of the Hopedale Inuit Community Government responsible for initiating the Agvituk Archaeology Project and Charlotte Wolfrey is the *AngajukKâk* of the Rigolet Inuit Community Government responsible for initiating the Double Mer Point Archaeology Project.
2. On 26 February 2020 the Newfoundland-Labrador Indigenous Tourism Association launched their *5-Year Strategy 2019–2024*. Unfortunately, the ensuing COVID-19 pandemic prevented discussion concerning the relationship of this new document to further partnership work in Nunatsiavut.

REFERENCES

Atalay, Soya. 2008. "Multivocality and Indigenous Archaeologies." In *Evaluating Multiple Narratives: Beyond Nationalist, Colonialist, and Imperialist Archaeologies*, edited by Junko Habu, Clare Fawcett, and John M. Matsunaga, 29–45. New York: Springer Press.

———. 2012. *Community-Based Archaeology: Research with, by and for Indigenous and Local Communities*. Berkeley, CA: University of California Press.

Arendt, Beatrix. 2013. "The Return to Hopedale: Excavations at Anniowaktook Island, Hopedale, Labrador." *Canadian Journal of Archaeology*, 37: 302–330.

Beck, Wendy Elizabeth, Dee Murphy, Cheryl Perkins, Tony Perkins, Anita Jane Smith, and Margaret Jean Somerville. 2005. "Aboriginal Ecotourism and Archaeology in Coastal NSW, Australia: Yarrawarra Place Stories Project." In *Indigenous Archaeologies: Decolonizing Theory and Practice*, edited by Claire Smith and H. Martin Wobst, 226–241. New York: Routledge.

Bird, Junius Bouton. 1945. "Archaeology of the Hopedale Area, Labrador." *Anthropological Papers of the American Museum of Natural History* 39 (2): 121–190.

Bradford, William, and William H. Pierce (photographer). 1864. *Iceberg in the Atlantic Ocean, off the Coast of Labrador*. Library of Congress, Prints and Photographs Division. https://www.loc.gov/item/2012645577/.

Bresner, Katie. 2010. "Othering, Power Relations, and Indigenous Tourism: Experiences in Australia's Northern Territory." *PlatForum* 11: 10–26.

Bunten, Alexis Celeste. 2018. "Deriding Demand: A Case Study of Indigenous Imaginaries at an Australian Aboriginal Tourism Culture Park. In *Indigenous Tourism Movements*, edited by Alexis C. Bunten and Nelson H.H. Graburn, 31–55. Toronto, ON: University of Toronto Press.

Bunten, Alexis Celeste, and Nelson H.H. Graburn. 2018. "Current Themes in Indigenous Tourism. In *Indigenous Tourism Movements*, edited by Alexis C. Bunten and Nelson H.H. Graburn, 1–27. Toronto, ON: University of Toronto Press.

Colton, John W. 2005. "Indigenous Tourism Development in Northern Canada: Beyond Economic Incentives." *The Canadian Journal of Native Studies* 25 (1): 185–206.

Colwell-Chanthaphonh, Chip, and Ferguson, T. J. 2008. "Introduction: The Collaborative Continuum." In *Collaboration in Archaeological Practice: Engaging Descendant Communities*, edited by Chip Colwell-Chanthaphonh and T. J. Ferguson, 1–32. Lanahm, MD: Alt Mira Press.

Colwell-Chanthaponh, Chip, T. J. Ferguson, Dorothy Lippert, Randall H. McGuire, George P. Nicholas, Joe E. Watkin, and Larry J. Zimmerman. 2010. "The Premise and Promise of Indigenous Archaeology." *American Antiquity* 75 (2): 228–238. https://doi.org/10.7183/0002-7316.75.2.228.

Fugmann, Gerlis. 2012. "Developing a Remote Region: Tourism as a Tool for Creating Economic Diversity in Nunatsiavut." *Études/Inuit/Studies* 36 (2):13–33. https://doi.org/10.7202/1015976ar.

Graburn, Nelson H.H. 2018. "Experiments in Inuit Tourism: The Eastern Canadian Arctic." In *Indigenous Tourism Movements*, edited by Alexis C. Bunten and Nelson H.H. Graburn, 198–221. Toronto, ON: University of Toronto Press.

Hamilton, Scott. 2013. "Archaeology, Tourism and Other "Marriages of Convenience": Examples from Western Canada." In *Tourism and Archaeology: Sustainable Meeting Grounds*, edited by Cameron Walker and Neil Carr, 165–180. London: Routledge.

Hall, C. Michael, and Jarkko Saarinen. 2010. "Tourism and Change in Polar Regions. Introduction: Definitions, Locations, Places and Dimensions." In *Tourism and Change in Polar Regions: Climate, Environments and Experiences*, edited by C. Michael Hall and Jarkko Saarinen, 1–41. New York: Routledge.

Higgins, Jenny. 2015. "Tourism before Confederation." Heritage Newfoundland and Labrador. https://www.heritage.nf.ca/articles/economy/tourism-pre-confederation.php.

Hinch, Tom D. 1995. "Aboriginal People in the Tourism Economy of Canada's Northwest Territories." In *Popular Tourism: Tourism in the Arctic and Antarctic Regions*, edited by Colin Michael Hall and Margaret E. Johnston, 115–130. New York: John Wiley and Sons.

Hinch, Tom, and Richard Butler. 1996. "Indigenous Tourism: A Common Ground for Discussion." In *Tourism and Indigenous Peoples: Issue and Implications*, edited by Richard Butler and Tom Hinch, 3–19. Oxford: Elsevier.

Inuit Tapiriit Kanatami. 2016. *National Inuit Suicide Prevention Strategy*. https://www.itk.ca/wpcontent/uploads/2016/07/ITK-National-Inuit-Suicide-Prevention-Strategy-2016-English.pdf.

Kelvin, Laura Elena. 2017. *There is More Than One Way to Do Something Right: Applying Community-Based Approaches to an Archaeology of Banks Island, NWT*. PhD dissertation, The University of Western Ontario.

Kelvin, Laura, Emma Gilheany, Denver Edmunds, Nicholas Flowers, Mackenzie Frieda, Claire Igloliorte, Halle Lucy, and John Piercy. 2020. "Strength-Based Approaches to Involving Inuit Youth in Archaeological Research." *Canadian Journal of Archaeology* 44: 83–104.

Little, Jack I. 2016. "Seeing Icebergs and Inuit as Elemental Nature: An American Transcendentalist on and off the Coast of Labrador, 1864." *Social History* 49 (99): 243–262. https://doi.org/10.1353/his.2016.0009.

MacGregor, Sir William. M. 1910. *Reports of His Excellency WM. MacGregor, G.C.M.G, C.B., M.D., &c., Governor of Newfoundland, of Official Visits to Labrador 1905 & 1908*. St. John's: Government of Newfoundland.

Maureira, Teresa Miranda, and Susanne Stenbacka. 2015. "Indigenous Tourism and Processes of Resilience – About Communicative Strategies among Tourism Workers in Québec." *Acta Borealia* 32 (2): 148–170. https://doi.org/10.1080/08003831.2015.1090204.

MQO Research. 2012. *Labrador Travel Survey Final Report*. St. John's: Government of Newfoundland and Labrador.

Notzke, Claudia. 1999. "Indigenous Tourism Development in the Arctic." *Annals of Tourism Research* 26 (1): 55–76. https://doi.org/10.1016/S0160-7383(98)00047-4.

Nunatsiavut Government. 2008. *Tourism Nunatsiavut Final Strategic Plan, February 2008*. Forerunner Creative Tourism Strategies Ltd. Nain: Nunatsiavut Government.

———. 2014. *Nunatsiavut's Tourism Strategy 2014–2020: Sharing Our Story, Our People, Our Land*. The Tourism Café Canada and Brain Trust Marketing and Communications. Nain, NL: Nunatsiavut Government.

———. 2017. *Nunatsiavut's Tourism Strategy 2014–2020: A 2017 Mid-Point Review and Tactical Update*. The Tourism Café Canada and Brain Trust Marketing and Communications. Nain, NL: Nunatsiavut Government.

O'Flaherty, Patrick. 1979. *The Rock Observed: Studies in the Literature of Newfoundland*. Toronto, ON: University of Toronto Press.

Plane, Mark R. 2010. "'Remarkable Elasticity of Character': Colonial Discourse, the Market Economy, and Catawba Itinerancy, 1770–1820." In *American Indians and the Market Economy, 1775–1850*, edited by Lance Green and Mark R. Plane, 33–52. Tuscaloosa, AL: University of Alabama Press.

Raibmon, Paige. 2005. *Authentic Indians: Episodes of Encounter from the Late-Nineteenth-Century Northwest Coast*. London: Duke University Press.

Reid, R.W. 1912. *Catalogue of Specimens Deposited by Sir William MacGregor G.C.M.G, M.D. (Aber.), etc. in the Anthropological Museum, Marischal College, University of Aberdeen, 1899–1909*. Aberdeen: University of Aberdeen.

Rompkey, Ronald, ed. 1996. *Labrador Odyssey: The Journal and Photographs of Eliot Curwen on the Second Voyage of Wilfred Grenfell*. Montreal, QC: McGill-Queen's University Press.

Rowley, Susan. 2002. "Inuit Participation in the Archaeology of Nunavut: A Historical Overview." In *Honoring Our Elders: A History of Eastern Arctic Archaeology*, edited by William W. Fitzhugh, Stephen Loring, and Daniel Odess, 261–271. Washington: Smithsonian Institution.

Steckley, John. 2009. *White Lies about the Inuit*. Toronto, ON: University of Toronto Press.

Stephen, Kathrin. 2018. "Societal Impacts of a Rapidly Changing Arctic." *Arctic Climate Change* 4 (3): 223–237. https://doi.org/10.1007/s40641-018-0106-1.

Tate-Libby, Julie. 2013. "Saving Punalu'u: Ka'ū as a Cultural Kīpuka." In *Tourism and Archaeology; Sustainable Meeting Grounds*, edited by Cameron Walker and Neil Carr, 181–193. London: Routledge.

Weetaluktuk, Daniel. 1978. "Canadian Inuit and Archaeology." Paper presented at the Canadian Archaeological Association Conference. https://canadianarchaeology.com/caa/about/awards/daniel-weetaluktuk-award/canadian-inuit-archaeology.

CHAPTER 4

NIPIVUT AND THE RESTORYING OF INUIT LIFE IN MONTREAL

Mark K. Watson, Christopher Fletcher, Donna Patrick, and Sara Breitkreutz

INTRODUCTION

26 January 2016: Nipivut Episode #8

In the basement of CKUT90.3FM, McGill University's campus community radio station, Annie sits behind a large analog control panel with big black headphones on. Stephen, the Inuk producer beside her, connects to the outside phone line – a second's pause and – "is that you Putulik?" Annie asks in Inuktut. "Ehh," he replies. Annie was born and brought up in Iqaluit but moved to Montreal in the early 1980s. She is a well-known social worker with Inuit in and around the city. Among other community-driven responsibilities, Annie is the main host of Nipivut, the Montreal Inuit radio show.

On the show, Putulik is talking to Annie about being on the local and national news. Originally from Cape Dorset, Putulik moved south with his mother over twenty years ago. Without employment or adequate housing, they both started to rely on shelters for support and ended up on and off Montreal's streets. Media interest in Putulik arose after he had seen a teenage boy huddled over begging for money in the city's downtown core. Feeling bad, he had crossed the street and offered the boy his own jean jacket. "Here, let's make you a little warmer," he told the boy as he put the jacket around him. Putulik tells Annie: "I did it because I'd been through that."

Putulik's kind gesture became mainstream news because the boy to whom he gave his jacket was not homeless. The boy and his friend were running a "social experiment," and his friend had discreetly caught Putulik's exchange on camera from the other side of the street. The video was uploaded to YouTube, and was then picked up by The Canadian Broadcasting Corporation (CBC) and other media, including the Aboriginal Peoples Television Network (APTN).[1] While Putulik had done several interviews that week, over the phone in the CKUT studio that morning Annie was the first to speak to him about it in Inuktut.

Annie's motivation for helping launch the Nipivut show in 2015 was so she could support Inuit in and around Montreal the best she could, whatever situation they found themselves in, and use the radio to connect people. That is why, as Putulik talked to Annie that morning on Nipivut, he got to tell his journey in his own words: of moving to Montreal aged 21, of life on and off of the city's streets with not only

DOI: 10.4324/9780429275470-4

his mother but also his brother. He spoke of some of the decisions he had made, the toll that different substances had taken on his spirit, and his pride in his hard-fought sobriety. For all its emotional difficulty, Putulik got to share *his* story of gratitude, resilience, and compassion for fellow Inuit, and to ask that people not forget Inuit in the city. It left Annie, and Putulik, in tears.

Nipivut and the southern extension of Inuit geography

Nipivut means "our voice" in Inuktut. The radio team aired its first show on 6 October 2015. Nipivut responds to a long-standing need identified by Inuit in Montreal for a radio program to better serve the growing population in and around the city (see Mesher 2000; Tungasuvvingat Inuit 2006).[2] The show highlights the diversity of Inuit experiences amidst the growing population in the Greater Montreal region, a figure that recent research puts at 2300.[3]

To listen to Inuit narrate their own experiences on the Nipivut show is to understand that Montreal is *not* a "somewhere else" that Inuit happen to end up, but an important and, now, permanent extension of Inuit geography and social life. In fact, a key principle of the show is its assertion that *Inuit are Inuit irrespective of where they may be*. This geographically blind approach is vitally important in Montreal as it naturalizes the diversity of Inuit from the four Inuit land-claims regions across the Arctic while also recognizing second and third generations of Inuit born and brought up in and around the city. In contrast to literature that stories Inuit as immutably linked to the "harsh" conditions of the northern tundra, in this chapter we follow Nipivut in understanding that an "Inuit world" is anywhere Inuit choose to be, and where they see themselves as Inuk.

Simply put, our intention in this chapter is to begin to restory the presence of Inuit in Montreal over the last seventy years. To achieve this we will be talking about Montreal differently: not in terms of dislocation but as an *extension* of Inuit life. There are three main reasons for this. First of all, since the 1960s, Montreal and other cities have come to play crucial roles as service hubs supporting northern infrastructure. To talk to someone today in Kangirsuk, Igloolik, or Cambridge Bay about their CAT scan, cancer treatment or university entry is inevitably to talk about their temporary visit or long-term relocation to Montreal or other cities like Ottawa, Winnipeg, or Edmonton. Over the last 60 years or more, different policy decisions and inter-governmental transfer agreements have forged expansive, integrated networks in which essential services unavailable in the North, such as second and third-line health care and post-secondary education, are provided in southern cities. The overall impact of moving people through these networks cannot be ignored. In 2017, for example, close to 8,000 Inuit from Nunavik (which has a population of approximately 15,000) traveled to Montreal for health care or as escorts for patients (Ross 2018). Notwithstanding the social stress these journeys place on individuals and family members, the financial costs and cumulative environmental impacts of these visits are also significant.

A second reason to talk about Montreal as an extension of Inuit geography and the four land-claims regions – and why it can be considered the "Fifth Region," as suggested by Inuit artist Barry Pottle (see Koperqualuk and Husain 2018) – is the rise

Figure 4.1 *Qulliq* (traditional oil lamp) on a table used for an outdoor broadcast of Nipivut. Photo: Sara Breitkreutz.

of permanent settled urban Inuit populations. In 2016, the national census recorded 17,690 Inuit living outside of Inuit Nunangat.[4] Notwithstanding statistical adjustments for undercounting, at least one in four Inuit (27 percent) now live in southern Canada, an important statistic that speaks to a range of mostly undocumented histories of Inuit (circular) migration and displacements into Montreal and other southern cities (Terpstra 2015; Tungasuvvingat Inuit 2006; see also Patrick et al. and Fletcher, this volume). This demographic also draws attention to the difficulties faced by Inuit in situations of homelessness in cities, particularly Montreal, which we will come to address.

Finally, the language of extension helps both to counter representations of Inuit as not belonging to or being "out of place" in Montreal, and to contest the general characterization of urban Inuit experiences as short-lived, marginal, and therefore unimportant. We articulate what has remained historically implicit for much of the last seventy years: that is, the Inuit enactment of their "right to the city." The "right to the city" concept was first coined over 50 years ago by the sociologist Henri Lefebvre (1968), but has since been refined and employed by a variety of (organizational) actors around the world to articulate different kinds of rights for mostly marginal and underprivileged groups and individuals to participate in the formation of cities (Attoh 2011; Quicke, Prout and Green 2017). In the 1960s, for Inuit in the eastern Arctic at least, this right was not about the physical space of the city per se, but about the right to access communal goods of the new liberal welfare state that the federal government was unable or unwilling to provide in Arctic regions. These communal goods included services such as advanced healthcare and postsecondary education that were generally located in and around southern metropolitan centers.

The right to access healthcare and educational opportunities in Montreal – and to stay in and move around the city – continues today for Inuit from the Nunavik land claim region in northern Quebec under the James Bay and Northern Quebec Agreement (1975). But, as we will discuss, the "right to the city" concept now encompasses many different aspects of Montreal Inuit life such as the challenges vulnerable Inuit face in finding adequate food and shelter in Montreal and the self-determined struggle of Inuit organizations to provide Inuit in the city with access to other communal goods such as country food and social opportunities for cultural exchange and language use.

CHAPTER OVERVIEW

There is no single reason why Inuit have chosen to live in Montreal: some are in the city for employment (particularly with Inuit owned entities such as the Makivik Corporation, Air Inuit, Kativik School Board, and the Avataq Cultural Institute, among others), quality health care, or educational opportunities. Some are just visiting, passing through, or following family members. Some may have chosen to move simply because they could, whereas others may be intentionally escaping circumstances in the North or may have ended up there as a result of the justice system. And then there is the increasing number of Inuit who were born and/or brought up in the city (Kishigami 1999). For the purposes of this chapter, we limit our focus to three facets of Inuit life in Montreal. As a means of linking the central themes to Inuit experiences in the city, we employ the Nipivut show as narrator by starting each section with a relevant ethnographic vignette from an episode.

In the first section, we focus on the historical provision of health and educational services in Montreal for Inuit from the eastern Arctic. We describe an important shift away from the ad-hoc and often traumatic medical evacuations of Inuit carried out by federal government agents for the treatment of tuberculosis, to the formal creation in the 1960s of a distributed infrastructural network for the delivery of health services anchored by institutions in Montreal. We discuss the role that McGill University's medical school network played in shaping and sustaining this essential structure. We go on to consider the continuing implications of this network for Inuit today but also how, for some Inuit, the historical legacies of family loss from the era of emergency evacuations continue to shape the emotional landscape of life in Montreal.

In the second section, we look at the association of Montreal with situations of Inuit homelessness. We contrast Inuit perspectives of troubled mobilities as a transregional and systemic issue rooted in the ongoing effects of settler-colonialism, against non-Inuit representations of homelessness as a localized "social problem." We describe key features that inform Inuit precarity in Montreal, including the misrepresentation of Inuit as not belonging and therefore having less right to the city than non-Indigenous citizens – a point we elaborate on with reference to the Villeray Incident, a discriminatory campaign launched in 2010 by an anonymous neighborhood group against an Inuit-led proposal to establish an out-patient residential center in the north Montreal borough.

In the third section, we look at Inuit self-organization. We discuss the creation of the Association of Montreal Inuit in the late 1990s before paying specific attention to the formation in 2017 of Inuit Siqinirmiut Quebecmi Illaujut/Southern Quebec Inuit Association (SQIA). SQIA's work for Inuit across the broader southern Quebec region exemplifies the creation of new opportunities for community action and the extension of Inuit sociality into everyday Montreal life.

We conclude this chapter by briefly contrasting the situation of Inuit in Montreal with Inuit in other cities through reference to Inuit participation on the Urban Realities panel at the Inuit Studies Conference held in Montreal in October 2019.

To begin then, we turn to city-based matters of health, education, and related infrastructures for Arctic communities via a Nipivut segment from February 2020.

HEALTH, EDUCATION, AND THE EMERGENT INUIT "RIGHT TO THE CITY"
18 February 2020: Nipivut Episode #114

"We're here to talk a little bit about tuberculosis tonight," Gabriel, the guest host, says as he opens the show. There had been a significant spike in tuberculosis cases among Inuit in Montreal in 2019. Jessika, a nurse, and Noemi, a physician, both from the provincial Department of Public Health, sit opposite Gabriel. They are in the studio to provide information about a large truck housing a portable chest x-ray lab and blood clinic parked next to Cabot Square to the west of downtown. For the next three days, the health workers were hoping to encourage as many Inuit as possible, particularly those in the most vulnerable situations, to board and get tested. The results were to be handed back with a gift voucher in a couple of weeks at Resilience, a new day shelter located on the other side of the square.

The interview is in English. Betsy, who also often hosts the show, is there too and spontaneously cuts in to provide Inuktut translation. The context of this conversation is not lost on anyone in the studio; the collective historical memory of the "TB evacuations" of Inuit to southern hospitals that started in the 1940s is not spoken of, but it resonates still. Jessika and Noemi know this. They are keen to reassure listeners and emphasize the department's ongoing collaborations with Inuit organizations. They also provide a vivid description of the truck's interior as well as an explanation of the 30-minute procedure patients are brought through. Based on the general feeling in the studio, the interview has gone well. Just as Gabriel draws the segment to a close, Betsy spontaneously decides it is time for a language lesson: "*Kinauvit? Kinauvit?* … What's your name? Everyone repeats; "Betsy *uvunga*, my name is Betsy, Betsy *uvunga*," everyone gives their name. Big smiles on everyone's faces. "*Tunngasugit, Tunngasugit.*" This one is a little trickier for the guests. "*Tunngasugit, Tunngasugit, Tunnga – su – git,*" Betsy breaks down the syllables. Many times the word goes back and forth across the table. It is important for Betsy that Jessika and Noemi get their pronunciation right. "What does it mean?" Betsy is asked. "This is what you say when you are welcoming Inuit," she says.

*****

Betsy's intervention on Nipivut that evening served as a modest reminder to the health workers in the studio that Inuit are individuals, with names, to be welcomed as Inuit, not objects of medical analysis. This way of testing for TB – with mobile equipment staffed by non-Inuit health workers parked for a brief period of time close to populations of Inuit – is a mirror image of how testing was done throughout the Arctic under the federal government program that ran between 1946 and 1969. Normally, a ship would arrive, people would be brought on board and given an x-ray, and those afflicted would be kept on board and taken away for treatment. By 1956, one in seven Inuit had already been relocated to the South, often for over two years and often without any contact with family members (Grygier 1994, xii). In Quebec, Inuit were placed in one of 22 hospitals or convalescent homes across the southern part of the province; ten of those institutions were on the island of Montreal.

At that time, those destined for Montreal hospitals were usually brought for an initial assessment to the hospital on the First Nations reserve at Kahnawà:ke just off the island. Some individuals would then find themselves moved back to Montreal, while others, particularly children, are known to have remained there. The increasing number of children at the hospital in Kahnawà:ke motivated a social worker to make an arrangement with the Protestant Children's Homes in Montreal to find foster homes for them in the city (Grygier 1994, 127). Other transit foster homes for adult Inuit waiting to return home were organized by a member of the Travellers' Aid Society in the town of Huntington close to the US border (Grygier 1994, 127).

The felt legacy of those evacuations – of loss, anxiety, and separation – still resonates in people's experiences of the city today. In 2011, 59 years after last seeing her mother (Galakkiq) boarding a Montreal-bound plane for treatment, Mary Kauki stood with her own daughter in the United Church graveyard in Kahnawà:ke with local congregation members. The previous year, the Mohawk church minister, Maureen Scott Kabwe, had led a memorial service to unveil a monument identifying the burial site of 15 Inuit at the edge of the graveyard (Standup 2010). Inuit had been buried there between 1950 and 1959 under the authority of the local Indian agent. The minister found that the burial records had only noted one name for each individual (the majority of the names were poorly transliterated) and one home community (for all but one). She was able to send what information she had to the different communities. Word reached Mary and her family – "Kauki (Fort Chimo)" had been on the list. "I always planned on finding [my grandmother]. That was my mission for years," Mary-Joanne, Galakkiq's granddaughter, would tell a *Nunatsiaq News* journalist, "but she found us" (Curtis 2011).

The ongoing attempts of family in the North to find those who went south without ever returning speaks to the enduring memory of that period, and the ambivalent connections it has forged between many Inuit and the city (see Stevenson 2014, 21). Mary's family search resonates today in every call, text, or visit made in search of a father, daughter, son, sister, or friend gone missing in the city. It resonates also with everyone tested at Cabot Square in February 2020.

Geographically distributed health infrastructures

From 2018 to 2019, on average 140 people a week traveled down from Nunavik to Montreal for specialized healthcare. While still fraught with the anxieties of separation from home, this urban shift in the provision of all second- and third-line healthcare services to Inuit brokers a new conversation about an Inuit "right to the city" distinct from the practical and political debate about the TB evacuations that preceded it.

In 1964, for example, the Department of Northern Affairs and Natural Resources Canada opened a General Hospital in Frobisher Bay (modern-day Iqaluit; hereafter, FBGH). Although it was the first such hospital in the Eastern Arctic, its limited operating capacity meant that the government had to contract out specialized medical services for the Baffin region to McGill University in Montreal (see Baxter 2006). Utilizing the network of scheduled flights to different Arctic communities out of Montreal's Dorval airport,[5] senior pediatric residents attended the FGBH on a monthly rotation and Inuit traveled to Montreal for specialized services. By the 1980s, the Inuit demand for consultants and services in the city was becoming significantly more complex, and so Inuit stays were lengthening. To address this, Baffin House was opened in Montreal to facilitate patient lodgings, appointments, and consultant referrals for all those traveling from the Northwest Territories (later Nunavut). This program lasted until 1997 when the Baffin Regional Health and Social Services Board – not without some controversy – transferred all southern specialist services to the Ottawa Heart Institute (Baxter 2006).

For northern Quebec, however, the Réseau Universitaire Intégré de Santé–McGill (University Integrated Health Network – McGill), a geographic zone of responsibility that encompasses Nunavik, continued to play an important role in Inuit health services. Section 15 of the James Bay and Northern Quebec Agreement (JBNQA) signed in 1975 established provisions for health and social services adapted to the region's needs, and a new Inuit institution, the Nunavik Regional Board of Health and Social Services (NRBHSS), was eventually formed. This new structure institutionalized travel to southern facilities for advanced medical care and effectively formalized what had been an ad hoc process (Grondin 1990). In 1978 the Montreal General Hospital (MGH) agreed to be responsible for Inuit patients and the Module du Nord Quebecois was created.

For Nunavimmiut, the right of access to the city for healthcare also extended to the provision of suitable accommodations. Experiences of traveling to Montreal were strongly tied to stays in a growing number of boarding homes run by people contracted by the MGH. These relaxed family-style lodgings fostered an important network of friendships and strong social bonds between Inuit and Montrealers that were not terribly different from the social norms that accompanied northern travel and visiting. People had favorite places to stay – Bob and Annie's house in Dorval, the Nolet's place in Notre-Dame-de-Grace, and Madeleine's in Lachine, were known throughout Nunavik, and those who came for repeated treatments were usually housed at their "favorite" places. As the number of people traveling grew, the boarding house system became unwieldy due in large part to the logistical challenge of getting the right people from the right boarding house to the right hospital clinic at the right time.

A dedicated facility for housing Nunavimmiut called Nunavik House was finally opened in 2000 on Rue St. Jacques in the borough of Notre-Dame-de-Grace. However, by 2005, due to overcrowding and other issues – this was not the "best" part of town and people reported feeling unsafe in the surroundings – many patients and their escorts were having to stay at different temporary locations. In 2011, when the lease for Nunavik House came to an end, the NRBHSS considered moving the new patient house to the northern Montreal borough of Villeray. However, public controversy surrounding that proposal (see the following section) persuaded the board to make other plans, and for the next six years, patients were housed downtown at the YMCA building near Atwater metro station, a stone's throw from Cabot Square.

In 2016, the NRBHSS opened its own dedicated facility. Called Ullivik (meaning "a place to stay or wait"), the accommodations are situated close to the Dorval airport. It currently operates on a 15-year lease at a cost of $2.5 million and has space for 125 beds. While Dorval has a sizable Inuit community and is a familiar place for most traveling Inuit, the fact that Ullivik is located on a sliver of land between two highways with no residential neighbors, is not an accident. The anxieties of the Villeray incident, discussed below, were not lost on the planners of Ullivik.

Within the context of the JBNQA (Section 17) Inuit "rights to the city" also extend to accessing postsecondary education. Due to the fact that there is no postsecondary institution in northern Quebec, Inuit wanting to pursue further education have always had to move south. Today, over 50 Inuit from Nunavik enter either CEGEP (Quebec college) or university level programs in Montreal each year. In 2017, in a bid to provide an Inuit-focused educational experience for students in an urban setting, and recognizing the success of the Nunavut Sivuniksavut in Ottawa (a bridge program between high school and university for Inuit youth from Nunavut, see Patrick et al., this volume), Kativik Ilisarniliriniq (the School Board of Nunavik) launched its own Montreal-based college program called Nunavik Sivunitsavut. Accredited through John Abbott CEGEP, an English language college on the west island of Montreal, the program is taught out of the offices of the Avataq Cultural Institute in downtown Montreal, and funded by the Quebec Ministry of Education with support from the Kativik Regional Government and Makivik Corporation. While this post-secondary level of education attracts the most attention, the needs of the growing number of Inuit children attending daycare and the mainstream school system in Montreal must also not be ignored. Indeed, this became a topic that garnered enough interest for the Kativik Regional Government to fund an impact assessment report in 2006 on Inuit early childhood education in the city (see Rowan 2006).

Recasting the city-based provision of health and education in terms of an Inuit right to the city underscores the vital role that Montreal plays as a service hub within a distributed infrastructural network anchored by the needs of Inuit in northern communities. However, redescribing the southern extension of an Inuit world into Montreal in terms of this right discloses a political if also intensely personal and contested conversation over identity claims – of who can(not) claim this right. Inuit who already live in southern Quebec, for example, generally cannot receive services from their northern institutions even when their problems are well known. This creates ironic situations where people living in Nunavik will be provided with more comprehensive and culturally adapted health care and educational opportunities in Montreal than the Inuit who actually live there. We do not have the space to interrogate the structural context of this inequality here. Instead, in the next section, we engage with what it implies: that the right to the city is never given but must be fought for (Quicke, Prout and Green 2017, 167), a reality particularly felt by Inuit in situations of homelessness.

TROUBLED MOBILITIES
23 February 2016 – Nipivut Episode #11[6]

A snowy yet dark February evening in the city. The Nipivut team is on the street under the CKUT tent outside of the Native Friendship Centre on the corner of Ontario and St. Laurent. In spite of the cold, making the outside broadcast happen has sparked an air of excitement among everyone huddled around the heater. This episode is part of the annual homelessness marathon organized by CKUT in conjunction with the national association of campus-community radio stations. The show is entirely in Inuktut and will be broadcast nationwide. Annie has spread the word and people begin showing up.

"For those women and men who sleep outside," Annie says into her microphone, but more so to the people gathered around her, "I'm going to ask some questions: who has a home or who doesn't have a home. I'll ask what's your name and where you're from."

Saila sits down and puts on the headphones. He is quick to share his struggle with alcohol over the last 20 years. "There were a lot of fights and a lot of violence when I was growing up," he explains. "I used to watch people get into fights, other people used to watch too. I was with people who weren't happy."

"When you get a home," Annie asks, "does that feel better?"

"Yes," he says. "I used to have a home, but I got kicked out. It was because of drinking too much, that's why I got kicked out."

Figure 4.2   Banner for the CKUT90.3FM Homelessness Marathon event. Photo: Sara Breitkreutz.

Others come by to talk with Annie before Lava sits down. Quietly, he says he has been in the city for three years. "Before I came to Montreal," he explains, "I didn't have a home. And when I came to Montreal, it was the same." Like others before him on the show, he talks about spending time at Projet Autochtones du Quebec (PAQ), a popular Indigenous homeless shelter in Montreal, where he has been refused entry of late because of his drinking.

"Do you get kicked out during the day, even if it's cold?" Annie asks him.

"Hmm ... when I do, in the winter, I usually go to a place where it's warm during the day," he replies. "Sometimes I stay away from people who are bad. When it starts to get violent, I move away."

Annie has to wrap up. Lava says, "Thank you for listening to me. I just want to say hi to all those people who don't have a home. If you're sleeping outside try to find a place, and if you can't go there, keep looking. I want to say hi to my friends and family too."

*****

Everyone who sat down with Annie under the CKUT tent that night spoke in their own way of hurtful relationships or difficult circumstances elsewhere, including lack of a home or a safe and decent place to live. Inuit account for over 40 percent of Montreal's Indigenous homeless population, a stark statistic considering that Inuit make up only 15 percent of the Indigenous population in the city (Kishigami 1999). Due to the visibility of Inuit on Montreal streets, situations of Inuit homelessness are all too often mischaracterized as a "social problem" based on discriminatory stereotypes of Inuit being "out of place" or not belonging in the city. Many organizations now draw on the idea of the "right to the city" in campaigns for more affordable housing and better arrangements for temporary shelter in cities (Quicke, Prout and Green 2017). However, for Inuit – and for Indigenous peoples elsewhere – it is important to recognize how the historical and contemporary processes of colonization mediate individual and collective experiences of the city (Peters and Andersen 2014; Quicke, Prout and Green 2017). As Jobie Tukkiapik, former president of Makivik Corporation has put it, "the causes of Inuit homelessness are rooted in northern regions" (Makivik Corporation 2012b), meaning that one cannot ignore the difficult relations with northern communities that individuals in the city may live with. Troubling situations in the North may motivate someone to physically leave that place, but the manifestations of such situations in and through interpersonal relationships inevitably affect people wherever they move. Sometimes, the material circumstances can follow.

In 2012, Makivik Corporation submitted a report to the Front d'action populaire en réaménagement urbain, identifying a range of social determinants in Nunavik linked to the reality of homelessness in Montreal. They included: a high cost of living, food insecurity, severe housing shortages, high levels of poverty, and unsafe domestic environments (Makivik Corporation 2012a, 6). The report also recognized the drift into Montreal homelessness of Inuit released from federal or provincial detention centers across southern Quebec, men and women who may either be forbidden by court order from returning to their home communities, or who may no longer be welcome at home (Makivik Corporation 2012a, 7).[7]

In spite of the fact that street-involved people likely constitute less than 20 percent of the total Inuit population in the city, many non-Inuit in Montreal associate Inuit with homelessness and poverty. This was epitomized by events in the northern Montreal borough of Villeray in 2010. At that time, the Nunavik Regional Board of Health and Social Services (NRBHSS) had submitted a proposal to the local council to turn a building that formerly housed a Chinese hospital into a dedicated Inuit out-patient center. Once news of the proposal spread, however, flyers with the headline "Danger-Imminent" suddenly appeared through neighborhood letterboxes. A key line read: "This [Inuit out-patient center] will lead to a major increase in crime in your neighborhood ... You only need to go to the corner of St. Laurent and Viger to see the magnitude of the disaster to come if we do not act quickly." The flyer conflated the Inuit health residence with Inuit homelessness, which was in turn equated with prostitution, drug abuse, and "the smell of urine." The flyers urged local residents to reflect on the consequences that Inuit moving into the area would have for personal safety and property prices.

During this moment of heightened community tensions, the local mayor, Anie Samson, only stoked the controversy further by appearing not to denounce the core message of the flyer in an interview with Radio-Canada (CBC 2010). Furthermore, NRBHSS meetings with the borough council left Inuit representatives shocked by the opinions held by some of its councilors – the chair of the NRBHSS would later describe those meetings as the coldest she had ever attended (CBC 2010). In spite of an upswell of support for the project and for Inuit from local citizens groups, the council rejected calls to lift its rezoning freeze and in September of that year the NRBHSS rescinded its application.

The so-called "Villeray Incident" highlighted how quickly representations of Inuit as a "problem" and as a people "out of place" in the city can be mobilized for local (political) ends. Effectively, the discriminatory campaign launched by the anonymous authors of the flyer contested any Inuit right to the city. It ignored the varying collective assertions to that right and the broader context of settler-colonial history within which the urban Inuit population has dramatically increased. We do not question the fact that Inuit homelessness is a difficult and multifaceted issue. Nevertheless, it is important to emphasize that from an Inuit perspective, understanding situations of homelessness requires storying the present through individual experiences – in both northern communities and southern cities – and in dialogue with the drastic transformations occurring within Inuit communities across the Arctic regions. Jobie Weetaluktuk's documentary *Qallunajatut: Urban Inuk* (2005) employs this lens to moving effect when storying the lives of different Inuit on the streets of Montreal. Robert Lewis' film *Be Smile* (2006), made in collaboration with Isaac Augiak and Thomas Paru Weetaltuk, adopts a similar approach.[8]

This relational framing of the issue also raises the question of Inuit-specific service provision. The emerging social infrastructure for vulnerable Inuit in the city is replete with local, agency-specific initiatives or projects. In fact, Jobie Weetaluktuk was one of the founding board members of the Association of Montreal Inuit, the first grassroots organization in the city that sought to support all Inuit in the city, including the homeless, by hosting monthly feasts with country food (Mesher 2000; also see below). In 2010, the Makivik Corporation – in collaboration with the Kativik Regional Government's Ungaluk program – implemented a strategic action plan in response to the acuteness of the situation. Primarily focused on access to health and social services and prevention, the plan has invested more than $3 million over the last ten years in creating and sustaining a service network for Inuit in partnership with different agencies in the city – including Chez Doris Women's Shelter, the Open Door, the Native Friendship Centre of Montreal, and Project Autochtones du Quebec.[9] While this funding is important, policymakers also understand – in relation to what we have discussed above – that any program evaluation is ultimately tied to the capacity of different stakeholders to work together in effecting a broader political vision to change the longstanding systemic issues affecting northern communities.

Building on these initiatives, it is important to recognize how Inuit have collectively organized in response to the overlapping social realities of Inuit in (and around) Montreal. In the final section, we turn to a brief history of Inuit self-organization. We consider how these collaborative efforts have mobilized the community in pursuit of social change, and we consider and the benefits of rethinking their role under the "right to the city" banner.

URBAN SELF-ORGANIZATION/SELF-DETERMINATION
14 May 2019: Nipivut Episode #94

The chatter of people catching up, others meeting for the first time. The sounds of a harmonica, guitar, and happy family gatherings. The shrill of children playing, spontaneous applause, and Gabriel's contagious laughter responding to something out of earshot, an Inuit game most likely. It is the Southern Quebec Inuit Association's (SQIA) spring community feast. We listen with Gabriel as people talk both about the *niqituinnaq* (country food) on offer, and about the connections with the community and families that this gathering makes possible. Thanks to SQIA, the feast is now a bi-monthly event. This one is being held at a new location, an evangelical church next to Cabot Square in downtown Montreal. In spite of the urban milieu, its ties to northern communities resonate strongly. "Where does the country food come from?" Gabriel asks Sarah, SQIA's wellness worker. This time, she says, the Arctic char has come down from Iqaluit, the caribou from Salluit, the seal from Inukjuak, and the ptarmigan from Quaqtaq.

Sarah herself is originally from Nunavut (Cape Dorset/Kinngait) and is one of the event's key organizers. "The purpose of the feast," she tells Gabriel, "is to allow for Inuit to get together and to eat country food … and for us to come together, just be together; but it's also open to everyone, an opportunity for us to show who we are as a community and how we are as a community."

Over a hundred people come that day – with tables overflowing, some people stand while others sit with their plates of food around the edge of the room. Just a couple of months prior, Sarah had been on Nipivut speaking to SQIA's commitment to wellness, talking about it through a community lens as a safe space where people can come to "feel good" – be it spending time with one another or sharing country food, speaking Inuktut or practicing craftwork or other skills, or just asking for information or support. Being well together is what is important she says.

* * * * *

Inuit self-organization in Montreal stretches back to the late 1990s. It represents an important, grassroots intervention in the deficit-based narrative of urban Inuit life. By focusing on the strength of collective organization – and, within it, the capacity of certain individuals – to reframe personal challenges, common interests, or cultural skillsets as aspects of a shared experience, self-organization serves to address specific, local Inuit needs. And, in a sprawling city such as Montreal, it brings collective exchanges into people's lives that may otherwise never occur due to time, distance, or lack of opportunity (cf. Watson 2014, 42). In this way, Inuit have sought to actively recognize and address the needs of the growing urban Inuit population and, in the process, advocate on behalf of those most marginalized by the exclusionary structures of city life.

The first such Inuit organization in Montreal was the Association of Montreal Inuit (AMI). Formally incorporated as a non-profit organization in March 2000, the group led by Victor Mesher, then a Makivik employee, had secured supplies of country food from different individuals and groups in northern communities, and prior to its official launch had already hosted several community feasts at St. Paul's Anglican Church in Lachine. Partly in response to recommendations for action made by the anthropologist Nobuhiro Kishigami in his work on Inuit homelessness in Montreal (see Kishigami 1999; Mesher 2000), AMI was established and run "by the Inuit in Montreal for Inuit" and set up around an ethos of volunteerism in order to try to "address the social concerns of southern Inuit" (Mesher 2000, 61). Following the successes of Tungasuvvingat Inuit, the largest and longest-running urban Inuit organization based in Ottawa, the original vision of the board of the directors had been to work with Makivik Corporation to secure a permanent building in Lachine, to the west of the city, to house the association, as well as provide space for a drop-in center. Local council politics at the time frustrated attempts to move forward on this (Mesher 2000, 59) but between 2000 and 2006, AMI consolidated its network of country food providers and put on over 65 monthly community feasts held the last Saturday of every month. The feasts themselves quickly became important focal points for social gathering and cultural exchange.

By 2010, the activities of AMI declined following both a change in leadership and the withdrawal of funding from Makivik Corporation, but community activities were still advertised on its Facebook page in the following years. In 2015 a renewed commitment to self-organize in Montreal arose after an engaged group of Inuit from southern Quebec participated in the National Urban Inuit Dialogue, an 18-month consultation exercise facilitated by Tungasuvvingat Inuit. The participants' engagement in that process compelled them to reflect on the role an Inuit-specific organization could play in addressing not only the needs of Inuit in Montreal but also the increasing number located across the southern region of Quebec. The key needs of Inuit in the region identified at that time included promoting cultural, social, and economic development, supporting the use and development of the Inuktut language, contributing to the improvement of living conditions, supporting good health and well-being, and navigating the justice system.

A new era: The Southern Quebec Inuit Association

In October 2017, a five-member Inuit governing board was voted in to formally establish the not-for-profit Inuit Siqinirmiut Quebecmi Illaujut/Southern Quebec Inuit

Association (SQIA). As a direct result of the national dialogue process, SQIA was supported in part by Makivik Corporation, and held its inaugural Annual General Assembly at a church in the borough of Verdun. For Tina Pisuktie, SQIA's executive director, the founding of this organization served to fill a significant gap in community resources and to help Inuit "no matter where they are, to feel connected to their community" (Edgar 2017). As a community organization, the SQIA became directly involved in the production and management of the Nipivut radio show. Furthermore, within its first two years of operation, the association had created several community programs and activities including bi-monthly feasts, wellness groups, and sessions addressing the grieving process for people in the South according to Inuit culture.

SQIA has also been working as the principal community partner with researchers at the Université de Laval on the Qanuikkat Siqinirmiut ("How are those living in the South?") project. Funded through the Canadian Institutes of Health Research (CIHR), the project is developing a comprehensive health survey and needs assessment for Inuit living in southern Quebec. What SQIA and the broader QS project are seeking to achieve is a long-term commitment to structural change, including the development of health care services in the city tailored for the population, based on this better understanding of Inuit health in the South.

The "right to the city" is not a given or natural right; it is ultimately struggled for (Quicke, Prout and Green 2017, 167). The work of Inuit self-organization in terms of applying for funding, organizing staff and volunteers, creating new opportunities for community action, and so forth, exemplifies the self-determining but also contested qualities of this process. What we mean by this is that under the right to the city banner, self-organization speaks to more than just the logistics of organizing community events for Inuit. Be it a feast, or a beading workshop, the provision of interpersonal counseling, or the opportunity for people to speak or practice Inuktut, the primary purpose of SQIA (and AMI before it) is about identifying and securing collective access to communal goods not otherwise provided for in the city, with the aim of improving a collective sense of well-being in Montreal.

CONCLUSION: URBAN INUIT REALITIES

The brief description of Inuit in Montreal recounted above is not *the* story of Montreal Inuit. On the contrary, it is part of an ongoing conversation about the (re)storying of Inuit experiences in and around the city from Inuit perspectives, one that we feel can be better mobilized under the right to the city banner. In October 2019, this conversation was enlivened by the voices of other Inuit from cities across Canada when Tina Pisuktie (SQIA) and Maxine Angoo from the Tunngasugit Inuit Resource Centre in Winnipeg, co-organized the "Urban Inuit Realities" panel with support from the Nipivut team at the 21st Inuit Studies Conference in Montreal. The event took place over three hours in a packed room and was streamed live on Facebook. Much of the panel spoke to the efforts of Inuit in Montreal, Edmonton, Winnipeg, Ottawa, and Toronto to foster positive Inuit community relationships and identities in cities and build wider institutional and political structures. Speakers on that panel expressed similar points of view about the need and capacity of Inuit to self-organize and to establish collective spaces for social and cultural exchange in their respective cities. As Jason LeBlanc, a long-time Ottawa Inuit leader, put it:

> What is important about identity and belonging for Inuit away from home? The most important resource is your fellow Inuk ... why are all these organizations [in different cities] coming together and being so successful? It's because people need a place to share common values, common space, a place to be Inuk without feeling the pressures of explaining it, defending it, making someone else understand the reality.

Maxine, drawing from her work in Winnipeg, elaborated on how there is a growing number of Inuit "who just want a sense of belonging and community and food." Joshua Stribbell, acting president of the National Urban Inuit Youth Council, spoke to his emotional journey of connecting to his heritage through meeting other Inuit in Toronto, and the positive impacts of getting involved in community organization, including helping to put on the first Inuit feast in that city in 2015. Well-being, it was often noted on the panel, is connected to one's sense of identity. As Tina, from a Montreal perspective, elaborated, community gathering is a crucial strategy for helping Inuit well-being that should not discriminate. Finding a "place to come together" needs to serve a broad swath of Inuit in the city, not only those "on the streets and dealing with complex trauma," she said, but all Inuit "searching for their identity" or just wanting to "be part of something" in the city.

As we have shown in this chapter, a large part of urban Inuit positive identity-building involves claiming and acting on the authority to voice direct individual experiences and to link these insights to new and collective possibilities for social change. It is about recognizing the key roles that southern cities have played historically in the workings of distributed infrastructural networks supporting northern communities and the settler-colonial context within which such transformations (of Inuit life and social geography) continue to be reproduced. It is about challenging and changing the stereotypical images of Inuit as "out of place" in Montreal by restorying historical narratives and asserting, individually and collectively, the Inuit "right to the city": that is, the right for Inuit to politicize their marginalization in the city and propose their own vision of collective belonging in the present and in the city's future.

The Nipivut radio show is one such project that is already asserting this right by amplifying Inuit experiences in the city. Of course, Inuit in southern cities and northern communities face distinct local challenges, but the social, political, and historical connections between people endure: An important relation that invites us to rethink "the South" and, more pointedly, Montreal, as a vital, vibrant, and permanent extension of Inuit life.

NOTES

1 See the story about Putulik and Nipivut on the Aboriginal Peoples' Television Network at: https://www.aptnnews.ca/national-news/radio-program-in-montreal-providing-inuit-a-place-to-tell-their-stories/ (last accessed 28 July 2020).

2 The Nipivut project has received support from a community-university partnership between the Southern Quebec Inuit Association/Inuit Siqinirmiut Quebecmi Illaujut in Montreal, Tungasuvvingat Inuit in Ottawa, CKUT 90.3FM, CKCU 93.1FM, and Concordia University (Montreal). It has been funded in part by two grants from the Canadian Social

    Sciences and Humanities Research Council (Watson, PI; an Insight grant [435-2013-1794] and a Partnership Development Grant [890-2017-0033]).

3. This statistic comes from census data collected and analyzed in 2019 in collaboration with the Southern Quebec Inuit Association/Inuit Siqinirmiut Quebecmi Ilaujut for the Canadian Institutes of Health Research grant entitled: *Qanuikkat Siqinirmiut? A Community-Based Study of Southern Quebec Inuit Health and Wellbeing* (Fletcher, PI; 2018–2022).

4. This figure of 27 percent comprises those Inuit identifying as "Inuk" in the 2016 Census. In the same Census, 40 percent of Inuit living outside of Inuit Nunangat claimed Inuit "ancestry." An ancestor is usually a person more distant than a grandparent and can include mixed (Inuit and non-Inuit) ancestry.

5. By 1959, Nordair, based out of Montreal, was already operating commercial routes to Fort Chimo (Kuujjuaq), Frobisher Bay (Iqaluit), and Cape Dyer. By 1971, its scheduled flights had expanded to other villages including Resolute Bay, Clyde River, Cape Dorset, and Igloolik. The introduction to Montreal of First Air (formerly Bradley Air Services) and then Air Inuit (both owned by Makivik Corporation) in the late 1970s, with routes throughout (what is now) Nunavik and Nunavut, were integral to the delivery of health services but, moreover, to the emergence of a settled if also transient Montreal Inuit population come the mid-1980s.

6. This episode was aired entirely in Inuktut. The translations featured here are by Akeeshoo Sataa.

7. Although measurements of Inuit in situations of homelessness are limited, the findings of anthropologist Nobuhiro Kishigami (1999; 2008; 2015) drawn from interview-based research with homeless individuals in collaboration with different Montreal-based shelters and Inuit organizations over a 15-year period, are the most comprehensive to date.

8. *Be Smile* (directed by Robert Lewis) is available for viewing on Vimeo at: https://vimeo.com/103911360 (last accessed 26 August 2021).

9. For his role in implementing this action plan, Jobie Tukkiapik, former president of Makivik Corporation (2012–2018), received the Ordre de Montreal from the Mayor of Montreal in 2019.

REFERENCES

Attoh, Katuf A. 2011. "What *Kind* of Right is the Right to the City?" *Progress in Human Geography* 35 (5): 669–685. https://doi.org/10.1177/0309132510394706

Baxter, James D. 2006. "Historical Overview of the McGill Baffin Program, 1964–1997." *International Journal of Circumpolar Health* 65 (1): 91–95. https://doi.org/10.3402/ijch.v65i1.17875.

CBC [Canadian Broadcasting Corporation]. 2010. "Montreal Inuit Housing Faces Opposition." 3 June. Available at: https://www.cbc.ca/news/canada/montreal/montreal-inuit-housing-faces-opposition-1.926523 (accessed 28 July 2020).

Curtis, Chris. 2011. "The Long Goodbye: From Nunavik to Kahnawake." *Nunatsiaq News*, 13 June. Available at: https://nunatsiaq.com/stories/article/987899_the_long_goodbye_from_nunavik_to_kahnawake/ (accessed 28 July 2020).

Edgar, Courtney. 2017. "New Group Formed to Represent Inuit of Southern Quebec." *Nunatsiaq News*, 1 November. Available at: https://nunatsiaq.com/stories/article/65674new:group_formed_to_represent_inuit_of_southern_quebec/ (last accessed 28 July 2020).

Grondin, Jacques. 1990. "Les Inuit en ville. Communication et fictions autour des soins interculturels." *Anthropologie et Sociétés* 14 (1): 65–81. https://doi.org/10.7202/015112ar

Grygier, Pat Sandiford. 1994. *A Long Way from Home: The Tuberculosis Epidemic among the Inuit*. Montreal and Kingston, QC: McGill-Queen's University Press.

Koperqualuk, Gabriel, and Aeyliya Husain. 2018. *The Fifth Region*. Moving Images Distribution, 47 minutes.

Kishigami, Nobuhiro. 1999. "Life and Problems of Urban Inuit in Montreal: Report of 1997 Research." *Jinbun-Ronkyu* 68: 81–109.

———. 2008. "Homeless Inuit in Montreal." *Études/Inuit/Studies* 32 (1): 73–90. https://doi.org/10.7202/029820ar

———. 2015. "Low-Income and Homeless Inuit in Montreal, Canada: Report of a 2012 Research." *Bulletin of the National Museum of Ethnology* 39 (4): 575–624.

Lefebvre, Henri. 1968. *Le droit à la ville*. Paris: Anthropos.

Makivik Corporation. 2012a. "Report on Inuit Homelessness in Montreal, Canada." Presented to the Front d'action populaire en réaménagement urbain. Available at: https://www.homelesshub.ca/resource/inuit-homelessness-montreal

Makivik Corporation. 2012b. "Press Release: Signing of a Partnership Agreement between Makivik Corporation and Projets Autchtones Quebec, a Shelter in Montreal for Homeless First Nations and for Inuit." 4 October. Available at: http://www.makivik.org/signing-of-a-partnership-agreement-between-makivik-corporation-and-projets-autochtones-quebec-a-shelter-inmontreal-for-homeless-first-nations-and-for-inuit/ (last accessed 28 July 2020).

Mesher, Victor Jr. 2000. "No Longer Alone: A Haven of Happiness with the Association of Montreal Inuit." *Makivik Magazine* 54: 57–63.

Peters, Evelyn, and Chris Andersen. 2014. *Indigenous in the City: Contemporary Identities and Cultural Innovation*. Vancouver: UBC Press.

Quicke, Prout, Sarah Prout, and Charmaine Green. 2017. "Precarious Residence: Indigenous Housing and the Right to the City." *Geoforum* 85: 167–177. https://doi.org/10.1016/j.geoforum.2017.07.023

Ross, Selena. 2018. "Quebec Inuit and the Impossible Dilemma." *National Observer*, 29 January. Available at: https://www.nationalobserver.com/2018/01/29/news/quebec-inuit-and-impossible-dilemma (last accessed 28 July 2020).

Rowan, Carol. 2006. *Needs Assessment Concerning Montreal Inuit and Aboriginal Head Start*. Kuujjuaq, QC: Kativik Regional Government.

Standup, Jordan. 2010. "In Mohawk Territory, a Memorial for Inuit Who Died Far from Home." *Nunatsiaq News*, 20 September. Available at: https://nunatsiaq.com/stories/article/200910_in_mohawk_territory_a_memorial_for_inuit_who_died_far_from_home/ (last accessed 28 July 2020).

Stevenson, Lisa. 2014. *Life Beside Itself: Imagining Care in the Canadian Arctic*. Berkeley, CA: University of California Press

Terpstra, Tekke Klaas. 2015. *Inuit Outside the Arctic: Migration, Identity and Perceptions*. Eelde: Barkhuis Publishing.

Tungasuvvingat Inuit. 2006. *National Urban Inuit One Voice Workshop, Ottawa, 26–27 October 2005*. Ottawa, ON: Tungasuvvingat Inuit.

Watson, Mark K. 2014. *Japan's Ainu Minority in Tokyo: Diasporic Indigeneity and Urban Politics*. London and New York: Routledge.

CHAPTER 5

URBAN INUIT IN CANADA
A case study of Ottawa

Donna Patrick, Marika Morris, and Qauyisaq Etitiq

INTRODUCTION

On an October afternoon, in a crowded university classroom in downtown Montreal, Inuit from Edmonton, Winnipeg, Toronto, Ottawa, Montreal, and communities across the North, came together for a conference panel called "Urban Inuit Realities." This panel, co-hosted by Inuit and non-Inuit researchers working with Inuit in Montreal and Ottawa over many years, was part of the 2019 Inuit Studies Conference – a conference at which Inuit living in northern and southern Canada could come together to share their perspectives, concerns, and successes, including about the realities of being Inuit and their "right to the city" (see Watson et al., this volume).

This chapter focuses on Inuit Ottawamiut ("Inuit in Ottawa") but straddles the concerns of all Inuit living, working, and thriving in southern Canadian cities. Many Inuit share the desire expressed by Joshua Stribbell (Toronto) "to tell our story as urban Inuit"; and it is these stories, as Tina Pisuktie (Montreal) put it, of "people understanding who we are – understanding [our] experiences … this is what moves us forward this is what forges our relationship with others" (see Watson et al., this volume). While this chapter does not presume to tell the stories of all urban Inuit, it does try to bring to light many aspects of Ottawa Inuit life that center on community, work, learning, sharing, health, and healing. In what follows, we address the history of Inuit arriving, living, and organizing in Ottawa. We seek to answer such questions as: What has drawn Inuit to Ottawa and made the city a center for southern urban Inuit?; what events and processes have been part of creative community-building and place-making in the city?; and how are Ottawa Inuit tackling the challenges of the present and future? Jason Leblanc, another conference participant who was also executive director of the local Ottawa social services agency Tungasuvvingat Inuit (TI), noted that Inuit want "a place to come and share culture; a place to be built up and feel good about being Inuk [and] that reflects who Inuit are and supports people to carve [their] own path." In Ottawa, as Leblanc also noted, "we have a big resident population, but we have a regular influx of Inuit from other regions every day for health services, for justice services, for education services … Inuit coming in for services and resources not available in Inuit Nunangat" (the Inuit homelands comprising four land claims regions – Nunavut, Nunavik (northern Quebec), Nunatsiavut (Labrador), and the Inuvialuit settlement area of the Northwest Territories (NWT)).

In this chapter, we trace the establishment of Inuit organizations founded on Inuit needs and priorities, but also shaped over time by government funding priorities. The tide is currently trying to reach "at-risk" populations. Although addressing housing, poverty, employment, childcare, and mental health is extremely important, Ottawa Inuit who are not "at-risk" also need spaces to keep Inuit language and culture alive and to socialize with one another.

As co-author Qauyisaq Etitiq explains, there are no longer as many opportunities in the city for "just happy Inuit families that want to get together." In the 1980s and 90s, even though the Inuit population was smaller, Ottawa had an all-Inuit hockey team that competed for the All-Native Cup, and all-Inuit softball league, floor hockey team, and social gatherings. There has been a shift over the past decades in the focus for Inuit community organizing, which has gone from place-making in order to foster belonging for all Inuit, to providing much valued and needed community resources such as housing, income, employment, and family supports. This transition, it is worth noting, has also involved a discursive shift in the public and government spheres, through which Inuit have gone from an identity-based community to a needs-based "at risk" community. The key factor driving this shift has been the need for state funding for Inuit programs, which has required them to orient towards a needs-based discourse about who Inuit are and what they want in the city. This needs-based discourse has portrayed a view of Inuit as a population "in need" among the dominant non-Inuit population. While we do not wish to diminish the real needs of many Inuit for support and assistance in transitioning from northern to southern life, we must at the same time avoid stereotyped and generalized representations that do not reflect the rich and diverse stories of urban Inuit.

In the following sections, we document Ottawa Inuit efforts to claim their "right to the city" (Lefebvre 1968; 1996; Purcell 2014) by following the flow of Inuit migration to Ottawa and noting the contributions ordinary Inuit made and are making to creating a thriving, welcoming, helpful, and safe urban community.

This chapter draws on ethnographic inquiry, in the form of interviews and stories recounted to us, as well as on our own experiences. Some of the interviews that we will be describing were conducted for this chapter, while others reflect research conducted over many years. We use digital ethnography to tap into the virtual community life of Inuit in Ottawa and the initiatives of Inuit organizations. Our focus is on two local Ottawa organizations, Inuuqatigiit Centre for Inuit Children, Youth, and Families, an Inuit-led community services provider that fosters strong Inuit children, youth, and families through programs and services focusing on the whole family, including family well-being, child care, youth programs, art, and education, and Tungasuvvingat Inuit, a comprehensive Inuit-led social services agency which runs a food bank, community kitchen, housing first and housing support programs, the Alluriarniq program to help Inuit who have been trafficked, and the Pisiksik program to help Inuit in conflict with the law. TI also provides support for mental health and quitting smoking, hosts weekly cultural activities, and founded and oversees the Mamisarvik Healing Centre, the only Inuit-focused trauma and addictions residential program open to all Inuit in Canada. TI helps Inuit in Ottawa access services such as health insurance coverage, helps protect Inuit rights in interactions with child welfare agencies, and collects and distributes the stories of urban Inuit through its Urban Inuit Knowledge Centre. TI also founded a medical service for Inuit, which became the Akausivik Inuit Family Health Team.

Inuit also occupy an increasing number of mainstream Ottawa spaces. We also outline the Inuit programming at St. Margaret's Anglican Church; the history and impact of the Inuit Non-Profit Housing Corporation; and the Inuktut[1]-English language show Uqallagvik on CKCU-FM, the community radio station based at Carleton University. There are other urban programs and events that we do not focus on but that are prominent in the city. These include Inuit Tapiriit Kanatami (ITK), the national organization representing Inuit, the head office of which is in Ottawa, which holds an annual gala called "A Taste of the Arctic" at the National Arts Centre a few blocks away. Inuit films have been featured during Ottawa's Winterlude festival. Less than a decade ago, Inuit art was found only in the basement of the National Gallery of Canada. Now it is integrated through the Indigenous and Canadian Gallery and the Contemporary Gallery. There is also Larga Baffin, an Inuit-run residence for Nunavut Inuit requiring health services in the city; the Inuit Non-Profit Housing Corporation; and Nunavut Sivuniksavut (NS), an Ottawa-based college program for students from Nunavut. NS students give presentations and demonstrations of Inuit culture and music throughout Ottawa.

Inuit now also have a small presence in Ottawa's decision-making spaces. Prior to 1979, no Inuk had ever been elected to Parliament. Mumilaaq Qaqqaq is currently the Member of Parliament (MP) for Nunavut, and Yvonne Jones is the MP for Labrador.[2] Although Inuit have not benefitted from the same socioeconomic investments as other Canadians since the Second World War, Inuit are working, organizing, and making a distinct space for themselves and other Inuit in Ottawa and in Canada.

A LOOK AT INUIT WHO COME TO OTTAWA

A good place to begin our story of Inuit in Ottawa is with some of the early arrivals of Inuit from various points in the North in the 1950s. One person who came to Ottawa during this period was Mini Aodla Freeman, an Inuk from the James Bay region of Northern Quebec, who arrived in 1957. According to her autobiography (Freeman [1978] 2015), Mini, like other Inuit in the 1950s, arrived in downtown Ottawa by train from the southern James Bay community of Moose Factory in Northern Ontario, a trip that was common then. The Ottawa to which Mini arrived was one with a federal Eskimo Affairs Committee, which operated between 1952 and 1962, with no Inuit on it (Clancy and Lackenbauer 2019).

Two Inuit sisters from Chisasibi, Quebec, Sarah and Maggie Ekoomiak, who are now Ottawa's oldest Inuit residents, took the same trip as Mini in 1958. They had been working at the hospital in Moose Factory, built in 1949 as a tuberculosis sanitorium. Sarah was a nurse and Maggie was a dental assistant.

The sisters left Moose Factory in their twenties. When they arrived in Ottawa, they stayed for a few weeks with their uncle and aunt, Elijah and Gracie Menarik, before Gracie put them in touch with a social worker. Elijah and Gracie had met each other at the same Moose Factory hospital where Sarah and Maggie worked. Gracie was a non-Indigenous nurse and Elijah, an Inuk from the Chisasibi area, was a hospital orderly. They eventually moved to Ottawa together (McCallum 2014). Elijah became the first Inuktitut-speaking radio and television host in 1960 – hosting the first CBC North program, Taqravut. His name continues to be remembered in the CBC's Elijah Menarik Award, which honors his work advocating for Cree and Inuit language broadcasting (CBC 2015; NTI 2010).

At first, Sarah and Maggie found employment as nannies, and lived in two different Ottawa households. Sarah continued to work with the same family until 1960, when her friend Annie Weetaltuk arrived at her door announcing that she was going to work on a ship that summer and that Sarah should apply too. As a result, Sarah was offered a position as an interpreter on the *C.D. Howe*, a medical ship run by the Canadian government from 1950 to 1969 to test and transport Inuit tuberculosis patients (Smith 2004; Wilton 1993). In the 1990s Sarah visited Annie's grave in Kuujjuaraapik to thank her for convincing her to take that job on the *C.D. Howe*. This job was pivotal in Sarah's life. It provided her with an opportunity to better learn English and the many dialects of the Inuit language spoken across the North, and it later evolved into a permanent government position. Sarah is now comfortably retired near Ottawa.

Sarah recounted her life history to Donna Patrick, a co-author of this chapter, and Maureen Flynn Burhoe in the early 2000s. For Sarah and Donna, common ties with people from Kuujjuaraapik and Chisasibi in northern Quebec as well as in the Ottawa area have been a key part of a friendship that has developed over almost 20 years. Both Sarah and Maggie were an important part of Donna's life in Ottawa. With her car providing transportation, Donna shared numerous trips with the sisters to various community events at Tunngasuvingat Inuit, the Ottawa Inuit Children's Centre (now Inuuqatigiit Centre for Inuit Children, Youth, and Families), and other gatherings, community meals, and Anglican church services.

Two more recent stories of arrival in Ottawa are reflected in the life stories of Aigah Atigutsiak and Qauyisaq Etitiq. Aigah was born in 1959 in Arctic Bay, on the northern end of Baffin Island, and "grew up in a large family." She came to Ottawa in 1998, and like many Inuit residents of Ottawa, started out working for TI, where her first job was to temporarily replace her sister, who was going on vacation. Since Aigah had some training and experience working as a substitute teacher in Nunavut, she was later hired to work at the Inuit Head Start program, then located at TI (see Figure 5.1).

The next phase of Aigah's work life in Ottawa revolved around St. Margaret's Anglican Church. This church, founded in 1886, has been conducting services in Inuktitut for some time. In the past, these were often presided over by Rev. Roger Briggs, who had worked for some fifty years with the Arctic Diocese before retiring to Ottawa. Briggs was instrumental in helping train Aigah to assist in the offering of Inuktitut-language services at St. Margaret's. She first worked as a lay reader in the early 2000s, having been raised in a family that was "pretty much involved with the [Anglican] Church all the time." In 2015, she was ordained as an Anglican minister and now serves as the assistant curate at the church, offering an 11 am service in Inuktitut every Sunday. She has also ensured that bannock is part of the after-church gathering ever since she first started working there. This was a warm memory from her childhood in Arctic Bay: "My mother always made bannock all the time to feed us all." Offering bannock was a way of making Inuit feel welcome at the church.

Figure 5.1 Aigah Atigutsiak outside St. Margaret's Anglican Church in Ottawa where she is Assistant Curate. Photo: Donna Patrick.

Qauyisaq came to Ottawa in 2004 from Iqaluit, Nunavut, where he had been working as a policy analyst for the land claims organization, Nunavut Tunngavik Incorporated (NTI). He came to Ottawa to work for Inuit Tapirisat of Canada (ITC) (meaning "Inuit will be united") which later became Inuit Tapiriit Kanatami (ITK), (meaning "Inuit are united in Canada"). He was attracted to Ottawa by the comparatively better education system, and moved here when his daughter was in grade 5 so she could later get a good high school education. Qauyisaq himself took the opportunity to study sociology and Indigenous studies at Carleton University. Although he eventually earned his degree, he had to stop mid-way because of a lack of funding to take a job in the Northwest Territories. He resents the fact that many Canadians think Indigenous peoples receive free education, when one-third of Inuit leave postsecondary studies because of lack of funds. After living in the NWT for two years, Qauyisaq received a student loan from the NWT government which he had to repay in full. Despite being an Inuk born in the NWT, the government deemed him not to be Indigenous because he had lived outside the NWT. "It's a crazy funding situation for Inuit [students]," Qauyisaq said. To make it more complicated, Qauyisaq was born in Iqaluit, which was a part of the NWT when he was born but is now a part of Nunavut. Qauyisaq's family were among the first Inuit to live in what is now Iqaluit. There was no permanent settlement there until the US military base was established at Frobisher Bay, as the area was officially known, in the 1940s. Qauyisaq's family members worked at the base.

At ITC/ITK, Qauyisaq worked on the employment and housing files. He took a job at Pauktuutit Inuit Women of Canada, and when his wife Paani got pregnant, shared the parental leave with her – each one taking the same job for a while the other partner stayed home. Eventually, Qauyisaq took a position as education policy advisor at TI, working with school boards and the Ontario Ministry of Education to better serve and reflect Inuit student needs, and the need for all students to be educated about Inuit contributions to Canada. From TI, Qauyisaq became a consultant, because throughout his career he had given Inuit cultural awareness classes and workshops. He then took a position in the private sector Baffinland Iron Mines Corporation as coordination manager for the Inuit Impact Benefit Agreement that the company has with the landowner, Qikiqtani Inuit Association. Qauyisaq works remotely from his home in the Ottawa area with a lot of travel, including to the North and to the company headquarters in Oakville, Ontario. Qauyisaq's job is to ensure that Inuit are trained for whatever jobs they are interested in at the mine, and to support Inuit businesses that wish to bid for supply contracts with the mine. Qauyisaq works on decreasing turnover of Inuit mining staff by creating supports for Inuit and preventing racism, as much of the workforce is non-Inuit from elsewhere. He brings the perspective of Inuit rights in Canada to his job, including the knowledge that the mine would not exist if Inuit had not agreed that it could be there under the mechanisms in the Nunavut Land Claims Agreement.

Of course, these short snapshots of Inuit life-stories of arrival and work in Ottawa represent just a few of the experiences of Ottawa Inuit residents. These residents, like people of any community, are tremendously varied in terms of age, identity, time, and place of residence in the city – and the reasons why Inuit arrive in Ottawa and decide whether to remain are equally varied. Yet whatever their situation, many Inuit in Ottawa have some sort of experience with an Inuit organization in the city, either as staff, program or event participants, or both.

These common threads are present in the life stories of many Inuit residents of Ottawa who were born or raised in the South, such as in the stories of two other long-term Inuit residents, Heidi Langille and Lynda Brown. Heidi was born and raised in Ottawa, although her family's roots are in Nunatsiavut (Labrador). Heidi's father worked for the federal government's Department of Indian Affairs and Northern Development (DIAND). After arriving in Ottawa in 1978, he later became president of the Inuit Non-Profit Housing Corporation (INPHC), which had opened in 1975. INPHC subsidized units in the NWT and Nunavut as well as Ottawa in order to provide low-cost housing for families (Carpenter 1993, 65). It is still active now, providing subsidized housing, with Inuit as the priority population, but also accepting

First Nations and Métis. Heidi's father also helped to set up and organize Inuit House (1976–1983), which would be a welcome point for Ottawa Inuit. In the mid-1980s, Inuit House transitioned into what is now Tungasuvvingat Inuit (Webster 1993).

As a child growing up in Ottawa, Heidi met Inuit visitors to her family's home from across the Arctic. In her early twenties, after spending a few years in Nova Scotia, she reconnected with Inuit in Ottawa in 2002, when she worked at TI and sat on the board of directors of INPHC. It was in these roles that she met Lynda, who at the time was also working for TI and sitting on the INPHC board of directors. Lynda was born in Nunavut but raised in the South. She had moved to Ottawa in high school and connected with TI in 1993. With help from TI she was able to find ways to help fund her post-secondary education away from the city, at Trent University. Lynda returned to Ottawa after graduating in 1998 and worked with the Ottawa Inuit community until 2018, when she took a position with a national Inuit organization.

When Heidi and Lynda met in 2002, they were both parents with young children. Lynda had been working at TI since 1998 and was splitting her time between their employment program and their Sivummut Head Start program, which had opened in 1997. Heidi was scheduled to replace Lynda, who was taking maternity leave from her position as the Head Start coordinator. Organizing the Head Start parent council meetings in 2003 brought Heidi and Lynda together with other parents to, as Lynda explained, advocate "to give parents more of a voice in the decisions around … programming."

Other Inuit arriving from the Arctic have different kinds of experiences, especially those arriving prior to the mid-1970s. Qauyisaq shared a memory about an Inuk who moved to Ottawa in the 1970s:

> I remember her telling me a story about the first time she ever cooked spaghetti noodles in the South. It was the first time she ever made it … she asked her husband, how do I know when the noodles are cooked? "Oh, you just throw it against the wall." So, she said she threw the whole pot of noodles. [laughing] And she was probably born on the land. She used tents and igloos until she was probably in her teens.

Technology, access to southern products, and mobility have reduced this degree of culture shock. Inuit moving to urban centers after the advent of television in Inuit communities in the 1970s, and the internet decades later, have at least some familiarity with what they may encounter. The high mobility of Inuit in and out of northern communities, who can share their experiences, and who keep in touch on Facebook and other social media, also serve to give northern Inuit a sense of urban life. Today, products from elsewhere, such as spaghetti, are flown or shipped into northern communities, and are available for high prices. However, even technology, mobility, and southern products do not completely prepare Inuit who are moving or visiting from northern communities. The urban experience involves being surrounded by white people, experiencing racism, being misunderstood because of cultural differences, and being overwhelmed by having to navigate urban bureaucracies and systems, and jump through hoops to access Inuit rights and benefits. All of these experiences are in addition to having to learn from scratch how to take transit in cities, how to find housing and jobs without community connections, and how to respond to experiences of discrimination. Especially for Inuit who are rather isolated when they arrive, life can be lonely, and opportunities to connect with other Inuit are important. Many of these stories can be accessed through TI's Urban Inuit Knowledge Centre.

WHO AND WHERE ARE THE INUIT OF OTTAWA?

So far, our chapter has focused on some of the individuals who make up the Ottawa Inuit community. This section places these stories in the larger context of the urban Inuit population and movement to the South. There are different figures for how many Inuit live in Ottawa, depending on how they are counted and who counts them (Morris 2016a). Statistics Canada (2016) uses two different definitions in the Canadian census to count the Inuit population living outside of Inuit Nunangat. The first figure is that 27 percent of people who identify as Inuit live outside of Inuit Nunangat, This is the figure that is normally used. The second figure is that 40 percent of people who have Inuit ancestors (where an "ancestor" is "usually more distant than a grandparent") live outside of Inuit Nunangat. Among this 40 percent, not all of the respondents would self-identify as Inuit, despite having Inuit ancestry (Statistics Canada 2016), and they may or may not use Inuit services. Whether one refers to the higher or the lower figure, they both indicate that a significant proportion of Inuit no longer live in the northern land claims regions. This has implications for the continuity of Inuit culture and language, and the importance of Inuit-focused services in urban areas (Morris 2016a). It also points to the need for Statistics Canada to consult with urban Inuit organizations, and not just with Inuit Tapiriit Kanatami. ITK is the national Inuit organization which has representation from all of the Inuit land claims regions but lacks urban representation (Morris 2016b).

The 2016 Canadian census records the Ottawa Inuit population as 1,280 people. However, Inuit community service agencies estimate the population to be "at least 3,700, and as large as 6,000" based on the demand for their services (Pfeffer 2017). A Tungasuvvingat Inuit study (Smylie and Firestone 2017) found that many Inuit in Ottawa did not respond to the census. Ottawa has a large Inuit homeless population, as Inuit come to Ottawa to look for work, or to flee violence at home, but cannot find an affordable place to live (Pauktuutit 2017). Others may not view themselves as residents, having come for medical care or for education (Morris 2016a) What is clear is that Ottawa's Inuit population is growing. Larga Baffin, a boarding home for Inuit from the Baffin region of Nunavut who need specialized medical care in Ottawa, had to expand to 225 beds. It had been operating over capacity for many years, having to house patients and caregivers in hotels (Edgar 2016). TI's monthly Inuit lunch was forced to move from St. Margaret's Anglican Church to a larger space (Gregoire 2013).

Many, but not all, Ottawa Inuit reside in Vanier, just east of downtown Ottawa across the Rideau River. This is because most of the units offered by the INPHC in Ottawa have been in Vanier and regular rental housing in Vanier is more affordable than in the rest of the city. Vanier was traditionally a francophone and working-class community. In the early 1990s, there were only 300 Inuit residing there (Carpenter 1993). Over time, the area gentrified to a certain extent, but its population decreased. However, the population of Inuit residing there increased. Vanier is now also home to a number of Inuit organizations and Inuit meeting places, including some TI services, Inuuqatigiit, Akausivik Inuit Family Health, Wabano Centre for Aboriginal Health, and St. Margaret's Anglican Church.

Although Vanier has a large Inuit population and hosts a number of Inuit services and meeting places, the common association of Vanier with Inuit – as *the* place where Inuit reside in the city – is not entirely accurate, since many Inuit live in other parts of Ottawa and in areas outside of the city limits. Such an association has contributed to negative stereotyping and stigmatization of Inuit. As former TI executive director Jason Leblanc observed (at the Urban Inuit Realities panel mentioned above), Vanier is "one of the most impoverished postal codes in the city, [with] high rates of crime, food insecurity, social housing." Inuit organizers are mindful of such stereotypes and are constantly working to prioritize education of the wider public about Inuit cultural and social identities and about Inuit diversity within the population.

OTTAWA INUIT ORGANIZING

Woven through the life stories and descriptions of Ottawa Inuit life is the prominence of local Inuit organizations. The 1970s and 1980s were the starting point for Inuit institution-building in Canada. It was during this period that Inuit created the various organizations that evolved into those that make up the current institutional landscape of Inuit in Canada. Among the original organizations were Inuit Tapirisat of Canada (1971), Inuit Non-Profit Housing Corporation (1975), and Inuit House (1976). This period also saw the creation of land claims organizations, such as Makivik Corporation, which grew out of the 1975 James Bay and Northern Quebec Agreement. Pauktuutit Inuit Women of Canada was formed in 1984 and chose Ottawa for its national office. Nunavut Sivuniksavut began in Ottawa in 1985 as the Tungavik Federation of Nunavut Training, affiliated with Algonquin College, to prepare post-secondary students for leadership in the land claims region. TI was formed in 1987 to respond to the needs of Ottawa's growing Inuit population. Larga Baffin was founded in 2000 to provide a place for Nunavut Inuit to stay when receiving medical treatment in Ottawa.

TI created the Mamisarvik Healing Centre in 2003, which is a renowned, culturally appropriate treatment program for Inuit adults recovering from trauma and substance-use issues, and the only one in Canada open to all Inuit. The Ottawa Inuit Children's Centre (now called Inuuqatigit) was established by Inuit parents in 2005. The Tungasuvvingat Inuit Family Health Team was established in 2011, becoming the Akausivik Inuit Family Health Centre in 2015 (TI 2019; Gregoire 2015a).

There are often synergies between local, regional, national, and international Inuit organizations based in Ottawa, with staff moving from one to another, and with different organizations sometimes located in the same building. For example, ITK occupies the eleventh floor of a building on Ottawa's Albert Street, while the NTI Ottawa office and the Inuit Circumpolar Council occupy offices on the tenth floor. One of the chapter's co-authors, Marika Morris, conducted her Canadian Institutes of Health Research (CIHR) postdoctoral fellowship as a partnership with Pauktuutit Inuit Women of Canada. She and Pauktuutit were able to access the in-person advice of Nunavut Sivuniksavut students for two entire class periods to shape and name the project, and partnered with Mamisarvik Healing Centre to develop and deliver a workshop for Inuit youth on violence prevention.

In what follows, we focus primarily on Inuuqatigiit and TI, the two "powerhouse" local (rather than national, regional, or international) Inuit organizations in Ottawa. They have both been successful in locating funding sources, lobbying governments, and setting up and maintaining programming and activities.

TI is the main Inuit service provider in Ottawa, has a rich and complex history, and has touched the lives of many of our oral sources. It also has a close connection to one of Ottawa's first Inuit organizations, Inuit House, which was set up in the mid-1970s as a welcome point for Inuit. Local Inuit were able to access funding from the Department of Indian and Northern Affairs Canada (DIAND), as it was then known, as the department's headquarters were just over the river in Hull (now Gatineau), Quebec. However, DIAND funds were cut back in the 1980s, leading Inuit House to close in 1983. After the closure of Inuit House, DIAND counselors Eileen McArthur, and later Brenda Conboy, proceeded to lobby the federal government to open a new Inuit center downtown, which in 1987 became TI, sharing space with ITC on Bronson Avenue (TI 2017). Qauyisaq theorizes that Ottawa was more successful than other cities in founding services for local Inuit for a number of reasons:

> Montreal was the larger Inuit community at one time but there's a different relationship between Inuit, Quebec, and Canada. There really is no Canada presence in Quebec, so, they would have to go through the Quebec government to get any support. I think that is probably a tougher thing to do. Plus, the [national Inuit] political leadership was here [in Ottawa] so you got people going to bat for urban Inuit at big meetings.

Over time, the role of TI has changed. Qauyisaq explains that whereas its role in the 1980s and 1990s was mostly to organize social gatherings and group sports activities, its focus has now turned more towards at-risk populations, reflecting funding availability. TI does not exclude Inuit who are not in need from its events, but the events are not structured with working Inuit in mind. "You know, they always hold lunches during the week ... if you're working, you can't go."

TI has also grown considerably in size, now including over 60 staff running over 20 programs, mainly housed in a much larger office building in Ottawa's west end. It also broadened its concern to helping urban Inuit throughout Canada by securing funding to consult with Inuit in Edmonton, Winnipeg, Toronto, Montreal, and St. John's to develop a National Urban Inuit Strategy (Gregoire 2015b).

TI has also branched into advocacy and representation of Ontario Inuit, signing a memorandum of understanding with the Ontario Ministry of Education. Co-author Marika Morris worked on a project that Qauyisaq spearheaded when he was education policy advisor at TI. The project involved developing Inuit history and culture curriculum resource materials for all Ontario students from grades four to ten.[3]

Although many good relationships and synergies exist among Ottawa-based Inuit organizations, this has not always been the case. TI used to run the Sivummut Head Start program. According to Lynda Brown, parents made use of the program's parent council meetings beginning in 2002 to voice their concerns, to demand a greater role in program decisions, and to broaden the program offerings. As Heidi observed, TI's response to these concerns "was never what the parent council wanted," resulting in considerable "friction, hurt feelings and all the rest of it."

Of course, such disagreements between an organization's bureaucracy and the community it serves are hardly new. In this case, however, the result was that Head Start split off from TI and in 2006 became part of the Ottawa Inuit Children's Centre (OICC), which was established in 2005. OICC took possession of the Head Start building in Vanier, which is still in use. This achievement was the work of about a half-dozen parents of Inuit children, experienced and vocal advocates, who reached out to the Public Health Agency of Canada, the federal government agency funding the program, and learned that the funding contributions agreement that supported Head Start allowed it to separate from TI. The parents, though, had to incorporate a new organization – "a big, big job," according to Lynda, that was done in the early 2000s with "many, many hours of meetings ... [some] that went until after midnight." Heidi recollects that meetings took place weekly "at people's houses ... at people's office buildings ... I think we even met at a park one time."

OICC/Inuuqatigiit added a daycare in 2008 and an afterschool program in 2009, followed by a kindergarten program and a bridging program between the community and school, with the latter providing in-class presentations and one-on-one tutoring for public school students. Since then, Inuuqatigiit has also offered language and literacy, art, and other programs, geared towards not only young children and youth but also Elders and parents. This expansion also led to the creation of new management positions and the acquisition of four buildings, with a fifth under consideration. The growth "falls in line with the growth of the community," although it has also presented many challenges. Among these, Heidi enumerates how to manage growth "and maintain the small community feel amongst the staff." Lynda adds that the challenge remains of how to continue working with TI so that they were not "at odds with each other." The appointment of new executive directors at each organization, including the first Inuk executive director of Inuuqatigiit in 2019, has provided opportunities for more cooperation between Ottawa Inuit organizations and programs. Challenges remain, however, in forging new relationships and in working with municipal, provincial, and federal governments, all of which have experienced political turn-over.

Lynda is proud to see children coming through Head Start to become youth workers engaged in the community and "to have ... lifelong friends that ... have similar experiences and those connections [that] last forever." Many Inuit in Ottawa, in fact, know one another through having worked in an Inuit organization, or participated in a program or event.

It is worth noting that Inuit organizing in Ottawa over the past 20 years has not been confined to efforts requiring government funds. Other sites of Inuit-focused organizing and representation in the public sphere include St. Margaret's Anglican Church, which has programming serving Inuit; and the Inuit community-based radio initiative, Uqallagvik, which was modeled on Montreal's Nipivut radio show (see Watson et al., this volume). These are the subject of the next section.

INUIT CLAIMING MAINSTREAM SPACES IN OTTAWA

Donna Patrick has seen the value of St. Margaret's Anglican Church programming. She recalls one chilly Ottawa spring day in 2007, when she went to the church with Maggie and Sarah Ekoomiak to attend the TI-hosted monthly lunch feast, where

Inuit could enjoy country food. When they arrived in the church's parking lot, they saw people standing in groups of two or three near the back entrance of the church hall. Going around to the main entrance, they met the reverend at the time, who encouraged Maggie and Sarah to enter the main hall and to take seats at the round tables at the front. Although non-Inuit were not invited to, Donna was assured that she could accompany Maggie and Sarah, who wanted her to join them.

Since Inuit country food is a rare treat in the city, it was probably no surprise that the hall was packed. On the main tables sat a big pot of *tuktu* (caribou) stew, arctic char, bannock, and plates of vegetables and cheese; a side table was laden with coffee, tea, and plates of cookies. Sarah and Maggie, speaking Inuktitut, met other Inuit they knew, as together with Donna they relished the camaraderie, food, and socializing. Over the last few years, TI's monthly lunches have changed significantly. Given the growth of the Ottawa Inuit community and the rising costs of country food, the lunches had to offer less country food and move to a larger space a few blocks away, at Our Lady of Assumption Church, where there are no Inuit services.

Although the TI lunches had to move from St. Margaret's, the church hall is still used for after-church Inuit gatherings on Sundays. These grew over the years from a few tables to a packed hall. Donna recalls first venturing into St. Margaret's in 2004, a time when the church was considering tearing down the hall to build social housing for Inuit that would extend into the parking lot. Although social housing was badly needed at the time, the church decided, after much deliberation, against this plan. The need for Inuit to have a space to socialize together weekly was also meeting a profound community need for connection. The church's food offerings have also expanded, Aigah observed, so that they are now the size of a "full meal," with "more Inuit ... bringing country foods if they have [it] so we're sharing the food here ... it's growing since we've been here."

The church is a safe haven for many Inuit, who consider it a familiar place that is open to them, and where they can hear Inuktut spoken. Although the church does not provide health and social services like TI or Inuuqatigiit, more and more people, in Aigah's experience, seek help at the church, reflecting the community's growing needs – turning to the church when they are "struggling with a family [issue], struggling with Children's Aid; struggling with housing issues; struggling with ... trauma and recovery issues," and where they find people who will listen to a problem "and try to work on it seriously, not just talking about it." In other words, in this setting as elsewhere in Inuit community settings, the focus is on action in the urban public realm to support, reshape, and restory Inuit histories and trajectories.

One can also see this support, shaping, and reshaping of Inuit stories in the public realm in a more recent Ottawa Inuit community initiative, Uqallagvik ("radio station"). This is an Inuit-language radio show produced at Carleton University's CKCU 93.1 FM station that aired its first show in May 2019. (CKCU once had a monthly Inuit hour, but it did not have the infrastructure to continue). Uqallagvik is an extension of Montreal's Nipivut ("our voice") radio show and the result of a similar community-university partnership. The show is produced every other week by Jessie Kangok, Janet Evic (both pictured below), and Angeline Ivalu, and managed by Leena Arreak at TI, with funds transferred to TI from a university project grant managed by Mark Watson at Concordia University (see Figure 5.2).

Figure 5.2 Jessie Kangok and Janet Evic, hosts of Uqallagvik at CKCU FM, Carleton University, Ottawa. 2019. Photo: Joël Lamoureux, Tungasuvvingat Inuit.

The show broadcasts for one hour per week and provides announcements and in-person and telephone interviews in Inuktut and English. Some of the material is pre-recorded, but most of the show is live, with immediate translation of announcements and interviews. Since the show is based in Canada's capital, it is, as Jessie Kangok noted, more political than its Montreal counterpart, given the access that the producers have to people involved in Inuit and national politics (Miron 2019). But the show's Inuit music and language offerings and its reflection of Inuit interests and perspectives on urban life are similar to those of Nipivut.

We might say that the community-university partnerships that have led to the Nipivut and Uqallagvik radio programs have, like Donna's research with urban Inuit over the years, provided a public platform for urban Inuit to tell their stories and express their views and concerns about their lives in the city. The two radio projects have also provided a more practical benefit: providing Inuit with roles as managers of project funds and activities, evaluators of the productivity of grants, and project co-creators, working with university-based researchers to find sustainable funding. The researchers involved in these projects have always pursued a collaborative approach to defining the research project, determining how best to carry out activities, and documenting, assessing, and presenting results. The radio program is an important contributor for Inuit exercising their "right to the city" and Inuit management of urban space and inclusivity in the public realm.

CHALLENGES AND ACTION FOR THE PRESENT AND FUTURE

During the writing of this chapter, Inuit organizations at every level have stepped up to deal with the challenges of the COVID-19 pandemic and communicated pandemic-related information to Inuit via Facebook, which is in popular use among Inuit across the North and in urban centers. At the national level, ITK has also provided leadership, intervening with the federal government on behalf of Inuit. ITK adapted its Strategy and Action Plan budget to, among other COVID-related activities, produce a publication on *The Potential Impacts of COVID-19 on Inuit Nunangat* (ITK 2020):

> Inuit may be at higher risk for contracting SARS-CoV-2 [COVID-19] compared to most other Canadians and may be at higher risk for experiencing severe illness from COVID-19 due to health and social inequalities. The poor living conditions experienced by our people have the potential to magnify the impacts of the COVID-19 pandemic in Inuit communities by accelerating the spread of the virus within overcrowded homes ... Some Inuit may also face unintended social impacts from preventative public health measures [e.g. isolating in the home, closures of workplaces, schools, and daycares], such as domestic violence, child sexual abuse, unemployment and mental distress.
>
> (ITK 2020, 4)

ITK also produced culturally appropriate posters and shareable infographics about safety measures. These each provide a simple message in English, Inuktut syllabics, and Roman orthography, and were available in various Inuit languages (see Figure 5.3).

At the local Ottawa level, Inuuqatigiit Centre for Inuit Children, Youth, and Families posts up-to-date information about changing City of Ottawa regulations concerning the use of public parks, facilities closures, physical distancing, and mask-wearing. Normally, the Inuuqatigiit Facebook page posts information about jobs available, support for children's schooling and adults returning to school, mental health resources, creativity contests for kids, awards, videos for learning Inuktut, messages from Ottawa-area school boards affecting Indigenous students, recipes for healthy eating, and upcoming Inuuqatigiit programming and community events. During the COVID lockdown, it also posted activities people could do at home with children (such as making your own Inuit bone and stick game out of materials such as pens and string) and information about COVID-related financial and mental health supports. It reposted ITK's COVID-19 infographics to ensure Ottawa Inuit had access to this culturally – and linguistically – appropriate information.

Challenges also remain for Ottawa-based Inuit organizations to work with other Inuit organizations across Canada. So far, there has been some significant work from TI, including consultations from 2014 to 2016 in six Canadian cities (St. John's, Montreal, Ottawa, Toronto, Winnipeg, and Edmonton) to develop a National Urban Inuit Strategy to support the increased participation of Inuit in the economy (TI 2016). Pauktuutit's consultations delved in much more detail into urban Inuit women's experiences in the same cities, except St. John's (Pauktuutit 2017). The Pauktuutit report is full of quotations from urban Inuit women that bring life to the needs that are documented and the solutions recommended. Consultations performed by these organizations differ from consultations by governments or pan-Indigenous organizations in that they are based on Inuit Qaujimajatuqangit principles (TI 2016, 10), are usually led by Inuit, and are usually located in places that are, or are made to feel, culturally familiar to Inuit.

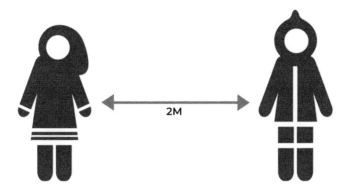

Figure 5.3 Inuit Tapiriit Kanatami Social media infographic, 2020. Courtesy of Inuit Tapiriit Kanatami.

Both reports highlight key issues such as housing insecurity, children taken into care, high rates of suicide, incarceration, and lack of access to culturally appropriate health and social services. In Ottawa, for example, 15.6 percent of the Inuit population is homeless, compared with less than 1 percent of the total population of Ottawa (TI 2016, 11). Almost a quarter of Inuit children and youth in Ottawa (23 percent) have had involvement with child welfare services (TI 2017, 18). Statistics such as these are very important to know and deal with, but can also serve to stereotype urban Inuit, the majority of whom are not homeless, addicted, or suicidal, and do not have children in care.

Whether Inuit in cities are experiencing these issues first- or second-hand, most Inuit are concerned about ensuring all Inuit, no matter where in Canada they live, have appropriate help if and when they need it, and ways to keep in close touch with Inuit culture, social and spiritual support and language. A strong and proud sense of culture and language can be a cornerstone of well-being, and part of a response to racism and stereotyping which seek to impose negative and narrow cultural misunderstandings onto Inuit. The long-term solution also involves public education and changes to public policies and institutions to eliminate socioeconomic inequalities between Inuit and other Canadians, and to promote Inuit well-being through knowledge of and pride in culture and language.

Qauyisaq notes that Inuit organizations do not follow Inuit traditional, decentralized forms of leadership and ways of working, but have taken on the model of hierarchical not-for-profit organizations that must operate in certain ways to maintain government funding. "They're a foreign environment ... for a lot of Inuit." A number of Inuit begin their careers working in Inuit organizations, which may give them both a broader sense of the issues affecting Inuit and how positive change can be made, as well as giving them experience in a mainstream-type of organizational structure that they would find elsewhere in the workforce. As such, Inuit organizations may be functioning as a bridge to employment for some Inuit.

Some organizations may still be dominated by non-Inuit in managerial roles, an area of some resentment and desire for change. Qauyisaq found that:

> the most challenging parts were always interacting with non-Inuit that worked for Inuit organizations with no experience with living in the North, no lived experience. Even if they do have the lived experience, they think that two years that they spent hiding in their apartment in Iqaluit is a northern experience.

Qauyisaq would like to see an Inuit-owned community center in Ottawa where larger events could take place, even national and international conferences. Most important for Qauyisaq is for Inuit to access their rights as Inuit no matter where they live. For this and for action on the continuing inequities faced by Inuit, governments need to keep up with the insights and recommendations of Inuit organizations who have consulted with Inuit and issued reports and recommendations on every priority issue.

CONCLUSION

Inuit in cities are beginning to affect and change wider social, economic, and political spaces, as well as providing Inuit-specific spaces where Inuit can regroup and recuperate. The impact of attempts to change broader systems is most evident in Ottawa, where Inuit had a head start through the earlier establishment of national and local organizations. Inuit organizations are on the front lines of educating governments and the public about the inequities facing Inuit at the national, regional, and local level, and local Inuit organizations such as Tungasuvvingat Inuit and Inuuqatigiit also provide direct services to Inuit. A challenge for these organizations has been changing governments, with changing funding priorities, and the need to operate in ways, and do only the things, that governments will fund. An advantage of the national and local organizations being based in Ottawa is the synergy of staff and occasional formal and informal partnerships between them. They respond together and separately, as the case may be, to emerging issues such as the COVID-19 pandemic. TI has also created spaces for urban Inuit across Canada to share experiences and strategies.

Inuit in Ottawa have not only established and expanded Inuit-specific services, but are making inroads in carving out Inuit spaces in non-Inuit institutions, like a local Anglican church and a radio station. Inuit are integrating into the larger community, but without compromising their identities and values as Inuit. Connections to Inuit culture, language, and social support remain a cornerstone of Inuit well-being in the city. Networks of Inuit, who may know each other from northern communities or through an Inuit organization, are working together to find services, jobs, and peace. In this chapter, we have highlighted the voices and experiences of a few of the many Inuit who came to Ottawa and stayed, made connections in the community, and worked toward continued inclusion, understanding, and community well-being.

NOTES

1. Inuktut refers to all varieties or dialects of the Inuit languages spoken in Canada. Inuktitut refers to an Inuit language spoken in the eastern Arctic; it is one variety among many.
2. It is notable that Mumilaaq Qaqqaq stated that she will not run again after her first term in office, citing her frustration in experiencing racism as an Inuk Member of Parliament, and lack of progress on the challenges facing Inuit and other Indigenous people in Canada.
3. As the provincial government changed during the course of this project, the status of these materials, and whether they are available or used, is unknown.

REFERENCES

Canadian Broadcasting Corporation (CBC). 2015. "Vintage CBC North: Celebrating 20 Years of Northbeat, Igalaaq." CBC, 10 November. https://www.cbc.ca/news/canada/north/vintage-cbc-north-celebrating-20-years-of-northbeat-igalaaq-1.3312666. Accessed 23 July 2020.

Carpenter, Mary. 1993. "Urban Inuit." *Inuktitut Magazine* 76 (1993): 62–69. https://www.itk.ca/wp-content/uploads/2016/10/1993-0076-InuktitutMagazine-IUCANS-IULATN-EN.pdf. Accessed 10 July 2020.

Clancy, Peter, and P. Whitney Lackenbauer. 2019. *Shaping Inuit Policy: The Minutes of the Eskimo Affairs Committee, 1952–62*. Calgary, AB: University of Calgary.

Edgar, Courtney. 2016. "Nunavut Patient Boarding Home Has Room to Grow in Ottawa." *Nunatsiaq News*, 19 July. https://nunatsiaq.com/stories/article/65674nunavut_patient_boarding_home_has_room_to_grow:in_ottawa/. Accessed 25 August 2020.

Freeman, Mini Aodla. 2015 [1978]. *Life among the Qallunaat*. [2015 edition edited by Keavy Martin and Julie Rak]. Winnipeg, MB: University of Manitoba Press.

Gregoire, Lisa. 2013. "Inuit Share Stories, Country Foods, at Ottawa Lunch." *Nunatsiaq News*, 21 October. https://nunatsiaq.com/stories/article/65674inuit_share_stories_country_foods_at_ottawa_lunch/. Accessed 24 August 2020.

———. 2015a. "Ontario's Only Inuit-Specific Clinic a Model of Patient-Centred Care." *Nunatsiaq News*, 16 February. https://nunatsiaq.com/stories/article/65674ontarios_only_inuit-specific_clinic_a_model_of_patient-centred_care/. Accessed 10 July 2020.

———. 2015b. "Ottawa Org Building National Urban Inuit Strategy." *Nunatsiaq News*, 13 October. https://nunatsiaq.com/stories/article/65674ottawa_org_building_national_urban_inuit_strategy/. Accessed 23 August 2020.

Inuit Tapiriit Kanatami (ITK). 2020. *The Potential Impacts of COVID-19 on Inuit Nunangat*. Ottawa, ON: ITK. https://www.itk.ca/wp-content/uploads/2020/06/itk_the-potential-impacts-of-covid-19-on-inuit-nunangat_english.pdf.

Lefebvre, Henri. 1968. *Le droit à la ville*. Paris: Anthropos.

———. 1996. *Writings on Cities* (trans. E. Kofman and E. Lebas). Cambridge, MA: Blackwell.

McCallum, Mary Jane Logan. 2014. *Indigenous Women, Work and History: 1940–1980*. Winnipeg, MB: University of Manitoba Press.

Miron, Kahlan. 2019. "Ottawa Inuit Get New Inuktitut Radio Show." *Nunatsiaq News*, 12 June 2019. https://nunatsiaq.com/stories/article/ottawas-first-inuktitut-radio-show/ Accessed 12 August 2020.

Morris, Marika. 2016a. "A Statistical Portrait of Inuit with a Focus on Increasing Urbanization: Implications for Policy and Further Research." *Aboriginal Policy Studies* 5 (2): 4–31. http://dx.doi.org/10.5663/aps.v5i2.27045

———. 2016b. "Statistics Canada Data Collection on Inuit: The Importance of Consultation and Context." *Aboriginal Policy Studies* 5 (2): 136–148. http://dx.doi.org/10.5663/aps.v5i2.25452

Nunavut Tunngavik Incorporated (NTI). 2010. "Jose Kusugak Receives the Elijah Menarik Award." NTI, 22 November. https://www.tunngavik.com/news/jose-kusugak-receives-the-elijah-menarik-award/

Pauktuutit Inuit Women of Canada. 2017. *Understanding the Needs of Urban Inuit Women*. Ottawa, ON: Pauktuutit. https://www.pauktuutit.ca/wp-content/uploads/358996508-Final-Report-UAS-Urban-Research-April-2017.pdf.

Pfeffer, Amanda. 2017. "'Woefully Inaccurate' Inuit Population Data Overwhelming Local Agencies." *CBC News*, 12 November. https://www.cbc.ca/news/canada/ottawa/woefully-inaccurate-inuit-population-ottawa-1.4391742. Accessed 25 August 2020.

Purcell, Mark. 2014. "Possible Worlds: Henri Lefebvre and the Right to the City." *Journal of Urban Affairs* 36 (1): 141–154. https://doi.org/10.1111/juaf.12034

Smith, Graeme. 2004. "Ship's Passage Opens Old Wounds for Inuit." *Globe and Mail*, 10 July. https://www.theglobeandmail.com/news/national/ships-passage-opens-old-wounds-for-inuit/article954390/

Smylie, Janet, and Michelle Firestone. 2017. *Our Health Counts: Urban Indigenous Health Database Project*. Ottawa, ON: Tungasuvvingat Inuit (TI).

Statistics Canada. 2016. "Aboriginal Ancestry." *Dictionary, Census of Population, 2016*. https://www12.statcan.gc.ca/census-recensement/2016/ref/dict/pop145-eng.cfm

Tungasuvvingat Inuit (TI). 2016. *National Urban Inuit Community Dialogue: Supporting Local Champions*. Ottawa: Tungasuvvingat Inuit. https://www.tungasuvvingatinuit.ca/wp-content/uploads/2017/06/National-Urban-Inuit-Community-Dialogue-EN.pdf. Accessed 23 July 2020.

———. 2017. "Tungasuvvingat Inuit Celebrates 30 Years of Serving the Inuit Community." News release, 10 March. http://tungasuvvingatinuit.ca/wp-content/uploads/2017/03/Press-Release-March-10-EN.pdf. Accessed 12 July 2020.

———. 2019. "About Us." TI. https://www.tungasuvvingatinuit.ca/overview/ Accessed 23 Aug. 2020.

Webster, Debbie. 1993. "Tunngasuvvingat Inuit: A Place Where Inuit Are Welcome." *Inuktitut Magazine* 76: 70–76. https://www.itk.ca/wp-content/uploads/2016/10/1993-0076-InuktitutMagazine-IUCANS-IULATN-EN.pdf. Accessed 10 July 2020.

Wilton, P. 1993. "'TB Voyages' into High Arctic Gave MDs a Look at a Culture in Transition." *Canadian Medical Association Journal* 148 (9): 1608–1609.

CHAPTER 6

BUILDING BOOMS AND SHIPPING CONTAINER HOUSING

Geographies of urbanization and homelessness in Nuuk, Greenland

―――・*・―――

Julia Christensen and Steven Arnfjord

INTRODUCTION

The summer of 2018 was a busy one in Nuuk, Greenland. In June, foreshadowing a trend that would last until August, a local newspaper ran the headline "Bygge-Boom" (building boom) across its front page. One evening, from Steven's balcony, we counted almost two hands' worth of cranes, busily assembling new residential high rises and government buildings across the Nuuk skyline. Yet that same summer, a cluster of shipping containers was unceremoniously deposited next to the garbage dump, and transformed into 12 low-cost housing units for single men and women in the community. These units were meant to immediately house those who could afford to pay a small amount in rent, but who had been unable to find housing through the public housing office. The program was intended to address in some small way what housing advocates in the community have described as a dramatic increase in the past 15 years in the number of Greenlanders living without housing in the city. In a participatory photography workshop with adult men and women experiencing homelessness, which we held as a part of our ongoing research on housing and homelessness in Nuuk, the topic of rapid development in the city was frequently discussed. Nothing was the same, and yet so much was: the rural-urban disparities driving the most recent wave of urban development was a familiar reflection of resettlement policies that have framed settlement geographies in Greenland since the earliest days of Danish colonization (see Figure 6.1).

While Nuuk experiences a rapid expansion, accounts of housing insecurity and homelessness are also abundant in local media coverage and public discourse. In 2017, a man identified in the media as homeless was found alive after 17 days in a warehouse where he had sought shelter but found himself locked in and unable to get out. Local media coverage of housing concerns and the plight of Greenlanders experiencing homelessness has increased steadily alongside the fervor of municipal expansion. Indeed, anecdotal reports from housing advocates and support providers in the city indicate the number of people experiencing acute, or visible, homelessness in Nuuk is on the rise. These are the Greenlanders most vulnerable to the current national and municipal social policy vis-à-vis housing insecurity and homelessness, which is to say the absence of any social policy at all. Thus far, there has been no

Figure 6.1 Construction cranes for new housing, Nuuk, summer 2018. Photo: Julia Christensen.

coordinated social policy effort at the national or municipal level to deal with the vulnerabilities that are exacerbated through contemporary Greenlandic urban strategy. Though state-owned public housing and housing cooperatives were, since the 1950s, the dominant housing tenure form, urbanization in Greenland has come hand-in-hand with efforts to develop housing markets in the regional centers, particularly Nuuk (Hansen and Andersen 2013). This has meant a growing neoliberalization of public housing in the capital in order to manage an increase in demand for what is ultimately a diminishing supply of public housing (Hansen and Andersen 2013). Exacerbating the disconnect between supply and demand for public housing is the fact that Nuuk is experiencing substantial population growth and yet, because many people fail to register officially with the municipality upon arrival, authorities are unsure of the actual total of current residents (Sørensen and Willumsen 2013).

This chapter emerges from our larger study aimed at understanding the social dimensions of homelessness in Nuuk, Greenland which began in 2015. What we see today in the city, and what we explore in this chapter, is the confluence of (re)settlement, urbanization, and acute housing need in the form of visible homelessness. We are interested in examining here how the trajectory of housing need and homelessness over time interconnects with the trajectory of resettlement and urbanization, and how both parallel developments can be understood as part and parcel of the welfare colonial experience in Greenland. In other words, homelessness in Nuuk does not emerge out of nowhere, but rather must be situated within the broader context of colonialism and urban development in Greenland.

We begin with a brief overview of the history of colonialism, resettlement, and urbanization in the Greenlandic context, with a particular focus on the capital city of Nuuk. The colonial experience in Greenland has been facilitated through the social welfare state, a process that involved significant manipulation of the ways in which Indigenous peoples organized themselves spatially and socially. Thus, the processes of urbanization cannot be disentangled from the larger context of welfare colonialism and its effects on the health and social geographies of the Greenlandic people. Yet the decolonization of Greenland through Greenlandic self-determination and self-governance has not resulted in a reversal of urban trends. In fact, the Self Rule government has turned to urbanization as a means towards increased autonomy from the Danish state, a policy that has had distinct consequences for those who are otherwise marginalized in contemporary Greenland. Finally, we examine the significance of a Greenlandic urban policy and the ways in which it brings into harsh light the absence of social policy on housing and homelessness.

URBANIZING GREENLAND

Today, Nuuk is a city of almost 18,000 and home to over 30 percent of the country's population, and is undergoing incredible expansion, building up and out at a pace that is almost impossible to track. The fervent push behind this rapid development, however, is not only to meet the needs of people who currently call the city home, but also the thousands of Greenlanders from rural settlements that the municipality of Sermersooq, the municipality in which Nuuk is located, and the Greenlandic government plan to resettle in the capital city in the coming years. Twenty minutes from central Nuuk, a new Sermersooq subdivision – Siorarsiorfik – will be the largest urban development project ever in Greenland, designed to address significant population growth and persistent housing need in the municipality, as well as draw young Greenlanders living abroad back to the country's capital. As we explore in this chapter, this latest urban expansion plan is part and parcel of a very long trajectory of (re)settlement and urbanization in Greenland. This trajectory was a core element in Danish colonial policy in Greenland, and has thus rendered urban and colonial forms and processes largely inextricable.

Over the early- to mid-20th century the Danish state actively pursued the centralization of previously nomadic Indigenous peoples in Greenland (Dahl 2010). Though (re)settlement policies were enacted to promote Greenlandic participation in the wage economy and facilitate administration by the colonial state, there were profound social and spatial implications as well. One of the key tools to promote settlement was the expansion of social welfare services, including the implementation of public health programs, education, public housing, and income support. The intention was to bring Greenlanders into the administration and culture of the Danish state – including language, and culturally rooted practices of home, health, family, and social organization. Indigenous languages, customs, and cultures were actively undermined through policies like "Danification" (Danish: *Danisering*), meant to erode Greenlandic language and even remove "promising" youth to boarding schools in Nuuk or to foster families in Denmark. These practices disrupted and dislocated Greenlandic homes, health, family, and community – the effects of which are ongoing today in what scholars articulate as the intergenerational effects of colonialism, namely negative effects on mental and physical health, family and community relations, sense of place, and cultural identity. Furthermore, these practices effectively produced the condition of chronic housing need, which underlies the emergence of hidden and visible forms of homelessness in Greenland.

As the Greenlandic people resumed self-determination over their own lands in the later part of the 20th century as part of a general process of decolonization and increased independence from the Danish state, questions of social administration and urban planning have remained key to the implementation of self-government. Today, Greenland is governed under a self-government arrangement, hereafter referred to as Self Rule.

While Greenland remains within the Kingdom of Denmark, the country has autonomy over its central governmental activities, including social policy, education, health, economy, and housing, while relying on Denmark for defense and foreign policy. Greenland has universal health care and is considered a welfare society in the Scandinavian model, meaning that taxpayers pay close to half their income in taxes in exchange for a wide spectrum of publicly administered services. At the same time, Greenland does receive considerable subsidies from Denmark to support its economy. In contemporary Greenland, an ever-sharpening urban focus has become central to the Self Rule government, and in this way, resettlement and urbanization have become entangled as key strategies towards self-determination and ultimately, total independence from the Danish state.

Greenland's 56,000 inhabitants are settled in 17 towns and some 60 smaller settlements (Danish: *bygder*) primarily along the west coast, which since 2009 have been administratively organized into four municipal regions. Notably there is no national road system, and therefore transportation between settlements is primarily by helicopter, small airplane, or boat. Not surprisingly, transportation is expensive, which further limits mobility between communities. About 90 percent of Greenland's population is ethnically Greenlandic (Inuit) while the remainder is mainly Danish (CIA 2017).

The population is highly urbanized, with well over 30 percent of Greenlanders living in the capital city, Nuuk, and over 85 percent living in the four largest settlements combined. Thus, towns and cities play a significant role in the lives of Greenlanders (Sejersen 2010). While Greenland's towns and cities are not large relative to urban centers in Europe or elsewhere in the world, its largest settlements constitute important administrative, political, economic, educational, and social centers. "The definition of a town in Greenland," according to Sejersen (2010, 167), "is thus not only related to its size, but moreover to its importance as a center." The trend towards urbanization in Greenland is only growing, with urban populations rising while the number of rural dwellers is on the decline (Hansen et al. 2013). This is due in part to the fact that Greenlandic towns have been singled out as drivers of the kind of social change sought after by the Self Rule government (Sejersen 2010). In a referendum in 2008, roughly 75 percent of the Greenlandic population voted yes to a law giving more self-rule to Greenland; a self-rule that was later approved by the Danish Parliament for implementation in 2009. This move necessitated an aggressive and clearly defined approach to self-determination and independence. At the same time, in order to finance greater independence from Denmark, the Self Rule government has largely looked to industrialization to lessen its dependency on financial transfer payments from Denmark (Nuttall 2008). The effects of climate change have led the Self Rule government to speculate about the potential for industrial development due to the country's strategic position globally vis-à-vis oil and gas development and the shipping industry (Larsen 2010). Despite what was traditionally a pessimistic and anti-urban attitude in Greenland, a Greenlandic way of life is no longer seen as incompatible with life in towns or cities (Sørensen 2008).

Yet while the Self Rule government plods ahead with its Sermersooq expansion plans in Nuuk, we are interested in what continued rural-urban migration, urbanization and resettlement mean for Greenlanders experiencing housing insecurity and ultimately, forms of homelessness. Much of the literature on Arctic rural-urban migration has identified this phenomenon as motivated by the pursuit of educational and employment opportunities. Yet in the pursuit of modernization and independence through urbanization, without adequate social policy responses to chronic housing needs and increasing visible homelessness in Nuuk, a significant number of Greenlandic citizens continue to be marginalized through resettlement. Though the policies and political powers have shifted over the years, the Self Rule government today has done very little to improve or plan for the housing and social welfare needs of socially marginalized Greenlanders.

The uneven geographies of social welfare institutions have a critical presence in Arctic homeless pathways, and Greenland is no exception. Those at particular risk of homelessness include low-income Greenlanders who face compounding life challenges, framed in large part by chronic housing need, poor mental health (including trauma), developmental disabilities, addictions, and breakdowns in intimate, family, and community relationships, risk factors that are indelibly tied to the sociocultural and material legacies of colonialism and modernization in the Arctic (Bjerregaard and Curtis 2002). The absence of key health and social supports in rural settlements and their concentration in urban centers is an important outcome of resettlement and one that directly affects the (im)mobility of Greenlanders experiencing housing insecurity and homelessness. However, it is critical to acknowledge that the condition of homelessness itself is produced and reproduced through the absence of housing – accessible, affordable, adequate housing that meets the needs of Greenlanders who may be living with a combination of the factors mentioned here.

COLONIALISM, RESETTLEMENT, AND URBANIZATION IN GREENLAND

Early colonization and settlements

Greenland was first colonized by Denmark in 1721. Yet despite Danish presence in Greenland, their influence was deliberately at arm's length. Historically, Greenlandic people lived largely nomadic lives, moving according to the seasons, the physical and spiritual bounds of their territories, and the availability of the animal and plant resources upon which their lives depended. At the beginning of the colonial period, trade was based primarily on whaling, but by the closing of the 18th century, the Royal Greenland Trade Company (a Danish state company formed in 1776) had established a large number of small trading posts along the west coast. The Company offered basic provisions to Greenlandic hunters in exchange for skins and furs. The Danish state favored this decentralized settlement pattern at the time, believing it supported a high level of self-sufficiency and facilitated trade in hunting products by still encouraging traditional subsistence lifestyles.

Though a Danish-Greenland relationship had been ongoing for over two centuries, it was the Second World War that brought about the most profound transformation for Greenland. Similar to experiences in Alaska and the Canadian North, the period around and following the Second World War thrust Greenland into the global spotlight and inspired renewed and intensified interests from the colonial (Danish) state. During the war, Greenland was entirely cut off from Denmark, and the United States, as well as Canada, established relationships with the colony which was positioned strategically between North America and Europe. After the war came to its conclusion, Denmark signed a new constitution which changed Greenland's status from a colony of Denmark to a Danish province, and gave Danish citizenship to all Greenlanders. As Stenbaek (1987) explains, this shift in relationship led many Danes to believe that Greenlanders (or "northern Danes") and Greenland should be remade into a northern Denmark – a social, spatial, and indeed cultural reflection of the state of Denmark. A shift in ideology thus occurred during and following the Second World War as the Danish state saw the economic, administrative, and geopolitical advantages of centralization, and of the assimilation of Arctic peoples into Danish cultural practices and modes of social organization.

Resettlement, modernization, and urbanization

The most aggressive resettlement and modernization period occurred from the 1950s to 1970s, under consecutive reform schemes launched in 1950 and 1964. These followed two parliamentary reports – the Report from the Commission for Greenland, published in 1950 and later referred to as G50, and the Report from the Greenland Committee of 1960, published in 1964 and referred to as G60 – authorized by the Danish government to review the possibilities for development in Greenland. Danish and Greenlandic politicians believed the industrialization of fish production to be an efficient way to improve Greenlanders' standards of living. In order to improve the level of welfare, education, living standards, and the labor market, movement to a handful of chosen towns along the west coast was encouraged by the Danish authorities. Though families were initially invited to relocate with promises of new housing and better economic prospects, many communities were closed down outright, or had investments withheld to encourage a concentration of the population in centers of industrial development, where modern educational, social, and health establishments were centralized.

Under G60, economic development in Greenland was concentrated in four towns – Nuuk, Sisimiut, Paamiut, and Maniitsoq. Between 1952 and 1963, approximately 3,000 households, which included families and extended families, were moved from smaller coastal settlements of roughly 100–200 inhabitants each, to these fast-growing towns as part of this modernization process. Substantial investments were channeled into infrastructure, housing, production facilities, and education as well as health institutions (Adolphsen and Greiffenberg 1998). Towns became centers of construction work on a previously unknown scale, resulting in abrupt changes to their physical layout, with the building of factories and concrete apartment buildings, known as the Bloks, as well as roads and other infrastructure (see Figure 6.2).

Although improvements to Greenlandic social welfare were the stated objective, this rapid resettlement had the effect of alienating people from their culture and

Figure 6.2 New apartments under construction behind Blok Q, a 1960s era concrete apartment block. Photo: Julia Christensen.

livelihoods, imposing living conditions that people were not used to and not culturally prepared for, and led to the increasing prevalence of health and social problems (Deth Petersen 1986). Housing needs were calculated as the total required to cover renewal, migration, and population increase (Deth Petersen 1986). The new apartment units built in the coastal towns were very small, and were designed primarily for small or nuclear families, a practice that continues today, despite the fact that many Greenlandic families lived (and continue to live) in multi-generational settings. Part and parcel of the resettlement strategies were the promises of housing and employment, including block housing projects in Nuuk. One of the infamous symbols of this period, these high-density apartment buildings, lined in rows in the center of Nuuk's downtown, were built to house the hundreds of families who were resettled from outlying settlements. The new housing and development plans emphasized high-density housing programs in regional centers alongside the expansion of social welfare services, which included the implementation of public health programs, education, and income support (Olsen 2005). These housing projects were modern (by the standards of that era) apartment blocks with sanitation, electricity, central heating, and larger indoor spaces. They were part of a broader modernization project in Greenland from 1950 to 1980 (Olsen 2005). The apartments were designed for families engaged in modern employment, and were established by Danish-organized political committees with little appreciation for the needs and wants of Greenlandic society. For example, the housing was not suitable for traditional subsistence activities like butchering a seal, although they had modern facilities like running water and electricity. Meanwhile, massive resettlement actually resulted in limitations in the employment and housing opportunities promised by the state, as migration increased competition for the limited supply of both (Deth Petersen 1986).

However, no strategies were in place to deal with the negative consequences of the resettlement, homelessness included. At this time, Greenland experienced what has been described as the period of its most direct colonial oppression, despite the fact that it was no longer legally considered a colony of Denmark, as the welfare system was developed, and Danish intervention was at its highest (Sørensen 1983). Towns became the symbolic, as well as concrete, manifestation of Danish cultural and political dominance and the arena for assimilation of Greenlanders into a Danish way of thinking and behaving.

CONTEMPORARY RESETTLEMENT AND URBANIZATION

Though the 1950s to 1970s brought about significant and unprecedented change to Greenlandic settlement patterns; prioritization of the urban and an encouragement of rural-urban resettlement persists today – the most recent examples can be seen in the 2002 public housing tenants rent reform (Danish: *huslejere*), and the municipal expansion in Nuuk. With the establishment of Home Rule in 1979, financial and political focus temporarily included a decentralized settlement structure, based on Greenlandic values – the so-called Greenlandization (Danish: *Grøndlandisering*) – and emphasizing a return to small places to compensate for years of neglect by the Danish state (Dahl 2000). However, efforts to manage the mounting challenges of an aging housing stock and at the same time bolster efforts towards increased independence from Denmark, led to renewed centralization and urbanization efforts.

Centralization now continues through both passive and overt policies meant to disincentivize rural life and encourage urbanization, which has a particular impact on Greenlanders who are marginalized through a lack of education or employment skills, or the presence of chronic health conditions such as addiction or trauma. Though the social welfare state has allowed the persistence of small settlements, the lack of economically sustainable local economies has meant that when services and investment are pulled back, there is little reason for local residents to stay. This kind of tactic has been employed time and again in Greenland in an effort to encourage migration to Greenland's largest centers, with little attention given to those who do not have the skills, resources, or social support to thrive in an urban economy. The promotion of an uneven geography of key health and social welfare services on the part of the Danish government, and now the Self Rule government is, we argue, a passive form of resettlement policy. Moreover, the present-day "bygge-boom" (construction boom) underway in Nuuk, with its new emphasis on private rental and owned housing, makes clear that urban life is not being envisioned for all Greenlanders, but only those who can afford such housing. A remarkable irony can indeed be found in a bygge-boom that does not include a diversification on the housing spectrum in order to meet the needs of all Greenlanders. In a country where public participation in policymaking has been emphasized, it is clear that participation does not include those Greenlanders experiencing acute housing need and homelessness.

Passive and overt centralization

Extension of the social welfare state to Greenland following the Second World War was a key strategy in what was effectively an ongoing Danish colonial interest in

Greenland. The centralization of key health and social services in Greenlandic towns and cities produced an uneven institutional geography across Greenland, one that is particularly important to the lives of marginalized Greenlanders who are at the highest risk of housing insecurity and forms of homelessness. Under the Self Rule government in Greenland today, urbanization is facilitated through deliberate policies. The most important change in this direction is probably that the 18 Greenlandic municipalities were merged into five large regional municipalities in 2018, and as a consequence, the majority of the city administration and associated jobs have been gathered in the five municipal center cities. Not only has there been a significant centralization of a number of public functions, where most publicly or semi-publicly owned corporate offices and administrations have gradually been gathered in the capital Nuuk, but there has been a significant impact on the centralization of post-secondary education, public housing and health, and social services. Parallel to the centralization of municipalities, a health facilities centralization has been ongoing since 2011. The former 16 health districts were combined into five health regions. This meant the closing of district hospitals and the centralization of health care services into the five largest Greenlandic centers, a move that was justified by dubious economic advantages and administrative arguments that it would improve the quality of health care.

While important social welfare functions have been concentrated in the core centers of these four municipalities, the implementation of a simultaneous "real costs" policy has also played a key role in encouraging rural-urban movement. While Hendriksen (2013) argued that the social welfare state previously served to facilitate small settlement dwelling due to subsidy programs that supported rural life, particularly the uniform price system, policy change in 2002 resulted in a partial reform of this system. The uniform price system subsidized electricity, heating, and water for the smaller communities, but since 2002 these have been gradually clawed back in order to create prices in the smaller communities that reflect "real costs" – a reform that is geared to benefit the economic dynamics in the towns and to promote a transfer of populations from local communities to the more competitive towns (Winther 2010). As a result, the high cost of living in the smaller communities has disincentivized rural life, and the resulting isolation of rural Greenlanders has been further compounded by changes in the transportation structure and the pricing system.

Framing the landscape of housing insecurity and homelessness in Greenland are the country's historical and contemporary dimensions of resettlement and rural-to-urban mobility. Though the resettlement plans of the mid-20th century were enacted to promote Greenlandic participation in the wage economy and facilitate administration by the colonial state, they also had profound social and spatial implications. Centralization policies then put into motion a distinct rural–urban geography in Greenland, a geography that frames the emergence of visible forms of homelessness in Greenlandic urban centers. The shifting spatial dynamics of the Greenlandic social welfare state have particular consequences for those who are without adequate education, or who are dependent on health and social services. The very institutions that are key in the lives of Greenlanders living with housing need or homelessness are precisely those that are increasingly centralized in urban Greenland: public housing, emergency shelters, the child welfare system, and the spectrum of health services.

HOUSING AND HOMELESSNESS IN GREENLAND

Homelessness as a Greenlandic social phenomenon is, with few exceptions, presented as predominantly urban, and largely Nuuk-centered (Arnfjord and Christensen 2016). A 2013 report cites an estimate of approximately 600 people living homeless in Greenland as a whole (Hansen and Andersen 2013). This number includes shorter homeless periods ranging from days to a few weeks; however, it says little about homelessness as a more chronic situation. In fact, the absence of a standardized definition of homelessness in Greenland makes it difficult to assess who is homeless and to draw meaningful comparisons between rural and urban communities, or to assess the scale and scope of homelessness within Greenland as a whole. Moreover, there is anecdotal evidence of significant numbers of people living homeless who are actually invisible in the system due to a lack of formal municipal registration. In the capital city of Nuuk, the conservative estimate of people living under a more permanent state of homelessness is 100–200 (Hansen and Andersen 2013). Our research however has uncovered anecdotal evidence from NGO-based support providers that the number of homeless individuals in Nuuk alone is upwards of 300 people. Moreover, we have found that there are four main experiences of homelessness that are most prominent: (1) men over 30 years of age who struggle with substance abuse; (2) youth with family, social, or economic problems who migrate from small settlements to larger centers in hope of new opportunities; (3) women who either are childless or no longer have custody of their children, and who have often been victims of domestic violence; and (4) men and women over 55 who have been evicted from their housing after failure to pay rent. It is predominantly the second and third groups whose experiences of homelessness are most affected by the kinds of passive and overt resettlement policy we describe in this chapter.

Urban housing landscape

Recent efforts on the part of the Self Rule government to promote resettlement to urban centers have included a steady decline in funding for housing in smaller settlements and the redirection of those funds towards public housing in the larger urban centers, mainly Nuuk (Hendriksen 2013). However, this redirection of funds has not resulted in an adequate increase in the number of public housing units. In fact, the infamous Blok housing is being dismantled, diminishing the overall public housing stock. Meanwhile, public housing in the Greenlandic context does not necessarily mean housing for low-income Greenlanders. In Greenland, housing is viewed as a matter of public responsibility and consists mainly of public housing. Thus, the bulk of rental housing in Nuuk, and in Greenland as a whole, is public with a private housing stock in 2010 of just 7,173 units compared to the public housing stock of 13,650 units (Greenland Statistics 2016).

Rental housing in Greenland is largely administered in one of two ways: through public housing or through public-sector employment. To access public housing, which is administered by Greenland's public housing authority, INI (Greenlandic: Inatsisartut Inissiaatileqatigiifik), one can add one's name to the housing list starting at age 18. These waiting lists, however, can be incredibly long. In Nuuk, for example, it can take upwards of 15 years to get an apartment on one's own. Meanwhile, certain jobs within the public sector (i.e., teacher, nurse, university professor) come with apartment assignments. As long as one maintains the post, one gets to keep the assigned rental apartment. Previously it was not uncommon to have employment-related apartment assignments, where rent was covered as part of one's salary, but this changed with the introduction of the "real cost" reform (Hansen and Andersen 2013).

There is currently no plan to support diversification of the housing stock, or to add to the housing spectrum. In fact, according to Hansen and Andersen (2013), the historical and continued dominance of the public housing market has contributed to this lack of diversity by discouraging or even preventing the development of a private housing sector. As a matter of social policy, rents were, prior to 2002, subsidized so significantly that the private rental sector did not have the incentive to build to a greater extent, as the market-determined rents would have been significantly higher than the rents for publicly owned rental housing. Meanwhile, savings were not accrued to cover the costs of public housing maintenance, which has led to a significant backlog in repairs and retrofitting.

Meanwhile, the challenges of providing subsidized housing to an increasingly urban population, where the urban public housing stock has not increased along the same trajectory, has led to the adoption of more punitive housing policies. The Self Rule government and Sermersooq municipality continue to pursue an aggressive urbanization program that does not include a robust strategy to address rising numbers of homeless adults and families in Nuuk, or Greenland as a whole. Moreover, these ambitious municipal expansion and centralization plans are being pursued alongside the neoliberalization of the housing market. For example, Hansen and Andersen (2013) reveal an increase in evictions from public housing between 2005 and 2013, which were due largely to increasing enforcement of rent and housing rules in light of diminishing housing stock. At the same time, evicted tenants may face great financial punishments not only due to unpaid arrears but also because the financial burden of repairs and renovations fall upon the tenants, a direct result of the Self Rule government not having a maintenance and renovation budget. Thus, public housing tenants currently subsidize the cost of building maintenance through the rents they pay, which results in higher rents and greater financial strain on the tenants themselves.

Alternatives to the public housing waiting list include (1) getting an education in order to find a job with an assigned apartment, or (2) purchasing a private house or apartment, which are both expensive and in short supply. In other words, the Greenlandic housing landscape can be highly problematic for those Greenlanders who do not have an advanced education or sustainable employment prospects. While Greenlandic is the country's official language, Danish is also widely spoken, and is the primary language of operation in the professional world, public administration, and postsecondary education – another remnant of Danish welfare colonialism in Greenland that leaves marginalized people behind. As several scholars have found, there is a distinct rural–urban disparity in Danish literacy, education levels, and employment outcomes (Hansen et al. 2013), leaving those who migrate from small settlements to larger centers at a significant disadvantage in the employment and housing markets.

Rural-urban geographies of homelessness

While the literature on Greenlandic homelessness, though sparse, touches on the dynamics of social marginalization, very little explicitly conceptualizes homelessness in Greenland within its specific geographical, cultural, or social context. For example, research suggests that rural-to-urban and Greenland-to-Denmark migration is a significant factor in Greenland homeless geographies, yet the dynamics of rural-to-urban mobility and their role in Greenlandic homelessness have not been well explored (Hansen and Andersen 2013). Rasmussen (2011) surveyed a representative sample of 1,550 people on the motivations behind their rural-to-urban moves. The top responses included education and employment, living conditions, social network, leisure opportunities, and access to public services. Furthermore, the majority of Greenlanders engaging in a rural-to-urban move were young people between the ages of 15 and 25, which reflects a similar observation by Hansen and Andersen (2013) that youth likely to engage in such a move were most at risk of homelessness.

With the lack of investment in economic and educational opportunities in many of the small settlements, young people in these communities are forced to seek these opportunities in regional urban centers or beyond. Our research echoes the findings of Hansen and Andersen's (2013) study, revealing a growing trend of youth migration to the cities, particularly Nuuk, without any secure housing arrangements in place. This results in unsustainable temporary housing solutions, such as staying with friends or family.

Another strategy is for people to leave the country entirely to seek opportunities elsewhere within the Kingdom of Denmark (including the Faroe Islands). This typically means traveling to Denmark, where Greenlanders hold citizenship, and where more than 14,000 Greenlanders currently reside (Baviskar 2015). Yet this kind of move does not always mean a brighter future. Recently, the Danish Council of Social Marginalization released a follow-up to a previous report on Greenlandic homelessness in Denmark. The report describes problematic conditions, such as language barriers, issues with access to education and employment, and disempowered social networks, as well as challenges with regards to Danish support staff who have limited understanding of Greenlanders' experiences and support needs. Thus far, there has been little joint effort between Greenland and Denmark to offer public help to prevent the homelessness of Greenlanders in Denmark, leaving them instead in the care of Danish NGOs.

This somewhat mirrors the situation in Greenland, where the continued lack of engagement by the public sector around homelessness issues has been enabled in some sense by the active engagement of the non-profit sector that has sought to fill the gap in programs and services for the housing insecure and homeless. In fact, these new forms of urban community and caring organizations are a positive outcome of the trends towards an increasingly urban Greenland. Local NGOs collaborate with one another to provide services to people living homeless in Nuuk, and they also express a common agenda to empower people living under homelessness and provide facilities for people within the environment to voice their concerns.

NoINI, Kofoeds Skole, the local chapter of the Røde Kors (Red Cross), and Frelsens Hær (Salvation Army) are filling the gaps in public sector support, and what is particularly interesting and problematic here is that much of the funding is either provided through foreign sources, local fundraising, or very, very few short-term pockets of funding from the municipal government. If the headquarters for these organizations determined different priorities and refocused their funds elsewhere, the consequences would be disastrous for Nuuk and Greenland as a whole. Already, the NGOs cannot provide a full slate of support services – for example, Frelsens Hær and NoINI offer the soup kitchen only one night a week. Furthermore, these NGOs are run by dedicated but overworked staff as well as volunteers, making the landscape of supports for urban Greenlanders experiencing homelessness even more precarious.

CONCLUSION

Several themes emerge to illustrate the ways in which resettlement and urbanization policies have, over time, laid the foundation for visible homelessness in Nuuk. In stark contrast to policy attention towards the encouragement of rural-urban movement stands the total absence of social policy on homelessness. There is currently no homelessness strategy in existence at the municipal or national level in Greenland. The limitations of the ideological belief that housing is a public responsibility are revealed in the absence of not only an official definition of homelessness, but a social policy directed towards Greenlanders experiencing homelessness.

There is reason for concern that homelessness will continue to rise in the capital. The intensified centralization, since 2011, of health and social services and facilities in Nuuk and the next four largest Greenland centers, as well as the urban concentration of employment and educational opportunities, make the regional centers a draw for all Greenlanders, including those at risk of homelessness. Meanwhile, the reality is that the municipality of Sermersooq, which includes Nuuk, is allocating more resources, including land, for housing, but not for the low-income groups, which suggests that ensuring a diverse housing spectrum is not a political priority. Yet while the Self Rule Government's urban focus is not limited to the facilitation of the wage economy, but also to the administration of health and social services, it has not implemented a social policy strategy to manage the consequences of centralization on marginalized Greenlanders. As a result, understanding homelessness as a distinctly urban issue becomes self-fulfilling or re-enforcing.

The rural–urban migration patterns of people living without secure housing in Nuuk are bound up in key institutional geographies, themselves significant in the lives of people experiencing homelessness through the complex dynamics of intergenerational effects of welfare colonialism. In particular, we have heard stories from youth who have been released from foster/boarding homes without housing in Nuuk, men and women who have been sent to Nuuk for psychiatric care and then released without housing, men and women sent to Nuuk for hospital care and then released without housing, men going to the jail but then released again without housing, and finally women who have migrated to Nuuk to escape violence at home, only to encounter tremendous difficulty in accessing housing once in Nuuk.

Significantly, there is very little funding and policy direction from the national government. This is a big concern because housing and other social supports are delivered by municipalities, and, with little to no coordination or follow-up between municipalities, there is a need for more leadership from the Self Rule government. With little national involvement, the onus falls on the municipalities and does not reflect the national geography of homelessness. This has resulted in the non-profit sector becoming increasingly involved in issues around homelessness, particularly in Nuuk. Some initial research has been conducted on the developing individual and collective actions of Nuuk NGOs, although it is still at an early stage (Arnfjord 2015).

In order to understand and ameliorate visible forms of homelessness in Nuuk, we must expand our focus outside urban bounds in order to fully attend to the significance of rural-urban dynamics. Moreover, Nuuk is enmeshed in rural–urban, Greenland–Denmark dynamics that extend beyond northern bounds, particularly along historical or contemporary (welfare) colonial-administrative relations. The Greenland–Denmark ties are incredibly significant when examining the mobility of Greenlanders experiencing homelessness. Yet, there is no integration of service delivery between the two countries, nor is there a coordinated policy approach to homelessness in general.

The ongoing legacies of (re)settlement are evident in Greenland, as the intergenerational effects of early resettlement policy and institutionalization underlie the service dependency of those Greenlanders experiencing housing insecurity and homelessness in Nuuk today. At the same time, resettlement and urbanization became representative of the welfare colonial process as Denmark sought to transform Greenland into a northern image of itself. Today, as Nuuk continues to expand at a fervent pace, and an urban Greenland is promoted to local and international audiences, there is an urgent need for social policy that directly addresses homelessness in Greenland at a national scale; one that recognizes the historical geographies that underlie what is commonly understood to be a contemporary phenomenon. In fact, housing insecurity and homelessness in Greenland today cannot be extricated from the broader, historical, welfare colonial context. State efforts to encourage resettlement to Nuuk must include comprehensive and robust efforts to ensure the inclusion of all Greenlanders in its urban self-image.

REFERENCES

Arnfjord, Steven. 2015. "Social udsathed og tuberkulose i Nuuk" [Social Marginalization and Tuberculosis in Nuuk]. *Tikiusaaq* 2 (23): 20–24.

Arnfjord, Steven, and Julia Christensen. 2016. "Understanding the Social Dynamics of Homelessness in Nuuk, Greenland." *Northern Notes* 45: 4–5.

Adolphsen, Jes Barsøe, and Tom Greiffenberg. 1998. *The Planned Development of Greenland 1950–1979*. Aalborg: Institut for Samfundsudvikling og Planlægning, Aalborg Universitet.

Baviskar, Siddhartha. 2015. *Grønlændere i Danmark: En registerbaseret kortlægning [Greenlanders in Denmark: A Census-Based Mapping]*. Copenhagen: SFI.

Bjerregaard, Peter, and Tine Curtis. 2002. "Cultural Change and Mental Health in Greenland: The Association of Childhood Conditions, Language, and Urbanization with Mental Health and Suicidal Thoughts among the Inuit of Greenland." *Social Science & Medicine* 54 (1): 33–48. https://doi.org/10.1016/S0277-9536(01)00005-3.

CIA (Central Intelligence Agency). 2017. *The World Factbook*. Greenland.

Dahl, Jens. 2000. *Saqqaq: An Inuit Hunting Community in the Modern World*. Toronto, ON: University of Toronto Press.

———. 2010. "Identity, Urbanization and Political Demography in Greenland." *Acta Borealia* 27 (2): 125–140. https://doi.org/10.1080/08003831.2010.527528

Deth Petersen, Marie-Louise. 1986. "The Impact of Public Planning on Ethnic Culture: Aspects of Danish Resettlement Policies in Greenland after World War II." *Arctic Anthropology* 23 (1–2): 271–280.

Greenland Statistics. 2016. *Aarsstatistik 2016 [Annual Statistics 2016]*. Nuuk, Greenland: Grønlands Politi.

Hansen, Klaus Georg, Søren Bitsch, and Lyudmila Zalkind, eds. 2013. *Urbanization and the Role of Housing in the Present Development Process in the Arctic*. Nordregion Report 2013:3. Stockholm: Nordregio.

Hansen, Knud Erik, and H. T. Andersen. 2013. *Hjemløshed i Grønland [Homelessness in Greenland]*. Aalborg: Statens Byggeforskningsinstitut, University of Aalborg.

Hendriksen, Kåre. 2013. *Grønlands bygder: Økonomi og udviklingsdynamik [Greenland's Settlements: Economic and Development Dynamics]*. Aalborg: Aalborg Universitet and Danmarks Tekniske Universitet.

Larsen, Joan Nymand. 2010. "Climate Change, Natural Resource Dependency, and Supply Shocks: The Case of Greenland." In *The Political Economy of Northern Regional Development*, vol. 1, edited by Gorm Winther, 205–218. Copenhagen: Nordic Council of Ministers.

Nuttall, Mark. 2008. "Self-Rule in Greenland: Towards the World's First Independent Inuit State." *Indigenous Affairs* 8 (3–4): 64–70.

Olsen, Tupaarnaq Rosing. 2005. *I skyggen af kajakkerne: Grønlands politiske historie 1939–79 [In the Shadow of Kayaks: Greenland's Political History 1939–79]*. Nuuk, Greenland: Atuagkat.

Rasmussen, Rasmus Ole. 2011. "Why the Other Half Leave: Gender Aspects of Northern Sparsely Populated Areas." In *Demography at the Edge: Remote Human Populations in Developed Nations*, edited by Dean Carson, Rasmus Ole Rasmussen, Prescott Ensign, Lee Huskey, and Andrew Taylor, 237–254. Farnham, UK: Ashgate.

Sejersen, Frank. 2010. "Urbanization, Landscape Appropriation and Climate Change in Greenland," *Acta Borealia* 27 (2): 167–188. https://doi.org/10.1080/08003831.2010.527533.

Sørensen, Axel Kjaer. 1983. *Danmark-Grønland i det 20. Århundrede- en historisk oversight. [Denmark-Greenand in the Twentieth Century: A Historical Overview]*. Copenhagen: Nyt Nordisk Forlag Arnold Busck.

Sørensen, Bo Wagner. 2008. "Perceiving Landscapes in Greenland." In *Nordic Landscapes: Region and Belonging on the Northern Edge of Europe*, edited by M. Jones & KR Olwig, 106–138. Minneapolis, MN: University of Minnesota Press.

Sørensen, Jane, and Ulla Willumsen. 2013. "Housing Issues in Nuuk (Greenland) and How to Get Students Involved." *Études/Inuit/Studies* 37 (1): 175–193. https://doi.org/10.7202/1025260ar.

Stenbaek, Marianne. 1987. "Forty Years of Cultural Change among the Inuit in Alaska, Canada and Greenland: Some Reflections." *Arctic* 40 (4): 300–309.

Winther, Gorm, ed. 2010. *The Political Economy of Northern Regional Development*, vol. 1. Copenhagen: Nordic Council of Ministers.

PART II

MORAL, SPIRITUAL, AND INTELLECTUAL WORLDS

CHAPTER 7

RESOURCE EXPLORATION AND EXTRAORDINARY HAPPENINGS IN GREENLAND'S COASTAL NORTHWEST

Mark Nuttall

INTRODUCTION

The Inuit world is more than the surficial appearance, formations, and textures of ice, snow, water, and land. Like all territory, it has depth and volume. It is a world of interspecies engagement and extraordinary happenings. People travel on sea and ice to hunt marine mammals and to fish, and they range far and wide on islands and land, from the tideline where they collect mussels, to further inland where they gather plants and bird eggs, hunt muskox and caribou, or head to rivers and lakes to fish. Yet they are also attentive to – and talk about – what lies below ground and above the earth, between the foreshore and the water's edge, within the sea, deep within hills and mountains, under the ice, and in the sky. Canada's national Inuit organization, Inuit Tapiriit Kanatami (ITK), uses the term Inuit Nunangat, which refers to land, water, and ice, as the most appropriate way to think about and describe the country's four Inuit homelands of Nunavut, Nunavik, Nunatsiavut, and the Inuvialuit Settlement Region. In doing so, ITK makes the distinction between the Inuktitut term *nunangat* and the Kalaallisut (Greenlandic) term Inuit Nunaat, which the ITK feels only refers to land and excludes water and ice. In Greenland (Kalaallit Nunaat), however, the world is not thought of and spoken about merely as terrain, water, or iciness, but as *pinngortitaq* – all that is around, above, below, underneath, and within; something continually coming into being, taking shape, dissolving, moving, merging, reforming, and reshaping (Nuttall 2017). Along with the world's surface, the subterranean, the ocean depths, and the atmospheric are enmeshed with the lives of humans, animals, and more-than-human beings and entities.

The underground and the geological have an imaginative force (cf. Bobette and Donovan 2019), and in Greenland the subterranean is also implicated in political discourse on future-making and sustainability. Deep time plays into and influences ideas about the kind of future to which Greenland aspires. A self-governing territory of the Kingdom of Denmark, Greenland is often at the forefront of scientific and media reports about global warming and the interest expressed by extractive industries in the resource potential of Arctic subsurface environments. Many Greenlandic politicians are also ambitious for political independence. Economic development policy in

Greenland has been shaped greatly over the past decade or so by the anticipation of a resource boom and the possibilities this might entail for achieving greater economic and political autonomy. Not all agree with this policy – for example, a number of grassroots organizations, NGOs, and communities have been critical of the regulatory processes surrounding resource extraction projects and are worried about the social and environmental impacts.

In this chapter, I illustrate this by drawing from some of my recent anthropological research in the Upernavik and Melville Bay area of northwest Greenland that is concerned with the effects of shifting and thinning ice, changing social worlds, mineral exploration, and environmentalist action on people's lives. Interspecies and multispecies encounters characterize the human history of the region and contemporary human-environment relations. Humans, animals, fish, snow, ice, water, rocks, wind, storms, wave action, and everything else that makes up and moves within and through these Arctic surroundings intermingle and share and shape them. Surprising things occur, but some extraordinary happenings may result, some people think, from the disturbance that resource exploration brings. Through an illustration of local concerns over seismic surveys investigating seabed geologies for the presence of oil and mining exploration carried out on land in recent years, I consider some of the ways people living in the region often think of and talk about their surroundings and their encounters with industry and with global processes, as well as the non-human entities which they say should also be included in participatory processes and considered in environmental impact assessments (see Figure 7.1).

Figure 7.1 Communities in northwest Greenland depend on hunting and fishing. During winter and spring, sea ice is vital for travel and movement, yet it is being disrupted by climate change. Melville Bay, northwest Greenland. Photo: Mark Nuttall.

SPECULATION AND EXPECTATION: MAKING THE GREENLAND RESOURCE FRONTIER

Greenland achieved Home Rule in 1979 and a greater degree of self-government with Self Rule in 2009. Significantly, ownership of subsurface resources was transferred from Denmark to Greenland in January 2010 and, to a considerable extent, much discussion has focused since then on how the country's economic prospects are tied to the extraction of minerals and hydrocarbons. Democratically elected Greenlandic parliaments and governments have, for a number of years, decided that oil, gas, and mineral exploitation should contribute to the overall sustainable development of Greenlandic society. As Greenland's government pushes forward with strategies for reducing the country's dependency on the annual block grant it receives from Denmark, and thinks about the possibilities for independence, developing a mining industry and, until recently, encouraging exploration for oil and gas have remained stated political aims. The geological mapping and representation of the vertical and volumetric dimensions (cf. Elden 2013), as well as the materialities, of the subsurface and the seabed and their hydrocarbon and mineral assemblages, are crucial elements of this policy (Dodds and Nuttall 2018; Nuttall 2017).

Under Greenland's Mineral Resources Act, prospecting, exploration, and exploitation licenses are only granted to public limited companies domiciled in Greenland. In effect, this means that foreign companies establish Greenlandic subsidiaries (which they mostly entirely own), often with offices in the capital, Nuuk, or other towns such as Ilulissat, Narsaq, or Qaqortoq. A number of resource projects are going through exploratory phases as well as the approvals process for exploitation and operational licenses. At the time of writing, a ruby and pink sapphire mine near Qeqertarsuatsiaat in southwest Greenland and an anorthosite mine southeast of Sisimiut were operating. An exploitation license has been granted to Australian company Ironbark Zinc Limited to develop a zinc-lead mine in Citronen Fjord in Peary Land in the country's far north, and recently to Tanbreez, another Australian company developing a rare earth metals project in south Greenland. Greenland Minerals (yet another Australian company), which has been planning for some years now to mine uranium and rare earth elements at Kuannersuit (Kvanefjeld) near Narsaq in south Greenland, is awaiting a decision related to its application for an exploitation license. The public hearings for the environmental and social impact assessments took place in February 2021, but the result of a snap election two months later put the project's approval and its future in doubt. The left-wing Inuit Ataqatigiit party (IA) formed a coalition government with the centrist-populist and pro-independence Naleraq party. While IA supports mining, it is opposed to the extraction of uranium and radioactive elements. A large ilmenite (an iron titanium oxide) "black sand" mine on the south coast of the Steensby Land peninsula near the closed settlement of Moriusaq, 42 kilometers northwest of Thule Air Base in northwest Greenland – known as the Dundas Ilmenite Project and being developed by Dundas Titanium A/S, which is registered in Greenland but 100 percent owned by the UK company Bluejay Mining, was given approval at the end of 2020. Dundas Titanium has been granted a 30-year exploitation license and is moving ahead with plans to develop the mine. Exploitation will see ilmenite extracted from coastal sand and shipped south along the west coast. The black sand under Moriusaq itself will also be mined for ilmenite, meaning that empty houses and other community buildings will be removed. Former residents who live elsewhere in the region – mainly in Qaanaaq – as well as others in the wider Qaanaaq region, use Moriusaq as a base for hunting (often for polar bear, walrus, and muskox), fishing, and overnight stays. Dundas Titanium points out that the local community is supportive of the project, and cites evidence for this in its social impact assessment report, but in the conversations I have had with people from Qaanaaq and Savissivik during recent fieldwork in northwest Greenland, it is clear that opinions are divided and that many have concerns over the environmental and social impacts and are concerned about being excluded from traditional hunting areas. Bluejay is also active with two projects in central west Greenland: in the Disko-Nuussuaq region (assessing prospects for nickel, copper, platinum, and cobalt mining) and at Kangerluarsuk (exploring the potential of zinc-lead-silver-copper deposits).

Mineral resources such as rubies, pink sapphires, uranium, and rare earth elements, and hydrocarbons, sand, and glacial rock flour have become objects of value for sustainable futures. This informs representations and impressions of Greenland as a dynamic extractive frontier that promises much to the companies and stakeholders that invest in the projects being marked out in it. However, despite this speculation, a number of projects have failed to materialize, including a much-hoped-for iron ore mine 150 kilometers northeast of Greenland's capital Nuuk, for which a production license had been granted in 2013 (Nuttall 2017). And while the waters of the west coast have been surveyed extensively for oil, none has been found. Assessments of the prospects for mining and oil development have caused Greenland's government to reflect on the danger of relying too heavily on the extractive sector. A fall in global markets has made some international companies cautious of working in Greenland for the time being, while the COVID-19 pandemic in 2020 disrupted that year's summer season's exploration plans for those who were still excited by the prospects and possibilities of an emerging resource frontier. In May 2020, Greenland's then-government announced a financial support scheme for mining companies whose plans had been put on hold by the restrictions imposed and the economic repercussions of the pandemic, as a way of encouraging them to stay invested in the country. However, as Bernauer and Slowey (2020) point out for Canada, researchers will need to pay careful attention to how the COVID-19 pandemic and the associated economic crisis is affecting and intensifying conflicts between Indigenous communities and extractive industries. Discussion over the future of extractive industry in Greenland is unlikely to escape similar scrutiny.

In July 2021, the new coalition government announced that it was suspending the granting of new licences for oil exploration, pointing out that Greenland was now committed to developing strategies for renewable energy. Despite this, the subsurface remains critical for Greenlandic notions of nation-building and state formation and ambitions for political and economic independence. This was underscored when, also in July, ICC-Greenland joined the Arctic Economic Forum (AEC), separately from its parent organization the Inuit Circumpolar Council (ICC; which was one of the founding members of the AEC in 2014), with the intent to promote Greenland's pro-mining stance and to argue that mineral extraction, along with tourism, was essential for diversifying the economy.

It may be more accurate to comment that Greenland's extractive sector is currently generating an economy of expectation characteristic of other resource zones, as well as being implicated in the dynamics, volatility, and turbulence of global markets (Watts 2015; Weszkalnys 2011; 2015). Speculative narratives about extraction and its economic potential abound and are often framed within a context of a rapidly warming Greenland in a "new" Arctic, where melting ice supposedly makes access to resources easier. The subsurface spaces involved in the making of this resource frontier are integral to a new earthly politics about Greenlandic autonomy (Dodds and Nuttall 2019). There is a geopolitical dimension to this as well. Foreign investment – including possible Chinese funding – is vital to the further development of Greenland's resource and infrastructural capabilities, while US interest in Greenland has been notable not just in the opening of a US consulate in Nuuk in summer 2020, but in the signing of a memorandum of understanding (MoU) in June 2019 that set out a framework for cooperation on mineral sector governance and technical engagement between Greenland's Ministry of Mineral Resources and the US Department of State. Among other things, the MoU has allowed for the joint Greenlandic-US funding of an aerial hyperspectral survey that was carried out over south Greenland in summer 2019. In October 2020, the US and Greenland signed a further agreement that constitutes a common plan for cooperation on bilateral trade and investment, science, minerals, and energy. Practices of envisioning and making the subsurface known are implicated in geopolitical imaginaries about the Arctic that inform strategy, contestation, and possibly conflict (e.g., Dodds and Nuttall 2018; Kama and Kuchler 2019). International interest in Greenland's resources shows that the strategic importance of the world's largest island has not diminished even if this interest is framed rather more in environmental, social, and economic ways, rather than a concern with potential military conflict, defense, and security, as it was during the Cold War. As Klaus Dodds and I argue, we can think of Greenland as a geo-assemblage (Dodds and Nuttall 2019), by which we mean a space where topological and topographical relationships and networks play their part in assembling and mobilizing discussions and narratives about Arctic sustainability, geopolitics, and environmental futures. Component parts of a geo-assemblage, we suggest, are engaged in, entangled with, and affected by, a complexity of processes that act to stabilize or destabilize them.

Resource talk in Greenland today illustrates how strata can be implicated in political life (Clark 2017) and how resources are made and given value (Bridge 2009; Li 2014). Whatever the economic possibilities, though, resource extraction and the nature of public participation in decision-making processes remain contested political, economic, social, and cultural affairs (Nuttall 2017). Mining companies promote their projects by emphasizing the uniqueness and scale of Greenland's geology and its mineral deposits (they are often described as being of the highest grade), and by arguing that mines will create economic opportunities – for example, Ironbark's website describes its Citronen zinc-lead project as "one of the world's largest undeveloped zinc-lead resources" while Bluejay claims the area it is prospecting for its Disko-Nuussuaq project has "potential to host mineralisation similar to the world's largest nickel/copper sulphide mine Norilsk-Talnakh ('Norilsk') in Siberia." Bluejay also stresses the uniqueness of the ilmenite deposit. Ilmenite is mined for its titanium – titanium dioxide is used as a pigment in paint, plastics, enamels, paper, and in cosmetics and in the making of a range of metal alloys, and the Dundas Ilmenite Project has been classified as the world's highest-grade mineral sand ilmenite deposit. Yet concerns are routinely expressed that such projects are in environmentally sensitive areas which are also (or are near to) cultural sites and vital places for hunting and fishing, and there are public anxieties over social and economic impacts. Exploration activities animate fraught political and public discussions concerning the future of Greenland, and include voices – ICC-Greenland and local non-governmental organizations have been especially critical – that wonder if a Greenlandic economy that includes an oil and mineral sector can be considered sustainable and proceed without major environmental disturbance and social disruption. Such critiques draw attention to Greenland, as a post-colonial territory and state in formation, being subject to a form of extractive colonialism characterized by what Leigh Johnson (2010) terms accumulation by degradation.

Along with speculative thinking, planning processes for extractive industries involve political, economic, abstractive, and calculative practices that define, mark off, and allocate value to resource spaces and extractive zones in what are defined as remote areas at a distance from human habitation. Subsurface geologies are assessed for their economic potential and classified as stocks of ore and hydrocarbons. The spaces – rendered as storehouses – in which these resources are situated and attributed value, though, are often places of multispecies encounters that are composed and brought into being through action and relations between the human and more-than-human. In resource company-speak and in impact assessments, however, they are described as frontier zones and are represented in reports and public hearings as empty wilderness areas with no human presence or imprint and low in biodiversity, yet filled with an abundance of subsurface resources that justify investment in lucrative mineral projects that promise to produce significant tonnage of commercial value. In narratives and discussions of both resource development and environmental protection, and in the processes that lead to environmental and social impact assessments, however, local people say they are rarely consulted and are often insufficiently informed about planned resource projects, especially in communities that would be close to or affected by extractive projects (e.g., Nuttall 2016). Also excluded, they say, are the more-than-human entities (including animals and other beings) that compose, configure, and animate the world along with humans. By way of illustration, I show how this is so in the Upernavik area of northwest Greenland.

EXTRAORDINARY HAPPENINGS IN NORTHWEST GREENLAND

About 2,800 people live in the Upernavik area, which is part of north Greenland's Avannaata municipality. The town of Upernavik has a population of around 1,100 and some 1,700 people inhabit nine smaller villages, ranging in size from about 50 in Naajaat to 450 in Kullorsuaq (Greenland's largest village). Many people are hunters and fishers. They utilize marine and terrestrial resources along and around the headlands, bays, islands, and fjords of a 450 kilometer stretch of coast, from the area close to the northern edges of Sigguup Nunaa (Svartenhuk) in the south to Qimusseriarsuaq (Melville Bay) in the northern part of Baffin Bay. Much of the catch shares – from seals, walrus, and Greenland halibut, for instance – circulate within and around families, households, and communities, but meat and fish products also find their way into and around local and country-wide distribution channels and provide the basis for a formal or cash economy (alongside the informal one of procurement, sharing, and reciprocity that is characterized by kinship and close social association) which gives people the opportunity to earn some of the money necessary for maintaining a hunting and fishing way of life. Local knowledge of the multilayered and textured places in which hunting and fishing activities occur, and through and around which people move and travel, is extensive, rich, and deep. Human–environment relations arise from, are given meaning, and are reproduced through the inter-weavings, entanglements, and trajectories of human and non-human entities, and the rhythms and flows, as well as the often difficult challenges and uneven turns, of everyday life on water, ice, and land. In some ways, Philip Hayward's (2012) idea of the aquapelago, an assemblage of marine and terrestrial spaces, seems apt as a description of the Upernavik area (as it does for Greenland as a whole). But for people who live in the region, this is *pinngortitaq*, a world that is always coming into being, forming and reforming – more than just the surface of the earth – encompassing water, ice, soil, rock, sky, and wind; surroundings which include the air, atmosphere, subsoil, mountain interiors, and earth processes; what is above and below and around, and how all of these things intersect, interact, and are entwined.

But climate change is rapidly affecting *pinngortitaq*. Sea ice is diminishing and the sea is warming. Glaciers are undergoing significant and often rapid melt at their fronts and on their surfaces; they are also retreating, and iceberg calving rates are on the increase (Box and Decker 2011; Cowton et al. 2018; van As 2011). Greenland's inland ice is experiencing mass balance loss, more surface melt, and increased run-off (van den Broeke et al. 2017), which also affects sea ice formation (Stroeve et al. 2017). The people who live in the Upernavik district observe, and are affected by, these environmental shifts, as are the residents of other parts of northwest Greenland (e.g., Hastrup 2018; Nuttall 2019a; 2019b). Over the last few years, I have spoken with many of those I know there about how they feel their surroundings are being reconfigured, and even disfigured, by abrupt climate change and rapid melt. The speed and extent of the changes they now experience around them present problems for travel, whether by dog-sled during winter and spring or by open boat during summer and autumn, and challenges their anticipatory knowledge (see Figure 7.2).

The last decade or so has also seen a number of activities in the area that have been related to oil exploration and the surveying and assessment of potential mining sites. These activities are often accompanied by technical reports and economic assessments of increasing accessibility to the region as the ice melts. License blocks in which exploration and exploitation can happen have been marked out in the coastal waters of the northwest by the Greenland government's minerals authority. For a few years, northern Baffin Bay was under the gaze of international oil companies and Upernavik was a busy place as a base for offshore activities and site surveys. Extensive seismic surveys took place in 2012 and 2013, but the seismic data were disappointing for the oil companies. No exploratory activity has been carried out since the last seismic surveys in 2013. However, some of those surveys encroached on a narwhal protection zone in Melville Bay. There is an annual hunting quota for narwhals in Upernavik district and Melville Bay which is adjusted each year. Most narwhals are hunted during the open-water season from August to September, which is the same period when seismic activities can operate in the area. I have written elsewhere about how,

Figure 7.2 Kangersuatsiaq, Upernavik district. Photo: Mark Nuttall.

following the surveys in 2012 and 2013, hunters from communities in the Upernavik district, as well as from Savissivik, reported that narwhal behavior was different and some felt that the hunt had been influenced negatively due to the seismic activities in the area (Nuttall 2016; 2017). The seismic survey vessels may have kept away from the coastal waters for a few years now, but even though they have been absent I am interested in how many people in Upernavik district still feel their presence in the lingering effects of their exploratory activities. Local observations, mainly by hunters, suggest that narwhals have remained restless since the ships were operating out at sea. In recent research, I have been listening to hunters' accounts of how, each spring and into the summer when narwhals arrive on their northward migration, they have been moving closer to the coast, swimming deeper into fjords and inlets that are choked with ice (which increases the risk of ice entrapment for narwhals when the sea eventually freezes in autumn or early winter). For example, hunters say that the seismic surveys made narwhals alarmed, restless, and agitated (*pikitsisivoq*) and they also observe that narwhals are sometimes confused or perplexed because they are frightened of something in the water (*uisanguserpoq*).

Local viewpoints and opinions vary about the prospects of the seismic survey vessels or exploration ships ever returning to northern Baffin Bay. Still, many people I know in the Upernavik area do worry that the oil companies will be back, despite the recent suspension of exploration, and they are concerned over an increase in mineral exploration and marine traffic. They talk about the necessity of communities being prepared to deal with industry, of being ready to express their thoughts and concerns, and for meaningful consultation to take place. Prior to the seismic surveys, visits to communities by the companies were short, and people said that they had received little information about exploration and its effects on the marine environment. They felt that the company executives and consultants had no interest in understanding the nature of *pinngortitaq* and the importance of animals for local livelihoods.

I have heard people remark in Upernavik that both indigenous use and knowledge of the sea, ice, and land, as well as the world below their feet, are overlooked and purposely ignored in discussions and decisions about resource development or environmental protection. Indeed, oil and mining companies get much of the information they think they need about northwest Greenland from the strategic environmental impact assessments and oil-spill sensitivity atlases compiled through the involvement of scientists based mainly at universities and research institutes in Denmark, as well as the occasional Nuuk-based expert. As Dransart (2013) puts it, vital powers emerge from the ways humans, animals, and other beings and entities come into contact and relate to each other (also, see Haraway 2008), but the social and environmental impact assessments carried out by consultants for particular projects do not consider those resource spaces or zones marked for conservation as places of textured human-animal-environment relations, or constellations of memories, narratives, stories, and possibilities. Instead, they are rendered remote places outside the human domain – rather than acknowledged as socio-natural worlds of interaction that are constantly in the making.

While people in the coastal northwest express concerns that marine mammals have been anxious or frightened in relation to seismic surveys, they also talk about how places – or ice, waves, and currents – appear agitated and disturbed. Such concerns are consistent with how mining activities and oil exploration, involving intensive seismic surveys and subsurface mappings, and large-scale industrial development plans such as hydropower and aluminum smelter projects have provoked fraught, heated political and social debates elsewhere in Greenland. People often say they feel excluded from decision-making processes surrounding plans for extractive industry projects, and that they have no opportunity to discuss the ways and nature of *pinngortitaq*, animals, and non-human beings with consultants. Much discussion about this in Greenland focuses on a desire to see a greater emphasis on the inclusion of local knowledge and local observations of change in social and environmental impact assessments (Nuttall 2017). Such talk raises questions about the nature of the "environmental" and the "social" in environmental and social impact assessments, but also about where the non-human – or more-than-human – fits in with how consultants go about their practice of gathering information.

A traveler arriving by air at the town of Upernavik may notice a large boulder located just within the airport's perimeter fence, close to the terminal building's entrance. It is a big enough rock, but it may also go unremarked, for the airport is located almost at Upernavik's highest point and there are other things that grab one's attention. Although it is only at an elevation of 126 meters, or 414 feet, in clear weather one walks out of the small terminal building to a dramatic view of mountains, islands, bays, and inlets, the Upernavik ice fjord, and, to the west, an iceberg-studded Baffin Bay. Given the grandeur, someone visiting Upernavik for the first time can be excused for not seeing or not paying too much attention to the boulder. However, like many things in the Upernavik area, it has a story that people tell in the town and throughout the district. Upernavik is situated on a small island and in the late 1990s, work began on the airport by leveling its mountaintop. Some two years of blasting and construction – and disruption to everyday life in the town – followed and the airport was completed in 2000. In one version of the story about the boulder, local people relate how, after a particularly intense day of blasting, the security guard keeping an eye on the site at night was visited by an *innersuaq* (plural: *innersuit*). *Innersuit* are human-like beings – some are smaller than humans, but they can also be the same size or even taller. They dwell underground and they live in ways that are similar to people on the surface. They hunt and they fish and their subterranean world is one of abundance. This night-time visitor was much smaller than the guard. Pointing to the boulder, he told him that it had been dislodged by the explosives and had landed on his brother, killing him instantly. The *innersuaq* warned that humans could not dislodge or move it, or disturb his brother's grave, otherwise misfortune would follow. The weather would turn bad and there would be difficult times ahead for hunters and fishers. There is a common thread in stories told about *innersuit* in Greenland. Misfortune can often arise if humans offend, injure, or kill them. But they can also bring good fortune and provide assistance and food to those in need (e.g., Rink 1875; Sonne 2017). Many of the dramatic shifts experienced in Upernavik and the wider coastal region in sea ice resulting from a warming climate have occurred over the last twenty years. Hunting and fishing have suffered, and many people have experienced difficult times (Nuttall 2019a; 2019b); the boulder has not been disturbed or moved, but sometimes people wonder about the coincidence nonetheless.

I relate this story about *innersuit* because in the work I do with communities in northwest Greenland, I hear people talk about their concerns that the underground is disturbed by seismic surveys, prospecting, and mining exploration, and *innersuit* figure in their accounts of extraordinary happenings that coincide with the investigative activities of oil and mining companies. In 2017, friends in Kangersuatsiaq told me that for the past two or three summers they had seen *innersuit*, who they thought would ordinarily live within the spaces along the coast and below the shoreline, moving inland to avoid disturbance. They attributed this to underground coastal *innersuit* experiencing continual shocks and sounds made by the airguns used by the seismic survey vessels, as well as the entrances to their subterranean homes being lashed violently by the waves they thought must follow. Also in Kangersuatsiaq, I organized a community workshop in June 2015 to talk about climate change – the discussion turned to the seismic surveys and one hunter spoke about holes in the ground and crumbling rocks:

> In 2012, we noticed that there was warm water coming up from unidentifiable holes in the land, near the old school building here in Kangersuatsiaq. It was at the end of February – it was cold, around −20 or −30°C, yet a lot of holes or geysers appeared with steam billowing from them. We had never seen it before. There was lots of steam coming from the warm water mixing with the cold. In 2013, there were scientists who came to study these things. But the people living here didn't get any information back about it. We've been noticing a lot of animals acting strangely or which seem to be frightened. We saw a harp seal without fur swimming nervously around an iceberg. There's got to be a connection because it was the exact same time seismic activities were going on.
>
> In 2012–2013, at the same time the holes were observed, we noticed that some rocks had fallen into the sea. We found a huge hole where the rocks fell from the

northeast part of the land. It was a circular hole and struck us as very odd. In Kangerlussuaq, we noticed parts of the slope of a big mountain crumbling away. We couldn't really see the source but the impact was certainly visible. A long time ago my father told me that he was out in the fjord and there was a helicopter travelling back and forth to the mountains. He heard sounds like explosions, as if there was some blasting going on. He had no idea what was happening up there because we never get information.

Hunters also talk about *qullugiarsuaq* – a great sea worm believed to live in Greenland's coastal waters – being disturbed and restless, as well as narwhals, other marine mammals, and fish. More hunters have said they were now either hearing or seeing it. In Kullorsuaq in the northern part of Upernavik district, a hunter I have known since the late 1980s told me he had seen *qullugiarsuaq* come close to his boat in 2013, shortly after the seismic vessels had been out at sea. It could be *qullugiarsuaq*, he and others said, that was also disturbing narwhals, making them nervous of being further out in open water, but *qullugiarsuaq* could first have been disturbed by the seismic surveys. To paraphrase van Dooren et al. (2016), it is important to recognize how people think about and consider such non-human beings as *qullugiarsuaq* as emerging from, growing, and making their lives within multispecies communities with deep, complicated, and entangled histories. Drawing on ethnographic work on mining encounters and negotiations in the Kono District of Sierra Leone, D'Angelo (2014) argues that people affected by mining sometimes interpret unexpected and mysterious events in terms of the acts of invisible beings. Emergent narratives about how they are connected to extractive intrusions into the realm of the non-human are, in fact, often highly politicized discourses and practices that cause necessary reflection on human action and responsibility.

CONCLUSIONS

Resource stakeholders (politicians, government bodies and institutions, local businesses, multinational companies) are imagining and making the resource frontier in Greenland. Global commodity prices may have fallen over the last few years, and other global processes – as well as growing pressure for countries to commit to decarbonization strategies and renewable energy projects – may be affecting plans for resource development in the Arctic, but the subterranean nonetheless remains critical for Greenlandic notions of state formation and ambitions for independence. Plans for mining and oil development projects in the Greenlandic underlands involve discourses about extraction and spatial technologies of power that privilege particular techno-centric and economic views of the Greenlandic environment. These views do not take into account local community perspectives on human-environment relations and the more-than-human nature of the surroundings in which resource extraction projects will be carved out. In northwest Greenland, people do not think of themselves and animals as living in divergent spaces or having ecologies that are mutually exclusive. And they often say animals are of the same opinion (Nuttall 2017). Yet, too often these surroundings are rendered wild and empty, or considered a region of ecological sensitivity, by those who continue to bring different perspectives to how they imagine and materialize the High Arctic.

How might we, then, seek to conceive of and understand the Arctic if we not only adopt more of a volumetric perspective (cf. Elden 2013) when thinking of territory, but proceed from understanding Indigenous ontologies and ways of being (e.g., Muller, Hemming and Rigby 2019) and take seriously the lifeworlds and agency of non-human beings and non-human entities (e.g., Kohn 2013)? How can the "environmental" and the "social" in environmental and social impact assessments be expanded beyond what is determined and defined by scientific institutional practices and processes? While animals play complex roles in the lives of humans, so humans have complex roles in the lives of animals. But how can the non-human be included (cf. Gray and Curry 2020; Starik 1995)? How can the non-human – narwhals, polar bears, *innersuit*, and *qullugiarsuaq*, for instance – be consulted, especially when people currently feel they have very little opportunity to be consulted themselves? How can and should non-human entities such as ice and water even be considered and accorded rights of representation (e.g., Strang 2020)? How does the non-human resist representations and classifications that render it inert, or as something that can be situated within political-economic spaces that are defined as resource zones? I have no easy answers to these difficult questions because they relate to ways of knowing that seek to account for the ontological dimensions of the interplay and entanglements of humans, animals, and environments. But such questions call for new ways of thinking about environmental and social impact assessment procedures and consultation processes for extractive industries in Greenland today, and how they should be redefined and reimagined (cf. Duarte and Belarde-Lewis 2015; Muller, Hemming and Rigby 2019) to take into account the ways in which the world is apprehended, perceived, and conceived by the people affected by resource exploration and development. However, this requires more than just acknowledging the need for the incorporation of Indigenous ways of knowing, but moving toward a greater understanding and awareness of relationality (see also, Strang 2020). This would allow for a deeper dialogue on the place of both the human and the more-than-human in a world of becomings, emergence, and extraordinary happenings.

ACKNOWLEDGMENTS

This chapter is based on research that has been funded by Project 6400 at the Greenland Climate Research Centre at the Greenland Institute of Natural Resources, and also draws on work done as part of the REXSAC (Resource Extraction and Sustainable Arctic Communities) Nordic Centre of Excellence funded by Nordforsk.

REFERENCES

Bernauer, Warren, and Gabrielle Slowey. 2020. "COVID-19, Extractive Industries, and Indigenous Communities in Canada: Notes towards a Political Economy Research Agenda." *The Extractive Industries and Society* 7 (3): 844–876. https://doi.org/10.1016/j.exis.2020.05.012.

Bobbette, Adam, and Amy Donovan (eds.) 2019. *Political Geology: Active Stratigraphies and the Making of Life.* Cham: Palgrave MacMillan.

Box, Jason E., and David T. Decker. 2011. "Greenland Marine-Terminating Glacier Area Changes: 2000–2010." *Annals of Glaciology* 52 (59): 91–98. https://doi-org.proxy.lib.sfu.ca/10.3189/172756411799096312.

Bridge, Gavin. 2009. "Material Worlds: Natural Resources, Resource Geography, and the Material Economy." *Geography Compass* 3 (3): 1217-1244. https://doi.org/10.1111/j.1749-8198.2009.00233.x.

Clark, Nick. 2017. "Politics of Strata." *Theory, Culture and Society* 34 (2–3): 211-231. https://doi.org/10.1177/0263276416667538.

Cowton, T. R., A. J. Sole, P. W. Nienow, D. A. Slater, and P. Christoffersen. 2018. "Linear Response of East Greenland's Tidewater Glaciers to Ocean/Atmosphere Warming." *Proceedings of the National Academy of Sciences* 115 (31): 7907-7912. https://doi.org/10.1073/pnas.1801769115.

D'Angelo, Lorenzo. 2014. "Changing Environments, Occult Protests, and Social Memories in Sierra Leone." *Social Evolution and History* 13 (2): 22–56.

Dodds, Klaus, and Mark Nuttall. 2018. "Materialising Greenland within a Critical Arctic Geopolitics." In *Greenland and the International Politics of a Changing Arctic: Postcolonial Paradiplomacy between High and Low Politics*, edited by Kristian Søby Kristensen and Jon Rahbek-Clemmensen, 139-154. New York: Routledge.

———. 2019. "Geo-Assembling Narratives of Sustainability in Greenland." In *The Politics of Sustainability in the Arctic: Reconfiguring Identity, Space and Time*, edited by Ulrik Pram Gad and Jeppe Strandsbjerg, 224–241. New York: Routledge.

Dransart, Penelope. 2013. "Living Beings and Vital Powers: An Introduction." In *Living Beings: Perspectives on Interspecies Engagements*, edited by Penelope Dransart, 1–16. London: Bloomsbury.

Duarte, Marisa Elena, and Miranda Belarde-Lewis. 2015. "Imagining: Creating Spaces for Indigenous Ontologies." *Cataloging and Classification Quarterly* 53 (5–6): 677–702.

Elden, S. (2013). "Secure the Volume: Vertical Geopolitics and the Depth of Power." *Political Geography* 34 (2): 35–51.

Gray, Joe, and Patrick Curry. 2020. "Ecodemocracy and Political Representation for Non-Human Nature." In *Conservation: Integrating Social and Ecological Justice*, edited by Helen Kopnina and Haydn Washington, 156–166. Cham: Springer.

Haraway, Donna. 2008. *When Species Meet*. Minneapolis, MN: University of Minnesota Press.

Hastrup, Kirsten. 2018. "A History of Climate Change: Inughuit Responses to Changing Ice Conditions in North-West Greenland." *Climatic Change* 151: 67–78. https://doi.org/10.1007/s10584-016-1628-y.

Hayward, Philip. 2012. "Aquapelagos and Aquapelagic Assemblages." *Shima: The International Journal of Research into Island Cultures* 6 (1): 1-10.

Johnson, Leigh. 2010. "The Fearful Symmetry of Arctic Climate Change: Accumulation by Degradation." *Environment and Planning D* 28 (5): 828–847. https://doi.org/10.1068/d9308.

Kama, Kärg, and Magdalena Kuchler. 2019. "Geo-Metrics and Geo-Politics: Controversies in Estimating European Shale Gas Resources." In *Political Geology: Active Stratigraphies and the Making of Life*, edited by Adam Bobbette and Amy Donovan, 105–145. Cham: Palgrave MacMillan.

Kohn, Eduardo. 2013. *How Forests Think: Toward an Anthropology Beyond the Human*. Berkeley, CA: University of California Press.

Li, Tania Murray. 2014. "What is Land? Assembling a Resource for Global investment." *Transactions of the Institute for British Geographers* 39 (4): 589–602. https://doi.org/10.1111/tran.12065.

Muller, Samantha, Steve Hemming, and Daryle Rigney. 2019. "Indigenous sovereignties: relational ontologies and environmental management." *Geographical Research* 57 (4): 399–410.

Nuttall, Mark. 2016. "Narwhal Hunters, Seismic Surveys and the Middle Ice: Monitoring Environmental Change in Greenland's Melville Bay." In *Anthropology and Climate*

Change: From Actions to Transformations, edited by Susan A. Crate and Mark Nuttall, 354–372. New York: Routledge.

———. 2017. *Climate, Society, and Subsurface Politics in Greenland: Under the Great Ice.* New York: Routledge.

———. 2019a. "Sea Ice, Climate and Resources: The Changing Nature of Hunting along Northwest Greenland's Coast." In *Climate, Capitalism and Communities: An Anthropology of Environmental Overheating*, edited by Astrid B. Stensrud and Thomas Hylland Eriksen, 57–75. London: Pluto Press.

———. 2019b. "Icy, Watery, Liquescent: Sensing and Feeling Climate Change on Northwest Greenland's Coast." *Journal of Northern Studies* 14 (2): 71–91.

Rink, Hinrich. 1875. *Tales and Traditions of the Eskimo*. Edinburgh and London: William Blackwood and Sons.

Sonne, Birgitte. 2017. *Worldviews of the Greenlanders: An Inuit Arctic Perspective*. Fairbanks, AK: University of Alaska Press.

Starik, Mark. 1995. "Should Trees Have Managerial Standing?: Toward Stakeholder Status for Non-Human Nature." *Journal of Business Ethics* 14: 207–217.

Strang, Veronica. 2020. "The Rights of the River: Water, Culture and Ecological Justice." In *Conservation: Integrating Social and Ecological Justice*, edited by Helen Kopnina and Haydn Washington, 105–119. Cham: Springer.

Stroeve, Julienne C., John R. Mioduszewski, Asa Rennermalm, Linette N. Boisvert, Marco Tedesco, and David Robinson. 2017. "Investigating the Local-Scale Influence of Sea Ice on Greenland Surface Melt." *The Cryosphere* 11: 2363–2381. https://doi.org/10.5194/tc-11-2363-2017.

Van As, Dirk. 2011. "Warming, Glacier Melt and Surface Energy Budget from Weather Station Observations in the Melville Bay Region of Northwest Greenland." *Journal of Glaciology* 57 (202): 202–220. https://doi-org.proxy.lib.sfu.ca/10.3189/002214311796405898.

Van den Broeke, M. R., J. Box, X. Fettweis, E. Hanna, B. Noël, M. Tedesco, D. van As, W. J. van de Berg, and L. van Kampenhout. 2017. "Greenland Ice Sheet Surface Mass Loss: Recent Developments in Observation and Modelling." *Current Climate Change Reports* 3 (4): 345–356. https://doi.org/10.1007/s40641-017-0084-8.

van Dooren, Thom, Eben Kirksey, and Ursula Münster. 2016. "Multispecies Studies: Cultivating Arts of Attentiveness." *Environmental Humanities* 8 (1): 1–23.

Watts, Michael J. 2015. "Securing Oil: Frontiers, Risk, and Spaces of Accumulated Insecurity." In *Subterranean Estates: Life Worlds of Oil and Gas*, edited by Hannah Appel, Arthur Mason, and Michael Watts, 211–236. Ithaca, NY: Cornell University Press.

Weszkalnys, Gisa. 2011. "Cursed Resources, or Articulations of Economic Theory in the Gulf of Guinea." *Economy and Society* 40 (3): 345–372. https://doi.org/10.1080/03085147.2011.580177.

———. 2015. "Geology, Potentiality, Speculation: On the Indeterminacy of First Oil." *Cultural Anthropology* 30 (4): 611–639. https://doi.org/10.14506/ca30.4.08.

CHAPTER 8

CHANGING TIMES FOR PEOPLE AND POLAR BEARS

Nina H.S. Lund

INTRODUCTION: POLAR BEARS EVERYWHERE

Melting ice and images of a lonely polar bear on a small ice floe have become icons of climate change (Bjørst 2014). The changing landscape does not just affect the large predator, but all the inhabitants of the Arctic and their relationships with each other. Particularly in East Greenland, the relationship between humans and polar bears has become problematic. The changing environment brings up the old debate about nature and society. Scholars such as Descola (2013 [2005]) argue that Western societies have an abyssal gap between society and nature, privileging humans as cultured beings who have created society to sit in opposition to nature. This dualism extends to the relationship between humans and non-humans (Pálsson 2004). This Western dualism is challenged by various ethnographic accounts (Ingold 2000). Recent attention in the form of multispecies ethnography considers the contact zones between humans and non-humans – in which the assumed dualism breaks down (Kirksey and Helmreich 2010). The breakdown of these ordering categories invites questions about how humans are affected. How do humans live with their changing environment? And how do humans connect to other animals, especially when the animals change the parameters of the relationship? In this chapter I explore how, for East Greenlanders, the traditional relationship to the polar bear as a prey animal has changed, and how a new security initiative to protect humans and bears from each other balances old and new perceptions of the polar bear.

On the east coast of Greenland, near the mouth of Scoresbysund, lies the small village of Ittoqqortoormiit. In 2017, I had the privilege of spending four months conducting fieldwork in this small hunting community. I lived with a local family whose heritage included polar bear hunting. I accompanied members of the polar bear patrol on their rounds, and I immersed myself in the everyday life of the village. The village was established as a colony in 1924 by the Kingdom of Denmark and was a manifestation of the Danish claim to the land. Long before the colony was created, the area was known for its rich hunting grounds and diversity of wildlife (Arke 2003). The area is still populated with a multitude of species, and now with a multitude of scientists who come to study them and their changing habitat. This chapter is no different, as it aims to illuminate the changing relationship between humans and polar bears. Today, Ittoqqortoormiit is the northernmost human settlement on the east coast of Greenland, with a national park as the closest neighbor. As in many arctic hunting villages, the brightly colored houses are oriented towards the sea, and hides are hung to dry outside the hunters' homes. The 71 Greenlanders who moved from Angmagssalik in 1925 to populate the colony survived mainly by hunting. The first settlers had left Angmagssalik due to starvation, but soon the same conditions found their way to Ittoqqortoormiit. Due to the short history of the village, the children of the first settlers are still alive. They are the oldest members of the community, and have children and grandchildren of their own. They take great pride in their heritage, and in telling stories of their childhoods. An elderly woman described to me the bushy eyebrows of Ejner Mikkelsen (the Danish colonial governor). Another told me that her grandmother was the first person to freeze to death in Ittoqqortoormiit. Even though the first years of the colony were in many ways brutal, residents look back on that era with nostalgia. They recall a simpler time, when a family could be fed simply by hunting, and there was little need for money. Paradoxically, the colonial rule that established the village is also held responsible for the end of these simpler times, as it introduced wage labor which many locals feel trapped by. Today, people in Ittoqqortoormitt express a difficult relationship with the west coast (the administrative center of Greenland), a continuation of long-held negative attitudes toward "outside authorities" (Lund 2019).

Since 2006, Ittoqqortoormiit, along with the rest of Greenland, has had a quota on the number of polar bears that can be hunted. It was further decided that they could only be hunted by occupational hunters. In 2017, the hunters of Ittoqqortoormiit shared a quota of 35 bears. The limitations on hunting have made it financially difficult to be an occupational hunter, and as a result, few young people today choose this profession. Most of the 375 residents have chosen a modern occupation (teacher, shopkeeper, etc.) and hunt part-time instead. They use their non-working hours to secure a substantial amount of their families' meat by hunting and fishing.

However, it is not just that humans have changed their behavior with respect to polar bears. Polar bears have also started to change their behavior with respect to humans. In Ittoqqortoormiit, polar bears have become invasive, wandering into the village. Often, they are looking for food, and although humans are not their preferred food source, they will attack if threatened. It poses a difficult situation for the locals. In 2018, their polar bear quota was already exhausted by 9 April, leaving a long wait before they could legally kill the intruders again. Many in Ittoqqortoormiit now fear for their children's safety and are themselves living with the constant prospect of being surprised by a polar bear. As a friend warned me,

> Don't go too far! There can be polar bears everywhere. It can come from here; it can come from there. It can climb, it can swim, it can run. You just have to remember: polar bears can't fly! All other directions are possible!
> (Ataata, interview 4 August 2017)

Inuit communities in Canada have recently faced similar conflicts with polar bears (Tyrrell 2006).

In order to mediate the conflict and minimize the number of human–polar bear conflict situations, the World Wildlife Fund (WWF), in collaboration with Greenland's

Department of Hunting and Fishery, set up a polar bear patrol. The patrol consists of two men who drive through the village on weekday mornings to scare away any potential polar bears before the children go to school. On days when there is polar bear activity, they follow up the morning patrol with additional trips, trying to locate the intruder. Furthermore, because they aim to handle all encounters between humans and invasive polar bears, the patrol staff is constantly on call to respond if a villager locates a polar bear before they do.

To illuminate how people in Ittoqqortoormiit relate to polar bears and their experience of living with invasive polar bears, I first describe the polar bear patrol and its efforts to keep the village polar bear free. I then review how the different experiences of the three now-living generations have created a generational gap in human–polar bear relationships. Lastly, I analyze the schemas that govern how people in Ittoqqortoormiit relate to polar bears, and I argue that rather than simply mediating between humans and polar bears, the polar bear patrol mediates different generational perceptions of polar bears.

The polar bear patrol

The patrol consists of two men, one local man who works with the local hunting official, each taking turns patrolling the village. Their aim is to "[keep] the village polar bear free" (WWF 2015). To this end, at 6 am, the patroller drives from the western end of Ittoqqortoormiit along one of the main roads through the village and down the steep road to the dump. He checks all the known entry points and hiding places used by previous intruder bears. There are plenty of such spots at the dump, where every piece of village trash, from tractors to toilet bags, ends up. Particularly in the winter when visibility is low and the watchman is aided only by a flashlight, his knowledge is key to finding the intruders. Various forms of trash light up when illuminated by the flashlight, making it difficult to distinguish a pair of glowing polar bear eyes from old electronics. Driving back towards the village, the patrolman uses the other main road, peering between the houses for polar bear signs before continuing out towards Walrus Bay. Along the way, he greets local hunters who are out early. He continues out of town for about ten minutes before returning back along the shore. There are no roads along Walrus Bay and the terrain is bumpy. In winter, he has to be mindful of the ice so that the ATV does not get stuck or fall through. There is no cellphone signal, making help a long, cold walk away (see Figure 8.1).

The morning patrol is a result of the local understanding of the invasive polar bears' tendency to respond to the rhythm of the villagers. By nature, polar bears seek to avoid human noise. During the night when Ittoqqortoormiit falls quiet, polar bears enter the village undisturbed, whereas the noise of the day usually keeps them at a distance. Often the noise of the patrol vehicle is enough to scare the unwanted visitors away. Other times the watchmen have to resort to firing warning shots at closer and closer range, putting themselves at risk. In very rare cases, a polar bear refuses to leave the village or worse, begins to attack. In these cases, the local hunting official requests authorization from the Department of Hunting and Fishery to kill the invasive bear.

Figure 8.1   Polar bear patrol at Ittoqqortoormiit garbage dump. Photo: Nina H.S. Lund.

Killing invasive bears is a last resort, and in the 2017 season, only two of 21 invasive polar bears were shot. On days where there are signs of polar bears (e.g., paw prints), the patrol adds extra rounds to make sure there are no intruders. If a bear is spotted in the village, the polar bear patrol can add extra circuits in order to find the intruder. The patrol team also warns the headmaster of the local school and spreads the word throughout the village. The patrol team aims to handle all interactions between humans and invasive polar bears in order to minimize the number of polar bears shot in self-defense. Therefore, it is vital that the polar bear patrol has the support of the community, rather than individual residents trying to take on an intruder. However, when it comes to supporting the polar bear patrol, generational differences are evident. The most difficult support to get is that of the grandparents' generation. The majority of people in this generation hold the opinion that invasive polar bears should be shot on sight, and that the meat should be distributed throughout the village, so everyone can get a taste. The parents' generation in general supports the patrol's work, however, they often argue that invasive polar bears should be shot on sight and deducted from the next year's quota. Further, they would allow individuals to respond rapidly themselves, instead of waiting for the polar bear patrol to arrive. The polar bear patrol's biggest concern is the children's safety. Children are aware of the safety procedures for encountering an invasive polar bear, but most of them admit that they would not know what to do if they ever were surprised by one. In order to maintain support from the village, the patrol team has to walk a fine line when handling invasive polar bears. On the one hand, they have to respect elderly hunters and their relationships with the bears, but on the other, they have to minimize the risk to children without killing the predators. Luckily, the patrol team members were both born and raised in the village, giving them the advantage of intimate knowledge of and relations with the community.

GENERATIONS OF POLAR BEAR RELATIONSHIPS

To understand Ittoqqortoormiit residents' relationships with the invasive polar bear, one must understand their relationship with polar bears in general. The grandparents' generation are the children of the first inhabitants of Ittoqqortoormiit. Their first memories of polar bears concern their fathers coming home with a dead bear on the sled. It was an important event, as it meant not just reuniting with their fathers, but also that there was food which was sometimes scarce. This generation usually followed a gendered division of labor, with women brought up to handle the polar bear meat and hides, and men joining the hunt as they grew up. Today, the old men reminisce about months-long hunting trips and tell tales of their youth. Many men from this generation and their fathers disappeared on those hunts. Therefore, to have lived a long life as a hunter and to have provided for one's family is a feat. Today, they are widely respected, and their opinions hold authority. As children, their first encounter with living polar bears often took place in the village. Before the quota system, hunters would sometimes kill a female bear and bring her cub back to the village where they would be kept in a cage and cared for until a colonial ship could pick them up and sell them to zoos around the world. The children loved having the polar bear cubs, as an old hunter recollects:

> I would go to the shop and buy two pieces of chocolate. One for me and one for the polar bear. Their lips were kind of like a monkey's, and they would use them to reach through the cage to take the chocolate out of your hand. Then they would lean against the cage, so we could scratch them. They loved that!
> (Svend, interview 19 October 2017)

Such interactions between children and polar bears served as a means of taming that helped the cub to get used to humans. Gender differences in hunting activities mean that the women of this generation are often more afraid of the invasive polar bears than men, who talk of knowing the animal and being used to interacting with it. For both the grandmothers and the grandfathers, the polar bear is a wild creature that humans can subdue for use as food and a commodity.

The parents' generation shares the grandparents' conceptualization of polar bears as food. Their fathers are the old men who now tell tales of hunting. However, very few in this generation are occupational hunters and instead hold wage labor jobs. They have grown up with the quota system that limits how many animals can be killed. Today, only occupational hunters are permitted to hunt polar bear, and the part-time hunters depend on a lottery for permission to hunt other large game. As a result, only a handful of men and women of this generation hunt polar bear, and access to polar bear meat has become increasingly uncommon. Few members of this generation are accustomed to handling polar bears. In general, this generation supports the quota system. Particularly those who benefit from tourism are concerned about maintaining the polar bear population. If a polar bear is spotted outside the village, members of this generation will often go to admire it at a safe distance. However, the prospect of being surprised by a polar bear in the village is inherently frightening to them.

Fear of invasive polar bears has also fundamentally changed what it is like to grow up in the village. The parents' childhood was full of freedom; they were allowed to play outside the village, and very few places were off-limits. Even in the dark winter months, they could stay out late. As Aviaja explained to me:

> It was after I lived in West Greenland and came back … after I had my children. Then [in 2007] you suddenly need to bring rifles and keep a lookout, and I thought, "Why?" People would say that there could be a polar bear here. I would ask: "But is there a polar bear?" It was strange to come back and suddenly have to be careful where you go and having to bring a rifle. When we were kids and teenagers, we were never careful where we went and never checked if there were polar bears.
> (Aviaja, interview 6 October 2017)

Now, however, the parents' generation restricts their children's movements because they fear for their safety. Children must be home before dark, giving them very little time with their friends during the winter. They are also not allowed to roam alone outside the village. Furthermore, it is only due to the polar bear patrol's morning drive that most children are allowed to walk to school unsupervised. For the parents' generation, the polar bear is a complex creature: It is meat that you long for, it is the main character in hunting stories of the past, and it is a source of income. But considerably more tangible is the immediate threat to their family and their property that comes from the everyday risk of living with invasive polar bears.

Not surprisingly, the children often see polar bears as an obstacle and complain about their curfews. They do, however, feel the danger themselves. Some children run home when the sun sets, particularly on days where there have been polar bears in the village. When children go hunting with their parents, they tend to stay close by and prefer to have someone with them if they have to urinate. Often, rumors of invasive polar bears circulate among the children, which brings a lot of excitement for them. However, once in a while, a child misbehaves by not being home at curfew, leaving their parents to drive from house to house searching for them. There is a general consensus that the young children are to be protected, so sometimes parents get a phone call from other residents informing them that their child has wandered out of the village. Concern for the children is why the majority across generations support the polar bear patrol's morning drive.

Teenagers find invasive polar bears to be a break from what might otherwise be a monotonous everyday life. They often plead with their teachers to cancel class, so they can all go see an invasive bear. Most children have tasted polar bear meat, but it is not a staple in their diet, and very few of them have been on a polar bear hunt or have learned to take care of the hide and meat. For the children, talking about polar bears means talking about invasive polar bears. They are considered dangerous, but it is a habitual danger dealt with in an everyday manner.

Each human generation has a different relationship with polar bears, reflecting its own history and experiences of everyday interactions with the bears. As human–polar bear interactions have changed with the emergence of invasive polar bears, so have the different generations' conceptualizations of both polar bears and humans' role in handling them. Whereas much of the literature on arctic Indigenous hunters identifies animism as the key to the hunter–prey relationship (e.g., Freeman and Wenzel 2006;

Ingold 2000; Willerslev 2007), in Ittoqqortoormiit this is not the case. When the first settlers were brought to the village, the Danish colonial administration baptized them and marked their traditional spirituality as evil. As a result, the grandparents' generation grew up with Christianity. The old men might tell tales of hunting that glorify both themselves and the polar bear, but they are not interested in the animal's soul. When asked about the spiritual side of hunting, many answer that they are not superstitious, or that if that is one's interest, they can read about it in a history book. Today, only a handful of the old animist practices that the first generation of settlers might have followed are remembered by anyone in the grandparents' generation. Their children (the second generation of children born in the village) appear unconcerned about the loss of heritage.

The grandparents were hunters seeking out and subduing the wild animal. For the children's generation, that relationship has now been inverted, and the wild animals are the ones seeking out human dwellings. As a result, men of the grandparents' generation often do not bring rifles with them on shorter trips. This was indeed the case when, in the winter of 2018, a villager was surprised by a polar bear and had to repeatedly punch it in the face to buy enough time to start his snowmobile and flee. Afterward, he was distressed by the encounter, as it was only by chance that his grandson was not with him.

The changes in the human–animal relationship have left the parents' generation both fascinated by the large animal and frightened for themselves and their families. The parents will often listen to the grandparents' hunting tales and respect their knowledge of the polar bears, but when it comes to their children's safety, they have no desire to take any chances. For them, the risk that the invasive polar bears pose is huge, and inherently frightening. On shorter fishing trips close to the village, members of this generation always bring their rifles, and many choose to stay close to their ATVs. For both of the older generations, the polar bear does not belong in the village. The polar bear is part of nature and should be found in nature, rather than in their village. The fact that the polar bear transgresses into the village troubles the borders between nature and society.

The children, on the other hand, are used to the invasive polar bears, and they are not generally frightened when walking about the village. However, the potential of being surprised by an invasive polar bear is inherently scary for them. In the children's generation, the human is the passive agent that reacts to the polar bear's actions, thereby reversing the traditional human–polar bear relationship of their grandparents' generation. Their grandfathers' hunting tales may be exciting, but are very far removed from their own everyday lives.

All three generations recognize that they now live with the constant possibility of meeting an invasive polar bear. This risk alone has made them alter their behavior to prepare for a potential polar bear encounter (e.g., keeping a lookout, bringing rifles, etc.). No one argues that the polar bears are not enacting a new kind of agency. What is being debated is how to deal with the intruders, and this is where the polar bear patrol steps in.

Intruders of space and mind

In order to function effectively and have the support of the community the polar bear patrol negotiates and mediates not only human–polar bear encounters, but also their own operational space. This mediating effort is embedded in the procedures that the polar bear patrol follows. It begins when a polar bear patrolman encounters an invasive bear. Often the polar bear does not pose an immediate threat; it has found a food source and is eating until it is disturbed by humans. This allows the patrolman time to assess the bear. First, he determines whether or not the polar bear is a repeat offender. The third time a polar bear enters the village, it is deemed habitual, and the polar bear patrol has a mandate to shoot it. The assessment is made based on recent polar bear activity, and whether or not the particular bear fits the size and description of previous intruders. Second, the patrolman assesses the polar bear's behavior by attempting to scare it away. If he is not immediately successful, the polar bear is categorized in one of two ways: aggressive or arrogant.

A bear is deemed aggressive if it attacks humans or property (usually dogs or food storage). If it attacks a human, the polar bear can be shot in self-defense. If the polar bear causes damage to property, it is usually discovered after the perpetrator has left the scene, and the victim is expected to inform the polar bear patrol, who can then kill the polar bear. The meat usually goes to the victim as compensation. An invasive bear is defined as arrogant if it appears to lack respect for humans and ignores attempts to scare it away. Arrogant polar bears present a different challenge than the immediate threat of the aggressive ones. They usually do not damage property, nor do they attack humans. So, there is no mandate to shoot them. Rather, the patrolman will move closer and closer to the animal, hitting it harder and harder with rubber bullets and hoping that the intruder will be compelled to move. Most arrogant polar bears eventually react and move on, but until the bear responds, the patrolman risks attack. Arrogant polar bears often become serial offenders as the normal noise of a human settlement does not bother them. An invasive polar bear can move between these categories and can be classified as both or either of them.

In the early hours of the morning on 8 November 2017, we (the patrolman and I) met a polar bear moving between the categories. On the morning patrol the day before, the bear had fled in a snowstorm when the ATV approached. It had been eating dog food and was startled by the human disturbance. On this morning, however, we had been awakened by the sound of the dogs before our normal patrol, and had driven directly to them. This time the polar bear was not surprised by us. It kept eating and lashing out at any of the dogs that dared to try to protect their food. We drove closer and closer, and suddenly a shot fired from behind us. It was the dogs' owner. The shot caught the polar bear's attention, and it began to move. The hunter shouted in Greenlandic to the patrolman, who resolutely positioned our ATV between the polar bear and the hunter, effectively using our bodies as shields as we herded the polar bear out of the village. I later learned that the polar bear had wounded one of the dogs, and the owner had set his mind on killing it. The next morning, the same bear returned to the village and was killed by the patrolman, as it had now shown aggression towards the dogs and had become arrogant enough to return for a third time (see Figure 8.2).

The dog owner is an occupational hunter in the grandparents' generation. To him, humans are hunters, and polar bears are to be hunted. He is accustomed to dealing with polar bears. The intruder injured one of his dogs, possibly a damaging loss of his investment. For all these reasons, he believes he should have the right to shoot the bear himself. On that morning, he was lucky that he did not manage to kill the

Figure 8.2   Polar bear and sled dogs, Ittoqqortoormiit. Photo: Nina H.S. Lund.

predator. Had he killed it, he would have been heavily fined. Furthermore, his first response was not to call the polar bear patrol but to deal with the situation himself. The patrolman put himself between the armed dog owner and the polar bear as a vivid assertion that the dog owner did not have the right to kill the polar bear.

After the bear was killed, the dog owner was given a portion of the meat as compensation for his dog's injury. These forms of compensation are part of efforts to win over the grandparents' generation to the patrol regime. The polar bear patrol ended up killing the polar bear as the dog owner wanted, though not because it was a polar bear in the village, but because it did not act as a normal polar bear should.

Paraphrasing Mary Douglas, Johannson (2009, 225) writes of transgressive wildlife as "subjects out of place." The invasive polar bears transgress spatially when entering human domains. The polar bears are expected to be out in nature, not in the village. Douglas (2002 [1966]) concludes that categories make the world meaningful to us, and that a transgression of categories threatens the world humans have constructed for themselves. Removing transgression is a way of stabilizing one's environment. Invasive polar bears bring chaos to the dog owners' world. In the traditional relationship between humans and polar bears (the relationship between hunter and prey), the humans are the active agents who travel out to the vast arctic nature and survive by courage and skill. They seek out polar bears who, in this view, are vulnerable, and who are the ones who must respond to the human's actions. The polar bear is assumed to fear humans and to be game for humans. The relationship with the polar bear is in a sense double-defining, producing both the nature of the polar bear and the hunter as well as their appropriate relationship. Invasive polar bears invert this relationship. When the polar bears seek out the village, they are the predators. Humans thus become the vulnerable ones, as they are exposed to attacks in their homes and must react to the polar bears' actions. Invasive polar bears are not just a threat to the dog owner's security and financial investment, but also to the occupational hunter's self-perception as a courageous hunter who knows wild animals and how to handle them.

This ambiguous position of polar bears between hunter and hunted also describes the perception of the parents' generation. As few of them are hunters, the identification of polar bears as game is more abstract, whereas invasive polar bears present a concrete and immediate threat. The connotation of polar bears as game animals has drifted even further into the background in the children's perception of polar bears. For this youngest group, the physical presence of invasive polar bears in the village is the dominant form of interaction between humans and polar bears.

The invasive polar bear transgresses not only spatially; it also disrupts what it means to be a polar bear and in doing so disrupts what it is to be a human in the village. Manifested through the change in everyday interaction of humans and polar bears, the spatial transgression of invasive polar bears makes humans react to them, and not the other way around. The immediate interaction has gone from hunting to protection and simultaneous effort to avoid killing the intruder. Furthermore, the risk of meeting an invasive polar bear has also brought changes to human behavior even when no polar bear is present (e.g., carrying rifles and adhering to restrictive curfews). The order of nature and society is under threat and with it the humans' world order.

The polar bear patrol also mediates the dog owner–polar bear conflict in a much subtler way than shooting the animal and offering its meat as compensation. The categorization scheme used to assess invasive polar bears as either aggressive or arrogant plays into the traditional human–polar bear relationship. The polar bear patrol staff talks about individual invasive polar bears, rather than defining all polar bears as invasive, as the children's generation has a tendency to do. In effect, this highlights the invasive polar bear as pollution of the normative category of "polar bear." In this way, the traditional perception of polar bears, and by extension their relationship to humans, is kept alive as the measuring stick of normative polar bear behavior. Polar bears as a species are still game animals that humans seek out in nature.

Invasive polar bears, in contrast to bears in nature, are individuals that do not represent their species. These individual polar bears can further be assigned as aggressive or arrogant, thereby constructing them as even less normal. Because the individual polar bears are abnormal, it follows that they should not be handled in the normal way (i.e., hunted as game). Even though humans in Ittoqqortoormiit ascribe otherwise human characteristics to invasive bears, they do not endow them with agency in either a classic anthropological sense (i.e., the ability to reflect upon one's actions) (Hylland Eriksen 2010 [1995], 52) or in a contemporary post-humanist sense (Kohn 2013). This stands in contrast to ethnographic reports of the spiritual powers of bears among Yup'ik (Fienup-Riordan 1990) and Koyukon (Nelson 1983) peoples in Alaska, and indeed, in contrast to polar bears' privileged position in Canadian Inuit cosmology (Saladin D'Anglure 1990). East Greenlanders deny that polar bears possess either spiritual powers or intentionality. The polar bear is seen as a reactive agent in the encounter, without intentionality or spirit. The locals "act" where the polar bear "behaves." Thus, the invasive polar bears are a pollution that is to be removed so there can once again be order in the local environment. With their removal, the disruption to the order of nature and society can be mitigated. and stability can be restored. In other words, identifying bears as either arrogant or aggressive serves as a way of containing and controlling the wild transgression. The application of these two characteristics that are normally associated with humans marks individual polar bears as unusual and designates the correct punishment for the perpetrator. Punishment in the form of banishment or death restores the balance between nature and society, as well as the balance of hunter and animal. It may seem paradoxical that a non-human without agency can constitute a threat that deserves punishment. However, because locals' perception of the environment and their place in it is linked to the Danish colonial heritage, they subscribe to the abyssal gap between nature and society. The polar bear belongs to the silenced nature and humans to the cultured society. The invasive polar bears transgress the abyssal gap and upset the ordering of the locals' world. Punishment of an invasive polar bear serves to restore order. Stabilizing the traditional categorization of polar bear and hunter allows the polar bear patrol an operational space where their efforts to avoid killing bears have merit with the grandparents' generation. By describing an individual invasive polar bear as either aggressive or arrogant, the polar bear patrol determines their course of action, but more importantly, they also remedy the threat to the eldest generation's self-perception as hunters.

The polar bear patrol, importantly, manages to mediate not just the human–polar bear conflict but also the generation gap in polar bear perceptions. The designation of invasive polar bears as individuals that transgress the norms of their species enables the three-generational perceptions to co-exist without directly opposing one another. It further provides an operational space for the polar bear patrol that has general support in the community. The example above is one of the rare occurrences in which an occupational hunter interfered with the polar bear patrol's work. As an occupational hunter in the grandparents' generation explained to me, "I wish we could shoot them [the invasive polar bears], but the patrol is good. It keeps the streets safe for my grandchildren" (Malik, interview 11 October 2017). His sentiment is the norm in the village, which ensures support for the polar bear patrol. With this support and the mediating effort described above, the majority of the polar bear patrol's work runs smoothly and keeps the village polar bear safe.

CONCLUSION

Much of the ethnographic literature concerned with Indigenous hunting practices and animal-human relationships focuses on the widespread prevalence of animism among arctic peoples (e.g., Ingold 2000). In Ittoqqortoormiit, this is not the case. The village is less than 100 years old and the residents have always had close ties to the colonial regime. Part of Denmark's effort to modernize Greenland was to baptize Indigenous people. With the change of religion, animism seems to have died out in Ittoqqortoormiit. Therefore, not surprisingly, the inhabitants have developed a perspective of society and nature that is much closer to the Danish, namely that the two are separate spheres. Nature is where you go for hunting and leisure, whereas the village is no place for undomesticated animals. Even the sled dogs are mostly kept on the outskirts of town. Invasive polar bears challenge this order. As a relatively new phenomenon, invasive polar bears are the latest incarnation of a continuously developing human–polar bear relationship. The relationship between people and polar bears has changed along with the everyday interactions between the two (Descola 2004). Members of the grandparents' generation see polar bears as game animals and see humans as hunters. From their perspective, humans are the aggressor in the relationship, and the polar bear simply reacts to human interference. The parents' generation shares the perception of polar bears as game animals, but also sees the invasive polar bear as an agent in the relationship. The children's generation usually only relates to polar bears as invasive. For them, the polar bears are the aggressor and living in the village means always living with the risk of being surprised by a polar bear. In the children's generation, the gap between nature and society has been eliminated when it comes to invasive polar bears. For them, the polar bears' transgression means that nature is also to be found in society. For the grandparents and the parents, the separation of the two spheres is violated by the intruders. I have illustrated how the grandparents' perspective is challenged by the presence of polar bears in the village. It is a form of pollution that upsets their categorization of the world. The polar bears are "subjects out of place" (Johannson 2009, 225). For the grandparents, the intruders turn the human–animal relationship on its head and construct humans as game instead of as hunters, making it difficult for the polar bear patrol to gain their support. Beyond simply mediating the security risk of living with invasive polar bears, the polar bear patrol also mediates the challenges the intruders pose to the order of nature and society and to hunters' self-perception as agentive and effective. Instead attributing invasiveness as a new feature of polar bears, the polar bear patrol always talks of invasive polar bears as individuals. The intruders are thereby seen as unusual and not representative of their species. The peculiarity of the invasive polar bear is further highlighted by the classification of polar bears as either arrogant or aggressive. The attributes are a contrast to normative polar bear behavior. The classification scheme does not just help the patrol follow protocol; it creates an operational space where their efforts not to kill invasive polar bears are rendered legitimate without challenging the traditional human–polar bear relationship. Furthermore, the classification of invasive polar bears as individuals, and as unusual, helps to restore the distinction between nature and society.

The three-generational perspectives are able to coexist without directly opposing one another. The grandparents are still understood as knowledgeable about polar bear behavior and continue to be respected. The children might see the polar bears as invasive, but also understand that there are other kinds of polar bears in nature. And the parents shift from one perspective to the other. The polar bear patrol effectively removes the disturbance by handling the invasive polar bears, keeping the inhabitants safe, and safeguarding their construction of the world.

ACKNOWLEDGMENTS

The research for this chapter was funded by the Oticon Foundation, the North2North Scholarship, and De Fynske Banker.

REFERENCES

Arke, Pia. 2003. *Scoresbysundhistorier: Fotografier, kolonisering og kortlægning – Med kartografiske afsnit af Stefan Jonsson.* [Histories of Scoresbysund: Photography,

Colonialization, and Mapping – With Sections of Cartography by Stefan Jonsson]. Copenhagen: Bogen Forlag.

Bjørst, Lil Randstad. 2014. "Arktis som budbringer – Isbjørne og mennesker i den internationale klimadebat." ["The Arctic as Messenger: Polar Bears and Humans in the International Climate Debate."] In *Klima og mennesker – Humanistiske perspektiver på klimaforandringer*, edited by Mikkel Sørensen and Mikkel Fugl Eskjær, 125–144. Copenhagen: Museum Tusculanums Forlag.

Descola, Philippe. 2013 [2005]. *Beyond Nature and Culture*. Chicago, IL: The University of Chicago Press.

———. 2004. "Constructing Natures: Symbolic Ecology and Social Practice." In *Nature and Society: Anthropological Perspectives*, edited by Philippe Descola and Gísli Pálsson, 82–103. London and New York: Routledge.

Douglas, Mary. 2002 [1966]. *Purity and Danger: An Analysis of the Concepts of Pollution and Taboo*. London and New York: Routledge.

Fienup-Riordan, Ann. 1990. "Original Ecologists? The Relationship between Yup'ik Eskimos and Animals." In *Eskimo Essays: Yup'ik Lives and How We See Them*, edited by Ann Fienup-Riordan, 167–191. New Brunswick, NJ: Rutgers University Press.

Freeman, M.M.R., and G.W. Wenzel. 2006. "The Nature and Significance of Polar Bear Conservation Hunting." *Arctic* 59 (1): 21–30. https://doi.org/10.14430/arctic360

Hylland Eriksen, Thomas. 2010 [1995]. *Small Places, Large Issues: An Introduction to Social and Cultural Anthropology*, third edition. London and New York: Pluto Press.

Ingold, Tim. 2000. *The Perception of the Environment: Essays on Livelihood, Dwelling and Skill*. New York: Routledge.

Johannson, Tino. 2009. "The Spatial Dimension of Human-Wildlife Conflicts: Discoveries of New Animal Geography." In *Celebrating Geographical Diversity: Proceedings of the HERODOT Conference in Ayvalik, Turkey, 28–31 May, 2009*, edited by Karl Donert, Yilmaz Ari, Maria Attard, Gerry O'Reilly, and Daneila Schmeinck, 255–263. Liverpool, UK: The Herodot Thematic Network. http://www.herodot.net/conferences/Ayvalik/papers/manuscript-v1.pdf.

Kirksey, S. Eben, and Stefan Helmreich. 2010. "The Emergence of Multispecies Ethnography." *Cultural Anthropology* 25 (4): 545–576. https://doi.org/10.1111/j.1548-1360.2010.01069.x.

Kohn, Eduardo. 2013. *How Forests Think: Toward an Anthropology beyond the Human*. Berkeley, CA: University of California Press.

Lund, Nina H. S. 2019. "Nanu – Bjørnen fra Bagsiden" ["Nanu: The Bear from the Backside"]. *Tidsskriftet Grønland* 67 (3): 112–120.

Nelson, Richard K. 1983. *Make Prayers to the Raven: A Koyukon View of the Northern Forest*. Chicago, IL and London: University of Chicago Press.

Pálsson, Gísli. 2004. "Human-Environmental Relations: Orientalism, Paternalism and Communalism." In *Nature and Society: Anthropological Perspectives*, edited by Philippe Descola and Gísli Pálsson, 63–82. London and New York: Routledge.

Saladin D'Anglure, Bernard. 1990. "Nanook, Super-Male: The Polar Bear in the Imaginary Space and Social Time of the Inuit of the Canadian Arctic." In *Signifying Animals: Human Meaning in the Natural World*, edited by Roy Willis, 178–195. London: Routledge.

Tyrrell, Martina. 2006. "More Bears, Less Bears: Inuit and Scientific Perceptions of Polar Bear Populations on the West Coast of Hudson Bay." *Études/Inuit/Studies* 30 (2): 191–208. https://doi.org/10.7202/017571ar.

Willerslev, Rane. 2007. *Soul Hunters: Hunting, Animism, and Personhood among the Siberian Yukaghirs*. Berkeley, CA: University of California Press.

WWF. 2015. "WWF Grønland og Arktis." ["WWF Greenland and the Arctic"]. Accessed March 16, 2018. https://www.wwf.dk/wwfs_arbejde/gronland_og_arktis/.

CHAPTER 9

SPEAKING THE INUIT LANGUAGE IN THE 2020s

Louis-Jacques Dorais

For some 40 years (1972–2011), part of my regular teaching included an Inuit language conversation class for undergraduate and graduate students in anthropology. During the 1960s, 1970s, and early 1980s, learning Iñupiaq (Alaska), Inuktut (Canada),[1] or Kalaallisut (Greenland) (hereafter IIK) was considered a requirement for social scientists eager to conduct research in the North, and especially in much of the eastern Canadian Arctic. Even if many young Indigenous people were bilingual, and spoke English (or Danish in Greenland) to at least some extent, older Inuit generally preferred to communicate in their native language. As years went by, however, bilingualism became the norm across the Arctic, so much that after the year 2000, when students would state their wish to learn IIK, I would half-jokingly tell them that they did not need to. Almost everyone was now fluent in English, and there were competent interpreters to help researchers communicate with the few remaining monolingual speakers.

Of course, my assertion – which was aimed at discouraging students who were not really serious about learning the language – was only partially true. Nowadays, even if the vast majority of Inuit are fluent in English or Danish, and even if, in some regions of their ancestral territory, Inuit Nunangat ("Land of the Inuit"), they no longer speak IIK, their Aboriginal tongue still constitutes a strong identity marker. In northern Canada, as well as in Alaska and Greenland, language is always highlighted – along with country food, traveling on the land, hunting for subsistence, and a few other elements – among the factors considered essential for defining who Inuit really are (Dorais 2010, Chapter 10). Hence, it is worthwhile to examine the nature and development of IIK in order to understand why Inuit still speak their language in the 2020s, despite the well-known global challenges to Indigenous language survival. In the following pages, I discuss some of the linguistic and social dimensions of the Inuit language. A short description of its historical and grammatical basis is followed by an analysis of the challenges to language retention, especially since the 1950s, and of the ways these challenges have been met by Inuit speakers. The chapter concludes with some reflections on the status of IIK at the beginning of the 2020s.

SOME HISTORICAL AND GRAMMATICAL DATA

Approximately 2,000 years ago, a population of arctic hunter-gatherers was living in western central Alaska, on and around the Norton Sound and Seward Peninsula area.

DOI: 10.4324/9780429275470-9

Their Asian ancestors had migrated across the Bering Strait two or three millennia earlier, and some of them (the Paleo-Eskimos) had carried on with their migration, progressively settling northern Alaska, Arctic Canada, and Greenland (see Friesen, this volume). The language spoken by the Norton-Seward people, the forbears of contemporary Inuit and Yupik, is called Proto-Eskimo by linguists. It is related to Unangam Tunuu (Aleut), and its speakers may have been in close contact, in a much more distant past, with speakers of the proto-Chukotkan and proto-Uralic languages, ancestors to present-day Chukchi and Finnish, among others (Fortescue 1998).

The Proto-Eskimo lexicon has been systematically reconstructed by three linguists, Michael Fortescue, Steven Jacobson, and Lawrence Kaplan, in their *Comparative Eskimo Dictionary* (Fortescue et al. 2010). Most of these words were transmitted to the linguistic children, so to speak, of the ancestral tongue: the contemporary Yupik languages and Inuit dialects. Their pronunciation and, sometimes, meanings were slightly modified along the way, but they largely preserved their original form and content (Dorais 2020, 13).

A major characteristic of Proto-Eskimo and its linguistic descendants is the ability to encode several meanings within a single word. This is due in large part to the "polysynthetic" grammatical structure, a term that describes a language that is able to include multiple different concepts into only one composite word. Most North American Indigenous languages are polysynthetic. By way of example, in some Inuktut dialects, a train is called *nunakkuujuukutaaq*. This term can be analyzed as follows: *nuna* ("land") + *kkuu* ("to go by") + *juu* ("that does it usually") + *kutaaq* ("long"). The literal meaning of "train" is thus "a long one that usually goes by land." A very large proportion of IIK words are constructed in this way.

As far as their syntactic structure is concerned, IIK words always start with a base (or stem) expressing their initial verbal, nominal, or adverbial meaning. A number of affixes (word parts that specify, qualify, or modify the meaning of the base) may optionally follow. The word must then end with a suffix marking its grammatical relationship with other words in the utterance, as with this three-word sentence:

umiarjuaraalungmik takulaurtunga avani
umiar-jua-raalung-mik taku-laur-tunga av-ani
"boat"-"big"-"very"-direct object "see"-past-1st. sing. indicative "away"-locative
"I saw a very big boat that is far away"

With this type of structure, a single word (i.e., base + affixes + suffix) often translates as a full English sentence, as in *illuliuqatigigumanngitara* ("I do not want to have him/her building a house with me").

During the 12th and 13th centuries, most ancestors of contemporary Inuit migrated northeastward to Canada and Greenland, replacing the Paleo-Eskimo populations that had formerly settled there. These migrants spread the Proto-Eskimo language all across the North American Arctic, where it progressively underwent linguistic change, splitting off into various dialects and subdialects.[2] Nowadays, linguists recognize the existence of 14–18 different IIK dialects, each belonging to one of four dialectal groupings: Alaskan Iñupiaq, Western Canadian Inuktun (in the Inuvialuit Settlement Region and the Kitikmeot region of Nunavut), Eastern Canadian Inuktitut (in the Kivalliq and Qikiqtaaluk [Baffin] regions of Nunavut, Nunavik, and Nunatsiavut), and Kalaallisut (in Greenland) (Dorais 2017). All these dialects are mutually intelligible to some extent, more so within each grouping. Despite its dispersion over the entire North American Arctic, IIK has thus preserved its linguistic unity.

CHALLENGES TO IIK

For centuries, IIK was the only language most Inuit ever heard during their lifetimes, with the exception of a minority who lived near the tree-line, at the boundary between Inuit and northern Athapaskan and Algonquian territories. Each regional group of speakers developed its own pronunciation, and the meaning of some words changed. For instance, the Proto-Eskimo word-base *aliga-* ("to be lonely or sad") preserved its original signification (under the form *alia-*) in a majority of dialects, but in the central Canadian Arctic (Inuinnaqtun dialect), Nunavik and Labrador, it took the opposite meaning ("to be glad"). In Alaska, the verbal base *tautuk-* ("to look") got a more general meaning ("to see"), while the Proto-Eskimo root for "seeing," *taku-*, the signification of which was preserved outside Alaska, took on a much more restricted meaning ("to check on something") among speakers of Alaskan Iñupiaq.

These changes were generally minor. In the absence of contact with speakers of other languages, and of social and cultural cleavages within Inuit society, there was no reason why IIK would have changed. There may have been some slight differences in the pronunciations of men and women, but their impact on language change was limited. Word lists and other linguistic data collected by explorers, traders, and missionaries during the 18th and early 19th centuries show that during that period, IIK was quite the same from Alaska to Greenland (Dorais 2010, 110–116). Nowadays, the grammatical suffixes remain essentially similar in all dialects, and, if differences in pronunciation are not taken into account, approximately 90 percent of the lexicon is common to all Inuit forms of speech.

Contact with alien languages only appeared when qallunaat (tan'ngit in Alaska and among Inuvialuit) started visiting Inuit Nunangat on a more or less regular basis. On Belle-Isle Strait in southern Labrador, as early as the late 17th century, local Inuit communicated in a trade jargon with the European fishermen and merchants who sailed there during summer. This pidgin language included words drawn from various tongues: Inuktut (*memek*, "drink," from *imiq*, "drinking water"), French (*troquo*, "let's barter!" from *troquons!*), Innu Algonquian (*monkoumek*, "knife," from *muhkumân*), and Basque (*makagoua*, "peace," from *bekagoa*, "peaceful").[3] When among themselves, however, Inuit had no reason to use these terms, except perhaps when joking about those hairy qallunaat (literally, "bushy eyebrows"). Actually, when traders, missionaries, and other Europeans came to live in the Arctic – from the 18th century onwards in Greenland, Labrador, and southern and central coastal Alaska, and from the late 19th and early 20th centuries elsewhere – it was they who learned to speak IIK. These newcomers often used a restricted vocabulary arranged in a European grammatical pattern, as with *uvanga auka taku ivvit* ("me no see you") instead of *takunngilagit* ("I do not see you").

For many decades, then, Inuit did not feel linguistically challenged. Some of them learned English – or Danish in Greenland – but they were not compelled to do so. On the contrary, contact with qallunaat, missionaries in particular, came with a bonus: the introduction of literacy in their own language. Chiefly aimed at enabling people to read the Christian scriptures and prayer books, literacy was rapidly appropriated by Inuit as a means for writing letters to each other and noting down important life events (see Nielsen, this volume). In Greenland and Labrador, IIK was the sole language of school instruction. Elsewhere, children learned to read and write within their families – by way of missionary-devised syllabic characters in Nunavik and eastern Nunavut.

Inuit culture was changing though, especially in terms of material goods (e.g., metal tools, guns, Euro-American staple foods), economy (trapping and hunting for trade), and religion (Christian ministers replacing shamans). But the language adapted brilliantly to change. Without any outside influence – except, in part, in the field of Christian terminology – Inuit speakers coined hundreds of neologisms: words denoting the objects, habits, and concepts newly introduced by qallunaat. Thanks to the polysynthetic structure of IIK, they were generally able to devise new terms which described the function or appearance of what was denoted.[4] In a limited number of cases, words already in existence were given new meanings. Here are a few examples, in the Nunavik dialect of Inuktut:

qukiuti	firearm ("a means for making a loud noise")
nunakkuujuuq	motor vehicle ("that usually goes by land")
kiinaujaq	money ("that looks like a face")
niuvirti	trader, merchant ("one in the habit of trading")
allatuq	he/she writes ("draws or sews decorative patterns")
pullaq	electric bulb ("bubble of air")

Only a small number of new words were borrowed from another language, usually English or Danish (e.g., *tii* for "tea," or *jaikaq* for "jacket"), and this in Canada and Alaska, as well as in Greenland. Over the years, the continued creation of neologisms allowed Inuit to express in their own language the near totality of new situations brought about by contact and, more generally, modernity.

In Greenland and eastern Canada, challenges to IIK only started to appear after 1945, when the Danish and Canadian governments became aware of the strategic value of their arctic territories. During World War II, these territories had served as aerial routes for transporting planes and other military material to the Allies fighting in Europe, and in the post-war period it became considered important to make the arctic lands an integral part of Denmark and Canada, respectively. The situation was the same in Alaska, where the Japanese attack – in 1942, Japan occupied two islands in the Aleutians and deported native Aleut islanders to Hokkaido – led the United States armed forces to build the Alaska Highway in order to facilitate the movement of troops.

In Alaska, however, Iñupiaq and several other Indigenous tongues, including the Yupik languages, were challenged as early as the first quarter of the 20th century, with the opening of missionary and government residential and day schools where instruction was conducted exclusively in English. In the western Canadian Arctic, two residential schools, one Anglican and the other Catholic, opened in 1929 in Aklavik. They taught an elementary English curriculum to Inuit and Dene children from the Arctic coast and Mackenzie Delta. In both regions, this intrusion of an alien tongue was amplified by the arrival of significant numbers of gold miners, muskrat trappers (especially in the Mackenzie Delta), fur traders, and other English speakers, several of whom settled permanently in the area. This explains why, contrary to most of their northeastern Canadian and Greenlandic compatriots, many Alaskan Natives and northwestern Canadian Inuvialuit, men in particular, had become bilingual by the 1940s. This early adoption of English probably helps explain the dominance of English in these two regions today.

After 1945, Denmark and Canada decided that Inuit under their administration should participate more fully in these two countries' economic, social, and legal systems. This implied the development of compulsory formal education in the national languages (Danish and English) and state-run economic and social planning (for Greenland see Arnfjord, this volume; Kuokkanen, this volume). Official interventionism was seemingly less important in Alaska, where development was left in the hands of the private and institutional sectors.

Greenland became an administrative province of Denmark in 1953 – until then, it had been a colony of the Danish Crown – and Greenlanders had been dubbed "Northern Danes." As concerns language, the low level of fluency in Danish among the Indigenous population was considered a problem to be solved:

> After 1950 it was decided that Danish should be taught in a much more systematic way because, educators believed, modern cultural and technical data could not be translated into Greenlandic [Kalaallisut]. This decision, which was rapidly enforced, entailed a severe setback for the aboriginal language. The reform of curricula conducted between 1961 and 1964 favored the production of Danish didactical material but left teachers of Greenlandic with a limited number of outdated manuals.
>
> (Dorais 2010, 190)

At the same time, schools were facing a severe shortage of Native personnel. Teachers were imported from Denmark, and promising Greenlandic students were sent to Denmark to complete high school. In 1967, a law stipulated "that school authorities could wait for up to three years before starting classes in Greenlandic but that Danish should be part of the curriculum from grade 1 on" (Dorais 2010, 190).

In Canada, the federal government established the Department of Northern Affairs and Natural Resources in 1953, renamed the Department of Indian Affairs and Northern Development in 1966. Besides economic development, one of its principal mandates was to provide Inuit of the Northwest Territories (NWT) (then including present-day Nunavut) and Arctic Quebec with formal education. Accordingly, between 1953 and 1965, some 40 federal day schools opened in population centers, into which nomadic families were strongly encouraged to move. Many of these settlements had never had a school before, except, in some places, sporadic classes taught by local missionaries. These teaching establishments offered an elementary – and, in a few communities, secondary – curriculum in English, taught by qallunaat teachers from southern Canada.

The social ideology that prevailed at that time was one of Euro-American conformity. In order to become useful, law-abiding citizens of Canada, Denmark (Greenland) and, implicitly, the United States (Alaska), Inuit and other Indigenous peoples had to give up their presumably outdated language and culture, replacing it with English (or

Danish), and modern western civilization. Of course, this way of thinking served to justify the economic, political, and intellectual (through schools) authority exercised over arctic lands by those in power in Canada, Denmark, and the US. According to anthropologist Robert Paine (1977), such a situation was part of a process of internal colonialism. In order to establish their control over the land, and exploit for their own financial profit the resources of outlying regions within the borders of their countries, politicians and business elite compelled local populations to assimilate to the majority society and, eventually, become cheap labor for the mining and other enterprises big companies wished to develop.[5] This type of hegemonic disrespect for Indigenous cultures and languages has been labeled cultural imperialism by the native Greenlandic scholar Robert Petersen (1977).

Inuktut suffered from this onslaught, aggravated in the early 1980s by universal access to television – with minimal content in Indigenous languages – and, later on, by the advent of the internet.[6] In Canada and Alaska, as a result of schooling, kids stopped being taught by their families to read and write in their mother tongue. Worse still, many parents believed that in order for their children to gain access to the opportunities increasingly available to Inuit for vocational training and wage work, families should leave education entirely in the hands of the English-speaking schools. This led to two unfortunate consequences. As concerns language, the level of proficiency in IIK – measured, for instance, in terms of mother tongue versus second language vocabulary available to speakers – started decreasing among youth with formal education (Allen 2007; Dorais 1989). And socially speaking, a cultural cleavage appeared between formally educated children and their often unschooled parents. The children's ability to understand their Elders and communicate with them diminished progressively. In the worst cases, bilingual parents stopped transmitting IIK to children. This had already been happening in the Iñupiaq-speaking regions of Alaska and among the Mackenzie Delta and Arctic coast Inuvialuit. It then extended to the central Canadian Arctic (the Kitikmeot region of Nunavut) and to Labrador, where provincial education in English replaced the Inuktitut-language missionary schools in 1949, the year Newfoundland joined the Canadian Confederation.

From a sociolinguistic perspective, the North American Arctic witnessed a situation of diglossia (Ferguson 1959). Diglossia refers to a situation in which a human group must resort to using two unequal languages in different contexts. Speakers of IIK had to resort to the predominant tongue (English or Danish) to gain access to formal education or post-elementary schooling, and to communicate (often through interpreters) with government administrators and non-Inuit organizations in general. The subordinate language (IIK) was mostly relegated to daily conversation. According to Ferguson, diglossia can endure for centuries, but Calvet (1974) has shown that in most contemporary cases of diglossia, the subordinate language is finally replaced or "swallowed" by the dominant one.

At the end of the 1960s, in Canada and Alaska at least, the eventuality of a full language shift toward English, entailing the final disappearance of IIK, seemed quite possible. However, it was not foreseen that instruction in English – Danish in Greenland – would bring the emergence of a first generation of young Inuit grounded in their Indigenous culture and still fluent in IIK, but also familiar with qallunaat cultural and social habits. They understood how the wider world operated and had acquired a high degree of fluency and literacy in their second language. In addition to future politicians, this generation produced people like Alaskan educator and linguist Edna Ahgeak MacLean, Nunavut language activist Jose Kusugak, Nunavik author and lecturer Zebedee Nungak, Greenlandic linguist Carl Christian "Puju" Olsen, among others. These people played an important part in meeting the challenges faced by IIK, thus contributing significantly to its preservation and development and ultimately averting a full language shift.

MEETING THE CHALLENGES

Thanks to this first generation of young, formally educated but linguistically and culturally grounded Inuit men and women conversant in qallunaat languages and concepts,[7] the period between the late 1960s and early 1980s saw the advent, all across the North American Arctic, of several Indigenous associations (e.g., the Inuit Circumpolar Council, founded in 1977). These organizations formulated very precise territorial, political and cultural demands, aiming at bringing Inuit Nunangat back under Inuit control. As a result, Aboriginal rights were progressively recognized, and this led to the signing of land claims agreements in Alaska and Canada. Greenlanders attained Home Rule in 1979 and more control with Self Rule in 2009.

Inuit claims included a strong commitment to measures for preserving Indigenous language and culture. A first step was to ensure that IIK is taught in local schools. In Greenland, Kalaallisut regained its position as the medium of instruction, right from grade one to the end of high school, with Danish taught as a second language. In Canada, from the 1970s on, the commitment toward Inuktut led to the emergence of bilingual education, which is still in effect in a majority of Nunavut and Nunavik schools (see Tulloch, this volume). This system allows the Indigenous language to serve as the unique or principal medium of instruction up to grades two, three, or four, after which it is replaced with English (or French in some Nunavik classes) for the rest of the elementary and secondary curricula – with the exception of occasional Inuit culture courses generally taught in Inuktut.

In communities where the native tongue has ceased to be transmitted to children, it may be taught as a second language. This is often the case in Alaska, although bilingual education also exists there. In 1972, popular pressure brought the state legislature of Alaska to pass a law requiring any school with at least 15 students whose mother tongue was not English to offer classes in these pupils' first language. The same law established an organization for linguistic research and teaching, the Alaska Native Language Center at the University of Alaska, Fairbanks. By the mid-1970s, the Center had endowed every Alaskan Indigenous language, including Iñupiaq, with a simple and accurate standard orthography. It also started to teach these languages to any Native person eager to learn their ancestral tongue.

Standardizing the orthography was considered essential in order to teach IIK in a systematic way. In Greenland, the local administration implemented orthographic reform in 1973. The official orthography, dating back to 1851, no longer reflected the pronunciation of the language. It was thus replaced by a much simpler writing system that corresponded more exactly to the way words were actually pronounced.[8] For example, *кavdlunâк* ("European") was now to be written "qallunaaq." This orthography, like the writing systems devised by the Alaska Native Language Center, was phonemic (or quasi-phonemic): each letter always symbolized the same phoneme (basic sound unit), and conversely, each different phoneme was represented in writing by only one specific letter. This ensured that the spoken and written languages were almost perfectly identical.

In Canada, after some unsuccessful governmental attempts at standardizing Inuktut orthography, native speakers decided to take the development of their written language into their own hands. In 1973, the newly established Inuit Tapirisat Canada (now Inuit Tapiriit Kanatami), set up a language commission, one objective of which was "to study the present state of the written language and recommend changes for the future" (Harper 1983, 54). In March 1976, an orthographic subcommittee proposed a dual (alphabetical and syllabic) writing system apt to allow any Canadian dialect of Inuktut to be transcribed in a precise and acceptable way. This system was phonemic, like its Greenlandic and Alaskan counterparts. It was formally adopted by the annual general assembly of Inuit Tapirisat Canada in September 1976, becoming the official orthography of the Canadian Inuit. After a few years, however, the speakers of some dialects decided to devise their own writing system (as was the case with the Inuvialuit), or to retain their former, non-phonemic orthographies (Inuinnaqtun and Labrador dialects).[9]

At the end of the 1970s, IIK had been endowed all over the Arctic with the basic tools (phonemic standard orthographies, Indigenous-language education) to enable it to survive and, hopefully, thrive. After two decades (the 1950s and 1960s) during which native language had been considered an obstacle to the personal and collective development of Inuit, IIK was recognized by governments and the general public as an essential component of the Arctic world and its identity. We already saw the important role played by the Alaska Native Language Center – established by the Alaska state legislature – in promoting and developing local languages. In Canada, Inuktut became an Indigenous official language of the NWT, and a growing number of services became available in Inuktut. When the NWT were partitioned in 1999, Inuktut, English, and French became the official languages of the new territory of Nunavut. A Languages Commissioner was appointed in order to ensure that linguistic rights were respected, an Official Languages Bureau was established within the Nunavut Government Department of Culture and Heritage, and an Inuit Language Protection Act was eventually voted in by the territorial legislature. Inuktut also received legal recognition in Nunavik in 1975, when the James Bay and Northern Quebec Agreement was signed, and in Labrador in 2005, with the advent of the Nunatsiavut Government.

When Greenland attained Home Rule in 1979, Paragraph 9 of the Home Rule Act stated that "Greenlandic [Kalaallisut] is the principal language of the land. Danish is to be taught thoroughly. Both languages may be used in matters of public concern" (Berthelsen 1990, 339). A Language Commission (Oqaasileriffik) was established in 1982 under the supervision of a Greenlandic Language Council. When Home Rule was replaced by Self Rule in 2009, Kalaallisut became the only official language in Greenland. A new law stipulated that all residents should speak it, whatever their origin, provided this would not be detrimental to their rights if their first language was Danish or another tongue (Dorais 2010, 245–246) (see Figure 9.1).

In Canada and Greenland, some parts of the private sector felt compelled to offer services in IIK. As early as 1978, Association Inuksiutiit Katimajjit, a not-for-profit organization devoted to the advancement and dissemination of knowledge concerning

Inuit, became involved in the translation and transliteration in syllabic characters of the Bell Canada telephone directory serving the Inuit communities of the NWT and Nunavik. More than forty years later, Inuksiutiit is still in charge of this task in Nunavik. Other businesses, such as the Northern stores, took similar initiatives. In Nunavut, the Languages Commissioner developed a language plan for ensuring that Inuktut-speaking customers are accommodated in their mother tongue in the private sector. Similar measures have been taken by the Self Rule government of Greenland.

After 1970, IIK became more prominent in the fields of musical arts and literature. Everywhere in the Arctic, people had always sung in their language, but over the last four or five decades – earlier in Greenland – singers increasingly availed themselves of the opportunity to record their music and to perform live in arctic festivals, as well as on the radio, television and the internet. Radio especially played – and continues to play in many communities – a crucial part in informing people in their own language and enabling them to express themselves, musically and otherwise. In Greenland, Kalaallit Nunaata Radioa, the national radio and television network, started radio broadcasting almost exclusively in Kalaallisut as early as 1926 (television broadcasting came much later of course).

Greenland also has a long-standing tradition of publishing in the native language. The newspaper *Atuagagdliutit*, still in existence, was founded in 1861. From 1900,

Figure 9.1   National Library and Ilisimatusarfik Institute in Nuuk, Greenland, 1985. Photo: L-J Dorais.

a significant number of Greenlandic essays, novels, poems, and other forms of literature have been published, all of them in Kalaallisut. By contrast, in Canada, mostly because of the late introduction of formal school literacy, it was only during the mid-1960s and early 1970s that Inuit authors started to publish[10] – principally in journals sponsored by the federal government or native organizations. Some of these texts are in Inuktut, but if classroom booklets are excluded,[11] a larger number of published works have been written or translated into English or, more rarely, French (on Canadian Inuit literature, see Martin 2012 and Duvicq 2019). As is the case elsewhere in the world, when they use their own language, Canadian Inuit creators generally prefer expressing themselves through music, film, and television (e.g., Zacharias Kunuk's Igloolik Isuma Productions), rather than the written word.

Thanks to these political developments, educational measures, and cultural initiatives, the situation of diglossia, described earlier, shifted by the end of the 1990s, and no longer threatened a full language shift in Greenland and northeastern Canada. All across the North American Arctic, IIK could no longer be considered a subordinate language. New linguistic markets had appeared – these are situations where each language or linguistic variety in presence is assigned a higher or lower value proceeding from the social and economic advantages it procures its speakers (Bourdieu 1991). Within these markets, IIK held a relatively strong position alongside English, Danish, and French. According to the anthropologist Donna Patrick (2003), this occurred because the increasing importance of IIK in its own sphere (village life and land-based activities) entailed the emergence of an alternative market, where IIK held a high social value. One language (English in Canada) was considered more useful in practical situations, the other (IIK) was principally efficient in the preservation of identity (see Figure 9.2).

Figure 9.2 Inuit culture class, Nunavut Arctic College, Iqaluit, Nunavut, 1999.
Photo: L-J Dorais.

Figure 9.3 Bilingual street signs in Iqaluit, Nunavut, November 2010. Simonie Michael was the first elected member of the Northwest Territorial Council, the precursor to the Northwest Territories and Nunavut Legislative Assemblies. Helen Maksagak was the first commissioner of Nunavut and the first woman and first Inuk to serve as commissioner in the NWT. Photo: Pamela Stern.

The coexistence of two languages means that Inuit Nunangat must now be considered as a fundamentally bilingual or even multilingual land, rather than an IIK-speaking region *stricto sensu*. In Canada, for instance, according to the 2001 census, 76 percent of people whose mother tongue was Inuktut could also hold a conversation in English. In 2016, this proportion had increased to 82 percent. Research conducted in the Qikiqtaaluk (Baffin) region of Nunavut in the late 1990s showed that in some communities (e.g., Iqaluit, the territorial capital), bilingualism seemed to favor the predominance of English. To be sure, most Inuit children were still taught Inuktut as their first language, but as soon as they had spent two or three years in school, many parents started addressing them in English. A majority of adolescents and young adults also preferred English – or a mix of English and Inuktut – for conversations with their peers (Dorais and Sammons 2002). In smaller villages, however, bilingualism was more equitable and less detrimental to Inuktut (Dorais and Sammons 2002; Tulloch 2004) (see Figure 9.3).

IIK IN THE 2020s

At the end of the 2010s, according to American, Canadian, and Greenlandic statistics, out of a world total of approximately 148,000 Inuit (including 112,000 living in Inuit Nunangat), some 109,000 (73.5 percent) spoke an IIK dialect as

Table 9.1 Geographic distribution of first language Inuktut speakers in Canada

Region	Inuit residents	Inuktut first language
Inuvialuit Region (NT)	3,100	500 (16%)
Nunavut Territory (NU)	30,600	27,000 (88%)
Nunavik (QC)	11,800	11,600 (98%)
Nunatsiavut (NL)	2,300	380 (16.5%)
Southern Canada	17,550	2,725 (15.5%)
Total	65,350	42,205 (64.5%)

Source: Statistics Canada (2018)

their first language.[12] However, percentages varied from one country or region to another.

In Alaska, according to the Alaska Native Language Center website (n.d.): "Alaska is home to about 13,500 Iñupiat, of whom about 3,000, mostly over age 40, speak the language." US government statistics (Siebens and Julian 2011) show that in 2010, there were 7,203 speakers of "Inupik" (Iñupiaq) in the United States, 5,707 of whom lived in their Alaskan native lands.[13] So, ten years later, in view of the fact that the language was almost never transmitted to young people, the total number of Iñupiaq speakers should have hovered around 5,000 individuals, with a plausible 3,000 to 3,500 residing in their Alaskan homeland.

In Canada, detailed language statistics for 2016 can be elicited from the Aboriginal Population Profile (Statistics Canada 2018). According to these data, knowledge of Inuktut was distributed as in Table 9.1.

Finally, *Greenland in Figures 2020*, a PDF document available online (Statistics Greenland 2020), states that in 2020, Greenland had a total population of 56,081, most of whom were of Greenlandic (Kalaallit) ancestry. Moreover, 16,770 persons born in Greenland were living in Denmark. It is generally considered that Kalaaallit account for about 90 percent of the population of Greenland, and that some 99 percent of them speak Kalaallisut as their first language, although no statistics seem to exist concerning these two points. This means that Greenland's native population amounted to some 50,500 individuals in 2020, with 50,000 speakers, plus 16,770 Kalaallit in Denmark, 12,000 of whom (but this is a guess) may have spoken Kalaallisut, considering that many young people raised in Denmark, especially in mixed families, were not fluent in the language.

Compared to several other Indigenous minority languages spoken in North America and around the world, IIK appears to be in good shape. It still constitutes the first language of almost three-quarters of all Inuit living in – or registered as residents of – their ancestral territories. Nowadays, the language is officially recognized as a bona fide teaching medium. Public funds are allotted for its preservation and development, and most people recognize that IIK forms an essential part of Inuit and, more largely, arctic identity. Kalaallisut has been retired from UNESCO's list of endangered languages. The Nunavut government wants Inuktut to become the main means of communication in the workplace, and in all Nunavik communities save one, it still serves as the default language. In areas like Labrador, the Inuvialuit Settlement Region, and Alaska, where the Indigenous tongue has stopped being passed on to children through the family, it is taught as a second language in a good number of schools, and some young people succeed in gaining relative fluency in it.

Despite these positive results, however, some caution is needed. In Greenland, there is now a movement to replace Danish with English as the country's second language. If this ever occurs, we are entitled to wonder if shifting linguistic allegiance from a local tongue spoken by some five million people to an economically and culturally attractive world language would not put an almost unbearable pressure on Kalaallisut.

In Nunavik and eastern Nunavut, where Inuktut is still used on a daily basis by a majority of Inuit, the most popular written language is English, and, with the exception of community radio, most oral and visual media speak the language of qallunaat. More dangerously perhaps, from grades three or four on, Inuktut is abruptly replaced by English – or French in some Nunavik classes – as the language of instruction. This means that after the age of eight or nine, children stop learning in their own language – except from what they can glean from their family and from sporadic "Inuktut language arts" courses. More advanced reading, writing, mathematics, science, and social skills are taught in an alien tongue.

As mentioned earlier, this bilingual education system has been in place since the 1970s (see Tulloch, this volume). In 2008, the Nunavut legislature adopted a law that would have extended the bilingual curriculum up to grade nine by 2019, but nothing was achieved due to a severe shortage of Inuit teachers. Consequently, on 4 June 2019, a new bill was tabled, postponing until 2039 the full implementation of an Inuktut-English curriculum up to grade 12. Such a failure in achieving the set goals illustrates the difficulty of protecting Inuktut efficiently, despite the best of intentions. Even if the language remains strong in most of Nunavut, its use is constantly declining, as shown in a statistical report released at the end of the 2010s (Lepage et al. 2019). In 2001, 72 percent of the territory's total population (Inuit and qallunaat combined) spoke Inuktut as their first language, but in 2016, this proportion had fallen to 65 percent, even though the proportion of Inuit residents remained constant at 85 percent. According to 2016 statistics, a large percentage of people were able to have a conversation in Inuktut – 77 percent in the Qikiqtaaluk region,[14] 88 percent in Kivalliq, but only 57 percent in the Kitikmeot region – and more individuals than before actually spoke it at home, but less so as their principal language. In bilingual Nunavut homes, Inuktut is increasingly superseded by English. This is congruent with the fact that in 2016, while the Indigenous language was the mother tongue of 97 percent of all Inuit residents of Nunavut aged over 64, only 72 percent of residents aged 20–24 spoke Inuktut as their first language. According to statistics from 2012 (Lepage et al. 2019, 33), one-third of Nunavut Inuit children and youth aged 6–24 admitted speaking Inuktut with effort or knowing only a few words. However, more than half of these non-fluent individuals (but 43 percent among those aged 6–14) said they understood the language well. Such figures are symptomatic of an asymmetry in linguistic abilities, typical of ongoing language shift (Alana Johns, personal communication).

Even though IIK brilliantly met the challenges of previous decades, when it was considered a nuisance rather than an asset, today it is still threatened even in some regions where it thrives. In order to survive and prosper, the language of the Inuit has to fulfill three basic conditions: (1) it must rest upon a reliable and efficient

Indigenous-language education system, yet to be implemented; (2) bilingualism must become stable and more symmetrical, as opposed to the seemingly ever-increasing predominance of English; and (3) Inuit speakers must realize that their mother tongue is as useful – albeit in a different way – as the language of qallunaat. In my opinion, it is only if these conditions are met that IIK will still be widely spoken by the end of the 21st century.

NOTES

1. Inuktut ("[speaking] like an Inuk") is the name adopted in 2016 by Inuit Tapiriit Kanatami to designate all Inuit dialects spoken in Canada.
2. A few centuries earlier, in southwestern Alaska and among people who had migrated back to present-day Russian Chukotka, Proto-Eskimo had started to evolve differently, giving rise to the four contemporary Yupik languages.
3. At the turn of the 20th century, an English-Iñupiaq pidgin (with some Hawaiian loanwords) also developed among American whalers and their Inuit crews, along the arctic coast of Alaska and Yukon.
4. Like most other North American Indigenous languages, IIK shows some reluctance to borrow foreign terms. This may be linked to the polysynthetic structure of these languages, which enables speakers to construct new words easily.
5. As opposed to the "classical" international form of colonialism, internal colonialism generally occurs under a paternalistic guise: it is for their own good that, under the guidance of a caring government, Inuit should abandon their "useless" language and "outdated" culture to adopt our modern civilization. During the 1960s, at the same time that the federal government of Canada was applying assimilative policies, it must be said to its credit that Ottawa genuinely encouraged and aided Inuit to develop local cooperatives, in order to enable them to become economically self-sufficient.
6. The internet was and still is prominently English-speaking. Nowadays, however, it is increasingly used by several Inuit organizations and governments to promote and reinvigorate IIK, or to convey information in the local language.
7. In Greenland, this generation was rather the second one. In the 1940s and early 1950s, a previous group of Native intellectuals and politicians educated, partly, in Denmark, (e.g., Robert Petersen, founder of the University of Greenland), also contributed to the movement.
8. Of course, because pronunciation can evolve quite rapidly, standard orthographies gain from being revised from time to time.
9. Some 20 years later, the Inuinnaqtun and Labrador speakers devised their own revised orthographies, both of them quasi-phonemic, but slightly different from the Inuit Tapirisat standard.
10. One notable exception is Salome Mitiarjuk Nappaaluk, a monolingual Nunavik woman literate in Inuktitut syllabics, who wrote a novel *Sanaaq* (after the novel's principal character) in the early 1950s. Unpublished until 1984 (when the original syllabic version appeared), it only became available in English thirty years later (Nappaaluk 2014). Another major Inuit author without formal education is Taamusi Qumaq, who compiled and published a voluminous (more than 15,000 entries) dictionary of definitions in Nunavik Inuktut (Qumaq 1991).
11. In Alaska, most texts published in Iñupiaq seem to be school booklets. At least one novel (*Elnguq*, after the principal character) has appeared in Yupik (Jacobson 1990).
12. These figures do not take into account some 30,000 Yupik individuals from southwestern Alaska and Russian Chukotka.

13 On top of that, 19,960 persons reported that they spoke a Yupik language.
14 The percentage of Inuktut speakers in the Qikiqtaaluk region is decreased due to the large proportion (approximately 40 percent) of qallunaat living in Iqaluit, the regional center and territorial capital.

REFERENCES

Alaska Native Language Center. [n.d.]. Languages: Iñupiaq. https://uaf.edu/anlc/languages/inupiaq.php.

Allen, Shanley E.M. 2007. "The Future of Inuktitut in the Face of Majority Languages: Bilingualism or Language Shift?" *Applied Psycholinguistics* 28 (3): 515–536. https://doi-org.proxy.lib.sfu.ca/10.1017/S0142716407070282.

Berthelsen, Christian. 1990. "Greenlandic in Schools." In *Arctic Languages: An Awakening*, edited by Dirmid R.F. Collis, 333–339. Paris: UNESCO.

Bourdieu, Pierre. 1991. *Language and Symbolic Power*. Cambridge, MA: Harvard University Press.

Calvet, Louis-Jean. 1974. *Linguistique et colonialisme: Petit traité de glottophagie*. Paris: Payot.

Dorais, Louis-Jacques. 1989. "Bilingualism and Diglossia in the Canadian Eastern Arctic." *Arctic* 42 (3): 199–207. https://doi.org/10.14430/arctic1658.

———. 2010. *The Language of the Inuit. Syntax, Semantics, and Society in the Arctic*. Montreal, QC and Kingston, ON: McGill-Queen's University Press.

———. 2017. *Inuit Languages and Dialects. Inuit Uqausiqatigiit*. Iqaluit, NU: Nunavut Arctic College Media.

———. 2020. *Words of the Inuit: A Semantic Stroll through a Northern Culture*. Winnipeg, MB: University of Manitoba Press.

Dorais, Louis-Jacques, and Susan Sammons. 2002. *Language in Nunavut: Discourse and Identity in the Baffin Region*. Iqaluit and Quebec City, QC: Nunavut Arctic College and Université Laval, Groupe d'études inuit et circumpolaires.

Duvicq, Nelly. 2019. *Histoire de la littérature inuite du Nunavik*. Quebec City, QC: Presses de l'Université du Québec.

Ferguson, Charles A. 1959. "Diglossia." *WORD* 15: 325–340. https://doi.org/10.1080/00437956.1959.11659702.

Fortescue, Michael. 1998. *Language Relations across Bering Strait: Reappraising the Archaeological and Linguistic Evidence*. London: Cassell.

Fortescue, Michael, Steven A. Jacobson, and Lawrence D. Kaplan. 2010. *Comparative Eskimo Dictionary with Aleut Cognates*. Fairbanks, AK: Alaska Native Language Center.

Harper, Kenn. 1983. "Writing Systems and Translations." *Inuktitut* 53, September: 3–103.

Jacobson, Anna W. 1990. *Elnguq*. Fairbanks, AK: Alaska Native Language Center.

Lepage, Jean-François, Stéphanie Langlois, and Martin Turcotte. 2019. *Evolution of the Language Situation in Nunavut, 2001 to 2016*. Ethnicity, Language and Immigration Thematic Series no. 89-657-X2019010. Ottawa, ON: Statistics Canada.

Martin, Keavy. 2012. *Stories in a New Skin. Approaches to Inuit Literature*. Winnipeg, MB: University of Manitoba Press.

Nappaaluk, Mitiarjuk. 2014. *Sanaaq: An Inuit Novel*. Winnipeg, MB: University of Manitoba Press.

Paine, Robert. 1977. "The Nursery Game: Colonizers and Colonized in the Eastern Arctic." *Études/Inuit/Studies* 1 (1): 5–32.

Patrick, Donna. 2003. *Language, Politics, and Social Interaction in an Inuit Community*. Berlin and New York: Mouton deGruyter.

Petersen, Robert. 1977. "On the West Greenlandic Cultural Imperialism in East Greenland." In *Cultural Imperialism and Cultural Identity: Proceedings of the 8th Conference of Nordic Ethnographers/Anthropologists*, edited by Carola Sandbacka, 187–195. Helsinki: Finnish Anthropological Society.

Qumaq, Taamusi. 1991. *Inuit Uqausillaringit* [*The Genuine Inuit Words*]. Quebec City and Montreal, QC: Association Inuksiutiit Katimajiit and Avataq Cultural Institute.

Siebens, Julie, and Tiffany Julian. 2011. "Native North American Languages Spoken at Home in the United States and Puerto Rico: 2006–2010." Report no. ACSBR/10-10. United States Census Bureau. https://www.census.gov/library/publications/2011/acs/acsbr10-10.html.

Statistics Canada. 2018. "Aboriginal Population Profile." In *2016 Census*. 98-510-X2016001 https://www150.statcan.gc.ca/n1/en/catalogue/98-510-X).

Statistics Greenland. 2020. "Greenland in Figures 2020." http://www.stat.gl/GFE2020/p1.

Tulloch, Shelley. 2004. *Inuktitut and Inuit Youth: Language Attitudes as a Basis for Language Planning*. PhD dissertation, Université Laval.

CHAPTER 10

INUIT BILINGUAL EDUCATION

Shelley Tulloch

A NOTE ON INUIT LANGUAGES AND DIALECTS

The Inuit language is commonly referred to as a continuum of dialects or closely related languages spoken over millions of square kilometers, from Kalaallisut in Greenland to Inupiaq in Alaska. Inuktut is used as an umbrella term by Canada's national Inuit organization, Inuit Tapiriit Kanatami, to refer collectively to all Inuit languages or dialects in Canada, including Inuktitut, Inuttitut, Inuktun, Inuinnaqtun, and Inuvialuktun etc.[1] Linguists and the Inuit Circumpolar Council generally claim that neighboring Inuit groups understand each other's language, but as geographic distance grows, inter-intelligibility declines (Dorais 2010). The Yup'ik languages in Alaska and Russia (e.g., Yugtun, Cup'ik) are closely related but not intelligible to speakers of Inupiaq, Inuktut, and Kalaallisut.[2]

The Inuit language has multiple written forms, some of them standardized. These include roman orthographic systems developed in Greenland, Labrador, and the western Canadian Arctic, and a syllabic system used in the eastern Canadian Arctic. Calls to develop a pan-Arctic auxiliary orthography have not come to fruition. Inuit Tapiriit Kanatami introduced an auxiliary written standard for Canadian dialects in 2019 that is not yet widely in use.

The vitality of Inuit and Yup'ik languages varies from region to region. Kalaallisut is considered viable, as it is learned as the mother tongue by almost all Greenlanders, and is used in media, schools, literature, and government. In some Canadian and Alaskan communities, Inuktut and Yup'ik are also being passed on in the home, and are widely spoken. In other communities, intergenerational transmission has ceased. In some, the only speakers are elderly, or second language learners. Across the Arctic, national languages threaten Inuit and Yup'ik languages.

BACKGROUND TO INUIT EDUCATION

The vitality of the Inuit languages is linked to language practices and ideologies in schools. Prior to formal schooling, Inuit raised children through *pilimaksarniq* – observation, practice, and individualized mentoring – through which youth acquired skills, abilities, values, and character. Children learned alongside family members, becoming equipped to contribute to and survive their society (Kuniliusie 2015).

DOI: 10.4324/9780429275470-10

The earliest missionary schools, starting in the 1700s in Greenland and Labrador, and more widely across the Canadian Arctic in the early 1900s, taught in Inuit languages. Inuit literacy spread quickly, as Inuit taught each other and sent letters to other areas of the Arctic. Dorais (1990) estimates that by 1950 (and much earlier in Labrador and Greenland) almost all Inuit could read and write in Inuktut (235, 237).

Changes in policies and practices from the early to the mid-20th century led to missionary, federal, or provincial/state/regional schools imposing the national language through deliberately assimilationist schooling. Many Inuit children were separated from their parents and siblings, forbidden to speak their language, and endured abuse. The Canadian Truth and Reconciliation Commission concluded that these residential schools were "always more than simply an educational program: it was an integral part of a conscious policy of cultural genocide" (TRC 2015, 55). Federal day schools of the time also pursued assimilationist agendas.

Even in schools where students had more positive experiences, Inuit educational leader Saimanaaq Netser (2013) reflected:

> [W]e were made to live like foreigners and became unrecognizable to our parents! We were being assimilated into the *Qablunaaq*[3] culture and civilized. During the time I was in Churchill, I enjoyed the experience, just like many others who attended this school. Unfortunately, as we attended this school, we were forgetting our Inuit heritage in every way, and we were losing our Inuit language as well.
>
> (10)

Inuit educational leader Sarah Townley explained that racism pushed her and her peers to abandon Inuktut in Labrador boarding schools, even if it was not explicitly forbidden in the school she attended:

> A lot of people lost their language when they went to the Dorm, 'cause they never kept it up. It would happen quickly. [How would they talk to their parents when they went home?] I have no idea. They couldn't really converse. But for me … I wouldn't speak Inuktitut in the dorm. I guess we were scared that people were going to make fun of us or that we would be bullied. I had a lot of relatives there but we still didn't speak Inuktitut. [Were you told not to?] I think it was just more us decided not to. A lot of us 'cause we went through that [racism] in our communities. 'Cause in Makkovik if I spoke Inuktitut and they didn't understand you would get degraded.
>
> (quoted in MacDonald 2015, 302)

Elder Rhoda Akpaliapik Karetak (2017) spoke to the shame, guilt, powerlessness, and pain Inuit parents felt as formal education alienated them from their children:

> It was very painful for us, as parents, when our children were taken away to residential schools to be educated in another culture and language … They didn't even consult with me or explain what was going to happen … When the realization came upon me that my children were to be taken from me, it became extremely unbearable for me as a mother.
>
> (186–187)

The schools took over the families' and the communities' role in educating children. They disrupted the close-knit bonds on which *inunnguiniq* – traditional child rearing – had been based and they undermined the language, knowledge, and proficiencies that Inuit valued.

Karl Kristian Olsen, Head of Department for the Ministry for Education, Culture, Research and Church in Greenland emphasized that early Inuit schooling was

> a universal system of the 'colonization of the mind' (Lynge 2011) through the use of Danish as the language of instruction, the use of Danish people as teachers and administrators over Greenlandic children, and instruction through the standard European curriculum.
>
> (Olsen and Tharp 2013, 101)

Settlers imposed the same cognitive imperialism (Battiste 2013) in Canada and Alaska through English and French language schools. Schooling was imposed alongside other policies and practices that devasted Inuit health, economies, families, homes, livelihoods, and ways of living. Mary Joanne Kauki (2015), an Inuit educational leader in Nunavik, wrote that understanding this history is part of achieving transformation in today's Inuit schools:

> The projects of retelling our history and acknowledging the impact of trauma and abuse are validating the confusion that many people, particularly our youth, continue to feel. Naming, discussing, and understanding our own history is starting to spark a decolonization of the mind.
>
> (156)

In Russia, while bilingual education in Yup'ik was favored in the 1930s and 1940s, "Russification" policies started in the 1950s, and essentially wiped out Siberian Yup'ik as a mother tongue (Morgounova 2004).

SELF-DETERMINATION AND BILINGUAL EDUCATION

In the second half of the 20th century, Inuit in Greenland, Canada, and Alaska used the tools they had acquired through schooling up to that point to advocate for their right to self-determination. The land claims they negotiated – the Alaska Native Land Claims Settlement Act in 1971, the James Bay Northern Quebec Agreement in 1975, Greenlandic Home Rule in 1979, the Inuvialuit Final Agreement in 1984, the Nunavut Land Claims Agreement in 1993, and finally the Labrador Inuit Land Claims Agreement in 2004 – addressed their right to protect, preserve, and promote their language and culture and to have greater control over the education of their children. In the words of Eben Hobson, Alaskan Inupiaq leader,

> Possibly the greatest significance of home rule is that it enables us to regain control of the education of our children …We must now begin to assess whether or

school system is truly becoming an Inupiat school system … [or if it] … continues to transmit white urban culture.

(1977, quoted in Harcharek 2005, i)

The creation of "truly Inuit schools" is an enduring vision that has been taken up by Inuit governments and land claims organizations and includes teaching in and through the Inuit language, offering opportunities for ongoing learning of the Inuit language and Inuit cultural practices, having schools that are grounded in Inuit values and worldviews, and that are led and taught by Inuit.

Colonial legacies and Inuit sovereignty clash in the creation of an educational system in accordance with Inuit ways of being, doing, and knowing. Although the James Bay and Northern Quebec Agreement (1975) specifically created an Inuit school board and mandated community-controlled, Inuktut bilingual education, Inuit leader Sheila Watt Cloutier (2011) questions whether a truly Inuit-centric educational system is attainable while Inuit work within imposed Eurocentric systems:

> Bringing about change … can be especially hard for us … because a lot of our institutions have been imported; we try to hook our cultural ways and language into them as add-ons rather than trying to build from a new foundation. The way to change these foundations is to get people inside the system who want to make real changes … It is like that in the education system: we have taken on somebody else's version of institutional learning and are trying to add on cultural and language classes, rather than starting with a model that makes sense to us culturally. And because we don't have hundred year-old institutional traditions, we have a golden opportunity today to create something new.
>
> (169)

The following sections explore the evolution and implementation of different models of Inuit bilingual education; curriculum and materials development; and Inuit teacher training, recruitment, and retention, and how these continue to shape the ways in which bilingual education takes place in the Inuit homeland (see Figure 10.1).

BILINGUAL EDUCATION MODELS AND OUTCOMES
Mother tongue education

Following Home Rule in 1979, Greenland adopted the strongest Inuit language education policies of any Inuit jurisdiction. The Greenlandic Home Rule government intended that Kalaallisut alone should be sufficient for any Greenlander to study, live, work, and thrive in Greenland, so Home Rule schools prioritized teaching in Kalaallisut. Kalaallisut is indeed thriving at home and at work, as well as at school. However, critics say that a monolingual school system, teaching only in the mother tongue, has negatively impacted young Greenlanders' opportunities for higher learning and future employment. Aviâja Egede Lynge, an Inuk human rights advocate speaking at the Inuit Circumpolar Council's 2018 Education Summit said, "there are many Greenlandic [Kalaallisut] only-speaking young Greenlanders; who are

Figure 10.1 Inuktut calendar currently in use in a Nain, Nunatsiavut (Labrador) classroom. The names of months and weekdays show the enduring influence of the German Moravian missionaries on Inuktut in this region. Photo: Kathy Snow.

often called the silent ones … and … are more often those that achieve very low grades" (ICC 2018, 21). Ivaaq Poulsen, a delegate to the Inuit Circumpolar Youth Symposium on the Inuit language explained, "Only one from my class went to college because the other students couldn't speak Danish or English well enough. This is a major problem. There are so many gifted Greenlandic people, but language is a big problem" (quoted in Tulloch and ICYC 2005, 7). Now, efforts toward "a reformed educational system for a decolonized Greenland" include earlier introduction of Danish and English, in order to achieve "internationally competitive trilingual students" (Olsen and Tharp 2013, 102). Greenland attempted a strong mother tongue model of Indigenous language schooling, and found it insufficient for the needs of its students.

Early-exit mother tongue bilingual education

In Canada and Alaska, the bilingual education model implemented in the 1970s is now known as an early-exit mother tongue bilingual program. In early-exit models, children learn in their mother tongue for the first few years of schooling, and then transition to learning in a national language. The model is grounded in UNESCO's 1953 Expert Report, which recognized that contrary to colonial systems of assimilationist education, children learn best when educated in a language and culture that reflects their home experiences. In contrast to the Greenlandic system, though, in Canada and Alaska the mother tongue, Inuktut, was used primarily as a bridge to familiarize children with schooling and introduce literacy, facilitating transition to schooling in the national language in Grades 3 or 4.

Anthropologist Donna Patrick and educational scholar Perry Shearwood (1999) track the emergence of Inuktut schooling in Quebec to awareness of UNESCO's recommendations and the Quebec Government's push, in 1964, to change the language of schooling from English to French in its northern communities: "The possibility of a language other than English – namely French – being used in the school sparked the idea that Inuktut, too, could become the language of instruction" (256). The Kativik School Board developed policies and programs to teach children solely in Inuktut from Kindergarten through to Grade 2, with English or French taught as a second language and gradually added as language of instruction starting in Grade 3 and through to the end of high school.

A similar model was introduced in the Northwest Territories starting in 1971.[4] The Northwest Territories *Learning Traditions and Change* report, chaired by Inuit leader Tagak Curley, recommended developing "Native Language programs in all subjects," starting with K-3 and building to Grade 10 (Recommendation 19, cited in Martin 2000, 27). In Alaska, too, early exit mother tongue programs started in the 1970s, particularly in communities where children still learned the Inuit/Yup'ik language at home.

In the 1980s and 1990s, strides were made towards improving Inuit bilingual education. Inuit parents were consulted about what they wanted for the education of their children, and their desire for an education system that would reflect their language and their culture started to be reflected in policies and practices. Regional school boards were established that could advance community-driven agendas. The Northwest Territories Education Act of 1995 allowed for schooling in Inuktut in cases where there was significant demand *and* enough teachers *and* enough materials. By this time, Inuit teachers were being trained and materials were being developed to meet the demand.

The Kativik School Board's research into bilingual education outcomes in Nunavik documented how bilingual education can enhance educational success, and foster a strong sense of identity and self-esteem in the children (Taylor and Wright 2003), which can help them persevere through to postsecondary (Fuzessy 1998). In addition, consistent with other research into the benefits of learning in one's first language, the level of proficiency in Inuktut at the end of Grade 2 correlated with subsequent achievement in the second language in Grades 3, 4, and 5 (Louis and Taylor 2001).

By the end of the 1990s, some schools in Inuit communities were using Inuktut as a language of instruction up to Grade 6, and Inuktut could be taught as a subject through to the end of high school, depending on the school and the availability of Inuktut teachers. Fiona Walton (O'Donoghue 1998), a long-term northern educator, educational consultant, and scholar of Inuit education described a feeling of optimism surrounding an educational system transformed by greater Inuit control:

> There are no easy answers ... however, school attendance and graduation rates have risen dramatically over the last ten years. This may be due to the growing sense of autonomy felt by Inuit ... It may also be related to the fact that the system is now more responsive to the needs of Inuit and that increasing numbers of Inuit teachers enable children to learn to speak, read, and write in Inuktitut and Inuinnaqtun. There is no doubt that very positive progress is taking place.
>
> (28)

Inuit hoped and expected that a bilingual education system would help sustain Inuktut, and in some ways it did. Children educated in Inuktut developed stronger conversational proficiencies than those who were only using it home. In addition, schooling in Inuktut was developing new, academic proficiencies in Inuktut that were not learned by children who attended schooling only in English or French (Louis and Taylor 2001). However, although students educated in Inuktut gained higher proficiency in Inuktut than their peers who were educated in English or French, as soon as they transferred to English or French language schooling as mandated by Grade 3 or 4, their proficiency in Inuktut started to decrease, eventually falling to levels even below what they had started school with, a process known as subtractive bilingualism (Louis and Taylor 2001).

In Nunavut, Inuit youths' stories show how the abrupt switch to English at school, without sustained teaching in or about Inuktut, corresponded to a loss of their mother tongue. This is particularly true in the larger regional centers like Iqaluit where a high number of non-Inuit live and work. In a 2004 study of Inuit youths' experiences learning and using Inuktut, Inuit youth said, "[I grew up speaking Inuktitut] until high school. That's when I started speaking more English than Inuktitut ... It seems like I lost it so fast, you know? Without realizing it" and "So, Grade 7 it all really happened with English. And I lost [Inuktitut] after that" (Two Inuit youth from Iqaluit, quoted in Tulloch 2004, 143–144). Dorais and Sammons (2002) conclude that "studies – including this one – have shown that both oral performance and literacy skills in Inuktitut decline in proportion to the number of years of formal education" (63), and this despite, at that time, 30 years of effort toward bilingual education.

Not only was the early exit model of bilingual education insufficient for protecting against language shift; it did not deliver on the promise of long-term educational equity for Inuit students. Students understandably struggled when, after learning in their first language for the first few years, they were abruptly thrown into learning exclusively in their second language without explicit support as emergent bilinguals. Corinna Kuluguqtuq (2012), an Inuk college student who grew up in Pangnirtung, Nunavut, remembers the difficulty she had at this transition:

> Probably, when I got to high school I didn't know a lot of English, maybe. That was one of one of the hardest [things] ... when I went to school, it was always all in my language all the time up until grade 5, and then we didn't have English classes until we got to grade 7, so going to high school and a lot of Qallunaat teachers and ... probably speaking English [was the hardest thing] ... Probably learning [English] at a little earlier age [would have helped].

The conciliator's report to the federal government concerning the implementation of the Nunavut Land Claims Agreement echoed what many parents were feeling: The abrupt shift to English and the early abandonment of Inuktut was blocking academic success and hindering the societal change and protection Inuit had envisioned in the creation of Nunavut (Berger 2006). These tensions are reflected in ongoing debates in Nunavut about the implementation of Nunavut's Education Act, and what balance of Inuktut and English instruction will best meet students' needs.

Two lessons can be taken from the experiences within the early-exit bilingual Inuit schools. The first is that schools alone cannot maintain the vitality of a language. Efforts beyond schools to provide lifelong opportunities for learning and using Inuktut are needed. The second is that in order to maximize the benefits of a bilingual program, both languages must be sustained throughout schooling, with both languages being taught as a subject, and being used as a language through which other subjects are taught and learned. Inuit parents have advocated for this strong use of Inuktut, and it was intended, but not implemented, in the earliest bilingual education models and subsequent education legislation.

Core second language

By the time bilingual education was gaining momentum, language loss was underway in the westernmost Canadian Inuit and Alaskan Inupiat communities, as well as in Labrador. In these communities, Inuktut was taught as a second language through core or immersion programs. In Russia also, Yup'ik children had the opportunity to learn Yup'ik as a subject. Core programs taught the language as a subject, usually for half an hour to an hour a day, three or four times a week. Although this provided a starting point, students said that learning was inconsistent, lacking clear progressions, and that it was not sustained in the higher grades. Katrina, a high school graduate from a western Canadian Inuit community, explained:

> And it [Inuktut courses] just kind of stopped as soon as we went into junior high. It was ... like we were learning, and then when we got to junior high it just went downhill and I think that's the main reason why I don't remember much of the Inuinnaqtun language.
>
> (quoted in Walton et al. 2013)

Efforts are being made to strengthen core Inuktut, especially in Nunatsiavut and the Northwest Territories.

Inuktut immersion

In immersion programs, children learn most subjects in and through a second language. The model was developed for (mainly white, middle-class) English students learning French in Montreal in the 1970s. Research into French immersion showed that the children learned very effectively in their second language, and by Grade 6 or 7, performed as well in both the first and second language as their peers who had only been educated in their mother tongue. Inuktut immersion was never offered for that long.

On the north coast of Labrador, immersion was offered irregularly, for Kindergarten and Grade 1 in Hopedale, and for Kindergarten to Grade 3 in Nain. Parents and teachers who were involved in the Inuit immersion programs said that they were excited that their children would have the opportunity to learn Inuktut at school. Anecdotally, community members said the strongest youth in Inuktut now are those who went through immersion. However, some parents chose to withdraw their children from the program, or not enroll them, because they were concerned about their children's progress in English. Teachers also expressed concerns that they were not supported in immersion teaching. Although Labrador at the time had fluent Inuktut teachers, with bachelor's or master's degrees in education, these teachers said they were left on their own to translate the English curriculum into Inuktut, and delivered immersion that way. It is possible the weak implementation, and gaps in communication about what to expect in immersion education, may have hindered commitment to the program.

Two-way/dual-language immersion

Two-way or dual language immersion programs use both languages side by side, with some subjects taught in one of the languages, and other subjects taught in the other, and both languages taught as subjects. This model was developed for Spanish-English learners in the southern United States, and was implemented in some Central Alaskan Yup'ik communities starting in 2011. An advantage of dual language programs is that they can support classes in which some children are stronger in one language when starting school, and others are stronger in the other. This is the case in larger Inuit communities that have a mix of Inuit and non-Inuit children in the school, such as Iqaluit or Kuujjuaq, as well as in many Inuit communities that are experiencing shift away from Inuktut and toward the national language. Dorais and Sammons (2002), for example, documented how siblings shaped home language use so dramatically that the family's first child might start school speaking only Inuktut, while the younger siblings might speak more English than Inuktut by the time they start school. This creates challenges for models focusing on "mother tongue" schooling. Another advantage of the two-way/dual-language immersion is that it allows communities, teachers, and learners to draw on bilingualism as an asset. A Yup'ik language teacher put it this way:

> Language shapes how we see the world. So when I speak in English my thinking is strictly on stuff that makes sense in the English language. And if I speak in Yupik there's different things in the Yupik language that does not make sense in the English language. So because of my experiences in both worlds, I've learned to take from each language.
>
> (YT3, quoted in Henke 2017, 77)

Inuit bilingual education has come a long way in the past 50 years. Inuit communities continue to pursue bilingual education as a tool for effective education and language revitalization. These dual goals and broader challenges in both offering excellence in education and in revitalizing Inuktut have sometimes been presented to Inuit as contradictory or mutually exclusive, and have contributed to confusion or ambivalence in the implementation of strong bilingual education policies (Aylward 2010). Still, Inuit persevere and innovate to make schooling more closely fit their communities' needs.

CURRICULA FOR BILINGUAL, INTERCULTURAL EDUCATION

Early in the implementation of bilingual education, regional school boards were established which operated with relative autonomy, developing curricula, materials, and policies reflective of the Inuit majority they were designed to serve. The processes of curriculum development centered Inuit knowledge and Inuit knowledge holders, and provided academic venues for Elders and younger Inuit educators to share knowledge as they documented what they considered important for Inuit children to learn. Naullaq Arnaquq (2008), who had a long career as a teaching assistant, then certified teacher, then teacher trainer, then Supervisor of Schools, then Director of Curriculum and School Services, and ultimately as an Assistant Deputy Minister in the Government of Nunavut, remembered, "Who we were as Inuit was finally being acknowledged by educational administrators and program consultants. Inuit teachers were finally given a space and opportunity to voice their ideas without it just being an afterthought" (115). It seemed the assimilationist climate was changing in Inuit schools.

In the Northwest Territories, the Piniaqtavut curriculum framework, and the Inuuqatigiit curriculum framework that followed and complemented it, were important initiatives for bringing Inuit language, culture, and worldviews into Inuit schools in the 1980s and 1990s. The Inuuqatigiit framework (Northwest Territories 1996) organizes learning about Inuit traditional knowledge into thematic groupings with core teachings from Elders, suggested activities, and targeted outcomes for four grade groupings. For example, a section on naming includes Elders' teachings, such as, "Inuit believe that a person's spirit never dies, that it is passed on through naming" (Northwest Territories 1996, 43). Outcomes for Kindergarten to Grade 3 children include learning about their own name, as well as basic kinship terms, and finding out who named them. In Grades 4 to 6, children would learn stories about important names in the community, as well as extended kinship terms, and they would write about their namesake. By Grades 7 to 9, they would be expected to appropriately use those kinship terms to refer to people in the community, and in Grades 10 through 12, they would describe how the importance of naming is seen in relationships, mourning, and describe inter-regional and international connections. Inuuqatigiit also provides guidance on school environment, language use, pedagogies, and assessment. For example, it recommends having the Inuit language visible and audible in the school environment, through posters, school announcements, student work, etc.

Piniaqtavut and Inuuqatigiit were not language curricula *per se*; the intent was to create space in the K-12 education for Inuit knowledge, culture, and language to be taught across the curriculum: "When an Inuuqatigiit topic or theme is integrated into all subjects, language is naturally integrated which provides a more meaningful context for the children" (Northwest Territories 1996, 18). Joanne Tompkins (1998) describes how the integrated Inuuqatigiit curriculum was used synergistically by Inuit and non-Inuit teachers, allowing for learning in one language to carry over into the other language:

> [T]each[ing] through themes had important implications for the Inuktitut program in the senior part of the school … When we began to have southern teachers use themes in the senior classes, it meant that there was something for Ooleepeeka [the Inuktitut instructor for Grades 4 to 9] to hinge her program on … It was a huge breakthrough for the way in which Inuktitut was taught and perceived in the school. Instead of merely doing puzzles, the students actually started reading and writing about real things in Inuktitut. (I had noticed

by looking at the students' work, and it was confirmed by both the Inuit staff and the students, that most of the older students felt uncomfortable writing in Inuktitut and had seldom been asked to write anything more than a sentence throughout their school careers. However, with persistence and encouragement and good pedagogy we saw amazing growth in even three months.)

(53–54)

Inuuqatigiit continues to be used in the Northwest Territories, however in Nunavut its implementation varied greatly from school to school as teachers and principals were not always equipped, or motivated, to deliver it (Aylward 2009). Implementation of Inuit-centered curriculum continues to be an issue, even where it has been developed (Inuit Tapiriit Kanatami 2017).

The momentum of developing culturally relevant curriculum and resources continued in the 2000s. Heather McGregor and Catherine McGregor (2016), a historian and the former director of curriculum development in Nunavut respectively, describe the Government of Nunavut as "adamant – even radical – about pursuing change during this period, as evidenced by hiring Elders as full-time staff, leading research on made-in-Nunavut educational philosophies, and integrating Inuit knowledge into dozens of projects" (110). Foundational documents guiding Nunavut schools have made space for Inuktut and Inuit knowledge across the curriculum. Early Inuktut literacy has been targeted through the publication of culturally relevant leveled readers. Using local photos, drawings, and stories, the book series moves through gradual progressions from early sound and word recognition to more complex fiction and non-fiction texts (see Figure 10.2).[5]

For teaching and learning Inuktut as a second language in schools, the Northwest Territories has developed a curriculum framework with learning resources, benchmarks, and assessment tools. The framework includes suggestions for culturally relevant pedagogies, including whole school and interactive approaches to learning, and online resources that can be adapted to specific dialects (www.ourlanguagesnwt.com). This program classifies indicators of oral proficiency from "pre-production" to "capable," however it does not set age- or grade-specific targets for language development.

Since the beginning of Inuktut bilingual education, teachers have been ingenious and industrious in creating and adapting materials to respond to students' needs. This is an added layer of work for which they are not compensated, and which can lead to burnout and feelings of Inuktut as a lower priority in their school system. On the whole, while a great deal of promising curriculum-related work has been done, there remains a feeling that more materials are needed, with more effective implementation, and that more recognition and accommodation is needed for the impromptu informal curriculum and materials development work that Inuit teachers are doing (Snow et al. 2018).

Inuit educators are also increasingly going back to the resources that educated Inuit children for centuries prior to and alongside formal education: the "land as teacher" (Obed 2017, 76). Inuk educational leader Rebecca Mearns (2017) writes, "The land is where our language and culture live, it is the source of knowledge, learning, and teaching" (107). Felicia, an Inuit bachelor's of education graduate operationalizes the potential of the land and Elders' stories in formal schooling:

Figure 10.2 Inuktut leveled reading curriculum and materials, developed by Nunavut-based publishing company, Inhabit Education. Nunavut teachers were trained on and used these materials starting in 2016. Photo: Kathy Snow.

We could learn about the growth and environmental surroundings of the berry bush in science class, engage students in reflecting on the activity and how they felt while they were doing it, or use it as an English-language arts project. We could create a history lesson, guided by the question, "How were these berries used before we had ovens and advanced cooking technology?" ... We hear so often about the lack of resources available ... Let us learn to think outside the box and look around us. Our environment provides endless resources that can easily be incorporated in every subject in the primary and elementary grade levels. Let us start taking these amazing resources that are readily available to us and create lessons that promote meaningful learning.

(Moore et al. 2016, 100)

Consistent with what was perhaps envisioned but not implemented in Inuuqatigiit, learning on and from the land and Elders creates rich opportunities for authentic language use and is consistent with community goals for bilingual education.

INUIT TEACHERS: THE HEART OF BILINGUAL INUIT EDUCATION

Inuit teachers are at the heart of bilingual Inuit education. They teach Inuktut both in the classroom and informally as they speak their mother tongue to each other in the hallways, the staff room, and the schoolyard. As long-term members of the communities in which they work, Inuit teachers contribute to excellence in education as they offer stability, consistency, and a cultural groundedness that is missing in the majority of short-term teachers from outside the Inuit homeland (Berger et al. 2016).

The development of northern teacher training programs has been central to the implementation of bilingual education since the 1960s and 1970s, with the Teacher Education Program in Labrador (TEPL), the Eastern Arctic Teacher Education Program (EATEP), and the Northern Teacher Education Program (NTEP) in the Northwest Territories and Nunavut, and others. Although teacher education has consistently been one of the more accessible postsecondary education opportunities available in the North, there are still too few Inuit teachers and educational leaders to meet demand. In Nunavut, for example, only about one in five teachers are Inuit (Berger et al. 2016). Recruitment and retention of Inuit in the teaching profession are hindered by barriers to completing postsecondary schooling and by systemic racism (Fyn 2014). Many Inuit teachers have experienced racism personally and all have experienced the marginalization of Inuit language and culture in the educational system (Snow et al. 2018). Also, there are fewer and fewer fluent Inuktut speakers available to become Inuktut teachers.

Inuit governments and their university partners have developed new training opportunities attuned to the needs of future Inuit educators and Inuit educational leaders in the 21st century. An innovative Nunavut Master's of Education program, for example, was co-developed by the University of Prince Edward Island and the Government of Nunavut and offered in two cohorts, from 2006 to 2009 and from 2010 to 2013 (see Figure 10.3). Delivery combined online and in-person learning in northern communities and on University of Prince Edward Island's Charlottetown campus. Students learned about educational theory and practice, as well as about the history and practice of education in the Arctic. Courses were taught by Inuit and non-Inuit co-instructors, and provided opportunities to use Inuktut in postsecondary. Graduates from the Nunavut Master's of Education explained how its deliberately decolonizing approach increased their willingness and ability to be agents of change. As one graduate explained:

Figure 10.3 Inuit educational leaders graduated in 2009 from the first Nunavut Masters of Education program, offered by the University of Prince Edward Island and funded by the Government of Nunavut. Photo: Steve Simon.

I am more willing to take risks, speak my opinion, trust my instincts, not simply be a people pleaser but work hard for what I believe in. I have a deeper knowledge and understanding of how the actions of the past have affected people today, and will continue to do so until we stand up and make a change. [Because of] my increased passion and dedication to the development of the Nunavut Education system, I am better able to understand systemic change and the process it requires to [make it] happen. I am more critically aware, I can detect the hidden messages in things and people now better than I could before and I also can make sense of what happened during colonization, how it affected Inuit people and the process and purposes of de-colonization and the fears of neocolonialism.

(quoted in Wheatley 2015, 22)

The Nunatsiavut Government and Memorial University of Newfoundland co-developed an Inuit Bachelor's of Education (first cohort, 2014–2019) which aimed at increasing the number of Inuit teachers in Nunatsiavut. Students followed Memorial University's core Bachelor's of Education courses, imbued with northern perspectives, and also took a parallel, intensive conversational Inuktut course. Nunatsiavut's education director, Jodie Lane explained her vision:

So we've got the Inuktitut Bachelor of Education program that we are infusing LITP [Labrador Inuktitut Training Program] with. So, these students, [...] will be taking Inuktitut in every semester as well as two Memorial University Inuktitut courses that are accredited [...] So, these people are being trained as educators with an Inuit specific curriculum that will also be having language, and important [knowledge] of our culture and traditions so it is just a full circle and I'm very very hopeful.

(quoted in Tulloch et al. 2017)

Graduates affirmed that having Inuktut in their program equips them to embed Inuktut into whatever they are teaching, even if they do not specifically as Inuktut teachers. Julie, one of the graduates explained, "[I'm] learning so much that I can just picture myself using that in the classroom. I'm by no means going to fluent at that, but I definitely want to incorporate as much as I can" (quoted in Tulloch et al. 2017).

In order to reach the potential of bilingual Inuit education, Inuit educators cannot carry the burden alone. In the 1980s and 1990s when Inuit bilingual education was gearing up, Inuit educators remember their southern Canadian colleagues making space for Inuktut in their otherwise English-speaking classrooms. A survey in the late 1990s of all teachers in what is now Nunavut identified a pressing desire among non-Inuit, as well as Inuit, for professional development opportunities to learn Inuktut (O'Donoghue 1998). Berger and Epp (2007) identified a willingness among non-Inuit teachers to adopt more culturally and linguistically relevant practices, and a need for professional development to do so. Inuit school boards have implemented cultural awareness training for incoming for teachers. Increasing opportunities for Inuit and non-Inuit educators to work across the curriculum, as a team, as was envisioned in the earliest years, holds promise for bilingual Inuit education.

The Second Language Acquisition Teacher Education (SLATE) program at the University of Alaska Fairbanks (first cohort 2007 to 2010) specifically created an opportunity for Indigenous (Inuit and Yup'ik) and non-Indigenous graduate students to learn side-by-side about bilingual Indigenous education. This program equipped both Indigenous and non-Indigenous teachers to contribute to changing the system:

> We decided to develop a ... program that would allow both heritage [Yup'ik] and English language teachers an important opportunity to develop common understandings concerning second language acquisition, language teaching, and bilingualism. Such understandings, we hope, will allow heritage [Yup'ik] and English language teachers to work together to foster their students' success in both languages.
>
> (Marlow et al. 2013, 2)

An important component of the Nunavut Master's of Education, Nunatsiavut's Inuit Bachelor's of Education, and SLATE was developing educational leadership, and fostering knowledge and use of critical and culturally nourishing pedagogies. These and other Inuit-specific training and professional development programs are promising for the future of Inuktut bilingual education as a new generation of teachers are trained to think and work outside of Eurocentric traditions, envisioning new Inuit-centric education in the North.

WHOLE SCHOOL, WHOLE COMMUNITY APPROACHES TO INUIT BILINGUAL EDUCATION

While challenges persist in the implementation of Inuit bilingual education, many examples also show bilingual programs in which students, staff, and communities are thriving. Two such examples come from Pangnirtung and Clyde River, Nunavut, where Lena Metuq and Jukeepa Hainnu were long-serving Inuit (co-)principals. A documentary film profiling their schools (Walton et al. 2011) shows what Inuit education could, in Principal Lena Metuq's words, "look like, sound like, smell like, feel like, taste like." An Elder joins a student who is sitting on the floor, cleaning a skin, and takes her traditional tool and joins the student in the work. An Inuk high school teacher, surrounded by Inuktut print and materials in his classroom, speaks fluidly in Inuktut as students follow along. Inuit teachers and principals converse with each other in Inuktut in hallways and staff rooms. Children and their families share breakfast in the gym prior to the start of the day. Students serve Elders caribou stew at lunch. A teenage mom pops in to see her toddler, cared for in the high school daycare. Elders, teachers, and students from Kindergarten through to Grade 12 go out on the land for an annual spring camp where they learn on the land, immersed in Inuktut, traditional ways of learning, and the values and strengths of their culture. Students speak of their struggles and their successes as they plan for the next steps of postsecondary or employment. Lena Metuq, Jukeepa Hainnu, and many other Inuit educational leaders have worked hard over many years to shape self-determined Inuit schools.

One key to success, as co-Principal Lena Metuq explains, is the deliberate confrontation of the hegemony of English, and efforts to balance the power of the two languages and cultures (and those who use them):

What I've seen most improved since I got here, is that the Inuit culture and language is at the same level as English subjects ... When we hire Qallunaat teachers, we try to prepare them [for] why we do things in a certain way in our culture. It has helped them tremendously and they come to realize they are here in Pangnirtung ... the English culture and language isn't the only way you can learn to look at life, they're here with Inuit on their own land. If they try to force students to learn just from their narrow point of view or opinions, it's not going to work, like it never had, so we have to incorporate Inuit values and principles in order to be productive in this school.

(quoted in Tulloch et al. 2016, 195)

As an Inuit educational leader, and with higher proportions of Inuit staff than in other Nunavut or Nunavik schools, she has been able to infuse Inuit language and culture throughout the school. She has engaged non-Inuit teachers to support Inuit language and culture across the curriculum, even if they do not speak Inuktut or practice Inuit cultures themselves. She has also created a context in which parents and other community members feel welcome and able to engage with the school, which helps to overcome the alienation of parents from schools that has persisted since the introduction of formal schooling (Anoee et al. 2017). Research in the Clyde River and Pangnirtung schools provides an example of the promise bilingual, intercultural education can hold, serving the needs of students and communities and equipping the next generation of capable Inuit adults, who are equipped to thrive as members of their communities, as well as in postsecondary education and future employment.

LIFELONG LEARNING

Education is a lifelong endeavor, extending well beyond the confines of Kindergarten to Grade 12 formal schooling. Grassroots, community-based initiatives that provide opportunities for Inuit of all ages to learn Inuktut before school (Inuktut preschools; language nests), beyond school (e.g., extracurricular activities that use Inuktut), and after leaving school (e.g., one-on-one mentor-apprentice learning) are also part of Inuit bilingual education. One promising "beyond school" model contributing to bilingual education is Ilitaqsiniq – the Nunavut Literacy Council's Miqqut program, a 12-week, full-time learning program for Inuit who are neither in school nor working. Elders and others teach a traditional skill (in this case, sewing), while embedding language learning and literacy into the practice. Adriana Kusugak (2013), who helped develop and teach the program, wrote:

The *Miqqut* program provided an opportunity to increase participants' skills in a variety of areas – including their Inuktitut language abilities ... Through exposure to the Elders' Inuktitut and encouragement to use Inuktitut on a regular basis, participants gained competence and confidence to use Inuktitut.

(14–16)

This program, and others modeled after it, has been a successful bridge to re-engagement with learning and work for many of the participants. At least one participant used Miqqut as a stepping stone toward becoming an Inuktut teacher, "I plan on taking NTEP [Nunavut Teacher's Education Program] so I want to improve my Inuktitut before I start that so I think this [Miqqut] will help prepare me for that" (Inuk youth, quoted in Kusugak 2013, 15). In other cases (e.g., in Nunatsiavut and Inuinnait communities), Inuktut teachers are benefiting from mentor-apprentice programs, where they are paired with a more fluent speaker, and learn one-on-one.

INTERNATIONAL COLLABORATION

The Inuit Circumpolar Council emphasizes the unity of Inuit and Yup'ik across the homeland. The first Inuit Circumpolar Council meeting, held in 1977, mandated:

> WHEREAS, the barriers of distance and national boundaries have prevented closer contact and communication among the Inuit of Alaska, Greenland and Canada; and WHEREAS, the Inuit desire to … shar[e] … the adoption of educational philosophy to promote Inuit academic excellence; … BE IT RESOLVED … to establish Inuit student and teacher exchanges … [and] to establish exchanges of educational and cultural and media materials.
> (Inuit Circumpolar Conference 1977, Resolution 77-04, quoted in Inuit Tapiriit Kanatami 2017, 18)

Following the ICC's 2018 Inuit Education Summit, delegates again affirmed their similar experiences and desire to learn from each other. The meeting's recommendations recognized the resilience of Inuit to date, and the importance of teachers, curriculum, and pedagogies. They emphasized, as mandates of national, regional, and international Inuit organizations and policies have before, that: "the Inuit language and the challenges it faces from second- or foreign- language speakers within our lands, territories, and culture is the key and most important component of any Inuit-focussed educational policies that Inuit may wish to further or develop" (ICC 2018, 37). Inuit have blazed a trail for Indigenous bilingual education over the past 50 years; Inuit in each country and region have developed and collaborated on innovative approaches, and are hoping to establish mechanisms to share these across borders to strengthen Inuit bilingual education.

CONCLUSION

There is an urgent need for schools that encompass Inuit languages, cultures, and worldviews, and support the next generation of Inuit. Educational equity for Inuit students has not yet been achieved and knowledge and use of Inuktut continue to decline.

Schooling, which has been used as a vehicle for assimilation, is now being used by Inuit as a means to reclaim what was being lost, and as a context for rebalancing power. Over 50 years of self-determination in education, Inuit have slowly been turning the institution and its goals around. Inuit governments and land claims organizations have created space for policies and practices that bring Inuit languages, knowledges, and pedagogies into schools. Governments, universities, teachers, Elders, and allies have worked to develop training programs, curricula, and materials that facilitate the transfer of Inuit languages and knowledges.

The Eurocentric origins of formal education and contact between Inuit and non-Inuit continue to shape the way education takes place. Decades of deliberate exclusion of Inuit language and knowledge, and of Inuit parents and community leaders, were followed by more covert racism and systemic barriers to their inclusion. But Inuit, who love their children and believe in a bright future for them through education, language, and culture; and youth, who believe in themselves and their agency to take hold of that future, have persisted in bringing about change, and are working to transform a colonial system from the inside out. As it was in the 1970s, the challenge remains to create truly Inuit schools. Inuit scholar Naullaq Arnaquq (2008) has now retired after decades of work in every area of Inuit bilingual education. Her *uqaujjuijjusiit* (words of advice) continue to be a call to Inuit, and a reminder to non-Inuit who influence the northern educational context: "We must make the education system our own. This is the task we have ahead of us for the future" (191).

NOTES

1 For the purposes of this chapter, Iñupiaq is included when referring to Inuktut.
2 Both Inuit and Yup'ik fall under the broader "Inuit" grouping as defined by the Inuit Circumpolar Council, https://iccalaska.org/about/.
3 Qablunaaq (also written Qallunaat) is an Inuktut word referring to non-Inuit.
4 At the time, the Northwest Territories included what is now Nunavut Territory. The territories formally separated on 1 April 1999.
5 Examples of approved resources can be viewed online at https://www.gov.nu.ca/education/curriculum/curriculum-database/inuktitut-language-arts-2.

REFERENCES

Anoee, Nunia Qanatsiaq, Shelley Tulloch, Jeannie Arreak-Kullualik, Kerri Wheatley, and Sandy McAuley. 2017. "(Re)invigorating Family and Community Leadership in Inuit Bilingual Education." *AlterNative: An International Journal of Indigenous Peoples* 13 (1): 2–10. https://doi.org/10.1177/1177180116689025.

Arnaquq, Naullaq. 2008. *Uqaujjuusiat – Gifts of Words of Advice: Schooling, Education and Leadership in Baffin Island*. Master's thesis, University of Prince Edward Island.

Aylward, M. Lynne. 2009. "Journey to Inuuqatigiit: Curriculum Development for Nunavut Education." *Diaspora, Indigenous, and Minority Education* 3 (3): 137–158. https://doi.org/10.1080/15595690902991022.

———. 2010. "The Role of Inuit Languages in Nunavut schooling: Nunavut Teachers Talk about Bilingual Education." *Canadian Journal of Education* 33 (2): 295–328.

Battiste, Marie. 2013. *Decolonizing Education: Nourishing the Learning Spirit*. Saskatoon, SK: Purich Publishing.

Berger, Paul, and Juanita Ross Epp. 2007. "'There's No Book and There's No Guide': The Expressed Needs of Qallunaat Educators in Nunavut." *Brock Education* 16 (2): 44–56. https://doi.org/10.26522/BROCKED.V15I1.27.

Berger, Paul, Karen Inootik, Rebecca Jones, and Jennifer Kadjukiv. 2016. "A Hunger to Teach: Recruiting Inuit Teachers for Nunavut." *Etudes/Inuit/Studies* 40 (2): 47–69. https://doi.org/10.7202/1055431ar.

Berger, Thomas R. 2006. *Conciliator's Final Report March 1, 2006 'The Nunavut Project' Nunavut Land Claims Agreement Implementation Contract Negotiations for the Second Planning Period 2003 – 2013*. Retrieved from Indian and Northern Affairs Canada website: https://www.rcaanc-cirnac.gc.ca/DAM/DAM-CIRNAC-RCAANC/DAM-TAG/STAGING/texte-text/nlc_1100100030983_eng.pdf.

Dorais, Louis-Jacques. 1990. "The Canadian Inuit and Their Language." In *Arctic Languages: An Awakening*, edited by Dirmid R. F. Collis, 185–289. Paris: UNESCO.

———. 2010. *The Language of the Inuit: Syntax, Semantics, and Society in the Arctic*. Montreal and Kingston, QC: McGill-Queen's University Press.

Dorais, Louis-Jacques, and Susan Sammons. 2002. *Language in Nunavut: Discourse and Identity in the Baffin Region*. Iqaluit, NU and Quebec City, QC: Nunavut Arctic College and GÉTIC.

Fuzessy, Christopher. 1998. "Biculturalism in Postsecondary Inuit Education." *Canadian Journal of Native Education* 22 (2): 201–209.

Fyn, Dawn E. L. 2014. *Our Stories: Inuit Teachers Create Counter Narratives and Disrupt the Status Quo*. PhD dissertation, University of Western Ontario.

Harcharek, Jana. 2005. *Defining the Role of the Iñupiaq Program: Recommendations for Initiating Reform*. Report to the Board of Education. Barrow, AK: North Slope Borough School District.

Henke, Kristin Sattler. 2017. *Effects of Dual Language Protocol on Literacy Proficiency of Yup'ik Students*. PhD dissertation, Oregon: Concordia University.

ICC. 2018. *Inuit Education Summit [Report]*. Nuuk, Greenland: Inuit Circumpolar Council.

Inuit Tapiriit Kanatami. 2017. *(Re)visioning Success in Inuit Education: A Report of the 2017 Inuit Education Forum*. Prepared by Melanie O'Gorman, Kathy Snow, Shelley Tulloch, and Heather Ochalski for Inuit Tapiriit Kanatami. https://www.itk.ca/wp-content/uploads/2017/10/inuitreport-web.pdf

Karetak, Rhoda Akpaliapik. 2017. "Healing Unresolved Issues." In *Inuit Qaujimajatuqangit – What Inuit Have Always Known to be True*, edited by Joe Karetak, Frank Tester, and Shirley Tagalik, 182–207. Halifax, NS and Winnipeg, MB: Fernwood Publishing.

Kauki, Mary Joanne 2015. "Reflections of an Emerging Inuit Educational Leader." In *Sivumut – Towards the Future Together: Inuit Women Educational Leaders in Nunavut and Nunavik*, edited by Fiona Walton and Darlene O'Leary, 141–162. Toronto, ON: Canadian Scholars' Press.

Kuluguqtuq, Corinna. 2012. *Full-Length Interview from Inuit Qaujimajatuqangit and the Transformation of High School Education in Nunavut [Fiona Walton, PI]*. Retrieved from https://www.youtube.com/watch?v=S2EmVjcpg8g.

Kuniliusie, Maggie. 2015. "Arctic Cotton and the Stratified Identity of an Inuk Educational Leader." In *Sivumut – Towards the Future Together: Inuit Women Educational Leaders in Nunavut and Nunavik*, edited by Fiona Walton and Darlene O'Leary, 57–70. Toronto, ON: Canadian Scholars' Press.

Kusugak, Adriana. 2013. "Pijunnautitaaqpaalliqsimaliqtut: Building Confidence through Cultural and Literacy Skill Development." Unpublished paper from master's of education research project, University of Prince Edward Island.

Louis, Winnifred, and Donald M. Taylor. 2001. "When the Survival of a Language is at Stake: The Future of Inuttitut in Arctic Quebec." *Journal of Language and Social Psychology* 20 (1/2): 111–143. https://doi.org/10.1177/0261927X01020001006.

Lynge, Aviâja Egede. 2011. "Mental Decolonization in Greenland." *Inter-Nord: International Journal of Arctic Studies* 21: 273–276.

MacDonald, Martha. (2015). *Inside Stories: Agency and Identity through Language Loss Narratives in Nunatsiavut*. PhD dissertation, Memorial University of Newfoundland.

Marlow, Patrick E., Marliee Coles-Ritchie, Sabine Siekmann, and Joan Parker Webster. 2013. "Introduction." In *Communities of Practice: An Alaskan Native Model for Language Teaching and Learning*, edited by Patrick E. Marlow and Sabine Siekmann, 1–5. University of Arizona Press.

Martin, Ian. 2000. *Aajiiqatigiingniq: Language of Instruction Research Paper*. A Report to the Government of Iqaluit, Nunavut, Canada. Nunavut Department of Education.

McGregor, Heather, and Catherine A. McGregor. 2016. "Behind the Scenes of Inuit Curriculum Development in Nunavut, 2000–2013." *Etudes/Inuit/Studies* 40 (2): 109–131. https://doi.org/10.7202/1055434ar.

Mearns, Rebecca. 2017. *Nunavut, uqausivut, piqqusivullu najuqsittiarlavu (Caring for Our Land, Language and Culture): The Use of Land Camps in Inuit Knowledge Renewal and Research*. Master's thesis, Carleton University.

Moore, Sylvia, Cheryl Allen, Marina Andersen, Doris Boase, Jenni-Rose Campbell, Tracey Doherty, Alanna Edmunds, Felicia Edmunds, Julie Flowers, Jodi Lyall, Cathy Mitsuk, Roxanne Nochasak, Vanessa Pamak, Frank Russell, and Joanne Voisey. 2016. "Inuit-Centred Learning in the Inuit Bachelor of Education Program." *Etudes/Inuit/Studies* 40 (2): 93–107. https://doi.org/10.7202/1055433ar.

Morgounova, Daria. 2004. *Language Contact on Both Sides of the Bering Strait: A Comparative Study of Central Siberian Yupik-Russian and Central Alaskan Yupik-English Language Contact*. Master's thesis, University of Copenhagen.

Netser, Saimanaaq Patricia. 2013. "Seeking Identity." Unpublished paper from master's of education research project, University of Prince Edward Island.

Northwest Territories. 1996. *Inuuqatigiit: The Curriculum from the Inuit Perspective*. Yellowknife, NT: Government of the Northwest Territories, Department of Education. https://www.ece.gov.nt.ca/sites/ece/files/resources/inuuqatigiit_k-12_curriculum.pdf

Obed, Diane. 2017. *Illiniavugut Nunami: Learning from the Land. Envisioning an Inuit-Centred Educational Future*. Master's thesis, Saint Mary's University.

O'Donoghue, Fiona. 1998. *The Hunger for Learning in Nunavut Schools*. PhD dissertation, University of Toronto.

Olsen, Karl Kristian, and Roland G. Tharp. 2013. "Indigenous Education in Greenland: Effective Pedagogy and the Struggles of Decolonization." In *Indigenous Peoples: Education and Equity*, edited by Rhonda Craven, Gawaian Bodkin-Andrews, and Janet Mooney, 95–118. Charlotte, NC: Information Age Publishing.

Patrick, Donna, and Perry Shearwood. 1999. "The Roots of Inuktitut-Language Bilingual Education." *The Canadian Journal of Native Studies* 19 (2): 249–262.

Snow, Kathy, Shelley Tulloch, Heather Ochalski, and Melanie O'Gorman. 2018. "Reconciliation, Resilience and Resistance in Inuit Teachers' Professional Development and Practices." *Education in the North* 25 (1–2): 108–134.

Taylor, Donald M., and Stephen C. Wright. 2003. "Do Aboriginal Students Benefit from Education in Their Heritage Language? Results from a Ten-Year Program of Research in Nunavik." *The Canadian Journal of Native Studies* 23 (1): 1–24.

Tompkins, Joanne. 1998. *Teaching in a Cold and Windy Place: Change in an Inuit School*. Toronto, ON: University of Toronto Press.

TRC. 2015. *Honouring the Truth, Reconciling for the Future: Summary of the Final Report of the Truth and Reconciliation Commission of Canada*. Ottawa, ON: Truth and Reconciliation Commission of Canada.

Tulloch, Shelley. 2004. *Inuktitut and Inuit Youth: Language Attitudes as a Basis for Language Planning*. PhD dissertation, Université Laval.

Tulloch, Shelley, and Inuit Circumpolar Youth Council. 2005. First Inuit Circumpolar Youth Symposium on the Inuit language. Symposium report prepared for the Inuit Circumpolar

Youth Council. http://www.inuitcircumpolar.com/files/uploads/ICYC-LanguageReport-English.pdf

Tulloch, Shelley, Lena Metuq, Jukeepa Hainnu, Saa Pitsiulak, Elisapee Flaherty, Cathy Lee and Fiona Walton. 2016. "Inuit Principals and the Changing Context of Bilingual Education in Nunavut." *Etudes/Inuit/Studies* 40 (1): 189–209. https://doi.org/10.7202/1040151ar.

Tulloch, Shelley, Mark Sandiford, Sylvia Moore, Jodie Lane, Doris Boase, and Tracey Doherty. 2017. *Formation of Inspiration: The Inuit Bachelor of Education Program* [documentary film]. Charlottetown, PE: University of Prince Edward Island. https://www.youtube.com/watch?v=eNfA7wuRKLE

UNESCO. 1953. *The Use of Vernacular Languages in Education*. Lucerne: C. J. Bucher AG.

Walton, Fiona, Alexander McAuley, Lisa MacDougall, Darlene O'Leary, K. Ross, and Mark Sandiford, producers. 2011. *Going Places: Preparing Inuit High School Students for a Changing, Wider World*. [Documentary video]. Charlottetown, PEI: University of Prince Edward Island. https://www.youtube.com/watch?v=81gyHsoHtw8

Walton, Fiona, Mark Sandiford, Kerri Wheatley, Naullaq Arnaquq, Alexander McAuley, and Rebecca Mearns. 2013. *Alluriarniq –Stepping Forward: Youth Perspectives on High School Education in Nunavut* [Documentary video]. Charlottetown, PEI: University of Prince Edwards Island and Beachwalker Films.

Watt-Cloutier, Sheila. 2011. "Pioneering Change." In *Arnait nipingit: The Voices of Inuit Women in Leadership and Governance*, edited by Louis McComber and Shannon Partridge, 157–170. Iqaluit, NU: Nunavut Arctic College.

Wheatley, Kerri. 2015. *"We are Building a Critical Voice Together": The Second Nunavut Master of Education Program 2010–2013*. A final research report presented to the Department of Education, Government of Nunavut, edited by Shelley Tulloch and Fiona Walton. Charlottetown, PE: University of Prince Edward Island.

CHAPTER 11

LITACY AND CHRISTIANITY IN GREENLAND

Flemming A.J. Nielsen

In an influential book, *The Construction of Nationhood*, the British theologian and historian Adrian Hastings showed that the development of literary languages and the production of Bible translations were key factors in the nation-building processes in medieval and early modern Europe (Hastings 1997). A similar point may be made as regards the first Inuit to be confronted with the Western world, the Greenlanders. The present-day self-confident Greenlandic nation, including its fully functional Indigenous language that is, as a matter of course, used in all aspects of life by the vast majority of the population, is hardly imaginable without the Christian missionaries' efforts to develop a literary language.

Due to the fact that literature produced by the Greenlanders themselves began to appear only in the mid-19th century, descriptions of Greenlandic-language literature[1] tend to skate over its beginnings in the 18th and early 19th centuries. The first novel written by a Greenlander in the vernacular was published in 1914 (Storch 1914). Before 1950, seven novels, a number of short stories, a songbook, some plays, and a collection of poems in Greenlandic had been published (Langgård 2011, 130–138). Since then, a national literature has developed comprising such a quantity of works in Greenlandic that "nobody keeps count of their total number anymore" (Langgård 2011, 123).

This remarkable development is due to a number of factors, a crucial one being Greenland's position in the Scandinavian sphere of influence since the Middle Ages. In 1721, the Norwegian missionary Hans Egede (1686–1758) arrived as the Danish-Norwegian king's representative and settled at the west coast of Greenland in order to educate and Christianize the Greenlanders and inform them of their status as subjects of the king of Denmark and Norway.[2] A decade later, in 1733, the Moravian Brethren from Germany, with permission from the king of Denmark-Norway, commenced their missionary work, which they continued until the end of the 19th century when they felt forced to leave Greenland because of increasingly hostile relations between Denmark and Germany (Kjærgaard and Kjærgaard 2003, 77–80). Until then, both the Danish state mission and the Moravian Brethren issued an abundance of religious and linguistic books in Greenlandic as well as other kinds of teaching material.[3]

BEFORE WRITING

One of the earliest attestations of Inuit being confronted with the medium of writing may be seen in the reports about Martin Frobisher's (c. 1535–1594) expeditions in search of the Northwest Passage. During all three voyages to Meta Incognita ("Unknown Limits") – the southernmost peninsula of Qikiqtaaluk (Baffin Island) – 1576–1578, he met locals that, judging by reports published as early as 1578 (Collinson 1867), were probably Inuit. In the same year, Frobisher also went ashore on the west coast of what later turned out to be Greenland, and as the first European to do so after the Norsemen disappeared from Greenland early in the 15th century, he realized that the cultures of the eastern and western shores of the strait that posterity would name the Davis Strait corresponded closely to each other. The year before, 1577, the seafarers had learned that the locals in Meta Incognita

> knewe very well the use we have of writing, and receyved knowledge thereof, eyther of oure poore captive countreymen whyche they betrayed, or else by thys oure newe captive who hathe seene us dayly write and repeate agayne such wordes of hys language as we desired to learne.
>
> (Collinson 1867, 146)

Violent confrontations, accordingly, had also taught the locals about writing as the Englishmen tried to learn their language and write down its words and their meanings. The result was a list of 17 Inuit words. Apart from four possible Greenlandic words in the Icelandic *Saga of Erik the Red* (Nielsen 2012, 118–120), the words collected during Frobisher's expedition were the first Inuit words that were ever committed to writing (Dorais 2010, 106–107).

"OUR TRUE BROTHERS IN ADAM": THE SECOND COMING OF CHRISTIANITY TO GREENLAND

Literacy and Christianity were interconnected from the very outset of the Christian missions to the Inuit world. Everywhere, Inuit learned to read and write through the efforts of Christian missionaries who thereby contributed to irrevocable changes in Inuit culture. As regards Greenland, the country had been part of Norway and, hence, the Danish-Norwegian empire since the Middle Ages.[4] The Norse populated the southwestern part of Greenland in the late tenth century when no other peoples resided there. Two hundred years later, the ancestors of today's Inuit entered the far north of Greenland from present-day Canada. The two cultures – the Inuit in the north and the Norse in the south – do not appear to have been on friendly terms with each other. For that and a number of other reasons, the Norse eventually disappeared early in the 15th century (Nedkvitne 2019).

Even though communications between Denmark-Norway and Greenland had ceased, it was known in Europe that the local population, at least in West Greenland, were no longer Christian Norsemen but a people that in the usage of the time were characterized as "barbarians" or "savages," by which was meant that they were not Christians, and that they were not aware that they, in the minds of the European sovereigns, were subjects of the king of Denmark-Norway. At the end of the 17th century, the learned Peder Hansen Resen (1625–1688), Danish historian, legal scholar, and mayor of Copenhagen, gave a comprehensive description of Greenland in a manuscript drafted in Latin (Resen 1688 [1987]). He characterized Greenland as a lost country that ought to be retrieved by the king of Denmark-Norway since the king was the country's rightful owner. Resen's main reason for writing so was the idea that the Greenlanders were born of the same blood as were all other people who were descendants of Adam, the first human being created by God, according to the Bible. Besides being "barbarians," immigrants, and hostile to Christians, the Greenlanders were also "our true brothers in Adam" who enjoyed the kingdom's guest-friendship by inhabiting Danish territory. Convinced that their alleged cruelty would be mitigated by their becoming Christians and familiar with the Christian way of life, Resen argued that they should be set free from the tyranny of the demons (Resen 1688 [1987], 156–158).

Arguing in much the same spirit as Peder Hansen Resen, the Norwegian clergyman Hans Egede submitted a proposal to the king that missionaries should be dispatched to Greenland, which had for centuries been part of Norway even though its inhabitants had been forgotten and neglected by the authorities. From his research, begun a decade earlier, Egede knew that Greenland's inhabitants were "savages."[5] According to a theory of his, when the old Norse were still living in the country, another people inhabiting northern Greenland (the "Skraellings" of the Icelandic sagas) had moved south, and an increasing number of violent confrontations had eventually exterminated Norse culture, even though some of the Norse had survived and had mixed with the newcomers (Egede 1745, 113). According to Egede's theory, then, the Greenlanders of his day were a mixed population, and for want of Christian teachers, these people were heathens. In 1719, Egede suggested that this nation gone astray should be reincorporated into the Kingdom of Norway and its people brought to acknowledge their God and their king (Nielsen 2019, 86–87). When this proposal was accepted by the king of Denmark and Norway, Frederik IV (1671–1730), the West Greenlanders became the first Inuit to be exposed to the Christian mission, and gradually, Greenland became reintegrated into the multicultural Danish-Norwegian empire.

THE FIRST GREENLANDIC TEXTS

In 1722, less than a year after his arrival in Greenland, Hans Egede wrote in his diary that the fact that the Greenlanders had observed him busy with "books and spiritual matters" was part of the reason why they considered him an *angakkoq*, a shaman (Egede 1738, 44-45). In autumn 1722, the first Greenlander, a young man called Kojuch (Hans Egede's spelling), came to stay at the new Danish colony. He had agreed to do so for payment as well as free board and lodging. His "job" was to learn religion, which would occur in tandem with learning to read. Another purpose of the paid stay was that the missionary hoped that he and his four children would be able to learn the local language by spending time together with Greenlanders. Things did not work out well with Kojuch, but in December 1722, two other young men, Kusach and Navia, agreed to stay at the Danish colony. For payment of one fishing hook per letter, they quickly learned the entire alphabet, and before the new year, they were able to reproduce the most important parts of Luther's Small Catechism in their own language (Nielsen 2019, 91–92).

That was only the beginning. Soon knowledge of elementary Christianity and stories from the Bible spread through the first Danish settlement situated at an island in the skerries of Greenland's present-day capital, Nuuk, that Egede had called The Island of Hope. In April 1723, Hans Egede had drafted his first written catechism in the Greenlandic language. It is easy to demonstrate its numerous linguistic shortcomings, but it was not utterly incomprehensible. Revised manuscript versions from the following years bear witness to a very steep learning curve as regards the missionary who was assisted by converts, his children who quickly became fluent speakers of Greenlandic, and a linguistically gifted Norwegian clergyman, Albert Top, Hans Egede's colleague in Greenland for four years (1723–1727).

Catechetic and biblical texts in Greenlandic produced by the Danish-Norwegian Christian mission were the first writings drafted in any of the Eskaleut languages.[6] From the earliest years of Hans Egede's residence in Greenland, a number of Greenlandic manuscripts have been preserved: lists of words and grammar notes, as well as continuous texts, the first of which was the aforementioned short catechism drafted as early as in spring 1723. Two slightly different, improved versions of this catechism were produced the following year, and during the fall of 1724, an ambitious project of translating all the basic texts of the Danish Evangelical-Lutheran state church of the day commenced. Within a few years, perhaps a hundred pages of Greenlandic text were written, even though the language had been all but unknown to the European world before 1721. A precious collection of manuscripts from 1725, in Egede's own handwriting, contain translations of substantial portions of the Bible, missionary sermons, catechetic texts, and prayers, as well as a comprehensive list of words, and the world's first attempt at describing the grammar of an Inuit language (Nielsen 2012).

However, even though the earliest production of Greenlandic texts was initiated by the Christian mission, and even though the mission's need for catechetic and other edifying texts was obviously the top priority, it has recently been demonstrated that a few traditional songs and a freshly composed drum song in the traditional style were also written down as early as the year 1725 (Nielsen 2014b). This was the year that Hans Egede received two questionnaires containing a total of 90 questions from his superiors in Denmark and Norway concerning all aspects of Inuit culture, most notably language, religion, oral tradition, eating habits, living and health conditions, as well as local wildlife, geography, and archaeology. In response to a question about the nature of Inuit songs, Hans Egede cited three traditional songs that he had written down at dictation (see Figure 11.1). The transcribed songs present numerous linguistic problems, which is hardly surprising given that nobody had ever before attempted to transcribe traditional poetry in this language that was still poorly understood by the Europeans. Nevertheless, two of the songs are recognizable from later collections of Inuit oral tradition (Nielsen 2014b). In addition to this traditional material, Egede also wrote down a freshly composed drum song made by Pooq, who was one of two Greenlanders ever to voluntarily board a European ship (Harbsmeier 2006, 356). He was also the first Inuk to return from Europe to his native land. After his journey in summer 1725, he composed his drum song telling fabulous news about Norway and

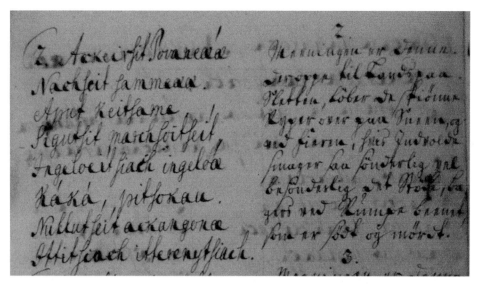

Figure 11.1 A traditional Greenlandic song written down by Hans Egede in 1725. Greenlandic text is in the left column, with the Danish translation on the right. Source: Royal Danish Library.

Denmark, with horse-drawn houses mounted on wheels and man-made mountains (towers) (Nielsen 2014b). Very early, the development of the Greenlandic literary language and the production of Greenlandic texts were progressing by leaps and bounds, and the production of literature was not strictly limited to the kinds of texts that the missionaries needed for their activities.

As has already been shown, the missionaries, from the very outset of their presence, insisted that the locals should not only internalize the values of Christianity, but that the converts should also learn to read Christianity's basic texts themselves. When Pooq went to Denmark in 1724, he brought along a small book that he had been taught to read. It was a short, hand-written Greenlandic catechism drafted by Hans Egede.[7] It may safely be assumed that Pooq was not the only convert to receive a hand-written catechism. Several such manuscripts must have been circulating in Greenland, even though very few have been preserved.

The first book printed in Greenlandic was a reading primer published in Copenhagen by Hans Egede in 1739 (Nielsen and Kjærgaard, forthcoming). It was soon followed by a comprehensive catechism containing catechetic texts, collections of hymns and prayers, as well as the rituals of the sacraments of baptism and Holy Communion (Egede 1742). Only two years later, the first portions of the Bible, the four Gospels, were printed (Egede 1744).

After another three years, in 1747, the Moravian Brethren issued their first printed hymns (Anonymous 1747), and in quick and rapid succession, both missions published several hymnals[8] and catechisms[9] throughout the remainder of the 18th century. These include the first book printed in Greenland, a Moravian hymnal (Brodersen 1793), issued more than half a century prior to the establishment of a proper printing press in Greenland (Oldendow 1957). It is a strong testimony to the missionaries' dedication to their task that two translations of the entire New Testament were printed within a few decades (Egede 1766; Fabricius 1794), both financed by the Danish government. In addition to these two translations of the New Testament, the Moravian Brethren issued a collection of biblical stories (Beck 1759) and a harmony of the Gospels (Anonymous 1778).

Almost the entire indigenous population in western Greenland had become literate by the end of the 18th century, a time when illiteracy was still widespread in Europe (Frandsen 1999). From the beginning, the texts drafted in Greenlandic by the missionaries were copied by hand and distributed by interested readers. Even when the first printed books appeared in Greenland, some of those books were copied by hand by the readers. So great was the attraction of the new medium of writing that about a thousand copies of books printed in Greenlandic were sent from Denmark and Germany to Greenland every single year during the first half of the 19th century, a time when there were hardly more than 10,000 people living in Greenland (Kjærgaard 2011, 143–144). This immense quantity of books in Greenlandic written or translated by missionaries and their helpers among the converts – catechisms, translations of the New Testament, hymn books, collections of stories from the Bible – were funded by the Danish-Norwegian king's government and the Moravian Brethren in Germany, and the books were enthusiastically received by the public they were intended for.

THE CATECHISM AND THE JOURNEY TO HEAVEN

When Hans Egede commenced his missionary work in Greenland on 3 July 1721, his intention was to preach Christianity in accordance with Martin Luther's Small Catechism. The contents of this catechism therefore constitute the beginning of Greenlandic literature. In the preface of his book, Luther says that every Christian should learn the Ten Commandments, the Apostolic Creed, and the Lord's Prayer by heart, and that every believer should recite the Creed and the Prayer several times a day, thereby internalizing their contents.[10] Soon after publication (1529), so-called "explanations" amplifying Luther's short primer began to appear in the Protestant world. In Denmark, the king ordered his Court chaplain Erik Pontoppidan (1698–1764) to prepare such a book to be used for religious instruction in the incipient public school system in Denmark-Norway (Thorkildsen 2017). Pontoppidan's book *Truth Leading to Godliness* (1737) remained popular in pietistic circles well into the twentieth century, and it became highly influential in Greenland as well.

Already in 1739, Hans Egede's son, Poul Egede (1708–1789), translated Pontoppidan's book. Later, the Icelandic clergyman Egill Thorhallesen (1734–1789) spent ten years in Greenland (1765–1775) and reported that every mission station in southern Greenland that he had visited had its own handwritten translations of the book. All these translations were painstakingly rewritten every year by teachers and pupils, and were at the same time "expanded and partly changed," as Thorhallesen puts it.[11] In this way, a welter of local versions of Pontoppidan's explanation of Luther's Small Catechism were developing before Thorhallesen printed his version (Thorhallesen 1777) in order to reduce the religious confusion caused by the existence of several, diverging Greenlandic versions of the Danish-Norwegian kingdom's official textbook of religion. Thorhallesen's book, however, was soon superseded by the prominent missionary Otto Fabricius' (1744–1822) version that came out in 1790, at a time when Pontoppidan's book was gradually falling into disrepute in Denmark where a new age of rationality was dawning. Nevertheless, Fabricius' pietistic work became the leading textbook of religion in Greenland for nearly a century. It was reprinted no less than six times, the latest version appearing in 1874.[12]

In Fabricius' explanation of Luther's Small Catechism, the Christian life is a journey beginning at baptism and ending in heaven. God's written word, when read and understood correctly, shows the way to the destination, while the classic texts of the catechism (The Ten Commandments, The Apostolic Creed, and The Lord's Prayer) show how the Christian person should live, what he or she should believe, and how faith should be internalized and appropriated.

Fabricius' exposition of The Ten Commandments is a detailed and clear guide for how to lead the Christian life with no room for shamans (*angakkut*) or witches (*ilisiitsut*). In accordance with Luther's own teaching, the commandments are given far-reaching interpretations. The prohibition of killing other people also prohibits merely annoying one's fellow human beings. Perhaps it was the interpretation and implementation of the fourth commandment ("honor thy father and thy mother") that had the most profound effect on Greenlandic society. The believer was instructed to respect and obey any person to whom the king had given authority as long as the official in question acted in accordance with the word of God, because it was God himself who had chosen the king. Such persons to be obeyed, of course, included the clergymen and the teachers (*ajoqersuisut*). Through the fourth commandment and the way it was taught, an awareness of being the king's subjects was created and disseminated, and Greenlandic society became increasingly hierarchical. Previously, the Inuit in Greenland had subsisted in scattered groups with a shared culture and language. There were no formal authorities. "The men tacitly followed the advice of the oldest, most experienced hunter in matters of fishing and hunting, and the *angákoq* had no power except in religious matters bearing on the existence of the whole community" (Sonne 1982, 24). Now those groups became a unified nation with formal authorities, and a Christian culture began to develop.

At the close of the first Christian century in Greenland, a new literary genre was introduced to an increasing number of readers when Poul Egede's translation of Thomas à Kempis' famous book on Christian devotion, *The Imitation of Christ*, was printed in Greenlandic in 1787. Originally written in the 15th century, this book was known and valued in the entire Christian world until at least the early 20th century. Apart from the Bible, no book has been translated into more languages. In agreement with the central motif of the Greenlandic catechisms, the title page emphasizes the journey to heaven: "Thomas à Kempis has written these words about the followers of Christ in order to encourage a holy life while going from these temporal things to Heaven" (my translation from Greenlandic). New Greenlandic versions were published twice, in 1824 and 1906.

INUIT REACTIONS TO CHRISTIANITY

Prior to the mid-19th century, we know about Inuit's reactions to the Christian mission only from the writings of Europeans, mostly the missionaries themselves who were not sparing with their reports of both the failures and successes of their efforts. Some of the most crucial early discussions between Inuit and missionaries concerned the Inuit's traditional figure *toornaarsuk*, the shaman's (*angakkoq*'s) helping spirit (Sonne 1986). From a Greenlandic glossary, Hans Egede had learned that *toornaarsuk* meant "devil" (Bartholin 1673, 76), which is why he made the same identification when he settled in Greenland. Being unfamiliar with shamanistic religious systems, Hans Egede and his fellow missionaries and successors believed that *toornaarsuk* was the Inuit supreme god, even though there were no temples or high places where this god was worshipped. While the missionaries conceptualized *toornaarsuk* as the antithesis of the Christian God, they did not believe that the *angakkut* really acted in collusion with the devil. In the eyes of the missionaries, the *angakkut* were skillful cheaters whose deceived audience did not question that the spirits falsely preached by the *angakkut* were real. It is no wonder, then, that the locals at first did not appreciate the missionaries' preaching that their precious figure *toornaarsuk* was a fallen, disobedient angel. They tried to convince Egede that *toornaarsuk* "was not evil and did not harm anyone but disclosed to their *angakkut* what would happen to them. If they took action accordingly, nothing evil would befall them" (Egede 1738, 158, my translation; Nielsen 2012, 132–133).

Other early discussions concerned aspects of Christian mythology. A number of such confrontations are mentioned in two published excerpts of diaries kept by Hans Egede's son Poul Egede throughout his long life since he came to Greenland as a 12-year-old boy with his family in 1721. In 1725, an *angakkoq* told the teenager – already well versed in the local language – a story about a virgin giving birth to a son who became a great *angakkoq* performing miracles, healing the sick, and resuscitating the dead, but the forefathers of the *qallunaat* had killed this marvelous man who subsequently revived and went to heaven. This is a typical example of how Christian mythology very early became part of local oral tradition. As a personal comment, the *angakkoq* added that if the virgin's son had come to the Greenlanders, they would have loved and obeyed him instead of foolishly killing such a great *angakkoq* that was able to resuscitate the dead (Egede 1788a, 20).

Poul Egede mentions a number of similar discussions of mythologies. When he served as a missionary in the Disko Bay Area (northern Greenland) in 1736–1740, his audience was trying to understand his preaching while also questioning aspects of it that they found illogical, and he himself asked questions about Inuit thinking while pointing out aspects that he thought were senseless. His central message was that God loved the Inuit and wanted them to be saved and to go to heaven. The way to heaven was belief in Christ and obedience to the Ten Commandments. According to the missionary, Christian doctrine did not have to be proved by miracles, since no sensible person would doubt anything sensible (Egede 1788a, 119). The concept of reason thus was an important part of the Christian message. The Inuit's non-Christian mythology, magic, and conceptions of the world were referred to as "superstition," and the missionary, in his own eyes, was fighting against this superstition with reason. In his diary, Poul Egede wrote that, confronted with his teaching, the Greenlanders, including the *angakkut*, actually did dissociate themselves from their earlier mythology and ways of thinking, while the *angakkut*, according to the missionary, had to admit that they were powerless and were not really able to heal, to communicate with invisible spirits, or to fly to heaven or to the moon (Egede 1788a, *passim*).

Very early, a local theological tradition began to evolve. Poul Egede reported that a group of converts once met a group of non-converts who were singing and performing drum dances in their traditional way. As one of the converts held that these singers and dancers belonged to the devil, another convert asked the missionary his opinion. Reluctant to judge the singers and the dancers, the missionary's reaction was that he felt more offended by the harsh speech of the believers than by the singing of the non-believers. As regards the latter, he declared himself convinced that some of them would eventually be praising God with the song of the chosen ones (Egede 1788a, 202–203). As regards literature, Poul Egede was assisted by local converts as he translated catechetic and biblical texts to Greenlandic. One of them, an intelligent young woman called Arnarsaq, wondered why he repeatedly revised and changed biblical texts that had already been translated, as if God's word needed medicine like a sick person. When the missionary explained why revisions of translations were needed, Arnarsaq replied that "what has already been written is understandable and adequate" (Egede 1741, 125, my translation). This remark shows that already at that early time (1739), a self-confident, local theological tradition based on the catechism had evolved for the missionary to take into consideration, in addition to a new culture of writing. The biblical stories were subjected to discussions and evaluated by the local converts who recommended that the missionary omit references to the patriarchs' polygamy from the translations of the Bible. They also questioned God's conduct in several biblical narratives (Egede 1788a, 117, 161–162).

As regards the Christian ethical code, women in general were more open-minded than men, since the harsh taboo regulations mostly affected women of childbearing age who also had to endure male propensities to polygamy and to treating their spouses violently (Egede 1788a, 123–124).

According to the reading of Poul Egede's diary by Aqqaluk Lynge, an influential Greenlandic politician and author, Inuit's initial opposition to the Christian mission was due to their sincere wish to understand the new ideas before accepting them. Aqqaluk Lynge emphasizes that "Christianity only gained a footing in Greenland after Inuit had understood it in full, and not least because they themselves had made up their mind that [becoming Christians] was the right decision to make" (Lynge 2018, 62–63; my translation). Early in the 19th century, the entire population in western Greenland had decided to become Christians, and when the Inuit began to express themselves in writing on a large scale in Greenland's first newspaper, *Atuagagdliutit*, founded in 1861 – edited by Greenlanders and published in Greenlandic from the very beginning – Christianity was the inevitable premise of everything that was printed, reported, and debated, even though the newspapers were from the beginning fundamentally secular. Christianity was no longer only the project of missionaries from abroad. Fully embraced by the West Greenlanders, Christianity had become their own project, which is why West Greenlanders served as missionaries in East Greenland and the Thule district from the beginning of the 20th century. The newspapers written and edited by the Greenlanders themselves show no indications of the old Greenlandic religion being still alive in West Greenland in the mid-19th century (Langgård 2018a, 150–152).

GREENLANDIC LITERATURE IN THE 19TH CENTURY

The number of publications in Greenlandic increased dramatically in the 19th century. The literary genres already introduced were still in use as catechisms, hymnals, translations of portions of the Bible, and other devotional literature continued to appear in great numbers. This includes the first children's Bible, with the first picture appearing in a Greenlandic book (Fabricius 1818). In the 19th century, all of the Old Testament books were translated and printed, and the entire Bible came out in 1900 (Anonymous 1900). The biblical book of Genesis was printed in 1822 (Fabricius 1822), but manuscripts of different versions of portions of this text had been circulating since autumn 1724 when Hans Egede first translated the story of the creation of the world (Kjærgaard 2011, 135–142).

In 1851, the first Greenlander published a book. His name was Wittus Steenholdt (1808–1862), head catechist in Aasiaat and teacher at the catechists' school in Ilulissat (northern Greenland). His book is a textbook about Christianity titled, *Man's Own Thinking and the Revelation of God* (my translation from Greenlandic). The title page informs its readers that it is written in *Inuttut* – the language that is, and was, usually called *Kalaallisut* in Greenland. He translated a number of schoolbooks from Danish to Greenlandic, as well as substantial parts of the New Testament before publishing his second book, this time at the newly established printing press in Nuuk: *Doctrine about Morality and Justice* (my translation; Steenholdt 1860). Steenholdt's enduring reputation is mainly due to famous missionary and linguist Samuel Kleinschmidt (1814–1886) who appreciated Steenholdt's contributions to his Greenlandic-Danish dictionary in its preface (Kleinschmidt 1871). The result was unsurpassed; Kleinschmidt's Greenlandic-Danish dictionary is the best one ever published – albeit necessarily obsolete now – because of its many details and nuanced explanations missing in later dictionaries. The contemporary Greenlandic standard orthography is but a light revision of that of Kleinschmidt and Steenholdt.

Very popular in Greenland was a book about morality printed in 1837, based on the German educator Joachim Heinrich Campe's (1746–1818) works. Campe was generally held in very high esteem at the time, and in a bilingual publication, his teachings were put into Hans Egede's mouth as the missionary had fictive conversations with so-called "disciples." Originally written by merchant Johan Christian Mørch (1768–1830), the book was published by missionary Peter Kragh (1794–1883) who added a long introduction about Hans Egede's missionary work (Mørch 1837). It is not known when Mørch drafted his work.

Apart from such edifying literature, fictional stories also began to appear in print. Noteworthy is a story about the eternal triangle, *Two Brothers*. This book is based on a German legend that missionary Knud Kjer (1802–1865) published in Greenlandic (Kjer 1838). The same missionary also provided Greenlandic versions of several Danish hymns and secular songs that highly influenced later poetry authored by Greenlanders.

Several other samples of popular European literature of the time were translated into Greenlandic, and much-circulated in the form of manuscripts that the readers themselves copied laboriously, but most of which have not been preserved. However, a few of these manuscripts were printed. In 1839, a collection of manuscripts was published which had originally been written by a clerk, Rasmus Jensen Brandt (1772–1818), as early as 1810. This collection contains material that Brandt had composed himself, such as a number of fictitious dialogues between Greenlanders about their own affairs as well as about the universe. There are also a number of moralizing fables and an abridged version of a Danish novel. This material was published by the above-mentioned Peter Kragh under the title *Oqaluttualiat*, "Tales," almost three decades after it had been written down by Brandt (Brandt 1839). In the meantime, several copies had been made by hand by anonymous readers. Another example is the popular epic poem "Oberon" (1780) by the German writer Christoph Martin Wieland (1733–1813). This epic was translated into Greenlandic by Johan Christian Mørch, and it circulated in manuscripts for many years before it was printed in the new Greenlandic newspaper *Atuagagdliutit* in 1863.

With one magnificent exception, all books published in Greenlandic before 1855 were printed in Europe, in Denmark in particular. The above-mentioned hymnal printed in Nuuk in 1793 by an inventive Moravian missionary, Jesper Brodersen, was an experiment, and Brodersen's old primitive equipment was rediscovered and used for a series of simple prints appearing from 1855 to 1857: a few pages of news from Europe, a small medical guide, a biography of Hans Egede, and a translation of the Lutheran Augsburg confession of faith (Oldendow 1957).

In 1857, no less than two printing presses were established in Nuuk, at that time a very small town of just a few hundred inhabitants. One printing press was an official one, established by the high-ranking Danish Government official Hinrich Johannes Rink (1819–1893),[13] and the other printing press was secured through the private initiative of the aforementioned Samuel Kleinschmidt.[14] Schoolbooks in Greenlandic, in addition to the catechisms, had begun to appear in the 1830s. Now Samuel Kleinschmidt issued his own series of schoolbooks, religious books, and translations of biblical books (see Figure 11.2).

From the official printing press established by Hinrich Johannes Rink, a number of richly illustrated books came out very early for entertainment and educational purposes. The literary counterpart of Kleinschmidt's editions of biblical books were four bilingual volumes containing traditional tales sent in by Greenlanders from the entire west coast (Rink 1859–1865). The four volumes were illustrated by woodcuts made on the basis of drawings by two Greenlandic artists who later became famous: Aron from Kangeq (1822–1869) and Jens Kreutzmann (1828–1899). These traditional tales printed in two languages may be said to be the beginning of proper Greenlandic fiction, even though the first novel written by a Greenlander did not appear until 1914. The preface of the first volume – written by a Greenlander, probably catechist Rasmus Berthelsen, who, according to the colophon, supervised the printing process – states a utilitarian purpose of the publication:

> It is useful to know about the lives of our ancestors because we may learn from them the consequences of their good and bad actions and lead our own lives accordingly. The old Greenlanders were brutish, cruel, and ignorant, but also more tough, strong, and brave as regards hunting than most people are nowadays. Since they were unacquainted with Christianity, many of their acts of cruelty are understandable.
>
> (Rink 1859, my translation)

Written versions of these stories from the oral tradition became immensely popular. Many of them were reprinted several times in *Atuagagdliutit*. The purpose of the newspaper was "to present role models for the Greenlanders, to give them

Figure 11.2   Two Greenlanders visiting Copenhagen in 1724: Pooq and his friend Qiperoq. Printed in Nuuk, Greenland, 1857.

some knowledge of the world outside Greenland and to allow Greenlanders to debate among themselves" (Langgård 2011, 123). From the beginning, the paper was issued only in Greenlandic, and it contained articles that were mostly written by Greenlanders: news, socio-political debates, articles about the world outside Greenland, and translations of European literature (books and articles from magazines) considered to be enlightening, entertaining, or edifying by the editors who were, from the outset, Greenlanders. In the earliest years, the paper came out five or six times a year. Later (from 1874), the periodical was published every month; today it is a weekly. In the early days, volumes containing the yearly production of newspapers were distributed all over the west coast, and they circulated among enthusiastic readers until they went to shreds. An expert on the early Greenlandic newspapers, Karen Langgård, declares to be "struck by the level of competence in the debate" documented by *Atuagagdliutit* before and especially after 1900 (Langgård 2011, 128) (see Figure 11.3).

Medical guides and books about the care of babies and midwifery also began to appear in Greenlandic in the 19th century, and in 1858, the earliest administrative texts and official announcements were issued. Most of the important literary genres were thereby represented in the local language by the end of the 19th century.

Figure 11.3 Front page of the first issue of Greenland's first newspaper, *Atuagagdliutit*, 1861.

THE EARLY 20TH CENTURY

In 1909, a group of prominent Danish citizens interested in Greenlandic affairs started a literary society with the aim of procuring literature in Greenlandic for the benefit of the Greenlanders. In the presentation of the society, the Greenlanders are described as a literate people who read every piece of literature at their disposal, which was not much if the Bible, schoolbooks, and devotional literature are left out of account.

The founders of the society regarded the provision of reading matters as an essential prerequisite for "developing the culture of the Greenlandic society" (my translation). Therefore, they held that books that were both informative and entertaining should be published.[15] The first "informative and entertaining" books provided by the new society were a description of the newly "discovered" Thule Inuit (Inughuit) (Rasmussen 1909), a collection of stories from the Icelandic sagas (Rasmussen and Rasmussen 1911), and two small books about non-European peoples all over the world (except Inuit!) whose traditional ways of life were threatened by the spreading of civilization, which, however, was seen as a good and necessary thing (Rasmussen and Olsen 1912–1913). The books became very popular in Greenland, some of the material having already been published in *Atuagagdliutit*.

The "discovery" of the Christian West Greenlanders' non-Christian kinsmen and women in East Greenland and in the Thule district made a huge impression on the reading public who admired their ancestors for their hunting competence while at the same time considering their culture to be "pagan and evil" (Langgård 2011, 131). When the Christian mission began in East Greenland in 1894 and in the Thule district in 1909, the paganism of the past virtually unfolded before the eyes of the West Greenlanders, especially as West Greenlandic missionaries were involved in both missions from the start. A highly interesting description of the East Greenlanders written by a West Greenlandic missionary came out in 1906 (Rosing 1906).

MODERNITY

Giving a thorough overview from a pointed postcolonial perspective, Karen Langgård (2011) divides the literary history of Greenland into six phases:

1) During the last decades of the 19th century, the Greenlanders began to write their own church hymns (Langgård 2011, 123–124). According to Karen Langgård, the newspaper articles of the time testify to "an ethnic-national discourse defining the ideal Greenlander as the competent seal-hunter and the pious Christian," and the same kind of discourse may be found in much of the written literature of the 20th century, too (Langgård 2011, 126). Often the newspaper printed articles about Hans Egede, his family, and their great importance to Greenland because they saved the Greenlanders from "the great darkness of ignorance," which is an often-quoted expression (*nalusuunerup taarsuanit*), synonymous with paganism (Langgård 2018a, 153).
2) Romantic nationalism and sociopolitical debate dominate the literature before 1953, including the aforementioned seven novels authored by Greenlanders (Langgård 2011, 130–138). There were no calls for "decolonization," but both Greenlanders and Danes were invited to work together in order to create a better future. Greenlandic authors were influenced by Danish national romanticism, and in their fictive portrayal of the past, they made their non-Christian ancestors anticipate Christianity by having them believe in one divine power and act on the basis of Christian ethic concepts such as mercy and neighborly love.
3) As a consequence of Greenland's conversion to a Danish county in 1953, a forced process of modernization and Danification characterized the next two decades, from the 1950s to the 1970s. The past became a dominant theme in

novels as romantic nationalism continued to dominate, while the heroes of the non-Christian past were depicted as supermen whose norms were fully in line with Christian morals and ethics (Langgård 2011, 138–143).

4) The process of modernization and Danification was accompanied by growing politicization of ethnicity and national feeling. From the late 1960s to the 1980s, the literature was characterized by ethno-national mobilization and the fight for Home Rule (Langgård 2011, 144–147). Highly influential was the politician and poet Moses Olsen (1938–2008) who created new ethno-national symbols and called for an awakening of the heritage of the ancestors as regards their songs and their sense of freedom. In many ways, Moses Olsen was the mastermind behind the process leading to Home Rule in 1979. In the late 1970s and in the 1980s, the poets campaigned for opposition against the Danes who were seen as capitalists profiting from the Greenlanders and ruthlessly suppressing them, whereas the Greenlanders were described as proletarians suppressed by capitalists.

5) The 1990s saw what Langgård has described as a literary crisis. The fight for Home Rule was long since over. The ethnic symbolism and discourse about the true Greenlandic way of life were generally toned down in everyday society, but were still important themes in the literature that was mainly produced by already-established authors or older men that did not really meet the demands of younger readers who felt – and still feel – that literature should be about everyday lives and problems in contemporary Greenland, and less bound to ethno-national issues and symbols (Langgård 2011, 147–152, 168).

6) In the first decades of the new millennium, Greenlandic literature has been increasingly focused on individual experiences and religious and spiritual issues at the expense of collective socio-political matters. Themes are addressed that until recently were taboo: alcoholism, violence, incest, child abuse, suicide, and the neglect of children. The literature thus unveils problems that are far too common in Greenland, but it describes, too, the happier experiences. In a continuation of oral tradition, the thriller genre has become very popular, and elements of the traditional, pre-Christian spiritual culture are used in new ways, even though Christianity is still the firm foundation in many Greenlanders' lives.[16] Today, according to the church's own numbers, 95 percent of the population in Greenland are members of the Evangelical Lutheran church.[17]

From the end of the 19th century, knowledge about the still non-Christian parts of Greenland – eastern Greenland and the Thule district – increased dramatically in the fully Christianized western Greenland where these two populations were soon considered to be compatriots of the West Greenlanders. At the same time, the West Greenlanders felt confronted with their own forefathers' non-Christian religion and culture. According to Langgård, the non-Christian past was transformed in works of fiction to make it compatible with the Christian norms of the 20th century. The aspects of the past that did not comply with Christianity, such as taboo regulations, blood feuds, and the activities of the *angakkut*, were toned down. It was not before the end of the 20th century, from the 1980s, that the spiritual aspects of Inuit's non-Christian past were used in the literature, and even then only to a limited degree because knowledge of this kind of spirituality is generally very limited in today's

Greenland. Conversion to Christianity is sympathetically described in Greenlandic fiction at the same time as the members of the pre-Christian society are praised for their work ethic, hunting skills, and their competence in handling the material world. Especially after World War II, there are also several secularized works of fiction that are more sympathetic to pre-Christian culture and beliefs. The Church and its people are also criticized for betraying the society by not fulfilling its Christian duties. However, Christianity and its norms constitute the inevitable premise of such criticism, even though in contemporary Greenlandic literature, Christianity and the Church no longer monopolize spirituality (Langgård 2018b).

CONCLUSION

The history of Greenlandic literature begins with the catechisms and their utopian journey to heaven. Since the entire western Greenlandic society was Christianized early in the 19th century, literacy has been used for many other purposes than strictly religious or utilitarian ones, but the missionaries' insistence on learning, using, and developing the local language for their specific purposes, and not least their invention of a literary language and their endeavors to teach Greenlanders to use it, are probably the main reasons why the Greenlandic language is still very much alive and used everywhere in contemporary Greenland. Today it is the language of literature, pop music, government, and legislation. No other Aboriginal language in the American hemisphere has a comparable status.

NOTES

1. Among the most important such descriptions are Berthelsen (1986; 1994) and Langgård (2011).
2. The best general introductions to the early Greenlandic church history continue to be Bobé (1952) and Gad (1973).
3. Kjærgaard (2011) gives a valuable overview of the literary production and its impact as regards the 18th century.
4. A description of this empire may be found in Kjærgaard (2016).
5. In his diary (Egede 1722 [1925], 3), Hans Egede wrote that his brother-in-law who was a sailor with experience from Greenland, had informed him that there were "savages" in West Greenland. He had no information about possible inhabitants in East Greenland.
6. As regards the term "Eskaleut," see Fortescue, Jacobson, and Kaplan (2010). The main Eskaleut branches are Aleut, Yupik, and Inuit languages.
7. The original is lost, but at least three copies were made shortly after Pooq's arrival in Denmark, and they have been preserved in libraries in Halle (Germany), Paris, and London – but, as a matter of fact, not in Denmark or Greenland (Nielsen 2014a).
8. Anonymous (1754; 1759; 1772; 1785); Bruun (1761); Thorhallesen (1776); Egede (1788b).
9. Egede (1756; 1772; 1780); Fabricius (1790; reprinted 1797).
10. For a full introduction and commentary to Luther's Small Catechism, see Peters (2009–2013).
11. Thorhallesen (1777, my translation). Kjærgaard (2011, 134–145) reviews all handwritten literary works known to have existed in Greenland in the 18th century. Very few of those thousands of manuscripts have been preserved. They were worn to shreds and then used for lighting fires.
12. Reprinted 1797, 1818, 1833, 1842, 1866, and 1874.

13 A comprehensive biography of Hinrich Johannes Rink is Rink (2019).
14 A comprehensive biography of Samuel Kleinschmidt is Wilhjelm (2013).
15 The presentation of the society is printed in Danish in Knud Rasmussen's Greenlandic book about the Thule Inuit (Rasmussen 1909).
16 Langgård 2011, 152–167, 170. The literature of the latest decade is not in conflict with Karen Langgård's description from 2011. The most important contemporary Greenlandic author is probably Niviaq Korneliussen whose novel *Homo Sapienne* was published in 2014. Even though the title is in a kind of French Latin (the word *sapienne* is Latin, but the female inflection is French), its contents are written in Greenlandic with several passages in English. The novel has been translated into a number of languages, British and American English included. Her latest novel, *Naasuliardarpi* (*The Valley of Flowers*), came out in 2020 and has suicide as its dominant theme. It has already been translated into Danish and will be published in English sometime in the near future.
17 https://www.folkekirken.dk/folkekirken-arbejder/mission/groenlands-apostel-hans-egede (accessed 27 August 2020).

REFERENCES

Anonymous. 1747. *Illei-inneit Ingverautikschengvoennik karalin okausiennik* [*Some Prayers To Be Sung in the Language of the Greenlanders*].

Anonymous. 1754. *Illeit Tuksiautit Tuksiutillo* [*Some Prayers and Psalms*].

Anonymous. 1759. *Illeit Tuksiautit Tuksiutillo* [*Some Prayers and Psalms*]. Utrecht: Pieter Muntendam.

Anonymous. 1772. *Illeit Tuksiautit Tuksiutillo* [*Some Prayers and Psalms*]. Berlin: Johannes Georg Boss.

Anonymous. 1778. *Nalegauta Jesusib Kristusib Annaursirsivta sullirsei* [*The Deeds of Our Lord Jesus Christ*]. Barby.

Anonymous. 1785. *Tuksiautit attuagæksit illageennut innuit nunænnetunnut* [*Prayers To Be Read by the Congregation in the Country of the Inuit*]. Barby.

Anonymous. 1900. *Atuagarssuit tássa agdlagkat ivdlernartut tamarmiussut, tastamantitorkamigdlo tastamantitâmigdlo* [*Great Books, Namely All the Holy Scriptures from both the Old Testament and the New Testament*]. Copenhagen: Rosenberg.

Bartholin, Caspar. 1673. "Vocabula Gróenlandica" [Greenlandic Words]. *Acta Medica & Philosophica Hafniensia*: 71–77.

Beck, Johannes. 1759. *Die lezte Mensch-Sohns-Tage* [*The Last Days of the Son of Man*]. Utrecht: Peter Muntendam.

Berthelsen, Christian. 1986. "Greenlandic Literature: Its Traditions, Changes, and Trends." *Arctic Anthropology* 23 (1–2): 339–345. https://www.jstor.org/stable/40316120

———. 1994. *Kalaallit atuakkiaat 1990 ilanngullugu* [*The Books of the Greenlanders until 1990*]. Nuuk: Atuakkiorfik.

Bobé, Louis. 1952. *Hans Egede: Colonizer and Missionary of Greenland*. Copenhagen: Rosenkilde and Bagger.

Brandt, Rasmus Jensen. 1839. *Okalluktualiæt* [*Tales*]. Copenhagen: Fabritius de Tengnagel.

[Brodersen, Jesper]. 1793. *Tuksiautit akioreeksautikset* [*Prayers for Antiphonal Singing*]. Nuuk.

Bruun, Rasmus. 1761. *Ivngerutit okko 119. Arsillyput Kalalin Opertut Attuægekseit Nalektarangamik* [*These 119 Psalms Are Written Down To Be Used by the Greenlandic Believers When They Attend Church Services*]. Copenhagen: Gottmann Friderich Kisel.

Collinson, Richard, ed. 1867. *The Three Voyages of Martin Frobisher, In Search of a Passage to Cathaia and India by the North-West, A.D. 1576-8 (The Hakluyt Society, 38)*. New York: Burt Franklin.

Dorais, Louis-Jacques. 2010. *The Language of the Inuit*. Montreal, QC: McGill-Queen's University Press.

Egede, Hans. 1722 [1925]. "Relation angaaende dend Dessein med dend GrønLandske Mission" [Report about the Project of the Greenlandic Mission]. In *Hans Egede. Relationer fra Grønland 1721-36 og Det gamle Grønlands ny Perlustration 1741 [Hans Egede. Reports from Greenland 1721-36 and New Description of Old Greenland 1741]*, (Meddelelser om Grønland, 54), edited by Louis Bobé, 1-29. Copenhagen: Bianco Luno.

———. 1738. *Omstændelig og udførlig Relation, Angaaende Den Grønlandske Missions Begyndelse og Fortsættelse [Detailed and Elaborate Report about the Beginning and Continuation of the Greenlandic Mission]*. Copenhagen: Johann Christoph Groth.

———. 1742. *Elementa Fidei Christianæ [Elements of Christian Doctrine]*. Copenhagen.

———. 1745. *A Description of Greenland*. London: C. Hitch.

Egede, Poul. 1741. *Continuation af Relationerne Betreffende Den Grønlandske Missions Tilstand Og Beskaffenhed [Continuation of the Reports about the Condition and State of the Greenlandic Mission]*. Copenhagen: Johann Christoph Groth.

———. 1744. *Evangelium Okausek tussarnersok [The Gospel, the Wonderful Word]*. Copenhagen.

———. 1756. *Catechismus Mingnek D. M. Lutherim [Dr. M[artin] Luther's Small Catechism]*. Copenhagen: Gottmann Friderich Kisel.

———. 1766. *Testamente Nutak [The New Testament]*. Copenhagen: Gerhard Giese Salicath.

———. 1772, 1780. *Katekismuse Mingnek D. M. Luterim [Dr. M[artin] Luther's Small Catechism]*. Copenhagen: Gerhard Giese Salicath.

———. 1788a. *Efterretninger om Grønland, uddragne af en Journal holden fra 1721 til 1788 [Reports about Greenland Excerpted from a Diary Kept from 1721 to 1788]*. Copenhagen: Hans Christopher Schrøder.

———. 1788b. *Ivngerutit Tuksiutidlo [Psalms and Prayers]*. Copenhagen: Hans Christopher Schrøder.

Fabricius, Otto. 1790. *Ajokærsutit illuartut Gudimik [The Holy Doctrines about God]*. Copenhagen: C. F. Skubart.

———. 1794. *Testamente Nutak [The New Testament]*. Copenhagen: C. F. Skubart.

———. 1818. *Bibelingoak merdlâinnut [Small Bible for the Children]*. Copenhagen: C. F. Skubart.

———. 1822. *Testamentitokamit Mosesim Aglegèj siurdleet [Moses' First Book from the Old Testament]*. Copenhagen: C. F. Skubart.

Fortescue, Michael, Steven Jacobson, and Lawrence Kaplan. 2010. *Comparative Eskimo Dictionary with Aleut Cognates* (Alaska Native Language Center Research Paper, 9). Fairbanks: University of Alaska Press.

Frandsen, Niels H. 1999. "Literacy and Literature in North Greenland." *Études/Inuit/Studies* 23: 69–90. https://www.jstor.org/stable/42870946

Gad, Finn. 1973. *The History of Greenland. II. 1700–1782*. London: Hurst.

Harbsmeier, Michael. 2006. "Pietisten, Schamanen und die Authenzität des Anderen: grönländische Stimmen im 18. Jahrhundert" [Pietists, Shamans and the Authenticity of the Other: Greenlandic Voices in the Eighteenth Century]. In *Das Europa der Aufklärung und die außereuropäische koloniale Welt [Europe in the Age of Enlightenment and the Colonial World outside Europe]*, edited by H.-J. Lüsebrink, 355–370. Göttingen: Wallstein.

Hastings, Adrian. 1997. *The Construction of Nationhood: Ethnicity, Religion and Nationalism*. Cambridge: Cambridge University Press.

Kjer, Knud. 1838. *Kattængutigeek [Two Brothers]*. Copenhagen: Fabritius de Tengnagel.

Kjærgaard, Thorkild. 2011. "Genesis in the Longhouse: Religious Reading in Greenland in the Eighteenth Century." In *Religious Reading in the Lutheran North: Studies in Early Modern*

Scandinavian Book Culture, edited by Charlotte Appel and Morten Fink-Jensen, 133–158. Newcastle upon Tyne: Cambridge Scholars Publishing.

———. 2016. "Danish Empire." In *The Encyclopedia of Empire, II*, edited by John M. MacKenzie, 651–657. Wiley Blackwell. http://doi.org/10.1002/9781118455074.wbeoe351

Kjærgaard, Thorkild, and Kathrine Kjærgaard. 2003. *Ny Herrnhut i Nuuk 1733–2003 [New Herrnhut in Nuuk 1733–2003]*. Nuuk: Ilisimatusarfik/Atuagkat.

Kleinschmidt, Samuel. 1871. *Den Grønlandske Ordbog [The Greenlandic Dictionary]*. Copenhagen: Louis Klein.

Korneliussen, Niviaq. 2014. *Homo Sapienne*. Nuuk: Milik Publishing.

Langgård, Karen. 2011. "Greenlandic Literature from Colonial Times to Self-Government." In *From Oral Tradition to Rap: Literatures of the Polar North*, edited by Karen Langgård and Kirsten Thisted, 119–187 Nuuk: Ilisimatusarfik/Atuagkat.

———. 2018a. "Kristendommen i de grønlandske aviser fra 1861 og ind i det 20. århundrede" [Christianity in the Greenlandic Newspapers from 1861 until the Beginning of the Twentieth Century]. In *Kristendom i Grønland [Christianity in Greenland]*, edited by Sven Rune Havsteen, Karen Langgård, Sofie Petersen, Hans Anton Lynge, Kennet Pedersen, and Aage Rydstrøm-Poulsen, 149–168. Copenhagen: Eksistensen.

———. 2018b. "Kirke, kristendom og den grønlandske skønlitteratur" [Church, Christianity, and Greenlandic Fiction]. In *Kristendom i Grønland [Christianity in Greenland]*, edited by Sven Rune Havsteen, Karen Langgård, Sofie Petersen, Hans Anton Lynge, Kennet Pedersen, and Aage Rydstrøm-Poulsen, 193–209. Copenhagen: Eksistensen.

Lynge, Aqqaluk, 2018. "Verdensanskuelsernes sammenstød" [The Clash of Pictures of the World]. In *Kristendom i Grønland [Christianity in Greenland]*, edited by Sven Rune Havsteen, Karen Langgård, Sofie Petersen, Hans Anton Lynge, Kennet Pedersen, and Aage Rydstrøm-Poulsen, 61–67. Copenhagen: Eksistensen.

Mørch, Johan Christian. 1837. *Grønlændernes første Præsts Hans Egedes Aften-Samtaler med sine Disciple [The Greenlanders' First Clergyman's Evening Talks with his Disciples]*. Copenhagen: Fabritius de Tengnagel.

Nedkvitne, Arnved. 2019. *Norse Greenland: Viking Peasants in the Arctic*. Abingdon-on-Thames: Routledge.

Nielsen, Flemming A. J. 2012. "The Earliest Greenlandic Bible: A Study of the Ur-Text from 1725." In *Ideology, Culture, and Translation*, edited by Scott S. Elliott and Roland Boer, 113–137. Atlanta, GA: Society of Biblical Literature.

———. 2014a. "En ukendt grønlandsk katekismus fra 1724" [An Unknown Greenlandic Catechism from 1724]. *Grønlandsk Kultur- og Samfundsforskning 2013-2014* (1): 123–144.

———. 2014b. "Fire gammelgrønlandske sange" [Four Songs in Old Greenlandic]. *Tidsskriftet Grønland* 62: 204–211.

———. 2019. "Det dansk-grønlandske kulturmøde fra middelalderen til Hans Egede" [The Danish-Greenlandic Encounter of Cultures from the Middle Ages to Hans Egede]. In *Grønlændernes syn på Danmark. Historiske, kulturelle og sproglige perspektiver [The Greenlanders' view on Denmark. Historical, cultural, and linguistic perspectives]*, edited by Ole Høiris, Ole Marquardt and Gitte Adler Reimer, 59–104. Aarhus: Aarhus University Press.

Nielsen, Flemming A. J., and Thorkild Kjærgaard. Forthcoming. Catechism Primers in Greenland. In *Catechism Primers in Europe*, edited by Britta Juska-Bacher, Wendelin Sroka, Tuija Laine, and Matthew Grenby.

Oldendow, Knud. 1957. *Bogtrykkerkunsten i Grønland og mændene bag den [The Art of Printing in Greenland and the Men behind It]*. Copenhagen.

Peters, Albrecht. 2009–2013. *Commentary on Luther's Catechisms*. 4 vols. St. Louis, MO: Concordia.

Pontoppidan, Erik. 1737. *Sandhed til Gudfrygtighed [Truth Leading to Godliness]*. Copenhagen: Gottmann Friderich Kisel.

Rasmussen, Knud. 1909. *Avángarnisalerssârutit [Tales of the People of the North]*. Copenhagen: Rosenberg.

Rasmussen, Knud, and Vilhelmine Rasmussen. 1911. *Kavdlunâtsiait kalâtdlit nunâliarκârnermingnik oκalugtualiaisa ilait [Some of the Tales about the Norsemen's First Journeys to Greenland]*. Copenhagen: Rosenberg.

Rasmussen, Knud, and Gustav Olsen. 1912–1913. *Silarssuarmiulerssârutit. Inuit κavdlunâjúngitsut inûsiánik ugperissáinigdlo univkât [Tales about the Denizens of the World. Stories about the Lives and Beliefs of the People That Are Not Europeans]* 2 vols. Copenhagen: Rosenberg.

Resen, Peder Hansen. 1688 [1987]. *Descriptio Færoarum, Islandiæ et Grönlandiæ [Description of the Faroe Islands, Iceland, and Greenland]*. Manuscript. The Royal Danish Library. In part translated to Danish: *Groenlandia* (Det Grønlandske Selskabs Skrifter, 28). Copenhagen: Det Grønlandske Selskab, 1987.

Rink, Hinrich Johannes, ed. 1859–65. *Kaladlit Okalluktualliait [Stories of the Greenlanders]* 4 vols. Nuuk: The Printing Office of the Inspectorate.

Rink, Pia. 2019. *Grønland blev hans skæbne. Om H. J. Rink og hans tid [Greenland Became His Destiny. About H. J. Rink and His Time]* 2 vols. Copenhagen: Det Grønlandske Selskab.

Rosing, Christian. 1906. *Tunuamiut. kalâtdlit Gûtimik nalussut ugperissáinik ilerκuinigdlo inûsiánigdlo [The East Greenlanders. About the Beliefs, Customs, and Lives of the Greenlanders Who Know Nothing about God]*. Nuuk: The Printing Office of the Teachers' College.

Sonne, Birgitte. 1982. "The Ideology and Practice of Blood Feuds in East and West Greenland." *Études/Inuit/Studies* 6 (2): 21–50. https://www.jstor.org/stable/42869352

———. 1986. "Toornaarsuk, An Historical Proteus." *Arctic Anthropology* 23 (1–2): 199–219.

Steenholdt, Wittus Frederik. 1851. *Innûb nangminek' isumaliornera Gudib'lo tekkotinera [Man's Own Thinking and the Revelation of God]*. Copenhagen: I. G. Salomon.

Steenholdt, Wittus Frederik. 1860. *Illerkuksamut imàlôneet illuarnermik ajokersout [Doctrine about Morality and Justice]*. Nuuk: The Printing Office of the Inspectorate.

Storch, Mathias. 1914. *Singnagtugaκ [A Dream]*. Copenhagen: Rosenberg.

Thomas à Kempis. 1787. *Christus-mik Mallingnairsut [Following Christ]*. Copenhagen: The Printing Office of the Orphanage.

Thorhallesen, Egill. 1776. *Tuksiutit ... Tuksiautillo [Psalms... and Prayers]*. Copenhagen: Gerhard Giese Salicath.

———. 1777. *Katekismus [Catechism]*. Copenhagen: Gerhard Giese Salicath.

Thorkildsen, Dag. 2017. "Luther og nasjonal identitet i Norden" [Luther and National Identity in Scandinavia]. *Teologisk tidsskrift* 6 (1).

Wilhjelm, Henrik. 2013. *Grönländer aus Leidenschaft. Das Leben und Werk von Samuel Kleinschmidt [Greenlander by Inclination Samuel Kleinschmidt's Life and Work]*. Neuendettelsau: Erlanger Verlag für Mission und Ökumene.

CHAPTER 12

EVERYDAY INTERSECTIONS OF INUIT HEALTH AND BIOMEDICAL KNOWLEDGE

Christopher Fletcher

The cultural frameworks through which people think about and experience health have broad repercussions for health systems and the work of the people who make them run. Inuit health is an intense inter-cultural field of knowledge, action, and surveillance that involves a range of actors in different levels of government, university-based researchers, Indigenous organizations, health system administrators, and northern residents, all of whose work is structured in a series of legal frameworks that include national Medicare policies, provincial health authorities, regional land-claim agreements, the scope of practice of professional orders (doctors, nurses, physiotherapists, social workers, etc.), union collective agreements, and so on. Studying the intersections of health models shows us how they are enabled and constrained by the structural contexts in which they are situated while also bringing our attention to the ongoing process of inter-cultural dialogue and struggles for meaning and social legitimacy that is occasioned through the provision of health services. In exploring these issues, I focus on how the intersections of distinct health knowledge systems play out in the everyday lives of people in Nunavik. This necessarily leads to questions what place does "tradition" have in the North today? How may Inuit epistemology receive appropriate consideration in contemporary medical and social systems, and through these how does suffering become tangible in interpersonal spaces?

    The profound disparities between the health of Inuit and that of the majority of Canadians are well described in the literature (Wallace 2014; ITK, 2014; Cameron 2011) and a pervasive feature of Inuit history in Canada. Indeed, it was concerns about the health of Inuit that provided the impetus for systematic state intervention, however imperfect, in the Canadian North in the post-World War II period. Today, knowledge of difficult living conditions, high suicide rates, and substance abuse problems are part of the common knowledge about Inuit in southern Canada. That, for most people, is the extent of their knowledge about Inuit health and well-being. Without negating the importance of the entrenched health disparities, symptomatic as they are of broad social and economic inequalities, it is important to recognize that stereotypes about Inuit may themselves be damaging and constitute an important determinant of health. For example, the stereotype of widespread alcoholism does not hold up to scrutiny – studies have shown that the proportion of people who have consumed alcohol in the past 12 months is significantly less in Inuit Nunangat than in southern Canada (Wallace 2014; Muckle et al. 2007). Likewise, there are areas where Inuit health is good and strengthening. Infant mortality was a serious problem in Inuit communities well into the 1970s, and while still high, has been steadily decreasing and is much closer to the national average than it once was. The rate of deaths from cardiovascular disease and cancer are significantly lower for Inuit than in the rest of Quebec (Duhaime et al. 2015). The prevalence of diabetes in Nunavik is comparable to that in southern Quebec although obesity and food insecurity – both harbingers of diet-related disease – are increasing. There is a protective effect associated with a traditional diet of marine mammals, fish, and caribou. The physical activity associated with hunting, fishing, and gathering food is good for the body and the mind. On the other hand, overcrowded housing is unacceptably common and brings with it a host of physical risks and social stressors that complicate mental health conditions. Overall, however, the health portrait for Inuit in Canada is still difficult. Life expectancy, the broadest indicator of population health, is still roughly a decade less for Inuit than the non-Indigenous population of Canada. Looked at from another angle, the average Canadian has a nearly 75 percent chance of reaching the age of 80; an Inuk just 50 percent (Tjepkema et al. 2019).

While doom and gloom statistics are easy to recite, they only tell a small portion of a story of Inuit resourcefulness, community engagement, and leadership in the face of profound historic challenges and their ongoing impacts. In my work as an educator teaching about the social determinants of health, I find it important to challenge the received wisdom about the nature of illness and disparity in Indigenous communities. Early on in fieldwork in Nunavik, I was strongly encouraged by community leaders to think about and frame my research around what is good in the world and not to dwell on the negative. This approach has subsequently become known as a "strengths-based" approach to health that seeks to counterbalance the distressing statistics and damaging stereotypes of Indigenous suffering. The latter have been roundly criticized as undermining the political aspirations of Indigenous people by questioning their competency to control their own affairs. However, while this argument is compelling, it was not the political impacts of representation that people were teaching me; rather they framed it within a cultural model of how illness and disease manifest in the world. In this view an excessive dwelling on the negative opens the potential for malevolent forces to bring those very things into existence (Fletcher and Kirmayer 1997). Inuit understand a model of health in which words create the very objects they describe. It is now relatively common in academic and research circles to take a similar view to understanding and describing health at a population level. What are the strengths that people access to help themselves? How have Indigenous peoples maintained their cultural and social integrity in the face of persistent efforts to force change? How can the practices, philosophies, and ontologies of Indigenous people shape systems of health and healing? In these questions we see a convergence between academic and Inuit understandings health, well-being, and disease. While the pathways each took to get to the same place are quite different, they are not incommensurate worlds. I have tried to take this lesson to heart and in working with Inuit health institutions, and in collaborating with communities on projects they create to encourage well-being at home, I think we have fostered some healthful words and actions.

The important health disparities between Inuit and non-Inuit are forged through time in systems of all kinds that together impact how people live and how they are cared for, what they can afford, and the experiences they, their parents, and grandparents have had. Inuit hear the more or less the same discourses about health from an ever-changing cadre of southern workers. A few stay and make their lives in northern communities, but the vast majority move on after a few years or even less. It is a sad irony that it is often easier to hire someone from southern Quebec for a job in Nunavik than it is to hire an Inuk from another community.[1] In this context of constantly changing outsiders, a near-continuous effort of education is required to bring health practitioners to some minimal understanding of the community and people with whom they now live and serve. The place of culture in shaping and responding to these health inequities is another of those conversations and it is certainly one that predates me and will surely continue long after I am gone.

MEANINGS AND MODELS IN INUIT HEALTH

In cultural understanding, historical records, and in contemporary practice we see health emerging in a series of tensions within the body, between peoples, in teachings and practices of Inuit and biomedical institutions. It is the question of the cultures of health and healing that ultimately underpin this chapter.

A number of Inuit authors and culture experts have made significant contributions to the description of health from the perspective of Inuit knowledge. Taamusi Qumaq the accomplished community leader, Inuktitut language expert, intellectual and advocate for Inuit political autonomy from Puvirnituq, worked with cultural linguist Michèle Therrien who published an insightful and broad-ranging interview with Taamusi (Therrien 1995). In it he describes the distinction between interior and exterior bodily states in the conception of illness by Inuit. Two major categories are identified: Wounds, broken bones, contusions, burns, and skin conditions are generally classed as *anniaq*, a semantic category that organizes around pain with an identifiable source as the common factor of the condition. Internal illness from headache, stomach pain, poor functioning body, bowel problems, unexplained weakness, and mental conditions are considered *qanima* – conditions that afflict the interior. The cause of these is less immediately known and requires consultation with particularly knowledgeable people, in the past with shamans, to determine the origin of the condition and course of action. It is interesting that health centers in the communities today are known are *aanniavik*[2] – the place for pain, and hospitals the place for large pain. There is no "qanimavik." People will go to consult with nurses and doctors for all sources of discomfort and disease, however it is often remarked by non-Inuit health professionals that preventative medicine and longer-term therapies are difficult for people to follow. It is also common to hear qallunaaq health professionals remark that people wait much too long to consult for what should be relatively simple medical problems. Why don't they come sooner? The reasons for this are complex and are found in the way people conceptualize health and also in their relationships with health care systems and providers. It is possible to see here the underlying distinctions between known and unknown, internal, and external, Inuit and qallunaaq coming to play. How people perceive health care providers is also relevant, as is how they believe they are seen by them. What may seem to non-Inuit to be indifference may, in fact, be a respectful attention by Inuit for whom it is culturally normative to not question people who have knowledge and authority.

With the signing of land claims agreements across the Canadian North the place of culture in health care was formalized and a certain leverage taken by Inuit. For example, in Nunavik, Inuit had long been concerned by the familial and social impacts of a policy that saw pregnant women sent to southern hospitals many weeks in advance of their due dates to be closer to hospital and biomedical services. In a strictly biomedical view, it is logical to anticipate and mitigate as much risk as possible from birthing. The social and familial impacts of such policies were not part of the equation and it is in these that Inuit experienced disruption and alienation from the otherwise joyous experience of birth. In the 1980s when a new hospital was planned for the Hudson Bay coast, Inuit women and allies advocated for a birthing center to be included so that once again Inuit may be born into the hands of other Inuit. The Inuulitsivik maternity was created and staffed by Inuit and midwives from the South; it continues to this day as a testament to Inuit capacity to provide culturally and medically safe services (Van Wagner et al. 2012). The growth of the maternity center is a clear example of how the Inuit and biomedical cultures of health and risk are animated by different meanings and significance for Inuit and qallunaaq. In a lived and cultural perspective birth is not a medical act but rather a social one. A new member of the family and community has arrived. In this example, we see how culture is not an abstracted set of rules, norms, and dispositions but rather a set of ways of doing and acting that are fundamental to institution building, administrative capacity building, and indigenization of the health workforce. The question of what place there is for Inuit culture in health care systems is an ongoing discussion that sometimes feels a bit cyclical.

With this preamble about the place of culture in health in mind I turn to some ethnographic examples that reveal a less formalistic and politically charged version of the cultural intersections of health models. These examples illuminate how differing models of health engage people in daily negotiations with each other and across cultures.

Let me begin with a little story. In 2017 the Nunavik Regional Board of Health and Social Services undertook a large-scale population health survey in the region. While certainly not the first population health survey to be undertaken in the Arctic, the Qanuilirpitaa project is remarkable because it was the first to be initiated and fully controlled by an Inuit organization. My role was to co-direct the Community Component of the survey. The Community Component was a new dimension and approach to conducting a northern health survey. My colleague Mylène Riva and I were given the mandate to explore and describe health from a community and cultural perspective, providing research results that were designed to be taken up by communities and Inuit organizations as part of a planned community health mobilization process (Fletcher et al. 2021). Part of our methods involved all too brief visits to the 14 communities of Nunavik with the CCGS Amunsden – a coast guard research vessel – as our living and traveling headquarters. On board was a mixed team of about 30 people, some from the North, many of them from Laval University in Quebec City where the research team is based. As the Amunsden made its way from southern Hudson Bay north to the Hudson Straits and then down to Ungava

Bay we spent from one to three days in each community; people came on board the ship, proceeded through a number of research stations giving blood, doing a spirometry (lung capacity) test, and answering a health questionnaire (see Figure 12.1).

The community component team were some of the only members of the crew who left the ship and went ashore into the communities. It was October which is not an ideal time to be piloting a ship around in the Hudson Street as the weather was tough, but each day we went into the community meet with people in municipal organizations, community leaders, and other interested people to gather a broad understanding of what health means and how it is manifested in the community on a daily basis.

In one community I got off the small barge that moved between the ship and the shore and ran into an acquaintance I hadn't seen a number of years. He asked me what I was doing there. I told him I was working on the health survey and that we were in town for only three days. He was aware of the survey and the reason the coast guard ship was in the bay. He told me he was selected to go on board as part of the recruitment for the survey but had decided not to do so. It is of course his right to not participate, but the reason he chose not to is, itself, an example of how cultural models of health come into play in cross-cultural encounters. There has been a resurgence of tuberculosis in several Inuit communities in the Canadian North and my acquaintance had recently had a number of tests to determine whether he was afflicted by the disease. It was not the research itself that he is hesitant about, rather he said he had had another blood test recently which left him feeling that he didn't really have more to give. In experiencing this form of lassitude, he embodied the Inuit understanding of blood as the vehicle through which the energy of the animal consumed by the human is transmitted. To be well is to have strong blood. Human

Figure 12.1 Hunting canoes and with CMS Amunsden in the distance, Kangirsuk, Nunavik, 2018. Photo: Marie-Claude Lyonnais.

blood enriched by the meat of animals provides plenty of energy to accomplish the tasks that need doing with skill and efficiency.

The blood energy complex has been described by researchers over the years (Borré 1994; Kirmayer et al. 2008), and the example here shows the persistence of the Inuit cultural model of health and its application in decision making in Nunavik. The near absence of any attempt to understand or talk about the quality of blood and energy in the survey tools developed by a large team of researchers, epidemiologists, and public health professionals[3] is a clear indication that cultural modes of experiencing health and illness are difficult to incorporate in an epidemiological survey of the state of health of a population. Perhaps it's good enough to rely on large scale culture-distant measures when we are trying to characterize the health of the population, but given that the promoters of the survey are Inuit themselves, it does make sense that we would want to deepen that understanding and see if the results of our work are ultimately effective in extending Inuit control over health care planning and provision. The simple exchange over going or not going on the ship to do the health survey reveals the social complexity of health and how describing the state of Inuit health is situated in historical relations with the state.

While we did not speak of it, it is likely the case that the arrival of the Amunsden, emblazoned with the color and maple leaf of the Canadian flag, invoked for people in the communities we visited the historical precedent of government ships traveling the North examining the health of Inuit since the 1930s. The CGS Nascopie had been patrolling the eastern Arctic since 1937 bringing mail, police, and medicine. It was replaced by the CD Howe in 1950. Both ships carried out increasingly sophisticated health investigations and in the case of the CD Howe, required people diagnosed with tuberculosis to remain onboard to be treated in southern sanitoria. Some

Figure 12.2 Running track marked out with candles in paper bags. Canadian Cancer Society Relay for Life, Puvirnituq, Nunavik, 2017. Photo: Marie-Claude Lyonnais.

4500 people were ultimately evacuated from the North, and many never returned (Qikitani Inuit Association 2014; Bonesteel and Anderson 2008). The medical evacuations were disruptive to Inuit families and traditional economies, essentially forcing people into dependency in emerging communities. The effects of this era are still felt today, and efforts are finally being made to determine what happened to those who never returned. In 2019, the Canadian government apologized for the racism and discrimination that Inuit faced throughout that era and launched the Nanilavut Initiative to locate the remains of those who died in the South (ITK 2018).

There is no doubt that the lives of Inuit today are profoundly influenced by their own and government responses to diseases particularly since the end of World War II. Epidemic diseases have, at various times, raged across the North leaving behind death and reshaping the lives of survivors, even resulting in the very communities that people live in today. Not all illness episodes however are as fraught with such devastation. As organizers of feeling and meaning of disease, cultural models of health are however significant in all illnesses (see Figure 12.2).

QUMAIT QALLUNANIIT

A second example comes from an experience early in my career. It's cold, it's January, and everyone is itchy. An infestation of scabies (*Sarcoptes scabiei*) has been making itself felt in the community for a couple of weeks. The parasite has made its way into almost every household and a community-wide public health intervention is required to eradicate it. By chance, the medical doctor in the community is an old friend and I've been staying with him and his family since arriving in the town. An outstanding communicator and devoted community-engaged physician, he has been working with regional health authorities, local community health workers, nurses, community leadership, and the mayor's office on a strategy to end this infestation of an innocuous yet irritating skin parasite.

To understand the complexity of this task it is important to know something about how municipal services are delivered in Arctic communities. While running water is essentially ubiquitous in the eastern Arctic communities, the water is supplied by truck and is stored in reservoir in a warm spot inside each building. Likewise, wastewater is kept in a reservoir that is regularly pumped out by a sanitation truck. The cold climate and permafrost make water delivery by pipe impractical and where it has been tried it is often very expensive and difficult to maintain. To deal with scabies the entire community needs to coordinate not only all members of the household, but the washing of all the clothing and bedding that people use. Keep in mind also that the number of people per household is generally higher in northern communities than it is in typical southern Canadian households. The quality and quantity of housing is an extremely important determinant of health. In the case of scabies, it's likely that the proximity of people in relatively small spaces contributes to the extent of the outbreak. The parasite is very opportunistic and has by this point infected pretty much everybody in the community regardless of the number of people in the household. To wash everyone and everything at the same time, water needs to be delivered and the waste taken away in a coordinated fashion for every single household in the town over a brief period of time, in this case about 24 hours. This requires the coordination of human and community resources with a medical intervention.

The doctor, along with the community health worker and people working at the health center in the town called a public meeting in the evening before the effort is to begin. The meeting is well attended primarily by women and girls who are normally in charge of the household and children. The presentation begins with a bit of a preamble by a community health worker and then it falls to my friend to describe the treatment. He is a bit of a natural ham and makes good light of how thoroughly one needs to wash their body with the prescribed cream in order to take care of the infection. The humor he brings to the public meeting is welcome and it seems to take some of the tension out of the room. An extra wrinkle in the treatment process is that the best cream for treating scabies is not recommended for pregnant women. There is an alternative but less effective cream available. In order to determine who is pregnant, women talk privately to the nursing staff and in cases where it's not certain whether or not they are pregnant, they take a pregnancy test. The pregnancy test lends a whole other dimension to the scabies outbreak adding complexity and perhaps anxiety to the process. To recap, there are two different possible creams depending on pregnancy that need to be applied to everyone in every household at roughly the same time. Then everybody needs to bathe and all the clothing washed and dried in a household where the water tank holds 250 gallons and is quickly depleted.

This complex set of events is not an insurmountable task and everyone seems to be getting along with it. At the end of the presentation on the treatment process people are given a chance to ask questions. The first of which was something I had not anticipated. A mother in her 20s raises her hand and asks quietly whether scabies is a fatal disease. The room is hushed and I feel a wave of sadness runs through the room. In her very reasonable question, we see how despite the very good practice of the physician and the excellent engagement of the nursing station staff and community health worker the presentation is situated by people in the community within a history of interaction between the health care system medical authority that is much more serious and complex than a simple scabies outbreak. In the history of Inuit communities, the most significant medical attention has been focussed on epidemic disease and this has certainly been the case in the community we are in. At various times tuberculosis, measles, smallpox, and influenza have impacted the communities in the North leaving considerable death, suffering, and social disruption in their wake. The pattern continues and the 2010 H1N1 outbreak had a much greater impact on Inuit and First Nations peoples than on the majority population (Helferty et al. 2010). As I write this, we are in the midst of the COVID-19 pandemic and the North is under unique and strict quarantine conditions including restrictions on movement between communities and between the North and South. The public health response to tuberculosis in particular was the impetus for the creation of many of the communities that exist today in the North. The provision of permanent fixed housing was a major response of the government to tuberculosis and in settling people and communities they, perhaps, effectively treated most cases. They did, however, create new conditions for disease and social suffering. While scabies is not a terribly worrying health condition, the way that it is dealt with is quite similar to these other more serious conditions and certainly in line with the history of medical intervention in the North. The woman was reassured that no this is not a fatal condition, it's really just an irritant, and it's one that can be dealt with relatively easily and with few consequences. The woman's question should not be seen as coming from a lack of knowledge, but rather as perfectly reasonable given the history of epidemic disease in the North. Moreover, the community resources mobilized to respond to the outbreak were, by necessity, substantial lending seriousness to the condition.

But the issue wasn't finished. The next question in the form of an extended monologue came from one of the few Elder men in the room. The man stood up and, as is normal, the room fell silent; people listening respectfully. He spoke in Inuktitut and the translation was forthcoming in fits and starts whenever he stopped to take a pause. He asked rhetorically but also seriously how it is that white people manage to bring so many different diseases with them to the North? How is it that this *qumait qallunaniit* – lice that live with qallunnaat – has come to bother Inuit in their daily lives? As with the question from the young woman before him, this man's discourse was one of historical depth and collective awareness of the history of disease and suffering that followed the contact between Inuit and outsiders. Clearly given his age this man had witnessed the suffering and deaths of people afflicted by epidemic diseases.

We were reminded by his passionate discussion of how different Inuit and qallunaat understandings of the health care system may be. For health care workers, governments and Eurocanadians generally, health care is socially constructed as a kind of gift from the state to those in need; while for Inuit it may be received as a necessity arising from the impacts colonization and globalization. He was not finished with his critique of the cleanliness of white people and went on to describe and perhaps critique the very treatment that was being offered in the gymnasium this evening. He said that Inuit know parasites well and have always had them in their hair and that they already have always had ways of dealing with these *qumait*. He described two kinds of lice that were common when people lived in igloos one a "good" kind and the other "bad." People would selectively physically remove the bad ones leaving the good ones. The different *qumait* were identifiable by their color. The good have the effect of cleaning the blood of the person they inhabited and should be maintained.

It's tempting to read a lot into the statement, and it appears to me to have been offered in part as a critique of the presumed superiority of medical treatments provided by southern health institutions in the North. For some conditions at least the traditional practices are already adequate, such as dealing with normal conditions like skin parasites. Presumably only trained entomologists in southern Canada would be able to identify different species of headlice and yet in the North this kind of information is a salient part of a local diagnostic and preventative health tradition, a clear demonstration of the depth of Inuit health knowledge. As this example shows, there is a historically and culturally informed way of understanding all afflictions. Further, there are very real everyday implications of these ways of knowing that can influence biomedical treatment, community uptake of an intervention, and ultimately the degree of health achieved. Whether there is in some abstract and absolute right or wrong way is of no consequence. What matters is that people are engaged in knowledgeable and respectful ways in the pursuit of health and healing.

HOW TO TREAT A DROWNING VICTIM

My attention is drawn to a post on "Your Voice on Nunavik," a popular public forum on Facebook, by a young man who is a first responder trained in techniques sanctioned by national first-aid organizations. With evident distress in his words, he says he is confused by the statements a well-respected Elder has just made on the regional community radio about how according to Inuit medical practice victims of drowning should be treated. The Elder's prescriptions are not only different from what he has learned in his work, they contradict his professional training entirely. He would not be able to stand by and observe the victim, as the Elder prescribed. If he was in a situation where he came across a drowning victim, he would follow his training and intervene. The posting is brief but evokes a range of responses that give insight on how models of health intersect in everyday life.

It is no small thing to disagree publicly with an Elder, social norms favor silence in the face of discord, particularly between generations, and it is from here that the tension comes. In expressing his confusion, he is engaging in a broader discussion occurring across Inuit Nunangat on the role of traditional knowledge and practice in contemporary society. (Laugrand and Oosten 2009; Karetak et al. 2017). The comments are numerous and pick up on his anxiety over the different treatment methods. Most people write to defend the traditional treatment as appropriate to the way Inuit live; *Do not question what has been offered* by the Elder, they implore. Several reinforce the Elder's knowledge, a couple going so far as to relate how this man's direct intervention and knowledge saved their own lives. Another commenter talks about how the Elder's treatments prevented the loss of his hands and feet to frostbite. Others relate drownings they have witnessed where the victim came back to life after appropriate care according to Inuit ways. A couple ridicule the poster for believing in the southern ways he has been taught. The subtext centers around the complex cultural politics of learning the "right" and white way to do things when they conflict with Inuit ways. The hegemony of biomedical practice is wrapped up in the internalization of colonial thinking is being driven through his "southern" training.

This debate on social media is another powerful example of how Inuit ways of health and healing are confronted by biomedical practice. That this debate happens exclusively among Inuit in both English and Inuktitut is also telling. The story of drowning is an interesting case where Inuit and biomedical methods conflict and draws our attention to the varying paths that health knowledge and models take into the daily lives of people in Nunavik. To put this in a broader ethnographic perspective, being a first responder is a prestigious and serious job with some cachet in northern communities. Primarily made up of young men, the responder role was created in the early 2000s to provide an initial level of care that would take some pressure off the staff in the small nursing stations in most of the communities. The program is financed by the Inuit-run regional health and social services board which is a public institution with authority over health care delivery. The first responders have nice equipment including snowmobiles, new ambulances, four-wheel all-terrain vehicles, and a specially designed sled to bring injured people in from the land. They are given a tailored training program by first responders based in southern Quebec and are part of a group of firefighters and search and rescue teams in each community. The nature of responding to rescues in northern communities requires them to also be competent navigators on the land and waters that surround the communities. These are skills that are part of the broader set of Inuit knowledge and for the most part the first responder role is seen as complementary rather than conflictual with Inuit practice. Responding to drowning draws on both Inuit and southern skills.

As in the past, drowning is relatively common today. In Nunavik, death by accidents and injuries occur at about 3.5 times the provincial average in Quebec (Duhaime et al. 2015, 39) and a significant portion of these are drownings. In part these are the kinds of accidents that occur when people are heavy users of a large and difficult landscape. In a cultural sense, drownings, while sad and regrettable, are a normal kind of accident and have always been part of a life that requires traveling on the land and water. Consequently, many more people in Nunavik have direct experience with drownings and their treatment than in the South.

As a form of accidental death, drowning is a serious and complex biological and cultural phenomenon. As the posts on Facebook describe, the status of drowning victims is in many cases not clear – are they dead or are they alive? It is often difficult to know. Drowning transcends the normal categories of life and death which are in most circumstances self-evident. I was involved in a project that ultimately resulted in a book published by Avataq Cultural Institute (Fletcher 2012) documenting Inuit first-aid treatments including drowning. During the research for this project people spoke about how those who have been submerged for long periods of time are hovering between two states, they have stopped breathing, may be in cardiac arrest, yet despite outward appearances they are alive and may survive. Thus, with drowning victims there is an extended ambiguous or liminal phase between life and death. It is in such fraught periods that we would expect cultural models to provide direction and solace. It is important to keep in mind that given the climate and terrain, effectively all northern drowning episodes take place in cold water and survivability is quite good under these conditions according to the people with direct experience of drowning. In mainstream medical practice there is growing awareness of the physiology of cold drowning an adage in emergency medicine is that the drowning victim is not dead until they are "warm and dead" (c.f. Copass et al. 2003).

While biomedical and Inuit nosologies recognize a prolonged period of near-death is possible and difficult to determine, the treatments prescribed in each medical tradition are quite different. The Inuit knowledge of drowning differentiates several types based on the particular ecological setting of the accident. There are differences in fresh water and saltwater drowning conditions as well as between moving versus standing water. River drownings are often complicated by contusions, head trauma, and fractures from the body being rolled downstream. Additionally, freshwater drowning victims tend to have inhaled more plant material than those who are submerged in seawater. People I worked with reported that it is possible to survive up to 24 hours of disappearance in the water, although it is not clear how much of this is spent actually submerged. Cases where someone recovered from up to nine hours underwater have been witnessed and I have heard similar stories from different communities in other contexts in the years since this research was undertaken. For example, remarkably similar observations were made by Inuit in Nunavut (Therrien and Laugrand 2001). All of this I take to indicate that there is an empirically verified basis to Inuit observations on drowning as well as in many other domains, and this knowledge base is widespread.

The western medical standard of cardio-pulmonary resuscitation (CPR) is a relatively recent phenomenon that only developed in the 1970s through the US army experience in Vietnam. The American Red Cross subsequently introduced training for the technique into its public education campaigns and it has since become an iconic life-saving technique of popular and medical culture. The CPR technique can be generalized as aggressive re-inflation of liquid-filled lungs accompanied by stimulation of the heart muscle and lungs through external compression of the chest. In all cases, biomedical treatment of near drowning is surrounded by the need for urgent care.

In contrast to the biomedical approach, the Inuit treatment of drowning victims focuses on a calm and gentle approach; the victim must be gently removed from the water and placed face down on a gradual slope or over a rock with the head lower than the rest of the body. Gravity will drain the water from the lungs and vomiting may occur just prior to breath returning. No warming or other physical intervention is required although a blanket may be used to protect the body in cold weather. Most importantly, people remarked that the froth that often comes out of the mouth of people who have drowned must not be touched, even if it is voluminous. This is a major point of contention for Inuit in their view of western medicine and one that speaks to particularly deeply held understandings of what constitutes existence.

In Inuit cosmology the *anirniq* or life-breath is one of three essences of a human being. *Anirniq* is a form of consciousness, an eternal soul/being that can in some instances like drowning become disengaged from the body it inhabits. The sometimes-copious foam exuded by drowning victims is a physical manifestation of the life-breath on the verge of departing the body and hence evidence of pending death. People are neither dead nor alive but somewhere in between as the life-breath that is normally inside has exited the body yet takes a visible form as foam and remains in contact with the person. Consequently, physically removing the foam is akin to removing the life-breath and hastening the person's death. It is this cultural logic that informs the behaviors required of people around a drowning victim. There should be little noise and no physical exertion around the body as the *anirniq* may "decide" to depart. The person who finds the drowning victim should be the only one to handle the body, getting it into proper positioning, and speaking gently with the victim if they regain consciousness. It is presumed that the person who finds a drowning victim will have no malice towards them – they could just leave the person in the water if they did – and will best be able to encourage the life-breath to return to the body. In several reports I have collected, Inuit reported watching qallunaat medical and first aid personnel removing the foam from the face in the process of delivering CPR to a drowning victim thus unnecessarily determining the fate of the drowning victim. Like in the young man's post in these accounts we see a sense of cultural dissonance at play in the relations between Inuit and qallunaat around the treatment of drowning. There is respect and gratitude for the services and skills that biomedicine has brought to the North, but there are times when the unexplored subtle cultural constructions of health, life, and death they carry are brought into focus bringing discomfort and contestation.

Lest I give the impression that Inuit practice is somehow cultural and biomedical practice scientific or correct, it is worth considering the physiology of cold-water drowning. As I have followed this issue over the years since the initial project, I have watched the biomedical practice develop situational nuances and ecologically adapted understandings and responses to drowning. In short, it is increasingly recognized that cold-water drowning poses unique conditions that require a specialized treatment. Victims of drowning are protected to some extent by the bodily response;

the "diving reflex" is a physiological reaction to submersion that stops breathing, slows the heart, and restricts blood circulation in the extremities. The effect of these reactions is to preserve and reduce the consumption of oxygen by the body while protecting the brain and vital organs. The response is particularly accentuated in cold water where a ten-degree reduction of temperature can double the amount of time the brain can survive (Szpilman et al. 2012: 2107). The Inuit observation that people can survive much longer periods of time than generally recognized in biomedical practice seems to be at least in part confirmed by new scientifically grounded understandings of drowning physiology. Additionally, it is now recognized that there is a high risk of circulatory collapse when drowning victims are removed from cold water. The coldwater effect coupled with the surrounding water pressure has the effect of increasing circulatory pressure which is suddenly released when the body is removed from the water (Harries 2003). This is the second instance where the Inuit technique of slow and gentle withdrawal of the body would be protective.

In this example there is the possibility that Inuit treatment methods for drowning are more appropriate to the particular ecology of injury than biomedical standards. The collective experience people in the North have with this form of accident and the ecological contexts in which it takes place are shared knowledge of considerable depth. Whether one ignores the possibility of circulatory collapse or the danger of removing the edema, survivability of drowning may be decreased. At the very least this example shows that cultural practice that differs in its explanatory content from biomedical rationality is not necessarily inefficacious. More to the point, Inuit medical practice is based on many generations of observational and direct experience in the northern environment. The lesson I take from the drowning example is that cultural models of health and healing are underpinned by real-world experience and should not be relegated to a folkloric or culturalist perspective.

CONCLUSION

The place of Inuit culture in the provision of health care in the Canadian North has been a complex facet of the relations between Inuit and qallunaat. In many instances in the historical record, culture appears as a problem that limits the effectiveness of treatment, patient "compliance" with medical instructions, and comprehension in general. For many practitioners, culture (and to a similar extent language) have been presented as black boxes that defeat good clinical practice and health promotion programs oriented to the population at large. Culture is mystifying, obscure, and beyond the grasp of most. The colonial project of the North was always about bringing culture to heel in the face of the state and its representatives. Fixing individuals in new socio-spatial and economic configurations that were at once about fostering health, defeating pandemic disease (especially tuberculosis), and making Inuit citizens of equal stature if not opportunity. Conversely, culture is also seen as the source of health well-being, and meaning for Inuit. It is common to hear from Inuit and non-Inuit alike that access to the land, traditional foods, camping, hunting, and being together away from the community is healthful and healing. Such configurations of health link time on the land with positive experiences of autonomy, self-sufficiency, and strong positive affective relations with kin. Of course, neither is necessarily wholly right or wrong; different ways of experiencing, understanding, and doing are difficult to comprehend and impact on how people do what they do and what they make of it. Culture is a powerful motivator for positive action, but it is not a panacea for all illnesses, individual and collective affliction, in a globally connected world where, for example, globally transported environmental contaminants are present in high quantities in northern food species. The capacity and authority to infuse all healing actions, whatever their origins, with cultural significance is a path toward health and well-being.

NOTES

1. In part this is because of the way housing is allocated. Inuit land claim beneficiaries and southern workers access different housing pools and there are very few private houses in Nunavik. Housing and jobs are intricately linked.
2. *aaniaq* – pain – *vik* dwelling of.
3. The survey tool is not entirely culture blind to Inuit practice. For example, among other sections, there are questions about food "cravings," which are culturally modulated and focused on specific preparations of northern foods.

REFERENCES

Bonesteel, Sarah and Eric Anderson. 2008. *Canada's Relationship with Inuit: A History of Policy and Program Development*. Ottawa, ON: Indian and Northern Affairs Canada. Retrieved from https://www.aadnc-aandc.gc.ca/DAM/DAM-INTER-HQ/STAGING/texte-text/inuit-book_1100100016901_eng.pdf.

Borré, Kristen. 1994. "The Healing Power of the Seal: The Meaning of Inuit Health Practice and Belief." *Arctic Anthropology* 31 (1): 1–15.

Cameron, Emilie. 2011. *State of the Knowledge: Inuit Public Health, 2011*. Vancouver, BC: National Collaborating Centre for Aboriginal Health. Retrieved from https://www.nccih.ca/docs/context/RPT-InuitPublicHealth-Cameron-EN.pdf

Copass, M., L. Gonzales, M. Eisenberg, and R. Soper. 2003. *EMT Manual 3rd edition*. Philadelphia, PA: W.B. Saunders.

Duhaime, Gérard, Sébastien Lévesque, and Andrée Caron. 2015. *Nunavik in figures 2015–full version*. Québec: Canada Research Chair on Comparative Aboriginal Condition, Université Laval, 133. Retrieved from https://www.nunivaat.org/doc/publication/Nunavik-in-Figures-2015-Full-Version-2016.pdf

Fletcher, Christopher. 2012. *Inuit Piusituqaqtigut Uimanarsijunik Aanniasiurusingit/Premier Soins Traditionnels Inuits/Traditional Inuit First-Aid*. Montreal, QC: Avataq Cultural Institute.

Fletcher, Christopher M. and Lawrence J. Kirmayer. 1997. "Spirit Work: Nunavimmiut Experiences of Healing and Affliction." *Études/Inuit Studies*, 21 (1–2): 189–208.

Fletcher, C., M. Riva, M.-C. Lyonnais, I. Saunders, A. Baron, M. Lynch and M. Baron. 2021. *Definition of an Inuit cultural model and social determinants of health for Nunavik. Community Component*. Nunavik Inuit Health Survey 2017 Qanuilirpitaa? How are we now? Quebec: Nunavik Regional Board of Health and Social Services (NRBHSS) & Institut national de santé publique du Québec (INSPQ).

Harries, Mark. 2003. "Near Drowning." *BMJ:British Medical Journal*, 327: 1336–1338. doi: 10.1136/bmj.327.7427.1336

Helferty, Melissa, Julie Vachon, Jill Tarasuk, Racel Rodin, John Spika, and L. Louise Pelletier. 2010. "Incidence of Hospital Admissions and Severe Outcomes During the First and Second Waves of Pandemic (H1N1) 2009." *CMAJ : Canadian Medical Association journal*

= Journal de l'Association médicale canadienne, 182 (18): 1981–1987. doi: 10.1503/cmaj.100746

ITK (Inuit Tapiriit Kanatami). 2014. *Social Determinants of Inuit Health in Canada*. Ottawa, ON: ITK. Retrieved from https://www.itk.ca/wp-content/uploads/2016/07/ITK_Social_Determinants_Report.pdf

———. 2018. Nanilavut [Press release] March 8, 2018. Retrieved from https://www.itk.ca/nanilavut/

Karetak, J., F. J. Tester, and S. Tagalik. 2017. *Inuit Qaujimajatuqangit: What Inuit have Always Known to be True*: Fernwood Publishing.

Kirmayer, Lawrence J., Christopher Fletcher, and R. Robert Watt. 2008. "Locating the Ecocentric Self: Inuit Concepts of Mental Health and Illness." In *Healing Traditions: The Mental Health of Aboriginal Peoples in Canada*, edited by Lawrence Kirmayer and Gail Valaskakis, 289–314, Vancouver, BC: UBC Press.

Laugrand, F., and J. Oosten. 2009. "Transfer of Inuit qaujimajatuqangit in modern Inuit society." *Etudes/Inuit/Studies*, 33 (1–2), 115–152.

Muckle, Gina, Olivier Boucher, Dominque Laflamme, Serge Chevalier, and Louis Rochette. 2007. *Nunavik Inuit Health Survey 2004: Alcohol, Drug Use and Gambling among the Inuit of Nunavik: Epidemiological Profile*. Québec: Institut national de santé publique du Québec & Régie régionale de la santé et des services sociaux de Nunavik. Retrieved from https://www.inspq.qc.ca/node/2580

Qikiqtani Inuit Association. 2014. *Qikiqtani Truth Commission: Thematic Reports and Special Studies 1950–1975*. Retrieved from https://www.qtcommission.ca/sites/default/files/public/thematic_reports/thematic_reports_english_aaniajurlirniq.pdf

Szpilman, D., J. J. Bierens, A. J. Handley, and J. P. Orlowski. 2012. "Drowning." *New England Journal of Medicine*, 366 (22), 2102–2110.

Therrien, Michèle. 1995. Corps sain, corps malade chez les Inuit, une tension entre l'intérieur et l'extérieur. Entretiens avec Taamusi Qumaq. *Recherches Amérindiennes au Québec*, 25(1): 71–84.

Therrien, Michèle and Frédéric Laugrand, editors. 2001. *Interviewing Inuit Elders: Perspectives on Traditional Health*. Iqaluit, NT: Nunavut Arctic College.

Tjepkema, Michael, Tracey Bushnik, and Evelyne Bougie. 2019. Life Expectancy of First Nations, Métis and Inuit Household Populations in Canada. *Health Reports*, 30 (12): 3–10. doi: 10.25318/82-003-x201901200001-eng

Van Wagner, V., Osepchook, C., Harney, E., Crosbie, C., and Tulugak, M. 2012. Remote midwifery in Nunavik, Quebec, Canada: outcomes of perinatal care for the Inuulitsivik health centre, 2000–2007. *Birth*, 39 (3), 230–237.

Wallace, Susan. 2014. *Inuit Health: Selected Findings from the 2012 Aboriginal Peoples Survey*. Statistics Canada. Retrieved from http://www.statcan.gc.ca/pub/89-653-x/89-653-x2014003-eng.pdf

PART III
INTIMATE AND EVERYDAY WORLDS

CHAPTER 13

"REAL NORTHERN MEN"
Performing masculinity and culture in Ulukhaktok, Canada

Peter Collings

INTRODUCTION

In June of 1993, I went on a hunting trip with Charlie Hanayi (a pseudonym). I had been in Ulukhaktok for nearly a year, working with my mentor, Rick Condon, to follow a sample of (then) young men, documenting their economic activities over the course of a year. One of the goals of the research was to identify the strategies these young men pursued as they negotiated an economic, social, and political environment that was quite different from the one their parents faced at the same age.

Charlie was one of our study participants, but we had become friends over the course of the year and hunted together fairly often. We'd left Ulukhaktok in the late evening, heading northwest on our four-wheeled ATVs, paralleling the coast. The temperature, around six degrees Celsius, was warm for the time of year, and the recent snowmelt left the trail very muddy. We were looking for musk ox, seeking a small herd that other hunters had spotted a few days before. We eventually found the animals, and Charlie shot a medium-sized male. After some difficulty driving the remaining musk ox away from the carcass, we set down to butcher the animal.

After nearly a year in Ulukhaktok, and multiple musk ox hunts, I had a pretty good idea about how butchering a musk ox should go. I knew at least enough that I no longer required constant supervision. So, when I realized that Charlie had stopped and was watching me work, I was a little self-conscious. I finally looked up after a few minutes, expecting a gentle critique, but he gave me his approval instead. "You're turning into a real Northern Man."

"What is a real Northern Man?" When I finally asked Charlie what he meant, he laughed, but he soon became thoughtful. "A Northern Man means you have to do two things. If you come to live in the North and you want to be a real man, you have to go out hunting. Then, you can't be lazy."

Charlie's observation hit on the very thing that Rick and I were so interested in investigating. How did men of Charlie's cohort, the first generation born and raised in a permanent settlement, manage to become "Real Northern Men" in an era when it was increasingly difficult to engage in the activities that had denoted manhood for the earlier generations? Hunting, fishing, and trapping, collectively part of what northern researchers label *subsistence*, was an expensive endeavor for young men, who often lacked not only cash for equipment and supplies but also knowledge and experience to become proficient food producers. Schooling and other aspects of settlement life also make it difficult for young Inuit to acquire hunting skills. These realities have made it even more challenging for the next generation to become hunters than it was for men of Charlie's cohort.

Charlie's observation about what it takes to be a Real Northern Man also addresses the heart of Inuit masculinity. In Arctic research, the problem of masculinity has been relatively straightforward. Most research understands masculinity as encompassing what men do. Inuit men hunt and fish. Arctic researchers have implicitly regarded masculinity as an economic domain, frequently measured in kilometers traveled and kilograms of meat produced. This understanding has historical roots in the theoretical underpinnings of scholarship about Inuit and other hunter-gatherer societies. We have, however, very little understanding of what masculinity means for Inuit, especially for younger men. These men face significant hurdles as they come of age and define themselves in the context of permanently settled communities where wage employment opportunities are limited and the costs of living are extraordinarily high.

This chapter addresses some of the ways that Inuit, especially younger Inuit, have understood and defined masculinity as something beyond the material production of food. Underneath the importance of masculinity being what men *do*, the prevailing theme of manhood revolves more broadly around productivity, which includes activities that emphasize social and cultural production. Younger men – those currently in their twenties – face numerous difficulties in becoming recognized as men. They are keenly aware of the expectations laid upon them by their elders, and their choices are driven both by necessity and by their need for validation.

After reviewing how men have been understood in Arctic research, I will turn to two examples that demonstrate the paths men pursue to become Real Northern Men. Their activities balance cultural, social, and financial capital in different ways to send messages to themselves, other men, and other community members about their intentions to be understood and accepted as Inuit men. Some of these activities remain thoroughly rooted in subsistence, while others, such as drum dancing, appear on the surface to be primarily expressive but are nevertheless equally productive.

MASCULINITY AND ARCTIC RESEARCH

Charlie's assertion that Real Northern Men hunt and fish reflects perhaps the historically predominant research interest in northern communities. Hunting, trapping, and fishing have long held the attention of outsiders, who have been drawn to the study of arctic foragers by Inuit's ability to survive and thrive in one of the planet's most challenging environments. A theory-driven interest in subsistence draws from traditions in cultural ecology, human behavioral ecology, and economic anthropology (some examples include Collings 2009; Damas 1969; Harder and Wenzel 2012; Kemp 1971; Natcher 2009; Ready 2016; 2019; Smith 1991). Subsistence research implicitly understands masculinity primarily as what men do, a conceptualization that also appears in more practical, applied research. Hunting and fishing remain important in northern settlements, where the cost of living is high. Documenting and assessing the contribution of subsistence hunting in these communities has also generated significant research attention related to wildlife management or to economic planning and development (see, for example, Burch 1985; Fall 1990; Lonner 1980; Magdanz, Utermohle and Wolfe 2002; Müller-Wille 1978; Wheeler and Thornton 2005).

Beyond research, of course, subsistence is clearly important to Inuit. Subsistence is a primary driver of Inuit identity, and Inuit across the Arctic depend on wild foods as an important component of their diets. The pervasive research focus on men's activities in subsistence has, however, almost certainly influenced how Inuit themselves define and understand masculinity. From the perspective of theory-driven subsistence research, researchers required a particular kind of study participant: the "expert" hunter. These were older men who came of age during the contact-traditional era (Helm and Damas 1963), who remained highly active hunters partly because their health and financial circumstances permitted it, and who were comfortable working with outsiders. These traits garnered the attention and resources of outside academics seeking either to reconstruct traditional lifeways or to answer questions about the adoption of imported technologies such as snowmobiles.

In the context of rapidly changing economic, political, and ecological climates, the significant focus on subsistence over the past half-century and more has meant that researchers and other outsiders have reinforced the idea that hunting and other land-based activities implicitly define men. The most appropriate pathway to manhood is predicated upon hunting and fishing, preferably full-time, despite the fact that Inuit hunters have for decades depended on family members' wage work to support their activities. Condon and I confronted the "masculinity equals hunting" problem almost immediately in our 1992–1993 research. We suspected that some of the men in our sample increased their hunting and trapping precisely because we were paying attention to those activities. Others in our sample deliberately exaggerated their knowledge of hunting, especially for me, the newcomer. The hyperbole about hunting only eased up when they realized I was onto them.

This body of inquiry likewise examined financial capital as the principal mechanism for understanding gender more broadly, concluding that the relative positions of Inuit men and women were complementary and interdependent (see, for example, Bodenhorn 1990; Briggs 1974; Guemple 1986; 1995). For academics, men and women were defined primarily, though not completely, by their economic roles and activities. Other research (Condon and Stern 1993; Fogel-Chance 1993; Jolles 1997; McElroy 1975; 1978) expanded on these ideas by investigating how changes in the North had consequences for how Inuit understood and constructed gender roles.

More recent work addressing women has gone beyond the gender-as-economics approach by examining the meaning and experience of womanhood in contemporary contexts. Bilsson, Mancini, and others (Bilsson 2006; Bilsson and Mancini 2007; Wachowich 1999; Dowsley 2014), for example, have all addressed the complexities of women's lives as they negotiate changing relationships with the land, their communities, and their families. Noteworthy, however, is that while women's lives and experiences have received increased attention, very little research attends to Inuit masculinity in the same way.

The domain of gender, and specifically masculinity, that addresses men's and women's lives beyond economic and social roles is frequently embedded in examinations of social and cultural identity. These works address the development and maintenance of Inuit identities in changing social environments and include research on Inuit adolescence (Condon 1987; O'Neil 1983), identity construction in relation to self-governance (Dybbroe 1996), and, of course, the links between identity and subsistence (Condon, Collings and Wenzel 1995; Rasing 1999; Searles 2002). Other research addresses identity as a form of personhood, paying attention to concepts of proper behavior and the interconnections between members of the community. These works examine concepts such as the Inuit ideal of the genuine person, or *inummarik* (Brody 1975; Collings 2014), links with the environment (Fienup-Riordan 1986; Stairs 1992; Stairs and Wenzel 1992), and identity construction in changing circumstances (Dorais and Searles 2001; Searles 2001).

The research trajectories briefly identified here reflect both trends in research related to gender and preconceptions about how researchers have understood men and women. Specific to Inuit masculinity, outsiders have understood it primarily as an economic domain, ignoring what it means to be Inuit and male. The approach of most research addressing Inuit manhood specifically examines what Gutmann (1997) outlines as the ideals and practices that make men *men*. In the example that opened this chapter, Charlie references some of the core concepts of what makes a "Real Northern Man." In the background of research on Inuit masculinity is an approach that asks how men are socially male – what are the roles that men must assume in society to be understood and viewed as men? What is less prevalent in this research is attention to performativity. What are the kinds of things men do to display their masculinity to others?

Briggs (1997) suggests one avenue of inquiry by focusing on the activities that Inuit recognize as emblematic of Inuit manhood. Hunting and fishing as emblems of both Inuitness and manhood are immediately apparent, but others may be less obvious to outsiders. Furthermore, while hunting resonates with both Inuit and non-Inuit as a masculine domain, activities such as drum dancing may serve as emblems of Inuit identity and manhood in opposition to qallunaat (white people) expectations of masculinity. Graburn (2006) likewise observes that activities like drum dancing are part of a larger process of cultural recovery. Although activities like drum dancing may provide some financial capital for the participants, their value lies primarily in social and cultural production. One learns the songs and dances via observation, interaction, and practice, further emphasizing and reinforcing the Inuitness of the activity to the participants while providing a public space, as Inuit might phrase it, to "participate in their culture."

In the remainder of the chapter, I focus on the core problems of asserting masculinity for younger men in Ulukhaktok, a settlement of about 400 Inuit in the Northwest Territories. I have been conducting research in the community since that first year of fieldwork in 1992–1993, focusing on both subsistence and on the life course and human development. The two domains are, unsurprisingly, intertwined, and the following addresses how each – subsistence and productivity, on the one hand, and the younger Inuit's struggle to conform to cultural models of human development, on the other – appears as both activity and performance. The examples I employ here derive from fieldwork conducted since 2014 exploring Inuit concepts of stress, well-being, and coping. These interviews have identified the stressors young men experience and provide insights into how these young men construct their identities as men. The interview narratives that follow have been lightly edited for clarity.

HUNTING AS MASCULINE PERFORMANCE

One afternoon in July 2018 – sunny and warm, with a slight breeze that kept the bugs away – I'd gone with a few friends to fish at one of the local lakes, Kunuk's Lake, perhaps a two-kilometer walk from town, and happily out of sight of the settlement. Nestled under cliffs, there is little ATV traffic in this direction, so it tends to be quiet. Since it was somewhat out of the way, my companions and I were a little surprised to see Stephen coming from the other direction, walking with a packsack and a fishing rod. There is something about being "on the land," even only a kilometer or two from town, that enhances sociality and friendliness. My interactions with Stephen in town, if I saw him at all, would normally be limited to a curt "hello" and nod. Out here, though, he stopped, chatted, and fished with us for a while. Stephen had already been out for much of the day fishing at Upstairs Lake, perhaps another two kilometers further east and, as the name implied, further up into the land. Stephen already had enough fish for himself, so he spent much of his time chatting with us.

I've known Stephen since he was small. His father was a participant in the 1992–1993 study. Stephen's father died when Stephen was very young, and his mother had long since moved to another community. Stephen had been back in Ulukhaktok for about five years, deciding to settle there because of the presence of a large extended family. Even so, as a 20-something male, he was having difficulty even finding a place to live. The public housing the government provides to Inuit residents was oversubscribed, and the waiting list was long. Being single and male, he had low priority for a house. Consequently, he was living in a self-built cabin behind his grandmother's residence. As with most cabins, it was constructed of recycled material – dimensional lumber and plywood repurposed from other projects, a recycled window providing light, and insulation scavenged from multiple sources. He heated his cabin through a combination of a Coleman stove and a portable electric heater, the power provided by an extension cord from his grandmother's house.

Our meeting at Kunuk's Lake was fortuitous, as it provided Stephen with some courage to come by my house and ask to be interviewed. He knew that I and Tim Murray (a graduate researcher) were conducting interviews, but only after our paths crossed while fishing did he come for a visit. Stephen was acutely aware of the problems young men faced in Ulukhaktok. With no father and a nonresident mother, he was especially dependent on collateral relationships. He had no hunting equipment save for a fishing rod and his lures, so his ability to produce country food was limited to walking out of town to fish. Which he did often, ranging as far as 15 kilometers in a day if the weather permitted.

One of the biggest problems that young men experience was, he felt, a lack of assistance from older men, whom he perceived as judgmental. He admitted that, like most men and women his age, his Inuinnaqtun fluency was minimal, but he knew enough to recognize when older men were making fun at him as he walked down the street:

PC: So what are the biggest stressors that people in town experience? What are the things that stress them out?
SK: Well, there's other families where the older generation picks on the younger generation, like teases them. Like about their old lifestyle, like their past.
PC: So that would be like people that would be your mum's age?

SK: Yeah. Like, just because we don't speak Inuinnaqtun doesn't mean that we can't understand what they're saying sometimes, you know? I even heard a couple of Elders talking around about me, thinking I didn't know what they were saying, but I heard them call me a "fucking dog."

PC: Gee whiz. Did you let them know that you knew what they were saying?

SK: [Smiling and laughing] I think they might have knew 'cause they quit and burst out laughing and then took off.

PC: Does that happen a lot?

SK: Um, it probably does for other people. But I don't really hang around Elders anymore. I mean, I fish for my *nanaq* [grandmother]. I tried to bring her a fish the other day and she said she just got some, so I just cooked that one up.

PC: Was she happy that you brought it by anyway?

SK: Yeah, yeah. She just said, as soon as I walked up to her, to her picnic area, I just caught the fish from King's Bay. I walked up and she's like "I just got a couple, and maybe someone else would want it, or make *piffi* [dry fish] or something." So I just made a *piffi* and cut a good three-plate fillet and cooked that up.

Stephen said he frequently hears that young people could solve their problems if they simply got jobs, but since jobs are scarce, the competition is severe. Stephen made it quite clear that he felt the pressure from older men:

PC: Do the Elders make fun of you, or is it just your parents' generation?

SK: I don't think they make fun of me, it's, I've only heard of other people, three other people like talk about me when I'm around.

PC: Yeah. So that's, that's a kind of stressor for young people, then?

SK: Yeah. I'd say the stressors would be a long list, not making money and being told that if they [young people] want money they should go and find a job, because there isn't much jobs up here. Like you got at least 60 other people trying to apply for this one position. And yet people are telling kids to go find a job instead of sitting around.

Stephen's economic situation is common for many other men in his cohort – 20-something, finished with formal schooling, but few prospects for getting a job simply because there are not enough jobs. Stephen's experience was reflected in the statements of several other men I interviewed that year. During one interview, another young man, Joseph, summed up the problem:

JK: A lot of guys are waking up and worrying about their life. They're realizing that this is how their life is going to be. Get up, have breakfast, maybe go for a drive, watch television, and try not to be bored.

Interviews with younger men over the past five years have reinforced these specific themes. Younger men are keenly aware that being economically productive is an important part of being a man, but their limited access to cash is a significant hurdle. As Stephen noted, there are very few jobs available for men in the settlement, and most of those are part-time, casual, or seasonal. These jobs do not provide enough income to either support a family or assemble the equipment profile necessary to support hunting. This is not to say that all young men are in positions identical to Stephen or Joseph, but it is worth noting that the young men who are productive hunters receive significant support from their parents and grandparents, who provide them with the equipment and supplies they need to travel on the land. As one older woman noted in an interview, "you really need a big family to survive up here." Her comments reference the ways that the senior members of the extended family, or *ilagiit*, allocate resources to their adult children (Chabot 2003; Wenzel 1981) while acknowledging the importance of family members as a pool of labor (see Dahl 2000).

Someone like Stephen, unemployed and limited in the ability to produce either money or game, must therefore find other means to establish his worth. His offering of a fish to his grandmother is one example. Inuit universally acknowledge the importance of giving and generosity, but it is noteworthy that Stephen offered fish to a woman who had no need for it. She fishes for herself, and her other adult children also provide her with country food. It is much more likely that Stephen's offering was more performative, for himself as much as his grandmother, than material. For many young men who have less to offer in actual productivity, it is the performance of productivity that serves as validation of their manhood.

One important venue for performing masculinity in this manner is during duck season. Duck hunting is a highly visible space in which young men demonstrate their commitment to the central themes of manhood. Duck season begins in May, when king eider ducks migrate along the coast, heading into Prince Albert Sound for nesting. Although the king eider (*kingalliq*) migrates in the largest numbers, other species are also taken at this time, including common eider, Canada goose, brant, and sandhill crane. *Kingaliiq* is, however, the most important. For the parents of adult children in Stephen and Joseph's cohort, the goal is to store enough ducks in the freezer to provide weekly meals for the remainder of the year, providing variety in the diet.

The most popular hunting location is Mashuyak, a camping spot approximately eight kilometers from the settlement. The migration flyway is especially close to the land there, and ducks arrive in very large numbers. There are numerous cabins, and families without cabins set up tents for the season. It is a high-traffic area, the buzz of snowmobiles marking the progress of those coming and going from town, and shotguns firing at all hours. Furthermore, the public nature of hunting at Mashuyak is generational. When Rick and I were working in 1992–1993, we were struck by the massive increase in activity associated with duck hunting. Some of the men in our study sample had been essentially idle during the previous ten months, yet from mid-May through the end of June, these men were hyperactive. They effectively moved to Mashuyak, returning to the settlement only to do laundry, bathe, and resupply, before immediately heading back out of town. A similar pattern exists today, with many young men pushing themselves to take as many ducks as they can.

A major attraction of duck hunting is that participation costs are relatively low. Mashuyak is close to town, and one does not require the full complement of traveling equipment to be successful. Those without a snowmobile can always catch a ride on someone's sled; those without gear can borrow a shotgun and stay in a relative's cabin or tent. And, just as in spring 1993, today's generation of young men are engaged in the same behavior, staying out all night on the ice, waiting for ducks, and enjoying the opportunity to perform what they view as an important socially and culturally validating activity.

And performance it is, in multiple ways. Although their parents and grandparents appreciate the ducks they provide – some older men openly state that they no longer hunt ducks because their kids take so many – the young men, as in 1993, do not seem to be very efficient. Asking a young man how duck season is going usually generates a response like "15 and 78." The first number refers to the boxes of shotgun shells used. The second refers to the number of ducks taken. Higher numbers establish their prowess, despite the fact that a high number of boxes of shells fired signals inefficiency with a shotgun.

The performance, however, may be as much for themselves as it is for others, a public demonstration of one's commitment to hunting in one of the few venues realistically available to them. Duck hunting, though both materially and culturally productive, does not carry the same prestige as an expedition hunt for caribou. The caribou hunt occurs later in the summer, and hunters travel by boat, sometimes several hundreds of kilometers, returning up to a week later, and arriving on the beach, in full view of the settlement, with a boat filled to the gunwales with highly prized caribou. Likewise, duck hunting does not approach the aura of manliness conferred upon men returning from a winter hunt, their faces frostbitten, skin peeling from the cold they endured on the trail.

I noted earlier that one of the additional values of duck hunting is that, in addition to being an emblematic performance of manhood, it is socially validating. People camp together, eat together, and engage with each other on the land in ways they would not in town.

Another, more specific example of subsistence as social production for young men appears later in the summer. For younger men with access to ATVs, the summer months provide opportunities for trips on the land to fish the nearby lakes for lake trout. Small groups of young men organize excursions and spend several hours, usually within 40 to 50 kilometers of the settlement, fishing at different lakes depending on weather and trail conditions. Although the overt goal is to catch fish, it is equally clear that these are social activities. They reinforce friendship and kinship bonds through common experience in a highly valued activity. Being "on the land," even minimally, is widely cited as an important mechanism for coping with stress and promoting healing, enhanced by the social nature of the engagement.

In a formal analysis, trout fishing is almost certainly uneconomic. The costs of trout in terms of fuel, time, and equipment are high, and lake trout are not as highly valued as other country foods taken during the summer, including musk oxen, ringed seals, arctic char, and caribou. The seemingly uneconomic nature of trout fishing suggests that such trips are better thought of as strictly leisure or recreational activities. They become valuable for younger men, however, by reinforcing social ties and developing social capital. They also provide young men with opportunities to develop skills in navigating the landscape, repairing equipment, and problem-solving, building a foundation for future subsistence activities.

DRUM DANCING AS MASCULINE PERFORMANCE

With more intense subsistence activities, such as expedition hunts and winter travel, closed to most young men, what is one to do during the remainder of the year? Duck season is, after all, less than six weeks in duration, as is summer trout-fishing. One solution to the problem of masculinity for younger men has reemerged in an arena that is predicated primarily on performance, and it has become an important pathway to manhood for the cohort of men born after 1980.

Drum dancing was frowned upon by the missionaries and the RCMP during the contact-traditional era, and while dancing persisted in the community, it did so out of the sight of most outsiders. Dancing re-emerged as a community-wide and public activity during the late 1990s. I first became aware of its re-emerging popularity during my dissertation research in 1997, when organized drum dancing sessions in the school gym or the community hall occurred twice and sometimes three times a week. The form was "Western" or "Inuvialuit" style, practiced in the other communities to the west. In Inuvialuit dancing, drummers sit in a row of chairs, playing the drums in unison and singing. Others without drums may stand behind them and sing. Dancers arrange themselves in front of the drummers. The songs and dances are a living catalog, with some songs attributed to specific Elders, and they tell stories and of activities from the past. In the late 1990s, the drummers were all Elders, led by Jimmy Memogana, a highly respected Elder who remained an active hunter into his late 80s. It was one of the few places in the settlement where people of all ages, from infancy to old age, interacted socially (see Figures 13.1, 13.2, and 13.3).

The western Arctic style of dancing reflects the unique nature of Ulukhaktok, which is a mixed community of Inuinnait (formerly called "Copper Eskimos" or "Copper Inuit") and Inuvialuit, people from the Mackenzie Delta region who settled in the community beginning in the late 1930s. Each group had its own style of drum dancing. What Ulukhaktomiut call "Central Style" descends from Inuinnait tradition and differs from the Inuvialuit Style. Central style is a solo performance. The dancer beats a drum while dancing and singing. Both the drum and the beater are different

Figure 13.1 Ulukhaktok Elder Jimmy Memogana setting fish nets under the fall ice at Fish Lake, 1997. Photo: Peter Collings.

Figure 13.2 Jimmy Memogana and grandson Buddy Allikamek drumming in the home Jimmy shared with his wife Nora, March 2000. On Friday evenings, Jimmy's and Nora's grandchildren and great-grandchildren often danced to Jimmy's drumming. Photo: Pamela Stern.

Figure 13.3 Inuvialuit style drum dancers practicing at the community hall, Ulukahktok, December 2019. Photo: Tim Murray.

in design and construction (see Conlon 2009 and Dewar 1990 for more detailed descriptions).[1]

Once re-established, both styles maintained their popularity, although the western style has become the predominant, more publicly visible, activity. By the mid-2000s, the composition of the western group had changed significantly. Jimmy and the other Elders were no longer actively participating by 2005, and several of Jimmy's grandchildren and great-grandchildren had become recognized as the leaders of the group. Leadership clearly carried a certain status for these young men. They were widely regarded as talented dancers, and they became stewards of the songs and keepers of the drums. The group also began traveling to other communities to dance, which conferred additional status while providing some modest opportunities to earn money.

One of these men, Danny, exemplifies a definition of masculinity as being about cultural productivity as much as economic productivity. Like Stephen, he has had difficulty achieving economic stability, and his entrée into hunting seemed as much about coping with stress as it was about producing food. He became more serious about country food production when he began following the advice of his grandfather:

DE: My grandpa was talking to me [about three years ago], he told me, "if you're feeling stress, just go on the land, it'll feel better." I had no transportation, and I was feeling bad, so I was getting all my traditional food by walking. And I probably put on maybe close to 100 miles in not even a month on my legs. I probably got like at least 100 birds down within a couple of weeks.

PC: Jeez. You were duck hunting on foot? And so you had to carry them back?

DE: Mm-hmm. My grandpa, this year, Pat, he's been feeling bad for me for going hunting and stuff like that by walking. He gave me a snowmobile to use this year, to help me out.

PC: Right on.

DE: But then I told him "this is how you guys did it long ago. Why can't I do it?" But then last year I just about fell through the ice when I was walking. I was jumping a crack and I ended up falling through the ice. I wasn't going "safety first," I just wanted to come back. I had a lot of ducks. So there's this crack to jump. I had this funny feeling as I was just gonna jump. So I stopped, I threw my ducks over, and my gun and my packsack, and then I jumped. That's when I fell through. I never told anybody up until maybe three weeks after it happened and I finally said something. If I told somebody, they'd tell me not to go hunting anymore by myself. They'd take more safety precautions. You know how like, they'd tell me to stay, wait for your cousin, they could go with you, and stuff like that. But me, I'm more independent, I do stuff on my own when it comes to hunting.

Danny seems to be referencing two important themes here. The importance of provisioning is clearly at the forefront, but also lurking in Danny's retelling of his involvement in duck hunting is the notion that Charlie, in the introduction, phrased as "you can't be lazy." Danny followed his grandfather's advice and went hunting with what he had. Danny's efforts eventually yielded a snowmobile to support his travel, though it is unclear if that investment was made because Danny demonstrated effort or because one of his trips nearly ended in disaster.

Despite Danny's activities as a duck hunter, he is an exemplar of a young man in that drum dancing has become the principal way he connects to his Inuit heritage and demonstrates his commitment to Inuit values. Danny is extremely proficient at drum dancing and, at 25-years-old, is one of the recognized leaders of the group. These values were instilled when he was very young, as Danny notes:

PC: So you've never been without it [dancing].
DE: Yeah. If I go without it I'd be too stressed. My brain would be like steam coming out of my ears.
PC: When did you start drumming as one of the leaders of the group?
DE: As soon as I learned all of the words to each song. It's kind of like a memory game, like maybe I'd say since I was 12 or 11, since then I started singing with my grandfather, and from there, from my grandfather to my uncle William, he's been passing it down, he says "keep it going, keep our youngest ones going."
PC: So I noticed the other night, that you were kind of running the show, you were the center drummer.
DE: Yeah.
PC: When does someone get to sit and drum? Because I think the other night there were five or six people, and a lot of other people moved in and out, moved in and out. When can, say, somebody sit and pick up the drum and drum with the leaders?
DE: As soon as the leader shows enough respect for you and he knows you have all the words and stuff like that, then he could let you take the lead, sing this and that, and say "I want this song sung."
PC: So when did that happen for you? When did you become the leader?
DE: Not too long ago, maybe about like 4 years ago.

Dancing goes beyond being a stress-reduction activity. Danny indicates the lessons he learned from his grandfather then by his uncle William, only a year older and the leader, to "keep it going" by performing the dances and passing them down to others. In a sense, membership in the group provides a sense of productive purpose for Danny, now responsible for transmitting cultural practices and values to another, younger, generation:

DE: There was funding through the school to teach the kids once a day. We'd go there. You know they have gym classes, but instead of their gym classes they said they'd like to learn drum dance. It was more of their choice to pick, and, and the whole school, I was surprised that the whole school gym class switched to drum dance instead of physical education.
TM [Tim Murray]: They wanted to do that more?
DE: Yeah, they were actually interested in learning. I was so amazed it made me feel good. So I had no choice, I just dropped what I was doing and went to teach the school. It made me feel good, like.
PC: And they come regularly now, some of them?
DE: Yeah, they come every Saturday, and they say "I can't wait for Saturday to drum dance!"

DE: And they still do it every year. Probably as soon as school starts again and the snow is on the ground, they'll probably come and ask our group again, "would you like to teach drum dance in school again?" We'll be teaching for about two or three weeks. And by the time, maybe the second and half week they got it going, they got the motions down, the songs down, and they've learned the whole thing. And by then it's, just keep growing and growing and growing. Our group used to be so small until we started teaching the kids in school. And now more and more kids are interested, and they know we can go to places like Toronto, like we went there last year, they know there's opportunities like that to get out of town and show what our culture is and what we do for a living. There's that more kids want to see the world, to show them what we can do, what we're a part of. We try to teach them so we can keep our traditions as long as we can. [Pause] It makes me feel good to see all those young people participating in our culture.

Dancing connects young men like Danny with an emblematic marker of being Inuit while being valued by others. Equally important, though, are the opportunities it provides for generating cultural capital. Danny indicates in the narrative that he had to "learn all of the words to each song," which means both the words and their meanings because he never properly learned Inuinnaqtun. The language was not spoken to him by his parents when he was growing up, a factor that accounts for UNESCO's classification of Inuinnaqtun as "definitely endangered" (Moseley 2010). Danny has extreme difficulty communicating with his father's parents, who are monolingual Inuinnaqtun speakers.

The language gap is significant. In 2016, I observed a practice performance of the Central style dancers as they prepared for the arrival of a cruise ship. Just as with teaching drum dancing at the school, performing for the tourists is an opportunity to earn money. During the rehearsal, dancers practiced singing and dancing specific songs, after which the senior male Elder provided instruction on the finer aspects of performance. His advice included guidance on holding the drum properly, emphasizing specific words in the song, and appropriate posture. After one of these brief lessons, one young woman, then 22, spoke up and asked, "could someone tell me what grandpa is saying? Because I can't understand him."

Inuinnaqtun, like all of the languages in the Eskimo-Aleut family, is polysynthetic, highly inflected, with utterances composed of multiple morphemes strung together to form single-sentence words. Like most young people in Ulukhaktok, Laura, Danny, and Stephen have some control of what we might call nouns or verbs, but they lack the ability to form anything beyond simple utterances. Learning the songs and their meanings is a potentially important vehicle for revitalizing the language, but there has been little support from the government in this regard. Younger people also face challenges from their fellow community members; their halting attempts to speak Inuinnaqtun are sometimes ridiculed outright by those with greater control of the language.

DISCUSSION AND CONCLUSION

The central problem of being a Real Northern Man is that what outsiders have long identified as the fundamental requirements of being a Real Northern Man are out of reach for most young men. While young men can and do make earnest attempts to follow the dictate that Real Men hunt and fish, their activities are limited simply because they lack access to the resources necessary to support those activities. Stephen aptly observed that there are far too many applicants for any job, and most of the jobs that are available are sub-optimal: part-time, seasonal, or casual. This reality may account for Joseph's observation that maybe "this is all there is." Becoming materially productive depends more on structural factors, like having a large family to provide economic support in the form of equipment, supplies, and instruction, than on individual motivation. The young Inuit briefly profiled here provide some evidence that masculinity, at least for these young men, is increasingly attained not through material production, but through cultural and social production. The kinds of subsistence engagements that Stephen and Danny can access produce minimally, at least in the material or economic sense. The value of participating in duck hunting lies more in the performative messages that it sends to other members of the community and to oneself.

The value of performance appears most prolifically in Inuvialuit-style drum dancing, an activity that today is the exclusive domain of young people. Drum dancing provides an opportunity for young men like Danny to emphasize masculinity as cultural production, demonstrating their considerable ability as drummers, singers, and dancers, in an activity that is highly valued by other members of the community, Elders and children alike. It is in some ways a reformulation of what it means to be a Real Northern Man, drawing on cultural performance as an important definition of what it means to be male and Inuit.

Even so, it remains unclear how much freedom these young Inuit have in defining cultural production and molding a practice like drum dancing to meet their own needs. Drumming songs are highly personal and reference "traditional" activities, and they are sung in a language, Inuinnaqtun, that few younger drummers have even minimal control over. The songs and dances represent the motions involved in activities such as setting a net, hunting seals, or, in one song, using a muzzleloader rifle while hunting. During part of our interview with Danny, we asked him whether he composed his own songs and sang them. He did, but the fact he could not compose them in Inuinnaqtun seemed to invalidate them as drum songs. Furthermore, there is a keen sense that a newly composed song lacks the validity of a song handed down from an Elder.

> Most of my songs are about nowadays and stuff like that, but my, my ancestors say, used to tell us not to bring our, the new ways into our old dances. That's why I don't like making new songs. It's a "don't bring that technology stuff into our old-time dances." Sometimes I make a song about smoking a cigarette. You know, waiting for ducks, I was sitting there patiently. I was doing that one time and my great grandpa kind of understood me about making a cigarette, but he kind of got mad at me, too, and said, "you don't bring those ways into our old ways." You know, bringing the new ways into our old ways, kinda mixing it up, like a remix. He kinda didn't like that.

I will close with a final observation on some of the tensions in the community that seem to exist between young men and their Elders. In the quote above, Danny highlights that his great-grandfather disapproved of introducing new elements into drum dances and songs. Stephen noted that young men were disparaged for (apparently) lacking initiative. These tensions may not be as severe as they seem on the surface.

In August 2019, Simon Ikpakohak (a pseudonym) was visiting my house, and we were making bannock, the traditional fried bread. While Simon was mixing up a batch of dough, the subject of drum dancing came up, and I asked Simon whether he knew any of the songs or dances that his father, a respected drum dancer, knew and performed. Simon said that he didn't know anything about drum dancing. As far as I knew, Simon had never been to the hall or gym to even watch the dancers. When I asked why, Simon simply said "that's because I always hunted and fished for my parents." At first, I thought that was a bit harsh of his parents, to expect that Simon would always be hunting and fishing for them, but Simon's meaning later became clear. Through hunting and fishing with his father, Simon possessed all of the important and necessary subsistence skills and knowledge needed to, effectively, be a Real Northern Man. Perhaps Jimmy Memogana's motivation in leading the re-emergence of drum dancing was to expose the generation younger than Simon's to a set of culturally and socially productive activities that would provide them with an appropriate path to manhood.

NOTE

1 The Central style of drum dancing has changed over the past 20 years, perhaps influenced by the more group-oriented performance of the western dancers. When the Central dancers perform today, multiple dancers, each with their own drum and beater, frequently perform in unison.

REFERENCES

Billson, Janet M. 2006. "Shifting Gender Regimes: The Complexities of Domestic Violence Among Canada's Inuit." *Études/Inuit/Studies* 30: 69–88. https://doi.org/10.7202/016150ar

Billson, Janet M., and Kyra Mancini. 2007. *Inuit Women: Their Powerful Spirit in a Century of Change*. Lanham, MD: Rowman and Littlefield.

Bodenhorn, Barbara. 1990. "'I'm Not the Great Hunter, My Wife Is': Inupiat and Anthropological Models of Gender." *Études/Inuit/Studies* 14 (1–2): 55–74. https://www.jstor.org/stable/42869683

Briggs, Jean. 1974. "Inuit Women: Makers of Men." In *Many Sisters: Women in Cross-Cultural Perspective*, edited by Leslie E. Sponsel and Thomas Gregor, 261–304. New York: Free Press.

———. 1997. "From Trait to Emblem and Back: Living and Representing Culture in Everyday Inuit Life." *Arctic Anthropology* 34 (1): 227–235. https://www.jstor.org/stable/40316435

Brody, Hugh. 1975. *The People's Land: Eskimos and Whites in the Eastern Arctic*. New York: Penguin Books.

Burch, Ernest S. 1985. *The Subsistence Economy of Kivalina, Alaska: A Twenty-Year Comparison of Fish and Game Harvests*. Technical Paper 128. Division of Subsistence. Juneau, AK: Alaska Department of Fish and Game.

Chabot, Marcelle. 2003. "Economic Changes, Household Strategies, and Social Relations of Contemporary Nunavik Inuit." *Polar Record* 39 (1): 19–34. https://doi-org.proxy.lib.sfu.ca/10.1017/S0032247402002711

Collings, Peter. 2009. "Birth Order, Age, and Hunting Success in the Canadian Arctic." *Human Nature* 20: 254–274. https://doi.org/10.1007/s12110-009-9071-7

———. 2014. *Becoming Inummarik: Men's Lives in an Inuit Community*. Montreal, QC: McGill-Queen's University Press.

Condon, Richard G. 1987. *Inuit Youth: Growth and Change in the Canadian Arctic.* New Brunswick, NJ: Rutgers University Press.

Condon, Richard G., Peter Collings, and George Wenzel. 1995. "The Best Part of Life: Subsistence Hunting, Ethnicity, and Economic Adaptation Among Young Adult Inuit Males." *Arctic* 48 (1): 31–46. https://www.jstor.org/stable/40511615

Condon Richard G. and Pamela R. Stern. 1993. "Gender Role Preference, Gender Identity, and Gender Socialization among Contemporary Inuit Youth." *Ethos* 21: 384–416. https://www.jstor.org/stable/640578

Conlon, Paula. 2009. "Iglulik Inuit Drum-Dance Songs." In *Music of the First Nations: Tradition and Innovation in Native North America*, edited by Tara Browner, 7–20. Urbana and Chicago: University of Illinois Press.

Dahl, Jens. 2000. *Saqqaq.* Toronto, ON: University of Toronto Press.

Damas, David. 1969. "Environment, History, and Central Eskimo Society." In *Contributions to Anthropology: Ecological Essays. Proceedings of the Conference on Cultural Ecology*, Ottawa, ON, August 3–6, 1996, 40–64. National Museum of Canada Bulletin 230.

Dewar, K. Patricia. 1990. *A Historical and Interpretive Study of Inuit Drum Dance in the Canadian Central Arctic: The Meaning Expressed in Dance, Culture and Performance.* PhD dissertation, University of Alberta. https://doi.org/10.7939/R3ZP3W59X

Dorais, Louis-Jacques, and Edmund Searles. 2001. "Inuit Identities." *Études/Inuit/Studies* 25 (1–2): 9–35.

Dowsley, Martha. 2014. "Identity and the Evolving Relationship between Inuit Women and the Land in the Eastern Canadian Arctic." *Polar Record* 51 (5): 536–549. https://doi.org/10.1017/S0032247414000564

Dybbroe, Susanne. 1996. "Questions of Identity and Self-Determination." *Études/Inuit/Studies* 20 (2): 39–53. https://www.jstor.org/stable/42869937

Fall, James A. 1990. "The Division of Subsistence of the Alaska Department of Fish and Game: An Overview of its Research Program and Findings: 1980–1990." *Arctic Anthropology* 27 (2): 68–92. https://www.jstor.org/stable/40316227

Fogel-Chance, Nancy. 1993. "Living in Both Worlds: 'Modernity' and 'Tradition' among North Slope Inupiat Women in Anchorage." *Arctic Anthropology* 30 (1): 94–108. https://www.jstor.org/stable/40316331

Fienup-Riordan, Ann. 1986. "The Real People: The Concept of Personhood Among the Yup'ik Eskimos of Western Alaska." *Études/Inuit/Studies* 10 (1–2): 261–270.

Graburn, Nelson. 2006. "Culture as Narrative." In *Critical Inuit Studies: An Anthology of Contemporary Arctic Ethnography*, edited by Pamela Stern and Lisa Stevenson, 139–154. Lincoln, NB: University of Nebraska Press.

Guemple, Lee. 1986. "Men and Women, Husbands and Wives: The Role of Gender in Traditional Inuit Society." *Études/Inuit/Studies* 10 (1–2): 9–24. https://www.jstor.org/stable/42869538

———. 1995. "Gender in Inuit Society." In *Women and Power in Native North America*, edited by Laura F. Klein and Lilian A. Ackerman, 17–27. Norman, OK: University of Oklahoma Press.

Gutmann, Matthew C. 1997. "Trafficking in Men: The Anthropology of Masculinity." *Annual Review of Anthropology* 26: 385–409. https://doi.org/10.1146/annurev.anthro.26.1.385

Harder, Miriam T., and George W. Wenzel. 2012. "Inuit Subsistence, Social Economy and Food Security in Clyde River, Nunavut." *Arctic* 65 (3): 305–318. https://www.jstor.org/stable/41758937

Helm, June, and David Damas. 1963. "The Contact-Traditional All-Native Community of the Canadian North: The Upper Mackenzie Bush Athapaskans and the Igluligmiut." *Anthropologica* 5 (1): 9–21. https://www.jstor.org/stable/25604554

Kemp, William B. 1971. "The Flow of Energy in a Hunting Society." *Scientific American* 225 (3): 104–115. https://www.jstor.org/stable/24923120

Jolles Carol Zane. 1997. "Changing Roles of St. Lawrence Island Women: Clanswomen in the Public Sphere." *Arctic Anthropology* 34 (1): 86–101. https://www.jstor.org/stable/40316426

Lonner, Thomas D. 1980. *Subsistence as an Economic System in Alaska: Theoretical and Policy Implications.* Technical Paper No. 67. Anchorage, AK: Alaska Department of Fish and Game.

McElroy, Ann. 1975. "Canadian Arctic Modernization and Change in Female Inuit Role Identification." *American Ethnologist* 2 (4): 662–686. https://doi.org/10.1525/ae.1975.2.4.02a00060

McElroy, Ann. 1978. "The Negotiation of Sex-Role Identity in Eastern Arctic Culture Change." *Western Canadian Journal of Anthropology* 6: 184–200.

Magdanz, James, Charles J. Utermohle, and Robert J. Wolfe. 2002. *The Production and Distribution of Wild Food in Wales and Deering, Alaska.* Technical Paper 259. Juneau, AK: Alaska Department of Fish and Game, Division of Subsistence.

Moseley, Christopher, ed. 2010. *Atlas of the World's Languages in Danger*, 3rd edition. Paris: UNESCO Publishing.

Müller-Wille, Ludger. 1978. "Cost Analysis of Modern Hunting among Inuit of the Canadian Central Arctic." *Polar Geography* 2 (2): 100–114. https://doi-org.proxy.lib.sfu.ca/10.1080/10889377809388644

Natcher, David. 2009. "Subsistence and the Social Economy of Canada's Aboriginal North." *The Northern Review* 30: 83–98.

O'Neil, John D. 1983. *Is It Cool To Be an Eskimo? A Study of Stress, Identity, Coping, and Health Among Canadian Inuit Young Adult Men.* PhD dissertation, University of California, San Francisco.

Rasing, W.C.E. 1999. "Hunting for Identity: Thoughts on the Practice of Hunting and its Significance for Iglulingmiut Identity." In *Arctic Identities: Continuity and Change in Inuit and Saami Societies*, edited by Jarich Oosten and Cornelius Remie, 79–108. Leiden: Universiteit Leiden.

Ready, Elspeth. 2016. "Challenges in the Assessment of Inuit Food Insecurity." *Arctic* 69 (3): 255–330. http://doi.org/10.14430/arctic4579

———. 2019. "Why Subsistence Matters." *Hunter-Gatherer Research* 3 (4): 635–649.

Searles, Edmund. 2001. "Fashioning Selves and Tradition: Case Studies on Personhood and Experience in Nunavut." *American Review of Canadian Studies* 31 (1–2): 121–136. https://doi-org.proxy.lib.sfu.ca/10.1080/02722010109481586

———. 2002. "Food and the Making of Modern Inuit Identities." *Food and Foodways* 10 (1–2): 55–78. https://doi-org.proxy.lib.sfu.ca/10.1080/07409710212485

Smith, Eric A. 1991. *Inujjuamiut Foraging Strategies.* New York: Aldine de Gruyter.

Stairs, Arlene. 1992. "Self-Image, World-Image: Speculations on Identity from Experiences with Inuit." *Ethos* 20 (1): 116–126. https://doi.org/10.1525/eth.1992.20.1.02a00050

Stairs, Arlene, and George Wenzel. 1992. "'I am I and the Environment': Inuit Hunting, Community, and Identity." *Journal of Indigenous Studies* 3: 212.

Wachowich, Nancy. 1999. *Saqiyuq: Stories from the Lives of Three Inuit Women.* Montreal, QC: McGill-Queen's University Press.

Wenzel, George. 1981. *Clyde Inuit Adaptation and Ecology: The Organization of Subsistence.* Mercury Series Ethnology Service Paper 77. Ottawa, ON: National Museum of Man.

Wheeler, Polly, and Tom Thornton. 2005. "Subsistence Research in Alaska: A Thirty Year Retrospective." *Alaska Journal of Anthropology* 3 (1): 69–103.

CHAPTER 14

KEEPING BUSY IN SAVISSIVIK
Women and work in Northwest Greenland

Janne Flora, Kirsten Hastrup, and Astrid Oberborbeck Andersen

Within Greenland and beyond, the Avanersuaq region is frequently distinguished from other areas of Greenland as a place where Inughuit hunters keep traditions alive. Not only is Avanersuaq located in the far northwest of the country and perceived as more or less out of reach, but it is also a region where hunters adhere to old hunting traditions, for instance by using kayaks, harpoons, and floats for narwhal hunting, and using dogsleds for transport and hunting in winter. Over the decades, the perceived isolation has been reinforced and broken in different ways. The establishment of the Thule trading station in 1910 introduced a monetary economy and placed the region within an international network of trade and exchange. Some of the most famous polar expeditions of the early 20th century set out from Avanersuaq, relying heavily on the wayfaring, skills, and knowledge of Inughuit. And more recently, the introduction of the internet and social media to all areas of Greenland has enabled the extension of social connectivity to people all over the country and the world. Still, there is a strong sense that the Inughuit are unique in Greenland, maintaining their own name and dialect, and depending predominantly on hunting as the societal mainstay, implicating men and women equally.

Our purpose in this chapter is to explore the work of "hunters' wives" (singular: *piniartup nulia*) in Savissivik, the southernmost village in Avanersuaq.[1] Hunters throughout the region maintain that their ability to be a hunter in the first place is contingent on having a wife who is willing and able to live and work as a hunter's wife, that is, to carry out the work appropriate to that particular economic and social position. As in other parts of the Arctic (see Bodenhorn 1990; Shannon 2006; Todd 2016; Vebæk 1990) hunting is not strictly a male activity, but a shared livelihood for married couples – husbands and wives – with each partner carrying out complementary work. The work of hunters' wives is frequently referred to as "busyness" – and the wife of a successful hunter is as an *ulapittoq*, or "someone who has a lot to do." This equilibrium is challenged by the phenomenon of so-called "female flight" occurring throughout the Arctic, whereby many women migrate southwards, away from traditional areas and modes of life, seeking education, professional employment, and new lives in urban areas (Hamilton et al. 1996; R. Rasmussen 2009). This phenomenon poses a challenge in Savissivik, where the departure of women leaves many men unmarried and unable to pursue certain kinds of hunting, affecting the livelihood and pride of individual hunters. The departure of women also peddles the idea that life and hunting may be better and easier elsewhere. Ultimately, this places Savissivik in a precarious situation of depopulation, which may one day, conceivably, lead to abandonment and closure – a prospect faced by many other villages in Greenland. The relative absence of women, thus, magnifies not only the importance of hunting, but also the crucial role that hunters' wives play in making hunting possible.

Using examples from anthropological fieldwork we conducted (both collectively and separately) in Avanersuaq, we locate busyness in gender and time. We situate busyness as a value that should be understood against the backdrop of Savissivik's relative isolation, economic neglect, and outmigration, and seen as a virtue that ties together and makes traditional hunting and gender relations meaningful in the present. Busyness therefore is an activity in and of itself. Being busy, we argue, is not merely something that hunters' wives are – it is something they *perform* as they go about their work in the everyday.

SAVISSIVIK: VILLAGE AND PEOPLE

Savissivik is the southernmost and most isolated of the four permanently inhabited villages in the region (see Figure 14.1). Qaanaaq, Siorapaluk, and Qeqertat are located near each other, some 200 kilometers north of Savissivik. Qaanaaq and Siorapaluk can be reached by weekly helicopter connections, or if weather and sea-ice conditions permit, by dogsled in winter and spring, or by motorized boats in summer. To the south, Savissivik faces the vast Qimusseriarsuaq (Melville Bay) where hunters in

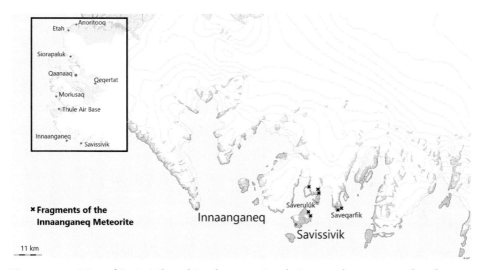

Figure 14.1 Map of Savissivik and its placement in relation to other towns and settlements in Avanersuaq. The map also shows the locations of the Innaanganeq (Cape York) meteorite fragments, that gave name to Savissivik as a *Place of iron*, and were at the center of some of the most important Inughuit trade networks, until the fragments were removed. They are now housed by museums in Copenhagen and New York. Base map: ASIAQ and GSD accessed through NUNAGIS (www.dk.nunagis.gl), with additions and edits by Janne Flora).

Savissivik usually hunt narwhal in summer, and travel by boat to reach their southern neighbors in Kullorsuaq in the Upernavik district, where many in Savissivik have relatives. Weekly helicopters between Qaanaaq and Savissivik go via Thule Airbase (established in 1953, and Savissivik's closest neighbor), for which all non-locals require security clearance to be allowed passage. Unlike Qaanaaq, serviced by a weekly plane from Ilulissat (via Upernavik), Savissivik is only rarely visited by tourists. Winter sea ice has been thinning in recent years, and glaciers retreating, thus rendering safe passage by dogsled between Savissivik and Qaanaaq difficult. Travel by outboard motorized boats during the open water season has likewise been difficult since 2011 with the closure of the settlement of Moriusaq, located halfway between Savissivik and Qaanaaq, which had previously provided travelers with an opportunity to refuel. In many ways, Savissivik orients its contact to the outside world southwards to the Upernavik area, located at the other end of Qimusseriarsuaq (Melville Bay), for hunting and for possible spouses.

As of January 2020, the entire registered population of all age groups in Avanersuaq consisted of 767 individuals. However precise these population statistics appear, there is a great deal of migration in and out of the region, and these figures should therefore be read merely as indicative. Around 650 individuals of the total population were registered inhabitants in the town of Qaanaaq, while 55 were registered as residing in Savissivik, making this the village in Avanersuaq with the largest population (Greenland Statistics 2020a). Looking closer at different age groups, we note that not only has the registered population in Savissivik declined in overall numbers, but the adult population of 17- to 64-year-olds has decreased by nearly half from 73 in January 1990 to 39 in January 2020 (Greenland Statistics 2020c). During the same period, the female-male ratio for the same age cohort went from roughly equal in 1990 (in fact, actually more women than men), to 65 percent male and 35 percent female (or 25 men per 14 women) today (Greenland Statistics 2020c). The most dramatic demographic shift, however, involves the population of children under the age of 17, which decreased dramatically from 39 individuals in 1990 to a mere 12 in 2020 (Greenland Statistics 2020c). This speaks to an overall decline in the current population, but also hints at a possible future for Savissivik in which the population may not be a given at all.

The decline may in part be linked to the centralization of Greenland's school system, set in motion in 2004, which in Savissivik means that schoolchildren move to Qaanaaq at the age of 12 or 13 to finish their primary education. While some may return to Savissivik afterward, for instance, to take up a life as an aspiring hunter or hunter's wife, most students, and especially young women, will continue their education in towns further away, in Ilulissat or Nuuk, and some may even travel abroad for education. Though family ties remain strong, and children and youth return to Savissivik for holidays, the path of education ultimately means that children in Savissivik, at least in theory, leave home at the age of 12 or 13. Many parents accompany their children to Qaanaaq to avoid separating schoolchildren from the rest of the family. Some parents return once their children are old enough to fend for themselves, but many do not. The abandoned houses these families leave behind are striking in otherwise picturesque Savissivik. They signal a void, and a loss of the time when Savissivik was abuzz with activity. But they also gesture to the hope and potential that people may one day return (see Figure 14.2).

Figure 14.2 Panoramic view of Savissivik towards Innaanganeq (Cape York) in the far distance. Above flocks of little auks fly in swooping movements between the cliff immediately adjacent to Savissivik where they nest, and the sea where they feed, 2014. Photo: Astrid Oberborbeck Andersen.

As with most small and isolated villages in Greenland, and in Avanersuaq in particular, life is only feasible in Savissivik if one actively engages with hunting, or if one has access to locally hunted food by being closely related to a hunting family. The few employment opportunities available are in the crucial infrastructure that secures the daily running of the village: the school, health station, service house, waste disposal, power and water station, church, and local council office. Aside from keeping the infrastructure of Savissivik running, these jobs also make a valuable supplement to household incomes, and they make it possible for families to maintain and invest in expensive hunting equipment such as motorized boats, rifles, etc. Unlike hunters in Qaanaaq, where Greenland halibut has emerged as a commercial resource over the past two decades and thrown a financial lifeline to many hunters in that area of Avanersuaq (Flora et al. 2018; Hastrup et al. 2018b), no such economic opportunities exist for hunters in Savissivik. Instead, the income generated by hunters in Savissivik is based primarily on sealskin, and on private sales of fresh foods, especially *mattak*[2] in spring and summer, when narwhal hunting takes place. They may also happen upon occasional opportunities to function as service providers in scientific projects or, more rarely, tourism.

Opportunities for monetary income are few. In 2018, the average gross household income in Savissivik was the lowest in Avanersuaq and among the lowest in Greenland.[3] Adding to the general financial pressure, the Greenlandic hunting laws state that occupational hunters must earn at least 50 percent of their gross annual income from hunting-related activities such as sales of catch, or from providing infrastructure to scientific projects or tourists. Failure to do so jeopardizes their right to renew their hunting licenses, which grants them access to hunt animals that are protected by quotas such as narwhal and polar bear. The latter play a significant role in Savissivik, from where polar bear hunting takes place in Qimusseriarsuaq (Melville Bay), but increasingly only by hunters who are married, and whose wives have the experience to clean and cure polar bear skins.

BUSYNESS: GENDER AND TIME

Busyness is not a concept one immediately associates with Arctic hunting societies, where popular images traditionally convey stillness, timelessness, and an equilibrium between the natural and the human world. Rather, we tend to see busyness as a concept that arises in modernity and the industrial world. Studies of busyness among North American working families, for instance, have shown that busyness arises from building pressures and responsibilities in work- and family-lives alike, technological time management, and a growing inability to separate work-life from family-life (Darrah 2007; Graesch 2009). In such studies, busyness often carries negative connotations and verges on what we have come to know and talk about as stress. Popular images of hunting societies in the Arctic, conversely, are characterized by images of so-called happy-go-lucky Inuit who live at the mercy of their natural environment, similar to the representation depicted by Robert Flaherty in his famous 1922 film, *Nanook of the North*. The film paints the hunter as a hardworking hero, while the activities of women are all but invisible (Fienup-Riordan 2003; Huhndorf 2000; Marcus 2006).

This popular image is echoed in anthropological literature relating to hunter-gatherer economies, where hunter-gatherer affluence comes to be measured not in money or goods, but in an abundance of leisure time (Sahlins 1972) – an argument which has since been widely critiqued (see Bird-David 1992; Kaplan 2000). Sahlins did not consider the effect of colonial processes that had, and have, pushed many hunter-gatherer societies into economic poverty, deprivation, and indeed into dependency on colonial and monetary economies. Nor did he explore what must be variable meanings of "work" and "leisure," or indeed take into account, the amount of work that goes into hunting *beyond* the hunting event itself – not least the work carried out by women. The women hardly spent much time in their hammocks, as in the image Sahlins provided for the leisurely hunting life.

On a conceptual level, owing in no small part to the popular proverb, "time is money,"[4] the notion of busyness implies some sort of relationship between production and the limitation of time. This is only to some extent the case with busyness in Savissivik. Though time is important, busyness here has less to do with its limitation, and more to do with the pressure and repetition of time that go hand-in-hand with the seasonal changes, and how the past is connected to the present and future through busyness. To be busy emphasizes the amount of work one has to do, or the fact that one even has something to do, much more than it does keeping with clock time. Moreover, busyness in Savissivik, or being "someone who has much to do" (*ulapittoq*) is gendered, and is associated with hunters' wives. Flensing animals, sharing, distributing, and selling meat, preparing food for storage, cleaning and curing skins and furs, sewing winter clothes and traditional dress for her husband and her family, keeping her husband's winter clothes in good condition, rearing the sled dog puppies: this is all part of the hunter's wife's work and her busyness. Economically, her work is inseparable from her husband's. He brings home the catch, after which, according to tradition, she takes over to process, distribute, or sell the food. Significantly, as we shall return to below, there is moral value ascribed to her work and busyness, rendering the notion of "being busy" not merely something one is, but something one does. Busyness is in many ways an activity in and of itself. Her distribution of food among relatives and households partly ensures that everyone has food to eat, but it also invokes social relations and recurrently makes these relevant. Her dexterity and knowledge to treat skins properly and transform these into clothing that dresses her husband, children, and frequently individuals beyond the household, meet the basic human need to stay warm in the High Arctic winter, while also generating financial income for the household. But her skills also bind people together in a way that is steeped in the knowledge and tradition that has been passed on to her from older generations of women.

One could argue that the busyness of a hunter's wife is a performative act through which she comes into being as a woman and as a hunter's wife – and that her busyness therefore reproduces gender roles (see Butler 1990). However, in some ways, it would be more accurate to say that the hunting couple, the wife and husband, produce each other's gender roles through their respective work. Hunters and their wives respectively hunt and are busy, for each other, their children, their extended families, and their dogs. When hunters' wives talk about being busy, it is generally an expression of appreciation. And when others describe a hunter's wife as an *ulapittoq* – someone who has a lot to do – it is similarly a compliment to the diligence with which she carries out her work. However, these are also implicit commentaries on her husband's ability and industry as a hunter, or even a "big hunter," a *piniartorruaq*.[5] Their respective work is intimately intertwined, and each is preconditioned by the other. The more he hunts, the busier she is; and the busier she is, the more he hunts.

In anthropological literature, subsistence hunting in the Arctic is frequently thought of as a circular economy, in which there are several human and non-human actors (e.g., Fienup-Riordan 1995, Laugrand and Oosten 2017). Animals, who are perceived as sentient beings, offer themselves freely to the deserving hunting couple who, by their proper treatment of the animal (non-human person), ensure its return, and ensure that the hunting couple will be deserving of animals in the future. These beliefs vary across the Inuit Arctic both as guiding principles and in the extent to which they are expressed. The proper treatment of an animal that has offered itself up to the hunter crucially includes not wasting it. All parts should be shared, used, and above all, appreciated. The appreciation of a hunter's wife, of her own busyness, is thus befitting to good behavior that helps secure the hunt in the future.

Before leaving the discussion of gender and time, it should be emphasized that the division of labor is not cast in stone. On the contrary, life in the region has always been remarkably flexible in the sense that work and responsibilities ascribed to gender and generation could sometimes change in accordance with individual choices, and other times out of necessity (e.g., Hansen 1986; Vebæk 1990). We shall briefly relate an example of this from a woman of our acquaintance, whose life began on the coast north of Innaanganeq (Cape York) where her family lived in a stone and turf house, "with a wooden floor," as she proudly noted. This was a token of her father's standing as a very capable hunter. When she was four or five years old, her mother died in childbirth, leaving her father with three children. He had to rely on her, the oldest, to tend the fire, trap hares, look after her siblings, mend clothes, etc. Later, when her father had remarried, she also took on some typical male tasks and became adept at using the rifle. Once, at the age of 12, she was asked to drive a dogsled laden with meat from their own settlement to Uummannaq, the central village at the time, where some of their relatives were suffering from hunger. She was still very young, and it took her about ten hours on the ice to get there, traveling with a rifle at hand to protect herself from roaming polar bears. She made it, and it also made her – in the sense that ever after, she felt invincible, mastering both genders' roles.

Later, as a hunter's wife, her confidence and daring grew. She participated in her husband's hunting trips – with young children of her own – and they became renowned for their hunting luck. Sometimes, she had to have other women help her, curing or boiling some of the meat, for which they were paid in kind. Accidents happened along the way, in the shape of fires, trichinosis, and the loss of a son, but she carried on, and in addition to being a busy hunter's wife, she also became a schoolteacher, and continued helping her children and (later) grandchildren with the hides they brought home. Her handicraft, not least her mittens and *kamiit*[6] made from sealskin, is highly praised. She is busy – in the particular sense of being always engaged in some kind of work, and finding time for everything. Her life has been varied, but she has constantly kept herself busy – at first because she had no choice, but later because her sense of self was invested in her activities.

The economic and moral value placed on busyness in Savissivik is owed to the fact that busyness is never given or constant. Some periods are busy, while others are not. Likewise, some families may be hit by spells of poor hunting, while others may not. In Savissivik's history, distant and recent, there are many examples where busyness comes and goes. Changes may be regular and expected, such as the changes of season, the arrival and departure of game animals, the formation and extent of the sea ice, and the weather – although these also sometimes surprise. Other times, there are sudden shifts, such as restrictions and opportunities set by the Greenland government based on biological surveys.[7] Sudden shifts may also be caused by the prospects and failures of projects, such as the attempt to establish production and storage facilities for hunters to trade their catch for sale in the urban centers of Greenland where hunting has become less common. Or quite crucially, the shifts can be ascribed to the gender imbalance in Savissivik, which as stated above, leaves a significant proportion of men unmarried, and thus effectively, unable to be very active hunters. Without a wife, these hunters have no one to be busy with their catch – and so, their catch is in a sense wasted. The economic and moral value ascribed to hunters' wives and to their busyness is thus one that goes hand in hand with the shifts of time itself, while also intertwining hunting traditions, gender relations, and economic needs in such a way that life in Savissivik is continually made possible, relevant, and meaningful.

THE IRON: A BUSYNESS THAT WAS

Savissivik, which means "Place of Iron" or "Place of Knives," takes its name after the famed Innaanganeq (Cape York) meteorite that crashed, fragmented, and dispersed into the area some thousand years ago. Two fragments landed on the Savissivik Island, while others landed on the mainland not far from Savissivik, and similarly came to inspire the names of these places: Saveqarfik and Saveruluk. Prehistoric Inuit (Tunit/Dorset) began extracting meteoric iron from here in the 7th century and continued after Thule culture Inuit arrived in Greenland around the 1200s until the arrival of American and European explorers in the 19th century. They shaped the iron into harpoon points, knives, and crescent-shaped women's knives (singular: *ulu*), inserted the iron into trade networks that also included soapstone, copper, and driftwood, and were oriented westwards into the Canadian Arctic (Appelt et al. 2015, 16–18). While the Inughuit of Northwest Greenland lived in isolation from the colonial activities in West Greenland, the activity around the meteorites at Savissivik made the place a hub of human, economic and social activity across Smith Sound for more than 1000 years.

John Ross's expedition, which arrived in the area of Savissivik in 1818, encountered a group of Inughuit, one of whom – a man by the name Meigack – explained to the expedition's Greenlandic translator, Hans Sakæus,[8] that they had traveled to the area with the intention to procure iron, which they used for knives and blades. The iron, Meigack explained, could be found in several locations near a place, which Ross registered as Sowallick – Iron Mountain (likely Savilik). They would collect especially durable stones found at a place Ross registered as Inmallick (Innaanganeq [Cape York]) located some distance from the sites of the meteorites, and use these to dislodge the pieces of iron, and flatten them into oval shapes appropriate for knives (Ross 1819, 103–105; lxxviii). Having since been claimed, first by Robert Peary and since by Danish explorers and scientists, the most impressive meteorite fragments are now on display in museums in the United States and Denmark. What remains at the meteorites' original locations today speaks to the human activity that once occurred in the area: shelters and dwelling structures, tent rings, meat caches, animal bones. Most impressive however are the sizable heaps of the so-called "hammer stones" from the Innaanganeq area, which Hans Sakæus had learned about from Meigack. The smallest of these weigh between three to four kilograms, and the largest between 25 to 30 kilograms. Archaeologists estimate that the entirety of hammer stones in one site alone, Saveruluup Itilliapalua (from where Peary removed the fragment called "Woman" in 1895), weighs a staggering 70 tons (Appelt et al. 2015, 26).

That the meteoritic iron became a resource at all is a testament to the ingenuity and hard work of the people who have lived and traveled to the area for millennia. The resources were not just "out there" waiting to be harvested. They were discovered, experimented with, worked on, used, and shared. The hammer stones now left at the places where the meteorites used to be speak to the astonishing intensity with which the meteorites were mined and the importance the meteorites must have had. Like the abandoned houses in Savissivik the hammer stones also bear witness to the busyness, social life, and human networks that once sprung from the area around Savissivik. They also, however, speak to a vacuum – a non-busyness – left by Americans and Europeans who arrived in the area claiming both meteorites and fame, and that continues to affect people in Savissivik today. There is a strong sense in which, the busyness of today, at least in part, occurs in the vacuum created by these stolen meteorites. Understanding the scientific and economic worth of the meteorites, and their potential to attract economic investment and thereby secure Savissivik's economic present and future, there now remains an air of suspicion among some people in Savissivik that scientific activities in the area may operate with the covert purpose of discovering and removing hitherto unknown fragments of meteorite.

THE VALUES OF BUSYNESS

Busyness generates economic value. But there is also a moral value to being busy. Busyness is something that hunters' wives perform. Rather than being something that merely happens to them, they make busyness happen. Much like the meteoritic iron that people traveled to, extracted, worked, and out of which tradeable objects, value, and social relations grew hundreds of years ago, so too are the resources that keep the hunters' wives busy today worked and made into commodities that can be sold, traded, worn, eaten, and shared. Our argument here is that resources are worked in order to generate economic value and, perhaps more importantly, to generate busyness itself.

One of the resources that generates both economic value and busyness itself is sealskin. The seal, and especially the ringed seal,[9] has been a mainstay resource in Inuit communities throughout the Arctic for millennia. Seal meat has sustained the lives of humans and dogs; the blubber was burned for heat and light until the introduction of kerosene and candles; and the versatile sealskin, which is warm, durable, and waterproof, was used for clothing, footwear, tent canvases, sleeping mats, kayak shells, water buckets, as well as rope and string used for a vast array of tools, until the introduction of fabrics and factory-made clothes which rendered the sealskin a by-product. Even the bones and claws of seals were transformed into tools and jewelry, until these too could be purchased in shops. Being widely available for most of the year, communities throughout the Arctic have perfected the seal hunt across different seasons and environments: at breathing holes, at the ice edge, on the sea ice, on ice floes, or in open water – all conditions require different methods and techniques and will yield a different catch. In Avanersuaq, where the ringed seal remains a mainstay food, the North Water polynya and sea ice define the hunting grounds for most of the year (cf. Hastrup et al. 2018a). Hunters hunt ringed seals[10] for most of the year, except summer, when they switch to hunting large sea mammals (cf. Flora et al. 2018; Gilberg 1984).

The busyness around sealskins is old, but it has changed over time. Scraping, cleaning, and curing sealskins, softening them by chewing on them, and eventually transforming them into clothing that would dress the entire family, was always women's work. With the arrival of the fur trade to the Arctic, sealskin transformed in value into a tradeable resource that fed the high demand of American and European fashion houses. By the mid-20th century, imported clothing and various tools and objects had become available in settlement stores throughout Greenland, thus transforming sealskin into a by-product that people no longer used for clothing. Only in the most active hunting families did the wives continue to sew winter clothes out of sealskin and other furs, needed especially by the hunter on his long hunting trips during winter. Most sealskins were cleaned, cured, and traded, and became a vital element in many Inughuit household economies. Talking to us about her childhood in Savissivik during the 1980s, a woman in Qaanaaq reminisced that as far back as she could remember, she knew not to disturb her mother when she worked on skins of so-called grade-A quality. Scraping and cleaning these skins, before tying them onto a wooden frame for drying, these skins required her mother's full attention. The slightest slip of her *ulu* would cause cuts or abrasions in the skin, and thus ruin its potential to fetch the highest price. Anti-sealskin campaigns, originally targeted at industrial sealing (Lynge 1993; Wenzel 1991) caused a crash in the sealskin market, which was felt by hunting families throughout the Arctic. Many were no longer able to sustain themselves by hunting alone, and were coerced away from villages and settlements into towns where they could find salaried employment or irregular wage labor.

Although the demand and financial value of sealskin is but a fraction of what it used to be, and the work involved in cleaning the skins for trading is substantially less time-consuming than it used to be, sealskin remains an important resource for economy and busyness in Savissivik today. Using only the best quality skins, the hunters' wives scrape the skins clean of blubber, rinse them in a salt solution, and pack them for freezing until they can be shipped out on one of the two supply ships that arrive in Savissivik each year during summer. Some of the most active hunters' wives keep some sealskins back, however. These are cleaned, cured, softened, and sewn into clothing using traditional methods. Sealskin clothing items include vital winter clothes for her husband, herself, and her children, while others are made to be sold to tourists and acquaintances. Just as skins from ringed seals and bearded seals vary in size and quality, and have different uses, so too do the seasons produce different results in curing these skins. Depending on the age and species of seal, and the size and quality of skin, some skins may be depilated. Because it is thick and durable, depilated skin from older bearded seals is well-suited for the soles of *kamiit* (boots) used for hunting. Meanwhile, the depilated skin of younger bearded seals is more supple and whitens when dried in winter, making it particularly suitable to *arnatuut*, the long and white boots characteristic of a woman's traditional dress in Avanersuaq.

Another no less important use of sealskin has nothing to do with clothing or sealskin trade at all, but with food. Together with its blubber, the skin of a freshly caught ringed seal can be used to ferment little auks, small sea birds that arrive in Savissivik each spring to nest in the towering talus slopes immediately behind the village (see Mosbech et al. 2018). The arrival of the little auks transforms not only the complex of food sources available, but also social life and activities (Mosbech et al. 2018); they bring a seasonal shift to busyness to Savissivik generally, and to the hunters' wives specifically. Not long after the birds arrive, the hunters' wives, their children, and elderly relatives, who now have independent access to food for the rest of the summer, ascend to the little auk colonies. They collect eggs and using an *ipoq*, a closed net woven onto a circular frame and attached to a long rod, they catch the birds as they fly in circular patterns over the mountainside.

The much-relished dish of fermented little auks, called *kiviaq*, was traditionally an important winter food and sustained many through the dark and frigid season when the sea ice in the Innaanganeq area made it difficult for hunters to access sea mammals (K. Rasmussen 1921, 530–540). Today the *kiviaq* is mainly a festive food enjoyed at christenings, weddings, confirmations, and so forth. Each *kiviaq* consists of as much as 500 freshly caught little auks, which, together with ample amounts of blubber, are packed into the coat of a freshly caught seal. The air is compressed from the package, before it is sewn up, sealed with blubber, buried underneath a pile of rocks, and left to ferment for some months. Each family has their own favorite places to catch and ferment the little auks, either immediately behind the village or on one of the adjacent islands where the little auks also come to nest. The hunters' wives keep track in their calendars of the dates at which their *kiviat* (plural) were buried, and how many little auks each of them contain. They also plan and adjust the amount of *kiviat* they make each year according to the celebrations they expect to occur during the year. Some may also sell their *kiviat* to families who live in Qaanaaq, where there are no little auk colonies, and where access to this delicacy therefore is hard to come by for many families who have no opportunity to catch little auks in the spring and summer, and therefore must purchase them.

The now widely available mobile telecommunications and social media technologies have come to play an important role in such transactions, since many hunters' wives use social media to sell their produce. The value rendered through the sales of *kiviaq*, sealskin, or polar bear fur clothing items crafted by hunters' wives in Savissivik, extends far beyond the money they earn from such transactions, encompassing the value of knowledge, tradition, and busyness itself. This may be exemplified by the many photographs on social media posted by women, depicting their own everyday lives as hunters' wives – that is, how they do their busyness. The photographs may show the arrival of little auks, the preparation of sealskins for trade, the curing of polar bear skins, which at some point become a pair of men's winter trousers (*nanut*); or even the stitches with thread made of dried tendon, and intricately placed in a pair of *kamiit* or *arnatuut* she is sewing. Other photographs display the flensing of animals, or the preparation of dishes. Their reception, particularly from

Figure 14.3 After scraping the blubber from the sealskin and cleaning it, Anike suspends the sealskin onto a wooden frame where it cures, 2015. Photo: Storm Odaq of his wife Anike taken for the *Piniariarneq Project* (see Andersen et al. 2017; Flora et al. 2018).

women who live elsewhere in Avanersuaq, Greenland, or even abroad, is characteristically joyful and full of admiration of the skills of the hunters' wives, and of Savissivik as a place where hunters' wives keep busy. Moreover, these displays of busyness online may also be taken as a sharing of the experience and moral value of busyness. For various reasons, many of the women who enjoy seeing the photographs do not have the means, time, skills, or opportunity to live these kinds of busy lives themselves. The busyness of hunters' wives therefore does not merely clothe and feed the many individuals throughout the country who cannot clothe or feed themselves by traditional means, it also helps keep old traditions and livelihoods alive in the present and possibly the future (see Figure 14.3).

KEEPING BUSY

In this chapter, we have attempted to highlight two things. First, that hunting in Savissivik and Avanersuaq is not exclusively a male activity, but rather an activity in which women are actively involved through the work and responsibilities they carry out as "hunters' wives." Second, that busyness (*ulapinneq*) in Savissivik is far removed from familiar connotations of stress, pressure, and obligation related to work and family life, being actually a virtue and something that hunters' wives perform rather than something that they simply are. We have located busyness in gender and time, showing that busyness relates to the work of hunters' wives, and that it changes over time, in form as well as content. The relative isolation and economically uncertain future of Savissivik contribute to the economic and moral value of busyness; both in the sense that it contributes to keeping life in Savissivik viable, but also in that it keeps alive old values, knowledge, and traditions related to hunting and, not least, related to the caring cooperation between the hunter and the hunter's wife. A hunter hunts for his wife, children, extended family, and dogs, and when he goes hunting, his wife tends to see him off. She carefully packs and helps him secure his supplies and equipment onto the sled. Some wives pack little tokens or ornaments into their husband's bags, which help attract certain animals that they long to taste. Frequently, the hunter's wife leads the dog team across the bumpy ice foot and onto the sea ice, from where the hunter sets off. She does so, by walking slowly in front of the dogs, the sled, and her husband, gently waving his whip into the air, so the dogs stay behind her. While her husband is gone, she may glance out onto the sea ice and the horizon several times a day, searching for signs of her husband's return, and for signs of changes in the weather. She may ask other hunters returning home, for news of her husband. In this way, she can be ready at the ice foot to welcome her husband home with their catch. And from there, she takes over the dog team, leading it, her husband, and their catch back home, where her busyness begins.

ACKNOWLEDGMENTS

We are grateful to the people in Savissivik and Avanersuaq generally, who have received us with hospitality and kindness during various research trips to the region. This chapter builds upon the authors' collaboration on the NOW Project (2014–2017) (www.now.ku.dk), funded by the Carlsberg Foundation and Velux Foundations.

NOTES

1. In Inuktun (the dialect spoken by Inughuit), Savissivik is pronounced "Havighivik." We use the official West Greenlandic (Kalaallisut) spelling for place names according to the Greenlandic Language Secretariat, Oqaasileriffik.
2. Skin with blubber of narwhal or beluga whale, usually consumed raw, but occasionally also boiled, fried, or fermented. This delicacy is the richest naturally occurring local source of vitamin C.
3. The average gross household income in Savissivik in 2018 was 255,984 DKK, which is around half of those in Greenland's capital, Nuuk (609,996 DKK) and the municipality capital, Ilulissat (498,248 DKK) (Greenland Statistics 2020b).
4. Coined by Benjamin Franklin in 1748.
5. Piniartorsuaq in West Greenlandic (Kalaallisut).
6. Traditional boots.
7. Large sea mammals such as narwhal, beluga whale, walrus, polar bear, and the land mammals muskox and caribou are all managed by hunting quotas and hunting seasons.
8. Hans Sakæus was from the Qeqertarsuup Tunua (Disko Bay) area.
9. In Inuktun ringed seal is known as *puihi*, as opposed to *natseq* as it is known in West Greenlandic and other areas of the Arctic.
10. To a lesser extent bearded seal (Inuktun: *ughuk*) and harp seal (Inuktun: *aataaq* (older), *aataaraq* (younger)), the latter of which rarely occur in the Qaanaaq area.

REFERENCES

Andersen, Astrid Oberborbeck, Janne Flora, Kasper Lambert Johansen, Mads Peter Heide-Jørgensen, and Anders Mosbech. 2017. Piniariarneq: From Interdisciplinary Research towards a New Resource Management. Copenhagen and Aarhus: University of Copenhagen and Aarhus University. https://now.ku.dk/documents/Piniariarneq_report.pdf.

Appelt, Martin, Jens Fog Jensen, Myrup Mikkel, Haack Henning, Sørensen Mikkel, and Michel Taube. 2015. *The Cultural History of the Innaanganeq / Cape York Meteorite*. Technical Report. University of Copenhagen, Natural History Museum of Denmark, the National Museum of Denmark, and the Greenland National Museum.

Bird-David, Nurit. 1992. "Beyond 'The Original Affluent Society': A Culturalist Reformulation." *Current Anthropology* 33 (1): 25–47.

Bodenhorn, Barbara. 1990. "'I'm Not the Great Hunter, My Wife Is': Iñupiat and Anthropological Models of Gender." *Études/Inuit/Studies* 12 (1–2): 55–74.

Butler, Judith. 1990. *Gender Trouble*. London: Routledge.

Darrah, Charles N. 2007. "The Anthropology of Busyness." *Human Organization* 66 (3): 261–269.

Fienup-Riordan, Ann. 1995. *Boundaries and Passages: Rule and Ritual in Yup'ik Eskimo Oral Tradition*. Norman, OK: University of Oklahoma Press.

———. 2003. *Freeze Frame: Alaska Eskimos in the Movies*. Seattle, WA: University of Washington Press.

Flora, Janne, Kasper Lambert Johansen, Bjarne Grønnow, Astrid Oberborbeck Andersen, and Anders Mosbech. 2018. "Present and Past Dynamics of Inughuit Resource Spaces." *Ambio: A Journal of the Human Environment*, 47: 244–S264. https://doi.org/10.1007/s13280-018-1039-6.

Gilberg, Rolf. 1984. "Polar Eskimo." In: *Handbook of the North American Indians, vol. 5: The Arctic*, edited by William C. Sturtevant, 577–594. Washington, DC: The Smithsonian Institution.

Graesch, Anthony P. 2009. "Material Indicators of Family Busyness." *Social Indicators Research* 93: 85–94. https://doi.org/10.1007/s11205-008-9408-3.

Greenland Statistics. 2020a. http://bank.stat.gl/pxweb/en/Greenland/Greenland__BE__BE01__BE0120/BEXST4.PX/table/tableViewLayout1/?rxid=60fff9aa-8b20-4c1f-81dd-91036f979b29 (accessed 2 April 2020).

Greenland Statistics 2020b http://bank.stat.gl/pxweb/en/Greenland/Greenland__IN__IN20/INXH3.px/table/tableViewLayout1/?rxid=INXH306-04-2020%2008:23:14) (accessed 2 April 2020).

Greenland Statistics 2020chttp://bank.stat.gl/pxweb/en/Greenland/Greenland__BE__BE01__BE0120/BEXST4.PX/table/tableViewLayout1/?rxid=5c9cb2c4-4ae2-48d4-a1c1-24debdcd992b (accessed 2 April 2020).

Hamilton, Lawrence C., Rasmus Ole Rasmussen, Nicholas E. Flanders, and Carole L. Seyfrit. 1996. "Outmigration and Gender Balance in Greenland." *Arctic Anthropology* 33 (1): 89–97.

Hansen, Keld. 1986. "Kvindelige Fangere [Female Hunters]." *Tusaat / Forskning* 2: 11–14.

Hastrup, Kirsten, Anders Mosbech, and Bjarne Grønnow, eds. 2018a. Special Issue: The North Water: Interdisciplinary Studies of a High Arctic Polynya under Transformation. *Ambio: A Journal of the Human Environment* 47 (Supplement 2).

Hastrup, Kirsten, Astrid Oberborbeck Andersen, Bjarne Grønnow, and Mads Peter Heide-Jørgensen. 2018b. "Life around the North Water Ecosystem: Natural and Social Drivers of Change over a Millennium." *Ambio: A Journal of the Human Environment* 47 (Supplement 2): 213–225. https://doi.org/10.1007/s13280-018-1028-9.

Huhndorf, Shari M. 2000. "Nanook and His Contemporaries: Imagining Eskimos in American Culture, 1897–1922." *Critical Inquiry* 27 (1): 122–148. https://doi.org/10.1086/449001.

Kaplan, David. 2000. "The Darker Side of the 'Original Affluent Society.'" *Journal of Anthropological Research* 56 (3): 301–324. https://doi.org/10.1086/jar.56.3.3631086.

Laugrand, Frédéric, and Jarich Oosten. 2017. *Hunters, Predators and Prey: Inuit Perceptions of Animals*. New York: Berghahn Books.

Lynge, Finn. 1993. *Arctic Wars, Animal Rights, Endangered Peoples*. Hanover, NH, and London: University Press of New England.

Marcus, Alan. 2006. "Nanook of the North as Primal Drama." *Visual Anthropology* 19 (3–4): 20–22. https://doi.org/10.1080/08949460600656543.

Mosbech, Anders, Kasper Lambert Johansen, Thomas A. Davidson, Martin Appelt, Bjarne Grønnow, Christine Cuyler, Peter Lyngs, and Janne Flora. 2018. "On the Crucial Importance of a Small Bird: The Ecosystem Services of the Little Auk (*Alle alle*) Population in Northwest Greenland in a Long-term Perspective." *Ambio: A Journal of the Human Environment* 47 (Supplement 2): 226–243. https://doi.org/10.1007/s13280-018-1035-x.

Rasmussen, Knud. 1921. "Beskrivelse af Thule Distrikt [Description of the Thule District]." *Meddelelser om Grønland* 60: 517–567.

Rasmussen, Rasmus Ole. 2009. "Gender and Generation: Perspectives on Ongoing Social and Environmental Changes in the Arctic." *Signs* 34 (3): 524–532. https://doi.org/10.1086/593342.

Ross, John. 1819. *A Voyage of Discovery, Made under the Orders of the Admiralty, in His Majesty's* Ships Isabella and Alexander, *for the Purpose of Exploring Baffin's Bay, and Inquiring into the Probability of a North-West Passage*. London: John Murray, Albemarle Street.

Sahlins, Marshall. 1972. *Stone Age Economics*. Chicago and New York: Aldine Atherton Inc.

Shannon, Kerrie Ann. 2006. "Everyone Goes Fishing: Understanding Procurement for Men, Women and Children in an Arctic Community." *Études/Inuit/Studies* 30 (1): 89–109. https://doi.org/10.7202/016147ar.

Todd, Zoe. 2016. "'This is the Life': Women's Role in Food Provisioning in Paulatuuq, Northwest Territories." In *Living on the Land: Indigenous Women's Understanding of Place*, edited by Nathalie Kermoal and Isabel Altamirano-Jimenez, 191–212. Edmonton and Athabasca: Athabasca University Press.

Vebæk, Mâliâraq. 1990. *Navaranaaq og Andre: De grønlandske kvinders historie* [*Navaranaaq and Others: Greenlandic Women's History*]. Copenhagen: Gyldendal.

Wenzel, George. 1991. *Animal Rights, Human Rights: Ecology, Economy and Ideology in the Canadian Arctic*. Toronto and Buffalo: University of Toronto Press.

CHAPTER 15

"I DON'T EVEN SEW FOR MYSELF ANYMORE"

The role of sewing in a northern Inuit economy

Tristan D. Pearce and Kristin Emanuelsen

INTRODUCTION

Inuit have undergone profound socio-economic changes in the last half-century including migration into settlements and the advent of the mixed subsistence-cash economy (Damas 2002; Irwin 1989). Inuit attachment to a subsistence-oriented economy remains strong but it is difficult, if not impossible, to live in an arctic community and participate in subsistence activities without a source of cash income (Condon et al. 1995). Wage employment is limited in most arctic communities, making the traditional economy important for its potential in terms of generating cash income as an alternative to wage employment (Freeman and Wenzel 2006). Many Inuit guide non-resident hunters, and sell animal skins, carvings, artist prints, and sewings, among other items, outside their local communities for income (Miller 1994; Oakes 1988). Inuit have capitalized on their subsistence skills and resources to earn cash income, which is often needed to continue to participate in traditional activities (Oakes 1995; Wenzel 1987).

Much has been written about mixed economies in the Arctic and the role that hunting can play in generating cash income (e.g., Collings 2011; Dombrowski et al. 2013; Harder and Wenzel 2012). Other studies have documented the contributions Inuit make to household and community economies through sewing (Miller 1994; Oakes 1995). They found that sewing provides an opportunity for women to use their traditional skills for income generation and to gain a sense of financial accomplishment and independence.

This chapter builds upon previous studies to discuss the role of sewing in a northern economy through a case study of Inuit women in Ulukhaktok, Northwest Territories, Canada. This chapter is distinct from other work on sewing and economy in the Arctic in that it includes women from different generations, ranging from women who were raised on the land to women who have lived their entire lives in the community. We focus on women because they are the predominant needleworkers in Ulukhaktok, but we acknowledge that some men also earn income from sewing. Rather than quantifying cash income earned through sewing, this chapter describes, with examples, the role of sewing in the local economy. Here we draw upon ethnographic data collected in Ulukhaktok between 2018 and 2020 about the role and importance of sewing to Inuit women (Emanuelsen 2019), as well as 16 years of research experience in the community by Pearce.

STUDY APPROACH AND METHODS

The research was conducted in collaboration with community members in Ulukhaktok and followed key considerations for conducting research with Inuit described by Inuit Tapiriit Kanatami (ITK) and the Nunavut Research Institute (NRI) (ITK and NRI 2007), Pearce et al. (2009), and consistent with the National Inuit Strategy on Research (ITK 2018). These include engaging Inuit to help define the research questions and involving Inuit throughout the entire research process including project design, data collection and analysis, and results dissemination. The research was part of the *Nunamin Illihakvia* project that is governed by the Ulukhaktok Community Corporation (UCC) and funded by Indigenous Services Canada, Climate Change and Health Adaptation Program (CCHAP). Study protocols were approved by the Human Research Ethics Boards at the University of the Sunshine Coast (S181208) and by the Aurora Research Institute (#16521), which oversees research in the Northwest Territories.

Ulukhaktok (70.7364° N, 117.7681° W) is a coastal Inuit community of approximately 440 people (91 percent Inuit; 216 men and 228 women) located on the west coast of Victoria Island in the Inuvialuit Settlement Region (ISR), NWT, Canada (GNWT 2018). Inuit in Ulukhaktok are largely descended from the northernmost groups of Inuinait (Copper Inuit): the Kangiryuarmiut of Prince Albert Sound and the Kangiryuatjagmiut of Minto Inlet (Condon et al. 1995). Several western Inuit (now called Inuvialuit) from the Mackenzie Delta region and several Puvilingmiut families from the Reid Island area also moved to the Ulukhaktok area during the settlement period (Condon et al. 1995). Ulukhaktok was selected as a study community because of its reputation for practicing culture and traditions, including sewing, and because the first author has established research relationships in the community.

Thirty interviews were conducted by the authors and two Inuit research partners (women aged 37 and 31) with a sample of Inuit women stratified by age (Table 15.1). A purposive sampling strategy was used to recruit interview participants ($n = 23$) between 18 and 80+ years of age who were involved in sewing. A snowball sampling strategy was then used in which participants helped identify people within the identified group who might be willing to participate in the research ($n = 7$). Interviews were audio recorded and mostly conducted at the participants' homes, with others conducted at sewing groups. The interviews conducted in Inuinnaqtun involved

Table 15.1 Demographic characteristics of interview participants

Cohort	Age	Totals
Adult	18–34	7
Young Elder	35–49	5
Elder	50–74	13
Oldest Elder	75+	5
Total		30

an experienced interpreter who translated to English during the interview and later verified the transcripts. The interviews were complemented with informal visits with needleworkers, participation in sewing groups, and involvement in daily life in the community. The authors recorded their daily experiences and observations as fieldnotes.

For the purpose of analysis, participants were divided into four general categories based on generation as advised by the Inuit research partners (see Table 15.1). The recorded interviews were transcribed and analyzed following the principles of latent content analysis to identify recurring or common themes related to the role and importance of sewing (Bernard 2012). Direct quotes are used in the presentation of the findings to illustrate how the information was originally shared by participants.

RESULTS

Oldest Elder and Elder participants explained that sewing had been more straightforward when they lived on the land: you got an animal and used it to make clothing for your family. Today, however, participants said that there is pressure to earn some income from the animals that are harvested, and selling sewing made from the skins is one way to generate income. All participants, to varying degrees, have sold items they have sewn, and/or have sewn items specifically to sell. In most cases, sewing work is sold to customers from outside the community, either through personal transactions (in person or online) or through the local co-op art shop. This section provides some background to the economy of sewing in Ulukhaktok, followed by a description of sewing as a commodity in the community today. Next, some differences between store-bought and homemade clothing and the process of purchasing skins to sew with are discussed.

The rise of the cash economy

Inuit in the Ulukhaktok area were introduced to the market economy in the 1930s through fur traders and missionaries. Inuit traded furs for imported goods like metal knives, canned foods, and later rifles, which forever changed Inuit lives (Condon and Ogina 1996). As time progressed, Inuit adopted many southern products into their daily lives, which required them to hunt and trade furs to acquire. This is significant as furs were now valued as a tradeable commodity. Oldest Elder and Elder participants shared that as men hunted, women fleshed, dried, and prepared seal skins to trade.

> Some of us would do 12, 13 or 16 [seal skins] and some would do more than that a day. Every day there is a harvest and sometimes I would say in my mind, oh, another 15 to do tomorrow, but it was a way of getting rifles, a canoe, paper or providing for the family.
>
> (Elder, 71 years old)

She explained that it was at this time that people learned that an animal skin (mostly seal, white fox, and polar bear) was valued as a trading item, which changed how people approached harvesting. In addition to trading furs, Inuit were later taught and encouraged by missionaries to carve, make stone-cut prints, and sew items specifically to sell to people outside the community (e.g., small animals like owls [okpiks[1]]).

> Father Tardy from France, he was the one who started so many things, even our artwork. The art shop used to be a really small building where he got all these women sewing and all the print work that Elders made.
>
> (Elder, 53 years old)

Today the community can be described as having a mixed economy including both subsistence and cash income.

Sewing as a commodity

All participants shared that they sew to earn income, and some participants said that sewing was a key source of their household cash income ($n = 24$). Sewing is considered by participants to be a practical way to earn cash income. For some, sewing complements the income they earn through wage employment, and for others, it constitutes a way to earn cash income without being constrained by a job. It is commonplace for sewing items to be available for purchase at the local art shop and at the homes of many needleworkers.

> I sew for a living. I don't even sew for myself. Everything I make is for somebody else … in-town or out-of-town. I make everything from head to toe. I mostly just sew for making money. I make way more money than when I am working, sewing.
>
> (Elder, 55 years old)

Since the establishment of the settlement and introduction of the social welfare system, there has been an increase in both single-female and single-male households and a subsequent decline in married couples (Collings et al. 2016). Although Inuit social organization has always been flexible, traditional conceptions of social structure stress the complementarity of men and women. Sewing as a commodity has empowered many women in the market economy as wage earners and they can now purchase many of the materials (i.e., animal skins) they need for sewing from the community stores or online (Figure 15.1).

Sixty percent of participants ($n = 20$) said that they take customer orders for their sewings. Social media platforms, mostly Facebook, are popular ways of matching needleworkers with customers. This technology has added a new dynamic to how people sew. Participants shared that sewing for someone they do not know limits creativity and can become repetitive. In particular, orders that requested certain colors and designs felt restrictive for the women. As one Adult (43 years old) shared:

> I know there are people that take orders, but I can't do orders. If somebody wants a certain colour flower or they say they want a purple rose for mitts or kamiks, I can't do those orders. It has to be something I feel inspired to do and I want to do.

Figure 15.1   An Ulukhaktomuit needleworker uses a sewing *ulu* to cut out a pattern from a tanned seal skin purchased from the Ulukhaktok Community Corporation (UCC). Photo: K. Emanuelsen.

Another Adult participant (32 years old) shared that taking orders makes her feel stressed. She described getting her first order in a long time, and how she felt stressed because the customer was so specific, and wanted natural seal skin, which was not available in stores at the time of the order. So, she bought some other material to keep her mind busy while she waited for the stores to stock the natural sealskin so that she could start the order.

Participants also said that it is difficult to calculate the price of an item sewn to be sold. Making a piece of clothing or a sewing item involves expenses including material costs and the needleworkers' time. Some participants said that they consulted with older family members when pricing an item, and expressed a gap in training among needleworkers regarding how to assess the value of their work. An Adult participant (48 years old) explained how she calculates the price of an item she wants to sell. She adds together the cost of all the supplies she had to buy, the supplies she already had (e.g., needles and thread), and the cost of her labor. She also has to calculate the price of the size of the fur or material used for the order. Another Adult participant (22 years old) also said that she finds it hard to price her artwork.

> I use sealskin mostly, my mom orders from online [catalog]. They got all kinds of furs and colours. They are about the same price as UCC [community corporation]. I have heard how many people say that they would sew more if it was cheaper. Some people make them too expensive, and some put it too low. Would be good to have someone come in, and teach how to price their artwork. I just ask my mom, and she will tell me the right prize. Gloves patched is $350, $250 normal, kamiks patched is $450. She sells a lot, she takes orders from people out

of town, usually Facebook. They hear from their friends. They would share their size and ask price.

Participants said that some women in the community sew differently, or not to the highest quality, when selling items or clothing.

> Some of them take short cuts when they are sewing for an order rather than for family. They would try to make big stiches, and that won't be good. You will feel air, the cold. The cold air can go through. When they rush it.
>
> (Adult, 22 years old)

Participants were careful to say that while they do sometimes sew differently for sale orders, they still take pride in their work. One Elder participant (64 years old) explained that when she sewed *kamiks* for someone living in the South, she didn't need to use extremely tight stitching or the best thread as the *kamiks* were never going to be used in extremely cold conditions. Others said that they sometimes needed to rush to complete orders in time, and that this meant taking shortcuts like sewing bigger stitches. Caribou sinew is mostly reserved for sewing clothing for family members because it is superior to manufactured sinew or cotton thread for making stitches flexible and air-tight, but these alternatives are deemed, by some needleworkers, to be suitable for sewing clothing for customers living elsewhere.

> Long ago, we used to have no artificial thread. Now that we got artificial thread, we use them for sewing, the only thing is when I made my own clothing like this I use real caribou sinew. I still got some. If I use something to sell I use this one, but if I make real clothing for my family I use real sinew.
>
> (Elder, 67 years old)

That said, an Oldest Elder participant stated that while she was aware that some people sewed differently for paying customers, including not using caribou sinew thread, she sewed the same for everyone, regardless if they were a paying customer or family member. She did so as a matter of principle and pride in her craftsmanship, knowing that other people would know that she sewed that item.

Store-bought versus homemade clothing

All participants said that they buy clothes for themselves and for their kids at the stores, mostly due to the labor and time that go into sewing clothing. The clothing that they do sew tends to be winter clothing like *attigi* (parka), *pualuks* (mitts) and *kamiks* (Inuit boots).

> The only one I ever made [caribou parka] and I don't think I will ever make another. The worst part is the scraping and softening. A lot of work ... I don't make parkas for myself, there are parkas at the store.
>
> (Elder, 55 years old)

Figure 15.2 A locally harvested *ugyuk* (bearded seal) skin being stretched and bleached in the sun. Once prepared, it will be used to sew *ipegaoteks* (seal skin waterproof boots) and *kihiks* (seal skin bottom shoes). Photo: K. Emanuelsen.

The sentiment that preparing skins and sewing took too much time and labor, however, was not shared by all participants, and most Oldest Elder and Elder needleworkers still prepare their own skins and sew clothing out of them (Figure 15.2). This is mainly because they grew up when this was the norm and living in close association with the environment and animals was integral to sewing and the production of clothing. Young Elder and Adult participants said that preparing and sewing with skins is a lot of work and that it is easier to buy synthetic material or prepared skins at the stores. However, although material and skins may be available at the stores, not everyone has the funds to purchase them and few people have credit cards, which limits their use of online shopping. Nearly all participants said they would sew more if the material and skins in the stores were more affordable.

> The seal skin that comes from the factories, those ones are soft but if you do them on your own, there are a little bit tougher. I'd rather use seal because its waterproof. I would sew more if it were cheaper.
>
> (Adult, 39 years old)

All participants said that the quality of store-bought clothes is not as good as homemade clothing. Living in the community necessitates that clothing be able to withstand cold temperatures, especially when traveling on the land. Oldest Elder and Elder participants stressed the importance of wearing homemade clothing when on the land because it was warmer and more reliable. However, as the summers are getting warmer in the Arctic, and people are spending more time at home and indoors during the winter, a shift has occurred regarding the necessity of wearing homemade clothing. One Adult participant (32 years old) shared that her son can wear store-bought parkas, but not when it is really cold: "My son wears his jacket from the store mostly, but on really cold days I tell him to wear his parka. Wear it or he stays home."

An Adult participant (22 years old) shared: "It just feels better to use traditional stuff, and they are warmer too than store bought." Not only is the quality higher, but participants explained that they could design and tailor a clothing item to the person wearing it. For example, one participant shared how she feels better when her kids wear homemade clothing, especially when traveling on the land. She also stressed the importance of knowing who made the clothing so that it has the proper insulation and protection.

> Everybody sews a bit different. I noticed that some people, when they are sewing their parkas, their hood is so tight that when you zip it up, wind can't come in. And others are a bit longer or bigger, different. They sew it the way they like it. I like when it fits right around the face, that way I know that my daughter is going to be warm, then I don't have to worry about her. Or even when we are travelling, I know that the hood is there, I won't have to worry. That's one thing I asked my grandma when she was cutting out a parka, to make her hood close to her face so she could be warm. I like knowing that my children will be warm… like knowing that it is made by us, you know how warm it is and that it will be good for the winter. Knowing that we made it, and that we all put into it, extra layers and stuff.
>
> (Adult, 32 years old)

Purchasing animal skins for sewing

All participants said that skins sold at the Ulukaktok Community Corporation (UCC) (Kayutak Centre) are reasonably priced compared to the local stores. Participants also shared that they buy material and skins when traveling to bigger cities for medical care, or when visiting to take advantage of cheaper commodity prices. The local availability of sewing materials and skins is restricted due to the remoteness of the community and the monopoly the stores have on setting prices (Table 15.2). An Elder participant (66 years old) shared her view on this:

> A lot of the material I use now, I buy from the Kayutak Centre, once in a while I order it from the catalog, or a store in Edmonton. Not seal skin, but all other material. I always look at the material and if it is in the price range that I am willing to pay for it, I will. But if they are too pricy, I will wait and find better. I look at the prices from Coop and Northern, but I will not buy from there, too expensive. The prices have changed, they are there for profit, double and triple of the price.

Most participants, apart from a few in the Oldest Elder cohort, now largely depend on purchasing sewing materials and supplies from the store. Needleworkers no

Table 15.2 Prices for selected sewing materials at the Northern Store in Ulukhaktok, February 2019

Materials	Price (Canadian dollars)
Harp seal hide	279,99
Dyed colored seal skin	254,99
Cow hide	62,99
Rabbit pelt	139,99
Fox pelt	299,99
Beaver pelt	179,00
Pile linings (inside mitts)	25,99
Sewing thread (one bundle)	5,89
Sinew thread (one bundle)	25,00
Commander fabric	99,00
Duffel (for inside mitts)	83,99 × 1m
Fleece	10,99 × 1m
White embroidery stroud	61,99 × 1m

longer have to rely on having a hunter in their household to supply them with skins, and those that do now have the choice of using locally sourced fur skin or purchasing pre-tanned skins that are ready to sew. That said, needleworkers continue to be resourceful, and often repurpose and reuse items that are readily available in the settlement for sewing. An Oldest Elder participant (80+ years old) shared how she uses the red dye from a bingo dapper to color the *attungak* on her *kamiks*.

Young Elder and Adult participants said that the limited availability and price of sewing materials at community stores, including types of fur, colors, etc., influenced what they sewed. There are limited materials available for purchase in the community. Not only do stores tend to be expensive, but they also tend to have low stock at certain times of the year. A few participants are able to order sewing materials online or from catalogs and have them shipped to the community. The ability to do this has greatly expanded what people sew, and the variety of materials they sew with. Needleworkers are increasingly using furs from animals harvested elsewhere, like beaver, muskrat, and cow, and have access to a wide variety of colored threads, dyed furs, and synthetic materials (Figure 15.3). Not everyone, however, can access these materials, and the ability to order from outside the community is exclusive to those with credit cards and employment income.

> When I go out of town for medical and I see material like stroud [embroidery fabric], I would get it, because it is cheaper down there than here and you will probably regret it if you don't buy it. I don't order it; I don't have access to internet or telephone.
>
> (Adult, 48 years old)

DISCUSSION

This research supports the findings of previous work that shows that sewing is an important source of income for many Inuit women, and makes a substantial

Figure 15.3 A pair of modern *kamiks* sewn using purchased materials that were sourced outside the community and include: dyed seal skin, dyed cotton thread, synthetic fleece, and cowhide. Photo: K. Emanuelsen.

contribution to their household economy (Bunce et al. 2016; Miller 1994; Oakes 1988; 1995). There are limited opportunities in Ulukhaktok to earn cash income, and the wage employment that is available often requires some degree of training and scheduled time commitment. Needleworkers can earn cash income at the time of sale instead of waiting for a paycheck, and they can also work flexible hours, which is compatible with participation in seasonal subsistence activities. The introduction of high-speed internet and online banking has provided needleworkers with access to global markets and marketing tools such as social media. Inuit needleworkers have actively participated in constructing a local sewing economy that is rooted in the traditional but adapted for participation in a modern global economy. This finding is consistent with Stern (2001) who argues that Inuit in Ulukhaktok have been active players in the development of a local economy that is uniquely Inuit.

Selling sewn items has empowered some needleworkers financially but also has implications for sewing itself. Sewing items for sale, particularly items made for custom orders, is very different than sewing for one's family. Needleworkers expressed positive feelings when sewing for their family, but they did not have the same feelings when sewing for customers. They often found it stressful to meet time and style demands, and to have to sew something that they do not feel like sewing. It is now common for needleworkers to take orders and sell their sewing on the internet rather than through the local art shop, which adds an individualistic element to a culture that has been more focused on the collective. This increasingly individualist approach to sewing could have ramifications for local sewing culture as needleworkers become more focused on their individual businesses. Others have documented tensions inherent in the commercialization of subsistence outputs, notably country foods (Collings et al. 1998; Ford et al. 2016). This research found, however, that selling sewing is socially acceptable in Ulukhaktok and a recognized source of income.

A major change in sewing since the introduction of the internet in the community has involved the ways people acquire sewing materials, including skins. With the internet, Inuit are now able to access international markets to purchase skins and sewing materials. This provides opportunities for women who are not in a partnership with a man to participate in sewing, because it enables them to purchase skins rather than relying on a hunter to get them. This has also enabled women to sew whatever item they choose at any time of the year because they are not limited by the seasonality of hunting. While the internet has provided more access to earning income from sewing, it also comes with problems. Store-bought skins come prepared, tanned, softened, and ready to sew, which means that women are not learning the skills of how to prepare skins for sewing. This is problematic, as Elders stressed that the importance of sewing includes the entire process of getting an animal, appreciating the value of the skin and the animal that gave it to you, and preparing it for sewing. In the past, every skin was extremely valuable, and needleworkers learned to never waste anything. The availability of skins for purchase also raises questions about cultural continuity, as it enables people to sew with the fur of animals other than those harvested locally. Inuinait traditionally sewed with caribou and seal, but today needleworkers use a range of skins harvested across Canada, which is changing how people sew and the skills needed to do so.

The finding that over half of the women interviewed were single is noteworthy. This finding is consistent with changes in household structure in Ulukhaktok, including the increase in both single female- and single male-headed households, and the subsequent decline in married couples (Collings et al. 2016). Sewing provides women with a source of income that makes it easier to support a single-headed household, and women are able to purchase all of their skins and materials independent of a hunter. The rise of the single female-headed household may also have consequences for sewing. As previously discussed, buying skins disconnects needleworkers from the animal, the hunter. Additionally, the skills involved in preparing skins and sewing for an income are different than sewing for one's family. The disengagement of needleworkers from the local subsistence economy may have consequences for male hunters who place value on their hunting activities for providing skins for sewing. In Inuit culture, hunting and sewing are connected, just as hunters and needleworkers are connected, but changes in household structure and opportunities for needleworkers to operate independent of local hunters are altering these relationships.

CONCLUSION

The results show that sewing is an important source of cash income for many women in Ulukhaktok. Inuit sewn clothing is highly marketable in a global market that is overwhelmed with low-quality, generic products. The combination of unique styles, high quality of sewing, and cultural elements put Inuit clothing – especially *kamiks*, *attigi*, and *pualuks* – in high demand by customers outside the community. Sewing to earn money is important to Inuit women, but it can also bring stress, frustration, and exhaustion to needleworkers, similar to most income-driven activities. The introduction of the internet to the community has transformed how needleworkers acquire pelts, and how they market and sell their products. Inuit needleworkers have demonstrated resilience to socio-economic changes and have adapted their traditional skills to prosper in a mixed subsistence-cash economy.

ACKNOWLEDGMENTS

The authors thank Donna Akhiatak, Susie Memogana, and Annie Goose for their assistance in data collection. A special thank you to the research participants. This research was possible because of the generosity and kindness of the people of Ulukhaktok. This research was supported by the *Nunamin Illihakvia* project, governed by the Ulukhaktok Community Corporation, and funded by Indigenous Services Canada, Climate Change and Health Adaptation Program (CCHAP).

NOTE

1. This and many of the Innuinaqtun words in this chapter have been anglicized in the plural form through application of the suffix -s. The use of English suffixes on Innuinaqtun nouns and verbs is common in the English vernacular in Uluhaktokmiut.

REFERENCES

Bernard, H.R. 2012. *Social Research Methods: Qualitative and Quantitative Approaches*. Thousand Oaks, CA. SAGE Publications.

Bunce, Anna, James Ford, Sherilee Harper, Victoria Edge, and IHACC Research Team. 2016. "Vulnerability and Adaptive Capacity of Inuit Women to Climate Change: A Case Study from Iqaluit, Nunavut." *Natural Hazards* 83: 1419–1441. https://doi.org/10.1007/s11069-016-2398-6.

Collings, Peter. 2011. "Economic Strategies, Community, and Food Networks in Ulukhaktok, Northwest Territories, Canada." *Arctic* 84 (2): 207–219.

Collings, Peter, Meredith G. Marten, Tristan Pearce, and Alyson G. Young. 2016. "Country Food Sharing Networks, Household Structure, and Implications for Understanding Food Insecurity in Arctic Canada." *Ecology of Food and Nutrition* 55 (1): 30–49. http://doi.org/10.1080/03670244.2015.1072812.

Collings, Peter, George Wenzel, and Richard G. Condon. 1998. "Modern Food Sharing Networks and Community Integration in the Central Canadian Arctic." *Arctic* 51 (4): 301–314.

Condon, Richard G., Peter Collings, and George Wenzel. 1995. "The Best Part of Life: Subsistence Hunting, Ethnicity, and Economic Adaptation among Young Adult Inuit Males." *Arctic* 48 (1): 31–46.

Condon, Richard G., and Julia Ogina. 1996. *The Northern Copper Inuit: A History*. Toronto, ON: University of Toronto Press.

Damas, David. 2002. *Arctic Migrants/Arctic Villagers: The Transformation of Inuit Settlement in the Central Arctic*. Montreal and Kingston: McGill-Queen's University Press.

Dombrowski, Kirk, Emily Channell, Bilal Khan, Joshua Moses, and Evan Misshula. 2013. "Out On the Land: Income, Subsistence Activities, and Food Sharing Networks in Nain, Labrador." *Journal of Anthropology* 2013. https://doi.org/10.1155/2013/185048.

Emanuelsen, Kristin. 2019. *The Role and Importance of Sewing to Inuit Women in the Canadian Arctic*. Master of Arts Thesis, Queensland: University of the Sunshine Coast, 68p.

Freeman, Milton M., and George W. Wenzel. 2006. "The Nature and Significance of Polar Bear Conservation Hunting in the Canadian Arctic." *Arctic* 59 (1): 21–30.

Ford, James D., Joanna Petrasek Macdonald, Catherine Huet, Sara Statham, and Allison MacRury. 2016. "Food Policy in the Canadian North: Is There a Role for Country Food Markets?" *Social Science & Medicine* 152: 35–40. https://doi.org/10.1016/j.socscimed.2016.01.034.

Government of the Northwest Territories (GNWT). 2018. *Statistical Profile: Ulukhaktok*. https://www.statsnwt.ca/community-data/Profile-PDF/Ulukhaktok.pdf.

Harder, Miriam T., and George W. Wenzel. 2012. "Inuit Subsistence, Social Economy and Food Security in Clyde River, Nunavut." *Arctic* 65 (3): 305–318.

Irwin, C. 1989. *Lords of the Arctic: Wards of the State: the Growing Inuit Population, Arctic Resettlement and Their Effects on Social and Economic Change*. Dalhousie University, Department of Sociology and Social Anthropology.

ITK and NRI. 2007. *Negotiating Research Relationships with Inuit Communities: A Guide for Researchers*. Edited by Scot Nickels, Jamal Shirley, and Gita Laidler. Ottawa, ON and Iqaluit, NU: Inuit Tapiriit Kanatami and Nunavut Research Institute.

Inuit Tapiriit Kanatami (ITK). 2018. *National Inuit Strategy on Research*. https://www.itk.ca/wpcontent/uploads/2018/03/National-Inuit-Strategy-on-Research.pdf.

Miller, Elizabeth Mary. 1994. *Sewing and Silence, Sewing and Struggle: Socializing Women's Work in Igloolik, Northwest Territories*. Master's thesis, University of Windsor.

Oakes, Jill E. 1988. *Copper and Caribou Inuit Skin Clothing Production*. Ottawa, ON: University of Ottawa Press.

———. 1995. "Climate and Cultural Barriers to Northern Economic Development: A Case Study from Broughton Island, NWT, Canada." *Climate Research* 5 (1): 91–98.

Pearce, Tristan D., James D. Ford, Gita J. Laidler, Barry Smit, Frank Duerden, Mishak Allarut, Mark Andrachuk, Steven Baryluk, Andrew Dialla, Pootoogoo Elee, Annie Goose, Theo Ikummaq, Eric Joamie, Fred Kataoyak, Eric Loring, Stephanie Meakin, Scott Nickels, Kip Shappa, Jamal Shirley, and Johanna Wandel. 2009. "Community Collaboration and Climate Change Research in the Canadian Arctic." *Polar Research* 28 (1): 10–27. https://doi.org/10.1111/j.1751-8369.2008.00094.x.

Stern, Pamela Rose. 2001. *Modernity at Work: Wage Labor, Unemployment, and the Moral Economy of Work in a Canadian Inuit Community*. PhD dissertation, University of California, Berkeley.

Wenzel, George. 1987. "'I Was Once Independent': The Southern Seal Protest and Inuit." *Anthropologica* 29 (2): 195–210. http://doi.org/10.2307/25605231.

CHAPTER 16

"WE ARE STARVING FOR OUR FOOD"
Country food (in)security in Inuvik, Northwest Territories

Cahley Tod-Tims and Pamela Stern

Three weeks into my fieldwork in Inuvik, I received an email from an Aurora College student responding to my Call for Participants poster inviting Inuvialuit (Inuit) adults to participate in a short interview about their consumption of country food. I arrived at Becky's (a pseudonym) door at the agreed upon time and was invited inside. After settling down on the sofa in her living room, I noticed a child's handprint Christmas tree artwork that took pride of place on her wall. Becky told me that she had one child in daycare and one in school and it was just the three of them in the house. After moving from Paulatuk – a fly-in hamlet of fewer than 300 people – when she was eight years old, Becky has no kin left in Inuvik; "the rest of my family split apart." She told me that her favorite country (or traditional) food is Arctic char because "it's really fresh, I guess. And the taste reminds me of Paulatuk." I asked how often she is able to eat it here and she replied, "not very often. There was a seafood guy that I bought Arctic char off of. I finally had it after so many years."

I was immediately struck by how different Becky's country food situation was compared to the staff volunteers I had been chatting with at Ingamo Hall Friendship Centre. People there seemed to eat country food at least three to four times a week, whereas Becky had not consumed any in months! Even though other community members had declared that "people share country food with single-parents" as well as with Elders and non-able bodied residents, it appeared that Becky, a single mother, working and going to college, lacked the time, money, harvesting skills, or the social networks needed to be able to eat country food and to provide it for her children.

(Adapted from first author's fieldnotes)

Hunger is not new to Inuit. Stories of starvations are part of both Inuit legends and recent oral histories. What is new is the extent to which hunger affects households differently, in large part owing to their different social and economic circumstances. The most recent statistics indicate that Northerners have the highest rates of food insecurity in Canada, with an average of 57 percent of households in Nunavut unable to consistently and reliably obtain adequate food for themselves. At 21.6 percent, the share of food insecure homes in the Northwest Territories is also well

DOI: 10.4324/9780429275470-16

above the proportion of food insecure households in Canada's provinces (Tarasuk and Mitchell 2020). The most widely accepted definition of food security, from the United Nations' Food and Agriculture Organization (FAO), includes having consistent and reliable access to safe, nutritious, and culturally preferred foods in sufficient quantities to permit an active and healthy life (FAO 2008). What is also new is that for some individuals and families, hunger for country foods specifically – those hunted, fished, and gathered from the land – is both chronic and beyond their abilities to effectively address.

Today, many Inuit throughout Inuit Nunangat rely on commercial sources for their food. Imported market foods are expensive in the Arctic due to both high shipping costs and retail monopolies. Despite federal government programs to subsidize some of the costs of shipping food, the prices for commercial foods have continued to rise in many Inuit communities (Fafard St-Germain, Galloway and Tarasuk 2019). Since 2012, an Inuit grassroots organization in Nunavut, Feeding My Family, has protested high prices for commercial food that are often more than double or triple the cost of the same items in southern Canada (Bell 2012). While price is a primary cause of food insecurity among Inuit, it is not the only one. In addition to being expensive, food imported to the North is often high in calories, low in nutritional value, and poor in quality. Importantly as well, not only does a diet dependent on processed foods cause substantial health problems (Myers, Powell and Duhaime 2004), it does not satisfy Inuit *hunger* for foodstuff that connects them to their culture and homeland (Cassady 2008; Nuttall 1992; Yamin-Pasternak et al. 2014). The deprivation of such foods leaves many Northern people feeling "hungry all the time." Thus, for many Canadian Inuit, being food secure necessitates having reliable access to country foods.

Although we are interested Inuit food systems broadly, this chapter discusses ethnographic fieldwork concerning access to country foods conducted by Cahley Tod-Tims in Inuvik, Northwest Territories during the first quarter of 2020.[1] While country food is available in Inuvik, its distribution is highly uneven. As we discuss, the traditional mechanism for distributing country food – sharing – misses a substantial number of contemporary households. At the same time, country food is not widely or consistently available for purchase. The situation is such that even households with enough money to purchase adequate quantities of nutritious food may not have regular access to culturally desirable country foods, a situation we label "country food insecurity." Indeed, Stephenson and Wenzel (2017, 50) question whether Inuit can "be considered food secure without access to [country foods]." Similarly, we argue that country food insecurity transcends standard epidemiological ways of understanding and measuring food security. Country food insecurity is better understood as an issue of food sovereignty or the "right of peoples to healthy and culturally appropriate food" (La Via Campesina 1996).

To borrow from Lévi-Strauss (1971 [1962]), food must nourish people's beliefs, traditions, and values in order to be "good to eat." In the Arctic, "good to eat" foods that connect people to cosmologies, collective identities, reciprocity, and conceptions of well-being are most assuredly country foods. Country foods are also understood by Inuit to nourish their bodies and spirits in a way that "white food" cannot (Borré 1994). The intense emotional attachment to traditional foods became clear in many conversations Cahley had with Inuvialuit. For example, one woman described being overcome by emotion when she got some caribou after going without it for a long period. "I teared up because I really needed Native food. I was starting to get sick from not eating Native food ... getting a stomachache and feel[ing] weak" (Julia). Another said that eating country food "makes me feel happy and my body feels energized again" (Sheena). Country food satisfies hunger in a way that store-bought food cannot. "If you eat Native food, you're fuller longer and everything else. And it's just good soul food, eh?" (Lori).

Government administrators and other outsiders have long suggested that a regulated market for country foods would both support harvesters and offer access to country food to people at all income levels. In other words, the claim is that if Canadian Inuit hunters could easily sell part of their catch, they could earn an income while supplying local (and perhaps regional) demands for country food. Although country food markets are well established in Greenland, similar efforts to enable Canadian Inuit hunters to sell part of their catch have been mostly short-lived or, like the hunter support program in Nunavik, have been met with mixed success (Gombay 2005). In the Canadian North, traditional foods are exchanged for cash through a small number of private and collectively owned businesses, hunter support programs (long-running and *ad hoc*), and recently, through informal or gray market sales between individuals and for local businesses.

FIELD SITE

Inuvik is one of the larger towns in the Canadian Arctic. Located in the Mackenzie River delta region of the Northwest Territories, it is home to 3,140 people, including 1,290 Inuvialuit, 740 Gwich'in and others who identify as either First Nations or Metis, and 1,010 non-Indigenous residents (Statistics Canada 2017).[2] Inuvik was created by the Canadian federal government in the 1950s to replace Aklavik as the administrative center for the western Arctic. Today, in addition to government offices and health and educational institutions, the town hosts the administrative offices of both the Inuvialuit Regional Corporation and the Gwich'in First Nation. Inuvik also has restaurants, hotels, shops, construction and transportation companies, grocery stores, churches, a mosque, a library, a large recreational facility, and a community greenhouse. A number of these institutions are operated by Inuvialuit and Gwich'in organizations. Inuvialuit and Gwich'in from smaller hamlets travel to Inuvik for healthcare or to attend workshops and meetings. Some relocate to Inuvik for education or employment, frequently leaving behind their social networks.

An initial impetus for the research reported here was a proposal from the Inuvialuit Community Economic Development Organization (ICEDO) to advance the capacity of Inuvialuit beneficiaries[3] to process, store, and sell country foods in the wake of widespread food insecurity and climate change (Sue McNeil personal communication). A Government of Canada press release called a pilot food processing course developed by ICEDO and funded by the government a "success" that provided participants with the knowledge and skills to meet the "growing demand for nutritious and affordable country foods in Inuvialuit communities" (CanNor 2016). Like many "proposal economy" development projects, this one appears to have been instigated without plans for post-training support for business development (Stern and Hall 2015). And although ICEDO created a purpose-built facility to teach Inuvialuit to process country food for commercial sale, it seems that no country food businesses were launched as a result of training courses that ran from 2016 to 2019. After having learned about the training course, Cahley, a non-Indigenous master's student from British Columbia, approached the director for the project, who encouraged her to make it part of her thesis research. Although the food processing training program was (temporarily?) suspended shortly before Cahley arrived in Inuvik, she incorporated questions about buying and selling country food into her study.

GETTING COUNTRY FOOD

According to the 2019 NWT Community Survey, two-thirds of Inuvik households (including non-Indigenous households) consumed at least some of their meat and fish from country food sources in the year prior. Hunted or fished protein, however, provided at least half of the meat or fish eaten by less than a quarter (22.4 percent) of households, and almost two-thirds of Inuvik households (60.6 percent) ate little or no country food (NWT Bureau of Statistics 2019a) (see Table 16.1). As the ethnographic data we report here show, some portion of the Inuvik households are without any consistent access to country foods are Inuvialuit.

In Inuvik, Inuvialuit rely on several different ways to get country food. It could be that they or a member of their household hunts and/or fishes. The 2019 NWT Community Survey indicates that 37.7 percent of Indigenous people aged 15 or older in Inuvik did some hunting or fishing during the previous year (NWT Bureau of Statistics 2019b). There are a small number of full-time subsistence hunters, but the majority of Inuvialuit who harvest do so in what they consider their "spare time." For many, obligations of paid employment mean that they have to fit in harvesting after work, on weekends, and on holidays. As one Inuvialuit wage worker put it, "when the Spring comes, I go to Husky Lakes after work and jiggle [ice fish] until 10 or 11 pm." Another told Cahley that her husband had just returned with a moose that he and his cousin had caught. "He texted me to come and help, but I am at work and the blood is still draining anyway, so I'll work on it tonight or tomorrow."

At the same time that wage work restricts the time that people have to engage in subsistence work, wage income is absolutely essential to effective harvesting (Irwin 1985; Todd 2010; see also Collings this volume). The high cost for boats, snowmobiles, and other subsistence equipment, as well as for ammunition and fuel, means that harvesters generally have to rely on others in their households or close networks

Table 16.1 Household consumption of country food in Inuvik, 2018. Includes Inuvialuit, Gwich'in, non-Indigenous, and mixed households*

All or most meat and fish is country food	Approx. half of meat and fish is country food	Approx. one-quarter of meat and fish is country food	Little or no meat and fish is country food
9.5%	12.9%	17.0%	60.6%

Source: 2019 NWT Community Survey (NWT Bureau of Statistics 2019a)
*Based on a response rate of 66.4% of 1,180 Inuvik households

to even attempt to capture game. Among the six communities of the Inuvialuit Settlement Region Inuvik residents have the highest rate of labor participation (75.8 percent) and highest employment rate (68.3 percent) (NWT Bureau of Statistics 2019c). While much of the harvesting of wild foods is done by men, women's labor is integral for processing game and for the wages that support harvesting.

Inuvialuit also receive country food as gifts, usually described as sharing. Sharing traditional foods is widely understood as a moral obligation without expectations of immediate reciprocity (Collings et al. 2015; Levesque et al. 2002; Searles 2002; Stern 2005; Wray and Parlee 2013). Part of this ideology of sharing is predicated on the belief that animals make themselves available to those who share generously (Bodenhorn 2000; Searles 2016). A conversation with an Inuvialuit Elder illustrates this:

> I just got back from Aklavik and I was given a caribou and I shared that with as many people as I could. Yeah, I do it so that I don't want to get anything in return. Otherwise, it doesn't give you as good luck as you can if you just give it away. Especially if you give it away anonymously.
>
> (LG)

In present-day Inuvik, people frequently give gifts of wild food. Cahley's fieldnotes are filled with examples of country food sharing she witnessed or was told about. In many cases sharing occurs between closely related households, but individuals also share with non-kin. A single mother said that her church pastor sometimes gives her meat.

> He gets meat, too, from other people in town, so whenever he has extra, he will bring some here. So, he gave us a [caribou] shoulder piece and a few leg bones for – you know you cook it and you eat the bone marrow in the legs.

Inuvik residents also receive gifts of meat harvested elsewhere. These almost always come through kin networks. For some like Anna (a pseudonym) who has a large extended family in Ulukhaktok, the deliveries of country food arrive regularly. Once a month, her relatives send a box with "muskox, trout, char, or seal depending on the season," which she then shares with local friends who are also from Ulukhaktok. For others, the deliveries may not be quite so regular, but are no less important. For example, the woman whose husband texted her to come home to butcher the moose, was thrilled when her adult daughter brought her caribou meat from relatives in Yukon. "My daughter ha[d] these two huge boxes of caribou for me! And they put in pemmican too, like always." Another described a trip Sachs Harbour when she "came home with this huge box of geese and fish and I can't remember ... there was two other things in there ... for my family and my grandma" (Raven). This gift of country food came from a relative of a family friend she calls "Auntie." Upon learning that Raven was in Sachs Harbour, "Auntie" instructed her Sachs Harbour relative to give Raven country food.

Several organizations in Inuvik distribute country food to Elders and others who are regarded as unable to provide it for themselves. The Inuvik Community Corporation, Nihtat Gwich'in Council, and Inuvik Native Band Office distribute uncooked wild foods, while the Ingamo Hall Friendship Centre, Parish Hall Community Kitchen, and Inuvik Native Band Office run weekly soup kitchens (in the Autumn and Winter) and host feasts where country foods are often served. In March 2020, as a response to COVID-19, the Inuvik Native [Gwich'in] Band Office announced over Facebook that they "have caribou meat for Seniors, Single Parent families, Elders, and health challenged individuals," but that "meat is a priority to Band member[s]." The freezer at Ingamo Hall contains donated country foods, including beluga muktuk, dry whale meat, moose ribs, and berries, which they serve at Elders luncheons, healing circles, and youth programs, as well as the soup kitchen "because they attract people" (Ruth). There are also some community-wide events at which country food is served. For instance, attendees at the IRC Cup Cultural Weekend in March 2020 received a free lunch of cooked beluga *muktuk*, moose dry-meat, dry-fish, "donuts" (fry bread), reindeer chili, and reindeer soup provided by the Inuvialuit Regional Corporation.

Organized country food distributions in Inuvik often take the form of community harvests, or "community hunts" as people in Inuvik refer to them. Community hunts are managed and funded by local Indigenous organizations such as the Nihtat Gwich'in Council (NGC), Inuvik Hunters and Trappers Committee (HTC), and the Inuvik Community Corporation (ICC) for their own members and beneficiaries.[4] Typically, an organization contracts with local hunters to supply meat or fish, which is then distributed to its beneficiaries, or rather to *some* of its beneficiaries. For example, on 12 November 2019 the Inuvik HTC posted on Facebook that they were "looking for 5 hunters to do the Community Caribou Harvest. They get 5 tags each and will be getting paid per caribou." On November 25 they posted a follow-up notice: "[t]o our Inuvik Hunters and Trappers Membership of ELDERS and SINGLE PARENTS, we are now taking names for our annual Caribou Meat distribution." And on 13 May 2020, the ICC announced over Facebook that:

> in partnership with the Inuvialuit Regional Corporation and contributions from Indigenous Services Canada ... the [ICC] is currently doing a Community Geese Harvest. We will purchase a total of 500 geese, a maximum of 20 geese per person at a rate of $25 per goose. The geese **must** be plucked and gutted before purchasing.

Inuvialuit beneficiaries were invited to put their names down to be included on the distribution list. Elders had high praise for community hunts. An Inuvialuit Elder who also receives country food from her daughter's household, explained: "when I got my caribou meat this year, I was so happy. I got a hindquarter, and I got an arm. And I'm all alone. So, I brought it to my daughters, and they cut it up and we had meat." (Shirley) The meat she received as an Elder allowed her to give meat to her kin. Elders, single parents, and the unemployed are recognized as being in need of country food, while others, without regular access to country food, are largely left out of community distributions. One full-time worker voiced her frustration at not being considered in need by local organizations, "I think people have to have a little different way of thinking you know? There are other people that do need some traditional foods. I get them as gifts very rarely."

The Inuvialuit Final Agreement confirms that Inuvialuit "may, without restriction, sell, trade, or barter fish and marine mammal products acquired in subsistence fisheries" to other Inuvialuit and other Native peoples whose traditional territories overlap with those of Inuvialuit (Indian and Northern Affairs Canada 2005, 44). Inuvialuit may also trade or barter for land mammals including moose, bear, muskox, reindeer, and caribou, though with greater restriction than on fish or marine mammals. Highly desired barren-ground caribou, which are designated as a species under threat may not be harvested commercially, and their subsistence hunting is restricted. The Porcupine Caribou Management Agreement established in 1985, permits First Nations, Métis, and Inuvialuit hunters to "barter or trade for caribou meat" (11) or receive a small amount of cash for reasonable expenses incurred while hunting from "native users who are unable to hunt by virtue of age, illness or other disadvantages" (11).

Country food was sold in shops in Inuvik in the past. Victor and Bertha Allen operated a small store that carried country foods in the 1950s, and in the 1980s, the Inuvialuit Development Corporation had a retail outlet that according to the *New York Times*, sold "caribou and whale meat, seal blubber and other 'country foods' on which the Inuvialuit traditionally relied" (Wren 1985, 9).[5] Today, the only retail outlet for country food is an upright freezer at the rear of the IRC's Craft Shop. In February 2020, a small variety of foods, including whole fish, dry-fish, beluga muktuk, reindeer dry-meat, and cloudberries were available for purchase (see Figure 16.1). Several research participants confirmed that they had bought country food at the craft shop, but more as special meals or luxury purchases rather than day-to-day needs.

Many people turn to informal markets and a process they called "bartering" to obtain country foods. As a category, bartering can take several different forms, but it is often conceptualized as similar to sharing. In some cases, bartering consists of providing gasoline, ammunition, or other materials to someone going out hunting, with the expectation of receiving part of the catch. It can also be a negotiated trade of different goods. An Elder explained, "My uncle in Old Crow might say 'Bring me a pail of muktuk, I got caribou in my cache for you.' Okay so we give them their pail of muktuk, they'll give us caribou" (Shirley). And Jessie (a pseudonym) described how she got some Arctic char through contacts in another town since that fish is not found near Inuvik. A woman in Paulatuk had char, which she was happy to send in exchange for some toiletries that she could not get in Paulatuk. Jessie put together a "care package" and sent it with someone who was traveling to Paulatuk.

Bartering, in the local parlance, also refers to purchasing country food from an individual harvester at a price that is perceived to be reimbursement for the hunter's time and expenses.

> So people from Holman [Ulukhaktok], every time those people come down here they'll bring – 'cause they don't need to bring anything here, but they can still bring X amount of weight on the plane – it's straight char. And they'll bring it here and trade with people or sell it, depends.
>
> (Harley)

Facebook has become an important site for the informal sales of country food. "Ground muskox meat for $40 in Ziploc bags" was a regular posting on Inuvik's Buy & Sell Facebook page. And someone preparing to travel to Inuvik, posted "looking for some muktuk, will be arriving Jan 21–22."

Oh, there's this lady from Aklavik who makes – who spends most of her time on the land, so she – and she makes really good dry-fish and stuff. So, she comes in by boat every, I don't know, throughout the summer she'll come maybe four times. And basically, it's posted on Facebook and there's this WHOLE line up of people who show up at the river waiting for her ... She's really good and literally SO much money gets exchanged at that time.

(Raven)

People also find sellers through word of mouth. This is especially true for caribou that cannot be sold legally. During a conversation with several women, one research participant explained that even though community members are "not supposed to

Figure 16.1   Freezer with country food for sale in the craft shop operated by the Inuvialuit Regional Corporation, Inuvik, February 2020. Photo: Cahley Tod-Tims.

buy caribou, people do because they want it, and the hunters need the money since gas is so expensive." When asked about how the hunters advertise that they have caribou available if the exchange is illegal, another woman added that "they call up people they know want it." This prompted another woman to share a story about a time that she and her husband almost bought a whole caribou for $400. "My husband said that was too much because it didn't even have the stomach or organs that he likes, but I would have bought it because caribou is so yummy!" She and many others are able to reconcile this sort of purchase as barter, something akin to sharing, "because they're just going to use that cash to buy gas."

It is important to note that although country foods circulate widely in Inuvik, not all residents have ready access, even if they have the money to make a purchase. "Barter" exchanges, other than those that are facilitated through Facebook, require a network of relationships that can be difficult to establish and maintain. This is especially true for people who have recently moved to Inuvik from one of the smaller communities. Moreover, even if a resident is able to afford a recently harvested moose or caribou, they may not be able to transform it into foodstuff. Butchering a whole animal requires time they may not have. It also requires specialized knowledge as well as a place to process the meat and a freezer to store it.

CHANGE IN THE INUIT FOOD SYSTEM

The move from self-governed camps to permanent towns like Inuvik as well as to smaller settlements in the 1950s and 1960s set many changes in motion for Canadian Inuit including changes to the food system. Prior to that time, Canadian Inuit met nearly all of their food and much of their clothing needs by hunting, processing, sharing, and consuming animals. Camps were comprised primarily of people who recognized themselves as related through descent, marriage, or other mechanisms (see Trott, this volume). Consequently, most day-to-day sharing occurred among kin. The government-administered towns and settlements brought together groups of unrelated people, and while an ideal of generalized sharing persisted, most sharing continued (and still continues) to occur between kin (Collings 2011). At the same time that there were suddenly groups of strangers living together, Inuit living in settlements had more opportunities to consume imported commercial food and other goods, and new pressures to do so.

The pressures on Inuit to eat differently included restrictions on mobility, loss of access to hunting and fishing areas, mandatory school attendance for children, high costs for hunting equipment, time constraints posed by wage labor and other southern institutions, and government campaigns to encourage Inuit to adopt southern ideas about nutrition (Condon, Collings, and Wenzel 1995; Piper 2016; Stern 2003; Usher 1965; Williamson 1974). Some of these factors such as restrictions on mobility and the loss of access to hunting and fishing sites forced Inuit to immediately shift their food practices. The effects of other changes on the food system, such as schooling and nutrition campaigns, only became apparent over time.

Access to game animals was not the criterion the government used when siting towns and villages on Inuit lands. Instead, the government, as well as missionaries and trading companies selected sites with deep water harbors or other features that supported long-distance transportation. The site of Inuvik on the east channel of the

Mackenzie River, for example, was chosen because the topography and soil conditions permitted construction of an airport. Indigenous and long-term non-Indigenous residents of Aklavik who were expected to relocate to the new town, objected to Inuvik's location precisely because the site did not afford access to productive fishing, hunting, or trapping areas. Government planners believed it was inevitable that northern Indigenous people would move away from subsistence hunting (Boek and Boek 1960). Although not everyone can or does participate in subsistence hunting and fishing today, these continue to be critically important for nutrition and for social well-being.

SHARING AND (COUNTRY) FOOD (IN)SECURITY

Sharing country food is widely reported in the ethnographic and popular literature as a deeply held moral imperative across Inuit Nunangat. Among Utqiaġvik (Barrow) Iñupiat, according to Bodenhorn, sharing constitutes "a complex of social actions all of which create and maintain morally valued relationships that extend well beyond hunting" (2000, 28). Searles reports that many Inuit residents of Nunavut's capital, Iqaluit, hold similar perspectives, and he adds that consuming and sharing country food is a way that young Inuit are able to distinguish themselves from *qallunaat* and reinforce their sense of themselves as Inuit (2016, 201). Similarly, one research participant declared that "sharing and eating [country food] is who we are; if we didn't do it, we would feel fake."

Among some contemporary Inuit, sharing country food has been elevated from a cultural trait reported in ethnographies, to an emblem of Inuitness (Briggs 1997). This is not to deny the real economic, nutritional, and social benefits of sharing and eating country food, but to also recognize its symbolic power in a period when so much of Inuit daily life is structured by external institutions. When Cahley mentioned to one country food secure Inuvialuk that she was hearing that some people in Inuvik were able to eat country just one or two times a month, the reply was, "No, everybody shares here … It's still common here, because it's our custom." Others, however, recognized that there is great variation in peoples' access to country foods. "Some people eat it every day and some people might go years without," acknowledged one local leader. In some cases, the emotional resonance of sharing seems to constitute a form of "structural nostalgia … for a time when everything was better: people were more generous and uncomplicated, kindness was more disinterested" (Herzfeld 2016 [1997], 140).

> Years ago the community used to look after itself, but compared to then, people don't look after old people the way that they should. Like I know my family's pretty close knit and we look after each other, but it's like we take care of our own and that's good enough. It's kind of sad because of the society we live in, but that's the way it is.
> (34-year-old male resident of Ulukhaktok, quoted in Collings 2011, 211)

People in Inuvik also offered explanations for perceived failures to share, such as the high cost of hunting or shortages of meat. "People share less now because it is so expensive, it stays in the family more" or "[It] depends on what I have left after I've made sure that my family has enough." Many forget, or never recognized, that prior to living in towns, most sharing was, by necessity, among kin.

The idealization of sharing is so pervasive, that most are unaware that unequal access to country food is not a new phenomenon among Inuit. Pryor and Graburn (1977), using data collected by Graburn in and around Salluit, Nunavik in 1959, showed that distributions of food, labor, and advice as well the loan of tools and sled dogs were far from egalitarian or generalized. Their analysis revealed that the Inuit community was stratified into two groups: one comprised of low-status families who gave generously, but rarely received gifts or assistance, and another comprised of high status and well-provisioned families who were only occasionally generous with their resources, but were effective in manipulating the symbols of sharing.

> Furthermore, conspicuous giveaways or successful families were long remembered, and what people said about the rules of sharing sometimes counted for more than what people did: For instance, the high-prestige persons always vehemently upheld the ethics of the system and the necessity of total generosity, whereas some of the poorest questioned the need to continue a distribution system that had been functional among much smaller traditional social groups [in other words, kin groups]. Yet, as our analysis indicates, some of the former were net takers (even after the giveaways had been taken into account) and some of the latter, net donors!
>
> (Pryor and Graburn 1977, 94)

As we noted above, in contemporary Inuvik various Indigenous organizations coordinate distributions of country foods collected through community hunts or from individual donations. For example, a staff member at Ingamo Hall brought in the arm of a caribou he had harvested for the next day's soup kitchen. His reason for the donation was that he "likes helping those in need." A volunteer mentioned that approximately once a month she takes uncooked wild food to the Long Term Care Unit in the hospital. In her words, she "like[s] to cook there because the smells make the Elders happy, and then they jig [dance]!" While some of the organizations' food programs, like the soup kitchen or the food bank, are specifically constituted to address the food security needs of the most vulnerable members of the community, all of the programs to distribute country food direct their distributions to Elders, the unemployed, the disabled, and to a lesser extent, to single parents (see Figure 16.2). One unintended consequence of this policy is that households with employed adults can be the most *country food insecure*.

Unlike standard food security paradigms, the concept of country food insecurity accounts for the nuance of a mixed traditional and cash economy whereby an individual or household can be affluent in one economy, but poor in the other. While they may not struggle to buy groceries, many wage-earning Inuvialuit are unable to regularly obtain country foods because they lack either the time or the knowledge required for subsistence hunting. A short excerpt from an interview with a young Inuvialuit mother elucidates the desire for country foods:

Shawna: It's kinda hard to get Native foods. If there's that seafood guy around, I'd be able to get char, but that's about it.

Cahley: That's about it? Okay. How do you feel about that?
Shawna: I don't know, I think it should be easier. I miss having Native food. It's really good.

Figure 16.2   Country food set out for Elders' lunch program, Inuvik, February 2020. Photo: Cahley Tod-Tims.

A number of country food insecure individuals voiced a mixture of frustration and sadness for their country food poor situation. At the same time, they are ambivalent about schemes to create formal markets for country food; like others, they express nostalgia for a time when "everyone shared," and they develop explanations for their own country food insecurity. Thomas (a pseudonym), a middle-aged maintenance worker, for example, said that he is able to eat country foods only about once a month despite having eaten it every day when he "lived on the land outside of town up until the age of twelve." It is "something you grow up on, something you crave." He noted that "people do still share, especially with Elders, single mothers, and children," but believes that they "do not share as much nowadays because of the cost of hunting." He then conceded that his participation in harvesting, and thus his access to country foods, was limited by wildlife regulations that restrict hunting caribou close to town. "Time and money" keep him from harvesting, and so, to get country foods he would have to "rely on handouts." In some sense, Thomas posits himself as less deserving than those who are eligible for community distributions.

The question of deservingness came up in other conversations Cahley had with Inuvialuit about unequal access to country foods. For instance, in response to a question about whether there are people who do not seem to have enough connections to be able to acquire country foods, an Elder affirmed,

> Yeah, there's lots of those. There's a lot of extended families that are ignorant to their own family when it comes to country food. They're not gonna share with them, they're gonna say "You got skidoo [snowmobile], you got whatever. Why don't you go out? You got big boys" ... that kinda attitude.
>
> (Shirley)

This assumption is that able-bodied "big boys" with jobs and snowmobiles should be capable of producing country foods themselves. Likewise, a full-time administrative worker suggested that sharing country foods today is different than in the past.

> People share with the ones that need it. But because I'm a person who has the means to get it, because I'm young and my partner is able, they expect you to get your own meat. But let's say you didn't have all the hunting gear and your partner's not interested in hunting or whatever, then you wish for it, you know.
>
> (Margaret)

These explanations are somewhat analogous to Katz's explication of the "undeserving poor" who are believed to be capable of providing for themselves and yet willfully elect not to (2013). In his examination of the western welfare state and the moralization of poverty, Katz argues that when resources are finite, lines are drawn between those considered deserving and undeserving of help. Support is to be afforded only to individuals whose poverty is regarded as beyond their control. In contrast, the undeserving poor are imagined to have "brought poverty upon themselves" through either their own actions or their failures to act (Katz 2013, 3).

In Inuvik, there is widespread agreement that Elders, single parents, the physically challenged, and the unemployed deserve gifts of country food regardless of their actual situations. The employed, able-bodied youth, and working-aged adults, in contrast, are imagined to be beyond "the limits of social obligation" (Katz 2013, 4). The analogy to Katz's undeserving poor is not a perfect one, but it does help us think about the strange situation in which the people starving for country food are often financially secure and employed. For the most part, however, they feel helpless to alter their country food poor situations. For many in Inuvik, deservingness has tangible impacts on country food (in)security.

It is difficult to overstate the extent to which Elders in Inuvik are prioritized for gifts of country food, both in formal programs such as Community Harvests and in informal sharing networks. For instance, the Inuvik Hunters and Trappers Committee (IHTC) announced on their Facebook page that "54 Elders, 15 single parents, and 3 members received caribou meat" from the Community Caribou Harvest in December 2019. A similar story of explicit Elder prioritization occurred in August 2019 when the IHTC posted on its Facebook page that "2 pails of muktuk, whale meat, and caribou were donated. 1 ziplock bag of each to Elders so put your name down." We include these examples not to criticize sharing practices that emphasize Elders as deserving, but to illustrate that with finite resources, the existing distribution model excludes quite a few country food insecure households. We also want to emphasize that not a single country food insecure research participant suggested that Elders should receive less, only that they wished for a way to increase their own access and to assuage their own hunger for traditional foods.

Elders are also prioritized in informal country food sharing by relatives or general community members. While most country food exchanges occur via close kin or social connections, providing for Elders appears to be recognized as a communal responsibility. For example, an Ingamo Hall Friendship Centre employee in her twenties described how she and her husband had recently caught 30 loche [burbot] and after keeping some for themselves, gave the rest to Elders. In fact, this practice is so taken for granted that it was two months into her research project before Cahley realized that she had yet to explicitly ask *why* Elders are considered most *deserving* of traditional foods.

Cahley: This might seem obvious, but why is it so important that Elders are shared with first?
Lori: Because they're – to me it's because it's their delicacy to begin with, they grew up with this food. And it's just always been taught, "Elders first, share with Elders, and make sure your granny eats."
Sheena: You respect your Elders because they were there for you as a child. When we were vulnerable as a child, they were there for us. And now it's time for us to give back our time and respect.

Sharing with Elders is described as necessary for the Elders' well-being. "Now that they're so old, they can't do very much so I tend to share with my grandparents, my aunties and uncles, my older cousins" (Julia). Elders deserve shared country food because of their assumed physical limitations. Working-aged adults, on the other hand, are imagined to be physically able to hunt and yet, due to their lack of harvesting knowledge, time, or equipment may, in some cases, actually be less capable than some Elders. An interlocutor also confirmed that younger people might feel a sense of obligation to share with a non-kin Elder who "respected your family or was good friends with your grandparents" (Sheena). In this way, social networks that assume responsibility for sharing with Elders are maintained across generations.

It is important to note that while Elders are indeed prioritized for country food sharing, they often redistribute country food or cook it for their families. For instance, after jesting that "a hug and a smile" is the pay that he receives for sharing caribou with Elders, a full-time hunter explained that "if an Elder gets meat, they're making dry-meat. And that dry-meat is going to the ones they love too!" (FS). A youth describing how her grandmother provides their family with traditional foods illustrates this point further:

> Like when I was growing up, we used to go there [grandmother's house] for lunches sometimes. And like I said, she'd make fried [caribou] meat and Kraft Dinner [*giggles*], like that was lunch. We'd just hang out with her during lunchtime and eat her food, we were really little like maybe four or five kinda thing. And otherwise now it's more of a "Oh, let me make you food" and so she'll make food and then we'll just pick it up from her. And sometimes we'll hang out there and eat [caribou] meat and we'll take the rest home.
>
> (Raven)

In fact, a few days after the interview, Raven texted, "my grandma gave me some dry meat today and I thought you might want to try some."

CONCLUSION

In her short article, "The Cooler Ring," anthropologist Molly Lee describes a habit of her Yup'ik collaborator, Flora Mark, as they travel from village to village in southwestern Alaska visiting and interviewing other Yup'ik artisans. Flora, who lives in Anchorage, "never [leaves] home without her battered red and white industrial-sized Coleman cooler" (2002, 3). As they go from place to place in bush planes and on sleds pulled by four-wheeled ATVs, the unwieldy cooler goes with them. Flora delivers day-old donuts and other urban supplies to friends and relatives in the Yukon-Kuskokwim (Y-K) Delta and picks up seal meat, caribou ribs, salmonberries, and other country foods, some of which she will share with friends in Anchorage. As Lee writes about her research collaboration with Flora elsewhere (Lee 2006), we learn that part of what makes Flora such an effective research partner for Lee is that she knows *everybody*, is aware of their situations, their expertise. Her outgoing personality helps her know who has what and who would appreciate receiving what she has to offer. She is able to eat and share country food in Anchorage because she works hard at maintaining her connections in the city and in the Y-K Delta. Although Flora makes sharing look uncomplicated, it is anything but.

Similarly, it is no simple matter to maintain an Inuvialuit food system in contemporary northern towns and villages. Nonetheless, sharing persists as both a deeply held Inuvialuit value and a living practice. Indeed, the Inuvialuit participant who stated that "sharing and eating [country food] is who we are; if we didn't do it, we would feel fake" emphasized that sharing country food is as vital an element of traditional foodways as the actual consumption. To paraphrase, sharing is not what Inuvialuit do but *who* Inuvialuit are.

Country foods are not only nutritious, but they "taste better when we eat together" (Emily). As Mintz observed, "the symbolic significance of people taking their food together" (2008, 516) imbues foods with more than nutrients. The affective, sensorial, and sociocultural associations of country foods make them by far the most desired and prized nutritional items. Furthermore, their production, distribution, and consumption are foundational to people's sense of kinship, community, well-being, and identity. People experience joy from eating country food because of the company in which it is eaten and likewise take joy in each other's company because of the foodstuff's sensorial qualities. The social and emotional value of sharing is strengthened when, as one Inuvialuk put it, they "would rather wait for company" than eat country foods alone. These and other comments suggest that the way to address food insecurity is through expanded forms of sharing rather than commercial markets.

Indigenous organizations have developed programs to get country food to those who are understood to be most in need. These go a long way toward alleviating food insecurity in Inuvik, but do not necessarily address issues of food sovereignty. Some Inuvialuit remain country food insecure. They continue to hunger for country foods – foods laden with memories, sociality, and cultural values. Much of the health and social science literature on the dietary conditions in Arctic communities examines the situation through a food insecurity lens (see Loring and Gerlach 2012). Survey data indicate that that over half of Inuit households in Canada are food insecure. Statistics, however, do not necessarily account for variations in access to the types of food that community members crave and leave them feeling health-*full*. The sociocultural and affective dimension of consuming these foods makes understanding barriers to access vital for the well-being of all community members. This issue goes beyond nutritional surveys and caloric intake data from classic food security models; it is about addressing people's hunger for foods that connect them to their culture, identity, and homeland.

NOTES

1. The research plan was reviewed and approved by the Simon Fraser University Office of Research Ethics and licensed by the Aurora Research Institute. Cahley's travel to Inuvik was supported by a Northern Scientific Research Training grant from the Government of Canada. We thank Ece Arslan, Cheyanne Connell, Marina Kadriu, Sam Lee, Madelyn Prevost, and Chantelle Spicer for comments on an earlier draft. Errors of interpretation or fact are our own.
2. These census figures obscure the reality that the town is home to many ethnically mixed households and individuals with mixed ethnic heritage.
3. Inuit participants in the 1984 land claims agreement known as the Inuvialuit Final Agreement are referred to as beneficiaries.
4. These are ethnically based organizations that were established to interact with the state. Inuvik Community Corporation and Inuvik Hunters and Trappers are Inuvialuit.
5. Ulu Foods also had a wholesale division that provided fish as well as salamis and other cured meats made from muskox for southern markets.

REFERENCES

Bell, Jim. 2012. "Nunavut Demonstrators Gather to Protest Food Prices, Poverty" *Nunatsiaq News*, 9 June 2012. https://nunatsiaq.com/stories/article/65674nunavut_demonstrators_gather_to_protest_food_prices_poverty/ (accessed 19 July 2020).

Boek, Walter E., and Jean K. Boek. 1960. *A Report of Field Work in Aklavik and Inuvik, N.W.T. for the Research Co-ordination Centre Department of Northern Affairs and National Resources*. Unpublished manuscript.

Bodenhorn, Barbara. 2000. "It's Good to Know Who Your Relatives Are But We Were Taught to Share with Everybody: Shares and Sharing among Inupiaq Households." *Senri Ethnological Studies* 53: 27–60. http://doi.org/10.15021/00002844

Borré, Kristen. 1994. "The Healing Power of the Seal: The Meaning of Inuit Health Practice and Belief." *Arctic Anthropology* 31 (1): 1–15.

Briggs, Jean L. 1997. "From Trait to Emblem and Back: Living and Representing Culture in Everyday Inuit Life." *Arctic Anthropology* 37 (1): 227–235.

CanNor. 2016. *Success Story: Preparing Inuvialuit Businesses and Communities for Economic Diversification Opportunities*. Canadian Northern Economic Development Agency. https://www.cannor.gc.ca/eng/1467053877439/1467053896347

Cassady, Joslyn. 2008. "'Eating for Outsiders': Cancer Causation Discourse among the Inupiat of Arctic Alaska." *International Journal of Circumpolar Health* 67 (4): 374–383. https://doi.org/10.3402/ijch.v67i4.18341

Collings, Peter. 2011. "Economic Strategies, Community, and Food Networks in Ulukhaktok, Northwest Territories, Canada." *Arctic* 64 (2): 207–219.

Collings, Peter, Meredith G. Marten, Tristan Pearce, and Alyson G Young. 2015. Country food sharing networks, household structure, and implications for understanding food insecurity in Arctic Canada. *Ecology of Food and Nutrition*, 55(1), 30–49. https://doi.org/10.1080/03670244.2015.1072812

Condon, Richard G., Peter Collings, and George W. Wenzel. 1995. "The Best Part of Life: Subsistence Hunting, Ethnicity, and Economic Adaptation among Young Adult Inuit Males." *Arctic* 48 (1): 31–46.

Fafard St-Germain, Andrée, Tracy Galloway, and Valerie Tarasuk. 2019. "Food Insecurity in Nunavut Following the Introduction of Nutrition North Canada." *Canadian Medical Association Journal* 191: E55–E558. http://doi.org/10.1503/cmaj.181617

FAO (Food and Agriculture Organization of the United Nations). 2008. *An Introduction to the Basic Concepts of Food Security*. EC-FAO Food Security Programme. http://www.fao.org/3/a-al936e.pdf (accessed 21 July 2020).

Gombay, Nicole. 2005. "The Commoditization of Country Foods in Nunavik: A Comparative Assessment of its Development, Applications, and Significance." *Arctic* 58 (2): 115–128.

Herzfeld, Michael. 2016 [1997]. *Cultural Intimacy: Social Poetics and the Real Life of States, Societies, and Institutions*, 3rd ed. New York: Routledge.

Indian and Northern Affairs Canada. 2005. *Inuvialuit Final Agreement as Amended*. Ottawa, ON: Government of Canada http://irc.ub8.outcrop.com/system/files/Inuvialuit%20Final%20Agreement-Amended.pdf

Irwin, Colin. 1985. "Lords of the Arctic, Wards of the State: The Growing Inuit Population, Arctic Resettlement and Their Effects on Social and Economic Change – A Summary Report." *CARC-Northern Perspectives* 17 (1): 2–12.

Katz, Michael B. 2013. *The Undeserving Poor: America's Enduring Confrontation with Poverty*, 2nd ed. Oxford: Oxford University Press.

La Via Campesina. 1996. *Food Sovereignty*. http://viacampesina.org/en/index.php/our-conferences-mainmenu-28/2-tlaxcala-1996-mainmenu-48/425-ii-international-conference-of-the-via-campesina-tlaxcala-mexico-april-18-21

Lee, Molly. 2002. "The Cooler Ring: Urban Alaska Native Women and the Subsistence Debate." *Arctic Anthropology* 39 (1–2): 3–9.

———. 2006. "Flora and Me." In *Critical Inuit Studies: An Anthology of Contemporary Arctic Ethnography*, edited by Pamela Stern and Lisa Stevenson, 25–34. Omaha, NE: University of Nebraska Press.

Levesque, Carole, Dominique De Juriew, Catherine Lussier, and Nadine Trudeau. 2002. "Between Abundance and Scarcity: Food and the Institution of Sharing Among the Inuit of the Circumpolar Region During the Recent Historical Period." In *Sustainable Food Security in the Arctic: State of Knowledge*, edited by Gérard Duhaime, 102–115. Edmonton, AB: CCI Press.

Lévi-Strauss, Claude. 1971 [1962]. *Totemism*. Translated by Rodney Needham. Boston, MA: Beacon Press.

Loring, Philip A. and S. Craig Gerlach. 2012. "Searching for Progress on Food Security in the North American North: A Research Synthesis and Meta-Analysis of the Peer-Reviewed Literature." *Arctic* 68 (3): 380–392. http://doi.org/10.14430/arctic4509

Mintz, Sidney. 2008. "Food and Diaspora." *Food, Culture & Society* 11 (4): 509–523. http://doi.org10.2752/175174408X389157

Myers, Heather, Stephanie Powell, and Gerard Duhaime. 2004. "Setting the Table for Food Security: Policy Impacts in Nunavut." *Canadian Journal of Native Studies* 2: 425–445.

Nuttall, Mark. 1992. *Arctic Homeland: Kinship, Community and Development in Northwest Greenland*. Toronto, ON: University of Toronto Press.

NWT Bureau of Statistics. 2019a. *2018 Households Eating Meat or Fish from Hunting or Fishing*. 2018 NWT Household Survey. https://www.statsnwt.ca/Traditional%20Activities/

———. 2019b. *2018 Indigenous Engagement in Traditional Activities*. 2018 NWT Household Survey. https://www.statsnwt.ca/Traditional%20Activities/.

———. 2019c. *Community Labour Force Activity, 1986–2019 Activities.* 2019 NWT Community Survey. https://www.statsnwt.ca/labour-income/labour-force-activity/.

Piper, Liza. 2016. "From Subsistence to Nutrition: The Canadian State's Involvement in Food and Diet in the North, 1900–1970." In *Ice Blink: Navigating Northern Environmental History*, edited by Stephen Bocking and Brad Martin, 181–222. Calgary, AB: University of Calgary Press.

Pryor, Frederic L., and Nelson Graburn. 1977. "Exchange and Transfer: A Case Study." In *The Origins of the Economy: A Comparative Study of Distribution in Primitive and Peasant Economies*, edited by Frederic L. Pryor, 69–101. New York: Academic Press.

Searles, Edmund. 2002. "Food and the Making of Modern Inuit Identities." *Food and Foodways* 10 (1–2): 55–78. https://doi.org/10.1080/07409710212485

———. 2016. "To Sell or Not to Sell: Country Food Markets and Inuit Identity in Nunavut." *Food and Foodways* 24 (3–4): 194–212. http://doi.org/10.1080/07409710.2016.1210899

Statistics Canada. 2017. *Census Profile.* 2016 Census. Statistics Canada Catalogue no. 98-316-X2016001. Ottawa, ON. Released 29 November 2017. https://www12.statcan.gc.ca/census-recensement/2016/dp-pd/prof/index.cfm?Lang=E (accessed 21 July 2020).

Stern, Pamela. 2003. "Upside-Down and Backwards: Time Discipline in a Canadian Inuit Community." *Anthropologica* 45 (1): 147–161. http://doi.org/10.2307/25606121

———. 2005. "Wage Labor, Housing Policy and the Nucleation of Inuit Households in Holman, NWT Canada." *Arctic Anthropology* 42 (2): 66–81.

Stern, Pamela, and Peter V. Hall. 2015. *The Proposal Economy: Neoliberal Citizenship in "Ontario's Most Historic Town"*. Vancouver, BC: UBC Press.

Stephenson, Eleanor, and George Wenzel. 2017. "Food Politics: Finding a Place for Country Food in Canada's Northern Food Policy." *Northern Public Affairs* 5 (1): 49–51.

Tarasuk Valerie, and Andy Mitchell. 2020. *Household Food Insecurity in Canada, 2017–18.* Toronto, ON: Research to Identify Policy Options to Reduce Food Insecurity (PROOF). https://proof.utoronto.ca/ (accessed 18 July 2020).

Todd, Zoe Sarah Croucher. 2010. *Food Security in Paulatuk, NT: Opportunities and Challenges of a Changing Community Economy.* Master's thesis, University of Alberta.

Usher, Peter J. 1965. *Economic Basis and Resource Use of the Coppermine-Holman Region, N.W.T.* Ottawa, ON: Department of Northern Affairs and National Resources.

Williamson, Robert G. 1974. *Eskimo Underground: Socio-Cultural Change in the Canadian Central Arctic.* Uppsala: Almqvist & Wiksell.

Wray, Kristine and Brenda Parlee. 2013. "Ways We Respect Caribou: Teetl'it Gwich'in Rules." *Arctic* 66 (1): 68–78. https://doi.org/10.14430/arctic4267

Wren, Christopher S. 1985. "Corporate Fever Hits the Eskimos." *The New York Times*, 26 May. Section 3, p. 9. https://www.nytimes.com/1985/05/26/business/corporate-fever-hits-the-eskimos.html

Yamin-Pasternak, Sveta, Andrew Kliskey, Lilian Alessa, Igor Pasternak, and Peter Schweitzer. 2014. "The Rotten Renaissance in the Bering Strait." *Current Anthropology* 55 (5): 619–646.

CHAPTER 17

SOCIAL RELATIONS AMONG INUIT
Tuqłuraqtuq and Ilagiit

Christopher G. Trott

To maintain itself over time, every society must reproduce itself. This not only refers to the reproduction of each individual, but also to the reproduction of the economic, social, and cosmic relations that constitute the society. All such processes are mediated through the structure of social relations among the members of the society that are frequently referred to in the literature as "kinship" relations. In small-scale, face-to-face societies such as the Inuit, people were taught and knew their relationship to every other person within their universe of social interactions. On those rare occasions when they encountered someone new, Inuit could ask three key questions to locate that person socially:

Kinauviit? Who are you?
Nami nunaqaqpiit? Where do you have land?
Kinamik angajurraqqaqpiit?[1] Who is your camp "boss"?

These may appear as familiar and perhaps innocuous questions but the specific Inuit cultural content behind them forces one to think in very different ways.

I conducted my original research in Arctic Bay, North Baffin Island between June 1979 and July 1981. Much of what follows comes from that encounter and is thus ethnographically specific to the North Baffin region (Arctic Bay, Pond Inlet, and Igloolik) (see Trott 1989). The questions above specifically came from the context of visiting Inuit friends in hospital in Montreal. For five years I was a visitor and advocate for Inuit in hospital in Montreal (1983 to 1988). I returned to Arctic Bay in the summer of 2000 and found that although many of the Elders with whom I had worked had died, their children and grandchildren certainly knew who I was and expected me to know and act following Inuit ways. From 2001 until 2011, I worked every summer (and one spring and one fall) in Pangnirtung in South Baffin Island and finally for one summer in 2014 in Igloolik. My research, reflections, and observations are thus particularly focused on the Qiqiktani (Baffin) region. There were variations between North Baffin Island and Pangnirtung, especially in the application of "cousin" *illu* terms, but overall there was consistency and coherency across the region. There are further important variations across the Inuit world, but I think the general high-level principles I will articulate apply even though the details will vary.

DOI: 10.4324/9780429275470-17

Over time, I noticed that as people increasingly speak English, what I am about to describe is rarely if ever translated and thus may appear to have disappeared. Not so if one is speaking Inuktitut. The richness and variety of terms continue to be used. A good example is once when I was working with a group of students in Pangnirtung, our interpreter introduced herself and her baby who was on her lap. In English she said, "My name is Maili, and this is my son Piita." In Inuktitut she said, "My name is Maili, and this is my mother Uqalik." This is a difference that makes a difference, and what this chapter is about to explore.

Maili began by answering the question, *kinauviit*? To think about what this question covers, one can begin by asking about the constituent elements of a person. There are two ways one can consider the makeup of a human being.

First, the human person is made up of four elements:

a) *timi* – the body
b) *anirniq* – the "breath soul"
c) *tarniq* – the "soul"
d) *atiq* – the name soul

In this context, I do not want to explore the dimensions of *timi*. Suffice it to say that the body constitutes a symbolic field for Inuit as much as for any other people. See the work by Michèle Therrien (1987) for a comprehensive analysis of the body.

Anirniq is the "breath soul." It is perhaps best understood as the animating life force that upon death simply disappears into the universe. In modern Inuktitut, *anirniq* is also used to speak of the Holy Spirit in the Christian sense.

Tarniq is the word usually used generally for "soul" but is also based on the root for "shadow." When a person or animal is born, a tiny miniature version of themselves is captured inside a bubble (*pullaq*) that floats around in the body, although it is generally located near the groin. Upon death the bubble bursts and the soul departs the body – this is the soul that in modern Christian discourse goes to either heaven or hell but can also hang around and cause trouble and problems for those who remain behind. When the bubble is formed at birth it captures a very small part of the atmosphere (*sila*) on that day. Each person is thus intimately connected with the weather, and a person born on a nice day can bring nice weather while one born on a stormy day can invoke bad weather. The reproduction of humans is thus closely connected with the cosmos (*sila*). In the modern period it is often suggested that the atmospheric disturbances created by climate change are linked to the breakdown in human social relationships because of this connection.

Atiq is the name soul that is received from someone who recently died. We will return to this shortly.

There is a second way we can understand the makeup of a human person. In the cycle of relations with animals, game animals give themselves up to the hunters in order to supply their flesh for humans, not only for people to live and remain healthy, but also to supply the flesh for fetuses as they develop (Saladin d'Anglure 1975). In the same way that the animals share their bodies with humans, women cut up and distribute the flesh, releasing the soul of the animal to come back as another animal. Humans and animals are mutually implicated in each other's reproduction and in the reconstitution of the universe. Together, through relations with *sila* – as constituted through the *tarniq* and the mutuality of the reproductive relations with the flesh – humans are deeply embedded within the process of reproduction of the entire universe. As we consider the narrower field of human social relations, we have to keep in mind that it does not only involve those who may or may not be "kin," but the whole world.

As the flesh of animals builds the body of the fetus, it combines with the *atiq*. When I was in Arctic Bay, one of the women had a miscarriage. I was trying to express my sympathy to the woman's mother, to be passed on to the woman, when the older woman replied, "Not to worry, there was no *atiksaq* (material for an *atiq*) and thus the fetus could not grow." I am not sure why there was no *atiksaq* in this instance, but clearly since one of the crucial elements of the fetus was missing, it would not have formed.

ATIQ

Both of these models of the human have pointed to the importance of the *atiq*. *Atiq* literally means "name" but usually "soul" is added on in translation to indicate the deeper repercussions of the naming relationships. From his work in Igloolik,[2] Saladin d'Anglure (2018) has shown through the narrative of Iqalliuq that when a person dies, the name soul rises up out of the body and goes in search of a woman in the process of becoming pregnant. The name soul enters the woman and joins with blood from the mother, the semen from the father, and the flesh from animals to form a fetus. The fetus finds itself inside an *iglu* where it grows and develops until the time for birth.

Inuit have a number of ways of ascertaining which name has formed into a fetus. The most common way is for the mother or grandmother to dream of someone who has recently died coming over to their home to visit or have tea (Kappianaq in Otak and Pitsiulak-Stevens 2014). In the past, and especially during difficult births, either the midwife or a shaman would call out the names of the recently deceased and the child would be born when its own name was called out. There were times when a mistake was made, and when this happened the newborn would be colicky and would cry a lot until the name was changed to the correct name soul. In any case, the child was usually named after the last person who had died in the community. If one thinks back to the past with small groups of people spread out over the land, information on who had died recently would be fairly restricted geographically and so there was a high probability that the child would be named after a person who was related.

While I was in Arctic Bay, I had a Swiss Army pocket-knife which I carried as a memento of my father who had died just before I went north. One day the knife was stolen, and I was lamenting the fact to my friend, Arnaujumajuq. Arnaujumajuq turned to me and said, "That is so typical of a *qallunaaq* (white man) to remember someone by a material object." Picking up a small child, he said, "We Inuit remember the dead through our children, this child is my [deceased] wife and every time I hold the child I think about my wife." In this exchange, there are two important points: First that the deceased are remembered and "memorialized" in the children. Second, it indicates that children are the dead ancestors returned and thus must be treated with the love, care, and respect that one would have shown those Elders.

It is possible for new names to enter into the system and for some names to die. Names from people who had some form of physical or mental disability, who were chronically ill, or who were particularly evil might not be passed on and would disappear. Names could be added into the system by shamans giving the names of their helping spirits (*tunngrait*) to a person to add a stronger life force or to heal illness (see Saladin d'Anglure 1997 for the relationship between helping spirits and names). In the modern period, new names have been added into Inuit social relations through Christian baptism – the Protestant missionaries insisting that Inuit take biblical names and the Catholic missionaries insisting on saints' names – all of which are now passed on in the same way as Inuktitut names. Most recently, names from popular television shows (e.g., *Hannah Montana*) are being introduced into the system.

The physical characteristics and behavior of the newborn child are closely observed to confirm which name has entered into the child.[3] I was told in Arctic Bay that a particular person who had died had been very good at playing the accordion and jigging, and now the child who had his name responded to tapes of jigging music by jumping up and down. Another man told me that his namesake was a shaman who had been attacked by another shaman in the form of a wolf and lost his lower leg in the attack. The man I knew had one leg shorter than the other and had a significant limp. Children are inspected for birthmarks that match injuries, wounds, or other physical anomalies that their namesakes might have had. All of these provide material evidence for which name has entered a child.

Inuit usually have more than one name from more than one person who has recently died. Inuit usually have a minimum of two names but there are often many more.[4] I know one young woman in Pangnirtung who carries 26 names. This means that she would be a different person depending on the social context in which she is interacting. Unlike the western notion of the person as an integrated, unified, autonomous individual, for Inuit, persons can be divisible and act as an entirely different person in different contexts. On the other hand, a single name can also be given to a number of different children. In Arctic Bay, when one very popular elder died, his name was given to eleven different children. Another Elder's name was given to seven children. There is a special relationship among those who share a name as they all share in the same substance of the person. In North Baffin Island, people who share names call each other *avva* (half), in South Baffin Island, *atikuluk* (dear sweet name), and in northern Quebec and the Belcher Islands, *sauniq* (bone). Usually, one of the children who share names will be particularly marked as the one in whom the name is reincarnated while the other children will be acknowledged but not emphasized.

ATIIT AND SOCIAL RELATIONS

The point of this discussion is that the child who receives a name is the name-giver come back to life. One might be tempted to use the word reincarnated, but I think we have to be careful not to import the eastern notions of reincarnation and karma into the Inuit context. While the great Igloolik shaman Ava spoke of seeing the line of shadows of the name souls behind each person (Rasmussen 1929), it is clear that the focus is much more on the transmission of the name from the last person who died to the current child. Inuit distinguish between *inuujunniqtuq*, "no longer alive," which is used until the name returns in a child, at which point the person is *tuqujuq*, "dead"

(Bordin 2011). One friend of mine in Pangnirtung was grieving deeply after his wife had died, until the day when one of the other Elders came to him and said, "your wife has come back in this child. You do not need to mourn any longer."

In Figure 17.1, a man called Ittuq (grandfather) has died and his name has been passed to his recently born grandchild. Remember that the names do not have to pass through existing family relations. This diagram is to help simplify the discussion for understanding. When the child is born, the people in the diagram will use the kinship term they used for Ittuq. So, the grandmother will call the child *uiga* "my husband," the father *ataataga* "my father," the mother *sakiga* "my father-in-law," and so on.

In other words, the "kinship term" that was formerly applied to the deceased person is now applied to the child that incarnates that person (see Kublu et al. 1999). When I was in Arctic Bay, I was adopted by an elderly woman. Her husband had died and his name had been passed on. One of the children who received the name was my second oldest sister's child. Every time I visited, she would hitch the child up in her *amauti* and say to the child "*Irnikutakli nauk?*" (Where is your tall son?). He would point to me, and I was taught always to call him *ataataga* (my father) (and give him gifts, but that is another story). While it is easy and tempting to translate *ataata* as "father," what does it mean to be calling a 15-month-old child *ataata*? Is such a translation adequate?

In the spring of 1981, I was out in camp with some of my Inuit friends. We were sitting on the beach drinking tea when a two-year-old child toddled over carrying a huge fried bannock for Arnaujumajuq. He cooed affectionately at the child and took the bannock. He explained that the child had his wife's name, and as his wife had always cooked for him and fed him, so now did this little girl "cook" and "feed" him

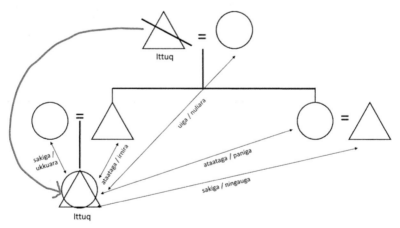

Figure 17.1 The passing of the name Ittuq from a recently deceased man in the senior generation to a newborn child. The child may or may not be a relative, but for the sake of clarity this diagram assumes they are related (grandchild). Living relatives call the child by the kinship term they used for the deceased person – the first of the paired terms are what the living relatives will call the child, and the second term, what the child (when it can speak) will call those relatives. In Inuktitut, this use of terms is called *tuqluratuq*. *uiga* = my husband, *nuliara* = my wife, *sakiga* = my father/mother-in-law, *ukkuara* = my daughter-in-law, *ataataga* = my father, *irnira* = my son, *paniga* = my daughter, and *ningauga* = my son-in-law.

as his wife. Similarly, one Sunday at church, one of the senior women stood up and invited everybody to her home because her husband had shot his first caribou and she wanted to feast the entire community with it. The woman was a widow and her husband had been dead for many years. She was referring to her 12-year-old grandson who had her husband's name and quite properly had now shot his first caribou and given it to his wife to distribute.

In Inuktitut, this way of applying terms is called *tuqłuraqtuq*. In the dictionary for North Baffin Island, *Uqausiit Tukingit*, it is defined as: "*Inuuqatminik qanutuinnaq tuqłurasunguvut atiruarnagu, surlu ilagijanga piqannarijangaluunniit*. They address whichever neighbour/companion without using their name frequently as if they were kin (*ila*) or a friend" (Ootoova 2000: 372).

The definition raises a couple of important points. *Tuqłuraqtuq* is a very broad term that encompasses the use of all the kinship terms for other people but may also include the use of nicknames. Thus, Catherine Asluluuq says, "my names were the ones that dictated my *tuqłurausiq*. There are only a few whom I call by *tuqłurausiq* through relationship" (Otak and Pitsiulak-Stevens 2014, 35). There is a priority given to the terms that are given through names and then other relations follow. It specifically refers to the terms of address that each person may use. Among Inuit it is very rude to call people, especially older people, by their proper names. The names are not secret, but it is always much more appropriate to use a kinship term when speaking with another person. Because of the dominance of this system, younger people will often not know what an older person's actual name is. Inuit start from what they actually call people in order to understand relationships (what has traditionally been called terms of address rather than terms of reference) rather than from an objective point of departure such as a genealogical grid.

This point brings us to one of the major perplexities in the study and analysis of Inuit social relations. Past studies have assumed that the set of genealogical relations among people form the basis of Inuit social organization (Trott 1982). The problem has been that at least 15 percent of the actual kinship terms used have been "skewed" or "incorrect" because of a cluster of "fictive" kinship relations such as the naming relationship (Graburn 1964; Guemple 1972). Such assumptions bear no relation to how Inuit understand their own relationships, which as we have seen begins from the core question, *Kinauviit?*, around the name.

For a westerner unfamiliar with the system, it can be very confusing to try and track these relationships. Earlier, I mentioned my friend in Pangnirtung who has 26 names. I love to go visiting with her because I am never very sure which name and therefore which relationship she will have with the people we are visiting. Jean Briggs (1998) describes how Inuit carefully teach children what their relationship is to each person they encounter.

NAMES AND LAND

How can we make sense of a system that is apparently so complex? I want to suggest five sets of data that move us towards an understanding.

First, I was working with an elderly woman in Arctic Bay and asking her the Inuktitut names of her grandchildren. She told me that one of the younger ones was called Puuqsimat. I had not encountered the name Puuqsimat anywhere else in my research, so I asked her who the name had come from. She replied that it had come from an old man in Qaanaaq, Greenland. This puzzled me even more until she explained that a long time ago (in 1865), a group of Inuit had migrated from North Baffin Island to the Thule district of Greenland (see Mary-Rousseliere 1991). Many (but not all) of the names had been lost to North Baffin Island and Puuqsimat was one of them. In recent years, the people of North Baffin and Qaanaaq had had a number of exchanges where the histories of this migration were shared from both sides. Puuqsimat had asked the people of North Baffin if they could they call one of their children after him when he died, so that his name could return to its proper land.

Second, I noticed that Inuit are strongly emotionally attached to the place where they were born.[5] The older people born on the land could tell me the precise square meter on the ground where their mother was located when they were delivered. I would hear rhapsodic accounts about how beautiful the land was where they were born (although I rarely noticed anything particular about it). In Pangnirtung, we visited a camp with a late-middle-aged woman and her granddaughter. She sat down on the ground within the circle of the remains of a *qammaq* with her granddaughter and began crying. I asked her what was the matter; she told me that this was the spot that she had been born. She had not been back to this site since she had left at the age of 18 to marry her husband. She proceeded to thank me profusely for bringing her to this place so that she could share it with her granddaughter.

I would suggest that this is closely related to two other ethnographic observations made in other areas of the Arctic. When anyone approaches Marble Island for the first time, they must crawl up the beach on their hands and knees crying out *ungaa ungaa*. Similarly, Saladin d'Anglure (1994) has observed in Igloolik that when people cross into territory that they have not been into before, they must get down on their knees and crawl onto the new land crying *ungaa ungaa*. *Ungaa* is the sound that a baby makes and the crawling on the land reflects the reversion to infancy in relation to the land.

The point here is that these locales reflect the place on the land where a name becomes incarnated. It establishes and/or continues the connection between the name and the land. Where the relationship has not been established by birth, a person must revert to birth to connect their incarnation of the name with the land.

Third, while I was working in Arctic Bay, I took side trips with Inuit friends to Pond Inlet and Igloolik – both communities within the North Baffin region but with larger populations than Arctic Bay. As I visited with my friends from Arctic Bay, there would be frequent exchanges of information about mutual relatives in Arctic Bay. I was often lost as to who we were talking about and would have to ask. The reply often came, "Oh, well they are called _____ in Arctic Bay, but here they are referred to as _____." This was often the context where I learned the second or third Inuktitut names of the people in Arctic Bay.

Fourth, I had carefully traced the movement of people over time across North Baffin Island, focusing particularly on the Admiralty Inlet region beginning in 1908 when the area had been reoccupied from Pond Inlet (Mary-Rousseliere 1982). I tracked the movement of people among the various camps throughout the region. I noticed that when a person with a particular name moved out of Admiralty Inlet, within a year they were replaced by someone else with the same name. Note that this is not a case of a person dying and the name being passed on, but rather that new person moved into the area. I had not noticed this initially; only when I realized that there were people of different genders with the same name, did I realize that they were in fact different people.

Fifth, in the historical material one can read accounts of "Sedna" ceremonies, the *tivaajut*. While this is a complex set of ceremonies that take place over a number of days, it ends with all the men lining up on one side and all the women lining up on the other side from the oldest to the youngest. Each person then calls out their name and the place where they were born (see point 2) (Blaisel and Oosten 1997; Boas 1964; Saladin d'Anglure 1993). After each person has done this, the shaman moves among the people, pairing them off to sleep together for the night. Unfortunately, much description and discussion of these events have been lost in the colonial tropes of savagery and primitive promiscuity, and so we have no idea what criteria were used to pair off couples for the night. I hypothesize that the couples were the husband/wife pairs who held the names in the previous generation.

What this evidence suggests is that there is a very strong connection between names and the land. In effect, the sets of relationships among the names provide a grid of social relationships over the land connecting particular groups of people to particular territories. Each of the names provides a node in that grid, and Inuit can tell where people belong, where they "have land" by which name node they fit into. To put it in other terms, the ownership of land for Inuit is mediated by the naming system.

This produces a rather peculiar effect. Because the names remain the same over land over time (or change slowly) it looks like the same people have occupied the same land since the beginning of time. In fact, we know that roughly 30 percent of the membership of various camps could change on an annual basis (Damas 1969). For ecological and other social reasons, Inuit must be highly mobile to take advantage of shifting resources. Yet the naming system gives the impression that no one ever moves, creating permanent relations between people and land.

This takes us back to the original question about what the kinship terms then reflect. In effect, using the kinship term for the person who last held the name reproduces the set of social relationships over the land of the previous generation. Rather than locating a person in the grid of genealogical relations as suggested by early approaches to Inuit social organization, this places each person within the history of social relations over the land. My 15-month-old *ataata* is not then my "father" but the progenitor of my social/economic hunting[6] relationships over land, and simultaneously, the successor to those relationships. Time, land, and kinship are all collapsed into a single moment.

ADOPTION

It is self-evident that the vagaries of human reproduction, illness, accidents, and death will not neatly line up each generation of newborns to replace those who have died. Inuit resolve this problem through the social practice of adoption. Research has shown that approximately 22 percent of Inuit children are adopted, and that this number has remained fairly constant over time (Guemple 1979). Adoptions are usually arranged among the mother and the adoptive parents just before the birth or shortly afterward. Growing up, an Inuit child would know both its birth parents and its adoptive parents, effectively doubling the number of parents and siblings that they would have. In conversation with many of my Inuit friends who were adopted, it is often difficult to tell which parent they are talking about without further elaboration. Linguistically, adoptive relatives were marked with the suffix *-ksaq* ("potential") as in *anaanaksaq* "adopted mother" or *paniksaq* "adopted daughter" but these terms were not always used in everyday discourse.

Most children were adopted by close relatives: usually, grandparents or uncles and aunts (Rousseau 1970). In part, this was because Inuit lived in small face-to-face communities over the land and the people physically close by would also be related. It was also because of the difficulty of feeding a newborn child anything but breast milk, which required the lactating mother to be nearby. Frequently, children were adopted by their grandparents in order for the children to care for the older people as they became less able to look after themselves. I often observed children withheld from school because of their responsibility to care for their grandparents on a day-to-day basis.

In terms of the couples that are giving up the children for adoption, families go through cycles of giving and receiving children. Young couples are most likely to give up children in the early stages of their marriages to older, more established couples. As couples age, they are more likely to adopt children. Part of the reasons have to do with balancing the number of children a couple can manage at any time. There are infertile couples who can and will adopt a number of children. I knew of one such couple in Arctic Bay who at the time I knew them had adopted six children. There are also other couples who do not seem to give up children for adoption in any case. I know of two couples in Arctic Bay and one in Pangnirtung who each had twelve children and no children were adopted in or out.

Saladin d'Anglure (1988) has argued that in the same way that in some societies people are exchanged in marriages to establish alliances between social groups, among Inuit children are exchanged among couples in order to establish and reproduce alliances. I find it difficult to imagine why couples that are already closely related need to establish alliances, but the close examination of the circulation of children over time does indicate that such a process is at play.

There is one feature of adoption that has not been commented on. If we return to Figure 17.1, suppose that the newborn child was adopted by the grandmother, then Ittuq would return to be with his wife. The name would return to the position that it held in the previous generation. In Inuktitut this is called *angirraqlaqpuq* – the name has returned to its home (Søby 1986). Through the name returning home, the actual social relations of the previous generations are reproduced not only through the names but through the physical proximity of the social relation. Not only can one recreate a husband-wife relationship, but sibling cohorts can be reconstructed on the death of any child. The most remarkable case is the rebuilding of the children of Attagutaluk in Igloolik after her first children died of starvation (see Saladin d'Anglure 1988). Not all cases need to be this extreme. In Arctic Bay I observed that couples would often adopt a niece or a nephew who had the name of one of their own deceased children.

Where I argued above that the naming system serves to reproduce social relations over time, over the land it can only do so at an abstract level. Adoption recreates those social relations in a concrete and visible way, giving them continuity in the short term.

MARRIAGE

On my last day in Arctic Bay in 1981, one of the Elders told me a story. When he was young, living close to what is now Igloolik, every spring another family would come and camp with his family. He was taught to call the daughter of this family *nuliaksaq* ("potential wife," i.e., fiancée) although it never occurred to him to ask why he called her by that term. When he was about fourteen, and the young girl was about thirteen, the family came to visit but this time when they departed, the young girl was left behind. Again, he did not think anything of it until he went to bed in the evening and his mother put him and the girl together in bed on the sleeping platform and announced from now on they were husband and wife. With a laugh, the Elder told me that he and his wife did not know much about sex, but they had a lot of fun finding out. Clearly, they worked it out as they went on to have 12 children.

This story points to a number of important issues. First, until the 1960s, most marriages were arranged. In a small face-to-face society, where most of the people in the surrounding area would be related, one of the functions of a "kinship system" was to create a category of people who were marriageable. Oddly enough, this did not seem to happen among Inuit. Marriage was based on much more pragmatic considerations such as the availability of partners who were not closely related. In a context with a high level of infant mortality, and high death rates among men due to hunting accidents, and among women due to complications in birth, even arrangements made by parents at birth could be fairly fragile. In surveying the marriages of sets of siblings, the only observable characteristic was that they tried to establish marriages with each of the various camps throughout the district, distributing alliances as broadly as possible. While one or other of the partners may have resisted certain marriages in the past, there was not really a whole lot of choice.

Until the arrival of Christian missionaries, marriages were unmarked affairs with no ceremony or recognition other than the couple living together and having children:

> In other words, all that was required for this kind of marriage was for a man and a woman to live together in the same house (which was usually shared with other relatives) and have sexual intercourse. Once these two conditions had been met even for a brief period, the relationship was considered established. The Eskimos[7] did not have any marriage ceremony and in fact there seems to have been no ritual whatsoever associated with the founding of a *ui-nuliaq* [husband-wife] relationship. Not only is this total lack of ceremonial embellishment unusual from a cross-cultural perspective, it was in distinct contrast to other aspects of Eskimo life. Taboos, rituals and ceremonies of various kinds were associated with almost every daily activity, and to me, their absence here is indicative of the rather unimportant place that the *ui-nuliaq* relationship had in the ideal Eskimo scheme of things.
>
> (Burch 2013 [1970], 105)

Why would marriage have a "rather unimportant place" in Inuit social relations? In any marriage, both the husband and the wife have a pre-existing set of social relations through their names that persist even after marriage. Inuit in Arctic Bay were very clear that names do not influence the choice of marriage partners (with the exception that female-sexed people with men's names always marry male-sexed people with women's names), which would make sense if marriages are based on the kinds of pragmatic considerations suggested above. At the same time, the naming relations turn the attention of the marriage partners outward rather than focusing entirely on the marriage relationship itself. Further, as I have argued above the entirety of social relations over land are already reproduced through the names.

Inuit are very clear though that marriage is critical for the mutual contribution of men and women to labor for each other (Briggs 1974; Guemple 1986). Men must produce the game to feed and support the women and children while women must produce the absolutely necessary clothing for the men so that they can hunt. Women also look after the children. Both men and women recognize the absolute necessity of the contribution of the other gender and also recognize that the labor of both genders is equally difficult. It is for this reason that a man without a wife (or vice versa) is virtually unthinkable among Inuit. In cases where a spouse dies, the other spouse will almost immediately begin searching out a new partner.[8] In cases where one spouse is incapacitated or infertile, couples in the past would exchange spouses until the labor balance could be equitably restored among all members of the exchange. Such exchanges also served to created alliances among couples belonging to distinct geographical camps and could be sustained over time.

ILA

Inuit draw all these relations together into a concept called *ila* (Tulugarjuk and Christopher 2011). This has frequently been simply translated as "kin," or in a more precise anthropological context as "kindred" – an ego-centered group of people related by blood, descent, or marriage (see Figure 17.2).

This is actually misleading as a translation. The word *ila* points more to being a member or part of something. Thus, when I was invited to join groups to go out hunting/camping, Inuit would ask, *ilaujumagavit*? "Do you want to be our *ila*?" or more generally, "do you want to be a part of our [hunting/camping] group?" This does not refer to an internally unified homogeneous whole out of which one is abstracting a part, but rather a group made up of a composite of individual parts (Dorais 2020: 104). This subtle distinction is important for two reasons. First, it upholds the incredible value Inuit place on the autonomy of each person. It is considered incredibly rude among Inuit to direct the activities or mind of another person. Second, it recognizes that whatever social group is formed it will always be internally divided by the cross-cutting external ties created by the naming relationships.

As Bodenhorn (2000) has pointed out, the combination of all the social processes described above creates an almost infinite array of possible relations for each Inuk. These are concretized and realized through two overlying sets of relations: space and food sharing. People who live together within a defined space are more likely to be regarded as *ila*. This can begin in the intimacy of the *igluqatigiit*, "those who share an iglu/house" to the neighboring *nunaqatigiit* "those who share land [camp]" to the surrounding camps in a region. When I was collecting family information in Arctic Bay I worked with two brothers. I never knew they had a sister until one day

Figure 17.2 Group of North Baffin Inuit at Uluksan, at the mouth of Arctic Bay, when the Hudson's Bay Company post opened in 1926. Left to right: Atuat, Attagutaluk, Iqlu, Dr. Livingstone, Nasaq, Akpaliapik, Qumangapik, and Alassuaq. Iqlu and Nasaq are Attagutaluk's parents, who in turn is married to Atuat. Qumangapik is shown with his first wife Alassuaq and his second wife Akpaliapik. Although not all these people are direct ancestors of the current population in Arctic Bay, all of these names continue to live on. Identification of people in the photo was done by Aglak Attitaq and Muktaaq Akumalik in 2000. Photo: Maurice Haycock, Department of Indian Affairs and Northern Development fonds, Library and Archives Canada, PA-102658.

a nephew came visiting from Igloolik and was welcomed into their homes. I asked why they had never mentioned their sister and they replied that she had moved away to Igloolik a very long time ago when they were very young, and they had never seen her again. Because they had lost the relation, they no longer counted her as a "sister." In the Belcher Islands, Guemple (1972) noted the opposite process at work – people who came to live together in camps (even affines) would gradually become called by the terms for siblings or other close relatives.

These spatial relations become drawn together under the *angajurraq*. The word *angajurraq* is based on the same root as *angajuq* "older same-sex sibling" and has the general meaning of "antecedent elder" (Dorais 2020). It can be used for one's parents but is more generally used to mean "camp boss" or senior person in a seasonal camp. People chose to follow a senior person who is competent and continues to demonstrate it through the prosperity of their camp. For a full discussion of Inuit leadership see Stevenson (1997). As Damas (1969) has pointed out, there is a tendency for the linking relations within camps to be between men, but it is not necessary.

The on-the-ground relationships within a camp are focused on those who can work together and can live together, and out of that, the "kinship" relations become actualized from all the potentialities of the naming relations.

The core value among Inuit is generosity in the sharing of meat. As noted above this flows from the generosity of the animals in sharing their bodies with humans. Across the Inuit homeland, there are a large number of different food sharing systems, from the most structured among the Natsilingmiut (see Balikci 1970), to much broader systems in Baffin Island (see Wenzel 1995). Whatever the system, it remains that if someone does not have meat and you do have meat, you are obliged to share it with them. Most of the literature suggests that a person shares meat with those who are kin. One of the most common forms of sharing is that the *angajurraq* and their spouse become the focal point for collecting the meat and then distributing it to those in need. The spatial boundaries of the camp, and those who are moving towards becoming "kin" by being members of the camp are thus more significant for meat sharing than a predefined sense of who is and who is not "kin." Bodenhorn (2000) makes this point clearly in the context of the distribution of whale *maqtaq* (skin) and meat in North Alaska. She argues that the relationship systems provide potentialities for "kin" that are realized in whom one shares meat with, making them *ila*.

Far from the stereotypes of Inuit wrenching a barely marginal subsistence from a harsh land, we find ourselves enmeshed in a rich, layered, and storied set of relationships. By setting the point of departure for the discussion from the *atiq* we are able to see the connections between the reproduction of the cosmos, the reproduction of the animals, and the reproduction of human social relationships over land. The sets of relations reproduced by the passing of the *atiq* lead to *tuqluraqtuq*, "how people refer to one another." In recent times, and in recent Inuit studies of their own "kinship systems" (see Otak and Pitsiulak-Stevens 2014; Owlijoot and Flaherty 2013), they have expressed concerns over the misunderstandings around *tuqluratuq* and the need to use this as a focal point for discussion. The concrete expression of these relationships appears as *ila*, which can then take on a number of day-to-day forms. The complexity of these systems opens up a world of interconnectivity among Inuit in their own land and with the animals.

NOTES

1 Thoughout this chapter I use the forms in the North Baffin dialect of Inukitut with which I am most familiar.
2 His work has also found similar intra-uterine narratives in northern Quebec and the Belcher Islands.
3 The astute reader will have realized that it is possible for the name of a man who has died to enter into a female child as is actually the case for Iqalliuq. Inuit names themselves are not gendered – there are no men's names and women's names. A female-sexed child who receives a name from a man will be brought up as a boy and a male-sexed child who receives a name from a woman will be brought up as a girl. This occurs in approximately 15 percent of the population. This question of gender nuances all of the discussion to follow, but it is beyond the scope of this paper. For full discussion see Saladin d'Anglure (1994) and Trott (2006). There are variations across the Inuit area on how these gender

relations are expressed. It is hard to tell how much of the variation is within the terms of Inuit culture and how much is a response to the pressures of colonialism forcing alignment with western gender categories. Further, many researchers have never thought to ask questions about Inuit gender categories and, thus, the data are very uneven. In teaching about gender to a class that included Inuit, one young Inuk woman criticized me for teaching nonsense. Across the table, another young woman pointed out to the first that she was a woman with a man's name and that she was pregnant with a child who was her grandmother (the child's sex was male). Even though the two women had been friends their entire lives, they had never thought to discuss this matter before and were mutually surprised by their own cultural misunderstandings.

4 This is one of the points where there is considerable variation across the Inuit world. In Greenland and Alaska, it seems that the number of names is much more restricted, often to one.

5 Nuttall's (1992) concept of "memoryscape" is particularly helpful here. Each place on the land is layered with stories from the personal to the cosmological.

6 I have expressed this in male terms because this is the actual situation in which I was involved. I trust it would not be difficult to translate this into broader more gender-inclusive terms.

7 Burch uses the term "Eskimo" in part because he is dealing with the Inupiat of North Alaska where the term is still in use, and also because he wrote the original text prior to the era when the term Inuit came into common usage.

8 This is less critical in the modern era with the provision of housing and old age allowances for older people, but was certainly the case in the past.

REFERENCES

Balikci, Asen. 1970. *The Netsilik Eskimo*. Garden City, NY: The Natural History Press.

Blaisel, Xavier, and Jarich G. Oosten. 1997. "La logique des échanges des fêtes d'hiver inuit." *Anthropologie et Sociétés* 21 (2–3): 19–44. https://doi.org/10.7202/015483ar

Boas, Franz. 1964 [1888]. *The Central Eskimo*. Lincoln, NB: University of Nebraska Press.

Bodenhorn, Barbara. 2000. "It's Good to Know Who Your Relatives Are But We Were Taught to Share with Everybody: Shares and Sharing among Inupiaq Households." In *The Social Economy of Sharing: Resource Allocation and Modern Hunter-Gatherers*, edited by George W. Wenzel, Grete Hovelsrud-Broda and Nobuhiro Kishigami, 27–60. Osaka: National Museum of Ethnology.

Bordin, Guy. 2011. "L'expression lexicale de la peur en inuktitut dans le nord de la Terre de Baffin." *Études/Inuit/Studies* 35(1–2): 223–244. https://doi.org/10.7202/1012843ar

Briggs, Jean L. 1974. "Eskimo Women: Makers of Men." In *Many Sisters: Women in Cross-Cultural Perspective*, edited by Carolyn J. Matthiasson, 261–304. New York: Free Press.

———. 1998. *Inuit Morality Play: The Emotional Education of a Three-Year-Old*. New Haven, CT: Yale University Press.

Burch, Ernest S. Jr. 2013 [1970]. "Marriage and Divorce among North Alaska Eskimos." In *Inupiaq Ethnohistory: Selected Essays by Ernest S. Burch Jr.*, edited by Erica Hill, 103–126. Fairbanks, AZ: University of Alaska Press:

Damas, David. 1969. "Environment, History and Central Eskimo Society." In *Contributions to Anthropology: Ecological Essays*, edited by David Damas. 40–64, Ottawa, ON: National Museums of Canada.

Dorais, Louis-Jacques. 2020. *Words of the Inuit: A Semantic Stroll through a Northern Culture*. Winnipeg, MB: University of Manitoba Press.

Graburn, Nelson H. H. 1964. *Tagagmiut Kinship Terminology*. Ottawa, ON: Northern Coordination Research Centre, Department of Northern Affairs and Natural Resources.

Guemple, Lee. 1972. "Kinship and Alliance in Belcher Island Eskimo Society." *Alliance in Eskimo Society*. Supplement. Proceedings of the American Ethnological Society for 1971, 56–78. Seattle, WA: American Ethnological Society.

———. 1979. *Inuit Adoption*. Ottawa, ON: National Museums of Canada, National Museum of Man.

———. 1986. "Men and Women, Husbands and Wives: The Role of Gender in Traditional Inuit Society." *Études/Inuit/Studies* 10 (1–2): 9–24. https://doi.org/10.7202/016149ar.

Kublu, A., J. G. Oosten, and C. H. W. Remie 1999. "Changing Perspectives of Name and Identity Among the Inuit of Northeast Canada." In *Arctic Identities: Continuity and Change in Inuit and Saami Societies*, edited by J. G. Oosten and Cornelius H. W. Remie, 56–78. Leiden: Research School CNWS, School of Asian, African, and American Studies, Universiteit Leiden.

Mary-Rousselière, Guy. 1982. "Gone Leaving No Forwarding Address, the Tununirusirmiut." *Eskimo* n.s. 24: 3–13.

———. 1991. *Qitdlarssuaq: The Story of a Polar Migration*. Winnipeg, MB: Wuerz Publishing.

Nuttall, Mark. 1992. *Arctic Homeland: Kinship, Community and Development in Northwest Greenland*. Toronto, ON: University of Toronto Press.

Ootoova, Elisapee. 2000. *Uqausiit Tukingit: Inuktitut Dictionary Tununiq Dialect*. Iqaluit, NU: Baffin Region Educational Council.

Otak, Leah, and Peesee Pitsiulak-Stevens, eds. 2014. *Inuit Kinship and Naming Customs in Baffin Region*. Iqaluit, NU: Nunavut Arctic College.

Owlijoot, Pelagie, and Louise Flaherty, eds. 2013. *Inuit Kinship and Naming Customs*. Iqaluit, NU: Inhabit Media.

Rasmussen, Knud. 1929. *Intellectual Culture of the Iglulik Eskimos*. Copenhagen: Gyldendalske Boghandel, Nordisk Forlag.

Rousseau, Jérôme. 1970. *L'Adoption chez les esquimaux Tununermiut (Pond Inlet, T. du N.-O.)*. Quebec, QC: Université Laval.

Saladin d'Anglure, Bernard. 1975. "Recherches sur le symbolisme inuit." *Recherches Amérindiennes au Québec* 5 (3): 62–64.

———. 1988. "Enfants nomades au pays des Inuit Iglulik." *Anthropologie et Sociétés* 12 (2): 125–166. https://doi.org/10.7202/015026ar

———. 1993. "The Shaman's Share or Inuit Sexual Communism in the Canadian Central Arctic." *Anthropologica* 35: 59–103.

———. 1994. "From Foetus to Shaman: The Construction of an Inuit Third Sex." In *Amerindian Rebirth: Reincarnation Belief among North American Indians and Inuit*, edited by Antonia Mills and Richard Slobodin, 82–106. Toronto, ON: University of Toronto Press.

———. 1997. "A New Look on Shamanism, Possession, and Christianization." *Études/Inuit/Studies* 21 (1–2): 5–36.

———. 2018. *Inuit Stories of Being and Rebirth: Gender, Shamanism and the Third Sex*. Winnipeg, MB: University of Manitoba Press.

Søby, Regitze M. 1986. "Angerdlartoqut: The Child Who Has Returned Home." *Études/Inuit/Studies* 10 (1–2): 285–296.

Stevenson, Marc G. 1997. *Inuit Whalers and Cultural Persistence: Structure in Cumberland Sound and Central Inuit Social Organization*. Toronto, ON: Oxford University Press.

Therrien, Michèle. 1987. *Le Corps Inuit (Quebec arctique)*. Paris: SELAF.

Trott, Christopher G. 1982. "The Inuk as Object: Some Problems in the Study of Inuit Social Organization." *Études/Inuit/Studies* 6 (2): 93–108.

———. 1989. *Structure and Pragmatics: Social Relations among the Tununirrusirmiut.* PhD dissertation, University of Toronto.

———. 2006. "The Gender of the Bear." *Études/Inuit/Studies* 30 (1): 89–109. https://doi.org/10.7202/016151ar

Tulugarjuk, Leo, and Neil Christopher. 2011. *Ilagiinniq: Interviews on Inuit Family Values from the Qikiqtani Region.* Iqaluit, NU: Niutaq Cultural Institute, Qikiqtani Inuit Association.

Wenzel, George W. 1995. "Ningiqtuq: Resource Sharing and Generalized Reciprocity in Clyde River, Nunavut." *Arctic Anthropology* 32 (2): 43–60.

PART IV
SOCIAL AND POLITICAL WORLDS

CHAPTER 18

INDIGENOUS WESTPHALIAN SOVEREIGNTY?

Decolonization, secession, and Indigenous rights in Greenland

Rauna Kuokkanen

INTRODUCTION

Greenland is undergoing a significant transformation as the result of the 2009 Self-Government Act. The new self-government era signifies much greater autonomy and decision-making for a country with an overwhelming Inuit majority. The Greenland Inuit are no longer subjugated by a colonial state and the constitutional protection of the rights of the Greenland Inuit exceeds that of most other Indigenous peoples in the world. Achieving extensive self-government in 2009 has compelled Greenland to explore new revenue sources and has created enormous pressure to develop the country's mineral resources, considered the main avenue for implementing Greenlandic self-government and a condition for full independence. The development of mineral resources creates a range of social, environmental, and political challenges compounded by complex circumstances characterized by climate change, global geopolitical tensions, and race for control of and resources in the Arctic.

This chapter considers Greenland's unique political state of affairs and discusses how it departs from and also contradicts the norm of Indigenous self-determination as non-secession. I discuss different conceptions of sovereignty and examine how they play out in Greenland. The chapter begins with a discussion of conceptions of sovereignty and self-determination and proceeds to consider the political context and implementation of self-government in Greenland. In conclusion, I propose that Inuit Greenlanders are advancing what I call "Indigenous Westphalian Sovereignty," a unique approach to self-determination in the Indigenous world. Notwithstanding that Greenland's aspiration for modern nationhood is not widely shared by most Indigenous peoples in the world, the chapter sheds light on the limits of the concept of Indigenous self-determination as non-secession, and on the enormous challenges and existing rifts that an endeavor for Indigenous independence poses. The chapter draws on interviews I conducted with 17 Inuit Greenlanders in Nuuk in March and April 2013, and is based on my comparative research on Indigenous self-determination in Canada, Greenland, and Scandinavia (Kuokkanen 2019).

SELF-DETERMINATION AS SOVEREIGNTY, NON-INTERFERENCE, AND DECOLONIZATION

The UN Declaration on the Rights of Indigenous Peoples (UNDRIP), adopted in 2007 by the General Assembly establishes self-determination as a collective human right that enables a group to determine its own political, social, cultural, and economic affairs. Indigenous self-determination is a foundational right and principle that gives rise to other central Indigenous rights, such as free, prior, and informed consent, as stipulated in a number of articles vis-à-vis development of Indigenous peoples' lands, territories and resources, forcible relocation, cultural and intellectual property, and states' legislative or administrative measures. The recognition of Indigenous peoples' right to self-determination in international law was a major struggle, and a significant effort by Indigenous representatives worldwide was put into convincing apprehensive states that the right to self-determination does not mean secession or independent nationhood. The Inuit, through their pan-Arctic NGO, the Inuit Circumpolar Council (ICC), were among the leading forces of the global Indigenous lobby that finally succeeded in the process that led to the adoption of UNDRIP.[1] Considering this history of Indigenous rights advocacy and the role of ICC, it might seem surprising that for the Inuit in Greenland (or Greenlanders), self-determination represents a transitional stage toward full political independence.

Divergent interpretations of the content of self-determination derive from different conceptions of sovereignty, which are highly contested and historically contingent (Barker 2005). The concept of self-determination as statehood within geographically separate territories and jurisdictions is rooted in the Westphalian concept of sovereignty and the related doctrine of non-interference in the domestic affairs of a state. The interpretation of self-determination as political independence, however, has been considered a misconception originating in the post-World War II decolonization framework, which "involved the transformation of colonial territories into new states under the normative aegis of self-determination" (Anaya 1996, 80). Further, state sovereignty conceptualized as non-interference and ultimate authority is being undermined by global capitalism and international law (Lapidoth 1992; Held 1995) and as a result, sovereignty is reconstructed at various levels, ranging from global and regional to sub-state settings (Sassen 1996). Some scholars even suggest that sovereignty may never have existed to the degree normally associated with the concept (Philpott 1995).

The concept of sovereignty is also complex and contested in Indigenous scholarship. Some emphasize how sovereignty for Indigenous peoples seldom calls forth independence or non-interference (Maaka and Fleras 2000, 93), whereas others maintain that there are Indigenous peoples that have always been sovereign and independent (Becker 1998). Others still suggest that the concept and ideology of sovereignty are incompatible with Indigenous ways of being, knowing, and relating in the world (Alfred 1999; Nadasdy 2017). For them, Indigenous sovereignty is a contradiction in terms and conceals the ways in which the hegemonic role of sovereignty in the world, dominated by a system of sovereign states, has profoundly negative impacts on Indigenous peoples and their social, cultural, and political organization. Even when Indigenous people do not seek independence, they nevertheless have to assume the trappings of sovereignty and the state if they wish to operate "in a universe of states and state-like political entities" (Nadasdy 2017, 7). This is particularly evident in contemporary Indigenous self-government institutions.

In today's interconnected world, the Westphalian view of the world as divided into mutually exclusive territories appears deficient. It disregards the reality of overlapping and multiple authorities and communities, and the interdependence that characterizes the human experience (Anaya 1996, 78). It also ignores Indigenous conceptions of self-determination and sovereignty, in which the notion of shared territories and jurisdictions and co-existing sovereignties are common (Borrows 2002; Macklem 2001). As an example, the historical Dish with One Spoon Wampum Belt covenant, an agreement between the Haudenosaunee Confederacy, the Anishinaabeg, and allied nations provided for peaceably sharing and caring for the hunting territories and resources around the Great Lakes (King 2007; Lytwyn 1997).

On the other hand, there are Indigenous people who support the principle of non-interference which, they argue, forms the foundation of the treaty agreements. Most notable is the Guswentah or Two-Row Wampum Treaty presented by the Haudenosaunee Confederacy to the Dutch in 1613. The Guswentah is a beaded belt consisting of two parallel rows of purple beads separated by three rows of white beads. The predominant interpretation focuses on the two rows of purple beads which represent two vessels going down the river. Some emphasize the meaning of the three rows of white beads which represent the principles of peace, friendship, and respect, while for others, the fact that the two rows never meet symbolizes and confirms the principle of non-interference (Hill 2017).

Many Indigenous peoples assert their pre-existing sovereignty, evident in the fact that at the time of contact they were politically independent societies or nations, governing themselves and their territories under their own laws. Their pre-existing sovereignty exists independent of constitutional, common, or civil law, and thus is not legitimated or validated by these legislative frameworks (Henderson 2008). Indigenous sovereignty was historically recognized by settlers through treaty-making but is frequently ignored and dismissed by contemporary states, even in cases where courts have recognized the existence of sui generis Indigenous sovereignty.[2] Yet, Indigenous sovereignty continues to be exercised collectively and individually, for instance, through hunting, fishing, or reindeer herding, or through the enactment of Indigenous governance and laws. Today, claims of Indigenous sovereignty are often synonymous with claims of Indigenous self-determination and the two terms are frequently employed synonymously (Barker 2005; Monture Angus 1998).

Notwithstanding Indigenous representatives successfully arguing for more accurate and inclusive interpretations of sovereignty and self-determination beyond separation and non-interference, they remain up against the international legal norms of state sovereignty and territorial integrity. Anaya (2009) reminds us, "The reach and application of the principle or right of self-determination… cannot be fully appreciated without attention to the doctrine of state sovereignty, which remains central to the international legal and political system" (194). This doctrine restricts Indigenous self-determination by restraining the ability of the international system to interfere with or influence affairs considered internal or domestic (such as policymaking).

That said, the argument according to which Indigenous people do not pose a "threat to the territorial integrity of states" (Pitty and Smith 2011, 127) is not fully accurate. Not all Indigenous people agree with remaining subordinate to the doctrine of state sovereignty. For some, the failure to question the legitimacy of state sovereignty over Indigenous peoples is a major deficiency of UNDRIP which, they point out, is a deeply compromised document and is not supported by all Indigenous representatives who participated in drafting it (Champagne 2012, see also Watson and Venne 2012; White Face 2013). Others stress the role and significance of the international system in adjudicating the question of Crown sovereignty vis-à-vis Indigenous sovereignty because of the partiality of the courts of the state (Manuel and Derrickson 2015, 167–168). For the Inuit in Greenland, self-determination is seen primarily as a transitional period towards independence, and as increased economic and political power to govern.

GREENLAND SELF-GOVERNMENT ACT, 2009

Passed in 2009, the Act on Greenland Self-Government grants extensive self-governing powers to the country. It contains 33 areas of jurisdiction to exercise legislative and executive authority, with Denmark retaining control of the constitution, citizenship, the Supreme Court, foreign affairs, defense, and currency. The Self-Government Act, as it is more commonly known, explicitly recognizes the right to an independent Greenland. Chapter 8 of the Act, titled, "Greenland's access to independence," provides that if a decision for independence is taken by the people of Greenland,[3] the governments of Greenland and Denmark shall negotiate an agreement subject to the consent of the Danish Parliament. If that stage is reached, "Independence for Greenland shall imply that Greenland assumes sovereignty over the Greenland territory" (2009, Article 21.4).

The vision of an independent Greenland is not new. It gained currency in the 1970s during the political mobilization of young Greenlanders, most of whom were studying in Denmark. According to former premier Lars-Emil Johansen, independence is a legitimate aspiration "deeply anchored in the Inuit soul" (AFP 2008). Most Greenlanders view self-determination as an important transitional stage to political and economic independence from Denmark. They agree that the transition will be long and challenging, but nevertheless, "at the very end of the road we can be our own nation" (interview with a preeminent municipal politician, 8 April 2013).

The three most significant aspects of the Act include the recognition of the people of Greenland as a people in international law; the exclusive right to subsurface mineral resources, and economic self-sufficiency in case of full independence. Currently, fishing is the main and the only considerable industry, accounting for over 90 percent of total exports. Greenland continues to be highly dependent on an annual grant from Denmark of 3.9 billion Danish kroner (US $600 million) which constitutes over half of the government budget (Schionning 2020). In the past, the grant amount was negotiated between the two countries every two or three years. With the Self-Government Act, the amount has been frozen and has presented itself as a double-edged sword. As it is no longer negotiated, the grant cannot be used as political leverage by Denmark in other negotiations, which apparently happened occasionally "if we didn't behave" (interview with government official, 3 April 2013).

IMPLEMENTING SELF-GOVERNMENT

The Self-Government Act and its accompanied fixed annual subsidy have created great pressure for the Greenland government to find new avenues for revenue. The most prominent option is the development of the country's extensive mineral resources and offshore oil and gas deposits. The first five years of self-government in particular were dominated by political debate and public discourse on mineral exploration and the entry of multinational corporations. One of the main reasons for this was the high commodity prices which resulted in a global rush by mining companies to conduct explorations in Greenland (see Nuttall, this volume). The warming of the Arctic due to climate change and the melting of Greenland's ice cap have also enabled more extensive explorations both on the land and offshore. Aleqa Hammond, the first female Premier, won a landslide victory in the 2013 Greenland national elections on promises to mine the country and put it on the path to independence. For her, climate change constituted an unprecedented opportunity for Greenland. She suggested that global warming is good for Greenland, enabling the exploitation of the country's large mineral resources.

Overall, the period after the national elections in March 2013 was characterized by considerable political instability. In October 2013, the Inatsisartut (the Parliament of Greenland) supported the controversial Siumut initiative to lift the 25-year-old moratorium on uranium mining, which enables the extraction of rare earth metals found trapped within uranium reserves. Rare earth metals are essential components of modern technology, from cell phones to weapons systems. The ban was overturned by a narrow margin of 15 to 14. During the parliamentary debate on the moratorium, a public protest was held in Nuuk against the lifting of the ban. A group called "Uranium: Maintain Zero Tolerance" petitioned the government with 1,200 signatures "to slow the process down, delay the vote, and bring it to a referendum to be voted on by all Greenlanders" (Weaver 2013). The leader of the opposition party Inuit Ataqatigiit, Sara Olsvig, expressed her dismay at the lack of citizen involvement in the decision-making. She referred to free, prior, and informed consent as a key norm of the UN Declaration on the Rights of Indigenous Peoples and maintained, "the process conducted by the government is the most anti-democratic process we have seen conducted in Greenland for a long time" (Olsvig 2013) (see Figure 18.1).

Another controversial decision by Hammond's government was the awarding of a license to London Mining for a USD 2.3 billion iron-ore open pit mine located in Isukasia, 150 kilometers from the capital in the Nuuk Fjord. Known as the Isua project, it was criticized for a number of reasons, including inadequate public consultation and considerable environmental, cultural, and socioeconomic impacts, including the importation of several thousand foreign laborers to construct and operate the mine. Commodity prices, however, collapsed in 2014 and led to the pullout of most oil and mineral exploration companies from Greenland, citing high infrastructure and operating costs in the remote Arctic region. The steep downturn in iron ore prices also led to the collapse of London Mining, putting the Isua project on hold (Hornby, Milne, and Wilson 2015).

The sudden downturn and departure of most multinational corporations dampened the political discourse of swift economic and political independence. Yet mining companies remain interested in Greenland, and some are currently developing mines

Figure 18.1 Protest in the southern Greenland town of Narsaq against lifting the ban on uranium mining in Greenland. An Australian mining firm has proposed to establish a uranium mine nearby. Photo: John Rasmussen, Narsaq Foto.

in the country that saw dramatic levels of melting of its ice sheet in 2019 (Davis 2020; Northam 2019; Peter 2019). The Government of Greenland also waived mineral exploration license obligations until the end of 2020 as a way of helping the mining sector operate in Greenland amid the COVID-19 pandemic (Naalakkersuisut 2020).

Apart from concerns about the environmental and social impacts of new mines, a number of questions arise regarding the importation of several thousand foreign laborers to construct and operate the mines, including questions of integration, working conditions, housing, and infrastructure (Kristensen 2008). As many participants pointed out, thousands of foreign workers in Greenland would take a significant toll on a sparsely inhabited country with a population of 57,000 and could have a negative impact on the status and use of the Greenlandic language. Some raised the risk of Greenlanders becoming a minority in their own country (cf. The Committee for Greenlandic Mineral Resources to the Benefit of Society 2014, 23).

One of the main critics of the rush to develop mineral resources has been the Inuit Circumpolar Council (ICC). In the 2011 Circumpolar Inuit declaration on resource development principles in Inuit Nunaat (the homeland of the Inuit), the ICC called for a balanced approach to extraction abided by "the free, prior, and informed consent of the Inuit of that region" (ICC 2011, Articles 2.1, and 2.3). In Greenland it is not, however, necessarily clear who is the appropriate constituent to give consent. Is it the government composed of Inuit Greenlanders, or the population at large? Both the government and the multinational companies have been criticized for their limited public engagement and shortcomings with regard to consultation and transparency. Information about the social, cultural, and environmental impacts of resource extraction has been hard to come by and is often clouded in technical jargon, or available only in Danish or English (Hansen 2013; Lund Sørensen 2008; Lyberth 2008; Nuttall 2008; Wilson 2015).

The pursuit of independence from Denmark is characterized by the risk of novel dependencies. Research shows that neoliberal, market-driven self-governance creates new forms of dependency and frequently widens socio-economic inequalities in Indigenous communities (see Kuokkanen 2011; Slowey 2008). Collaboration between Indigenous peoples and corporations also often mimics colonial relationships (Irlbacher-Fox 2009). A more recent concern for Greenland is the growing interest by the world's most powerful countries. China has already signed mining deals with Greenland and the United States announced the opening of a consulate and a multimillion economic aid package (after its offer to purchase Greenland from Denmark in August 2019 was swiftly spurned) in order to curb Russian and Chinese influence in the Arctic (Lynch 2020).[4]

Greenland's geopolitical significance has grown greatly amid the global race for rare earth and other mineral resources, but also due to Arctic waters becoming increasingly navigable as a result of climate change. The global interest has been met with mixed feelings in Greenland, generated consternation in Denmark, and led to the placing of Greenland on the top of the Danish national security agenda, as well as raising concerns about the Arctic's growing security disputes (Peter 2019). Regardless, none of this has swayed Greenlanders' ambitions for future independence. According to current premier Kim Kielsen, more than 70 percent of people in Greenland support this political endeavor.[5] The concern for new dependencies, however, looms as large as ever. In addition to potential economic dependency on transnational exploration companies, the new question is whether an independent Greenland would end up as a protectorate of the US (Breum 2020).

This is not to patronizingly suggest that Greenland and Greenlanders are not able to take care of their own affairs. Rather, my intention is to point out that considering the country's highly strategic geopolitical location together with its increasingly accessible mineral resources, it is relatively easy for other actors – whether states or corporations – to take advantage of the combination of Greenland's desire for political independence and its dire economic circumstances. The great dilemma for Greenland, on which nearly all Greenlanders agree, is finding the balance between the pressing need for new revenue sources, for diversifying the country's struggling economy, and for engaging in resource extraction, while meeting high environmental and social standards so that the Inuit hunting and fishing culture (dependent on healthy natural resources) is not jeopardized.

MULTIPLE SOVEREIGNTIES

In the Indigenous world, Inuit Greenlanders are in a unique position to push for full political independence. This is primarily for two reasons, beyond the matter of Indigenous peoples' right to self-determination. First, self-determination in Greenland takes the form of a public government and applies to the aggregate population of the country – not only to Inuit Greenlanders. Yet even if it is not de jure Indigenous self-government, thanks to demographics, it is de facto Indigenous self-government with an Inuit-controlled legislature.

Second, for a brief post-war period (1945–1954) Greenland was a "non-self-governing territory" under Chapter XI of the United Nations Charter. During that period, Denmark was required to report on Greenland to the relevant UN decolonization bodies. Greenland, as a former overseas colony, is a unique case among Indigenous peoples because at least in theory, it qualifies and is entitled to independence under the decolonization framework that provided for the creation of new states in Asia and Africa in the so-called decolonization era. Accordingly, the legal term "the people of Greenland" (the entire population of the country) is considered a colonial people for the purpose of the right to self-determination. If Inuit Greenlanders will indeed one day be sovereign in the Westphalian sense of the term, it is not because of their indigeneity but because of the country's history and demographics. This is also partly why the Inuit Greenlanders tend not to emphasize the discourse of Indigenous sovereignty; for most people, it is simply irrelevant. Notably, however, the pursuit for independence is complicated by Greenland's civil society, especially by the ICC which seeks to decouple Inuit self-determination from Westphalian sovereignty.

As an organization representing all Inuit people across the Arctic, the ICC focuses on the concept of Indigenous self-determination as an Inuit control over Inuit affairs but does not advocate for independence. According to the ICC, static conceptions of sovereignty (i.e., independence) do not adequately recognize Inuit rights "gained through international law, land claims and self-government processes" (2009, Article 4.1). Instead, the organization calls for greater recognition of the contested, overlapping nature and the unfixed meaning of sovereignty, including recognizing that sovereignties "are frequently divided within federations in creative ways to recognize the right of peoples" (ICC 2009, Article 2.1).

Independence would make Greenland the first Inuit state, and would make Greenlanders the arguably first Indigenous people in the world to achieve statehood.[6] As such, Greenland would be radically pushing the limits of Indigenous self-determination, defined by the international Indigenous political discourse as non-secession. At the same time, Greenland has also been presented as an example for other Indigenous peoples to follow. For former premier Kuupiq Kleist, the Greenland self-government agreement with Denmark represents "a de facto implementation" of UNDRIP, and a leading example to "Indigenous peoples everywhere" (Kleist 2009a; 2009b). However, in Greenland, Indigenous rights discourse has been, by and large, replaced by discourses of the nation-state and modern nationhood. Nationhood in Greenland is premised less on Indigenous identity, governance, or rights than on western conceptions of autonomy, the nation, and the nation-state. Rather than a matter of Indigenous self-determination and rights, the development of autonomy and self-government in Greenland has largely been a project of mainstream, standard nation-building. First home rule (1979–2009) and now self-rule have served as progress and evolution toward that goal.

Nation-building – and the nation itself – is commonly considered a process of constant mediation between modern and traditional (Canovan 1996; Chatterjee 1986; 1989; Nairn 1975). In the process of nation-building, the Greenlandic language (Kalaallisut) is a critical signifier in the delicate balancing act between traditions and modernity. Promoting the status of the Greenlandic language has become a central means of maintaining Greenlandic identity and culture while being part of the modern world. According to one participant, the right to one's own language is imperative, but so is being "part of the whole of the world," which implies thinking globally and following "what's going on with the rest of the world." Paying attention to the outside world is necessary, the participant argued, because "we cannot just look inside ourselves and have the idea that we can develop our country only of our own premise" (interview with a municipal leader, 8 April 2013). As a newly elected premier, Hammond offered the metaphor of an airplane to describe the way she wanted to run Greenland: one wing of the plane is Inuit identity, traditions, and values, and the other wing is global influence and interaction with various partners (interview, 11 April 2013). According to the metaphor, finding the compatibility (and thus balance) between the Inuit identity and global influence will make Greenlanders globalized, modern people.

In some ways, the political situation in Greenland, with its deep-seated aspiration for independence, corresponds more to the overseas colonies of Asia and Africa that gained independence in the 1960s and 1970s than other Indigenous peoples.[7] This is particularly evident in its current political discourse which in a number of ways resembles postcolonial, modern nation-building. Greenland resembles the classic scenario of postcolonial nationalism. For postcolonial nationalism and nation-building, the biggest enemy is not "foreignness" but rather "backwardness" (Zubaida 1988).

The common colonial portrayal of non-western peoples involves representing them as stuck in timeless tradition and therefore unable to meet the (western) standards of governance and statehood. In order to justify independence, the political elite of emerging nations are required to present themselves as modern (Chatterjee 1986). Greenland is no exception, and the performance of modernity is particularly clear in the way in which the growing divide between urban and rural Greenland is highlighted by elites in the capital. In popular discourse, a dichotomy is created in which Nuuk and a handful of other larger towns represent modernity while small settlements are symbols of timeless tradition if not backwardness (cf. Petersen 1995). Several participants shared a view according to which people in small communities were used to "waiting for someone to come and tell them what to do."

There are two Inuit discourses of sovereignty in Greenland: the discourse of shared, overlapping sovereignties emerging from the global Indigenous self-determination movement, and the Westphalian conception of sovereignty predicated on statehood, modern nation-building, and exclusive jurisdiction of territory. The first is promoted by Inuit NGOs, particularly the ICC, with an emphasis on the fact that the Inuit are an Indigenous people across the Arctic. The second is advanced by the formal political apparatus including the Parliament and Government of Greenland. Both discourses represent decolonization that for some Inuit Greenlanders signifies formal separation from Denmark and for others, a more profound transformation of colonial norms and values.

For some Greenlanders, the two discourses of sovereignty are mutually exclusive. When asked about the absence of the discourse of Indigenous rights in Greenlandic political discourse, the ICC Greenland representative remarked: "Because they are mistakenly taking Greenland as a state… But I think it's a wrong approach." For him, "nationalism and Indigenous rights are two completely different things" evident, for example, in the leading party's (Siumut) nationalistic ideology of independence which is "not compatible with the principles of the UNDRIP" (interview with

ICC Greenland representative, 22 March 2013). A central UNDRIP principle frequently overlooked by Greenland's political elite is free, prior, and informed consent, which is essential if Greenland is successfully going to develop its mineral resources for the benefit of the entire country, including the remote settlements and individuals at risk of marginalization or oppression.

The approval and endorsement of UNDRIP in 2007 undoubtedly represented the Indigenous challenge to Westphalian sovereignty, as suggested by Pitty and Smith (2011). I contend that Greenland poses yet another Indigenous challenge to Westphalian sovereignty – Indigenous Westphalian sovereignty where the two Inuit discourses of sovereignty converge. By no means it is a straightforward undertaking and there certainly are incongruities, but in many ways, it has already been unfolding for decades. Ultimately, the success of Indigenous Westphalian sovereignty will be measured in Greenlanders' ability to reconcile their endeavor for independence with Indigenous rights and self-determination which stress sustainable development of resources and promotion of cultural heritage, traditional knowledge, and economies.

CONCLUSION

This chapter has examined conceptions of sovereignty and implementation of self-determination in Greenland. The political vision of an independent Greenland has long animated Greenlandic society. Negotiating an agreement with Denmark and passing the Self-Government Act in 2009 has made the widely shared vision of independence a concrete prospect that can be achieved through a referendum in Greenland. Another significant aspect of the Self-Government Act is Greenland securing exclusive subsurface rights to its territory. Political independence requires economic self-sufficiency. In Greenland, this implies an aggressive push for developing its extensive mineral resources, which are becoming more accessible due to accelerating climate change melting Greenland's ice sheet.

Yet there are considerable concerns about public engagement, consultation, and the transparency of the government and multinational companies. Greenlanders, their organizations, and NGOs have called for greater compliance with the norm of free, prior, and informed consent. Greenland has also become a subject of global geopolitical tensions and power struggles by major states racing to control and access the Arctic's resources and increasingly navigable waters. In this context of contested Arctic sovereignty, Greenlanders are advancing their own form, what I have called "Indigenous Westphalian Sovereignty," a unique approach to self-determination in the Indigenous world. This is a difficult endeavor with internal dissensions and complications, including the risk of new forms of dependencies. Indigenous Westphalian sovereignty also challenges the notion that Indigenous self-determination is limited to non-secession.

NOTES

1 An NGO established in 1977 to represent the Inuit across the Arctic with regional offices in Greenland, Canada, Alaska, and Chukotka, Russia, the ICC's key policy areas have included Inuit rights and self-determination and the protection of Arctic environment.

Through the ICC, the Inuit have also been at the forefront of the international advocacy for Indigenous self-determination since the 1970s, including the drafting and passing the 2007 UN Declaration on the Rights of Indigenous Peoples (UNDRIP).

2. On the qualified recognition of tribal sovereignty in the United States, see, for example, Wilkins (1998).

3. The legal term "the people of Greenland" refers not only to the Inuit but encompasses the entire population of the country, although Inuit form a great majority of Greenland's population (88 percent).

4. On Chinese influence in Greenland, see Simpson (2018). On Russian influence in the Arctic possibly behind the US interest in Greenland, see Breum (2019).

5. Following an election upset on 6 April 2021, Kim Kielsen (Siumut Party) ended his term as premier and was replaced by Múte Bourup Egede (Inuit Ataqatigiit). Mining of uranium and rare earth minerals was a major election issue.

6. There are other states such as Bolivia where Indigenous peoples form a majority. Bolivia, however, became independent when it was still ruled by a small non-Indigenous elite.

7. Ironically, the Danish leadership is not keen on placing Greenland on the same plane as the postcolonial countries of the global South. Upon learning about the US aid package, some Danish MPs were outraged by the foreign aid, which suggests that Greenland is a developing country, stating "But Greenland is not a developing country. It is a western democracy. I think [the aid] is reprehensible" (*The Guardian* 2020).

REFERENCES

AFP. 2008. "Greenland Votes Massively in Favour of Self-Rule." *Canada.com*, 25 November 2008. Accessed 8 April 2016. http://www.canada.com/topics/news/world/story.html?id=878988d2-a6e1-49e78e4a-cf684ba0989d.

Alfred, Taiaiake. 1999. *Peace, Power, Righteousness: An Indigenous Manifesto*. Toronto, ON: Oxford University Press.

Anaya, S. James. 1996. *Indigenous Peoples in International Law*. New York and Oxford: Oxford University Press.

———. 2009. "The Right of Indigenous Peoples to Self-Determination in the Post-Declaration Era." In *Making the Declaration Work: The United Nations Declaration on the Rights of Indigenous Peoples*, edited by Claire Charters and Rodolfo Stavenhagen, 184–198. Copenhagen, IWGIA.

Barker, Joanne. 2005. "For Whom Sovereignty Matters?" In *Sovereignty Matters. Locations of Contestation and Possibility in Indigenous Struggles for Self-Determination*, edited by Joanne Barker, 1–31. Lincoln, NB and London, UK: University of Nebraska Press.

Becker, Mary Druke. 1998. "We Are an Independent Nation: A History of Iroquois Sovereignty." *Buffalo Law Review* 46: 981–1000.

Borrows, John. 2002. *Recovering Canada. The Resurgence of Indigenous Law*. Toronto, ON: University of Toronto Press.

Breum, Martin. 2019. "Russian Hypersonic Missiles May Be the Reason for Donald Trump's Wish to Buy Greenland." *High North News*, 28 November 2019. Accessed 26 April 2020. https://www.highnorthnews.com/en/russian-hypersonic-missiles-may-be-reason-donald-trumpswish-buy-greenland.

———. 2020. "Greenland's Premier: "We Must Work towards Independence." *High North News*, 20 January 2020. Accessed 26 April 2020. https://www.highnorthnews.com/en/greenlands-premier-we-must-work-towardsindependence.

Canovan, Margaret. 1996. *Nationhood and Political Theory*. Cheltenham and Northhampton, UK: Edward Elgar.

Champagne, Duane. 2012. AISA Presidential address. *13th Annual Conference of the American Indian Studies Association: "Making the UN Declaration on the Rights of Indigenous Peoples Work for Tribal Communities."* Tempe, AZ: Arizona State University.

Chatterjee, Partha. 1986. *Nationalist Thought and the Colonial World.* London: Zed Books.

———. 1989. "Colonialism, Nationalism, and Colonialized Women: The Contest in India." *American Ethnologist* 16 (4): 622–633. https://doi.org/10.1525/ae.1989.16.4.02a00020.

Davis, Nicola. 2020. "Scientists Confirm Dramatic Melting of Greenland Ice Sheet." *The Guardian*, 26 April 2020. https://www.theguardian.com/science/2020/apr/15/scientists-confirm-dramatic-meltinggreenland-ice-sheet.

Government of Greenland. 2009. *Act on Greenland Self-Government.* Act no 473 of 12 June 2009.

Hansen, Anne Merrild. 2013. "Community Impacts: Public Participation, Culture and Democracy." In *Background Paper for the Committee for Greenlandic Mineral Resources to the Benefit of Society.* Aalborg and Nuuk: University of Copenhagen and University of Greenland.

Held, David. 1995. *Democracy and the Global Order.* Cambridge: Polity Press.

Henderson, James (Sa'ke'j) Youngblood. 2008. "Treaty Governance." In *Aboriginal Self-Government in Canada: Current Trends and Issues*, edited by Yale Belanger, 20–38. Saskatoon: Purich.

Hill, Susan M. 2017. *The Clay We Are Made Of: Haudenosaunee Land Tenure on the Grand River.* Winnipeg, MB: University of Manitoba Press.

Hornby, Lucy, Richard Milne and James Wilson. 2016. "Chinese Group General Nice Takes Over Greenland Mine." *Financial Times*, 8 Jan. 2016, from http://www.ft.com/cms/s/0/22842e82-9979-11e4-a3d7-00144feabdc0.html#axzz3wg2p8jX6.

ICC. 2009. *The Circumpolar Inuit Declaration on Sovereignty in the Artctic.* Tromsø, Norway: Inuit Circumpolar Council.

ICC. 2011. *A Circumpolar Inuit Declaration on Resource Development Principles in Inuit Nunaat.* Nuuk: Inuit Circumpolar Council. https://www.arctic-report.net/wp-content/uploads/2012/01/Inuit-Declaration-on-Resource-Development-May-2011.pdf

Irlbacher-Fox, Stephanie. 2009. *Finding Dahshaa: Self-Government, Social Suffering, and Aboriginal Policy in Canada.* Vancouver, BC: UBC Press.

King, Joyce Tekahnawiiaks. 2007. "The Value of Water and the Meaning of Water Law for the Native Americans Known as the Haudenosaunee." *Cornell Journal of Law and Public Policy* 16 (3): 449–472.

Kleist, Kuupik. 2009a. Celebration Speech by Premier Kuupik Kleist on Inauguration of Greenland Self-Government, 21 June 2009.

———. 2009b. "Statement by Mr. Kuupik Kleist, Premier of Greenland, 2nd session of the Expert Mechanism on the Rights of Indigenous Peoples, Genera, 10–14 August 2009." In *Making the Declaration Work. The United Nations Declaration on the Rights of Indigenous Peoples*, edited by Claire Charters and Rodolfo Stavenhagen, 248–251. Copenhagen: IWGIA.

Kristensen, Kurt. 2008. "Maniitsoq får sin egen Chinatown" [Maniitsoq gets its own Chinatown]. *Sermitsiaq*, 28 March 2008, page 3.

Kuokkanen, Rauna. 2011. "From Indigenous Economies to Market-Based Self-Governance: A Feminist Political Economy Analysis." *Canadian Journal of Political Science* 44 (2): 275–297. https://doi-org.proxy.lib.sfu.ca/10.1017/S0008423911000126.

———. 2019. *Restructuring Relations: Indigenous Self-Determination, Governance and Gender.* New York: Oxford University Press.

Lapidoth, Ruth. 1992. "Sovereignty in Transition." *Journal of International Affairs* 45 (2): 325–346.

Lund Sørensen, Freia. 2008. "Sub-Surface and Self-Government." *Journal of Nordregio* 3 (8): 19–20.

Lyberth, Juaaka. 2008. "At gøre op med fortiden – eller hvorhen Grønland" [To do away with the past – or wherever Greenland]. *Tidskiftet Grønland* 2 (3): 66–79.

Lynch, Suzanne. 2020. "Trump Eyes Resource-Rich Greenland Again with $12bn Aid Package." 25 April 2020. Accessed 26 April 2020. https://www.irishtimes.com/news/world/us/trump-eyes-resourcerich-greenland-again-with-12bn-aid-package-1.4237371.

Lytwyn, Victor P. 1997. "A Dish with One Spoon: The Shared Hunting Grounds Agreement in the Great Lakes and St. Lawrence Valley Region." In *Papers of the 28th Algonquian Conference*, edited by David H. Pentland, 210–227. Winnipeg, MB: University of Manitoba.

Maaka, Roger C. A., and Augie Fleras. 2000. "Engaging with Indigeneity: Tino rangatinaranga in Aotearoa." In *Political Theory and the Rights of Indigenous Peoples*, edited by Duncan Ivison, Paul Patton and Will Sanders, 89–111. Cambridge: Cambridge University Press.

Macklem, Patrick. 2001. *Indigenous Difference and the Constitution of Canada*. Toronto, ON: University of Toronto Press.

Manuel, Arthur, and Grand Chief Ronald M. Derrickson. 2015. *Unsettling Canada: A National Wake-Up Call*. Toronto, ON: Between the Lines.

Monture Angus, Patricia. 1998. *Journeying Forward: Dreaming First Nations' Independence*. Halifax, NS: Fernwood.

Naalakkersuisut. 2020. "Adjustment of Exploration Obligations for 2020 to Zero." 2 April 2020. Accessed 26 April 2020. https://govmin.gl/2020/04/02/adjustment-of-exploration-obligations-for-2020-to-zero/.

Nadasdy, Paul. 2017. *Sovereignty's Entailments. First Nation State Formation in the Yukon*. Toronto, ON: University of Toronto Press.

Nairn, Tom. 1975. "The Modern Janus." *New Left Review* 1 (94): 1–28.

Northam, Jackie. 2019. "Greenland Is Not For Sale. But It Has Rare Earth Minerals America Wants." *NPR*, 24 November 2019. Accessed 26 April 2020. https://www.npr.org/2019/11/24/781598549/greenland-is-not-for-sale-but-it-has-the-rare-earth-minerals-america-wants.

Nuttall, Mark. 2008. "Climate Change and the Warming Politics of Autonomy in Greenland." *Indigenous Affairs* 1-2: 44–51.

Olsvig, Sara. 2013. "Parliamentary Uranium Vote: A Democratic Failure." *Arctic Journal*, 28 October 2013. Accessed 23 April 2016. http://arcticjournal.com/opinion/215/parliamentary-uranium-vote-democratic-failure.

Peter, Laurence. 2019. "Danes See Greenland Security Risk amid Arctic Tensions." *BBC News*, 29 November 2019. Accessed 26 April 2020. https://www.bbc.com/news/world-europe-50598898?intlink_from_url=https://www.bbc.co.uk/news/topics/c302m85q1dot/greenland&link_location=live-reporting-story.

Petersen, Robert. 1995. "Colonialism as Seen from a Former Colonized Area." *Arctic Anthropology* 32 (2): 118–126.

Philpott, Daniel. 1995. "Sovereignty: An Introduction and Brief History." *Journal of International Affairs* 2: 353–368.

Pitty, Roderic, and Shannara Smith. 2011. "The Indigenous Challenge to Westphalian Sovereignty." *Australian Journal of Political Science* 46 (1): 121–139. https://doi.org/10.1080/10361146.2010.546336.

Sassen, Saskia. 1996. *Losing Control? Sovereignty in an Age of Globalization*. New York: Columbia University Press.

Schionning, Bjorn. 2020. "As the Ice Melts, Greenland Considers its Future." *BBC News*, 9 January 2020. Accessed 26 April 2020. https://www.bbc.com/news/business-51014148.

Simpson, John. 2018. "How Greenland Could Become China's Arctic Base." *BBC News*, 18 December 2018. Accessed 26 April 2020. https://www.bbc.com/news/world-europe-46386867.

Slowey, Gabrielle. 2008. *Navigating Neoliberalism. Self-determination and the Mikisew Cree First Nation*. Vancouver, BC: UBC Press.

The Committee for Greenlandic Mineral Resources to the Benefit of Society. 2014. *To the Benefit of Greenland*. Nuuk and Copenhagen: Ilisimatusarfik (University of Greenland) and University of Copenhagen.

The Guardian. 2020. "Greenland Wary of US Plans for Aid Projects in its Territory." *The Guardian*, 23 April 2020. Accessed 26 April 2020. https://www.theguardian.com/world/2020/apr/23/greenland-cautiously-welcomesreports-us-investment.

Watson, Irene, and Sharon Venne. 2012. "Talking up Indigenous Peoples' Original Intent in a Space Dominated by State Interventions." In *Indigenous Rights in the Age of the UN Declaration*, edited by Elvira Pulitano and Mililani Trask, 87–109. Cambridge and New York: Cambridge University Press.

Weaver, Ray. 2013. "Power to the People." *Arctic Journal*, 24 October 2013. Accessed 8 January 2016. http://arcticjournal.com/oil-minerals/209/power-people.

White Face, Charmaine. 2013. *Indigenous Nations' Rights in the Balance: An Analysis of the Declaration on the Rights of Indigenous Peoples*. St. Paul, MN: Living Justice Press.

Wilkins, David E. 1998. "Tribal-State Affairs: American Indian States as 'Disclaiming' Sovereigns." *Publius* 28 (4): 98–123. https://doi.org/10.1093/oxfordjournals.pubjof.a030001.

Wilson, Emma. 2015. *Energy and Minerals in Greenland: Governance, Corporate Responsibility and Social Resilience*. London: International Institute for Environment and Development.

Zubaida, Sami. 1988. "Islam, Cultural Nationalism and the Left." *Review of Middle East Studies* 4: 302–321.

CHAPTER 19

INUIT NUNANGAT

The development of a common Inuit territorial and policy space in Canada

Nadine C. Fabbi and Gary N. Wilson

Inuit Nunangat is a phrase policy-makers would be wise to comprehend. It's how Inuit view the Canadian Arctic. It's how Inuit would like to be viewed by Canada and Canadian governments. Understanding it is just the start of enlightened policy in the Arctic.

(Mary Simon 2012)

INTRODUCTION

Inuit in Canada have made considerable progress in strengthening their autonomy on a regional level through land claims agreements and the governance structures that arise from them (Wilson, Alcantara and Rodon 2020, 3). However, the progress they have made at the national level, while significant, is less understood and appreciated. Over the last several decades, Inuit have built a national presence in Canada – one that is arguably unique in the world – through Inuit Tapiriit Kanatami (ITK), the national Inuit organization. Since it was established in 1971, ITK has championed the rights of Inuit in Canada at all levels of government. It has supported regional Inuit organizations in their efforts to negotiate land claims agreements and has lobbied the federal government on a range of important and challenging policy issues that affect Inuit communities, including education, healthcare, and housing. ITK has also promoted the idea of Inuit Nunangat ("homeland") as a common Inuit territorial and policy space to replace earlier, more general, concepts of "Arctic" or "North."

This chapter examines the emergence of Inuit Nunangat and the steps Inuit have taken to establish a national presence in Canada. It begins with an overview of the scholarship on cartography from both western and Inuit perspectives, followed by the ways in which successive Canadian governments sought to reshape the North in the decades after the end of the Second World War. It then discusses the rise of ITK, the unique methodology of Inuit land use and occupancy, and the efforts of ITK to develop the concept of Inuit Nunangat as a common territorial and political space. The second part of the chapter focuses on how ITK is represented at the federal level, its success in establishing government-to-government relations, and how this supports and advances the notion of Inuit Nunangat. Drawing on current theories of mapping, this chapter argues that ITK's success is, in part, the result of remapping and reframing the Arctic region to ensure the voice and interests of Inuit are represented in all future policies that will affect the region and its people.

CARTOGRAPHY: ART, SCIENCE, AND A PROJECT OF SELF-DETERMINATION

Recent efforts by ITK to establish Inuit Nunangat as a territorial and political space for Inuit in Canada is both a cartographic and political means of redefining the relationship between Inuit peoples and the Canadian state. Cartography is the study and practice of making maps for the purpose of communicating spatial information; it allows us to tell the story of the physical world and our relationship to it. Cultures around the world have made maps for thousands of years: carving them into clay tablets, inscribing them onto paper, setting them around a sphere or globe, or holding them in memory and invoking them as part of oral history. Art has also been used to embellish maps and to convey stories and values. Indeed, cartography is an art and a science, but it is also a process that can be used for political purposes including for self-determination.

Beginning in the 1990s, western scholars began to challenge how we think about maps by analyzing the political agendas and biases inherent in them (Harley 1989; 2001; Harley and Woodward 1987; MacEachren 1995; Monmonier 1991; Wood 1992; 2010). Theorists argued that maps express specific points of view and can serve as instruments of power. They can also represent particular realities while omitting others. As noted in a recent article on mapping and philosophy, "it matters whether you are on the map or not: mapping in language is about claiming, making a statement, controlling, representing, and purporting to know the world" (Perkins 2009, 385). "Counter-mapping" (Peluso 1995) is another theory developed to understand how Indigenous and other communities use mapping to push back against dominant powers and to assert their rights. However, decades prior to these new modes of thinking by western scholars in geography, political science, and sociology, Inuit in Canada were engaging in large-scale counter-mapping projects that would lay the foundation for future land claims and change the map of Canada. This mapping methodology – Inuit land use and occupancy – became a model for Indigenous mapping internationally and provided a new policy space for Inuit at the national level.

Until the mid-20th century, Inuit mapping was part of oral tradition. "Like other peoples in the world," explains Inuk author Michael Kusugak, "we have always carried maps in our minds" (2019). For Inuit, such maps were localized and reflected the ways in which the land, water, and ice were traditionally used for hunting, gathering, and traveling. However, Inuit mapping went through a major transformation in the post-war period, due in large part to resource development and government policies that would transform Inuit society. As a result of these political, economic, and socio-cultural changes, Inuit's sense of themselves and their place in Canada, and even the world, would take on new dimensions. In this changing environment, the local identity would still persist, but it would be influenced significantly by the need to settle land claims that would create new regional identities and ultimately establish a pan-Inuit homeland in Canada.

THE IMPACTS OF COLONIALISM AND STATE INTRUSION IN INUIT NUNANGAT

Until the mid-20th century, successive governments in Canada (federal and provincial) had neglected the North, including the territory now known as Inuit Nunangat. The remoteness of Inuit Nunangat meant that it did not undergo the same type of settlement that occurred in southern Canada; although it is important to acknowledge that Inuit and their territories were impacted by colonization and colonial policies and practices, such as the trauma and assimilation caused by the residential school system (Anawak 2009). The status and jurisdiction of the various regions that comprise Inuit Nunangat were also altered by southern-based governments without the consent or knowledge of Inuit. A case in point is the region of Nunavik in northern Québec. Between 1870 and 1912, it was transferred twice from the jurisdiction of Rupert's Land to the Northwest Territories to, eventually, the province of Québec. Despite "acquiring" this vast territory the Québec government did not play a role in the administration of the region for at least another 50 years and even successfully took the federal government to the Supreme Court in 1939 to avoid being responsible for the welfare of the Nunavimmiut, the Inuit of northern Québec (Desbiens 2013; Nungak 2017).

However, beginning in the late 1950s, governments at the federal and provincial levels began to take a greater interest in the North. This was largely driven by two processes: the need for resources for the country's economic development; and, the expansion of government intervention in the economy and society as a result of the development of the post-war welfare state. In terms of resource development, the federal government envisioned "a Canada of the North," and one that would be achieved by "the opening of Canada's Northland" to development (Diefenbaker 1958). For example, the government partnered with industry to create Panarctic Oils Ltd., a company that oversaw dozens of exploratory drilling projects across the Arctic Islands (Masterson 2013). It supported drilling for natural gas in the Mackenzie River Delta, and for oil and gas in the Canadian Beaufort Sea. The latter project would lead to a proposal for the Mackenzie Valley pipeline, linking the High Arctic with southern Canada and the United States. Provincial governments also become involved in this rush for resources. For example, the development of hydroelectric energy in northern Québec led to the James Bay hydroelectric project (Desbiens 2013). Collectively, these and other projects would reshape and redefine the North. They contributed to the massive alteration and destruction of the northern landscape and the colonization of the peoples living there. At the same time, they also prompted a reaction from Indigenous peoples, including Inuit. The political mobilization that followed in the wake of large-scale resource development projects like the Mackenzie Valley pipeline and the James Bay hydroelectric project would have a significant impact on the Canadian political landscape in the decades that followed.

At about the same time as the northern resource boom was getting started, governments across Canada were extending their political reach into the North. While some of this activity was connected to resource development (for example, providing critical infrastructure to assist and service new development projects), it was also connected to the expansion of the welfare state, a series of reforms aimed at improving the lives of Canadians as a whole. Inuit were impacted in both positive and negative ways by these developments. Sedentarization led to the relocation of Inuit into settled communities to facilitate government provision of services such as healthcare and education. Although these services were not to the same standards as those enjoyed in the South, they were a marked improvement in terms of what had existed before. Sedentarization, however, also negatively impacted Inuit by drawing them closer into the wage economy and separating them from their traditional nomadic lifestyle and culture. This, in turn, would cause many of the social challenges that affect Inuit societies to the present day.

The combination of political, social, and economic changes in Inuit communities in the 1960s and 1970s had a profound effect on Inuit society. Reflecting on this transition, Inuit leader and diplomat Sheila Watt-Cloutier commented:

> The Arctic is a different place than it was when I was a child. And while many of the changes are positive, the journey into the modern world was not an easy one—and it has left its scars. In a sense, Inuit of my generation have lived in both the ice age and space age.
>
> (2015, viii)

One of the most important and positive consequences of these changes was the effort on the part of Inuit to fight for self-determination, first through the negotiation and settlement of land claims agreements and later through political and economic reforms that would gradually enhance the autonomy of their individual regions in relation to other governments (Hicks and White 2015; Wilson, Alcantara and Rodon 2020). Central to these developments was the establishment of a national organization that would provide a unified voice for all Inuit.

ONE VOICE, ONE PEOPLE: THE FOUNDING OF A NATIONAL INUIT ASSOCIATION

From early on, Inuit leaders had a vision that was clear and consistent – Inuit would speak with a unified voice, and a clearly defined Inuit homeland would provide the foundation for future policy development. That unified voice was first articulated at the inaugural meeting of Inuit in Canada held in the summer of 1970 – the Coppermine Conference of Arctic Native People. At the conference, 33 delegates representing 22 communities in Arctic Canada discussed a number of concerns including oil and other mineral exploration, the testing of new shipping routes, housing, education, and hunting. Throughout the conference the main issue was white encroachment into Inuit communities and its influence on the lives and welfare of Inuit as well as the impending loss of Inuit freedom and self-determination. The meeting enabled Inuit to learn about the issues faced in the various regions and to realize the commonalities of their struggles. The creation of an organization to represent all Inuit was mentioned a number of times during the conference. One of the delegates, Noah Qumak argued: "If we only communicate in small separated groups, we will never become strong or get what we want. If we become one organization, well-known and strong, we can preserve our ways" (iv–2). The meeting concluded with a note summarizing the need for further communication and conferences that would contribute to "the goal of an organized voice" (x–2).

Importantly, the Coppermine Conference marked the first time Inuit would address the Government of Canada as one people (Bonesteel 2006, 43). During the conference, a telegram was drafted to Prime Minister Pierre Elliott Trudeau and Minister of Indian Affairs and Northern Development, Jean Chrétien, outlining key issues. The telegram, sent 16 July 1970, included six resolutions.[1] It was signed by all of the delegates who made the point that they represented "All of the Eskimo people of the North" (Coppermine Conference, Telegram, 2). In addition, the delegates requested that the "government recognize our rights as Aboriginals in the lands of the North" (Coppermine Conference, Telegram, 2). This telegram marked the beginning of the Inuit-Crown relations that have grown in scope in the 50 intervening years.

Three of the representatives at the Coppermine Conference, Noah Qumak, Jacob Oweetaluktuk, and Mary Cousins, would meet the following year to discuss a number of issues including, again, the need to form a national association. On 18 February 1971, seven Inuit representatives met in Toronto and Peterborough, Ontario. One of the results of this five-day meeting was the establishment of a national association. At that first meeting Jacob Oweetaluktuk took the lead on describing the current situation for Inuit and articulating the pressing need for a national organization:

> During the early stages when the government first came into our communities, it was quite all right for them to look after our own problems, administration, and so on … In the past there was nothing bothering us, but right now at this very moment there is something interfering with us Inuit … we have to find an organized voice amongst ourselves so we may direct our lives the way we want them to be. Maybe we should have something like an Inuit organization.
> (Inuit Tapirisat of Canada 1971)

The next day, Noah Qumak suggested Inuit Tapirisat of Canada (ITC, "Inuit Brotherhood of Canada") as the name for the new association. Further decisions were made regarding the structure of the organization and funding. Officers were elected and the first meeting was scheduled to include representatives from across the North.

The primary role of the new national association was to lobby for and support a land claims settlement for the entire Inuit region – a goal that would later be realized although somewhat differently than originally envisioned. In addition, the national association championed a number of issues and policies for Inuit that have made a marked contribution to the preservation of Inuit culture, language, and enhanced self-determination in Canada. ITC lobbied for inquiries into oil and gas development projects and sought injunctions against several natural resource development projects in the Arctic. It also initiated the Inukshuk Project in 1980 that ensured Inuit control over communications and led to the founding of the Inuit Broadcasting Corporation (*Inuktitut* 1980, 14–19). In 1989, ITC took over production of *Inuktitut*, a national tri-lingual magazine dedicated to Inuit culture, language, and life (ITK 1989, 2–5). It conducted studies and reports that have resulted in apologies from the federal government and compensation for Inuit who were victims of the High Arctic relocation and residential schools (ITK website). ITC also lobbied for full representation at constitutional talks.

In 1982, Canada patriated its constitution from Britain but not before an 18-month period of considerable political and legal struggles. Of concern to Indigenous peoples was the inclusion of Section 35 that would recognize and affirm Indigenous rights. Thanks to a grassroots movement that swept the nation, national support, and even international pressure, Aboriginal rights were enshrined in the Constitution Act of 1982. Inuit played a key role in the constitutional process (McInnes 1981). ITC assisted in the establishment of the Inuit Committee on National Issues (ICNI) to represent Inuit in the constitutional discussions. This committee also lobbied the federal government to sit as equals with the federal, provincial, and territorial governments represented at First Ministers' meetings (McInnes 1981, 57). While unsuccessful in this effort (representatives of Indigenous peoples were provided observer status), the efforts of the ICNI nonetheless paved the way for the future role of Inuit in constitutional matters. Later, during the constitutional reform process to amend the Canadian Constitution, Inuit, First Nations, and Métis were recognized as *full* participants in all constitutional matters – a marked development in Inuit-Crown relations. At that time Rosemary Kuptana, president of ITC, noted, "Inuit believe that this historic decision signifies a turning point in Canadian history, with the inclusion of aboriginal peoples as meaningful and equal partners in Canada" (1992, 40). It was also during Kuptana's presidency that ITC lobbied the government for the development of an Arctic Council to provide a forum where Arctic Indigenous peoples would sit as "equal participants with the eight circumpolar governments" to address "all issues of importance to Arctic peoples" (Kuptana 1992, 40).

In 2001, at the 30th anniversary of the founding of ITC, the association was given a new name – Inuit Tapiriit Kanatami (ITK, Inuit United in Canada) – to reflect the settlement of land claims agreements between the four Inuit regions and the Crown.[2] Today ITK is the "national voice" for Canada's 65,000 Inuit who live in 51 communities across the Arctic and outside Inuit Nunangat. The eight-member governing board includes the president and the presidents or chairs of each of the four Inuit land claims organizations (Inuvialuit Regional Corporation, Nunavut Tunngavik Incorporated, the Makivik Corporation, and the Nunatsiavut Government), all as voting members. The board also includes non-voting members: representatives from the Inuit Circumpolar Council Canada, Pauktuutit Inuit Women of Canada, and the National Inuit Youth Council. The president is elected for a three-year term by voting members of the board.

In a post-land claims era, as will be outlined later in this chapter, ITK has released national strategies on a range of policy issues from education and climate change to Canada's international obligations with regards to the rights of Indigenous peoples. While ITK has worked on a variety of levels to further the self-determination of Inuit in Canada and internationally, its most important roles were to support the negotiation of comprehensive land claims agreements and, following this, to define a common Inuit homeland that encompassed all the Inuit regions in Canada. In the words of Mary Simon, that initial "meeting of the minds in 1971 … kickstarted the land claims process" (*Nunatsiaq News* 2011). Almost 35 years later, an Inuit homeland would be put on the map and presented as a new policy space for all matters pertaining to Inuit. This homeland would be defined according to a unique Inuit mapping methodology.

INUIT LAND USE AND OCCUPANCY: A UNIQUE APPROACH TO LAND CLAIMS

Comprehensive land claims are also referred to as modern treaties. They are land claims based on traditional use and occupancy of lands that were not ceded to a government or settlers. Comprehensive land claims are settled through negotiation between an Indigenous group, a territory or province, and the federal government. The concept of comprehensive land claims was initially developed by the Government of Canada in response to the Calder Case of 1973, a Supreme Court case filed by the Nisga'a Nation of British Columbia for recognition of title to their ancestral lands. While the court ultimately ruled against the Nisga'a, the government nonetheless recognized the need for a policy to guide negotiations with Indigenous peoples where no treaties existed. In the months following the Calder Case, Minister of Indian Affairs and Northern Development Jean Chrétien issued a "statement of policy" on Aboriginal title. In addition to existing treaties and other agreements with Indigenous peoples, the policy recognized a *new* approach to land claims – land claims based on the "continuing use and occupancy of traditional lands" (Munro 1981, 11).

In the spring following the 1973 release of the "statement of policy," the Government of Canada held the Arctic Corridor Conference in Churchill, Manitoba. At this conference, ITC gave a presentation on the importance of Inuit land claims to the fabric of Canadian society. Tagak Curley, president of ITC, thanked the government for its recognition of Aboriginal rights earlier that year, pointing out that there had been no recognition of non-treaty rights for Inuit prior. He also thanked the government for its funding for the ITC land claims project in the Northwest Territories and research for an Inuit land use and occupancy study, noting that "[t]hese two mentioned projects are two of the significant building blocks for any and all policy in relation to the Inuit for some years to come" (ITC 1973, 2). Throughout the presentation, Curley argued that a freeze must be put on all exploration and development projects until Inuit land claims are settled. Of particular importance was the way in which Curley positioned ITC as an advocate, not just for Inuit but for Canada and all Canadians.[3] In the presentation, he described the United States as "out of control" in regards to its treatment of the environment and its over-consumption of resources. In response, he offered Canada a different way forward, an Inuit way:

> We believe the Inuit have a great deal to contribute to Canadian society. The Inuit wish to participate in the development of a Canada which properly considers "development" within a much broader context and one which includes Inuit values. The Inuit are not prepared to stand quietly on the sidelines and passively accept the destruction of their environment and identity, and the loss of what may well be the last opportunity for a better and different Canada.
>
> (ITC 1973, 5)

Curley effectively argued that Inuit land claims would play a key role in contributing an Inuit perspective on land use and development within Canada. Over the course of the next four decades, ITC would continue to work with Inuit organizations across Canada in the settlement of their land claims (see Figure 19.1).

Figure 19.1 Inuit Tapiriit Kanatami map of the four Inuit land claims settlement regions in Canada. Map: ITK 2005.

Inuit settled a total of five land claims agreements with Canada in accordance with the new government policy. These include the James Bay and Northern Québec Agreement (1975); the Inuvialuit Final Agreement (1984); the Nunavut Land Claims Agreement (1993); the Labrador Inuit Land Claims Agreement (2005); and the Nunavik Inuit Land Claims Agreement which came into effect in 2017 and includes the offshore region of Nunavik and northern Labrador. These new borders were created on the basis of culture, use and occupancy, and have provided the foundation for the development of a variety of regional governance models (Wilson, Alcantara and Rodon 2020). Inuit land use and occupancy studies played an important role in the settlement of these agreements.

In 1971 the Government of Québec announced the "project of the century," the James Bay Hydroelectric Development Project, one of the largest hydroelectric projects in the world. This was done without prior consultation with Inuit or Cree whose traditional lands would be dramatically impacted. In response, the Inuit created the Northern Québec Inuit Association (NQIA) to represent Inuit rights and to apply for an injunction to stop development. In what has been likened to the battle of David versus Goliath in Zebedee Nungak's book *Wrestling with Colonialism on Steroids: Québec Inuit Fight for Their Homeland* (2017, 64), Superior Court Justice Albert Malouf ruled in favor of the Cree and Inuit, effectively halting all construction for one week. Although Malouf's decision was overturned by the Québec Appeal Court, the process eventually resulted in an out-of-court settlement, the 1975 James Bay and

Northern Québec Agreement (JBNQA). During the settlement process Inuit employed a land use and occupancy methodology to define their territory, though according to Nungak, a member of the NQIA, it was a rushed and contentious process that resulted in significant divisions between Inuit communities (2017, 91). Nevertheless, the agreement was signed and celebrated as the first major comprehensive land claims agreement in Canada. According to the Makivik Corporation, the official representative of Inuit in Nunavik, the agreement heralded in a "new era in aboriginal land claims" (Makivik Corporation 2020).

By far the largest Inuit land use and occupancy study was the one that occurred in the central and eastern Arctic under the leadership of ITC. This was a three-year process from inception to the production of the final report. In 1973, ITC President Tagak Curley proposed the project to the Minister of Indian and Northern Affairs. Milton Freeman, a biologist and an anthropologist, was commissioned to direct the study. Dozens of researchers were involved in the project resulting in a three-volume report, *The Inuit Land Use and Occupancy Project* (ILUOP) (Freeman 1976). The report, which covered the Northwest Territories and the northeastern portion of Yukon Territory (Freeman 1976, 21), was used during negotiations for both the Inuvialuit Final Agreement (1984) and the Nunavut Land Claims Agreement (1993) (Freeman 2011, 20). Initially, ITC's plan was to present a single land claim for all Inuit in the Northwest Territories. However, pressures caused by impending oil and gas development in the Western Arctic led the Inuvialuit to pursue their own land claims agreement. In 1984, the Committee for Original Peoples' Entitlement (COPE)[4] which represented the Inuvialuit, and the Government of Canada, signed the Inuvialuit Final Agreement, the first comprehensive land claims agreement signed north of the 60th parallel. The Inuvialuit Regional Corporation was formed to serve the new Inuvialuit Settlement Region.

The methodology used for the land use and occupancy studies in both regions was called a "map biography" a process developed and tested by geographer Peter Usher years earlier (Freeman 2011, 23). Map biographies are individual recollections of activities and memories on the land. According to Usher (1992, 46), as Inuit left "no recognizable imprint on the landscape," evidence had to be found of "Inuit property and tenure systems in Inuit social organization, ideology, and values." This was accomplished by interviewing about 1,600 individuals in 34 communities across the Arctic (Freeman 2011, 22). Each map biography was then aggregated to create a "composite map" (Freeman 2011, 22).

What makes the Inuit land use and occupancy studies in Canada unique is that they rely solely on interviews and fieldwork conducted in the communities. For example, this approach differs from the methodology used as a basis for the Alaska Native Claims Settlement Act in the United States where references to published materials and other secondary sources were employed rather than the use of direct interviews (Freeman 2011, 22). The Inuit land use and occupancy process melds Inuit oral tradition with western mapping practices. This unique methodology serves to create new borders and embodies cultural values and a relationship to the world that is uniquely Inuit.

The Nunavut Land Claims Agreement, Canada's largest land claims agreement, received Royal Assent in 1993. The agreement included a promise for the creation of a new territory, Nunavut, established in 1999. The land use and occupancy study was integral to the agreement and subsequently used as a model for the subsequent Inuit land claims process in Labrador.

In 1973 the Labrador Inuit Association (LIA) was formed to advance Inuit land claims. In 1975 the LIA entered into an Agreement with the Department of Indian and Northern Affairs to conduct a use and occupancy study that would complement the ILUOP. The goal was to provide a "comprehensive, verifiable record of past and present Inuit use and occupation of the land and marine environment" (Brice-Bennett 1977, vii). The study, aptly titled *Our Footprints Are Everywhere: Inuit Land Use and Occupancy in Labrador* (1977), would lay the foundation for land claims in the region. The report includes early archaeological evidence, community land use practices, and perspectives on the importance of land in defining Inuit identity. In 1977, the LIA filed a land claim with the federal government which would eventually result in the Labrador Inuit Land Claims Agreement and the establishment of the region of Nunatsiavut in 2005.

As noted by Freeman, "the individual map biography and community composite map approaches" became "the accepted methodology used in land claims" (2011, 28). Inuit mapping has not only changed the map of Canada but has also changed how Canada thinks about itself as a country. When the final Inuit land claim was settled in 2005, ITK would immediately move to create a new map of Canada that would encompass all four regions and serve to challenge conventional concepts of the North and maps of the region.

ESTABLISHING AN INUIT HOMELAND IN CANADA

Once the land claims were either settled or in the final stages of negotiation, Jose Kusugak, then president of ITC, oversaw a number of initiatives in an effort to re-envision the place of ITC in relation to Canada. Kusugak first announced the new motto – "First Canadians, Canadians First." In the president's message in *Inuktitut* in 2001, Kusugak described how Inuit are different from other Indigenous peoples in that they identify as both Inuit and Canadian. "As Italian Canadians, Chinese Canadians and Jewish Canadians are proud of their ethnic background, so are Inuit," notes Kusugak, "and we want our partnership with Canada to continue to grow" (2001, 4). He spoke about the first 30 years of ITC as being dedicated to settling land claims and the next stage as "get[ting] Inuit to an equal starting point with the rest of Canada" (4). In early 2002, a new logo was unveiled depicting four Inuit, two males and two females, each representing one of four regions and creating, out of the empty space between them, the maple leaf of Canada and an ulu, a traditional Inuit cutting tool. Whit Fraser, who worked as executive director of ITK alongside Kusugak, credited him with making a "remarkable contribution towards instilling Inuit identity in Canada's collective consciousness" and for convincing the Government of Canada to distinguish Inuit from other Indigenous peoples (Fraser 2011).

Importantly, when the last Inuit land claim was settled in Canada in 2005, ITK created the first map that encompassed all of the Inuit regions into one unit. The map replaced provincial and territorial boundaries with cultural borders, effectively challenging conventional notions of territory in Canada. This would be the first time that the "political and jurisdictional boundaries within Canada—or, for that matter, between Arctic states—[were] drawn up with any attention to the linguistic and cultural unity of Inuit" (Simon 2012). Inuit Nunaat ("Inuit land") was initially chosen as the name for the new Inuit homeland. A few years later, in 2009, ITK adopted a new name, Inuit Nunangat, for the region. According to ITK, the reason for the change was twofold: first, they wanted to use a Canadian Inuktitut word; and second, the new name was more encompassing of how Inuit understand the notion of territory:

> "Inuit Nunaat" is a Greenlandic term that describes land but does not include water or ice. The term "Inuit Nunangat" is a Canadian Inuktitut term that includes land, water, and ice. As Canadian Inuit consider the land, water, and ice, of our homeland to be integral to our culture and our way of life it was felt that "Inuit Nunangat" is a more inclusive and appropriate term to use when describing our lands.
>
> (ITK nd., Maps of Inuit Nunangat)

The creation of Nunavut changed the map of Canada by adding a new territory; Inuit Nunangat changed how we understand Canada with cultural borders mapping over political ones. The change in name has potentially far-reaching implications not only within Canada but also internationally. If Inuit concepts of land are broadened to include ice and water, what might this mean for foreign policy, including the application of the United Nations Convention on the Law of the Sea to the current dispute over the Northwest Passage? In *A Fair Country: Telling Truths about Canada* (2008), John Ralston Saul provocatively asks the question – If Canada were to conceptualize territory from an Inuit perspective, how might this influence international law or for that matter, the border between Canada and Greenland?

> [I]f we were to take on our Northernness and argue from the position of Inuit legitimacy and Inuit concepts – of stable life involving a joining together of land and ice or water, how would the rest of the world react? Would international tribunals and courts have trouble with this rectification of names? Of course they would ... [b]ut they would be obliged to consider it and therefore to consider differently the very nature of the opposing arguments.
>
> (Saul 2008, 302)

While we do not yet know how Inuit concepts of territory may play out in the international legal realm, more recent events have demonstrated the impact that the map of Inuit Nunangat has had on Canadian policy and how Inuit conceptions of their collective territory are creating a unique Inuit policy space within the country.

In July 2009, *Canada's Northern Strategy: Our North, Our Heritage, Our Future* was released. The document included a conventional political map of Canada's North, featuring the three territories but excluding the Inuit regions of Nunavik in northern Québec and Nunatsiavut in northern Labrador. Although the strategy did feature a map of the modern treaties in the North, which included the four treaties signed by Inuit regional bodies and the Crown, it did not specifically refer to these regions by name (Government of Canada 2009). When the strategy was released, ITK President Mary Simon criticized the government for using a map that did not include all Inuit regions in a policy framework that directly affects Inuit (Boswell

2009). The government immediately acknowledged the oversight, apologized, and promised to reprint the document. This issue drew attention to the significant differences in how the federal government and ITK (and Inuit more generally) viewed the North in spatial terms.

Natan Obed, the current president of ITK, has noted that navigating the "current bureaucratic regions" is inefficient and that the current political/territorial landscape "by its very structure fails Inuit" (2019). These sentiments echo those expressed by Mary Simon in 2012 when she said that living at the geographic margins of Canada means that policies applying to Inuit Nunangat are often made elsewhere and are ineffective. As Obed later pointed out: "[a]cknowledging Inuit Nunangat's unique political and cultural primacy and expertise within our existing democratic governance structure is paramount to us in the North. It would be cost-effective, efficient, and a sign of genuine reconciliation" (2019).

INUIT NUNANGAT AS A COMMON TERRITORIAL AND POLICY SPACE

The previous section outlined the development of ITK and its articulation of Inuit Nunangat, a common territorial space comprising the different Inuit regions in the Canadian Arctic. This section will explore the ways in which ITK has positioned itself politically and collectively to represent Inuit interests at the national level. In recent years, ITK has reinforced the links between the different Inuit regions and their varied governance structures and, in doing so, has also presented a united front in policy discussions with the federal government, specifically through the establishment of the Inuit-Crown Partnership Committee (ICPC). ITK has also promoted the notion of Inuit Nunangat as a new and unified policy space by undertaking initiatives in several policy areas that are of critical importance to Inuit. As noted earlier, ITK has represented Canadian Inuit interests at the regional, national, and international levels for many decades. This section will focus specifically on its efforts since 2015 to engage with the federal government and to move its policy agenda forward.

One of the most significant developments to date is the creation of the Inuit-Crown Partnership Committee (ICPC). In 2017, Prime Minister Justin Trudeau and Inuit leaders signed the Inuit Nunangat Declaration which established the ICPC and represented a "shared commitment to a renewed Inuit-Crown relationship between ITK and the Government of Canada, and underscore[d] the common goal of creating prosperity for all Inuit, which benefits all Canadians" (Prime Minister 2017). As a permanent bilateral body, the committee works to address the challenges facing Inuit communities in Inuit Nunangat in areas such as education, health, housing, and economic development, as well as the full implementation of Inuit land claims agreements and redressing of past injustices. It is one of three separate bodies to manage the relationships between the federal government and Canada's three constitutionally recognized Indigenous groups. The ICPC, along with separate tables for First Nations-federal and Métis-federal relations, provide a direct means for the representatives of Indigenous groups to convey their priorities and concerns to the federal government and, in doing so, influence the policy development process (see Figure 19.2).

Figure 19.2   Prime Minister Justin Trudeau and Inuit Tapiriit Kanatami President Natan Obed sign the Inuit-Crown Partnership Declaration, Iqaluit, 9 February 2017. Photo: Adam Scotti, Prime Minister's Office.

The ICPC includes the prime minister, select federal ministers, the president of ITK, representatives of each of the Inuit land claims organizations, and the Nunatsiavut Government. The presidents of the National Inuit Youth Council, Pauktuutit Inuit Women of Canada, and the Inuit Circumpolar Council Canada also take part as observers (Prime Minister 2017). Since 2017, the committee has met once or twice a year, either in Ottawa or in Inuit Nunangat. In terms of quantity, this may seem like a limited number of meetings, but it is important to emphasize the quality of the interactions taking place. The structure and design of the ICPC follow a long-established Canadian tradition of executive federalism, a system of intergovernmental relations that focuses on the relationship between members of the provincial, territorial, and federal executive branches in high-level policy discussions (Wilson and Selle 2019).

ITK has embarked upon a comprehensive policy development process that serves as both a basis for discussions with the federal government through the ICPC and a way to demonstrate that Inuit across Inuit Nunangat are united, politically and territorially, in their policy positions. All policy documents are approved through ITK's broadly representative governance structure. They include position papers on the *Development and Implementation of the Arctic Policy Framework* (ITK 2018) and the establishment of an Indigenous Human Rights Commission through Federal UN Declaration Legislation (2020a), as well as a submission to the Canadian Arctic and Northern Policy Framework (ITK 2019a), an *Inuit Nunangat Housing Strategy* (ITK 2019b), the *National Inuit Climate Change Strategy* (2019c), and an *Inuit Post-Secondary Education Strategy* (ITK 2020b). In 2019, ITK, in partnership with Inuit regional government and territorial government partners, launched the National Inuit Health Survey.

These documents provide important insights on Inuit perspectives and priorities across several policy areas, and a comprehensive vision for a common policy space for Inuit Nunangat. For example, in response to the federal government's efforts to co-develop a new Arctic Policy Framework (APF), later referred to as Canada's Arctic and Northern Policy Framework (ANPF) with Indigenous, territorial, and provincial partners, ITK produced an overview paper entitled *Arctic and Northern Policy Framework: Inuit Nunangat* (ITK 2019a). The paper would later be included as an appendix chapter to the ANPF, along with other chapters representing the positions of the governments of the Northwest Territories and Nunavut, and a pan-territorial chapter (Government of Canada 2019).

The Inuit Nunangat chapter focuses on several key points. The first is that Inuit Nunangat is a distinct political, geographic, and cultural region and that Inuit are one people with a common language and cultural practices who "seek to participate fully in the national and global economies" (ITK 2019a, 4). It argues that "Canada currently lacks a policy which recognizes Inuit Nunangat. Implementing an Inuit Nunangat policy is the means to ensure respect and support for the right to Inuit self-determination" (ITK 2019a, 5). The second point is that Canada has failed to address the social and economic inequities that exist between Inuit and other Canadians. Indeed, "[a]ddressing social and economic inequity, both between Inuit Nunangat [and other parts of Canada] and within Inuit Nunangat itself, is a necessary pre-condition to the development of a healthy, resilient and secure Canadian Arctic" (ITK 2019a, 2). While such inequities stem from a long history of colonialism and neglect, the chapter also mentions other factors such as a lack of investment in social and physical infrastructure, the impacts of climate change, and the political and administrative division of Inuit Nunangat by provincial and territorial jurisdictional boundaries. From a governance perspective, this latter point is particularly important because these externally imposed divisions challenge the territorial unity of Inuit Nunangat and create program and funding disparities across this region (ITK 2019a, 5).

Of course, Inuit recognize that the existing administrative divisions of the Canadian federal system are part of the jurisdictional landscape that influences Inuit Nunangat and its political and economic development. In its *Development and Implementation of the Arctic Policy Framework* (ITK 2018), ITK called for a shared governance framework that operates at two different levels: within each Inuit region and across all Inuit regions. The paper went on to encourage the federal government to "build on existing trilateral mechanisms by facilitating and participating in intergovernmental forums between each province and territory, Inuit and the federal government" (ITK 2018). Such specific language is missing from the later document, but it does emphasize that the future prosperity of Inuit Nunangat is dependent not only on Inuit self-determination, but also on intergovernmental cooperation between Inuit and various levels of government. For example, it encourages the federal government to work with the provinces and territories in areas such as on tracking data in order to avoid exacerbating inequities that exist within Inuit Nunangat (ITK 2019a, 2). Such intergovernmental cooperation is necessary because many of the policy areas that are important to Inuit either fall under the constitutional or administrative jurisdiction of the provincial and territorial governments or involve those governments in other substantial ways.

Another underlying current within the Inuit Nunangat chapter of the ANPF is the idea that Inuit are best positioned to address the challenges facing their communities. Given the failures of paternalistic colonialism, one can understand why the Inuit would advocate for subsidiarity, a governance principle that emphasizes local control over policy decisions and administration. Ensuring coordination and equity across the region, as well as accountability to Inuit are important considerations. So too is the principle of universal access; many Inuit do not live in Inuit Nunangat but still need to access programs. Inuit also see local control as a way "to improve the coordination of related programs and strategies, minimize administrative burdens and build Inuit organizational capacity" (ITK 2020b).

In many respects, the Inuit Nunangat chapter of the ANPF presents an overarching set of perspectives that are reflected and elaborated in other policy-specific documents produced by ITK. The messaging across these various documents is consistent and this demonstrates a concerted effort to reinforce the notion that Inuit speak to other governments with one voice. This makes perfect sense given the small number of Inuit in Canada relative to other Indigenous groups and the fact that they are scattered across remote communities in four different regions and in other communities throughout Canada (Arriagada and Bleakney 2019). By presenting Inuit Nunangat as a unified territorial and political space, Inuit are maximizing their collective influence and confronting the externally imposed political and administrative barriers that divide them between different jurisdictions in the Canadian federation (Wilson, Alcantara, and Rodon 2020).

What has been the response of the federal government to these efforts to create a unified territorial and policy space? The initial signs have been cautiously positive. The establishment of the ICPC and the commitment of the federal government to meet on a biannual basis with Inuit leaders in that forum demonstrated a significant change from previous government practices. The fact that these meetings involve senior officials on both sides, including the prime minister and the president of ITK, gives them added weight. Over the last several years, the ICPC has discussed a variety of important issues, ranging from historical grievances (forced relocations and the treatment of Inuit during the tuberculosis epidemic of the 1940s to 1960s) and contemporary challenges (health and wellness, housing, early learning and childcare, education and skills development, and land claims implementation).

In 2018, the government took some further steps towards recognizing Inuit Nunangat as a distinct region when the Department of Fisheries and Oceans (DFO) and the Canadian Coastguard, in collaboration with ITK, announced the creation of "a stand-alone Arctic Region inclusive of the four regions of Inuit Nunangat" (Government of Canada 2018). Although this represented an important progression in terms of showing the federal government's formal recognition of Inuit Nunangat and its commitment to co-developing its Arctic and Northern Policy Framework in partnership with Inuit, there has been some criticism of the federal government's approach to co-development. The above-mentioned position paper on the Arctic Policy Framework (ITK 2018), for example, criticizes the government for not meeting Inuit expectations for co-development. Moreover, the Inuit Nunangat chapter was supposed to be fully integrated into the ANPF, but in the final version, this chapter, along with the other stakeholder chapters mentioned above, were only included as appendices (IWGIA 2020). As Kikkert and Lackenbauer (2019) have pointed out, "[w]hile these partner chapters formed an "integral part of this process," the framework concedes that "they do not necessarily reflect the views of either the federal government, or of the other partners."

The recent activities of ITK are part of a broader strategy to unify Inuit in Canada and speak with a common voice to government. None of this, however, would have been possible without the important work that ITK and its predecessor ITC carried out in support of the land claims process. At the heart of this work were the land use and occupancy studies that informed the negotiations around the land claims and provided evidence of a continuous and extensive Inuit presence throughout Inuit Nunangat. This work provided a necessary foundation on which Inuit have built a common territorial and policy space.

CONCLUSION

In 2018, the *Indigenous Peoples Atlas of Canada* was published, produced in partnership with the Assembly of First Nations, ITK, the Métis National Council, the National Centre for Truth and Reconciliation, and Indspire, in response to the Truth and Reconciliations Commission's Calls to Action. In his article, "De-Indigenizing and Re-Indigenizing Our Territory," Métis scholar Adam Gaudry discusses the power of maps, observing that:

> Cartography has long been an imperial enterprise used to claim territory and to imagine the geographic reach of empires. In its imperial usage, map-making is an instrument of Indigenous erasure ... But empires aren't the only ones who draw maps. Indigenous peoples also use maps ... to replace the lines of nation-states, provinces and other boundaries with borderlines and edges of their own ... Map-making is therefore a deeply political process, as it is a process of world creation ... how we draw maps goes hand-in-hand with how we understand the world we live in.
>
> (2019)

In Michael Kusugak's forward to the same volume, he explains that *nunannguaq*, or "representation of the land," is the Inuit word for "map," and that maps were always held in the mind of Inuit. Quoting the words of his uncle, Kusugak describes that the mental map provided a way to "look behind you so that you will know how to get back" (2019). By creating the map of Inuit Nunangat, ITK has taken the land claims that were settled based on Inuit use and occupancy and defined not only a new political region but a cultural and an historic one as well. Subsequent efforts to articulate a common policy approach and build a respectful and direct relationship with the federal government have advanced a common Inuit view of their place in Canada that is consistent with the idea of Inuit Nunangat as a homeland for all Inuit. In turn, the idea of Inuit Nunangat as a common territorial and policy space is changing how Canadians view themselves and also how the Government of Canada will understand the Arctic in the years to come. As John Ralston Saul asked, what if we were to understand the world from a northern perspective? Inuit have indeed taken important steps to answer that question from an Inuit perspective.

ACKNOWLEDGMENTS

This chapter was made possible in part by a grant from Carnegie Corporation of New York. The statements made and views expressed are solely the responsibility of the authors.

NOTES

1. The resolutions included objections to oil and gas exploration, hunting and trapping rights, safety concerns, the transfer of constitutional responsibility for the Inuit in northern Québec to the Government of Québec, education, and an acknowledgment of funding support for the Conference.
2. Although the Nunatsiavut land claims agreement was not signed until 2005, the Agreement-in-principle was signed in 2001.
3. What makes ITC unique among Indigenous organizations is its vision to situate Inuit as part of Canada. This is exemplified by the change in name to Inuit Tapiriit Kanatami (Inuit united in Canada) and new motto in 2001, "First Canadians—Canadians First."
4. COPE represented the Indigenous peoples of the western Arctic, including the Inuvialuit.

REFERENCES

Anawak, Jack. 2009. "The Impact of Canadian Residential Schools on the Inuit who Attended Them." In *Orality in the 21st century: Inuit discourse and practices. Proceedings of the 15th Inuit Studies Conference*. Edited by Beatrice Collignon and Therrien Michele (eds). 2009. Paris: INALCO.

Arriagada, Paula, and Amanda Bleakney. 2019. *Inuit Participation in the Wage and Land-Based Economies in Inuit Nunangat*. Ottawa, ON: Statistics Canada.

Bonesteel, Sarah. 2006. *Canada's Relationship with Inuit: A History of Policy and Program Development*. Ottawa, ON: Minister of Indian Affairs and Northern Development and Federal Interlocutor for Métis and Non-Status Indians.

Boswell, Randy. 2009. "Inuit Communities Left Off Ottawa's Map." *Vancouver Sun*, 29 July. www.vancouversun.com/news/todays-paper/Inuit+communities+left+Ottawa/1839846/story.html (accessed 25 September 2020).

Brice-Bennett, Carolyn. 1977. *Our Footprints Are Everywhere: Inuit Land Use and Occupancy in Labrador*. Nain, NL: Labrador Inuit Association.

Coppermine Conference of Arctic Native People. 1970. Community Centre, Coppermine, NWT.

Coppermine Conference Telegram. 1970. *Cape Krusenstern, (Nubuk)*, NWT (NU), 1 July http://capekrusenstern.org/research.html (accessed 8 September 2020).

Desbiens, Caroline 2013. *Power from the North: Territory, Identity, and the Culture of Hydroelectricity in Quebec*. Vancouver, BC: UBC Press.

Diefenbaker, John. 1958. "Opening Campaign Speech," 12 February. Winnipeg, MB. https://diefenbaker.usask.ca/1957-58-elections/7.php (accessed 7 September 2020).

Fraser, Whit. 2011. "Jose Kusugak, Nunavut's Cheerful Muse, Dies at 60." *NunatsiaqNews*, 19 January. https://nunatsiaq.com/stories/article/987898_jose_kusugak_nunavuts_cheerful_muse_dies_at_60/ (accessed 28 June 2019).

Freeman, Milton. 1976. *Inuit Land Use and Occupancy Project*. Ottawa, ON: Department of Indian and Northern Affairs Canada.

———. 2011. "Looking Back – and Looking Ahead – 35 Years after the Inuit Land Use and Occupancy Project." *The Canadian Geographer* 55 (1): 20–31. https://doi.org/10.1111/j.1541-0064.2010.00341.x

Gaudry, Adam. 2019. "De-Indigenizing and Re-Indigenizing Our Territory." *Indigenous Atlas of Canada*. https://indigenouspeoplesatlasofcanada.ca/forewords/ (accessed 20 July 2020).

Government of Canada. 2009. *Canada's Northern Strategy: Our North, Our Heritage, Our Future*. http://publications.gc.ca/collections/collection_2009/ainc-inac/R3-72-2008.pdf (accessed 23 September 2020).

———. 2018. "Fisheries and Oceans Canada, the Canadian Coast Guard and Inuit Tapiriit Kanatami Announce New Arctic Region." https://www.canada.ca/en/fisheries-oceans/news/2018/10/fisheries-and-oceans-canada-the-canadian-coast-guard-and-inuit-tapiriit-kanatami-announce-new-arctic-region.html (accessed 16 September 2020).

———. 2019. "Canada's Arctic and Northern Policy: Partner Chapters." https://www.rcaanc-cirnac.gc.ca/eng/1567801878530/1567801893671 (accessed 15 September 2020).

Harley, Brian J. 1989. "Deconstructing the Map." *Cartographia: The International Journal for Geographic Information and Geovisualization* 26 (2): 1–20. http://doi.org/10.3138/E635-7827-1757-9T53

———. 2001. *The New Nature of Maps*. Baltimore, MD: Johns Hopkins University Press.

Harley, J. Brian, and Woodward, D. 1987. *The History of Cartography*. Chicago, IL: University of Chicago Press.

Hicks, Jack, and Graham White 2015. *Made in Nunavut: An Experiment in Decentralized Government*. Vancouver, BC: UBC Press.

International Work Group for Indigenous Affairs (IWGIA). 2020. "Indigenous World 2020: Inuit Nunangat." 11 May. https://www.iwgia.org/en/canada/3634-iw-2020-inuit-nunangat.html. (accessed 14 September 2020).

Inuit Tapiriit Kanatami (ITK). 2005. Inuit Communities of Canada (map). https://www.itk.ca/inuit-communities-of-canada-map/ (accessed 28 June 2019).

———. 2018. *Development and Implementation of the Arctic Policy Framework*. Ottawa, ON: ITK.

———. 2019a. *Arctic and Northern Policy Framework: Inuit Nunangat*. Ottawa, ON: ITK.

———. 2019b. *Inuit Nunangat Housing Strategy*. Ottawa, ON: ITK.

———. 2019c. *National Inuit Climate Change Strategy*. Ottawa, ON: ITK.

———. 2020a. *Establishing an Indigenous Human Rights Commission Through Federal UN Declaration Legislation*. Ottawa, ON: ITK.

———. 2020b. *Inuit Post-Secondary Education Strategy: Raising Education Attainment Rates*. Ottawa, ON: ITK.

———. nd. Maps of Inuit Nunangat. https://www.itk.ca/maps-of-inuit-nunangat/ (accessed 12 October 2020).

Inuit Tapirisat of Canada. 1980. "Inukshuk Project." *Inuktitut* 46: 14–19.

———. 1989. "Editorial." *Inuktitut* 70: 2–5.

———. 1971. Transcript of the First ITC Meeting. https://www.itk.ca/timeline-item/7009-2/ (accessed 8 September 2020).

———. 1973. *Presentation to the Arctic Corridor Conference*, Churchill, Manitoba, 7–10 May. http://capekrusenstern.org/research.html (accessed 8 September 2020).

Kikkert, Peter, and P. Whitney Lackenbauer. 2019. "A Better Road Map Needed for Arctic and Northern Policy Framework." *Policy Options Politiques*, 17 September. https://policyoptions.irpp.org/magazines/september-2019/a-better-road-map-needed-for-arctic-and-northern-policy-framework/ (accessed 16 September 2020).

Kuptana, Rosemarie. 1992. "The Canadian Inuit and the Renewal of Canada." *Études/Inuit/Studies* 16 (1–2): 39–42.

Kusugak, Jose. 2001. "Canadian-First or First-Canadian?" President's Message. *Inuktitut* 90: 2–4. https://www.itk.ca/inuktitut-issue-90/ (accessed 12 October 2020).

Kusugak, Michael. 2019. "Forewords, Nunannguaq." In *Indigenous Peoples Atlas of Canada*. Canadian Geographic. https://indigenouspeoplesatlasofcanada.ca/forewords/ (accessed 20 July 2020).

MacEachren, Alan M. 1995. *How Maps Work*. New York: Guildford Press.

Makivik Corporation. 2020. "JBNQA." https://www.makivik.org/corporate/history/jbnqa/

Masterson, D. M. 2013. "The Arctic Islands Adventure and Panarctic Oils Ltd." *Cold Regions Science and Technology* 85: 1–14. doi:10.1016/j.coldregions.2012.06.008

McInnes, Simon. 1981. "The Inuit and the Constitutional Process: 1978–81." *Journal of Canadian Studies* 16 (2): 53–68. https://doi.org/10.3138/jcs.16.2.53

Monmonier, Mark. 1991. *How to Lie with Maps*. Chicago, IL: University of Chicago Press.

Munro, John C. 1981. *In all Fairness: A Native Land Claims Policy—Comprehensive Claims*. Ottawa, ON: Indian Affairs and Northern Development.

Nunatsiaq News. 2011. "ITK Plans "From Eskimo to Inuit in 40 years" Conference this November." 14 September. https://nunatsiaq.com/stories/article/65674itk_plans_from_eskimo_to_inuit_in_40_years_conference_this_november/ (accessed 6 October 2020).

Nungak, Zebedee. 2017. *Wrestling with Colonialism on Steroids: Quebec Inuit Fight for their Homeland*. Montreal, QC: Véhicule Press.

Obed, Natan. 2019. "Opinion: Inuit Nunangat Policy Space Would Be a Sign of Genuine Reconciliation." *The Hill Times*, 10 June. https://www.hilltimes.com/2019/06/10/203177/203177 (accessed 6 July 2020).

Peluso, Nancy. 1995. "Whose Woods Are These? Counter-Mapping Forest Territories in Kalimantan, Indonesia." *Antipode* 27 (4): 383–406. https://doi.org/10.1111/j.1467-8330.1995.tb00286.x

Perkins, C. 2009. "Mapping, Philosophy." In *International Encyclopedia of Human Geography*, volume 6, edited by Rob Kitchin and Nigel Thrift, 385–397. Elsevier.

Prime Minister. 2017. "Prime Minister of Canada and President of Inuit Tapiriit Kanatami Announce Inuit-Crown Partnership Committee." 9 February. https://pm.gc.ca/en/news/news-releases/2017/02/09/prime-minister-canada-and-president-inuit-tapiriit-kanatami-announce (accessed 10 September 2020).

Saul, John Ralston. 2008. *A Fair Country: Telling Truths about Canada*. Toronto, ON: Viking Group Canada.

Simon, Mary. 2012. "How do Canada and Inuit Get to Win-Win in the Arctic?" *Policy Options*, 1 August. Institute for Research on Public Policy. https://policyoptions.irpp.org/magazines/policy-challenges-for-2020/how-do-canada-and-inuit-get-to-win-win-in-the-arctic/ (accessed 14 July 2020).

Usher, Peter J. 1992. "Property as the Basis of Inuit Hunting Rights." In *Property Rights and Indian Economies: The Political Economy Forum*, edited by Terry L. Anderson. 41–66. Lanham, MD: Rowman and Littlefield Publishers, Inc.

Watt-Cloutier, Sheila. 2015. *The Right To Be Cold: One Women's Story of Protecting Her Culture, the Arctic and the Whole Planet*. Toronto, ON: Allen Lane.

Wilson, Gary N., and Per Selle. 2019. *Indigenous Self-Determination in Northern Canada and Norway*. IRPP Study: Canada's Changing Federal Community, no. 69. Montréal, QC: Institute for Research on Public Policy.

Wilson, Gary N., Christopher Alcantara, and Thierry Rodon. 2020. *Nested Federalism and Inuit Governance in the Canadian Arctic*. Vancouver, BC: UBC Press

Wood, Denis. 2010. *Rethinking the Power of Maps*. New York: Guilford Press.

Wood, Denis. 1992. *The Power of Maps*. New York: Guilford Press.

CHAPTER 20

ENERGY EXTRACTION, RESISTANCE, AND POLITICAL CHANGE IN INUIT NUNANGAT

Warren Bernauer and Jonathan Peyton

Extractive capitalism has always been a driving force in the colonization of the Canadian Arctic. In the late 19th and early 20th centuries, commercial whalers and fur traders established economies based on the extraction and export of natural resources, which disproportionately benefitted external interests. Many Inuit families participated enthusiastically in these new activities, and they are now remembered as important aspects of Inuit heritage. However, participation in the whale hunt and fur trade left Inuit dependent on unstable and crisis-prone economies (Ray 1990; Ross 1989). When the market for fox furs collapsed after World War II, the economic circumstance of many Inuit camps became dire (Tester and Kulchyski 1994).

The Canadian state responded to the social crisis created by the collapse of the fur trade by applying a new policy of assimilation to Inuit (Tester and Kulchyski 1994). Mineral exploration and mining were central to this new approach to arctic governance. Inuit – who up to this point had mostly escaped the colonial state's interventions – were coerced into moving into the permanent settlements that dot the map of the Arctic today. Policymakers expected that mineral and energy extraction would be the new basis of the arctic economy, and that Inuit would give up their hunting and trapping lifestyle to become wage laborers in mines and on oil rigs (Tester and Kulchyski 1994; QTC 2013). At the same time, the extraction of energy resources from the Arctic became central to the federal government's definition of Canada's "national interest." In line with this new policy, the federal government began promoting mining and energy extraction across the Arctic as a development strategy for Inuit and a nation-building project for Canada (Duffy 1989; Nassichuk 1987). The provincial governments of Newfoundland and Quebec adopted similar programs for the development and "modernization" of the arctic regions in those provinces (Desbiens 2013; Procter 2015).

By the end of the 1960s, Inuit from all parts of Inuit Nunangat began to resist extraction with petitions, litigation, and interventions in environmental assessment and planning processes. Conflicts over the extraction of energy resources – oil, natural gas, uranium, and hydroelectricity – were the sites of the most intense and passionate Inuit resistance. This resistance was driven by several factors. Inuit hunters began to observe serious negative effects on caribou, marine mammals, and fish as a result of mining and mineral exploration activities. It also quickly became clear to

Inuit that most of the economic benefits from non-renewable resource extraction – jobs, profits, royalties, and contracting opportunities – were captured by non-Inuit living outside of Inuit Nunangat. Moreover, the growth of mining and energy extraction posed fundamental questions about the ownership of land and resources in the Arctic that previous forms of extraction (commercial whaling and the fur trade) had not raised (Bernauer 2015; Cameron 2015; Nungak 2017; Procter 2015).

In this chapter we provide summary histories of political conflicts over energy extraction in each of the four regions of Inuit Nunangat – the land claims jurisdictions of Nunavik, Nunavut, Inuvialuit Nunangat, and Nunatsiavut. These regional histories show that resistance to energy extraction has shaped Inuit political development in several ways. The formation of Inuit political organizations, the recognition of Inuit rights and title by the courts, and the negotiation of modern treaties were all driven by conflicts with extractive industries. These histories also show that the recognition of Inuit rights by the courts and in treaties has resulted in an increased willingness to collaborate with extractive industries, especially on the part of Inuit political organizations. Indeed, many Inuit have come to see resource extraction as necessary for self-determination. However, in all four regions Inuit organizations continued to resist specific types of extraction they consider to be especially risky or otherwise run contrary to their interests. Because of the unique risks and impacts associated with the extraction of energy resources, these forms of extraction continue to be especially controversial. Moreover, it remains uncertain whether the strategy of relying on investment from multi-national corporations to drive economic development – a strategy now embraced by the Canadian state and Inuit organizations alike – will have the desired outcomes of facilitating community well-being and Inuit self-determination.

NUNAVIK

Conflicts over energy extraction in Nunavik have mostly focused on hydroelectric development. In 1971, Quebec Premier Robert Bourassa announced plans for a hydroelectric project in the James Bay region of northern Quebec. For Bourassa, hydro development was an important nation-building project for Quebec, helping drive economic development and modernization (Desbiens 2013). The James Bay Hydroelectric Project called for the diversion and damming of several river systems flowing into James Bay: the La Grand, Rupert, Broadback, and Nottaway rivers in Cree territory, as well as the Great Whale River which flows through both Cree and Inuit territory.

Inuit, represented by the Northern Quebec Inuit Association, joined the Cree in launching litigation to block hydroelectric development on their territories. An injunction granted by Justice Malouf of the Quebec Superior Court in 1973 recognized that Inuit and Cree possessed unextinguished Aboriginal title to northern Quebec. However, the injunction was suspended and later overturned by the Quebec Court of Appeal, based on legal details unrelated to Cree and Inuit title claims. Cree and Inuit appealed this Appeals Court ruling to a higher court (Craik 2004; Feit 2004).

However, while the Cree and Inuit case continued to work its way through the courts, construction on the James Bay project continued. This put considerable pressure on the Indigenous plaintiffs to settle out of court. Comprehensive land claims negotiations involving the Cree, Inuit, Government of Canada, Government of Quebec, and Quebec Hydro began in 1974 (Nungak 2017).

In 1975 the James Bay and Northern Quebec Agreement (JBNQA) was signed by representatives of the James Bay Cree, Nunavik Inuit, the Government of Quebec, the Government of Canada, and Hydro-Québec. The agreement was the first "modern treaty" negotiated in Canada. Cree and Inuit agreed to "surrender" their Aboriginal title to northern Quebec and withdraw their legal challenges to the James Bay project. In exchange, they received money, guaranteed hunting and trapping rights, title to small tracts of their traditional territory, and new provisions for environmental assessment and political development in northern Quebec. The agreement also committed to reduce the scope of hydroelectric development, which resulted in the first phase of development taking place only on the La Grande and Eastmain river systems, which lay entirely in Cree territory (Nungak 2017).

The JBNQA changed the structure of governance in Nunavik. The Northern Quebec Inuit Association was dissolved and replaced by the Makivik Corporation as the representative of Nunavik Inuit. The Kativik Regional Government was established as a public government responsible for delivering social services for all residents of Nunavik (Nungak 2017).

The JBNQA was incredibly controversial among Indigenous peoples in Canada, primarily because of the "extinguishment" clause it contained. Two Inuit communities in Nunavik initially refused to be parties to the JBNQA, in large part because of the provisions that extinguished Aboriginal title. Inuit politician Zebedee Nungak, one of the signatories to the agreement, explained that Inuit negotiators only agreed to this provision because they felt they had no other choice – construction on the project was proceeding regardless of their protests and litigation, and government negotiators were unwilling to discuss alternatives to the "surrender" of Aboriginal title (Nungak 2017).

By the late 1980s Quebec began to plan for the next phase of the James Bay Hydroelectric Project. The plan for "Phase Two" of the project was to include a massive hydroelectric complex on the Great Whale River. The Cree quickly resolved to fight the Great Whale project. Under the leadership of Matthew Coon Come, the Cree initiated legal challenges, conducted a public campaign that involved alliances with environmental groups like Greenpeace, and refused to negotiate a benefit agreement with Hydro-Québec (Craik 2004; Feit 2004).

Many Inuit participated in the campaign against the Phase Two expansion of the James Bay project. The most notable example of joint Cree-Inuit resistance was the Odeyak tour of the northeastern United States. As a symbol of Cree and Inuit unity, Billie Weetaltuk, an Inuit Elder from Kuujjuarapik, with the assistance of several Cree and Inuit, built a boat that combined design features of the Inuit kayak and Cree canoe. Their creation was called an "Odeyak" – a portmanteau of the Cree word for canoe and the Inuit word *qajaq*. In 1990, Cree and Inuit paddled the Odeyak from the mouth of the Great Whale River at Kuujjuarpik to the Hudson River in New York City. The Odeyak tour was focused on convincing American municipal and state governments – the main market for the power to be generated from Phase 2 – to cancel purchasing agreements for hydroelectricity from Quebec. The journey involved several public events along the way, culminating in Cree and Inuit participation in the Earth Day rally in New York City (Posluns 1993).

The position of Makivik Corporation – the successor of the Northern Quebec Inuit Association – was not clear. While Inuit leaders publicly claimed to support the Cree position, they nonetheless participated in negotiations with Hydro-Québec. In 1994, Makivik signed the "Kuujjuarapik Agreement-in-Principle" with Hydro-Québec, a move that led to tensions between Cree and Inuit (Martin 2008).

However, before Makivik's negotiations on the Great Whale project could continue, the Cree-Inuit campaign succeeded in convincing several American jurisdictions to cancel electricity purchasing agreements with Quebec. As a result, the economic rationale for the project disappeared, and the Government of Quebec announced its cancellation in 1995 (Craik 2004). Since that time, discussion about hydroelectric development in northern Quebec has focused on the Rupert and Broadback Rivers in Cree territory. As a result, there has been no significant debate in Nunavik over large-scale hydroelectric development for more than two decades.[1]

Nunavik Inuit and their Cree neighbors have also become embroiled in debates over uranium mining in Quebec. In 2008, a company called Strateco applied to conduct advanced exploration for uranium near the Cree community of Mistassini. The community opposed the proposal, and the Grand Council of the Crees of Quebec announced a moratorium on uranium mining on all Cree lands in Quebec (Council of the Cree Nation of Mistassini 2014).

Due in large part to Cree activism, the Government of Quebec imposed a moratorium on uranium mining in that province in 2013. The government also directed its public watchdog for the environment – Bureau d'Audiences Publiques sur l'Environnement (BAPE) – to conduct an inquiry into uranium mining in Quebec. During the BAPE process Nunavik Inuit supported the Cree position and opposed uranium mining in Arctic Quebec. Jobie Tukkiapik, then president of Makivik, told the press:

> There is consensus among Nunavik Inuit that development of the uranium industry in our region is not acceptable. Uranium is radioactive and can harm wildlife. The risk of contamination would cut us off from our traditional country foods. The negative impacts would be *nungujuittuq*, meaning something that will never perish.
>
> (Makivik Corporation and KRG 2014)

As a result of these and other submissions, in 2015 the BAPE panel concluded that it would be "inappropriate" to authorize uranium mining in Quebec due to the lack of social acceptability of uranium mining and problems with containing uranium tailings over the long term (BAPE 2015).

INUVIALUIT NUNANGAT

Conflicts over energy extraction in Inuvialuit Nunangat have focused almost entirely on hydrocarbons. Exploration for oil and natural gas began in the 1950s. By the late 1960s several significant discoveries led to the rapid expansion of activity in the Mackenzie Delta and Beaufort Sea (BREA 2016).

Inuvialuit opposition to the encroachment of the oil and gas industry began to mount in the early 1970s as the communities of Tuktoyaktuk, Sachs Harbour, and Aklavik resisted seismic surveys. While their protests did not stop exploration activity, the Inuvialuit did succeed in pressuring the government to impose stricter regulations on arctic oil and gas exploration (*Inuvialuit Magazine* 1975; Arnold et al. 2011; Zellen 2008).

In 1970, Inuvialuit led the creation of the Committee for Original People's Entitlement (COPE). COPE supported community-driven resistance to oil and gas exploration. However, it did not oppose the oil and gas industry in principle. Instead, it took the position that oil and gas extraction could only proceed if it was done responsibly with the full participation of Inuvialuit. COPE was especially critical of proposals for offshore drilling due to the unique risks associated with offshore oil and gas production (*Inuvialuit Magazine* 1976a; Arnold et al. 2011)

In 1974, debate erupted over a proposal to build a pipeline down the Mackenzie Valley. The proposed Mackenzie Valley Pipeline was intended to transport natural gas from Alaska and the Mackenzie Delta to markets in southern Canada and the United States. In response to backlash from Dene, Metis, and Inuvialuit, the Canadian government launched the Mackenzie Valley Pipeline Inquiry with Justice Thomas Berger as chair. Berger was given a broad mandate to examine all aspects of the proposed pipeline.

COPE's position was that the pipeline should not be approved until the Government of Canada settled land claims with the Inuvialuit. While COPE did not oppose the pipeline on principle, it insisted that it not proceed until Inuvialuit were provided with the legal means to participate in the decisions and benefits related to oil and gas development (*Inuvialuit Magazine* 1976b). The Dene Nation adopted a similar position (Watkins 1977).

Berger's report was released in 1977. He endorsed the Indigenous organizations' positions and recommended that no pipeline be built until the government settled land claims with northern Indigenous peoples. Berger suggested a ten-year moratorium on pipeline construction to provide time for negotiations (Berger 1977). These recommendations caused a firestorm of controversy. Berger's report was dismissed by industry and the Government of the Northwest Territories (Zellen 2008; Nuttall 2010). COPE embraced Berger's findings (*Inuvialuit Magazine* 1977) and ultimately used them as leverage in negotiating a land claim for the Western Arctic (Arnold et al. 2011).

In 1984 Inuvialuit signed the Inuvialuit Final Agreement (sometimes called the Western Arctic Agreement). As with the James Bay agreement, the Inuvialuit agreement extinguished Aboriginal title in exchange for a range of benefits and specific rights.

Like the Inuit of Nunavik, the Inuvialuit signed their modern treaty due to pressure from impending resource extraction. The Inuvialuit were originally part of the negotiations for the Nunavut agreement, but decided to withdraw and negotiate a separate agreement due to pressure from anticipated energy extraction. In the early 1980s, large-scale hydrocarbon extraction in the Beaufort Sea seemed imminent, although it ultimately never came to fruition.

The agreement led to the dissolution of COPE and its replacement by new organizations to represent Inuvialuit. The Inuvialuit Regional Corporation (IRC) was created to assume responsibility for Inuvialuit social and economic interests. A parallel government structure, the Inuvialuit Game Council (IGC), was created to represent Inuvialuit interests in wildlife harvesting and conservation.

The Inuvialuit Agreement led to a change in approach to the oil and gas industry as Inuvialuit organizations began to enthusiastically promote arctic hydrocarbon extraction. The Isserk Drilling Program – the first new proposal for offshore drilling after the claim was settled – received widespread political support from both the IRC and IGC. The proposal was so uncontroversial that it was approved by the Inuvialuit Environmental Impact Review Board (EIRB) in 1989 without a formal public hearing (EIRB 1989).

Nonetheless, even after signing a land claim, Inuvialuit support for the oil and gas industry was not unconditional. The 1989 Exxon Valdez oil spill off the coast of Alaska inspired people across the globe – including the Inuvialuit – to re-evaluate arctic oil and gas development. When the EIRB considered a proposal for offshore drilling in 1990 (the Kulluk Drilling Program), the IGC vocally opposed the project because of what it believed were serious deficiencies in the ability of industry and government to respond to an oil spill in the Arctic. The EIRB ultimately recommended the project not be approved due to the concerns raised by the IGC (Zellen 2008).

Industry interest in Inuvialuit Nunangat's hydrocarbon resources waned in the early 1990s due to a low market value of natural gas. Exploration slowed in the delta, drilling ceased in the Beaufort, and plans for a pipeline down the Mackenzie Valley were once again shelved (BREA 2016). By the end of the decade, however, there was a resumption in exploration activity in the Mackenzie Delta. Inuvialuit-owned businesses were playing a substantial role in the oil and gas economy by this point (Abele 2004). The Ikhil Natural Gas Project – the first commercial extraction of hydrocarbons from the Inuvialuit homeland – came online in 1999. Ikhil was a small project spearheaded by Inuvialuit-owned businesses that supplied the local heating and energy needs in Inuvik. The community anticipated that expansion of the natural gas sector in Inuvialuit Nunangat would ensure a steady supply of cheap heat and electricity (AMAP 2007).

When discussion of a natural gas pipeline down the Mackenzie Valley was renewed in the late 1990s, the IRC negotiated an equity stake in the project as a member of the Aboriginal Pipeline Group – a coalition of indigenous groups that included the Inuvialuit, Gwich'in, and Sahtu Dene (Abele 2004; Nuttall 2010). A joint-venture partnership, led by Imperial Oil and including the Aboriginal Pipeline Group, submitted a formal proposal to government regulators in 2004. An environmental assessment panel recommended the pipeline be approved in 2009, and the National Energy Board issued permits in 2010. However, rising cost estimates and low natural gas prices caused the consortium to put the project on hold. In 2017, Imperial Oil announced that the pipeline project was canceled (Imperial Oil 2017).

The delay and ultimate cancellation of the Mackenzie Valley Gas Project struck a significant blow to the Inuvialuit economy. Beyond the obvious loss of anticipated jobs, business contracts, and revenues, the cancellation of the pipeline caused local heating and electricity bills to skyrocket in Inuvik. When the small Ikhil project came online in 1999, most of the buildings in Inuvik were converted to natural gas heating. This was done under the assumption that a pipeline down the Mackenzie Valley would be built and ensure a sustained supply of natural gas after Ikhil was inevitably exhausted. The Ikhil well ran dry in 2012, and with the Mackenzie Valley Gas Project on hold, the community was forced to import propane at a much higher price (Bernauer 2019b).

Even though the Inuvialuit have enthusiastically supported the development of onshore and near-shore hydrocarbons, deep offshore drilling in the Beaufort Sea continues to be a source of controversy. The 2010 Deepwater Horizon disaster in the Gulf of Mexico, like the 1989 Exxon Valdez disaster, caused the Inuvialuit to re-evaluate their position on offshore drilling. One month after the Gulf of Mexico spill began, IRC Chair Nellie Cournoyea called for a halt to drilling in the Beaufort Sea, until concerns raised by Deepwater Horizon were addressed. One week later, ITK President Mary Simon echoed Cournoyea's call for a halt to arctic offshore drilling (Porta and Banks 2011). Partially in response to these concerns, the federal government initiated the Beaufort Regional Environmental Assessment, a collaborative process designed to address issues with offshore drilling in the Beaufort Sea (BREA 2016).

In 2016, Prime Minister Justin Trudeau announced a five-year moratorium on offshore hydrocarbon exploration and extraction in the Arctic. While the Inuvialuit have approached offshore drilling with caution, some Inuvialuit politicians have reacted to the moratorium with anger and frustration. The IRC was especially outspoken in its criticism of the moratorium, which it argued was unilateral and announced without any prior consultation (Government of Canada 2017; IRC 2019).

NUNAVUT

Nunavut Inuit have been involved in conflicts over the extraction of several types of energy resources. In the 1970s and 1980s Inuit in all three regions of Nunavut (Kitikmeot, Kivalliq, and Qikiqtani) were involved in conflicts over hydrocarbon exploration and extraction. The three regional Inuit Associations all supported community resistance to oil and gas exploration and extraction. Major flashpoints from that era include resistance to proposed exploratory drilling in Lancaster Sound (FEARO 1979; Jacobs and Palluq 1983), as well as opposition to the proposed export of natural gas from the High Arctic Islands by pipeline and icebreaking tankers (Bernauer 2020; Wilt 2020).

However, struggles against uranium mining have arguably had a greater impact on the political development of the Eastern Arctic than have hydrocarbons. Exploration for uranium in Nunavut began in the 1960s, with most activity taking place in the Kivalliq region near the community of Baker Lake. By the end of that decade, the federal government had leased vast swaths of Baker Lake Inuit hunting grounds to uranium exploration firms (McPherson 2003).

Baker Lake Inuit repeatedly petitioned the Canadian government to halt uranium exploration in the 1970s. When these petitions failed, the municipality of Baker Lake Inuit, the Baker Lake Hunters and Trappers Association, and the Inuit Tapirisat of Canada (ITC) sought a court injunction blocking exploration activity near Baker Lake. A federal judge issued an interlocutory injunction in the spring of 1978, prohibiting the government from issuing permits for new exploration projects that summer. The court's final decision, issued in 1979, was only a partial victory for Nunavut Inuit – while the judge recognized their Aboriginal title (a major milestone in land claim negotiations), he ruled that uranium exploration could continue in the Eastern Arctic (*Hamlet of Baker Lake v Minister of Indian Affairs* 1980). The petitions and legal action successfully pressured the federal government to develop new seasonal restrictions on mineral exploration to limit disturbance to caribou during sensitive calving and post-calving seasons (Bernauer 2015).

In the late 1980s, the uranium mining company Urangesellschaft proposed the Kiggavik uranium mine west of Baker Lake. Baker Lake Inuit, under the leadership of community organizer Joan Scottie, formed the Baker Lake Concerned Citizens Committee to give a unified voice for their opposition to the project. In a 1990 community plebiscite in Baker Lake, slightly over 90 percent of voters said "no" to the Kiggavik proposal. Regional organizations – including the Keewatin Inuit Association and Tunngavik Federation of Nunavut – formed a coalition to coordinate regional opposition to uranium mining. In the face of firm Inuit opposition and low prices for uranium – the latter due to the influence of the Chernobyl disaster on public perceptions of the nuclear industry – Urangesellschaft withdrew its proposal for the Kiggavik uranium mine (Bernauer 2015; McPherson 2003).

In 1993 Nunavut Inuit signed the Nunavut Land Claims Agreement (Nunavut Agreement). Like the Nunavik and Inuvialuit agreements, the Nunavut Agreement is a modern treaty that extinguished Inuit Aboriginal title in exchange for cash benefits and specified rights. However, the signing of the Nunavut Agreement was not motivated by impending resource extraction. Instead, pressure for Nunavut Inuit to sign the agreement in the early 1990s came from major concessions offered by federal negotiators. Reeling from the public relations fallout of the Oka Crisis in Quebec, government officials were desperate to show progress in its recognition of Indigenous land rights. As a result, the federal government agreed to the Inuit demand that the treaty provide for the division of the Northwest Territories and the creation of the new Nunavut Territory (Hicks and White 2015).

The agreement led to the dissolution of the Tunngavik Federation of Nunavut and its replacement by Nunavut Tunngavik Incorporated (NTI) as the organization representing all Nunavut Inuit. NTI shares this responsibility with the three regional Inuit associations: Kitikmeot Inuit Association, Kivalliq Inuit Association, and Qikiqtani Inuit Association. The agreement also led to the creation of the Government of Nunavut (GN) as a public government that all residents of Nunavut can participate in (Hicks and White 2015).

After the Nunavut Agreement was signed, Nunavut's Inuit organizations initially remained opposed to uranium mining. NTI and the Kivalliq Inuit Association refused to allow companies to explore for uranium on lands where Nunavut Inuit-owned mineral rights. However, this position was reversed in 2007 when NTI released a policy supporting uranium mining. Shortly afterward, NTI entered into a series of agreements with uranium companies for exploration on Inuit-owned lands (Bowman 2011; Göcke 2013). These decisions were criticized by Nunavummiut Makitagunarningit – a grassroots citizens group founded in 2009 to encourage critical debate about uranium mining in Nunavut – which argued that NTI's support for uranium mining was uninformed, irresponsible, and made without meaningfully consulting Inuit (Rodon 2018; Scobie and Rodgers 2013).

The Kiggavik uranium project was eventually acquired by the French company, AREVA Resources, which submitted a new proposal for the Kiggavik mine in 2008.

Their proposal was reviewed by the Nunavut Impact Review Board (NIRB) – a co-management environmental assessment board created by the Nunavut Agreement. At the final hearings, the Kiggavik project was opposed by the Baker Lake Hunters and Trappers Organization, Nunavummiut Makitagunarningit, and several Dene communities from northern Saskatchewan and the Northwest Territories. NTI and the Kivalliq Inuit Association, however, recommended the proposal be approved with terms and conditions that would allegedly protect the arctic environment (NIRB 2015a). The NIRB decision, issued in 2015, nonetheless recommended the project not be approved due to unacceptable levels of uncertainty in AREVA's impact assessment (NIRB 2015b). The following year, the federal government announced that it had accepted NIRB's recommendation and closed the file on AREVA's proposal (Bernauer 2019a).

While Nunavut's Inuit organizations supported uranium mining after signing the Nunavut Agreement, they have been much less enthusiastic about the prospect of oil and gas development in the new territory. The Qikiqtani Inuit Association (QIA) supported community opposition to proposed seismic surveys in Lancaster Sound in 2010, which were eventually abandoned in the face of litigation (*Qikiqtani Inuit Association v Canada* 2010). NTI and QIA also opposed a proposal to conduct seismic surveys in Baffin Bay and Davis Strait, arguing that offshore oil and gas exploration should not take place until a strategic environmental assessment is conducted. However, when the project was approved by the National Energy Board in 2014, neither NTI nor QIA challenged the decision (Johnson et al. 2016; Rodgers and Ingram 2019). The community of Clyde River ended up initiating litigation, which resulted in a precedent-setting victory for the plaintiffs at the Supreme Court of Canada in 2017 (*Clyde River v Petroleum Geoservices* 2017).

Unlike the Inuvialuit Regional Corporation, Nunavut's Inuit organizations did not react negatively to the 2016 federal moratorium on offshore oil and gas development in the Arctic. When the moratorium was first announced, they did not issue any public statements. However, during a strategic environmental assessment intended to determine if the moratorium should be lifted, representatives of NTI recommended the moratorium remain in place beyond its original five-year lifespan (NIRB 2019a). These submissions, along with ongoing community opposition to offshore oil and gas development, led the Nunavut Impact Review Board to recommend a minimum ten-year extension to the moratorium (NIRB 2019b).

NUNATSIAVUT

Conflicts over energy in Nunatsiavut have revolved around the extraction of uranium and the development of hydroelectric potential. Uranium was first identified in Labrador in 1954. The origins of uranium exploration are directly related to the provincial government's push to develop hydroelectric infrastructure as a statement of provincial autonomy in the fraught years after Newfoundland's entry into Canadian confederation in 1949 – hydroelectricity was extolled as a source of cheap power, an industrial icon bringing Newfoundland into modernity, and a nationalist badge of honor (Bannister 2012; Feehan 2011). The charismatic premier Joey Smallwood tied the new province's industrial fortunes to the British Investment Company, or Brinco, granting the company resource rights to a huge swath of Labrador. This was the legal basis for Brinco's eventual construction of the Churchill Falls Dam (1974), creating the initial infrastructural conditions that re-engineered provincial hydrology and resulted in the construction of the Muskrat Falls Dam, discussed below. A subsidiary, Brinex, first identified Labrador's uranium potential and began plans for extraction at several locations in the Central Mineral Belt, with most attention directed at the Kitts site near Makkovik. This attention was short-lived, as the market price for uranium collapsed in 1958 and plans for extraction were shelved.

The fleeting promise of a uranium economy still had profound effects on the lives of Labrador Inuit as the state sought ways to bring the peoples of the coastal hamlets into its vision of a settled, industrial society. Approximately 200 Inuit were relocated to Makkovik from Nutak and Hebron, nominally to access better services, but also at least in part to provide a labor base for the potential mine at the Kitts site (see Evans 2012). This relocation established a pattern of Inuit-government relations in Nunatsiavut: lack of consultation, disregard for Indigenous rights and territory, and inadequate material support in the wake of state-driven changes.

There was another push to develop Labrador's uranium resources in the 1970s. Brinex resumed exploration at the Kitts-Michelin site and developed a proposal for a uranium mine. However, Nunatsiavut Inuit successfully resisted the project. In 1980, an environmental assessment panel found that Brinex's did not demonstrate that the environmental effects of its mine would be limited to acceptable levels. Organized Inuit opposition, regulatory hurdles, and low prices for uranium (the latter due to the shadow the Three-Mile Island disaster cast over the nuclear industry) caused the company to shelve the proposal indefinitely (Procter 2015).

This newly organized Inuit political resistance was the result of several factors. The creation of the Labrador Inuit Association (LIA) in 1973 forced recognition of the "connections between settler colonialism and resources development," using this historical relationship to argue for land claims negotiations (Procter 2016, 290). Moreover, the LIA mobilized around the question of uranium, "to foster a sense of collective identity and vision among people on the north coast" (ibid.). A more pronounced community resistance to uranium mining also began to coalesce around this time, as individuals began to report changing ecological and health conditions in areas near the exploration sites. At a community health workshop in Nain in 2002, several community members reflected on the changing environmental conditions in their community in the 1970s, including changes in water levels, observations of sick wildlife, and cancers and other illness in their families (The Communities of Ivujivik, Puvirnituq and Kangiqsujuaq et al. 2005; see also Schiff et al. 2015). While the participants could not state with certainty whether uranium exploration was the cause of these problems, their comments show that the uncertainty of risk and contamination became a powerful narrative force in Nunatsiavut Inuit perceptions of the uranium industry.

The question of uranium mining re-emerged with the establishment of formal (albeit limited) Inuit authority over the lands of Nunatsiavut in 2005, with the signing of the Labrador Inuit Land Claims Agreement (Nunatsiavut Agreement). Like the treaties in Nunavik and Inuvialuit Nunangat, the negotiations for the Nunatsiavut Agreement were driven by proposed resource extraction – in this case, the prospect of the Voisey's Bay nickel mine (Lowe 1998).

Like all other Inuit land claims, the Nunatsiavut Agreement effectively extinguished Inuit Aboriginal title in exchange for money, title to smaller tracts of land, specified rights, and political development. Rather than creating co-management boards and corporate Inuit organizations, the Nunatsiavut Agreement established the Nunatsiavut Government as a regional Inuit government. Under the terms of the agreement, the newly formed Nunatsiavut Government was responsible for governance decisions over resource development on Inuit lands.

The signing of the Nunatsiavut Agreement coincided with another global upturn in the uranium mining industry, as the nuclear industry rebranded itself as a "clean" solution to climate change. Mining companies reignited interest in the Kitts-Michelin site. In response to development pressure and ongoing community concerns, the Nunatsiavut Assembly froze uranium exploration on Inuit lands in 2008. This moratorium was meant to provide the new government with adequate time to develop a legislative platform around resource development and environmental protection. It could also be interpreted as an expression of sovereignty. As Nunatsiavut Government leader Tony Andersen said when the moratorium was being debated:

> We are the decision body, we will make the rules that apply to our land. It is our land and we will continue to protect it and we have newfound powers that we will use to ensure that development that takes place will be done so on our terms ... Let [the mining companies] go do their work now. Let them find the techniques that will give us the confidence that perhaps, someday, uranium mining could be accepted in Labrador Inuit Lands.
> (Andersen 2008, quoted in Procter and Chaulk 2013, 26)

Clearly, the moratorium was an assertion of Inuit control over territory and decision-making, signaling a desire to control the pace, scale, and type of development that takes place on their land and pass the burden of certainty on to mining companies themselves (Procter 2015; 2016).

The moratorium had the intended effect of stifling exploration. Mining interests again stopped drilling and construction activity at the Kitts-Michelin locations, while several other companies abandoned exploration work at adjacent properties. The exploration freeze also revealed a lack of consensus in Inuit communities in Nunatsiavut over the economic potential of a nascent mining industry and the environmental and health threat to land and livelihood that came along with extraction.

The moratorium was lifted in late 2011 with the introduction of the Nunatsiavut Environmental Protection Act, which came into force in March 2012 and now governs resource development in the region (Procter 2015; 2016). Yet the question of uranium remains shrouded in uncertainty. As the case of Nunavut shows, local activists are capable of stopping uranium mining regardless of formal support from regional organizations. The ebb and flow of resource commodity markets has also generated its own set of politics in Nunatsiavut. Perpetually low prices for uranium in the wake of the Fukushima disaster make it unlikely that uranium mining will proceed in Nunatsiavut in the near future.

The institutional resource governance approach taken in response to uranium development can be contrasted to the bold activist response to the Muskrat Falls dam on the lower Churchill River. Even if the risks of uranium mining were uncertain, the potential health, social, and environmental harms of dam construction are clear and profound. The possibility of methylmercury contamination to fish, bodies, and food, alongside spiraling cost overruns, potential dam safety issues, methane released from the reservoir at Lake Melville, and order-of-magnitude heating and electricity bill increases have galvanized resistance among the people of Nunatsiavut and the people of Newfoundland and Labrador in equal measure (Cox 2019a; 2019b).

A Joint Review Panel was established to coordinate Federal and Provincial assessment processes for the Muskrat Falls hydroelectric proposal. The panel's 2011 report did not clearly recommend whether or not the project should proceed. However, it concluded that the project would have significant negative effects on arctic ecology and society, and was skeptical of the economic benefits Nalcor (the crown corporation behind the project) claimed the project would deliver. The panel recommended further studies to inform government decisions, as well as a host of additional mitigation measures to reduce the project's negative effects (Joint Review Panel 2011).

The Government of Newfoundland and Labrador issued permits for the Muskrat Falls project in 2013, ignoring many of the recommendations in the Joint Review Panel's report. In response, the Nunatsiavut Government applied to provincial courts to quash the permits, arguing that the government had breached its duty to consult Nunatisavut Inuit. In 2015 the litigation was dismissed, and the project was allowed to proceed (*Nunatsiavut Government v Government of Newfoundland and Labrador* 2015).

The Nunatsiavut Government has maintained its political opposition to the project despite the failure of litigation. Its "Make Muskrat Right" campaign harnessed the power of social media to place specific demands into the public domain. Using the hashtag #makemuskratright, the Inuit government has provided a platform for information about maps, scientific studies, and activism around the dam. As the short viral video that accompanies the campaign homepage claims, "There's a high cost in doing Muskrat Falls wrong; there's power in doing it right" (Nunatsiavut Government 2019). This campaign has focused directly on Inuit health and Indigenous rights. It has also been backed by multiple scientific studies, including research on the relationship between hydroelectric development and methylmercury contamination (Goodyear 2016).

There has also been more direct-action protest by Inuit residents of Nunatsiavut who fear the contamination of the fish and country foods that many rely on. In an effort to forestall flooding, October 2016 witnessed a two-week occupation of the Muskrat Falls site, alongside a protest march on the Trans-Labrador Highway and a hunger strike led by Inuk artist Billy Gaulthier. These events succeeded in shifting the narrative around the dam from one centered on the economic potential of energy generation to one focused on the long-term social, environmental, and health effects of mega dam construction (Brake 2018). More recently, in the summer of 2019, multiple protestors were arrested on Parliament Hill in Ottawa while delivering a petition signed by 15,000 people to the federal government. The imminent crisis of methylmercury is at the center of this activist momentum.

In response to Indigenous resistance, the Government of Newfoundland committed to new mitigation measures to reduce the threat of methylmercury contamination. However, the government failed to follow through with these promises in a timely manner. This prompted a hardening of rhetoric from the Nunatsiavut Government. In the words of Nunatsiavut President Johannes Lampe:

> We are extremely disappointed with how the premier has handled the whole Muskrat Falls fiasco. He has repeatedly betrayed our trust by refusing to address our concerns, opting instead to place the health, culture and way of life of Labrador Inuit at risk. In the spirit of reconciliation, we call on the premier to do the right thing and direct Nalcor not to flood the reservoir until the concerns of Labrador Inuit are meaningfully addressed.
>
> (quoted in Behrens 2019)

Despite these appeals, flooding of the Muskrat Falls reservoir began in the summer of 2019. By this point, frustration with the Government of Newfoundland and Labrador's handling of the Muskrat Falls project had spread beyond the affected communities in Labrador. A key source of public anger was related to the costs of the project, which had risen exponentially since it was first proposed.

The Government of Newfoundland and Labrador responded to growing public frustration with the Muskrat Falls project by initiating a public inquiry. The inquiry's report, released in March 2020 and titled *Muskrat Falls: A Misguided Project*, was highly critical of the government's handling of the project. Notably, the inquiry found that the government did not act fairly in its consultations with Inuit (Muskrat Falls Inquiry 2020).

DISCUSSION: EXTRACTION, DEVELOPMENT, AND SELF-DETERMINATION IN INUIT NUNANGAT

Most proposals for energy extraction in Inuit Nunangat were ultimately abandoned in the face of poor markets and Inuit resistance. Nevertheless, the debates around these proposals had important political effects which continue to shape the political terrain in northern Canada.[2] The development of extractive "mega projects" in the Arctic in the 1970s and 1980s was tied up in a colonial process of "nation-building" for Canada and Quebec (Desbiens 2013). The cases examined in this chapter show that Inuit resistance to these proposed projects drove a parallel process of Inuit political development. Nunavik Inuit opposition to hydroelectric development, Inuvialuit resistance to offshore oil extraction, and Nunavut and Nunatsiavut Inuit opposition to uranium mining, all played important roles in the recognition of Inuit rights in land claims and Canadian common-law.

The negotiation of land claims has tied Inuit organizations to economies based on extraction. Each treaty is premised on the assumption that royalties from extraction would fund Inuit governance, social services, and cultural development (Rodon 2014). This has led to several well-publicized conflicts between Inuit organizations and community groups like Hunters and Trappers Organizations, especially the aforementioned conflicts over uranium mining in Nunavut. The cases examined in this chapter show that Inuit organizations continue to oppose proposed extraction that they consider particularly risky or otherwise contrary to their interests, including deep offshore oil and gas production in Inuvialuit Nunangat, offshore oil and gas production in Nunavut, uranium mining in Nunavik, and hydroelectric development in Nunatsiavut. These examples notwithstanding, Inuit political organizations have largely accepted the premise that mining and energy extraction will drive economic development in their communities.

As Arn Keeling and John Sandlos note, the history of extraction in northern Canada is complex and shot through with contradictions. On the one hand, mineral and energy extraction are associated with the disruption of subsistence economies and community relationships. Moreover, most of the wealth produced by extraction has tended to flow out of the North. On the other hand, many Indigenous communities have responded to these challenges with resilience and creative adaptation (Keeling and Sandlos 2015).

Because of modern treaties and Indigenous-proponent agreements, northern Indigenous peoples now capture a larger share of the wealth produced by extraction than was previously possible (Huskey 2018; Mills and Sweeney 2013; Slowey 2008). These agreements have also provided new opportunities for Indigenous communities to participate in decisions about extraction, most notably through the co-management boards created by modern treaties (Notzke 1995; White 2006). Today, many Inuit see extraction as an important part of their heritage, identities, and aspirations for self-determination (Abele 2004; Cater and Keeling 2013; Nuttall 2010; Procter 2016). While extraction can damage or destroy the wildlife resources Inuit hunt, the wages northern Indigenous peoples earn at mining projects are frequently reinvested into subsistence production (Southcott and Natcher 2018). Moreover, as this chapter has shown, Inuit have succeeded in stopping some of the most destructive proposals for energy extraction in their homeland, therefore limiting the negative effects of extraction on northern communities and environments.

That said, the economic development record of arctic extraction has been disappointing, even in the era of modern treaties and "reconciliation." As in the past, the majority of wealth produced by extraction does not remain in Inuit Nunangat (Bernauer 2019b; Rodon 2018). Nor has formal support for extraction closed the development gap between Inuit and the dominant Canadian society. Inuit continue to lag behind the rest of Canada with regards to most statistical indicators of human development and well-being (Hicks and White 2015). There are serious questions to be asked about the ability and willingness of multi-national mining and energy companies – which function first and foremost to represent the financial interests of their shareholders – to deliver sustained development throughout Inuit Nunangat. Given the industry's track record in the Arctic, as well as the unstable "boom-bust" nature of extractive economies, the goal of driving arctic economic development through capitalist extraction remains very much uncertain.

There are also several outstanding political questions about the way decisions are made about extraction in Inuit Nunangat. While co-management processes allow northern Indigenous peoples to participate in decisions about extraction, real authority mostly remains in the hands of federal, provincial, and territorial governments. The co-management framework has also tended to privilege the interests of extractive industries over subsistence hunting (Kennedy Dalseg et al. 2018; Parlee, Sandlos and Natcher 2018; Scobie and Rodgers 2019). Similarly, despite attempts to incorporate Indigenous cultures into co-management, decision-making processes tend to privilege technical knowledge and western epistemologies over Indigenous knowledges and ways of knowing (Dokis 2015; Nadasdy 2003).

More fundamentally, the final decisions for most extractive projects are not made by Indigenous communities or public governments, but by private corporations. Countries in the Global South that rely on extractive industries to drive economic development are vulnerable to manipulation by foreign mining and energy companies (Gordon and Webber 2016; Gudynas 2010). As a result, even governments controlled by Indigenous politicians have been forced to make decisions that favor extractive industries over Indigenous interests (Andreucci and Radhuber 2015; Radhuber 2012). Indigenous organizations in Canada face similar pressures. It therefore remains unclear whether Inuit will be able to exercise meaningful self-determination under the current development framework, or if dependency on multinational capital will constrain and circumscribe their ability to define their own future.

NOTES

1 While there has been some conflict over a recent proposal for a small-scale hydro project near Inukjuaq (*Nunatsiaq News* 2019), the fact that the project is for local use makes it fundamentally different from the projects discussed in this chapter.
2 See Peyton (2017) for further discussion on the role of these "unbuilt environments" in the political and social development of northern Canada.

REFERENCES

Abele, Frances. 2004. "The Smartest Steward? Indigenous People and Petroleum-Based Economic Development in Canada's North." In *Canadian Energy Policy and the Struggle for Sustainable Development*, edited by G. Bruce Doern, 223–245. Toronto, ON: University of Toronto Press.

Andreucci, Diego, and Isabella M. Radhuber. 2015. "Limits to 'Counter-Neoliberal' Reform: Mining Expansion and the Marginalization of Post-Extractivist Forces in Evo Morales' Bolivia." *Geoforum* 84: 280–291. https://doi.org/10.1016/j.geoforum.2015.09.002

Andersen, Tony. 2008. Speech to Nunatsiavut Assembly. 5 March 2008. Nunatsiavut Hansard. http://www.nunatsiavut.com/pdfs/March_3_Hansard_Revised_08.pdf

Arctic Monitoring and Assessment Program (AMAP). 2007. "Oil and Gas Activities in the Arctic – Effects and Potential Effects: Vol 1." Oslo: AMAP.

Arnold, Charles, Wendy Stephenson, Bob Simpson, and Zoe Ho, eds. 2011. *Taimani: At That Time*. Inuvik, NT: Inuvialuit Regional Corporation.

Bannister, Jerry. 2012. "A River Runs through It: Churchill Falls and the End of Newfoundland History." *Acadiensis* 41: 211–225.

Beaufort Regional Environmental Assessment (BREA). 2016. "Key Findings: Research and Working Group Results." March 2016. www.beaufortrea.ca

Behrens, Matthew. "Mercury Poisoning, Muskrat Falls and Canada's Toxic Divide." *Rabble.ca*, 24 July 2019. https://rabble.ca/columnists/2019/07/mercury-poisoning-muskrat-falls-and-canadas-toxic-divide

Berger, Thomas R. 1977. *Northern Frontier, Northern Homeland – The Report of the Mackenzie Valley Pipeline Inquiry: Volume 1*. Ottawa, ON: Minister of Supply and Services Canada.

Bernauer, Warren. 2015. "Land Claims and Caribou Habitat Management: The Case of Nunavut." *Canadian Journal of Native Studies*. 35 (1): 5–32.

———. 2019a. "Land Rights and Resource Conflicts in Nunavut." *Polar Geography* 42: 253–266. https://doi-org.proxy.lib.sfu.ca/10.1080/1088937X.2019.1648582

———. 2019b. "Limits to Extraction: Mining and Colonialism in Nunavut." *Canadian Journal of Development Studies*. 40 (3): 404–422. https://doi.org/10.1080/02255189.2019.1629883

———. 2020. "Producing Consent: How Environmental Assessment Enabled Oil and Gas Extraction in the Qikiqtani Region of Nunavut." *Canadian Geographer*. 64(3): 489–501.

Bowman, Laura. 2011. "Sealing the Deal: Environmental and Indigenous Justice and Mining in Nunavut." *RECIEL*. 20 (1): 19–28. https://doi.org/10.1111/j.1467-9388.2011.00699.x

Brake, Justin. 2018. "'It's Cultural Genocide': Labrador Land Protectors in Court on Anniversary of Muskrat Falls Occupation." *APTNNews.ca*. 23 October 2018. https://aptnnews.ca/2018/10/23/its-cultural-genocide-labrador-land-protectors-in-court-on-anniversary-of-muskrat-falls-occupation/

Bureau d'audiences publiques sur l'environnement (BAPE). 2015. *Les enjeux de la filière uranifère au Québec: Rapport d'enquête et d'audience publique*. Rapport No. 308. Québec.

Cameron, Emilie. 2015. *Far Off Metal River: Inuit Lands, Settler Stories, and the Making of the Contemporary Arctic*. Vancouver, BC: UBC Press.

Cater, Tara, and Arn Keeling. 2013. "That's Where Our Future Came From." *Études/Inuit/Studies* 37 (2): 59–82. https://doi.org/10.7202/1025710ar

Clyde River (Hamlet) v Petroleum Geoservices Inc. 2017 SCC 40

The Communities of Ivujivik, Puvirnituq and Kangiqsujuaq, C. Furgal, S. Nickels, Kativik Regional Government – Environment Department. 2005. *Unikkaaqatigiit: Putting the Human Face on Climate Change: Perspectives from Nunavik*. Ottawa, ON: Joint publication of Inuit Tapiriit Kanatimi, Nasivvik Centre for Inuit Health and Changing Environments at Université Laval and the Ajunnginiq Centre at the National Aboriginal Health Organization.

Council of the Cree Nation of Mistissini. 2014. "No Uranium Development without our Consent." Brief Presented to Bureau d'Audiences Publics sur L'Environnement. 30 October 2014.

Cox, Sarah. 2019a. "A Reckoning for Muskrat Falls." *The Narwhal*. 16 May 2019. https://thenarwhal.ca/a-reckoning-for-muskrat-falls/

———. 2019b. "Mercury Rising: How the Muskrat Falls Dam Threatens Inuit Way of Life." *The Narwhal*. 22 May 2019. https://thenarwhal.ca/mercury-rising-muskrat-falls-dam-threatens-inuit-way-of-life/

Craik, Brian. 2004. "The Importance of Working Together: Exclusions, Conflicts, and Participation in James Bay, Quebec." In *In the Way of Development*, edited by Mario Blaser, Harvey A. Feit, and Glenn McRae, 166–186. London: Zed Books.

Kennedy Dalseg, Sheena, Rauna Kuokkanen, Suzanne Mills, and Deborah Simmons. 2018. "Gendered Environmental Assessment in the Canadian North: Marginalization of Indigenous Women and Traditional Economies." *Northern Review* 47: 135–166. https://doi.org/10.22584/nr47.2018.007

Desbiens, Caroline. 2013. *Power from the North: Territory, Identity, and the Culture of Hydroelectricity in Quebec*. Vancouver, BC: UBC Press.

Dokis, Carly A. 2015. *Where the Rivers Meet: Pipelines, Participatory Resource Management, and Aboriginal-State Relations in the Northwest Territories*. Vancouver, BC: UBC Press.

Duffy, Quinn. *The Road to Nunavut: The Progress of the Eastern Arctic Inuit since the Second World War*. Montreal/Kingston: McGill-Queen's University Press.

Environmental Impact Review Board (EIRB). 1989. "Public Review of the ESSO Chevron et al Isserk I-15 Drilling Program."

Evans, Peter. 2012. "Abandoned and Ousted by the State: The Relocations from Nutak and Hebron 1956–1959." In *Settlement, Subsistence, and Change among the Labrador Inuit: The Nunatsiavummiut Experience*, edited by David C. Natcher, Lawrence Felt and Andrea Procter 85. Winnipeg, MB: University of Manitoba Press.

Federal Environmental Assessment and Review Office (FEARO). 1979. *Report of the Environmental Assessment Panel: Lancaster Sound Drilling*. Ottawa, ON: Environment Canada.

Feehan, James P. 2011. "Smallwood, Churchill Falls, and the Power Corridor through Quebec." *Acadiensis* 40 (2): 112–127.
Feit, Harvey A. 2004. "Hunting and the Quest for Power: The James Bay Cree and Whiteman Development." In *Native Peoples: The Canadian Experience*, edited by R. Bruce Morrison and C. Roderick Wilson. New York: Oxford University Press.
Göcke, Katja. 2013. "Uranium Mining in Nunavut." *The Yearbook of Polar Law Online* 5 (1): 119–142. https://doi.org/10.1163/22116427-91000121
Goodyear, Sheena. 2016. "Scientists Back Inuit in Efforts to Limit Mercury Poisoning Risk from Muskrat Falls Hydro Project" *CBC.ca*. 26 October 2016. https://www.cbc.ca/news/technology/muskrat-falls-labrador-mehylmercury-1.3821827.
Gordon, Todd, and Jeffrey R. Webber. 2016. *Blood of Extraction: Canadian Imperialism in Latin America*. Halifax and Winnipeg, MB: Fernwood.
Government of Canada. 2017. *Arctic Policy Framework Regional Roundtable Discussion in Inuvik*. Crown-Indigenous Relations and Northern Affairs Canada.
Gudynas, Eduardo. 2010. *The New Extractivism of the 21st Century – Ten Urgent Theses about Extractivism in Relation to Current South American Progressivism*. Americas Policy Program. 21 January 2010.
Hamlet of Baker Lake v Minister for Indian Affairs. 1980. 1 FC 519.
Hicks, Jack, and Graham White. 2015. *Made in Nunavut: An Experiment in Decentralized Government*. Vancouver, BC: UBC Press.
Huskey, Lee. 2018. "An Arctic Development Strategy? The North Slope Inupiat and the Resource Curse." *Canadian Journal of Development Studies* 39 (1): 89–100. https://doi.org/10.1080/02255189.2017.1391067
Imperial Oil. 2017. "Mackenzie Gas Project Participants End Joint Venture." News Release. 22 December 2017.
Inuvialuit Magazine. 1975. "Tuktoyaktuk Land Freeze." November/December, 1975: 10–11.
———. 1976a. "Offshore Drilling Approved." March/April 1976: 6–7.
———. 1976b. "The Berger Inquiry." January/February 1976: 1.
———. 1977. "Mackenzie Valley Pipeline Decision." June 1977: 4–5
Inuvialuit Regional Corporation (IRC). 2019. "Re: The Committee's Study of Bill C-88, An Act to Amend the Canadian Petroleum Resources Act." Standing Committee on Indigenous and Northern Affairs.
Jacobs, Peter, and Jonathan Palluq. 1983. *Public Review: Public Prospect, The Lancaster Sound Regional Study*. Ottawa, ON: Indian and Northern Affairs Canada.
Johnson, Noor. Shari Gearheard, Jerry Natanine, Shelly Elverum. 2016. "Community Actions to Address Seismic Testing in Nunavut, Canada." *Practicing Anthropology*. 38(3): 13–16.
Joint Review Panel. 2011. *Report of the Joint Review Panel for the Lower Churchill Falls Hydroelectric Generating Project*. CEAA Ref No. 07-05-26178.
Keeling, Arn, and John Sandlos, eds. 2015. *Mining and Communities in Northern Canada*. Calgary, AB: University of Calgary Press.
Lowe, Mick. 1998. *Premature Bonanza: Standoff at Voisey's Bay*. Toronto, ON: Between the Lines.
Makivik Corporation, and Kativik Regional Government (KRG). 2014. "Makivik and the KRG Oppose Uranium Development in Nunavik." News Release. 3 December 2014.
Martin, Thibault. 2008. "The End of an Era in Quebec: The Great Whale Project and the Inuit of Kuujjuarapik and the Umiujaq." In *Power Struggles: Hydro Development and First Nations in Manitoba and Quebec*, edited by Thibault Martin and Steven M. Hoffman, 227–254. Winnipeg, MB: University of Manitoba Press.
McPherson, Robert. 2003. *New Owners in Their Own Land: Minerals and Inuit Land Claims*. Calgary, AB: Arctic Institute of North America.

Mills, Suzanne, and Brendan Sweeney. 2013. "Employment Relations in the Neostaples Resource Economy: Impact Benefit Agreements and Aboriginal Governance in Canada's Nickle Mining Industry." *Studies in Political Economy* 91 (1): 7–34. https://doi-org.proxy.lib.sfu.ca/10.1080/19187033.2013.11674980

Muskrat Falls Inquiry (Commission of Inquiry Respecting the Muskrat Falls Project). 2020. *Muskrat Falls: A Misguided Project.*

Nadasdy, Paul. 2003. *Hunters and Bureaucrats: Power, Knowledge, and Aboriginal-State Relations in the Southwest Yukon.* Vancouver, BC: UBC Press.

Nassichuk, Walter. 1987. "Forty Years of Northern Non-Renewable Natural Resource Development." *Arctic* 40 (4): 274–284.

Notzke, Claudia. 1995. "The Resource Co-Management Regime in the Inuvialuit Settlement Region." In *Northern Aboriginal Communities: Economies and Development*, edited by P. D. Elias, 36–52. North York: Captus Publications.

Nunatsiaq News. 2019. "Some Inukjuak Residents Remain Concerned about Hydro Project." 12 November 2019.

Nunatsiavut Government. 2019. "Make Muskrat Right." http://makemuskratright.com

Nunatsiavut Government v Government of Newfoundland and Labrador. 2015. NLTD(G) 1.

Nunavut Impact Review Board (NIRB). 2015a. *Final Hearing Transcript.* AREVA Resources Kiggavik Project. Vol. 11. NIRB File No. 09MN003.

———. 2015b. Final Hearing Report. AREVA Resources Kiggavik project. NIRB File No. 09MN003.

———. 2019a. Final Public Meeting Transcript for the Strategic Environmental Assessment in Baffin Bay and Davis Strait. NIRB File No. 17SN034.

———. 2019b. Final Report for the Strategic Environmental Assessment in Baffin Bay and Davis Strait. NIRB File No. 17SN034.

Nungak, Zebedee. 2017. *Wrestling With Colonialism on Steroids: Quebec Inuit Fight for Their Homeland.* Montreal, QC: Vehicule Press.

Nuttall, Mark. 2010. *Pipeline Dreams.* Copenhagen: International Working Group for Indigenous Affairs.

Parlee, Brenda L., John Sandlos, and David C. Natcher. 2018. "Undermining Subsistence: Barren-Ground Caribou in a 'Tragedy of Open Access.'" *Science Advances* 4 (2): e1701611. http://doi.org/10.1126/sciadv.1701611

Peyton, Jonathan. 2017. *Unbuilt Environments: Tracing Postwar Development in Northwest British Columbia.* Vancouver, BC: UBC Press.

Porta, Louie, and Nigel Banks. 2011. *Becoming Arctic Ready: Policy Recommendations for Reforming Canada's Approach to Licensing and Regulating Offshore Oil and Gas in the Arctic.* PEW Charitable Trusts.

Posluns, Michael. 1993. *Voices from the Odeyak.* Toronto, ON: Dundurn.

Procter, Andrea. 2015. "Uranium, Inuit Rights, and Emergent Neoliberalism in Labrador, 1956–2012." In *Mining and Communities in Northern Canada*, edited by Arn Keeling and John Sandlos, 809–849. Calgary, AB: University of Calgary Press.

———. 2016. "Uranium, and the Boundaries of Indigeneity in Nunatsiavut, Labrador." *The Extractive Industries and Society* 3 (2): 288–296. https://doi.org/10.1016/j.exis.2015.08.001

Procter, Andrea, and Keith Chaulk. 2013. "Our Beautiful Land: Challenges in Nunatsiavut Land-Use Planning." In *Reclaiming Indigenous Planning*, edited by Ryan Walker, Ted Jojola and David Natcher, 809–849. Montreal and Kingston: McGill-Queen's University Press.

Qikiqtani Inuit Association v Canada (Minister of Natural Resources). 2010. NUCJ 12.

Qikiqtani Truth Commission (QTC). 2013. *Nuutauniq: Moves in Inuit Life.* Iqaluit, NU: Qikiqtani Inuit Association.

Radhuber, Isabella M. 2012. "Indigenous Struggles for a Plurinational State: An Analysis of Indigenous Rights and Competences in Bolivia." *Journal of Latin American Geography* 11 (2): 167–193.

Ray, Arthur J. 1990. *The Canadian Fur Trade in the Industrial Age*. Toronto, ON: University of a Toronto Press.

Rodgers, K. and Ingram, D. 2019. "Decolonizing Environmentalism in the Arctic? Greenpeace, Complicity and Negotiating the Contradictions of Solidarity in the Inuit Nunangat." *Interface*. 11 (2): 11–34.

Rodon, Thierry. 2014. "Working Together: The Dynamics of Multi-Level Governance in Nunavut." *Arctic Review on Law and Politics* 5 (2): 250–270.

———. 2018. "Institutional Development and Resource Development: The Case of Canada's Indigenous Peoples." *Canadian Journal of Development Studies* 39 (1): 119–136. https://doi.org/10.1080/02255189.2017.1391069

Ross, Gilles. 1989. "Whaling, Inuit and the Arctic Islands." In *Interpreting Canada's North*, edited by Ken Coates and Bill Morrison, 235–251. Toronto, ON: Copp Clark Pitman.

Schiff, Rebecca, Anatu Sarkar, Mathilda Choi, and Zachary Anstey. 2015. *Community Perspectives on Uranium Exploration, Mining and Health Impacts in Makkovik, Labrador*. Division of Community Health and Humanities, Faculty of Medicine, Memorial University of Newfoundland.

Scobie, Willow, and Kathleen Rodgers. 2013. "Contestation of Resource Extraction Projects via Digital Media in Two Nunavut Communities." *Études/Inuit Studies* 37 (2): 83–101. https://doi.org/10.7202/1025711ar

———. 2019. "Diversions, Distractions, and Privileges: Consultation and the Governance of Mining in Nunavut." *Studies in Political Economy*. 100 (3): 232–251.

Slowey, Gabrielle. 2008. *Navigating Neoliberalism: Self-Determination and the Mikisew Cree First Nation*. Vancouver, BC: UBC Press.

Southcott, Chris, and David Natcher. 2018. "Extractive Industries and Indigenous Subsistence Economies: A Complex and Unresolved Relationship." *Canadian Journal of Development Studies* 39 (1): 137–154. https://doi.org/10.1080/02255189.2017.1400955

Tester, Frank J. and Peter Kulchyski. 1994. *Tamarniit (Mistakes): Inuit Relocation in the Eastern Arctic, 1939–63*. Vancouver, BC: UBC Press.

Watkins, Mel. 1977. Dene Nation: The Colony Within. Toronto, ON: University of Toronto Press.

White, Graham. 2006. "Cultures in Collision: Traditional Knowledge and Euro-Canadian Governance Processes in Northern Land Claim Boards." *Arctic* 59 (4): 401–414.

Wilt, James. 2020. "'The Ice Can Be Conquered': Scientific Knowledge and Mobilizing Arctic Gas." Unpublished Master's Thesis. University of Manitoba.

Zellen, Barry Scott. 2008. *Breaking the Ice: From Land Claims to Tribal Sovereignty in the Arctic*. Lanham, MD: Lexington Books.

CHAPTER 21

ATSUNAI ("BE STRONG")

Inuit women's leadership in Labrador

Andrea Procter, Peggy Andersen, Beverly Hunter, and Tracy Ann Evans-Rice

Leadership in Labrador Inuit society has been the focus of much research over the past two centuries. Missionaries and scholars have discussed the role of individual male leaders, *katimât* (men's meetings), and *angakkuit* (shamans) – mostly male – in pre-settlement camps (Kleivan 1966; Taylor 1968, 1974). In studies on Moravian Inuit society, they have examined the function of Inuit chapel servants, elected *AngajokKauKatiget* councils ("men meeting together"), and the male church elders of the Moravian Church (Brice-Bennett 1981; Evans 2013; Jenness 1967; Kleivan 1966; Peacock 1963). More recently, academics have explored the dynamics of modern government, from the community councils founded in the 1970s to the Nunatsiavut Government established in 2005 (Brantenberg 1977; Procter 2012; Procter and Chaulk 2013). Although these modern institutions are not explicitly gendered, since the 1970s, most of the elected Inuit officials in northern Labrador have been male. The leadership of Inuit men has been well established and well examined. The role that Inuit women play as leaders, on the other hand, has not garnered the same attention.

This chapter aims to contribute to this conversation by exploring Inuit women's leadership in Labrador, as described by Inuit. By listening to a collection of tributes made by Nunatsiavummiut about inspirational women in their lives, we examine how Inuit understand and value the role of female leaders in Labrador Inuit society today. As we shall see, this collective narrative depicts a distinct style of leadership that differs fundamentally from both the historical descriptions of Inuit leaders and mainstream society's individualized and institutional ideal.

DAUGHTERS OF MIKAK: CELEBRATING INUIT WOMEN'S LEADERSHIP IN LABRADOR

In 2014, women in Nunatsiavut proposed a project to document the leadership roles of Inuit women in Labrador. Charlotte Wolfrey of Rigolet, among others, noted that while many women have had a tremendous impact, most had not been publicly acknowledged. Charlotte worked with Andrea Procter to organize the Daughters of Mikak[1] project through the SSHRC-funded research partnership, *Tradition and Transition Among the Labrador Inuit*. They created an advisory group of women that included us (Beverly Hunter, Peggy Andersen, and Tracy Ann Evans-Rice), and over the course of a year, we encouraged people throughout Labrador to record digital stories about inspirational Inuit women in their lives. People were free to decide whom to celebrate, as well as to decide on the content of their stories. We recorded their tribute, and then we made digital stories by combining the audio with photographs. Much of coastal Labrador had slow internet at the time, so the relatively small digital files made the stories accessible online. The digital stories are posted on the Daughters of Mikak Facebook site and have enjoyed many thousands of views and shares.[2]

The 44 digital stories that were created are each unique, but together, they provide a strikingly coherent portrait of a distinct type of leadership. While a few of the women featured are prominent figures in Labrador who have worked in the political or public sphere, many more are women whose names may not be recognizable to those outside their own communities. They represent all ages and professions, but all of them have impacted those around them significantly.

By listening to the stories, we are able to examine how people in Labrador see Inuit women's leadership. The narrators of these digital stories made conscious decisions about which characteristics and experiences to bring to the foreground when celebrating these inspirational women. So what have they chosen to highlight? As tributes, the stories focus on the admirable and the ideal, but they nonetheless present a full and complex description of leadership. In this chapter, we analyze the narratives thematically by examining the content for common themes (Riessman 2008). We have tried to include almost complete transcripts of the stories, in order to appreciate the full storyline of the narrative. We have also tried to incorporate as many stories as possible to build a comprehensive picture of Inuit women's leadership, as understood and as celebrated by Labrador Inuit themselves/ourselves.

We will start with three stories. The first is told by Charlotte Wolfrey of Rigolet:

> I wanted to write a piece on a lady that had a great influence on my life as a child growing up in Rigolet. I want to honour a woman who is now deceased who deserves a part of her story to be told.
>
> Her name is Eva Palliser, an Inuk lady who lived all of her life practicing her culture, traditions and lifestyle. In addition to raising her children, I had the privilege of tagging along on many of their going out on the land expeditions. I remember being able to go with them for sometimes weeks at a time to hunt seals in the spring, to hunt ducks and geese in the fall.
>
> ... I was as free as a bird when I was with Eva and her family, I can't remember having to help with chores, I could play as long as I wanted, I learned to do things by watching. We would just watch her cleaning seal skins, preparing meat for supper, picking ducks, cleaning and drying fish. She was in her element, never complaining, always grateful and to me, it seemed that her husband and children and their wellbeing was all that mattered. And I guess some little girl who wanted to tag along and be a part of their lives.
>
> One thing funny that I would like to share is this, like I said I used to speak Inuktitut when I was small and especially when I was with Eva and her family.

It was in the spring of the year and we were over to a place called Kanijuk. We were all in tent in the evening and a big mosquito was buzzing around. I yelled "*tika, tika*" and I realized I never knew what a mosquito was in Inuktitut so I said "nipperee!" Everyone laughed hard and from then on we all called mosquitoes "nipperee."

... She was kind, she was patient, she was strong, and with all those big traits she stood a mere four foot ten if she stood that tall. This was a woman who had her own family, who had very little earthly possessions and absolutely no money (like everyone else at the time) yet she still made room for me in her boat, in her tent, in her life in every way. Nakummek Eva, *nulligivagit* or in Rigolet style, *nugligivagiit*.

The second story is from Sandra Dicker of Nain:

When I was growing up, the most important Inuit woman in my life was my mom. Her name is Jessie Wyatt. She was born in Hebron and she had three daughters. She had a lot of patience ... She's very kind, she taught us how to be good members in the community. She was a teacher. She got her degree in education. She taught in Inuktitut.

... She helped in our community by always being there to help others. If there was a tragedy, she always made sure she had time for those families who were suffering ... I remember her always bringing leftovers to our neighbours, little small gestures she always did what she could to help other people. She has influenced my life in instilling qualities in me as a parent, like to be a good mom. She taught me that family is always first, so ... to be kind to people, to take care of people that you love, and to help others who aren't so fortunate, and to just always make sure that your children know they are very loved by you.

The third story is from Nancy Ikkusek of Nain, who talked about her mother, Jenny Ikkusek:

My mother was the most important. I found her really special. She was always kind, and she always shared whatever she wanted to with other people that were hungry, or needed help. She would always share whatever she had with other people, and she cared about people. She always sewed, she knew how to sew. Before Christmas, she would always make our sealskin boots – a lot of time they were white-bottomed boots – and she would make our clothes with a sewing machine. She would make our dresses and our coats.

She was important to me because she taught me right from wrong, and she said, she always used to say, would you like to be treated like that? And she would say it in Inuktitut, and that would make me think that if I did something bad, I wouldn't want someone to do that to me.

I found she helped the community because she always helped people and she always tried to be there for everyone, and she cared what happened to the other person .... She improved my life because I tried to do what she used to do in all – I try to share what I can with low-income families, and I try to listen or see who's hurting because that's what she would do.

These three stories share some common themes about the women's traits: their generosity to others, their ability to connect people in their community, and their patience. The women all have a strong awareness of how those around them are doing, and a quick willingness to care for others when needed. In being acutely aware of others, they situate themselves in a social web of mutual responsibility towards family, neighbors, and community. They also influence others by modeling caring and moral behavior.

These social traits have a long history in Labrador. Moravian missionaries, who had arrived in the region in the 1770s, were constantly frustrated by the Inuit insistence on sharing food, materials, and labor with each other, and felt that such widespread generosity conflicted with their attempts to instill Protestant ethics of industry, providence, and frugality (Brice-Bennett 1990). The anthropological literature about Inuit society likewise echoes the importance of sharing and generosity as fundamental practices across Inuit Nunangat (Bodenhorn 2000; Wenzel 2000). Inuit women, as the ones who often are in charge of preparing and sharing food, actively create and strengthen social networks of interdependence (Bodenhorn 1990). These social networks connect almost everyone in Inuit communities through relationships based on kinship, fostering, friendship, Moravian church institutions, and "fictive kinship" such as namesakes, ritual sponsors, and midwives (Bennett and Rowley 2004; Damas 2002; Guemple 1988; Maggo 1999). In being sensitive to the needs of others within these social networks and spontaneously offering help, the women in the Daughters of Mikak stories demonstrate two closely connected core Inuit values: *nalli* (*nagli, naklik*) and *isuma* (*ihuma*). Jean Briggs' (1970) work on Inuit socialization has defined *nalli* (or love, nurturance) as the motivation for taking care of the ill, helping others, or adopting orphans, for instance. *Isuma* (or the ability to reason) is the defining feature of adultness (Briggs 1970). When a person has developed *isuma*, he or she acts with self-restraint and thoughtfulness. "Well-socialized persons were keenly aware of others," as Wim Rasing (1994, 113) notes in his work with Inuit in Igloolik.

Many other stories echo these themes, including Caroline Nochasak's tribute to her grandmother, Sarah Nochasak:

> She's always willing to help, no matter what. My *anânsiak* Sarah always had room in her home for family members and children, and loved them as her own, including me ... Being able to love everyone, no matter what, and being willing to help people just like that.

Miriam Brown also tried to help people in her community by acting as a foster parent and by being involved in many initiatives:

> She was instrumental in so many things, with the women's group, helping getting the daycare started ... She was an *Illusivut* [Inuit lifeskills program] teacher for the school, she was a midwife, she was involved with our Nain choir. Everything she did in life was an achievement, and she excelled at whatever it was she did.
>
> She was not educated and she didn't mind saying that, but she never let that get in the way. She always pushed herself to do things that other people were afraid to do. She was a humble woman, and when you look at it now, everything

was kind of quiet, like whenever there was stuff that was happening that she should be recognized for, it just passed. She was happy to just let it pass, no matter how big an achievement or hard work she did …

She was a foster parent, traditionally. Back in the day, there was a lot of people who, some of them had families who were too big, and so a lot of families couldn't take care of each other, so some of them would just go to live with other people in the community. There was a lot of people who would do this – it was a way of life. And so there was some people, and they'd go and live with *Anânsiak*. I didn't know that they lived with her, because a lot of the time, this happened before my time, cause they're all older people, and they'd be on the road – "Hey, mom," "Hi, mom!" And to auntie, "Hi, sis!" [I would ask,] "Is that our family??" "No. They went to live with mom years ago." And I'd be like, "Gee, there's a whole other side to *Anânsiak's* life that I didn't know about!" She took a lot of people in. A lot of times, it was because of hard times, and families help each other out in times of need. So she was really good that way.

Fran Williams recalled how her grandmother, Kitora Boase (see Figure 21.1), took care of her and taught her similar values:

My grandparents had a lot of influence on me. They taught me patience, to love the land, to be good to other people. They used to *KaKak*³ me all the time. She always used to make my tea in the morning although I was old enough to make it myself.

Similarly, Gwen Watts admired how her mother, Beatrice Watts, always tried to support people:

Figure 21.1 Kitora Boase, Hopedale. Photo used with permission of Nigel Markham.

> What I noticed about Mom was that she always had a kind word and the time to chat with people. She was the type of person who lifted people up. She didn't put people down, she didn't go around gossiping or saying mean things. She always saw the good in people. She always wanted to be there for people … She was really always aware of other people … She focused on the good in people, and brought out the best in people … When I think of my mother, I remember the love.

The women's commitment to their community is unmistakable. They are admired for their willingness to become involved, to help, and to develop positive relationships with the people around them. As Joe Dicker and Mary Adelaide say about their mother, Mary Dicker: "Most of all, I think, it was her involvement in the community." Jessie Wyatt taught her family "how to be good community members," and Fran Williams observed that people see being a community member as an important type of leadership:

> Mrs. [Sybilla Pamak] Nitsman I admired too, because she was really good at crafts, and she was a good community person, everybody looked up to her. She was really involved in the church. Those days it was so much being involved in the church, either through community elders, or in the choir. Not so much being a leader. But being a community member, involved in those types of things.

Good community members are much admired. The participants in this project celebrated women who "are always willing to help, no matter what," whether or not this involved a public or political role. A research team led by Kirk Dombrowski recently explored how Inuit in the northern Labrador town of Nain rely on these community leaders to provide assistance. Using social network analysis, the research illustrated how almost everyone in the community was connected through reciprocal sharing networks, and identified key individuals who acted as central sources of food, housing, employment, advice, and other supports (Dombrowski et al. 2013).

LEADERSHIP THROUGH RELATIONSHIPS AND ROLE MODELING

When we were developing the Daughters of Mikak project, the advisory group felt that Inuit women would not feel comfortable talking about themselves, so we decided to ask people to make digital stories about inspirational women instead. Given the importance of humility in Inuit society, people often do not want to appear boastful or pretentious (Briggs 1974; McGrath 1997). Inuit socialization has traditionally focused on learning self-restraint and sensitivity towards others as a way of maintaining group harmony (Briggs 1970; Condon 1992). Boasting about one's accomplishments is seen as immature, as it potentially highlights the relative failure of others and triggers aggression.

This reluctance to call attention to one's successes was extended to others in the Daughters of Mikak tributes. Most narrators did not list the women's personal achievements, perhaps in order not to embarrass them or provoke envy; instead, they described how the women impacted others. Their stories highlight relationships and the positive influence of the women on the narrators and on others. By embodying and displaying good values, the women acted as role models and indirectly taught others how to behave. Julie Dicker, for instance, outlined the influence that her grandmother, Sue Harris, has had on her by demonstrating impressive mental and physical strength:

> Hi, I'm Julie Dicker, and I'm from Nain, Nunatsiavut. Another inspirational Inuit woman to me would be my Ma, Sue Harris, and she's my mom's mom.
>
> When I think of my Ma, I think of her as a pillar of kindness, a pillar of truth, and a pillar of strength, because no matter what happens in her life or in her family's life, it could be a time of celebration, it could be a time of hardships, it could be a time of triumphs, it could be times of tragedy, there could be good times, bad times, ugly times, but no matter what happens, she kind of rides the waves right on through, and comes out standing on top as if nothing happened – it's just like normal.
>
> She always keeps herself grounded, and she remains steadfast and true to everything. No matter what happens, she never strays far from her normal. Always very grounded.
>
> Being true to herself and to everyone else around her is important. Growing up, say we – or even now, say we do something wrong, or something she knows isn't right. She'd be the first one to tell us that, "Okay, don't do that, that just isn't right. You got to do it the right way."
>
> Just an example of how strong she is ... [Julie describes how Sue fell and broke her hip but did not get medical help immediately]. And when she [finally] walked in to see the orthopedic specialist, she walked into his office, and he looked at her and he said, "She's walking?!? That woman must be made of nails!" Because all that time, for like a week and a half or two weeks, her hip had been fractured! So my Ma, Sue Harris, is one strong woman who never gives up.

Sue is inspirational because of the strength that she demonstrates in so many ways – in persevering through pain, but also in maintaining equanimity in difficult times, in ensuring that those around her act with integrity, and in being courageous enough to speak up against wrongdoing. These characteristics are reflected in Jean Briggs' research into the central role of *isuma* in Inuit society. As she describes, the ideal person in Inuit society is defined as being protective, helpful, generous, and even-tempered (Briggs 1970, 323). A mature adult should demonstrate rationality, control over impulsive behavior, and an ability to respond to problems calmly. Similarly, Wim Rasing's (1994) research with Iglulingmiut highlights how self-control and equanimity formed the basis of social control.

Despite the value placed on equanimity and self-control, Inuit leaders are not unassertive. Instead, the ability to exercise restraint can result in measured, thoughtful, and candid advice (Bennett and Rowley 2004). The Daughters of Mikak narrators see courage in women who reprimand others for their wrongdoings. Like Sue Harris, Eva Palliser also had the courage to speak the truth, as her granddaughter, Carlene Palliser recounted, and she found her strength by being grounded in her culture and identity:

> She wasn't ashamed of their language. It was a large part of who she was and where she came from. Being there through all the changes in the culture and

language, she never lost who she was. She always spoke the truth, even it if was something that someone didn't want to hear or agree with.

A similar image of strength permeates Tyler Edmunds' tribute to his grandmother, Silpa Sillett Edmunds:

> One of the strongest memories that I have of my grandmother, she was very tenacious, she was very strong, she always spoke her mind – she was very blunt. If there were any injustices, anything she felt wasn't fair, she would be the first to speak out against it, and she would invest all of her time and energy into ensuring that she did what she could to try to rectify that, to try to fix it. Right until her dying day, she had that passion, that energy to try to speak out against injustices.
>
> And she always said, the well-being of the Inuit was always of the biggest importance to her. It was a very beautiful thing. She always spoke out for what mattered, and what was important to her – her culture, her family, and her communities ... I just remember her as being a fighter, and I always respected that. I think anyone who came across her respected her for being that as well.
>
> She spoke Inuktitut ... [It] was a vital piece of who she was. She was very passionate about the language, and she was a very strong advocate ... She was one of the individuals who fought for the language, and fought for the language's rights.
>
> I was energized and I got a bit of passion from my grandmother for the need to pursue the language. And anytime that she would see that I had some interest in the language, she would throw herself behind it, 100 percent. You could see it in her eyes, when something was pronounced just right! She would become so proud. It's definitely one of my fonder memories, just that little connection that you would have in that moment, just sharing the language, and having that little bond.

Beatrice Watts was also fiercely outspoken about issues that impacted her community:

> She was an advocate on so many levels. She certainly fought all the time for anything to do with Inuit, and making sure that Inuit were treated fairly. And also that went for women, and Labradorians in general ... I think of my mother as a kind, patient woman, but when she thought that people were being treated unfairly or that there was some injustice or prejudice, she became angry and she spoke up ... She wouldn't stand for anything that put down other people, particularly based on race, and she always stood up. So in general, kind and patient, but with injustices, she had a steel backbone, I tell you.

In speaking up, however, Beatrice Watts did not aim to position herself as better than others or as an individual who stood out from the crowd. She "didn't like being praised up or made to be wonderful," Gwen Watts said. In the same way, Ruth Flowers "wasn't looking for rewards," recalled her daughter, Sharon Edmunds. "She wasn't looking for praise or admiration. She was just trying to make people's lives better. She didn't want any acknowledgment or fanfare – that wasn't her. She knew she made a difference." Miriam Brown also did not want accolades for her work:

— Atsunai *("be strong")* —

Figure 21.2 Miriam Brown, Nain. Photo used with permission of Candace Cochrane.

"She was a humble woman, and when you look at it now, everything was kind of quiet, like whenever there was stuff that was happening that she should be recognized for, it just passed. She was happy to just let it pass, no matter how big an achievement or hard work she did." Again, humility is a much-admired trait in these tributes, echoing Steenhoven's (1962) description of an Inuit leader in the central Arctic: "Everything he did was done quietly and without pretensions but with natural poise and dignity" (cited in Bennett and Rowley 2004, 96). One's positive impact on others is what is important, not the praise that might come with it (see Figure 21.2).

EMBODYING STRENGTH AND CREATING STRENGTH IN COMMUNITY

A broad definition of strength seems to tie the Daughters of Mikak stories together. These women embody physical and mental strength in their perseverance, courage, and ability to remain composed, patient, and humble in the face of challenges. They also create strength in others by binding people together, helping those in need, and inspiring others to follow their lead. The narrators' shared experiences with the women, whether through speaking Inuktitut together, as Tyler and Silpa did, or spending time together on the land, as Charlotte and Eva did, create bonds and memories. In their tributes, the narrators identified these memories and shared cultural experiences as giving them strength in their own lives. Joanne Voisey of Makkovik, for instance, illustrated how her grandmother's example gives her strength to overcome her own challenges:

> Ever since I've been a little girl, I've really looked up to my grandmother, my mother's mother, Rhoda Voisey. I've picked my grandmother because to me, she

is a woman of great strength and courage ... My grandfather passed away, and my grandmother raised her children on her own. She didn't remarry, so she had to work hard in a time when there wasn't a lot of modern conveniences and she had to do a lot of hard work on her own. She had to provide for her children outside of the home, she had to work, as well as do everything that you'd have to do to raise a family of 10 children ... I feel her influence in my life. I can see it in the lives of my family and in my mother, as she goes through her own struggles and needs to persevere – I can see that strength from my grandmother in her and in her being. I can feel her influence in my life as I pursue my education degree, and I know that when I go through hard times, or I'm struggling with things, trying to raise my children, that I draw on the strength of my grandmother. I hope that if I can be even a shadow of a woman that she is, that I will have achieved a great thing in my life as a Labrador woman.

Salome Jararuse from North West River identified her mother's strength as one of her most admirable qualities. She described how Selma developed this strength by experiencing times of hardship:

My mother, Selma Jararuse, is one of the most inspiring women that I know. I've heard stories of her past, and the trials and triumphs that she has went through as a women growing up in the community of Nain. She went through a lot of abuse, a lot of very negative things, but still to this day, she's very strong, she's very resilient, she's very happy-go-lucky. She has a lot of wisdom, and a lot of knowledge.

She's the rock of our family, she keeps us all together. She makes us stick together – she's very keen on that. Family is a very big thing to her. She likes to keep us all together and to lean on each other, to make sure we're always there for each other, to always love each other and to watch out for each other.

My mother has seven children and seven grandchildren ... She has taught us how to be strong, how to overcome things. She's very strong in her culture. She's taught us, her family, and a lot of the community of Goose Bay, she's taught us a lot about our culture, and about keeping our traditions alive, and how to respect our culture.

My mother is somebody that takes things that happen to her and learns from them in order to better her life and to make her a happier person. That's another thing that I really love about her. She don't let her past or the negative things define her. She learns from it and moves on.

... She likes to participate in a lot of things in the community, to volunteer, to be a part of traditional things, and to mingle with people. It just brightens her up. You see it in her when she's around people and helping people. It really does good to her soul, I believe.

My mother, Selma, is one of the biggest role models that I know. She is somebody who always leaves a mark, no matter where she goes. She'll leave a mark wherever she's to. For that, I believe, she is very wise, very knowledgeable, very smart. I love her very much.

BECOMING STRONG

In going through difficult times, Salome celebrated how Selma emerged stronger and wiser. As she said, Selma does "not let the negative things define her." Instead, she learns, develops, and teaches others to do the same. Other stories also celebrate how the women have learned and changed through their life as they developed into someone that people now admire. The narrators focus on how people are dynamic – our characteristics are fluid and we are able to transform ourselves through life. Sharon Edmunds, for example, admired how Ruth Flowers developed a deep sense of responsibility towards others after going through hard times herself:

> She experienced a lot of difficulties in her life that led her down the path that she lived. One of the things that came from that was a real desire to try to help people … It came from not a good place, but it directed her on a path of forever being there, stepping forward, and helping people the best way she could.

Rosina Brown of Nain also outlined how Miriam Brown developed as a person:

> She made herself go places where other people were afraid to. She didn't mind taking that extra step. And she grew from that. I saw her process, how it evolved … All of this really made her blossom, and made her more sure of herself.

Jim Goudie described Shirley Goudie's "progression as a woman" in his tribute, as she transformed herself from being a fisher raising six children to becoming the town manager for Postville. "I had this impression of her – and I think most people would see her as a very loving woman, very kind – but someone who was physically and mentally just impressively strong." In a similar way, Jodie Lane admired how her grandmother, Mary E. Andersen, dealt with difficulties in her life, including treating her two-year-old son after he was mauled by dogs in Makkovik:

> Would I have been able to be as strong as my Gram? In the face of tragedy, would I have been able to stand up and do what was needed? She did. They all did. We are here because of those strong women who were resourceful, courageous, smart, and brave. They were heroes and we must continue to honour them. Let us be resourceful and courageous and smart and brave. Let us be like them. Strong and beautiful.

STRENGTH AND WISDOM THROUGH HARDSHIP

These stories celebrate strength. The women have gained strength in their lives by going through difficult times, and they continue to create strength in those around them. In paying close attention to how others are doing and helping when needed, they bind people together and strengthen the social fabric of their community. They give others strength by sharing experiences, often based around the Inuit language and cultural activities. They work to strengthen their community by speaking out, correcting people's behavior, and tackling injustices, but without self-aggrandizement or appearing "proud," as they say in Labrador. By modeling generous, thoughtful, courageous, and persevering behavior, they inspire others to follow their example. They demonstrate how to confront difficult times with patience and equanimity, remaining grounded in their culture and identity.

These stories celebrate the strength and wisdom that come from experiencing difficulties, but the narrators do not describe those challenges in much detail, if at all. The Daughters of Mikak stories are almost universally positive and focused on celebrating the women's strengths, rather than dwelling on the hardships they have faced. The women are seen as role models rather than victims. This commitment to strength-based narrative and research was an important part of the project. Although we encouraged narrators to tell their stories as they wished, the goal of Daughters of Mikak was explicitly to honor the women in a positive light. As Tuck and Yang (2014, 231) argue, moving away from pain-based or victim research narratives towards desire-based narratives "does not deny the experience of tragedy, trauma, and pain, but positions the knowing derived from such experiences as wise."

Despite this emphasis on celebration, the social context of these stories and the challenges that the women have overcome are remarkable. In addition to the harsh physical environment and difficult living conditions of the region, Labrador Inuit have endured centuries of colonialism. Epidemics have torn families apart, relocations have evicted people from their lands, and foreign overfishing has destroyed local livelihoods (Brice-Bennett 2017; Budgell 2018). Residential schools and provincial education policies have resulted in a decline in people's proficiency in the Inuktitut language, and the child welfare system continues to separate families (Procter 2020). Intergenerational trauma and its resulting violence, substance abuse, suicide, and sexual abuse continue to plague many communities (Kavanagh 2019). All of these destructive and violent processes threaten to sever the connections between people, their families, and their communities. As Maori scholar Linda Tuhiwai Smith (2012, 28) argues, colonialism brings "complete disorder to colonized peoples, disconnecting them from their histories, their landscapes, their languages, their social relations and their own ways of thinking, feeling, and interacting with the world." Everyone in Labrador Inuit communities has been affected by these issues. But in these digital stories, the narrators have chosen to leave this context unspoken. The focus is firmly on the women who emerge as strong, inspirational leaders, and who demonstrate how to persevere and how to create strong, positive, and healthy communities.

Fran Williams' tribute to Kitora Boase is a prime example of this unspoken context. In her story, Fran does not mention that Kitora was a survivor of the Spanish flu epidemic in northern Labrador in 1918. Of the 263 people in her community of Okak, only 59 women and children survived the influenza outbreak (Budgell 2018, 209). After almost complete devastation, Okak was abandoned, and the 20-year-old Kitora moved with other survivors to Hopedale. Her new community witnessed her resiliency, as she rebuilt her life after the deeply traumatic experience. She became a strong role model for other women, opening her home and her heart to others, carrying on with day-to-day chores as needed, keeping up the traditions of craft-making, sewing, and cooking, and ensuring that family values were strong and visible. In her tribute, Fran describes how grateful she is for Kitora's kind nurturing, and for creating a home where Fran felt safe and loved. It is Kitora's impact on others that is celebrated; her traumatic experiences may or may not be already known by the audience, but the devastating details are not shared. Instead, her strength and her influence on the community are the focus of the story.

RE-THINKING LEADERSHIP

Anthropologists and missionaries have historically understood Inuit leadership in Labrador to comprise solely of political or institutional roles, most of which were assumed by men. With an eye only for conflict management and power, they did not recognize non-hierarchical and non-authoritative roles as constituting leadership. But the mainstream definition of leaders as solitary, powerful, and competitive individuals is too narrow. As this chapter has illustrated, Inuit in Labrador employ a vastly different definition. The style of leadership that has emerged from the Daughters of Mikak narratives values community, relationships, and the strength of social networks over individual authority and acclaim. Amy Hudson, an Inuk scholar from NunatuKavut in southern Labrador describes how this decentralized form of leadership is prominent among Inuit of NunatuKavut:

> Leadership in governance ... is not about the knowledge, power, or charisma demonstrated by a single leader (female or male). Rather, leadership can perhaps be best defined or recognized in those who are committed to shared knowledge and community and cultural preservation.
>
> (2020, 153)

In similar fashion, Indigenous scholars across Canada are challenging mainstream leadership theories, and highlighting instead the importance of relationships, responsibilities, and cultural values (Archuleta 2012; Pidgeon 2012).

Rather than understanding leadership as a quality that is reserved only for the elite few, the participants in the Daughters of Mikak project depict Inuit women's leadership as inclusive and accessible to anyone. While this project has centered on women's leadership, it does not exclude the possibility that men also assume this style of leadership. None of the tributes claimed that these roles were exclusive to women, and we did not pose the question. The cultural values that foster community solidarity, in fact, encourage everyone to assume these leadership roles. Leadership is shared rather than invested in a single authority figure. Inuit social organization is "inclusional (that is, calculated to pull people in)," as Guemple (1988, 146) observes, providing everybody with both membership and obligation. The importance of being generous and being mutually responsible for each other prompt people to act in the community's interest. At the same time, the cultural values of humility and patience discourage people from assuming too much authority over others or acting simply to gain recognition and acclaim. The importance of these values is apparent in the Daughters of Mikak project in the outpouring of admiration towards the women who embody them. At last count, Labradorians and other Canadians have watched the Daughters of Mikak digital stories over 150,000 times, and have shared them hundreds of times. These women and the roles they play have a profound impact on Inuit society, and Labradorians have been enthusiastic in their appreciation.

The stories told by Nunatsiavummiut through this project differ in some respects from the stories traditionally told by anthropologists. Anthropological research on Inuit social organization and socialization has focused on the combination of *ilira* (fear) and *nalli* (love, nurturance) in developing *isuma* (the ability to be rational) in children (Briggs 1970; 1998). By teaching young children that the people around them could be both loving and aggressive, they learn to be careful, uneasy, and controlled in their relations with others. Anthropologists have given much attention to *ilira* (fear) as a central controlling influence on Inuit behavior, often with the observation that the effectiveness of these traditional means of social control has crumbled with colonialism (see, for instance, Condon 1992; Rasing 1994). This focus on *ilira* and conflict management emphasizes restrictive power and the role of cultural values in inhibiting and restraining social behavior. In contrast, the Daughters of Mikak highlight the role of *nalli* (love, nurturance) in inspiring behavior and community solidarity. The narratives have an unwavering focus on positive influences and on the role of cultural values that support and strengthen social behavior. In dealing with the disruptive impacts of colonialism, these Inuit leaders foster values that encourage rather than limit as they aim to create positive change.

At their core, the Daughters of Mikak stories describe the women's strength in counteracting the fragmenting effects of colonialism. In the face of social challenges that threaten to tear communities and families apart, these Inuit leaders build relationships with those around them. They champion kindness, patience, humility, and strength, and emphasize relationships and responsibility over individual recognition. Many demonstrate courage by speaking up against injustice, and all have a fierce commitment to their communities. They are admired for their capacity to both learn and teach. They have learned and developed by experiencing hard times, and now act as role models for those who are going through the same thing. As leaders in the struggle against colonialism, these women heal fractured relationships by both modeling strength and strengthening others.

One hundred years ago, at the time of the Spanish Flu, the common Inuktitut greeting used in Labrador for goodbye was *atsunai* (Erdmann 1864). The word's literal translation takes on a new meaning in light of this discussion on women's leadership – "be strong," people told each other: "*Atsunai*."

NOTES

1 Mikak was an 18th-century Inuit woman whose leadership in negotiating with the Moravian Mission in Labrador has had lasting impacts. See https://www.facebook.com/DaughtersofMikak/videos/1735593536673054/

2 See www.facebook.com/DaughtersofMikak/ to view and listen to the digital stories.

3 Fran Williams defines *KaKak* as "a way of showing your love to a baby or a child with words that describe how much you love them – mimicking, loving words."

REFERENCES

Archuleta, Michelle. 2012. "Approaching Leadership through Culture, Story, and Relationships." In *Living Indigenous Leadership: Native Narratives on Building Strong Communities*, edited by Carolyn Kenny and Tina Ngaroimata Fraser, 162–178. Vancouver, BC: University of British Columbia Press.

Bennett, John and Susan Rowley. 2004. *Uqalurait: An Oral History of Nunavut*. Montreal, QC: McGill-Queen's University Press.

Bodenhorn, Barbara. 1990. "'I'm Not the Great Hunter, My Wife Is': Inupiat and Anthropological Models of Gender." *Etudes/Inuit/Studies*, 14 (1–2): 55–74.

———. 2000. "'It's Good to Know Who Your Relatives Are, But We Were Taught to Share with Everybody': Shares and Sharing among Inupiaq Households." In *The Social Economy of Sharing: Resource Allocation and Modern Hunter-Gatherers*, edited by George W. Wenzel, Grete Hoversrud-Broda, and Nobuhiro Kishigamis, 27–60. Osaka: National Museum of Ethnology.

Brantenberg, Terje. 1977. "Ethnic Commitments and Local Government in Nain, 1969–1976." In *The White Arctic: Anthropological Essays on Tutelage and Ethnicity*, edited by Robert Paine, 376–410. St. John's, NL: ISER Books.

Briggs, Jean. 1970. *Never in Anger: Portrait of an Eskimo Family*. Cambridge: Harvard University Press.

———. 1974. "Eskimo Women: Makers of Men." In *Many Sisters: Women in Cross-Cultural Perspective*, edited by Carolyn Matthiasson, 261–304. London: Free Press.

———. 1998. *Inuit Morality Play: The Emotional Education of a Three-Year-Old*. St. John's, NL: ISER Books.

Brice-Bennett, Carol. 1981. *Two Opinions: Inuit and Moravian Missionaries in Labrador 1804–1860*. Masters thesis, Memorial University.

———. 1990. Missionaries as Traders: Moravians and Labrador Inuit, 1771–1860. In *Merchant Credit and Labour Strategies in Historical Perspective*, edited by E. Ommer, 223–236. Fredericton, NB: Acadiensis.

———. 2017. *Dispossessed: The Eviction of Inuit from Hebron, Labrador*. Montreal, QC: Isberg.

Budgell, Anne. 2018. *We All Expected to Die: Spanish Influenza in Labrador, 1918–1919*. St. John's, NL: ISER Books.

Condon, Richard. 1992. "Changing Patterns of Conflict Management and Aggression among Inuit Youth in the Canadian Arctic: Longitudinal Ethnographic Observations." *Native Studies Review* 8 (2): 35–49.

Damas, David. 2002. *Arctic Migrants/Arctic Villagers: The Transformation of Inuit Settlement in the Central Arctic*. Montreal, QC: McGill-Queen's University Press.

Daughters of Mikak Digital Stories. 2014–2015. *Tradition and Transition among the Labrador Inuit*. Social Sciences and Humanities Research Council. http://www.facebook.com/DaughtersofMikak/

Dombrowski, Kirk, Bilal Khan, Emily Channell, Joshua Moses, Kate McLean, and Evan Misshula. 2013. "Kinship, Family, and Exchange in a Labrador Inuit Community." *Arctic Anthropology*, 50 (1): 89–104. http://doi.org/10.3368/aa.50.1.89.

Erdmann, Freidrich. 1864. *Eskimoisches Wörterbuch [Inuit Dictionary], vol. 1*. Budissin: E.M. Monte.

Evans, Peter. 2013. *Transformations of Inuit Resistance and Identity in Northern Labrador, 1771–1959*. PhD dissertation, Cambridge University.

Guemple, Lee. 1988. "Teaching Social relations to Inuit Children." In *Hunters and Gatherers, vol. II: Property, Power and Ideology*, edited by Tim Ingold, David Riches, and James Woodburn, 131–149. Oxford: Berg.

Hudson, Amy. 2020. *Reclaiming Inuit Governance: Planning for a Sustainable Future in NunatuKavut*. PhD dissertation, Memorial University.

Jenness, Diamond. 1967. *Eskimo Administration, vol. III: Labrador*. Technical Paper No. 16. Calgary, AB: Arctic Institute of North America.

Kavanagh, Jacqueline. 2019. *A Long Wait for Change: Independent Review of Child Protection Services to Inuit Children in Newfoundland and Labrador*. St. John's, NL: Office of the Child and Youth Advocate.

Kleivan, Helge. 1966. *The Eskimos of Northeast Labrador: A History of Eskimo-White Relations 1771–1955*. Oslo: Norsk Polarinstitutt.

Maggo, Paulus. 1999. *Remembering the Years of My Life: Journeys of a Labrador Inuit Hunter*, edited by Carol Brice-Bennett. St. John's, NL: ISER Books.

McGrath, Robin. 1997. "Circumventing the Taboos: Inuit Women's Autobiographies." In *Undisciplined Women: Tradition and Culture in Canada*, edited by Pauline Greenville and Diane Tye, 223–233. Montreal, QC: McGill-Queen's University Press.

Peacock, Frederick William. 1963. "Local Government Among the Eskimos of Northern Labrador." Unpublished paper. Memorial University, Centre for Newfoundland Studies.

Pigeon, Michelle. 2012. "Transformation and Indigenous Interconnections: Indigeneity, Leadership, and Higher Education." In *Living Indigenous Leadership: Native Narratives on Building Strong Communities*, edited by Carolyn Kenny and Tina Ngaroimata Fraser, 136–149. Vancouver, BC: University of British Columbia Press.

Procter, Andrea. 2012. Nunatsiavut Land Claims and the Politics of Inuit Wildlife Harvesting. In: *Settlement, Subsistence, and Change among the Labrador Inuit*, edited by David Natcher, Lawrence Felt, and Andrea Procter. Pp. 189–208. Winnipeg, MB: University of Manitoba Press.

———. 2020. *A Long Journey: Residential Schools in Labrador and Newfoundland*. St. John's, NL: ISER Books.

Procter, Andrea and Keith Chaulk. 2013. "Our Beautiful Land: The Challenge of Nunatsiavut Land Use Planning." In: *Reclaiming Indigenous Planning*, edited by Ryan Walker, Ted Jojoba, and David Natcher, 436–453. Montreal, QC: McGill-Queen's University Press.

Rasing, Wim. 1994. *"Too Many People": Order and Nonconformity in Iglulingmiut Social Process*. Nijmegen: Katholieke Universiteit.

Riessman, Catherine Kohler. 2008. *Narrative Methods for the Human Sciences*. London: Sage Publications.

Smith, Linda Tuhiwai. 2012. *Decolonizing Methodologies: Research and Indigenous Peoples*, 2nd edition. London: Zed Books.

Steenhoven, Gert Van Den. 1962. *Leadership and Law among the Eskimos of the Keewatin District, Northwest Territories*. La Haye: Uitgeverij Excelsior.

Taylor, James Garth. 1968. *An Analysis of the Size of Eskimo Settlements on the Coast of Labrador during the Early Contact Period*. PhD dissertation, University of Toronto.

———. 1978. *Labrador Eskimo Settlements of the Early Contact Period*. Ottawa, ON: National Museum of Man.

Tuck, Eve, and K. Wayne Yang. 2014. "R-Words: Refusing Research." In *Humanizing Research: Decolonizing Qualitative Inquiry with Youth and Communities*, edited by Django Paris and Maisha Winn, 223–247. London: Sage.

Wenzel, George. 2000. "Sharing, Money, and Modern Inuit Subsistence." In *The Social Economy of Sharing: Resource Allocation and Modern Hunter-Gatherers*, edited by G. Wenzel, G. Hovelsrud-Broda, and N. Kishigami, 61–85. Osaka: National Museum of Ethnology.

CHAPTER 22

CHALLENGES FOR GREENLAND'S SOCIAL POLICIES

How we meet the call for social and political awareness

Steven Arnfjord

THE CURRENT STATE OF AFFAIRS

Greenland is a welfare society where the well-being of the citizens is both a public concern and a political priority. In this chapter, I argue that the nation's social and political focus needs tuning and adjustment to combat individualistic tendencies in Greenlandic society. Inspired by Mencher (1967), I distinguish between a welfare state and a welfare society. I conceptualize a welfare state as a political organization put in place to create a welfare society: a society that prioritizes social and humanitarian principles of universal help and resource distribution, as opposed to individualism and economic self-interest. When we listen to recent political speeches delivered at the opening of the Greenlandic parliament (Inatsisartut), or when we celebrate International Workers' Day on 1 May, the concept of welfare always comes up. In a 2019 speech, former Premier Kielsen said that he wanted Greenland to keep improving upon the welfare of its citizens (Redaktionen 2019). But, what Kielsen calls improving citizen welfare is not the same as maintaining a welfare *society* that evolves from a welfare state[1] (Robertson 1988). Harold Wilensky once posed the question: "How does a welfare state, go about creating a welfare society?" (Wilensky 1975).

In this chapter, I discuss this question in the context of Greenland, beginning with a quick survey of the Greenlandic welfare society. Greenland has a universal healthcare system. This system includes medicine and dentistry as well as more complicated medical procedures that are handled by the Rigshospitalet in Denmark. In the cities, there are several hospitals, and in some smaller towns, there are health clinics. The clinics and hospitals are operated by a staff of nursing assistants, nurses, and doctors. For the most part, nursing professionals are trained in Greenland, and the doctors are trained in Denmark. There is a long tradition of importing Danish professionals to fill positions that have been vacant for a long time. Greenland does not have an abundance of health care professionals; nowadays, few countries do. Therefore, it is not unusual to see many seasonal Danish workers during June, July, and August. The health care system has a budget of 1.5 billion Danish Kr (US $200 million), with around 6–7 percent (US $14 million) spent on transportation alone (Grønlands Selvstyre 2019).

When it comes to social services, Greenland has a welfare system with tax-financed pensions, childcare, maternity leave, and other social supports, such as housing costs subsidies and rent-controlled public housing.

The educational system is likewise publicly financed from kindergarten all the way through graduate school. In addition to free education, the country provides a stipend to students above the age of 18. It also supplies them with inexpensive student dorms that are heavily subsidized.

To finance these expenses, Greenlanders pay taxes amounting to nearly 50 percent of their incomes. These include the general state and municipal taxes (approximately 42 percent) as well as automobile taxes and other fees. Greenlanders accept this high level of taxation, which has been consistent since the 1990s. It is rarely a subject of discussion, and unlike other jurisdictions, tax rates, and taxation are generally not political issues. On this matter, Greenlanders are aligned with the Danes, who, in large part, consider themselves to be happy taxpayers.

So far, we have established that Greenland is a welfare state in the sense that it is a political order that focuses on maintaining a universal welfare system based on democratic citizen rights. Greenland's population and the Greenlandic political body consider it a public responsibility, a "state-like" responsibility to care for its citizens. In that respect, Greenland has only a few privatized care institutions in the form of a few private kindergartens and one private school. The rest is a public matter from cradle to coffin. Greenland is, however, seeing a small rise in private health insurance for services received in Denmark. Thus far, private health insurance is only for the middle and upper classes.

In this chapter, I report on the main social issues in Greenland. When it comes to social issues, Greenland looks to Denmark to understand and compare the development of education level, life expectancy, general health, and other social issues. I elaborate on this below, through a discussion of the historical development of the Greenlandic welfare state over 50 years.

I discuss the Greenlandic welfare state from a perspective that considers that the majority of the challenges to current welfare policy are manageable. I do not claim to have the solution to Greenland's social worries. But I do claim from a critical perspective that the issues Greenland is facing could be improved through responsible social policies and research that goes beyond monitoring the current state of social affairs. From a shortage of affordable housing, a high suicide rate, increasing rates of poverty, and rising unemployment in remote towns, Greenland is facing problems that have solutions. We will return to this later after we have gone over the key themes in the Greenlandic welfare state.

SOCIAL POLICY AREAS

Core social policy themes in Greenland typically include social security, labor market policies, housing, healthcare, pensions, disabilities, and childcare. Sometimes one can locate education in the mix as well. Education has a monumental effect on the well-being of a country's citizens. The OECD has documented how education plays a significant role in promoting welfare and social progress (OECD Publishing 2010). However, education is not a standalone solution; it requires healthy communities and engaged families in order to work on an overall level (OECD Publishing 2010).

In Greenland, creating free and easy access to education for all citizens has been a priority. Education is universal and free all the way to master's-level studies. In this section, I briefly cover the core social policy themes mentioned above.

SOCIAL SECURITY

A social safety net is at the core of a welfare society. In Greenland the official concept is "public help" and consists of economic support together with rent control and other subsidies. It helps insure citizens under circumstances where they cannot provide for themselves. In Greenland, like most other welfare societies, assistance varies upon evaluations of need, including considerations such as whether a recipient has dependents or a spouse.

We see a significant variation in payouts from people receiving close to 8,000 Dkr. (US $1200) to 1350 Dkr (US $200) per month. Figure 22.1 shows the number of people receiving "public help" between 2015 and 2018. The graph shows a decline in people receiving "public help." This positive trend is due to a corresponding drop in unemployment (see Figure 22.2).

The two graphs look almost identical. The drop in recipients of "social help" corresponds with an increase in people entering or returning to the labor market. Other factors include some recipients of social help leaving Greenland, and some retiring as pensioners.

HOUSING

Housing is an essential aspect of social policy. By international convention, all humans are entitled to housing, and governments should provide their citizens with ample housing, as noted in the Universal Declaration of Human Rights, Article 25:

> Everyone has the right to a standard of living adequate for the health and well-being of himself and of his family, including food, clothing, housing.

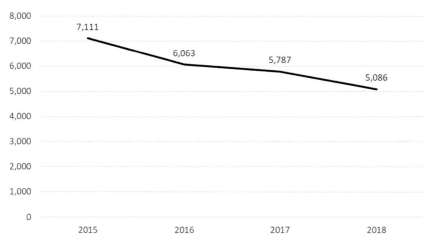

Figure 22.1 Number of people nationwide receiving "public help," 2015–2018. Greenland Statistics.

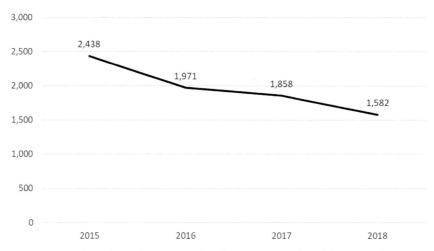

Figure 22.2 Number of people nationwide who were unemployed for more than a month, 2015–2018. Greenland Statistics.

Land is not privately owned in Greenland. Officially, it is the people's land. When one buys a property, they are purchasing only the structure, while the land on which it sits remains public land that has been allotted to the buyer through the land use and planning act. The act is primarily set up to protect the natural environment and ensure a socially responsible distribution of land and man-made installations. During the early-20th century, many Greenlanders transitioned from traditional stone huts, replacing them with prefabricated kit houses that they purchased by mail-order from Denmark and constructed themselves. The transition followed recommendations from a sanitary committee in 1947 and subsequent legislation in the national congress (Landsråd) which initiated the first real housing act. The legislation stated that the construction of housing required approval from a public planning board (Ministeriet for Grønland 1953 nr.3, p.114). Housing was, thus, transformed from a necessity to a commodity that was firstly approved and then owned. The transformation reflected the capitalization and bureaucratization of housing during the "modernization" of Greenland. This development drastically changed the housing situation from traditional houses to more modern homes, which, for the most part, still stand. In the 1950s and 1960s, we saw large steps towards population concentration brought about by forced re-settlements. During this period result of rapid modernization, many brutalist-style apartment blocks were built (see Figure 22.3).

Whereas the apartment-style housing of the earlier period was intended to modernize and equalize, the housing market today is informed by different parameters rooted in capitalism and less concerned with eliminating economic disparity. Mortgage loans are available only in Nuuk, Sisimiut, Ilulissat, and Qaqortoq, cities in which the banking sector believes that houses will maintain or increase their value. It also clearly signals the capitalist view of where future developmental areas are located in Greenland. The vast majority of public housing stock is administered by an organization called INI (Greenlandic for "room"), which administers the national housing stock. In Nuuk, ISERIT is the public housing administration. Housing is a widely discussed and heavily regulated area in Greenland. In Nuuk, which is the administrative and educational hub, house prices are soaring, making it very expensive to buy a house even though it sits on public land. The waiting list for citizens wishing to rent through INI in Nuuk is 15–20 years, and one cannot get onto the list until after the age of 18.

Nuuk is currently seeing a huge increase in new housing construction. The regional municipality of Sermersooq, of which Nuuk is the largest city, has laid out an aggressive new city expansion plan called Siorarsiorfik, which anticipates that Nuuk will be home to 30,000 inhabitants by 2030 – a 62 percent increase from the current population of 18,500 inhabitants. Yet the population of Greenland is not growing. The implication is that this increase in urban population will entail a widespread and vast depopulation of smaller cities and towns. Despite this building boom, homelessness is becoming a serious problem. Homelessness is a new phenomenon in Greenland, and affects all segments of the population – men, women, youth, and families (Christensen, Arnfjord, and Aastrup forthcoming). No legislation exists around emergency housing, transitional housing, or homelessness, leaving local municipalities to deal with these issues without any legislation.

Figure 22.3   Older apartment housing in Nuuk. Photo: Frank Sejersen.

HEALTHCARE

Healthcare is universal and covers every aspect of health from birth to old age, including medicine, cancer treatment, and dentistry. There are two private dentists in Greenland, both located in Nuuk. A small part of the population has purchased private health insurance that covers them when they are in Denmark. Greenlandic health standards are monitored closely in national surveys every four years. Over the past 20 years, healthcare and prevention programs have been handled by the ministry of health within the area of public health. Greenland has national health programs called Inuuneritta, which aim to keep the population of Greenland healthy. There are public health concerns around the birth rates and the abortion rate, which have remained at similar levels since the start of this century (Bjerregaard 2001). From a social policy perspective, the population is not growing but it is aging. And aging population is an international trend, but according to Grønlands Økonomiske Råd (Greenland's Economic Council) (2020), this trend will place significant strains on the national budget and the welfare state when the population begins to exit the labor market in high numbers.

Greenland is still dealing with some tuberculosis, but has a rather low level of sexually transmitted diseases (STDs). HIV/AIDS was a problem in the 1980s and 1990s, but now there are only few cases every other year. Suicide has been at an alarmingly high rate for decades. Greenland sees, on average, 47 suicides per year (82 per 100,000 people), one of the highest rates in the world. Suicide is mainly discussed as a public health concern. Health perspectives have previously focused on professionalizing help and supporting the individual through counseling, helplines, and individualized therapy, as well as focusing on family dynamics (Lynge and Bjerregaard 2000; Naalakkersuisut 2013). This focus on the individual has not produced any statistically significant change to the high level of suicide. A socially oriented approach as an alternative to the individualistic focus has had promising results in Finland (Upanne 2002) and northern Canada (Burke 2018; Kral 2019). Similar to other western societies, there is a clear correlation between health and educational levels in Greenland. A large public health study showed a correlation between smoking and obesity and educational levels (Bjerregaard, Dahl-Petersen and Larsen 2018). This underlines the importance of collaborations between social and public health policymakers for ensuring a healthy and educated population.

DISABILITIES

This policy area is one in which Greenland is getting more active. It used to be the case that most people with disabilities were cared for in central institutions that were not specialized, and a significant number of people were sent to Denmark for care. In 2016, an advocacy institution for people with disabilities (Tilioq) was created. Tilioq is responsible for monitoring and promoting the rights of people with disabilities. Presently, they are in the process of examining the public perceptions of people with disabilities.

Greenland has a rather high number of people who are on disability leave. While the country's ability to provide for people in this category is viewed positively, there is also a risk of people being permanently reliant on a fixed income. Disability allowances may be disempowering in the long term, and there are several public health issues that are connected with receiving passive benefits such as disability benefits. This area is important to monitor because this group historically has been hidden away. The political class is not accustomed to listening to them. The prime function of Tilioq is to listen and advocate on the behalf of people with disabilities as an overlooked group in society.

POVERTY

Living in economic poverty is understood as having lived for three years on an income that is 50 percent of the median income. In recent years, median income has risen as shown in Table 22.1.

In 2018, the poverty rate was 78,635 Dkr, 50 percent of the median income. The rise in median income means that the poverty rate is also rising. This seeming paradox is a result of growing income inequality driven by the concentration of employment in a few urban centers.

As Figure 22.4 shows, some parts of Greenland are prospering. Nuuk and Ilulissat are experiencing falling unemployment and rising income levels, while other cities such as Nanortalik and Tasiilaq are struggling with low income and high levels of unemployment.

Members of one of Greenland's largest political parties, Siumut, have argued that the country cannot operate with a definition of poverty derived from Europe because the situation in Greenland is very different from that in Europe. In particular, they argue that Greenlanders have easy access to food from hunting (Hussain 2013; Netredaktionen 2007). This argument ignores that hunting is itself expensive. It requires ammunition, fuel for a boat, or food for the sled dogs, and these expenses are hard to meet with a monthly income below 6,553 Dkr. Historically, as with Inuit elsewhere, meat and fish were distributed by sharing (Daugaard-Jensen 1911), but there was no centralized distribution system that could protect local groups from starvation in periods of unproductive hunting. Sharing still exists among hunting families, but it cannot take the place of centralized social welfare programs which ensure welfare distribution among citizens. A welfare model rests on bureaucratic principles of even treatment and transparency in the decision-making process. Nonetheless, the current model is borrowed directly from Denmark without consideration of its cultural appropriateness for an Arctic country with an Indigenous population.

Greenland's broad social safety net has not fully alleviated social problems, as reflected in the low birth rate, the high unemployment rate in remote towns, and the rising percentage of Greenlanders living below the poverty line. The increase in poverty, in particular, suggests that the gaps in the safety net are large. Some families,

Table 22.1 Median annual income, 2014–2018

	2014	2016	2018
Median annual income in DKr.	137,220	151,744	157,271

Source: Greenland Statistics

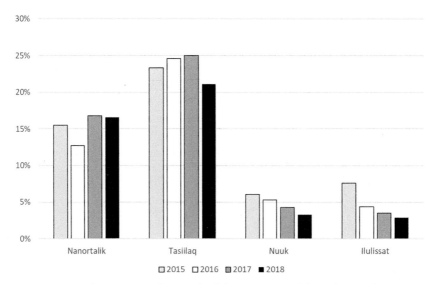

Figure 22.4   Unemployment rate for Nuuk, Ilulissat, Nanortalik, and Taasiilaq, 2015–2018. Source: Greenland Statistics.

for instance, are not able to survive on public benefits (Brøns 2020; Egede 2009; Schnohr, Nielsen and Wulff 2007). If Greenland is to preserve its "welfare society," the political leadership must make changes to the welfare system to make sure it reaches the target groups. While some politicians may regard current social problems as rooted in colonial history, it is essential to recognize that Greenland has had full authority over its social policies for the past 50 years.

In the next section, I present a brief overview of Greenland's socio-political history.[2] Understanding decisions made in the past might help us learn from them and gain a sounder understanding of future social and institutional planning.

A SHORT HISTORY OF GREENLANDIC SOCIAL POLICY

Colonialism is not always a clear-cut case of white rule over an Indigenous population. When looking back on Greenlandic social history, it is usually understood that Greenland moved towards semiautonomous governance with the Home Rule Act in 1979. While it is correct that the Home Rule Act stipulated sovereignty in areas such as education and social policy, Greenlanders had already been able to make independent social policy decisions since 1968, eleven years before Home Rule. In theory, Greenlanders were part of the decision-making process as early as 1850 via the local administrative boards which consisted of Danish members such as a priest, a colonial administrator, a doctor, and an assistant from the colonial administration. The Greenlandic members were elected by the people. Greenlandic historian Jens Heinrich (2012) showed that the Danish government sought approval of the Greenland National Congress before proposing that Greenland be incorporated as a province of Denmark in 1953. The National Congress consisted of elected members, most of whom were prosperous Greenlandic men from the ruling class. Heinrich's work brought nuance to classical post-colonial analysis, moving beyond a dichotomous analysis of colonial power versus powerlessness (Bonfil Batalla 1996; Memmi 1991). Post-colonial theory presents very valuable analytical aspects of colonial history. However, if only that theoretical aspect is used to understand history in Greenland, we run the risk of overshadowing cleavages within the Greenlandic population, such as class differences.

SETTING UP LOCAL ADMINISTRATIVE BOARDS

The Danish Rigsdagen organized Greenland into municipalities in 1908 (Rigsdagen 1908, 4239). Before this, in 1856, the idea of *forstanderskaberne* (local administrative boards)[3] was introduced by Heinrich J. Rink, Samuel Kleinschmidt, Jacob Lindorff, and Carl Janssen, directors of Greenland who had been appointed by the Danish King. Rink, who initially trained as a geologist, wrote about social issues, which he observed while working in Greenland (Rink 1877). I have categorized him as a humanist and a stark opponent to the then prevailing degrading attitudes toward Greenlanders. Rink was the most senior colonial official during a period when the population of around 10,000 faced high rates in child mortality and periods of hunger in some communities. Rink told of an episode in which he was conducting an inspection and came across a family that had run out of supplies, and had lost children to hunger. He provided an early description of what we would today call stratification, both concerning securing enough supplies for families to survive but also concerning what Rink more directly called lazy hunters or hunters with poor hunting skills (Rink 1884). Rink's analysis did not attempt to romanticize hunting culture. His goal was to obtain a mandate to establish procedures to intervene in the social system (Rink 1857). The focus of this pre-municipal administrative organ was to ensure some measure of social security when hunger struck, when children were at risk of losing their families, or when families had elderly family members for whom they could not provide.

MUNICIPALITIES

While the local administrative boards functioned in some areas, they were also criticized for not being democratic enough. Social services did not always reach the parts of Greenland where the needs were highest. The *forstanderskaber* relied on groups of appointed Greenlandic officials whose job it was to patrol their districts and see to it that people received care. The officials were respected male hunters without any formal training scattered all over what was then called the southern and northern districts of Greenland.[4]

In this process, we observe the beginning of the governmental social organizations of Greenland. At the time, although Greenland did have the *forstanderskaber*, the majority of important decisions were made in Denmark at the Ministry of Greenland. This was understood as a very unsatisfactory arrangement, and was extensively criticized: How could informed decisions be made from 3,500 kilometers away? A more localized decision-making body was needed.

The early initiatives, such as the municipalities, were predominantly Danish. To some degree, the imported social system fit the Greenlandic context because of the

Scandinavian emphasis on solidarity and the already well-established practice of income redistribution that resembled the Greenlandic cultural practice of distributing/sharing the hunt.

This is a clear example of how a formerly colonized country does not get the opportunity to develop its own welfare system. Robert Paine wrote about welfare colonialism in Canada's Northwest Territories, where local communities were excluded from participating in the decision-making process of setting up a system of welfare (Paine 1977). Welfare colonialism is an appropriate way of describing what took place in Greenland during Rink's tenure. Greenlanders did participate in aspects of the decision-making process, and also participated in implementing decisions made by the local administrative councils. However, the governing structure itself was approved in Denmark.

During the early 1900s, a municipal structure for Greenland was discussed in Denmark and later sent to a vote in Greenland. After some amendments to the proposal text, it was enacted in 1911 with little debate.[5] By today's standards, the text itself is filled with racist and paternalistic claims. When we read past that, they ended up deciding to create 62 municipalities. At the time the Greenlandic population consisted of 11,000 people. To make the colonial relation very clear, the law, translated into English, was called "The law about the ruling of the colonies in Greenland from 1908." These were local assemblies for which members of one of the 62 now municipal communities could seek election, provided they were male and respected members of society.

A central statement from the Danish Rigsdagen[6] said:

> When seeking self-rule in Greenland, it will be about putting the responsibility into the institutions up there such as the municipal council and the country council, but also the administration, to equip them with a capacity to work independently and reform the country on their own, the social division up there. The majority, therefore, finds that it would be unjust to create legislation that is too strong and underline that which we think should follow as a development.

The key agenda of the municipality system was to strengthen the bureaucracy around social welfare and social help. The law distinguished between benefits and poverty assistance. The latter is very close to what the Europeans at the time understood as poor laws.

A NEW ADMINISTRATION, 1925–1945

In 1919, the Danish Ministry of Interior Affairs set up a commission to revise the 1908/1911 law (Indenrigsministeriet 1924). The committee consisted of 23 members, of which only a handful were from Greenland. It was chaired by the former inspector of Greenland, Jens Daugaard-Jensen. At the time, Daugaard-Jensen was the director of the Board of Colonies in Greenland. The purpose of the new 1925 law was that Greenland should be prepared for a more open connection to the outside world, including more open trade. There was also a focus on education and the need to attract Danish teachers to Greenland (Sveistrup 1953).

In the 20 years leading up to the end of the Second World War, the new law of the administration of Greenland set in motion an administrative body called Sysselråd. These were administrative councils with a wide range of powers to offer help, including loans for housing, business supplies, hunting supplies, disability services to the blind and deaf, and pensions. The Sysselråd also supervised the church and schools. A key social policy text from this period is Knud Oldendows *Social forsorg i Grønland* (*Social Care in Greenland*) from 1930. Oldendow provided a future-oriented outline of the country's social history from a colonial administrative perspective. He compared the course of Greenlandic welfare with European social welfare, which is based on the various poor laws that emerged in the 18th century (Oldendow 1930).

G50/G60

From a social policy perspective, three drastic events happened after World War II. Denmark signed the declaration of the United Nations (UN), Greenland was enrolled as a formal region within the state of Denmark, and the Greenlandic commissions called G50 and G60 were put in effect.

By signing the United Nations declaration in 1945, Denmark promised that it would honor all chapters in the UN Charter, including Chapter 11, titled "Declaration regarding non-self-governing territories." This chapter addresses the responsibility of countries with colonies to ensure a long list of rights within their colonies, and to demonstrate due respect for the cultures of the peoples concerned, as well as their political, economic, social, and educational advancement. Additionally, this chapter addresses the responsibility to develop self-government and report regularly to the UN on these conditions (United Nations 1945). Chapter 12 of the charter includes a subparagraph, which discusses ensuring equal treatment in social, economic, and commercial matters.

On a fundamental level, this was interpreted as the Danish state's responsibility to equalize the level of well-being throughout the Kingdom of Denmark. The Danish administration had discussed this before, and I do not believe that they intended to deviate from that plan. But well-being is one thing, and cultural respect and protection are something else entirely. Thinking back to Chapter 11 of the Declaration, critical historians have suggested that the requirement to report regularly to the UN pushed Denmark to suggest that Greenland be made a full county within the Danish state (Kjær Sørensen 1983).

What followed were two distinct processes. The Danish administration, along with a select group of Greenlandic representatives, were joined in what was called the Greenlandic Commission of 1948 (Grønlandskommissionen 1950), abbreviated to G50. The general focus of G50 was to improve Greenland's commercial independence and overall economy and health. G50 had a vast impact on infrastructure. The Danish administration built ports for fishing boats. By this time, the majority of Greenlandic men were engaged in the fishery and the fishing industry. The country also saw improvements in general infrastructure, sanitation, and new hospitals. At the same time, it witnessed the forceful closure of settlements and forced relocations of residents, with a devastating effect on local communities and the national culture.

People began to feel a rapid transformation of society and a transformation that they, in general, did not think that they had chosen (Goldschmidt 1964; Udvalget vedrørende Grønlandske Kvinder 1975).

The Commission of 1964 focused on education and language (Grønlandsudvalget af 1960 1964), abbreviated to G60. Denmark's imposition of the Danish language onto Greenland has been widely discussed, and the evidence indeed seems to point in that direction. There were Greenlandic academics in the decision-making process, and plans were made to convert the language of instruction from Greenlandic to Danish (Lynge 1977, 2009). Parents were encouraged to let their children speak Danish, a language with which most parents were not familiar.

In the same period, the Danish government set out plans to experiment on an elite group of school children. A small, select group was sent to Denmark to learn Danish culture and language. The result was very negative, and the event is regarded as state kidnapping and a dark moment of Danish colonization. Even though the general understanding is that Greenland ceased to be a colony after 1953, this experiment was textbook colonial behavior in that it assumed that Greenlanders would simply become Danes. The period of G50 and G60 is in general looked on very critically, and rightfully so. There have been outspoken critics in many fields, including politicians such as Aqqaluk Lynge, and political artists such as Aka Høegh and Anne-Birthe Hove. Political parties such as Siumut and Inuit Ataqatigiit ran their first campaigns that were critical of decisions made in the 1950s and 1960s (Lynge 1993, 2002; Viemose 1977).

Until recently, few historians have paid attention to what else was going on during that time. A number of social transformations took place, concerning social help, housing policies, and an overall need for a more fine-tuned social administration. Landsrådet (the Greenlandic National Council) put in motion plans to employ a professional social worker (Atuagagdliutit 1955; Ministeriet for Grønland 1957). When, for economic reasons, that did not get resolved, plans were made to institute a social work education, with the aim to educate Greenlandic social workers who spoke Greenlandic and could connect with clients on an equal level.

Another key moment was the establishment and centralization of the country's social administration. By the mid-1950s, a new form of public servant emerged, the kæmner (city treasurer; in practice, municipal director). The kæmner resembled contemporary municipal directors: an unelected bureaucrat who was responsible for overseeing social services such as public help (unemployment subsidies, family allowance), care of children in need, and pensions. The kæmner deferred to a local welfare committee (*forsorgsudvalg*) that consisted of municipal elected members all working full-time jobs. The local welfare committee deferred to a national council. In order to further improve upon the welfare state, the Danish State and the Greenlandic National Council decided that a more centralized social administration was necessary, one that connected the social administration on a local community level and referred it to a national level. Therefore, the Office of Social and Labor Affairs was created in 1968 (Ministeriet for Grønland 1968 no. 2b, appendix 56). In practice the Office of Social and Labor Affairs functioned as Greenland's ministry of social affairs until the area of social affairs was formally transferred to Greenland through the Home Rule Act.

HOME RULE, 1979

The signing of the Home Rule Act is rightly celebrated as a significant event in the political history of Greenlanders and of Indigenous peoples globally. Greenlanders were the first arctic Indigenous people to achieve authority for nationwide domestic governance. Indigenous self-government processes occured much later in other parts of the circumpolar north, and none have been quite as sweeping as the governmental authority that was transferred to Greenlanders with Home Rule in 1979 and with the Self Rule Act in 2009. The historic nature of this achievement by an Indigenous people overshadowed other events, and thus little scholarly attention has been paid to the social needs in Greenland at the time. Although welfare policies were a substantial part of the Home Rule Act, there were few negotiations around these themes. Welfare was understood as an area that had been settled long before Home Rule itself. The first order of business from a sociopolitical perspective was the establishment of Greenland's first social commission, which was mandated to analyze what areas needed coverage in terms of social policies, and to create legislation for social policies.

Below, I briefly summarize the content of the three commissions that have been conducted to date.

THE FIRST SOCIAL REFORM COMMISSION IN 1980

The first commission was created with the purpose of creating Greenland's first social policy (Chemnitz 1980). The recommendations from the commission were used to create social legislation and establish a Greenlandic-run welfare state. The first commission consisted of iconic figures like Sofus Joelsen, who was a Greenlandic director of social services from Qaanaaq (Thule). Even more iconic was the south Greenland politician and women's rights activist Agnethe Nielsen, who worked together with other elected members and a few Danes working for Greenland, including the doctor Jørgen Bøggild. The commission had a big job to do. It had to create a full proposal for Greenland's first social policies while simultaneously trying to modernize perceptions of social policy and social administration. The commission was given a clear mandate from the Home Rule government to focus on areas such as children and youth, social benefits, worker's compensation, the elderly, and disabilities and housing (Socialreformkommissionen 1981). A year after the commission's report was published, the first outcomes emerged. A wide range of new welfare laws were passed in the Greenlandic parliament. The new legislation covered pensions, child support (alimony), public help (unemployment subsidies), and social help aimed at children and youth: all themes that the commission of 1980 worked on directly. In addition, the commission emphasized the importance of a more professionalized social administration in municipalities. To this end, the commission strongly underlined the importance of increasing social services, proposing a shift from social services based on objective criteria to more subjective criteria (their wording). This shift would secure a more even distribution of social services, and instill a more active approach to social service, rather than a passive support system. Other proposals included: creating an independent social review board, creating legislation that would differentiate between rights-based and needs-based help, and increasing preventive social work with children and families. The commission also stated that in order to achieve a more smoothly run social service system, more Greenland-educated social workers were needed. The commission's suggestions constituted the first Greenlandic take on social policies, offering a democratic perspective that aimed to improve the collective welfare of citizens of Greenland. In its closing statement, the commission wrote:

> Great emphasis has been placed on the fact that the proposals are expected to significantly improve conditions for the disadvantaged. The Commission considers it essential that a social reform will also lead to a better quality of life. (...) Further work should be made on proposals with a view to changes to the safety net and the services that can be made available to the population by the social services.
>
> (Socialreformkommissionen 1981, 213)[7]

During the same period, Greenland created social work education as part of Ilinniarfissiaq (Teacher Training College), which was initially a teacher training college but came to function as a college of teachers, preschool teachers, and social workers. The first class of social workers graduated in 1988. Previously, Greenlandic social workers and political icons like Aqqaluk Lynge, Martha Labansen, Kuupik Kleist, and Asii Chemnitz Narup had traveled to Denmark to train as social workers. Their educational training in Denmark may have played a part in maintaining the idea of Greenland as a welfare nation built on the model of rights-based universal benefits. All returned home and worked as either public servants or teachers, and many eventually sought careers in politics.

THE COMMISSION OF 1996

The second commission was formed during a complicated and turbulent time in Greenlandic political life. The country was facing a severe economic crisis and was dealing with issues of political corruption.

Like the first commission, the commission of 1996 was comprised of political leaders. However, it made little change to social policy. The main mandate was to look at policies regarding the elderly and the disabled, even though the overall understanding was that a vast modernization of social policies was needed to update legislation that was over 15 years old (Grønland Hjemmestyre 1997). The commission of 1996 did not fully succeed with either policy revisions or the much-needed improvement of social policy areas such as economic welfare services (unemployment subsidies, rent subsidies, family allowance, and updated pension system), or children's welfare. Nor did it achieve a restructuring of the public administration in order to simplify rules, legislation, and casework. It did make a number of recommendations however: revising the former passive unemployment subsidies (welfare) to a more workfare oriented approach; including more educated personnel within nursing homes; increasing child services through better-educated personnel; achieving closer cooperation between different public social organizations working on children and family issues; and implementing wholesale and cross-sectional solutions to benefit parents, schools and daycare institutions. When we compare the Greenlandic trends in the mid-1990s with neoliberal policies like activation and workfare orientation, Greenland followed paths similar to Canada and Scandinavia.

The commission report of 1996 contained political focus statements like: "[we need to] ensure a basic minimum subsistence for all who are seeking help." The previous prophylactic philosophies seem to have disappeared. The statement continues in the following: "The help shouldn't be so high that the families' current living standard could be maintained" (Grønland Hjemmestyre 1997). It signals that if a family runs into misfortune, it should have to experience that misfortune to some degree, and it is not the public's role to lift the family up to its previous standard of living. The commission basically outline an idea of the undeserving. In that sense, the commission of 1996 was something of a contradiction: understanding individuals to be responsible for lifting themselves out of the need for social security. This understanding, in fact, correlates with older understandings of the European poor laws (Dean 2019) which conceptualized poverty as a personal issue rather than a public responsibility. To a certain extent, Greenland is caught in a paradox between a governmental focus on maintaining a welfare system, and popular attitudes that consider individuals experiencing hardship to be at fault (Greenlandic Red Cross 2018). Some of the conclusions in the second social reform commission of 1996 correlate with values dating back to early colonial times, when poor law legislation included passages stating that individuals labeled as "lazy" should only receive the bare minimum. The second commission thus went against the trend in Scandinavia at the time, of trying to integrate people back into society and increasing levels of welfare services (Petersen, Petersen and Christiansen 2014).

During the end of the 1990s, the minister of social affairs, Benedicte Thorsteinsson, was relieved of his office. Thorsteinsson had issued the commission report from 1996 as a tool for how to improve different welfare areas, but very little work was accomplished in terms of creating new social legislation or updating on the suggestions made in the report. It was a long time before Greenland saw a politician who held the office of social affairs for a prolonged time. This turnover affected the general development of Greenland's social policies, delaying new legislation around child protection, pensions, and early retirement. A low level of social and political focus created an atmosphere where issues around child and family welfare were dealt with reactively. Things changed in the early 2000s with more proactive strategies towards teenage pregnancy (Hansen and Skafte 2009) and the creation of the spokesperson for children's rights: MiO. The institution continues to produce policy reports on children's well-being (Børnerettighedsinstitutionen MIO 2014). However more work still needs to be done when it comes to adults and the elderly.

THE PROFESSIONALIZED SOCIAL COMMISSION IN 2011

With the latest commission, the self-rule government chose to combine the tax reform and social reform commissions into one joint "welfare and tax commission." The commission was also professionalized with a professor of economics as the head. The professor was Danish, a circumstance that would have been unthinkable in Denmark: having a non-resident lead something as critical and influential as a welfare and tax commission. The idea of a professionalized commission was recently proposed by politicians to achieve more speedy processes and less public mistrust (Schultz-Nielsen

2019). The commission was technocratic by design and operated at arm's length from the political system. In recent years, this has been the trend, informing the establishment of the Greenlandic Fishery Commission, the Economic Council, and the health commission in 2020 (Naalakkersuisut 2020). This has shifted the discussion of the councils and commissions from politics to academic discretions around the core assignment of the commissions. The report from the welfare and tax commission echoes an economic understanding of social policy. The fundamental takeaway from the vast and comprehensive report, titled *Vores velstand og velfærd – kræver handling nu* (*Our Wealth and Welfare – Demands Action Now*), was affordability and public economic responsibility. The commission concluded with the goal that "as many as possible provide for themselves and contribute to the development of the society." It stated that maintaining the status quo was not a sustainable economic option (in terms of the tax level, welfare level, health level, and proportion of the population employed in the public sector) (Skatte- og Velfærdskommissionens betækning 2011, 14).

MEETING THE CALL FOR MORE SOCIAL-POLITICAL AWARENESS

A shortage of affordable housing, a high suicide rate, an increase in poverty levels, rising unemployment rates in remote towns – these are social issues that can be countered. The issues need to be addressed by clear political strategies and action plans. The statistical data suggests that these issues will grow worse if left unaddressed. If Greenland is to avoid further individualistic tendencies and keep moving on a path towards a healthy welfare society, then we need to see social policies and political action on both a national and a municipal level. At the time of writing, only one out of Greenland's five municipalities has formulated a social policy on the community level. But community-level social policies are important to create dynamics within the bureaucracy as mentioned above, and also to connect visions of Greenland's social policies with the everyday realpolitik.

As an overall plan Greenland can start dealing with these challenges by formulating social policies on a national level.

A change to future social policies in Greenland is no easy task. We are still seeing remnants of a colonial understanding of welfare. Still, conditions such as social history, different social needs, and political understandings of the purpose of a welfare society, change when transferred across the North Sea and the Atlantic. So, to meet the call and create policies that address the needs of the public, a central challenge for the Greenlandic government is to create a Greenlandic understanding of welfare. It will have to be a political strategy in order for the public to hold the leaders accountable for creating a social system that is true to the label "welfare society." This is a call for politicians to get to work on developing culturally appropriate Greenlandic social policies.

NOTES

1 When I write about the Greenlandic welfare state, the readers should bear in mind that I do not refer to Greenland in general as a state – it is still a semi-autonomous part of the Kingdom of Denmark, to which the concept of a nation-state is ascribed. Still, for

simplified reasons, I refer to the Greenlandic governments, and its dispositions as acts one would combine with a welfare state. In this chapter, I will also distinguish between the welfare state (Greenlandic political body/ruling body) and its ability to supply welfare for the people in Greenland.

2 A more detailed treatment can be found in Arnfjord (2017a, 2017b).
3 *Forstanderskaber* doesn't translate to English. The historian Søren Rud uses the phrase "local boards" (Rud 2018). I have added administrative to the translation to emphasize that the boards were a stepping stone to the current municipal boards.
4 In this historical summary, the east is not covered; for that, I apologize. It is due to the fact that East Greenland was ruled partly by Denmark and, to a small degree by Norway until 1967 (Perry and Arnfjord 2019).
5 Some historians say that the year is 1908. Both are correct; I choose to refer to later date because that is the year that the law came into practical use.
6 The name for the parliament of Denmark just after the Danish monarchy ended in 1848 and before *Folketinget* became the official name of the parliament in 1953.
7 Author's translation from Danish.

REFERENCES

Arnfjord, Steven. 2017a. "50 År Med Socialadministration Og Socialfaglighed: 2. Del – Socialpolitik, Kommissioner Og Socialrådgivere Med BA. [50 Years of Social Administration and Social Professionalism: Part 2 – Social Policy, Commissions and Social Workers with BA.]" *Tidsskriftet Grønland* 65 (4).

———. 2017b. "50 År Med Socialadministration Og Socialfaglighed– Del 1. [50 Years of Social Administration and Social Professionalism: Part 1]" *Tidsskriftet Grønland* 65 (2).

Atuagagdliutit. 1955. "Fra 'Droning Ingrids Sanatorium.' [From 'Queen Ingrid's Sanatorium]" *Atuagagdliutit*, February.

Bjerregaard, Peter, ed. 2001. "Abort i Grønland. [Abortion in Greenland]" *INUSSUK Arktisk Forskningsjournal*, 2.

Bjerregaard, Peter, Inger Katrine Dahl-Petersen, and Christina Viskum Lytken Larsen. 2018. "Measuring Social Inequality in Health amongst Indigenous Peoples in the Arctic. A Comparison of Different Indicators of Social Disparity among the Inuit in Greenland." *SSM Population Health* 6: 149–57. http://doi.org/10.1016/j.ssmph.2018.08.010.

Bonfil Batalla, Guillermo. 1996. *Mexico Profundo: Reclaiming a Civilization*. Austin: University of Texas Press.

Børnerettighedsinstitutionen MIO. 2014. *Fra Lov Til Praksis – En Undersøgelse Af Vilkårene for Det Sociale Arbejde Med Børn* [From Law to Practice – A Study of the Conditions of Social Work With Children]. Nuuk: Børnerettighedsinstitutionen MIO.

Brøns, Malik. 2020. "Mangel På Arbejde i Tasiilaq: Vores Børn Går Sultne i Seng. [No Vacant Positions in Tasiilaq: Our Children Go to Bed Hungry]" *KNR.Gl*, November 1.

Burke, Ashley. 2018. "Youth Suicides, Violence: Nunavut Community of Pangnirtung Calling out for Help amid 'Sense of Desperation.'" *CBC News Canada*, 18 May. https://www.cbc.ca/news/canada/north/pangnirtung-crisis-crime-suicide-prevention-1.4666470

Chemnitz, Jørgen. 1980. "Grønland Får Sin Helt Egen Socialpolitik. [Greenland Get's Its Very Own Social Policy." *Atuagagdliutit*, 12 June.

Christensen, Julia, Steven Arnfjord, and Marie-Louise Aastrup. Forthcoming. "Welfare Colonialism and Geographies of Homelessness in Nuuk, Greenland." In *Housing, Homelessness and Social Policy in the Urban North: Perspectives from Alaska, the Canadian North and Greenland*, edited by Julia Christensen, Sally Carraher, Travis Hedwig, and Steven Arnfjord. Toronto, ON: University of Toronto Press.

Daugaard-Jensen, J. 1911. Om Grønlands Administration [About the Administration of Greenland]. I C. Gulmann, ed. Gads Danske Magasin 1910–1911. København: Forlaget af G.E.C GAD.

Dean, Hartley. 2019. *Social Policy*. 3rd edition. Cambridge: Polity Press.

Egede, Elna. 2009. "Fattigdommen Breder Sig i Grønland – Nordisk Samarbejde. [Poverty Is Spreading In Greenland – Nordic Cooperation]" *Fattigdom i Norgen*. Nordisk Ministerråd.

Goldschmidt, Verner. 1964. "Udviklingen i Sociologisk Belysning. [Development in a Sociological Perspective]." In *Grønland i Udvikling*, edited by Guldborg Chemnitz and Verner Goldschmidt. Copenhagen: Fremad.

Greenlandic Red Cross. 2018. *Sårbare Grupper i Grønland – Kalaallit Røde Korsiats Sårbarhedsundersøgelse 2017–2018 [Vulnerable Groups in Greenland: Kalaallit Røde Korsiats Vulnerability Study 2017–2018]*. Nuuk: Greenlandic Red Cross.

Grønlands Hjemmestyre. 1997. *Socialreformkommissionens Betænkning 1997 [Report of the Social Reform Commission in 1997]*. Nuuk: Socialreformkommissionen.

Grønlands Økonomiske Råd. 2020. *Grønlands Økonomi – Foråret 2020* [Greenland's Economy: Spring 2020]. Nuuk: Grønlands Økonomiske Råd.

Grønlands Selvstyre. 2019. *Forslag Til FINANSLOV for 2020 [Suggestion for the Law of Finance]*. Nuuk: Naalakkersuisut.

Grønlandskommissionen. 1950. *Grønlandskommissionens Betænkning. Bd. 1–6 [Report from the Greenland Commission, vol. 1–6]*. Copenhagen: Gad.

Grønlandsudvalget af 1960. 1964. *Betænkning Fra Grønlandsudvalget Af 1960 [Report from the Greenland Committee of 1960]*. Copenhagen: S. L. Møllers Bogtrykkeri.

Hansen, Birgit, and Ina Skafte. 2009. *Tidlig Indsats Overfor Gravide Familier [Early Prevention for Pregnant Families]*. Nuuk: PAARISA.

Heinrich, Jens. 2012. *Eske Brun Og Det Moderne Grønlands Tilblivelse [Eske Brun and the Rise of a Modern Greenland]*. Nuuk: Naalakkersuisut.

Hussain, Naimah. 2013. "Det delte Grønland: tørkloset eller jacuzzi. [The Divided Greenland: Dry Toilet or Jacuzzi]" *Information*, 9 March: 10–11.

Indenrigsministeriet. 1924. *Beretninger Og Kundgørelser Vedrørende Styrelsen Af Grønland 1918–1922 [Reports and Announcements Regarding the Government of Greenland 1918–1922]*. Copenhagen: J. H. Schultz Forlag.

Jørn Henrik Petersen, Klaus Petersen, and Niels Finn Christiansen. 2014. "Det Socialpolitiske Idelandskab [The Social Political Landscape of Ideas]." In *Dansk Velfærdshistorie – Hvor glider vi hen, perioden 1993–2014. Vol. 6 [Danish Welfare History – Where are we drifting to, the period 1993-2014. Volume 6]*, edited by Jørn Henrik Petersen, Klaus Petersen and Niels Finn Christiansen. Odense: Syddansk Universitetsforlag.

Kjær Sørensen, Axel. 1983. *Danmark-Grønland i Det 20. Århundrede: En Historisk Oversigt [Denmark-Greenland in the 20th Century: A Historical Overview]*. Copenhagen: Nyt Nordisk Forlag.

Kral, Michael J. 2019. *The Return of the Sun : Suicide and Reclamation among Inuit of Arctic Canada*. New York: Oxford University Press.

Lynge, Aqqaluk. 1993. *Inuit: Inuit Issittormiut Kattuffiata oqaluttuassartaa [The Story of the Inuit. Circumpolar Conference]*. Nuuk: Atuakkiorfik.

———. 2002. *The Right to Return: Fifty Years of Struggle by Relocated Inughuit in Greenland, Complete with an English Translation of Denmark's Eastern High Court Ruling*. Nuuk: Atuagkat.

Lynge, Finn. 1977. *Tanker i et Bulldozerspor [Thoughts in a bulldozer trail]*. Nuuk: Det Grønlandske Forlag.

———. 2009. Kolonitid før og nu [Colonial Times then and now]. In B. K. Pedersen, F. Nielsen, K. Langgård, K. Pedersen, & J. Rygaard, ed. *Grønlandsk kultur- og samfundsforskning 2008-09*. Nuuk: Forlaget Atuagkat.

Lynge, Inge., & Bjerregaard, Peter. 2000. *Selvmord, Selvmordsforsøg Og Selvmordstanker I Grønland Suicide, Suicide Attempts And Suicidal Thoughts in Greenland]*. Nuuk: Unpublished paper.

Memmi, Albert. 1991. *The Colonizer and the Colonized*. London: Beacon Press.

Mencher, Samuel. 1967. "Ideology and the Welfare Society." *Social Work* 12 (3): 3–11.

Ministeriet for Grønland. 1953. *Beretninger Vedrørende Grønland 1951–52 [Reports Concerning Greenland 1951–52]*. Copenhagen: Nielsen & Lydiche.

———. 1957. *Beretninger Vedrørende Grønland 1956 [Reports Concerning Greenland 1956]*. Copenhagen: Nielsen & Lydiche.

———. 1968. *Beretninger Vedrørende Grønland 1967 [Reports Concerning Greenland 1967]*. Copenhagen: Nielsen & Lydiche.

Naalakkersuisut. 2013. *National Strategi for Selvmordsforebyggelse i Grønland 2013-2019 [National Strategy for Suicide Prevention in Greenland 2013–2019]*, Nuuk.

———. 2020. "Naalakkersuisut Har Godkendt Kommissoriet for Sundhedskommissionen. [The Minister Has Approved the Terms of Reference of the Health Commission]" 28. February. https://naalakkersuisut.gl/da/Naalakkersuisut/Nyheder/2020/02/2802_sundhedskommission

Netredaktionen. 2007. "Leder: Politisk Ukorrekt Rapport. [Editorial: A Politically Incorrect Report]" *Sermitsiaq.Ag*.

OECD Publishing. 2010. *Educational Research and Innovation Improving Health and Social Cohesion through Education*. Paris: Organisation for Economic Co-operation and Development.

Oldendow, Knud. 1930. *Socialforsorg i Grønland [Social Care in Greenland]*. Copenhagen: Det Grønlandske Selskab.

Paine, Robert. 1977. "The Path to Welfare Colonialism." In *The White Arctic: Anthropological Essays on Tutelage and Ethnicity*, edited by Robert Paine, 3–28. University of Toronto Press.

Perry, Kevin Anthony, and Steven Arnfjord. 2019. "Det Er Langt Fra Tasiilaq Til Nuuk – Perspektiver På Socialt Arbejde På Distancen. [It's a Long Way from Tasiilaq to Nuuk: Perspectives on Doing Social Work at a Distance]." *Tidsskriftet Grønland* 67 (4): 263–271.

Redaktionen. 2019. "Kim Kielsen: Velfærdsmæssig Udvikling Skal Aldrig Stoppe. [Kim Kielsen: The Development of Welfare Should Never Stop]" *Sermitsiaq*.Ag.

Rigsdagen. 1908. *Forslag Til Lov Om Styrelse Af Kolonierne i Grønland m.m. [Proposal for a Law on the Management of the Colonies in Greenland, etc.]* Copenhagen: Rigsdagen.

Rink, Hinrich. 1857. "Forslag Til Oprettelse Af et Slags Forstanderskaber Ved Kolonierne i Grønland Til Bestyrelse Af de Indfødtes Fællesanliggender. [Proposal for the Establishment of a Kind of Administrative Local Board at the Colonies in Greenland for the Directory of the Common Affairs of the Natives.]" *Departementstidende* no. 42. Denmark.

———. 1877. *Nogle Bemærkninger Om de Nuværende Grønlænderes Tilstand: Et Foredrag [Some Comments about The Current Conditions of the Greenlanders: A Lecture]*. Copenhagen.

———. 1884. *Om Grønlænderne [About the Greenlanders]*. Copenhagen: Det Grønlandske Selskab.

Robertson, Alex. 1988. "Welfare State and Welfare Society." *Social Policy & Administration* 22 (3): 222–234. https://doi.org/10.1111/j.1467-9515.1988.tb00305.x

Rud, Søren. 2018. *Colonialism in Greenland: Tradition, Governance and Legacy*. Cham. Palgrave Macmillan.

Schnohr, Christina, Sissel Lea Nielsen, and Steen Wulff. 2007. *Børnefattigdom i Grønland: En Statistisk Analyse Af Indkomstdata for Husstande Med Børn [Child Poverty in Greenland: A Statistical Analysis of Income Data per Household with Children]*. Nuuk: MIPI.

Schultz-Nielsen, Jørgen. 2019. "Doris: Erstat Politikere Med Fagfolk. [Doris: Replace Politicians with Profesionals]" *Sermitsiaq.Ag*, 25 November.

Skatte- og Velfærdskommissionens betænkning. 2011. *Vores Velstand Og Velfærd – Kræver Handling Nu. [Our Prosperity and Welfare Demands Action Now*. Nuuk: https://naalakkersuisut.gl/da/Naalakkersuisut/Departementer/Finans/Skatte-og-velfaerdskommissionen/Betaenkning

Socialreformkommissionen. 1981. *Betænkning Fra Socialreformkommissionen [Report from the Social Reform Commission]*. Nuuk: Socialreformkommissionen.

Sveistrup, Poul Peter. 1953. *Rigsdagen Og Grønland [Rigsdagem and Greenland]*. Copenhagen: J. H. Schultz Forlag.

Udvalget vedrørende Grønlandske Kvinder. 1975. *Kvinden Og Samfundsudviklingen = Arnaq Inugtaoqatigîngnilo Ineriartorneq [The Woman and the Development of Society]*. Copenhagen: Det Grønlandske Kvindeudvalg.

United Nations. 1945. *Charter of the United Nations and Statute of the International Court of Justice*.

Upanne, Maila. 2002. "Implementation of the Suicide Prevention Strategy in Finland." In *Suicide Prevention: A Holistic Approach*, edited by D. De Leo, A. Schmidtke, and R. F. W. Diekstra, 219–223. Dordrecht: Springer Net.

Viemose, Jørgen. 1977. *Dansk Kolonipolitik i Grønland [Danish Colonial Policy in Greenland]*. Copenhagen. Demos.

Wilensky, Harold L. 1975. *The Welfare State and Equality: Structural and Ideological Roots of Public Expenditures*. Berkeley, CA: University of California Press.

CHAPTER 23

RE-CLAIMING INUIT GOVERNANCE AND REVITALIZING AUTONOMY IN NUNATUKAVUT

Amy Hudson

INTRODUCTION AND BACKGROUND

Indigenous peoples were self-governing long before European and British assertions of sovereignty on Indigenous lands. Traditional forms of Indigenous governance were often associated with land and family, and emphasized the interconnection of multiple spheres including the familial, political, spiritual, economic, and environmental (Borrows and Rotman 1998, 673). Indigenous women were often integral to these forms of governance, wielding authority, voice, and vital knowledge. Inuit, in particular, adhered to governance principles that ensured their own survival. Traditional knowledge documented from Inuit Elders illustrates traditional governing practices, understood as "what had to be followed, done or not done" (Oosten et al. 2017, 1).

Colonialism threatened to destroy Indigenous autonomy (Borrows and Rotman 1998). The impact of colonial imposition on Indigenous sovereignty and power was destructive to Indigenous forms of governance, and over time, Indigenous peoples' "powers were annexed by the Crown" (Nikolakis et al. 2019, 57). Like other colonial governments throughout the world, colonial governments in what is now Canada consistently disempowered Indigenous peoples and, in particular, Indigenous women, by disregarding Indigenous forms of governance and refusing to include women in negotiations (Lawrence and Anderson 2005). As Huhndorf and Suzack (2010, 5) argue, "colonization has reordered gender relations to subordinate women, regardless of their pre-contact status."

Despite centuries of colonial rule, Indigenous nations in Canada have survived and maintained their own governance systems and processes, and have fought for the recognition of their political rights (Borrows and Rotman 1998). Aboriginal rights and title are communal rights that are inherent to Indigenous peoples in Canada, as they have occupied lands in what is now known as Canada since before European colonization (McNeil 2016). Under the constitutional framework of Canada, "Aboriginal peoples have rights to continue to exist as peoples with the right to self-determination" (Olthuis et al. 2012, 1). These rights were never extinguished, despite British and French assertions of sovereignty and the establishment of governmental authority in what is now Canada (Borrows and Rotman 1998). Indigenous peoples' inherent right to self-government was affirmed in the Constitution Act of 1982, Section 35, but Canadian courts have consistently failed to include Indigenous perspectives in law and analysis (Napoleon and Friedland 2016). Today, Canada purportedly considers self-government negotiations between Indigenous peoples and the state as opportunities to work with Indigenous nations towards self-determination (CIRNAC 2019). In practice, however, modern self-government negotiations continue to reinforce colonial rule of law and Euro-western forms of dominance. In response, this chapter presents an approach to governance that is Inuit-centered, based on values and perspectives that challenge the hierarchies, gender inequities, and recognition politics inherent in state-led governance in Canada.

SITUATING THE INUIT OF NUNATUKAVUT TODAY

There are approximately 6,000 Inuit who belong to southeastern, southern, and central Labrador. Over half of this population still resides on the traditional lands of their Inuit ancestors, now referred to as NunatuKavut. Translated from Inuttitut, NunatuKavut means "our ancient land." Inuit in southeast Labrador have practiced seasonal migration since time immemorial (Stopp 2002), and until the 1960s and 1970s shifted between seasonal homes, living in headlands in the summer and fall months, and in interior bay areas in the winter and spring (Martin et al. 2012; Procter 2020b). This seasonal shifting allowed Inuit to hunt and harvest, sustaining themselves and their families throughout the seasons. Inuit did not begin to live in permanent settlements until the 1960s, when the church and state sought to permanently settle southeast Labrador for the purposes of schooling and other service deliveries (Mercer and Hanrahan 2017). Many Inuit from this region, like other Inuit to the north, attended residential schools in Cartwright, North West River, and St. Anthony (Procter 2020b). These forms of outside interference brought many changes to Inuit life in southeast Labrador (e.g., provincial laws and regulations, western education, and wage labor economy). Yet, Inuit continued to practice their culture and traditions, and today they remain deeply connected to the lands of their ancestors. Many, if not most Inuit families in this region still maintain seasonal homes, and continue their traditions of hunting, harvesting, fishing, trapping, and educating children in the ways of their ancestors. Maintaining strong connections to traditional lands is integral to Inuit society today.

The Aboriginal rights of NunatuKavut Inuit are represented by the NunatuKavut Community Council (NCC). Although the political mobilization of Inuit in relationship with colonists in this part of Labrador can be traced back to the 18th century (i.e., the British-Inuit Treaty of 1765), in a modern context, Inuit from this region have been working since the early 1980s to gain formal recognition of their rights and filed a statement of intent with the Federal government under the comprehensive land claims policy in 1991. In 2015, the federal government began moving beyond the CLC process, working with Indigenous peoples through Recognition of Indigenous Rights and Self-Determination (RIRSD) processes. On 14 February 2018, Canada announced that it would work towards developing a "Recognition and Implementation of Indigenous Rights Framework consisting of legislation and policy" as part of its commitment to recognition of and reconciliation with Indigenous peoples (Government of Canada 2018). Also, in 2018, Canada accepted NCC (representing NunatuKavut Inuit) into the RIRSD process, and a Memorandum of Understanding (MOU) guiding the relationship was formalized between the Canadian government and the NCC in September 2019. Through this process, Canada and NCC will negotiate self-government agreements for NunatuKavut Inuit.

This chapter illustrates the active role that Inuit continue to play in advancing their future. To assist Inuit on their path to self-government and self-determination, I led a collaborative research study with NunatuKavut Inuit that sought to identify, reclaim, and reconstitute Inuit governance practices for the future, derived from the values and perspectives of Inuit from this region. As the NCC looks toward self-government and self-determination in a modern era, this research creates space for Inuit to share their knowledge and identify key areas of interest.

I am from NunatuKavut and maintain a strong connection to my home community of Black Tickle, specifically, and to NunatuKavut generally. This study reflects my approach to research as extending beyond social justice to include community and cultural preservation. Borrowing from the work of Indigenous scholar Shawn Wilson (2008), I undertake research that is both context-specific and accountable to the communities participating in this study. Wilson contends that relational research is an essential form of respect for participants. I have sought to enact this principle by representing Inuit in NunatuKavut from a place of strength and autonomy, recognizing their Inuit rights, and highlighting the social, cultural, and economic contributions of Inuit women. The following is part of my doctoral research, which included a Community Governance and Sustainability Initiative (CGSI)[1] in three pilot communities (Black Tickle, Norman Bay, and St. Lewis) which I led in collaboration with NunatuKavut Inuit. The pilot communities are indicated on the map in Figure 23.1.

To engage Inuit in discussions about their interests, perspectives, and visions for self-governance, I employed qualitative and Indigenous research methods, including individual and group interviews, storytelling sessions, surveys, and community gatherings. Many of these formats provided opportunities for networking, sharing, relationship-building, and learning, consistent with Indigenous methodologies. Additional data came from written submissions (storytelling and poetry) from 50 individual participants from the Community Governance and Sustainability Initiative (CGSI) pilot communities. In the submissions, participants described their most valued aspects of home and community. This approach encouraged positive thinking, connection, and reflexivity among participants. The submissions also provided in-depth insight into the values and priorities of participants that are integral to discussions about governance. Additionally, I analyzed relevant secondary data sources (e.g., NCC reports, archival documents, and community engagement notes) to support and enrich the study findings. I also used participant observation over a three-year period. Detailed notes and journaling, as well as my own experiences and knowledge as a result of my belonging to one of the study communities inform my findings.

Overall, the data collection activities resulted in a compilation of rich knowledge and expertise from Inuit in this study. I organized this knowledge into four themes and two principles of Inuit governance. I present them in this chapter following a review of modern treaty-making in Canada. The review helps situate a history of colonially rooted governance practices in Canada generally and its impact on the potential for Inuit self-determination in NunatuKavut today. This is followed by a discussion that illustrates the importance of Inuit-centered governance.

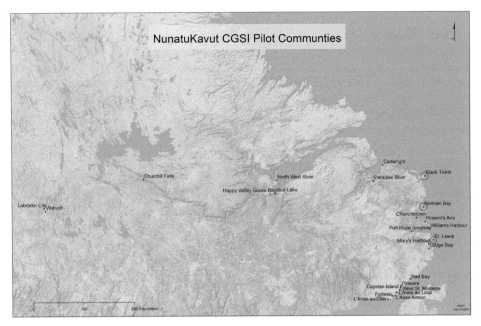

Figure 23.1   Location of the three NunatuKavut communities (circled) that participated in the CGSI pilot study. Map: Bryn Wood, NunatuKavut Community Council, 2020.

MODERN TREATY-MAKING IN CANADA

Early relations between the British Crown and Indigenous peoples in northeastern North America must be understood in their particular time and context. From "commercial compacts" to the Peace and Friendship Treaties of the 17th century and onwards, early agreements were largely borne out of commercial relations and the colonial desire for land and resources (Miller 2009). In NunatuKavut territory in southern Labrador, the British Crown made early attempts to seize control of coastal riches, negotiating with Inuit in order to exclude other competitor European nations.

Along the Labrador coast, Inuit violently resisted the growing numbers of European whalers, traders, and fishers who had exploited the region's rich marine resources each summer since the 15th century (Pope 2015). When Britain assumed colonial jurisdiction of Labrador from the French in 1763, the violence continued. The British Crown tried to pacify the coast by making a "peace and friendship" style treaty with Inuit in southern Labrador in 1765. The Crown also invited Moravian missionaries to establish trading posts and mission stations in northern Labrador in an attempt to draw Inuit to the north, and away from lucrative fishing grounds along the south coast (Hiller 1971). Despite the missionaries' efforts to limit their territory, Inuit continued to live along the entire Labrador coast. In the 21st century, the historical divide between the Moravian-influenced territory to the north and the non-Moravian territory to the south is reflected in the modern Inuit territories of Nunatsiavut along the north coast and NunatuKavut along the south coast (Procter 2020a).

The British-Inuit treaty of 1765 promised that "Inuit would have the protection of the British Crown and would have treaty rights, including those of self-government, harvest of wildlife and natural resources and a commercial right to trade" (Hanrahan 2014, 7). However, these treaty promises were not kept. Violence continued to erupt between Europeans and Inuit in the years following the treaty, and the exploitative policies and practices that characterized colonization undermined Inuit political, social, and economic society in southern Labrador for generations. Labrador remained a British colony until 1949, when Newfoundland and Labrador joined the Canadian Confederation. Even after that, the federal government did not immediately recognize its constitutional responsibility towards Indigenous peoples in Labrador (Hanrahan 2003).

While these earlier treaties referenced Indigenous sovereignty, autonomy, and self-governance, the interpretation of treaties has not always supported these ends in practice. In Canada, the courts have historically reduced the importance of treaties, especially in circumstances where treaty promises conflict with federal and/or provincial legislation (Coyle 2017). Even though the Crown entered into treaty relationships over two centuries ago, "Canadian law governing these treaties remains in its infancy" (Coyle 2017, 41). In their critical analysis of the legitimacy of modern treaty relationships between Indigenous nations and the state, Ivison and colleagues (2000) argue that the very practice of modern treaty-making rests on the premise that Indigenous peoples were sovereign, as did the earlier treaties. In 1982, Aboriginal treaty rights became entrenched in Canada's constitution (Coyle 2017). Yet, Ivison and colleagues (2000) explain that problems in treaty interpretation continue to arise, as states often use the treaties themselves as grounds to further state sovereignty.

The Canadian government introduced a comprehensive land claims (CLC) policy in 1973 to "negotiate settlements with Indigenous groups in those areas of Canada where Indigenous rights based on traditional use and occupancy of the land had not been dealt with by treaty or superseded by law" (Crowe 2019). The CLC process became the state's vehicle through which *some* Indigenous peoples could negotiate with Canada on matters related to land.

At the time that the CLC process was introduced, Indigenous claims to self-determination were heightened in response to the White Paper of 1969 (Coulthard 2014). Alcantara (2013) argues that the CLC process allowed Indigenous peoples to reassert power and authority over their lands and resources by formalizing a relationship with a state that recognized their jurisdiction on their lands. The CLC process can be seen as a vehicle for the recognition of Indigenous peoples by the state. However, some Indigenous scholars problematize the state's politics of recognition as another form of colonialism. Coulthard (2014, 3) states: "The politics of recognition in its contemporary liberal form promises to reproduce the very configurations of colonialist, racist, patriarchal state power that Indigenous people's demands for recognition have historically sought to transcend." To date, CLC agreements have been criticized as failing to materialize into fulsome agreements with broad and encompassing understandings of Indigenous self-government (Dalton 2006). Instead, as Alcantara (2013) describes, the state retains power and control in the modern treaty-making process. This view is consistent with analyses that implicate the state in their efforts to sustain their sovereignty through modern treaties (Ivison et al. 2000), and with the assessment that recognition politics constitute another form of colonialism (Coulthard 2014).

NunatuKavut Inuit have experienced many frustrations with the CLC policy, which has not been updated since 1986. Even though their land use and occupancy in their homeland is extensive and long-standing, a self-government agreement has not been finalized. Recently, the federal government implemented a new process to recognize and negotiate Indigenous self-determination (Recognition of Indigenous Rights and Self-Determination (RIRSD). While RIRSD does not technically replace the CLC policy on treaty-making, NunatuKavut Inuit have been asserting their Indigenous rights through the RIRSD process. However, if NunatuKavut Inuit are to achieve satisfactory results, it is critical that the RIRSD process be guided by Inuit governance principles and aspirations. In other words, it is imperative that the RIRSD process operates according to the principles that the government of Canada purports to espouse. It must be guided by principles of reconciliation and the recognition of rights and self-determination, rather than the denial of Indigenous rights.

WHAT WE LEARNED FROM NUNATUKAVUT INUIT

NunatuKavut Inuit have been deeply engaged in discussions about collective and community priorities, with a view towards advancing self-governance and self-determination on their lands. Extensive community engagement about Inuit governance and sustainability planning resulted in knowledge sharing and priority-setting. Four key themes emerged from the focused discussions, writing, and visioning exercises, as well as from informal conversations: (1) Place-based decision-making; (2) Intersections of health and governance; (3) Self-determined education; (4) Relationships to land, water, and ice inform our future. These four themes highlight how Inuit can be a part of (and already are) reclaiming and reconstituting their own governance practices as pathways toward self-determination. Discussions and engagement with NunatuKavut Inuit illustrate that there is an intensely felt need for individual and collective responsibility and accountability in reclaiming and re-constituting governance practices relevant to Inuit. These themes intersect and overlap, highlighting the holistic nature of Inuit society in NunatuKavut. The discussion of findings that follows provides insight into the determination of Inuit to govern themselves through values and practices that are grounded in their own perspectives and worldviews.

Overwhelmingly, NunatuKavut Inuit expressed their values in relation to their right to live in freedom, safety, health, and happiness upon the lands of their ancestors, according to their own vision for the future, and rooted in their traditional way of life. Furthermore, participants emphasized the importance of values associated with home and community, kinship, education, economic security, and health (of humans and of the environment). These ideas came up repeatedly throughout conversations and in written submissions. The key themes below are imbued with core values that are integral to rebuilding and reconstituting modern Inuit governance practices in NunatuKavut. As a whole, they reflect the need for a holistic and Inuit-centered approach to governance that is grounded in the places, histories, cultures, and realities of Inuit themselves.

Theme 1: Placed-based decision-making

Place-based decision-making refers to the autonomy of Inuit to make decisions that are rooted in the core values, interests, and goals of the people who live on their lands. This concept is paramount to Inuit ways of knowing and being and is evident across all four themes. Many Inuit maintained that this form of decision-making was important given their Indigenous rights, and the multifaceted connections (social, familial, economic, spiritual, physical, political) they maintain to their ancestral homeland. In this context, place-based decision-making is derived from people who live in and remain connected to their place of origin, and to their ancestors over many generations. This form of decision-making is informed from a place of strength, that privileges the knowledge and values that communities deem central to their future survival. As one community member stated: "We should be able to make the decisions about our own community that will impact us." This process does not necessarily ensure that decisions or actions will always be right. However, when informed by a commitment to the interests and priorities of the people, it may help to ensure that decision-making will be just and relevant to Inuit themselves.

During a community engagement exercise that brought Inuit from across NunatuKavut together, some participants drew a line of connection between land claims and community survival and autonomy. Inuit in this region strongly feel that they have a right to their lands and resources (connected to generations and ancestors before them) and that the freedom to exercise their rights (through a land claim) would equip them with additional resources to sustain their communities into the future (i.e., job opportunities, control over resources, good environmental decision-making, etc.). One participant stated: "We should have control of our resources. It is the right thing to do. It is our right." Another participant stated that "there are many reasons why we should have rights and title [recognized and affirmed by colonial governments] … Right now it means the very essence and survival of our small communities. Absolutely necessary for their survival."

Place-based decision-making can also be understood through Inuit values associated with community connections. Participants openly discussed the importance of one's connection to place and how the knowledge and expertise gained through such connections are vital for community and cultural life. One participant stated: "my family are linked through a desire to live off the land and sea [...] passed on through generations." Some participants discussed how they often felt as though outsiders have made decisions for them and about their community, without their consent or knowledge. Many people still feel the impact of residential schools in their lives. As young children, they or their relatives were forced to leave their families and communities to attend a distant and foreign school, under the strict discipline of outside authorities (Procter 2020b). Participants described how outsider decision-making has often negatively impacted communities through policies, programming, and regulations that do not align with community interests and realities. In other cases, they noted the absence of programs and other opportunities altogether. Participants were clear that they are best positioned to know what works for their respective communities because they are the ones who continue to live on their lands.

The participants' determination for place-based decision-making was also fueled by the numerous barriers that they continue to find imposed on their path to self-government and self-determination. Focused discussions on governance were useful for learning from participants as they expressed their concerns for the future of their communities in the face of issues such as declining population, lack of or loss of industry, and inadequate health and infrastructure. Many of these participants, the majority of whom were women, perceived that they have had little autonomy or influence to effect change. They understood that power and control over their communities were largely held by outside actors, in particular the federal and provincial governments.

As a way of navigating the barriers to self-governance, participants engaged sustainability as both a method to achieving place-based decision-making, and as a concept consistent with their own ways of knowing and being to help them think about and plan for the future (Hudson and Vodden 2020). To Inuit who participated in the CGSI process, sustainability meant the preservation and survival of community and culture, whereby Inuit lead decision-making on their lands informed by their own values, knowledge, and expertise (Hudson and Vodden 2020). One participant explained that she has a role to play in community sustainability as things continue to evolve and change. Her concern for the future was directly connected to her interests in the continuation of an Inuit way of life and the continued survival of her community:

> This is the lifestyle I wanted. I can't imagine being somewhere else now. I've seen so many changes and I want to be a part of creating sustainable communities. Want to be a part of keeping the communities for future generations.

While communities currently have a governance apparatus for control and decision-making, such as municipalities or volunteer committees, the former tend to mirror colonial governance structures. Volunteer governance committees, in contrast, often lack the necessary capacity in terms of funding, resources, time, or training to participate in governance in a meaningful way. Place-based decision-making is vital to the rebuilding and reconstitution of Inuit governance today, particularly in priority areas identified by Inuit.

Theme 2: Intersections of health and governance

Participants identified health as a matter of immediate urgency and priority across NunatuKavut. Inuit in this region understand health and governance as interconnected. Many participants explained that existing health services in the region often fail to respond to their needs and interests, particularly in ways that are culturally relevant. While the regional health authority in Labrador aims to build internal capacity to deliver more culturally sensitive care and services, this work is still in its infancy and does not translate into actual programming for NunatuKavut Inuit. Thus, place-based decision-making is necessary for positive health outcomes in NunatuKavut.

Place-based decision-making is useful for understanding the connections between health and governance. Participants prioritized a range of health needs ranging from mental health, broader health access, and specialized care, including culturally relevant community-based health supports. In a conversation about the importance of self-governance and self-determination to Inuit, NunatuKavut president Todd Russell observed: "Well-being and governance are connected. If we are to be healthy, if our communities are to be healthy, we must make decisions for ourselves and from our own place" (personal communication 2019).

Other participants explained that they lacked access to vital programming such as the Non-Insured Health Benefits (NIHB) provided to many Indigenous peoples in Canada, which they felt would alleviate the extreme costs associated with medication and improve overall health care access and outcomes. Such programming is afforded to other Inuit in Canada who have settled land claims agreements. Responsive health care and supports for Elders and seniors in NunatuKavut were also identified as areas requiring immediate attention. Participants maintained that health initiatives should be community-based and locally driven, and that the NCC should play a leading role in health programming with and for communities.

Many NunatuKavut communities face inequities in access to health services and programming. Travel to other regions of the province or country is often necessary to access vital health supports. For example, the nearest shelter for women facing violence is located hundreds of kilometers away, and accessible only by air from some communities. The same is true for hospital access and specialized medical care, which require travel to Newfoundland or to another province entirely. Participants, and in particular women, described how challenging this situation was for them, especially those who were primary caregivers for children and other relatives. Additionally, participants explained how traveling to an urban region for health care can cause anxiety, which may be further exacerbated for those who have never traveled outside their home region or province.

In some cases, individuals simply do not receive the care they need because the barriers to access in terms of costs, time, or transportation are too much for them to bear (Darlene Wall, personal communication 2020). Overall, NunatuKavut Inuit see a leadership role for the NCC in collaborating with various levels of government to ensure increased health access, and in leading the development of culturally relevant community health programming and support in NunatuKavut that respond to community needs.

Theme 3: Self-determined education

Participants' priorities around education were multifaceted. Overall, participants described education as a way to further self-determination efforts. They understood education as a tool to re-connect to culture, whether through culturally relevant curricula and land-based learning, opportunities to acquire skills and credentials, or strengthened community capacity as post-secondary graduates return home to live and work. And, equally important, many recommend privileging traditional forms of education in NunatuKavut, such as the role of grandparents and storytelling in Inuit education. All of this is understood to contribute to community and cultural sustainability.

Discussions around education led to conversations about culture, autonomy, and the strengthening of the community. People are seeking to rebuild and re-institute Inuit language and lifeways that have been stolen or pushed to the margins, while also revitalizing and privileging the traditional lifeways that remain today. Inuit in this region see education as an opportunity to ensure that culture and tradition are preserved and passed onto future generations. Traditions like survival skills, hunting and harvesting, language, crafting, and maintaining knowledge of the land, water, and ice are all valued forms of education and knowledge that are important for the sustainability of culture and community life.

Participants talked about how the secondary school system should be more inclusive of Inuit culture and heritage as well. They cited the need for developing curricula that reflect Inuit culture, history, and values. One participant stated:

> If we do not teach our children/grandchildren about our past and culture then this is a huge loss or failure. I think we can look to other Aboriginal groups and see how the loss of culture affected their lives. Everyone needs to know where they came from and keeping our culture alive is very important.

Participants also recognized a need for locally trained and educated teachers so that knowledge could continue to be passed on in ways that reflect and validate Inuit culture and history. One participant stated: "People from the outside have a role, too. But for influencing children, it's important to have local people [teaching our children in our schools]." This was further illustrated while I (in my role as NCC Director of Research, Education, and Culture) collaborated with communities during the development and early roll-out of an Inuit Education Program (IEP), led by NCC and carried out in seven schools across NunatuKavut. The program responded directly to community interest in culturally relevant curricula by teaching skills and strengthening capacity in areas like preparing traditional foods, working with sealskin, and learning Inuttitut, among others. Community members were eager to support the inclusion of knowledge holders and Elders from within the community as instructors in this program, and explained that where possible, IEP students should be taught by people from their respective communities (see Figure 23.2).

Currently, the provincial curriculum does not accurately reflect the history and culture of NunatuKavut (Moore et al. 2018). Instead, it perpetuates colonial narratives about Inuit in this region. Inadequate curriculum materials and a lack of cultural awareness training for teachers have resulted in a situation where Inuit in NunatuKavut do not see themselves reflected in what they are learning about Indigenous peoples. Teachers are also often ill-equipped to supplant the existing curriculum materials with content that is culturally relevant. Lessons learned from the collaborative development of the IEP indicate that parents and caregivers want to see their children educated in areas that advance cultural skills, knowledge, and pride. To date, the IEP has responded to community interest in culturally relevant education by providing opportunities for youth to learn how to make snowshoes, *kamutet* [sleds], sew sealskins and make clothing, and prepare and preserve traditional foods, as notable examples. In discussing the importance of culture to education, one participant stated: "When I have kids, it will be very important. They will need to know about their past and how their culture links us all."

Inuit women illustrate the central role storytelling plays in education, knowledge exchange, and connectivity. In this region, Inuit value connecting with each other through stories, ensuring that youth learn from stories passed down across generations, and partake in the sharing and knowledge exchange that keeps stories alive (Hudson et al. 2015). One participant stated (with agreement from others) that "grandparents are the best education." Another participant explained how passing on knowledge like traditional cooking (bread, pies, jams) can be used to teach

Figure 23.2   Zachary Keefe (left) and Brady Morris (right) from Black Tickle participate in NCC's Inuit Education Program and learn to make sealskin mittens. Photo: NunatuKavut Community Council.

patience and to reduce stress. There was a concern that if storytelling was not prioritized by future generations, then the loss of Elders would result in the loss of stories. As one participant put it: "Once we're gone, the stories will be gone." Storytelling was also seen as important for strengthening survival skills, which was identified as an important area of education for children. Some participants explained that without storytelling, youth would not learn how to survive out on the land, navigate in stormy weather, or hunt and harvest. Overall, the participants described the loss that they would feel if stories were not passed down through generations, and how this would negatively impact the interconnectedness of community members.

In NunatuKavut, education is seen as a pathway to both community and cultural survival. These lessons are vital to NCC as leadership continues to pursue and privilege Inuit education in NunatuKavut as a matter of self-government and self-determination.

Theme 4: Relationships to land, water, and ice inform our future

Finally, participants described a strong connection to the land, water, and ice around them, and they expressed how this connection continues to sustain a balanced life in NunatuKavut. In discussions around governance, participants connected the importance of local control, knowledge, and autonomous decision-making to issues including developments on their lands, marine species and wildlife harvesting regulations, monitoring, conservation, and youth involvement in the fisheries. Furthermore, the discussions revealed that people's sense of health, freedom, safety, and economic security are interconnected to the way they continue to live in relation with the natural environment and those around them. There is a deeply rooted sense of respect and concern for the health and well-being of not only humans, but all life forms, including land, water, ice, and animals. The ability of Inuit to survive over generations is highly valued, as hunting, trapping, harvesting, and other land-based forms of survival have been central to Inuit lifeways throughout history in NunatuKavut. Not only are these lifeways indicative of Inuit survival and adaptability, but in a modern context, they provide a continued connection to ancestors and values associated with intergenerational knowledge (see Figure 23.3).

Historically and still today, community connection is embedded in peoples' relationship to the land, water, and ice around them. When asked what she values about her community, one participant demonstrated a deep connection to land:

> I love how the ground thaws, in the spring of the year. When you get to go for that first ride on bike [all-terrain vehicle or ATV] so far in over the land. The sea, land and snow mixes together in the air and creates a scent that is like no other. I take big breaths in and sometimes I try to eat it.

Living on and with the land is still an important part of life in the study communities. Participants further understood that their knowledge and observations are vital to ensure the survival and renewal of the natural environment. Overall, participants described their connection to the lands, water, and animals around them in ways that demonstrated a deep emotional and personal attachment. For example, one participant stated:

Figure 23.3 Left to right: Taylor Keefe, Zachary Keefe, and Tegan Keefe of Black Tickle enjoying a day on the land in Porcupine Bay, Labrador. Porcupine Bay was once the winter home of many Inuit families prior to resettlement. Black Tickle residents maintain a strong connection to this area today. Photo: Tara Keefe, Black Tickle.

> The way the bog smells in the spring when everything is starting to thaw, sitting out on the point and watching flock after flock of birds flying by. The smell of sweetness in the air as you go in over the land berry picking. The beautiful colors of bright green grass has [as] you climb the hills in July, the sound of seagulls going crazy for a feed of fish when the fishermen come in with their catch. The way the lights dance on the water on a beautiful calm summer's night.

Another participant (whose family recently had to move to a larger community in Labrador) explained her enduring connection to her community:

> I can still smell the saltwater and seaweed from around the coves and, whenever I close my eyes, I can picture the northern lights or the bright stars. There's so much I miss about home. I'd love to see everyone playing soccer ball or tag in the middle of the night and I want to hear the crackling sounds of the wood burning during bonfire night.

The value that participants placed on home, culture, and community are integral to conversations of Inuit governance, including matters around hunting and harvesting regulations, fisheries, the conservation of species, economic development opportunities, etc. These same values and forms of intergenerational knowledge are also vital to informing policy and regulations on issues that impact the ability of Inuit to live according to their worldviews in relationship with the lands, water, ice, and animals around them. The following principles (discussed below) connect the importance of Inuit lifeways, values, and perspectives to the reclamation of Inuit governance.

DISCUSSION: EXPLORING VALUE-BASED PRINCIPLES OF INUIT GOVERNANCE IN NUNATUKAVUT

The key themes described above illustrate Inuit priorities and values as they pertain to self-governance matters. These priorities and values are integral to the reclamation and reconstitution of Inuit governance practices in NunatuKavut today. In analyzing the key themes and relevant secondary data, I have identified two emergent principles of Inuit governance that are derived from the expressed values, priorities, and perspectives of Inuit in this study: (1) Relational governance: accountability to the past, present, and future, and (2) Governance that is holistic, gender-balanced, and shared.

Relational Governance: Accountability to the past, present, and future

Throughout Canada, traditional forms of Indigenous governance have often been supplanted by colonial governance structures that privilege Euro-western perspectives (Borrows and Rotman 1998; Lawrence and Anderson 2005). In NunatuKavut, colonial interference has meant the imposition of foreign governance processes that are antithetical to Inuit perspectives and values. Despite this, Inuit from this region are asserting their right to self-government and self-determination, in ways that are culturally meaningful, as illustrated in the four themes described above. These themes translate into an Inuit-centered, culturally relevant approach to governance that is relational and accountable to the past, present, and future.

Such an approach differs fundamentally from state-centered governance. This approach seeks to imbue governance processes with the knowledge, expertise, perspectives, and values of Inuit themselves, including knowledge that has been passed down over generations through storytelling. Participants in the study discussed in this chapter see the need for relational accountability in decision making and as that which respects and honors ancestors, youth, Elders, lands, water, and ice. They recognize the importance of learning from both the past and the present. This is important for advancing good governance on their lands and for building a future that is accountable to their relations. Inuit understand that a deep and enduring relationship to place is central to decision-making, informed by the knowledge and expertise of all who live on their lands, including those who have come before them. Additionally, Inuit understand that good governance can only derive from an approach that seeks to strengthen the health of communities and individuals.

Relational governance in an Inuit context seeks to dismantle the hierarchies and power relations that persist in state forms of governance, and that impede Inuit self-government and self-determination. Relational governance does this by exercising inclusivity, fairness, and transparency. This includes recognizing multiple sites of knowledge and expertise, valuing the roles and contributions of community members, including Inuit women as experts, knowledge holders as educators and leaders, and embracing the values and knowledge that connect people with the lands, water, ice, and animals around them. For example, Inuit described their interest in education that reflects their culture and traditions, including those that privilege their relationship with the land. Storytelling is central to achieving these efforts and reflects how Inuit see themselves as responsible and accountable for the education of children and youth. Learning from the past equips Inuit with the skills and knowledge to navigate the present, imbued with values that continue to encourage the dissemination of knowledge to future generations. These qualities are central to relational governance in NunatuKavut.

Relational governance is also committed to a future that is informed and led by those who will be most impacted by it. This approach requires that knowledge and wisdom from previous generations are available and drawn upon. It responds directly to the desire of Inuit in this study to make decisions about matters that impact them and their communities directly (see theme one). Borrowing from Wilson (2008), a relational approach in this study context respects those who hold knowledge in the context of their own place and time and approaches them as experts and knowledge holders. Accountability is an integral and related function of responsibility in this governance context. Accountability measures that are Inuit-informed and led and decided upon by consensus, will aid in maintaining good governance practices and just decision-making that is considerate of the past, present, and future.

Governance that is holistic, gender-balanced, and shared

Prior to the imposition of state governance on the lives of Inuit in NunatuKavut, Inuit were self-governing and adapted to their world, and made decisions that supported their survival (NCC 2020). Today, Inuit from this region maintain a deeply rooted connection to their home and territory (NCC 2020; Hudson and Vodden 2020). Inuit describe how their connection to place situates them to best make decisions regarding their lands. In this study, place-based decision-making is borne from generations past, and includes individual and collective life experiences that are wrapped up in one's sense of belonging to a place. Furthermore, it privileges the primary role of Inuit women in everyday life. For example, as described in theme two above, health is a community-wide issue connected to governance, and women play a key role in caring for both family and community. Inuit women are demonstrated leaders and healers in advancing community well-being and sustainability. Women have also been integral to ensuring that traditional knowledge, skills, and stories are passed on, and they continue to identify intergenerational knowledge-sharing as a priority (Hudson et al. 2015). A history of colonization has silenced women's voices and virtually displaced them from the historical record. Some participants recalled that although women shared similar realities as the men, they were often not the ones telling the stories. One participant said: "It was almost a little bit like they were seen and not heard." Women were also originally excluded from Crown negotiations with Indigenous peoples (Lawrence and Anderson 2005). Yet the resilience, determination, and cultural expertise that Inuit women continue to demonstrate in NunatuKavut communities are central to the revitalization of place-based decision-making.

Throughout this research, the commitment of Inuit women to their community and culture was pronounced. Women play a key role in leading and organizing social facets of community life in NunatuKavut. These activities promote togetherness, storytelling, and sharing. Collaborative work and dialogue with Inuit women created opportunities for women to have their voices heard in diverse and holistic discussions about governance from Inuit perspectives. Euro Canadian structures do not always privilege or highlight the work of women in Inuit communities and thus, their contributions are not always apparent in observations drawn from Euro Canadian ways of knowing and being. Therefore, a perspective that is gender-balanced in this context does not intend to dismiss the important role or place of men in Inuit society. Rather, an enduring history of oppression and marginalization faced by Indigenous women broadly, and Inuit women in NunatuKavut specifically, means that we must be cognizant of these colonial legacies in reclaiming and reconstituting Inuit governance today.

The role of storytelling in knowledge-sharing across generations in NunatuKavut is key to holistic and place-based decision making (see theme three). Inuit describe storytelling as central to shaping the way that Inuit live, and as a tool for community and cultural survival. Participants shared that storytelling is valued for the way it can assist in the physical, social, and mental well-being of Inuit families in harsh geographic and isolated areas of Labrador, where survival depends on local knowledge and expertise. As described above, Inuit in this region are committed to ensuring that their children and grandchildren learn from the past and seek to pass on the knowledge of their ancestors. Intergenerational knowledge-sharing is a priority and has important implications for the revitalization of Inuit governance in the territory. Leadership in governance, in this context, is not about the knowledge, power, or charisma demonstrated by a single leader (female or male). Rather, leadership can perhaps be best defined or recognized in those who are committed to shared knowledge and community and cultural preservation.

CONCLUSION

As many Indigenous scholars have illustrated (Borrows 2010; Napoleon and Friedland 2016), Indigenous governance has been invariably influenced by Euro Canadian forms of governance. In order to reclaim and reconstitute Inuit governance practices, NunatuKavut Inuit need to develop practices and processes that are culturally relevant, responsive to Inuit priorities, and reflective of Inuit principles of governance, including measures of responsibility and accountability. As inherent rights holders belonging to the land, water, and ice of their ancestors, Inuit have the legitimate and unwavering jurisdiction and autonomy to make decisions that impact them directly. Governance, in this place, should be upheld and legitimated by and for those who are responsible and accountable to all of their relations.

The key themes identified and discussed above, while by no means exhaustive, serve to inform areas of life that are of significant importance to Inuit in NunatuKavut today. We must remember however, that as society changes and evolves, Inuit adapt and respond to a changing world around them. As a result, governance priorities must be flexible and adaptable. Inuit in NunatuKavut share with other Inuit groups in Canada concerns and interests around self-governance in areas such as the environment, education, health, and well-being. NunatuKavut Inuit differ in their ability to exercise self-governance, however, as they do not have a settled land claim. Given the complex history of state-Indigenous relations in Canada, from early treaties and assimilation policies, to modern land claims, NunatuKavut Inuit have faced many obstacles on their road to self-government. But they do now have a formal relationship with the state that will guide self-government interests and discussions into the future. And as this study has demonstrated, their determination for self-governance is strong.

In reflecting on the future in NunatuKavut, this study offers an understanding of Inuit governance that challenges the hierarchies and power relations inherent in the colonial practices and worldview of the Canadian state. Inuit perspectives on governance emphasize that autonomy and authority originate from the enduring connections between people and place, and not from the dispossession of Indigenous peoples from their places, which, as Coulthard (2014) and Cardinal (1999) contend, is emblematic of colonial governance structures. McGregor et al. (2020) maintain that global and national forms of governance have consistently failed Indigenous peoples around the world. State governance in Canada tends to reflect a western style of dominance characterized by "formal, hierarchical, and state-centered policy processes" (Alcantara and Nelles 2014, 188). This approach to governance is often rigid, unchanging, and unable to efficiently adapt to growing and evolving societies.

By contrast, evolving discussions in NunatuKavut make clear that Inuit governance is concerned with the social, political, and cultural preservation of communities and people, including all facets of society regarded as important by Inuit, such as family, water, animals, and land. Governance must rest on a foundation that is compatible with the worldviews and perspectives of the people who live in NunatuKavut. This study illustrates the multifaceted role of Inuit in informing decision-making on their lands. Individuals in positions of western authority, and those who express a commitment to reconciliation, need to take a step back to assess and critically analyze concepts of leadership and governance. Diverging worldviews and perspectives on governance bring attention to the need to achieve an alternative reality regarding Inuit-state relations in Canada, whereby EuroCanadian forms of governance and Inuit-centered place-based decision-making are negotiated in ways that create space for the expression and self-determination of all Inuit.

NOTE

1 The CGSI refers to a community-driven research study (part of Hudson's doctoral research). The CGSI used a strength-based approach while working collaboratively with Inuit in three pilot communities in NunatuKavut (Black Tickle, Norman Bay and St. Lewis). The CGSI identified culturally relevant pathways for sustainability planning that privilege the knowledge and expertise of Inuit. In addition, community sustainability goals across all three pilot communities were identified. This study helped to inform best practices in inclusive and culturally relevant community engagement that continue to be used by NCC in their consultations with Inuit throughout NunatuKavut. More information can be found about this study and the three pilot communities in Hudson and Vodden (2020).

REFERENCES

Alcantara, Christopher. 2013. *Negotiating the Deal: Comprehensive Land Claims Agreements in Canada*. Toronto, ON: University of Toronto Press.

Alcantara, Christopher, and Jen Nelles. 2014. "Indigenous Peoples and the State in Settler Societies: Toward a More Robust Definition of Multilevel Governance." *Publius: The Journal of Federalism* 44 (1): 183–204. https://doi.org/10.1093/publius/pjt013.

Borrows, John. 2010. *Drawing Out Law. A Spirit's Guide*. Toronto, ON: University of Toronto Press.

Borrows, John, and Rotman, Leonard Ian. 1998. *Aboriginal Legal Issues: Cases, Materials and Commentary*. Toronto and Vancouver: LexisNexis Canada.

Cardinal, Harold. 1999 [1969]. The Unjust Society, 2nd edition. Vancouver: Douglas and McIntyre.

Coulthard, Glen Sean. 2014. *Red Skin, White Masks: Rejecting the Colonial Politics of Recognition*. Minneapolis, MN: University of Minnesota Press.

Coyle, Michael. 2017. "As Long as the Sun Shines: Recognizing that Treaties Were Meant to Last." In *The Right Relationship: Reimagining the Implementation of Historical Treaties*, edited by John Borrows and Michael Coyle, 39–69. Toronto, ON: University of Toronto Press.

Crowe, Keith. 2019. "Comprehensive Land Claims: Modern Treaties (2019). *The Canadian Encyclopedia*. https://www.thecanadianencyclopedia.ca/en/article/comprehensive-land-claims-modern-treaties.

Crown Indigenous Relations and Northern Affairs Canada. 2019. *Self-Government*. https://www.rcaanc-cirnac.gc.ca/eng/1100100032275/1529354547314#chp2.

Dalton, Jennifer E. 2006. "Aboriginal Title and Self-Government in Canada: What is the True Scope of Comprehensive Land Claims Agreements?" *Windsor Review of Legal and Social Issues* 22: 29–78.

Government of Canada. 2018. *Overview of a Recognition and Implementation of Indigenous Rights Framework*. https://www.rcaanc-cirnac.gc.ca/eng/1536350959665/1539959903708.

Hanrahan, Maura. 2003. *The Lasting Breach: The Omission of Aboriginal People from the Terms of Union between Newfoundland and Canada and its Ongoing Impacts*. St. John's, NL: Royal Commission on Renewing and Strengthening our Place in Canada.

———. 2014. "A People of Nation Caralit and their Southern Inuit Descendants: Exploring the Inuit Presence in the 'Unknown Labrador'" In *KITASKINO: Key Issues, Challenges and Visions for Northern Aboriginal Communities in Canada*, edited by Herman J. Michell and Cathy H.G. Wheaton, 1–22. Vernon, BC: J Charlton Publishing Ltd.

Hiller, James. 1971. "Early Patrons of the Labrador Eskimos: The Moravian Mission in Labrador, 1764-1805." In *Patrons and Brokers in the East Arctic*, edited by Robert Paine, 74–97. St. John's, NL: ISER Books.

Hudson, Amy, Sylvia Moore, and Andrea Procter. 2015. *Culture Carriers*. Internal Report. Happy Valley-Goose Bay: NunatuKavut Community Council (NCC).

Hudson, Amy, and Kelly Vodden. 2020. "Decolonizing Pathways to Sustainability: Lessons Learned from Three Inuit Communities in NunatuKavut, Canada." *Sustainability* 12 (11): 4419. https://doi.org/10.3390/su12114419.

Huhndorf, Shari M., and Cheryle Suzack. 2010. "Indigenous Feminism: Theorizing the Issues." In *Indigenous Women and Feminism: Politics, Activism, Culture*, edited by Cheryle Suzack, Shari M. Huhndrof, Jeanne Perreault and Jean Barman, 1–17. Vancouver, BC: UBC Press.

Ivison, Duncan, Paul Patton, and Will Sanders. 2000. *Political Theory and the Rights of Indigenous Peoples*. Cambridge: Cambridge University Press.

Lawrence, Bonita, and Kim Anderson. 2005. Introduction to "Indigenous Women: The State of Our Nations." *Atlantis* 29 (2): 1–8.

McGregor, Deborah, Steven Whitaker, and Mahisha Sritharan. 2020. "Indigenous Environmental Justice and Sustainability." *Environmental Sustainability* 43: 35–40. https://doi.org/10.1016/j.cosust.2020.01.007.

McNeil, Kent. 2016. "Aboriginal Title and Indigenous Governance: Identifying the Holders of Rights and Authority." *Osgoode Legal Studies Research Paper Series* 12 (14).

Martin, Debbie H., James E. Valcour, Julie R. Bull, John R. Graham, Melita Paul, and Darlene Wall. 2012. *NunatuKavut Community Health Needs Assessment: A Community Based Research Project*. Happy Valley-Goose Bay, NL: NunatuKavut Community Council Incorporated.

Mercer, Nicholas and Maura Hanrahan. 2017. "Straight from the Heavens into your Bucket": Domestic Rainwater Harvesting as a Measure to Improve Water Security in a Subarctic Indigenous Community." *International Journal of Circumpolar Health* 76 (1): 1312223. http://doi.org/10.1080/22423982.2017.1312223.

Miller, J. R. 2009. *Compact, Contract, Covenant: Aboriginal Treaty-Making in Canada*. Toronto, ON: University of Toronto Press.

Moore, Sylvia, Amy Hudson, and Erika Maxwell. 2018. *Review of NunatuKavut Southern Inuit Education Program*. Internal document commissioned by NunatuKavut Community Council.

Napoleon, Val, and Hadley Friedland. 2016. "An Inside Job: Engaging with Indigenous Legal Traditions through Stories." *McGill Law Journal* 61 (4):725–754. https://doi.org/10.7202/1038487ar.

NCC. 2020. *Who We Are*. NunatuKavut Community Council. https://nunatukavut.ca/about/who-we-are/

Nikolakis, William, Stephen Cornell, and Harry W. Nelson, eds. 2019. *Reclaiming Indigenous Governance: Reflections and Insights from Australia, Canada, New Zealand, and the United States*. Tuscon, AZ: University of Arizona Press.

Olthius, John, Nancy Kleer, and Roger Townshend. 2012. *Aboriginal Law Handbook*, 4th edition. Toronto, ON: Thomson Reuters.

Oosten, Jarich, Frédéric Laugrand, and Willem Rasing. 2017. *Inuit Laws. Tirigusuusiit, Piquujait, and Maligait*, 2nd edition. Iquailut, NU: Nunavut Arctic College Media.

Pope, Peter. 2015. "Bretons, Basques, and Inuit in Labrador and northern Newfoundland: The Control of Maritime Resources in the 16th and 17th Centuries." *Études/Inuit/Studies* 39 (1): 15–36. http://doi.org/10.7202/1036076ar.

Procter, Andrea. 2020a. "Elsewhere and Otherwise: Indigeneity and the Politics of Exclusion in Labrador's Extractive Resource Governance." *The Extractive Industries and Society*. https://doi.org/10.1016/j.exis.2020.05.018.

Procter, Andrea. 2020b. *A Long Journey: Residential Schools in Labrador and Newfoundland*. St. John's, NL: ISER Books.

Stopp, Marianne P. 2002. "Reconsidering Inuit Presence in Southern Labrador." *Études/Inuit/Studies* 26 (2): 71–106. https://doi.org/10.7202/007646ar.

Wilson, Shawn. 2008. *Research Is Ceremony. Indigenous Research Methods*. Halifax, NS and Winnipeg, MB: Fernwood Publishing.

CHAPTER 24

THE PREDICAMENT OF SUSTAINABILITY

Solutions in Greenland

Frank Sejersen

INTRODUCTION

Faced with the global challenges of climate change, the loss of biodiversity, the interference with the nitrogen cycle (Rockström et al. 2009), and the ambitions of the United Nations (UN) Sustainable Development Goals to improve the living standards of people around the world, the need to find sustainable solutions and transitions is more pressing than ever. The linking of sustainability and development is indeed necessary. However, it confronts us with several predicaments. It not only challenges our basic understandings of the relationships between nature, man, and development, it also challenges our very understanding of what we are dealing with, who we are, and who we want to become. When people discuss how to focus, organize, and mobilize sustainable development, there are often underlying cultural processes taking place which relate to phenomenon-making, people-making, and community-making. It is these processes of making the social world that are the focus of this chapter. The predicament of sustainability relates to the fact that these productive processes are seldom addressed directly, and in some cases are actively excluded, in order for involved actors at all scales to control representations and understandings of the problem (Bacchi 2012), and thus, to configure conflicts (and divert voices) in particular ways (Sejersen 2019a).

In the Arctic, discussions of sustainable development exude conflicts over, and negotiations of, the basic units of life and ways of understanding the web of relations. Furthermore, processes of people-making and person-making (the creation of social imaginaries) are weaved into the creation of nature-making and animal-making. These productive acts of creative world-making mean that sustainability is about *more* than just changing, installing, managing, and controlling human activities. It also implies that sustainability issues are used as tools to think with because sustainability as a political project stirs everything up for critical reflection. This implies that discussions of the long-term consequences of local users' applications of certain technologies in, for example, salmon fishing or bird hunting, are entangled with discussions of what kind of life and what kind of society can and should exist.

In this chapter, three cases of management conflicts in Greenland are analyzed with special analytical attention to the negotiations of the social life and imaginaries that take place. In all three cases, the Greenlandic state plays an important role in the reconfiguration of how social identities are perceived, and thus also in how the Inuit world should be organized. The chapter focuses on the ways that sustainability discourses and the regulatory practices of the Greenlandic authorities work to reconfigure the economic lives and identities of resource users (hunters and fishermen) and enhance processes of nation-building and the legitimacy of the Inuit self-government.

SUSTAINABILITY: APPROACHED AS ACTIVE WORLD-MAKING

Sustainability as a concept is associated with ideas of balance and stability that can be maintained into the future. In the report of the World Commission on Environment and Development (1987, 8) the most circulated definition of the concept stipulates that the balance between sustainability and development can be understood as follows: "Humanity has the ability to make development sustainable to ensure that it meets the needs of the present without compromising the ability of future generations to meet their own needs."

When sustainable development is directly linked to human needs, a number of dimensions of what constitutes "needs" may emerge. Rasmussen (2002, 40), for example, points out that economic, social, technological, political, and cultural "needs" are important to take into consideration when evaluating regulations formulated on the basis of the ideas laid out in the concept of sustainable development. With this list of dimensions, we see the contours of conflict and the tough decisions that have to take place. Furthermore, we see that those decisions may create winners and losers. A lot of research, for example within the field of political ecology, focuses on these important aspects (Robbins 2012).

The purpose of this chapter is to engage in an investigation of some of the predicaments that emerge when we talk about "sustainability." Hence, the chapter relies on a discursive approach rather than an investigation of whether or not an "optimal balance" between the abovementioned dimensions of sustainability has been obtained. Whenever sustainability is talked about and becomes the center of discursive attention, people also invest in and evoke ideas about space, time, subjectivities, and communities. Sustainability is, indeed, an open signifier, which different discourses try to fill with meaning. The concept of sustainability is not only given content by different discourses, but the concept itself is mobilized and used to make a difference in the world. Therefore, the chapter approaches "sustainability talk" as active world-making and the creation of spaces of legitimate identities and voices. When sustainability talk is turned into concrete regulations by the authorities, some livelihoods, communities, skills, and resource practices are banned or marginalized, while others may be reinforced. Because sustainability talk has real-life impacts, we need to understand in more detail what is invested in this talk.

"Sustainability" is not only linked to identity politics (who is allowed to do what?) but also linked to politics of ontology (what/who are and should we be regulating?). Discussions of sustainability take place between different groups (communities, usergroups, etc.) with different identities, interests, perspectives, and visions. Inherently, the discussions and conflicts themselves configure and demarcate these groups as well as the phenomena and units they evoke as important parts of reality. This chapter thus challenges the ontological status of community, and by doing so, opens up space for a more dynamic understanding of community-making. In such a perspective, social imaginaries are enacted. Furthermore, this approach acknowledges more openly that discussions of sustainability also involve ontological insecurity. Often, Inuit and other Indigenous peoples have suggested that their non-western worldviews offer a different ontology and epistemology (Fienup-Riordan 1990; McGrath 2011; Nadasdy 2007; Østmo and Law 2018). Discussions about the usefulness of "Traditional Ecological Knowledge" or "Indigenous Science" are examples of how the politics of ontology may play out and how claims of a particular ontology have political and practical ramifications. In Greenland, the politics of ontology are very much linked to conflicting mobilizations of social imaginaries (Sejersen 1998; 2003).

In this chapter, I analyze sustainability discussions in Greenland as a politics of ontology. I investigate how sustainability can be seen as related to the conceptualization, recognition, and reconfiguration of groups and communities with practical implications in terms of representation and the distribution of rights, responsibilities, and resources (Bertelsen 1996; Sejersen 2019a). Narratives of sustainability have a value because they work as persuasive pointers to potential action in the fields of development and identity (Bertelsen 1996, 14) for certain groups. The chapter analyses how "groupness" is configured, communicated, facilitated, and legitimized when sustainability is addressed and mobilized as a political issue.

In discourses of sustainability, the demarcation of groups themselves seem to pose few problems. What is often pointed out as the main problem is the lack of, or even inaccurate representation of, particular groups' interests and perspectives. The perspective of this chapter challenges this taken-for-grantedness of groups, and focuses on how groupness and social imaginaries are productively evoked and how political voices play an important role in the re-configuration of social identities. In this perspective, social identities are not carved in stone; they are constantly being (re)negotiated. Sustainability discussions constitute a very productive arena for such negotiations. The chapter shows how sustainability discussions in Greenland are closely related to community-making and processes of community re-imagination at different scales. In particular, it shows how the pursuit of Inuit nation-building not only becomes an important dimension in discussions about sustainability, but a pivotal driver of the discussions and the direction they take.

GREENLAND AND THE LEGAL FRAMEWORK FOR SUSTAINABILITY

The regional population in Greenland attained Home Rule in 1979, and because the majority of the population is made up of people who consider themselves Greenlanders (of Inuit descent), it is fair to say that the Inuit of Greenland took a huge step in pursuing increased self-determination and reshaping the (post)colonial relationship with the former colonial power (Denmark). The regional government structures set up in Greenland (Dahl 2005) can be seen as an extensive model for the fulfillment of Indigenous peoples' rights. The Home Rule Act laid the groundwork for the creation of a Greenlandic government and a Greenlandic parliament. Important areas of responsibility and public interest, like the health care system, environmental management, and the educational system, were transferred from Denmark to Greenland, including an annual block grant to finance the work. Thus, environmental issues have been managed by the Greenlandic authorities, and regulations have continuously been adopted by the Greenlandic parliament. Furthermore, Greenland fleshed out its own system of knowledge production used to underpin its decision-making. In 2009, the Act on Greenland Self-Government increased the powers and responsibilities of the Greenlandic authorities. The Act also makes it possible for Greenland to declare full independence from Denmark. Quickly after the passing of the Act, Greenland took over the responsibilities of mineral development. However, the increased powers of self-government that came in 2009 did not directly influence the management of renewable resources because Greenlandic authorities already had full responsibility over environmental management, since 1979.

The Greenlandic authorities have introduced an armory of regulations as part of the implementation of a sustainability management regime. To underpin decision-making, the authorities receive scientific advice from the Greenland Institute of Natural Resources, established in Nuuk in 1995, replacing advice from institutions located in Denmark. Hence, knowledge production and expertise were brought closer to Greenlandic political realities. Biological research plays an important role in the management decisions taken by the government, and biologists often put forward issues that require the attention of authorities. The Greenlandic government pursues a clear and outspoken framework with respect to its management of natural resources and applies international principles of sustainability, control, and transparency.

However, hunters and fishermen who participate in management discussions often disagree with biologists' population estimations, as well as management regulations proposed by the government. Frequently, these discussions configure around different knowledge claims. Similar management conflicts are found elsewhere in the Arctic (Fienup-Riordan 1990; Huntington 1992; see also Lund, this volume). In 2015, Jimmy Stotts (cited in Hoag 2015), president of Inuit Circumpolar Council (Alaska section), explained the controversy in the following way:

> We feel that science and scientists today are dismissive of the value of indigenous knowledge. Indigenous knowledge is actually based in indigenous culture and that has its own worldview and its own way of looking at what's important.
>
> For example, when you talk about biodiversity, the perspective from the outside world is very often focused on protection and conservation. We believe in protecting and conserving the biodiversity so we can use it. We utilize these animals for food and so on and so forth. If you're aware of Inuit culture, you know that we're a coastal hunting people – that's our existence. When we talk about biodiversity, we're a part of that environment and we are part of that ecosystem. We have a relationship with these animals, but we are not there to protect them from everybody. That is a cultural difference that sometimes is hard to get beyond.

However, the production of knowledge claims in Greenland often differs from how claims are made in Canada and Alaska with respect to environmental management. In the North American region, knowledge claims about environmental management are often linked to concepts of "Indigenous" and "traditional." This connection emphasizes that these claims are part of a knowledge regime that is epistemologically and ontologically distinct from western-based science. In the North American context, the knowledge conflict frequently becomes a conflict between different worldviews and the asymmetrical (colonial) relationship that exists between them. By underlining the "Indigeneity" of the knowledge regime, its proponents also underline its location outside of the apparatus of the state, and the importance of recognizing the dominance of the state through a colonial perspective (Sejersen 2015). In Greenland, the idea of "Indigenous knowledge" is not often asserted in management conflicts (Sejersen 2004; Thisted 2019). Rather, hunters and fishermen rely on claims of "local knowledge." By doing so, they accentuate their intimate relationship to the resources, as well as the (local) communities in which production, distribution, and consumption take place. In this discourse, local resource users position scientific experts as *distanced from reality* and coming from *another (external) social group*. As a consequence, the Greenlandic government is represented as being alienated from its own population if it listens too much to the scientists. Sometimes, this discourse of distance and alienation is accentuated by conceptualizing expert and government statements as Danish even though the statements have been put forward by Greenlanders. However, this alienated and asymmetrical position of the state is *seldom* seen as colonial. Rather, it is seen as undemocratic, narrow-minded, and a form of governance from a distance (mentally, physically, culturally, economically, and practically). Thisted (2019, 189) mentions that local resource users can view governance from a distance as illegitimate; one could also say that distance is creatively used to underpin arguments about illegitimacy.

Increasingly, biologists work with local resource users in Greenland in order to improve their scientific work (Sejersen 2002). This tendency is seen increasingly across North America (Huntington et al. 2011). Working together enables different knowledge claims to be explored as a positive resource for all involved. One potential benefit is that cooperation can lead to a keen awareness of the differences and similarities in how a) data is produced, b) how data is interpreted and c) how interpretations are linked to action (Nadasdy 2003; Sejersen 2002). Experimentation with new cooperation between scientists and local resource users, as well as experimentation with new management ideas in Greenland, have resulted in a prize-winning monitoring project where local people monitor and manage chosen resources with the application of simple methods (citizen science and local knowledge). The project created a Natural Resources Council in the community of Attu on the west coast of Greenland. In 2018, when the council won the Nordic Council Environment Prize, the Greenland Minister for Nature, Environment, and Research, Siverth K. Heilmann, stated that "[t]he Natural Resources Council has shown how citizens, authorities, and researchers can combine their knowledge and work closely together, to achieve the best results for the benefit of nature and living resources" (cited in Nordeco 2018).

However, science retains a privileged position in government decisions. Frequently, hunters and fishermen have to live with restrictions and regulations that they find frustrating and wrong. In North America, Indigenous peoples have, for a long time, worked to develop stronger systems of co-management where different knowledge claims are put forward and discussed in more transparent ways. Furthermore, in North America, Indigenous peoples are working systematically to establish practices, collaborative methods, and structures that support their knowledge regimes. Among other things, initiatives focus on a) documenting knowledge that is necessary to engage in dialogue about development or determine the proper course of development, b) providing knowledge and tools through guides, manuals, or plans to support meaningful participation in development, and c) reclaiming knowledge and reimagining self-determined human development (Carroll 2019).

Indigenous and local knowledge claims are not only claims that are made to point at a) political asymmetries in decision-making, b) the existence of non-western epistemologies and ontologies, or c) the value of integrating other ways of learning, knowing, and communicating. Knowledge claims can also be understood as the evocation of communities and of relations between communities. Claims of local knowledge, for example, are also claims to what and who is considered "local." Hence, knowledge claims are important in the production of locality (Appadurai 1996) as well as in nation-building (Whyte 2018). Furthermore, knowledge claims are a way to underpin and legitimize particular worldviews, needs, obligations, responsibilities, and perspectives that are associated with particular communities (see Figure 24.1).

As the three cases below will show, management conflicts emerge due to different perspectives and knowledge claims. However, they also evolve due to different visions of the social (social imaginaries). Hence, management conflicts challenge the understandings of objects of reality but also re-configure social relations and social identities. The three cases explored in this chapter (guillemot, beluga whale, and Greenlandic halibut) have been chosen because they are all highly controversial management conflicts that have evoked widespread public discussion and concern in Greenland.

Figure 24.1 The town of Maniitsoq had its life nerve cut when the fishing industry moved elsewhere. The town is now trying to reorganize and find new avenues for development. People in Maniitsoq often complain about how the authorities in the capital of Nuuk seem to bypass their needs and interests. Photo: Frank Sejersen.

GUILLEMOT

In Greenland, Brünnich's Guillemots (*Uria lomvia*), also called thick-billed murres, are a treasured bird species celebrated for their tasty meat. In some regions, the guillemots make up a substantial proportion of the supply of meat and thus are important in the subsistence economy. In other parts of the country, they are also an important source of income when sold on the local meat market (Falk and Kampp 2001, 9). At the end of the 1990s, biologists argued that the bird population was decreasing and that something drastic had to be done. This announcement was followed by an intense discussion of how to protect the birds and how to regulate the human activities that have a negative impact on their population dynamics. Biologists pointed out the problems faced by the bird: it is a slow breeding species with slow population growth (Falk and Kampp 2001).

Guillemots become mature when they are four to five years old. They breed on small stone shelves on vertical cliff sides. Here, breeding couples create huge colonies, and the females lay only one egg. They do not build nests, which leaves the chance that inexperienced young birds might push their egg off the shelf. Furthermore, two out of three young birds die of natural causes. Historically, the breeding colonies contained thousands of birds, and hunters recall how foreign visitors and salmon fishing boats stressed and killed the birds (Falk 1998). Thus, hunters point at "foreign" people as the problem. At the breeding cliff called Salleq in the Uummannaq area, the population was estimated to be 200,000 in 1940. During a bird count in 1994, no breeding guillemots were observed (Egevang and Boertmann 2012, 42–45). Along the west coast of Greenland, many former breeding cliffs are now empty. Biologists point out contemporary hunting as a critical human activity endangering the population. Hunt reports in the 1990s indicated an annual hunt of 187,645 in 1994 and 253,286 in 1996 (Denlinger and Wohl 2001, 27). The guillemot case became one of the more troublesome conflicts in Greenland because the decline in stock took place so rapidly and because the hunt was considered so important, culturally.

The hunting primarily takes place during winter in the overwintering areas in the southern part of Greenland. Large groups of adult and young birds from Greenland, Canada, Svalbard, and Iceland gather at the sea. Thus, the large number of birds hunted stem from multiple populations in the Arctic and contains many juvenile individuals. In the spring, the birds start to migrate to their respective breeding grounds in the Arctic. Birds traveling north along the coast of Greenland are primarily mature adults on their way to breeding colonies in Greenland. These birds were also subject to hunting during their spring migration up north. It is this spring hunt that was the center of focus in the conflict. Because the spring hunt focuses solely on birds using colonies in Greenland, it was identified as the main threat to the overall population of guillemots, and tools in a new bird regulation (2001) were suggested to limit it. The regulations caused an outcry by hunters along the coast, because the regulations hit a valued life-nerve of their hunting culture. Many letters to the editor, community meetings, campaigns, hearing processes, protests to politicians, and so forth, followed in the wake of the introduction of the new bird regulation. The regulation protected the breeding population in the Upernavik area, in the northern part of Greenland by prohibiting the spring hunt. For people in Upernavik it was seen as an intervention based on the government's lack of knowledge of local conditions, needs, and traditions. A relation of care and intimacy was linked to the birds by people in Upernavik, and the bird was configured as entangled in relations that were evoked as local and special. Thus, hunters cast the birds as game, which was essential if one cared for the wellbeing of people in Upernavik. Some critical comments in the public debate also positioned hunters south of Upernavik (who were still allowed to hunt the guillemots) as only caring for themselves, and marginalizing others in their pursuit of self-interest. The regulation was seen as an act of (national) standardization prioritizing the politically and demographically strong population in the south, who intervened in local matters in irresponsible ways and without any meaningful consultation. The conflict emerged as a conflict between north and south, between community wellbeing and national interest, between hunting for a living and hunting for leisure. Critical arguments configured people in different demarcated groups and in particular, the north-south demarcation was accentuated to a point not seen very often. The hunters conjured (shifting) groups of legitimate users by the integration of birds in different socio-cultural-economic group configurations. Different regimes of legitimization not only made up birds in different ways but also conjured and installed the social entities that were thought to make up the system.

Seen from the state's point of view the birds were recast into a *national population* to be cared for. When the flying, breeding, eating, and dying birds in Greenland were designated as a "national population," it created a new set of attentions, relations, and bureaucratic practices within a different kind of space-time frame (Nadasdy 2008). This (re)framing of birds also changed the frame in which responsibilities emerged, as well as the political effects of scarcity and depletion. The depletion of guillemots meant something different for the state than it did to hunting communities. For the state, international responsibilities, as stipulated in different agreements and cooperation, enveloped the guillemot in a regime where rationalities are (inter)national. Ideas of scarcity and depletion of the resources configure temporality around the time frame of the nation (bureaucratic as well as political). The international cooperation that Greenland has become engaged in entangles the birds in new relations of attention and obligation.

Due to different entanglements, the guillemot was approached as primarily *a breeding bird* (related to the nation) while the hunters understood them as primarily *a bird of prey* (related to the hunter communities). Often these diverse configurations were understood as different and conflicting perspectives on the *same* bird. What I am arguing is that it is different kinds of bird-making (resource-making) that entail different ontologies and social points of attention. The Greenlandic government enacts itself as a state of a particular kind by its bird-making processes, which involve the integration of birds in its bureaucratic apparatus.

The predicament of sustainability in this case is not only related to understanding a) what the problem is, b) how to solve it, c) what the consequences of management interventions are, and d) who can partake in the discussions. I claim that the predicament is also related to the fact that the birds are configured in quite different ways – and in some cases so differently that the real conflict is also about the subject matter itself. That is why the discussions are not only about different perspectives. They are political struggles about different ways of understanding what the world is made up of and how entities are related. Therefore, it is a political struggle to enforce one's ontology as dominant. In this case, we also see a state that increasingly promotes and conjures itself through the rationalities of (inter)national rights, obligations, bureaucratic tools, and responsibilities. The tasty birds so important for families suddenly find themselves entangled in a regime of legitimization where they are represented as belonging to national breeding populations under international attention. Thus, the birds also become spearheads in the nation-building ambitions and processes pursued by the Inuit of Greenland, despite the fact that many Greenlanders were excluded from hunting the birds by the state's initiatives.

The birds are brought into a relationship with the Greenlandic state, which resembles a kind of ownership and thus commitment and responsibility. Birds are translated into populations that are appropriated by the state/nation. This process can be seen as an act of nationalism and thus the creation of resources as "natural" and "belonging" to a certain territory can be approached as a part of nation-building. The argument is that nation-building is mobilized by acts of resource enactments of a particular kind. The dynamics of political struggles of ontology are not only related to the objects in question (i.e., birds), but also to the social entities that can claim a relation to those objects (e.g., hunting communities or states). These social entities are conjured, (re)produced, regulated, and tested through discussions of sustainability.

Inspired by Lévi-Strauss (1969, 162) one can say that in order for a substance (entity) to be "good to eat" (*bon à manger*), the substance must also be "good to think" (*bon à penser*). A substance (e.g., guillemot) can by acts of translation (Sejersen 2019b) be turned into a "resource" for a particular human community. When a "resource" is creatively made up, it is promoted by social entities that in the very same process (re)produce and imagine the social entity itself in time-space. Migrating birds are good to eat but indeed also good to think the social with.

BELUGA

At the beginning of the 1990s, hunters, biologists, and wildlife managers were challenged to a great extent when research indicated that something drastic had to be done about the management of beluga whales (*Delphinapterus leucas*, also called white whales). The Greenland–Canada Joint Commission on the Management and Conservation of Narwhal and Beluga (JCCMNB) kept on urging Greenland to limit the hunt and to create elaborate management regulations. Based on Home Rule government-sponsored biological surveys, the JCCMNB announced, that "the rate of decline of the stock requires that the effective implementation of such measures should take place on an urgent basis" (JCCMNB 1993). If one wanted the beluga population to reach its 1981 size, a full cessation of hunting for 23 to 46 years would be required (JCCMNB 1994, 6).

For Greenlandic whale hunters, this came as a shock. However, the hunters had also experienced changes in hunting practices over the years. These changes had given rise to several conflicts and cleavages within and between communities. To understand the growing predicament, it is important to understand the way beluga whale hunting as a cultural complex takes place.

The beluga whale is a highly valued prey and is especially celebrated for its tasty skin. In the economy of hunters, the catch of a beluga whale can be seen as a strategic resource for the household because it generates large quantities of culturally valuable meat/skin and a good potential income within a relatively short period (Dahl 1989).

Beluga whales hunted off the west coast of Greenland belong to the two Baffin Bay populations. Biologists note that the migration pattern makes the beluga whale population especially vulnerable to over-exploitation due to the whales' coastal habits:

> During the autumn they move south along the west coast of Greenland, passing near a number of settlements with intensive white whale hunting and where especially females are taken in large numbers ... These coastal areas may act as "bottlenecks" for the whale population.
>
> (Heide-Jørgensen 1994, 148)

Beluga whales often migrate and move in groups. Hunting practices differ from region to region and season to season. However, one hunting practice has been the center of attention. Communities have long practiced what has been labeled cooperative hunting, where all skilled hunters participate. All participants get an equal share of the catch. However, the emergence of larger boats and an increasing number of hunters from outside the communities have challenged the system of distribution and the orchestration of the hunt as well as the distribution of meat (Dahl 2000; Sejersen 2001). Hunters in bigger boats (or boats with several hunters) started to require a larger share of the total catch, and in some cases, though the hunt was cooperative, the whales secured were claimed by individual boats, even though others had been part of the hunt. The flensing scene was increasingly turned into a battlefield of interests and constant negotiation between different hunters, who started to relate to each other in terms of socio-economic background, home community, hunting license, use of technology, role in the hunt, and final use of the catch. At the flensing scene, hunters had to negotiate which rule to apply and thus decide upon which socio-economic group to favor. Such decisions are political, ethical, and for some hunters potentially devastating economically. Questions of social sustainability soon became the central issue. Who should have access rights, including user rights and distribution rights? Similar conflicts are found in Inuit communities in Canada and Alaska (Sejersen 2001).

In 1992, the Home Rule government of Greenland started to implement the first of many attempts to reduce the harvest. At the local level, these new regulations soon became entangled in the already complex setting. The technology of government excluded and included different user groups' possibilities to go beluga hunting. One of the political questions was how the whale should be interpreted. The whale was taken out of local regulations and controls and appropriated by the state via the new Home Rule management regime (Dahl 1998; 2000). All citizens in Greenland were allowed user rights because belugas were seen as a resource belonging to Greenland. The government did not want to restrict user rights to particular communities because it saw Greenland as *one* hunting territory open to all *citizens*. This act of national resource appropriation can also be seen as an act of nation-making and citizen-making – of Inuit nation-building. However, in order to limit the hunt, the Home Rule government had to install an arsenal of different criteria for users to get access to the resource (beluga) and for users to distribute their catch. In that process, whale hunters suddenly saw themselves distributed in new bureaucratically defined socio-economic entities. Hunters were whirled into a new people-making process initiated by the state (but already played out in a variety of ways at the flensing sites).

Hunters creatively tried to escape the categories they were locked into by changing their technology, for example. Many hunters protested against the categories they were fixed in (e.g., suddenly the size of their boat demarcated their hunting rights) as much as the rights ascribed to the different categories.

In a thorough investigation of the conflict, anthropologist Jens Dahl (1998, 76–77) concluded that:

> When Home Rule took over the management of hunting and fishing a completely new type of discrimination was institutionalized. This was the association of rights with specified social groups, such as full-time hunters and fishermen; part-time hunters and fishermen; owners of certain types of boats or owners of special licenses ... The social and territorial control as exerted by the local communities has been exchanged with centralized political control.

The case shows how discussions of sustainability also establish new social entities that cross-cut existing ones, rearranging the social reality and challenging what is considered stability. It is important to note that the making up of new social entities is part of many management initiatives around the world. The point is that sustainability is not only a matter that existing social entities have to relate to, influence, and deal with. Rather, issues of sustainability often involve the reconfiguration of the social itself and the conjuring of new social entities that suddenly have to think of themselves as political subjects (Sejersen 2019a). Frequently, sustainability conflicts initiate processes whereby old and newly created social entities (ontology of the social) become subject to planned management. The predicament of sustainability is that discussions often have to take place and have to navigate between the existing stable and the unstable new. In this gap, questions of ontology become of paramount political importance and much effort is invested in promoting one's social ontology as hegemonic. The social itself is at stake.

GREENLANDIC HALIBUT

The Greenlandic economy is extremely dependent upon the income from fishing activities. 91 percent of Greenland's export value, and 25 percent of value creation in society, stem from fisheries (Fiskerikommissionen 2019). The income from fishing is primarily generated from the shrimp fisheries. However, since the 1990s, the fisheries of Greenlandic halibut (*Reinhardtius hippoglossoides*) have increased in importance, and are now the second most important fishery. For communities, families, and businesses/companies, the fisheries play a paramount role. Many households are economically dependent upon access to Greenlandic halibut and the possibility to sell the catch in order to sustain the household. Contrary to shrimp, the fishing of Greenlandic halibut can also be pursued by the use of small-scale technology (a dog sled, a dingy, and long lines). The fishing industry generates a number of land-based jobs in fish processing plants, and communities are often eager to be integrated with the industry in order to be part of the income-generative activities of fishing.

Therefore, sustainability in the fisheries is of paramount importance, and every year controversies emerge about Total Allowable Catch (TAC), quota sizes, distribution of quotas, demarcation of seasons, requirements that vessels land their catch at land-based plants, technological requirements, etc. Due to the economic importance of fisheries, the industry is eager to make its strategies for sustainability transparent, and many of the Greenlandic fisheries have now received the MSC certificate. However, the economic importance of fisheries and the many dependent fishermen also make quota politics a highly political matter. Sometimes, quotas are distributed in order to satisfy the electorate. The Fishery Commission (Fiskerikommissionen 2019, 21) shows how the quota (close to the coast) for Greenlandic halibut exceeded the TAC by 11 percent in 2013. Every year the TAC was exceeded, and in 2019 the excess amounted to 76 percent. With respect to cod, the TAC was exceeded by 25 percent (2013) and 308 percent (2019). The commission pointed out that there is not enough fish to meet the demands of fishermen (see Figure 24.2).

The Greenlandic Self-Rule set up fishing commissions to advise the government. The latest of several reports was published in 2019. In this report, the commission urges the government and industry to make improvements in the governance of fisheries through the introduction of Individual Transferable Quotas (ITQ) to make the fisheries more efficient, sustainable, and to optimize the income to society (maximize the resource rent). In effect, the report proposes to configure the fisheries around neoliberal ideas (for an introduction see Pinkerton and Davis 2015).

Already in 2009, the commission came to the conclusion that the fishing sector was becoming *less* work-intensive and *more* capital-intensive. Furthermore, the commission noticed a general trend in the overall job market. Due to estimated future job prospects in the mining and aluminum industries, the commission argued that the ITQ system could make the fisheries more economically sustainable for a reduced number

Figure 24.2 Management regulations decided upon in the capital Nuuk are often criticized by people living elsewhere in Greenland using arguments that stress Nuuk's cultural and economic detachment from the rest of Greenland. Photo: Frank Sejersen.

of people engaged in the industry (Fiskerikommissionen 2009, 147); the "leftover" manpower could be absorbed by the new mineral industries. Hence, sustainability in the fishing sector and important systemic decisions were based on prospective developments in other sectors. What seemed sustainable from the point of view of a small fisherman's household became judged as rather unsustainable from the state's multisectoral point of view. In the state government system, fish became translated into resource rents for society as a whole. Thus, the value of the fish is not the fish itself (quality, price, and quantity), but rather what the Greenlandic society as a whole can generate on the basis of catches. The commission changed the interpretation of the meaning of common resources. From being resources that many had access to with little overall profit, common resources became resources that few should have access to in order to generate the maximal profits to underpin the state's economy to the benefit of the population. The government wanted the fisheries to be managed effectively, and the commission interpreted this as a wish to *increase* the market-based income of *full-time* fishermen. Put differently, the commission concluded the number of fishermen should be minimized in order to increase the income of the remaining fishermen, who were to fish on a full-time basis (Fiskerikommissionen 2009, 144), and that the government should decrease its economic interventions in order to usher the fisheries into the dynamics of the market. According to the commission (Fiskerikommissionen 2009, 83–85) too many people in the halibut fisheries earned too little to make a contribution to society, and the recruitment of new fishermen into the sector should be limited (144). A Social Impact Assessment (Delaney et al. 2012) unsuccessfully tried to draw the government's attention to the importance of small-scale fishing for the maintenance and resilience of households in communities where cash income possibilities were limited.

Jacobsen (2013a; 2013b) has pursued extensive research in Greenland and analyzed the transformations that took place in the Greenlandic fisheries when ITQ systems were introduced. Because the ITQ system was deliberately installed to centralize the fisheries into fewer hands, the consequence was that the number of fishermen and boats decreased. When the ITQ system was introduced in the shrimp fisheries in 1990, the number of boats was reduced from 46 to 12 (Det Uvildige Udvalg 2005, 58–59). Therefore, the ITQ system raises questions related to social fairness and effectiveness (Jacobsen 2013b, 3).

In 2012, the ITQ system was also introduced into the Greenlandic halibut fisheries. Part of the transformation was discursively created by considering *local boats* and *vessels* as belonging to a *national fleet*. In 2009, the licensed fleet consisted of 151 vessels above eight meters and about 1100 small entities (Jacobsen 2013b, 5). With respect to production, the trade in fish in 2009 showed that 89 percent of the license holders (n = 1116 persons) earned very little, while 10 percent (n = 142 persons) earned a medium income, and just 1 percent (n = 10 persons) earned a substantial income. The commission's ITQ idea challenged the many fishermen, who integrate fishing into multi-activity lifestyles.

The introduction of the ITQ resulted in the expected buying and selling of quota licenses because many fishermen did not find the ascribed quota economically feasible. One of the fundamental rationales behind ITQ is that the few fishermen allowed to fish would protect investments and resources better, due to personal interests. For the state, this mentality is attractive and it will supposedly increase the resource rent and thus the overall benefits to society. In 2019, a new commission published a discussion paper arguing for ITQ. The paper was titled "Our Fish, Our Welfare," and it clarified the connection between ITQ, fish as a common resource, and the welfare of society. By introducing ITQ, the state not only limits citizens' access to fish as a common resource but translates the common resource into common welfare (of all citizens). In this perspective, sustainability is about underpinning a particular citizen-state relation, and a way that the state governs its population and formulates promises of state-supported security, development, and prosperity. For fishermen, who are left without a license and unable to provide for their families, this strategy can appear quite abstract. The alternative employment possibilities for these former fishermen are not as plentiful as suggested by the commission (indeed, the possibilities are rather non-existent). A proposed solution is to increase mobility (people have to move to jobs), and the ITQ system can, thus, also be seen as a tool to reconfigure the job market and as part of a regional reorganization of the population (see Figure 24.3).

There are several interesting points in the ITQ case. First, it clearly shows that neoliberal ideas of management are not necessarily imposed on Inuit societies from "the outside," subsequently forcing Inuit to adapt. Neoliberal ideas of management are used strategically as a strong driver of nation-building, people-making, and social engineering in Greenland. Second, the introduction of ITQ indicates how questions of sustainability are scaled in quite different ways and how the resource and the value itself may be translated differently (is the management focus fish or the resource rent?). The predicament of sustainability is that the referent objects (Gad et al. 2019) are slippery and become objects of political and social strategizing.

Figure 24.3 With the number of boats and resource users increasing, the demand for new management regulations is a heated topic of debate. Photo: Frank Sejersen.

CONCLUSION

In the three cases explored in this chapter, the socio-cultural and economic stakes are high, and divergent perspectives are at play. In this way, these conflicts share similarities with many other management conflicts worldwide. However, the analysis shows how the growing Inuit nation-building process is a pivotal driver in how sustainability discussions take place in Greenland and in the choices of management rationales pursued by the Inuit authorities.

On a broader analytical level, the analysis shows how Inuit nation-building in Greenland conjures itself through discussions and how the entities of the world (categories of the social as well as the natural) are reimagined, re-arranged, and reconfigured as part of this nation-building process. Often, management conflicts involving Indigenous peoples focus on how Indigenous peoples' local perspectives clash with the perspectives of non-Indigenous state authorities. In this case, the emerging Indigenous self-government authorities are in conflict with local Indigenous resource users. What is especially interesting is how the state and local resource users have (and rely upon) different concepts of sustainability: the state is concerned with "national resources" that statecraft can be brought to bear on to create and sustain citizens and state institutions through bureaucratic and scientific values and practices, while local resource users are interested in "common resources" that sustain local communities, families, and intimate social relations through local values and practices.

The Greenlandic authorities evoke a management situation, where birds, whales, and fish not only become the focus of political attention but also become problematized in particular ways. The important and, as the cases show, necessary political debate of implementing management mechanisms to ensure sustainable use also involves working with the social categories and the associated user rights. The sustainability discussions related to the wise use of birds, whales, and fish become issues that have to integrate all citizens as beneficiaries of the resources. This way of problematizing the sustainability discussions elevates concrete user perspectives (hunters and fishermen) to more abstract national users (citizens). This upscale in social attention is also an upscale of the ideas of the community (from small-scale, local, to large-scale national). Living organisms (birds, whales, and fish) that have underpinned local households and communities are through the sustainability talk translated into national "populations," "resources," and "rents." In that process, something happens.

The predicament of sustainability is that the reference objects (Gad et al. 2019) (be they social or natural) can be unstable and under constant negotiation, during discussions. A fish may be reconfigured from a "local resource" to a "national resource rent," and in this process also change the social imaginaries (e.g., who is a fisherman and what is the purpose of fishing?). Thus, the Greenlandic national authorities create alternative understandings and particular truths of the social as part of making sustainability governable. The social is not self-evident.

Sustainability is about altering, legitimizing, and constructing the social world and paving the road for particular social formations to take place. The predicament is that the way sustainability talk works with the social world is not addressed directly. When sustainability efforts align people in particular relationships and positions (e.g., as hunters or citizens), these efforts can be seen as part of the politics of people-making. Hence, resistance to sustainability initiatives is not only about promoting alternative kinds of knowledge and management ideas, but can moreover be seen as a resistance to the reworking of the social world that is taking place. The predicament is that social categories are normally considered evident (e.g., a hunter is a hunter). The categories of the social world are seldom identified as an inherent aspect of the so-called "gaps of knowledge" that have to be filled in management discussion. And for good reason, because it is rather gaps in political processes that camouflage how sustainability talk and subsequent discussions in fact remake and rework the social when the talk is about sustainable use of natural resources.

REFERENCES

Appadurai, Arjun. 1996. *Modernity at Large*. Minneapolis, MN: University of Minnesota Press.
Bacchi, Carol. 2012. "Why Study Problematization? Making Politics Visible." *Open Journal of Political Science* 2 (1): 1–8. http://doi.org/10.4236/ojps.2012.21001.
Bertelsen, Kristoffer B. 1996. *Our Communalized Future*. PhD dissertation, Aarhus University.
Carroll, Jennifer L.L. 2019. "Development Dilemmas: Rural Development Students Imagining a Sustainable Future in Alaska." *Paper presented at the Northern Political Economy Symposium*, Nov 14, Rovaniemi.
Dahl, Jens. 1989. "The Integrative and Cultural Role of Hunting and Subsistence in Greenland." *Études/Inuit/Studies* 13 (1): 23–42.
———. 1998. "Resource Appropriation, Territories and Social Control." In *Aboriginal Environmental Knowledge in the North*, edited by Louise-Jacques Dorais, Murielle Nagy, and Ludger Müller-Wille, 61–80. Québec City, QC: GÉTIC.
———. 2000. *Saqqaq. An Inuit Hunting Community in the Modern World*. Toronto, ON: University of Toronto Press.
———. 2005. "The Greenlandic Version of Self-Government." In *An Indigenous Parliament?*, edited by Kathrin Wessendorf, 150–177. Copenhagen: IWGIA.
Delaney, Alyne E., Rikke Becker Jakobsen, and Kåre Hendriksen. 2012. *Greenland Halibut in Upernavik. A Preliminary Study of the Importance of the Stock for the Fishing Populace*. Aalborg: Aalborg University.
Denlinger, Lynn. and Wohl, Kenton, eds. 2001. *Seabird Harvest Regimes in the Circumpolar Nations*. CAFF technical report no. 9. Akureyri: Conservation of Arctic Flora and Fauna.
Det Uvildige Udvalg. 2005. *Omsættelige kvoter og andre metoder til regulering af rejefiskeriet [Transferable Quotas and Other Methods to Regulate the Shrimp Fisheries]*. Nuuk: Grønlands Hjemmestyre.
Egevang, Carsten, and David Boertmann. 2012. *De grønlandske fuglebeskyttelsesområder – en statusrapport [The Greenlandic Bird Protection Areas – A Status Report]*. Teknisk rapport 87. Nuuk: Grønlands Naturinstitut.
Falk, Knud. 1998. "Review of Seabird Bycatch in Greenland." In *Incidental Take of Seabirds in Commercial Fisheries in the Arctic Countries*, edited by Vidar Bakken and Knud Falk, 18–22. CAFF Technical Report 1. Akureyri: Conservation of Arctic Flora and Fauna.
Falk, Knud, and Kampp, Kaj. 2001. *Lomvien i Grønland: Mulige effekter af forskellige bestandspåvirkende faktorer, og praktiske grænser for ressourceudnyttelse [The Guillemots in Greenland: Possible Effects of Different Factors Affecting the Population and Practical Limits of Ressource Use]*. Teknisk rapport no. 38. Nuuk: Grønlands Naturinstitut.
Fienup-Riordan, Ann. 1990. *Eskimo Essays*. New Brunswick: Rutgers University Press.
Fiskerikommissionen. 2009. *Fiskerikommissionens betænkning [Report by the Fisheries Commission]*. Nuuk: Fiskerikommissionen.

———. 2019. *Vores fisk – vores velfærd [Our Fish – Our Welfare]*. Nuuk: Fiskerikommissionen.

Gad, Ulrik Pram, Marc Jacobsen, and Jeppe Strandsbjerg. 2019. "Introduction: Sustainability as a Political Concept in the Arctic." In *The Politics of Sustainability in the Arctic: Reconfiguring Identity, Space and Time*, edited by Ulrik Pram Gad and Jeppe Strandsbjerg, 1–18. London: Routledge.

Heide-Jørgensen, Mads Peter. 1994. "Distribution, Exploitation and Population Status of White Whales and Narwhals in West Greenland." In *Studies of White Whales (Delphinapterus leucas) and Narwhals (Monodon monceros) in Greenland and Adjacent Waters*, edited by Erik W. Born, Rune Dietz, and Randall R. Reeves, 135–150). Copenhagen: MoG, Bioscience 39.

Hoag, Hannah. 2015. "Q&A: Inuit Priorities and Indigenous Knowledge." *News Deeply*, 16 December. https://www.newsdeeply.com/arctic/community/2015/12/16/qa-inuit-priorities-and-indigenous-knowledge

Huntington, Henry P. 1992. *Wildlife Management and Subsistence Hunting in Alaska*. London: Belhaven Press.

Huntington, Henry P., Shari Gearheard, Andrew R. Mahoney, and Anne K. Salomon. 2011. "Integrating Traditional and Scientific Knowledge through Collaborative Natural Science Field Research: Identifying Elements for Success." *Arctic* 64 (4): 437–445.

Jacobsen, Rikke Becker. 2013a. *Power and Participation in Greenlandic Fisheries Governance*. PhD dissertation, Aalborg University.

———. 2013b. Small-Scale Fisheries in Greenlandic Planning – The Becoming of a Governance Problem. *Maritime Studies* 12 (2). https://doi.org/10.1186/2212-9790-12-2.

JCCMNB (Joint Commission on the Management and Conservation of Narwhal and Beluga). 1993. Press Release, August 26.

———. 1994. *Report of the Joint Commission on the Conservation and Management of Narwhal and Beluga, Meeting of the Scientific Working Group June 20–23, 1994*.

Lévi-Strauss, Claude. 1969. *Totemism*. Harmondsworth: Penguin.

McGrath, Janet Tamalik. 2011. *Isumaksaqsiurutigijakka: Conversations with Aupilaarjuk towards a Theory of Inuktitut Knowledge Renewal*. PhD dissertation, Carleton University.

Nadasdy, Paul. 2003. *Hunters and Bureaucrats*. Vancouver, BC: UBC Press.

———. 2007. "The Gift in the Animal: The Ontology of Hunting and Human-Animal Sociality." *American Ethnologist* 34 (1): 25–43. https://doi.org/10.1525/ae.2007.34.1.25.

———. 2008. "Wildlife as Renewable Resource: Competing Conceptions of Wildlife, Time and Management in the Yukon." In *Timely Assets: The Politics of Resources and Their Temporalities*, edited by Elizabeth Emma Ferry and Mandana E. Limbert, 75–106. Santa Fe, NM: SAR Press.

Nordeco. 2018. "Nordic Council Environment Prize Winner." 2 November. https://www.nordeco.dk/single-post/2018/11/02/Nordic-Council-Environment-Prize

Pinkerton, Evelyn, and Reade Davis. 2015. "Neoliberalism and the Politics of Enclosure in North American Small-Scale Fisheries." *Marine Policy* 61: 303–312. https://doi.org/10.1016/j.marpol.2015.03.025.

Rasmussen, Rasmus Ole. 2002. "Bidrag til en bæredygtig udvikling i Grønland." [Contributions to a Sustainable Development in Greenland] In *Aspekter af Bæredygtig Udvikling i Grønland [Aspects of Sustainable Development in Greenland]*, edited by Rasmus Ole Rasmussen and Klaus Georg Hansen, 11–42. Sisimiut: Sisimiut Museum and NORS.

Robbins, Paul. 2012. *Political Ecology: A Critical Introduction*. Malden, MA: Blackwell Publishing.

Rockström, Johan, Will Steffen, Kevin Noone, Åsa Persson, F. Stuart Chapin III, Eric F. Lambin, Timothy M. Lenton, Marten Scheffer, Carl Folke, Hans Joachim Schellnhuber, Björn Nykvist, Cynthia A. de Wit, Terry Hughes, Sander van der Leeuw, Henning Rodhe, Sverker Sörlin, Peter K. Snyder, Robert Costanza, Uno Svedin, Malin Falkenmark, Louise

Karlberg, Robert W. Corell, Victoria J. Fabry, James Hansen, Brian Walker, Diana Liverman, Katherine Richardson, Paul Crutzen, and Jonathan A. Foley. 2009. "A Safe Operating Space for Humanity." *Nature* 461: 472–475. https://doi.org/10.1038/461472a.

Sejersen, Frank. 1998. *Strategies for Sustainability and Management of People. An Analysis of Hunting and Environmental Perceptions in Greenland with a Special Focus on Sisimiut*. PhD dissertation, University of Copenhagen.

———. 2001. "Hunting and Management of Beluga Whales in Greenland." *Arctic* 54 (4): 431–443.

———. 2002. *Local Knowledge, Sustainability and Visionscapes in Greenland*. Copenhagen: University of Copenhagen.

———. 2003. *Grønlands naturforvaltning. Ressourcer og fangstrettigheder [Greenland's Environmental Management. Resources and Hunting Rights]*. Copenhagen: Akademisk Forlag.

———. 2004. "Local Knowledge in Greenland: Arctic Perspectives and Contextual Differences." In *Cultivating Arctic Landscapes*, edited by David G. Anderson and Mark Nuttall, 33–56. New York: Berghahn Books.

———. 2015. *Rethinking Greenland and the Arctic in the Era of Climate Change*. London: Routledge.

———. 2019a. "Scaling Sustainability in the Arctic." In *The Politics of Sustainability in the Arctic: Reconfiguring Identity, Space and Time*, edited by Ulrik Pram Gad and Jeppe Strandsbjerg, 94–107. London: Routledge.

———. 2019b. "Brokers of Hope." *Polar Record*. https://doi.org/10.1017/S0032247419000457.

Thisted, Kirsten. 2019. "'How We Use Our Nature': Sustainability and Indigeneity in Greenlandic Discourse." In *The Politics of Sustainability in the Arctic: Reconfiguring Identity, Space and Time*, edited by Ulrik Pram Gad and Jeppe Strandsbjerg, 176–194. London: Routledge.

Whyte, Kyle. 2018. "What Do Indigenous Knowledges Do for Indigenous Peoples?" In *Traditional Ecological Knowledge and Sustainability: Learning from Indigenous Practices for Environmental Sustainability*, edited by Melissa K. Nelson and Dan Shilling, 57–83. Cambridge University Press

World Commission on Environment and Development. 1987. *Our Common Future*. United Nations.

Østmo, Liv, and John Law. 2018. "Mis/translation, Colonialism, and Environmental Conflict." *Environmental Humanities* 10 (2): 349–369. https://doi.org/10.1215/22011919-7156782.

AFTERWORD
Inuit worlds in a global Arctic

Peter Schweitzer

First of all, let me position myself and the few words below in the context of this book and the Inuit worlds and lives described in it. I am a non-Inuit academic currently living and working thousands of kilometers from the Arctic, in the central European city of Vienna. I had, however, the privilege of living in Alaska for more than 20 years, and have been working with Inuit and Yupik individuals and groups, primarily in Alaska and Chukotka (and to a rather limited degree in Greenland and Canada) for the last 30 years. Thus, I propose this be understood as an intervention from a "friendly outsider," someone who has been fascinated, awed, and – at times – scared by developments in the Arctic in recent decades. After this multitude of inspiring articles, I want to add a few considerations about the history, present, and future of Inuit worlds. I use the expression "Global Arctic" here, a notion that has become prominent in recent years, but which has its shortcoming in addition to its obvious advantages. The expression becomes problematic when it implies that the Arctic – and Inuit worlds – have only become global recently. Anyone familiar with the broad sketches of arctic colonial histories knows, however, that Inuit worlds and their resources have been familiar to – and connected with – European worlds for close to a millennium. But leaving the notion of the "global" tied exclusively to episodes of western colonial history is misleading as well. Inuit have been agents of world history in Asia, North America, and Greenland long before the notion of the "West" even existed.

A BRIEF LOOK BACK

Writing at the beginning of the third decade of the 21st century, one should not forget that most Inuit worlds looked radically different for most of the last century. The editor of this volume has reminded us in her introduction that "the Inuit worlds we know today began to take shape in the nineteenth century" (Stern, this volume). While it is true that in some parts of the Inuit world traumatic colonial interventions had started earlier (e.g., in Greenland and Alaska), the colonial period – and thus a period with a certain amount of documented oral and written testimonies – had enveloped all Inuit lands by the end of the 19th century. Friesen's essay on "Ancestral Landscapes" (this volume) sketches a 2,000-year history from Inuit origins in the

Bering Strait region to the so-called Thule migration to the 19th century. These thousands of years of development did not come to a halt then but were severely constrained by the new southern masters who gradually took control of many aspects of life. Inuit creativity and ingenuity, which had guaranteed their survival in the High North in the first place, were considered no longer relevant by many of the new colonial agents.

The colonial worlds through which the Inuit lived impacted all spheres of life, from subsistence activities to religious beliefs, and from language practices to legal procedures. Not surprisingly, the study of Inuit lifeways and traditions, a field originally known as Eskimology and later as Inuit Studies, reflected these relationships. Recent publications critically interrogate the trajectory of these studies. While Krupnik (2016) has provided a valuable collection of "early Inuit studies," highlighting both its achievements and shortcomings, Stern and Stevenson (2006) have collected examples of newer approaches, so-called "critical Inuit studies." Part of these newer approaches has been a stronger involvement of Inuit communities in the research. On the one hand, this has been achieved through more participatory ways of doing research, that is different strategies of co-producing knowledge and research agendas. On the other hand, the fact that many Inuit have joined the field has of course led to dramatic changes and improvements in Inuit studies. We see this trend reflected in this volume as well, where a significant number of Inuit authors have joined non-Indigenous ones and one Sámi author. This mix seems most productive, as Inuit studies need not only Inuit perspectives but non-Inuit ones as well. While the view from the inside has often been missing in the past, the absence of outside perspectives can be counter-productive as well. That is, while Inuit studies without Inuit should be a thing of the (colonial) past, Inuit studies without non-Inuit would impoverish the field and diminish important comparative possibilities regarding Indigenous and global developments elsewhere. In the following, I briefly highlight three important domains that seem to define – but not exhaust – Inuit and non-Inuit concerns regarding the Arctic.

CLIMATE CHANGE

The impacts of global climate change in the Arctic are well known and much talked about. Not only are the environmental changes triggered by climate change in the High North "amplified," and thus more noticeable than in other regions of the globe, but these changes affect people who depend a lot on subsistence activities – like the Inuit – in a much more noticeable way than city dwellers who are often far removed from the process of harvesting and producing food. The Arctic has not only been the "canary in the coal mine" for climate change research in general but also one of the first areas for regional climate assessments (ACIA 2004). Since then, a multitude of research case studies about climate change in the Arctic, including the Inuit world, have been conducted. Inuit knowledge about sea ice and other forms of ice have played a central part in these studies, in many of which Inuit traditional knowledge holders and Inuit scholars have appeared as authors and contributors (see, for example, Gearheard et al. 2013; Krupnik et al. 2010). Inuit have also used the dramatic impacts on their livelihoods for political activism, such as a recent book by

— *Afterword* —

Sheila Watt-Cloutier, a former chair of the Inuit Circumpolar Council (Watt-Cloutier 2018).

Apart from the ecological consequences of climate change, there are significant social and economic impacts. One of the effects of the receding sea ice cover in the Arctic Ocean has been the increase in arctic marine shipping. While the so-called Northern Sea Route, above arctic Russia, has received most academic and business interest, the passage above Canada, the so-called Northwest Passage, will be most felt within the Inuit world, from West Greenland along the Canadian Coast to the Inuit areas of northern Alaska. While the international transportation options via the Northwest Passage are still limited, sustained climate change might eventually open up the so-called Trans-Polar Route (Melia et al. 2016), which would bypass most Inuit areas except for the Bering Strait.

GLOBAL ECONOMIC INTERESTS

The above-mentioned rise in arctic marine shipping is one obvious indicator of the increased economic interests in the High North. These interests are not fueled by northern consumer demands but by southern demands for northern resources and services (arctic passage being just one of them). Inuit lands and sea-beds contain a multitude of valuable non-renewable resources that have not been exploited yet due to exorbitant costs and insufficient technologies. The fact that many of these resource extraction endeavors are being negotiated now, and were not implemented in the distant past, has the advantage that in most cases Inuit must be consulted before such activities can proceed. This is not the case in Chukotka, or, if so, on paper at best. In Greenland, on the other hand, the aspiration of state sovereignty, an expensive project, might lead to the disregard of local Inuit concerns if state interests are at stake. Canadian projects are characterized by a variety of benefit-sharing agreements, the positive or negative impacts of which will be seen more clearly in the future. A mostly positive example with a certain history concerns oil production on the Alaskan North Slope. The Inuit (Iñupiaq) communities of Utqiaġvik (formerly Barrow) and surroundings have certainly benefitted financially (Huskey 2018) and it seems that part of the proceeds has been invested in strengthening subsistence and cultural domains. While resource extraction will for many Inuit communities remain one of the few options for economic development, new opportunities have arisen in some places. One of them is tourism, a field that has been addressed by several chapters in this volume (see Rankin et al., this volume). Another one is science and education that is becoming an increasingly more important revenue source in the North; a recent spectacular example is the Canadian High Arctic Research Station (CHARS) in Cambridge Bay, Nunavut.

SOVEREIGNTY

While political sovereignty and cultural sovereignty are important topics throughout the Inuit world, there is no denying that conditions on the ground vary significantly from country to country and, sometimes, from region to region. While the Inuit of Greenland and eastern Canada are relatively close to political self-determination, the western part of the Inuit world looks less promising in that respect. As Kuokkanen (this volume) has argued, Greenland is advancing "Indigenous Westphalian sovereignty," while the politics of the Canadian territory of Nunavut is largely determined by its Inuit majority population. Other parts of northern Canada with forms of Inuit self-governance reach from Nunatsiavut (based on the Labrador Inuit Land Claims Agreement Act) in the east to the Inuvialuit Settlement Region in the Yukon and Northwest Territories in the west. There is also the notion of Inuit Nunangat, the homeland of the Inuit in Canada, which comprises the Inuvialuit Settlement Region, Nunatsiavut, Nunavik (in northern Quebec), and Nunavut, and which is being promoted by the national organization Inuit Tapiriit Kanatami (Fabbi and Wilson, this volume). Still, there are parts of Canada, such as NunatuKavut (Hudson, this volume) in central and south Labrador, that are still fighting for such land claims agreements (and, thus, for being seen as part of Inuit Nunangat).

Things are more dire in Alaska and Chukotka. In Chukotka, the small number of Inuit (mostly Yupik speakers and under 2,000 people in total) makes things complicated to begin with, but the political developments within the Russian Federation of recent years toward centralization and authoritarianism have destroyed many of the advances toward self-determination made during the 1990s. While land claims by Alaskan Indigenous groups, including Inuit and Yupiit, were supposed to be solved by the Alaska Native Claims Settlement Act (ANCSA) in 1971, Inuit and Yupik struggles for more self-governance continue today. The fact that ANCSA was passed earlier than comparable Canadian settlements might be part of the reason that most Alaskan Indigenous groups seem to be further from self-determination than their counterparts to the east. Finally, while Greenland might be closest to state sovereignty, this might not prevent the marginalization of certain cultural Inuit traditions and identities, such as those of East Greenlanders, who are a small minority within the country, spatially and linguistically removed from the political and economic centers in West Greenland.

THE INUIT WORLD VERSUS INUIT WORLDS

This volume has developed a productive tension between the singular (Inuit world), which seems to be the standard for individual volumes within the "Routledge Worlds" series, and the plural (Inuit worlds), which more properly reflects the different lived Inuit realities within and across for different arctic countries (Canada, Greenland/Denmark, Russia, the USA). Where the format of previous overview works (e.g., Damas 1984) had accentuated an impression of unity in diversity by cataloging all regional, linguistic and social Inuit groups, this volume follows a different rationale. It provides glimpses into different aspects of Inuit realities, from housing to geopolitics, from sewing to sovereignty, from country food to tourism, and from bilingual education to energy extraction, to name a few. These represent not only different topics, but also different perspectives, authored by a wide array of scholars ranging from academic specialists to traditional knowledge holders and practitioners. There is also no attempt to cover all "sub-groups" of the Inuit world, as the classic anthropological handbooks of the 20th century had routinely done. For example, the relatively small group of Inuit (primarily Yupik speakers) residing in Chukotka in the Russian Federation receives hardly any attention in the book, apart from a few comments regarding archaeology and linguistics. It is a similar situation regarding the more

— *Afterword* —

numerous Inuit groups of Alaska, although Alaskan examples and references can be found throughout. Neither Alaska nor Chukotka, however, are at the center of any of the individual chapters. I am mentioning this not to invoke pedantically what is missing but in order to point to one quality of this treatment of the Inuit world, namely to present a variety of Inuit worlds without claiming that there can be an exhaustive and authoritative list of all Inuit worlds. We clearly understand that this multitude of worlds speaks to the creativity of the Inuit under often difficult (post) colonial conditions.

The notion of one Inuit world is of course also a political one. Ever since Inuit from Alaska, Canada, and Greenland met in Utqiaġvik (Barrow), Alaska, in June of 1977 to found the Inuit Circumpolar Conference (ICC) – and left an empty seat for an Inuit/Yupik delegation from the Soviet Union – has the idea of one Inuit world gained political and symbolic relevance. In 2006, ICC renamed itself the Inuit Circumpolar Council and has become one of the strongest Indigenous voices within the Arctic and beyond.

THE FUTURE OF THE INUIT WORLD(S)

A number of recent and current developments in the Arctic seem positive, while others seem less so. Will climate change radically alter arctic ecologies and thus endanger Inuit subsistence activities? Will climate change push millions of climate refugees up North and make Inuit minorities in their own lands? Or will climate change enable Inuit to expand their economic, political, and cultural options? Will the increased demand for arctic resources bring prosperity and well-being to the North or will the so-called resource curse haunt the Inuit world? Will increased political independence, in Greenland and elsewhere, be a positive development for individual Inuit and their quality of life, or will it lead to new economic and political dependencies? Finally, will the unique cultural achievements of the Inuit survive the 21st century or be replaced by an anonymized and globalized consumer culture? Obviously, I cannot answer these questions nor can anyone else at this point. Actually, the tone of these questions might be wrong. They imply that the future of the Inuit world will solely be determined by external forces. While there is no denying that the future of the Arctic cannot be understood without reference to external factors in a globalized world, Inuit history has taught us that external forces alone can never explain the course of events. Likewise, Inuit futures will first and foremost depend on Inuit agency and actions. While the challenges will be many, new opportunities will arise as well. Some of these opportunities and challenges will be regional or local in scale, which will further contribute to the emergence of multiple Inuit worlds. At the same time, the notion of one Inuit world continues to be a powerful symbol of unity across these multiple lived realities.

REFERENCES

ACIA. 2004. *Impacts of a Warming Arctic: Arctic Climate Impact Assessment.* Cambridge: Cambridge University Press.

Damas, David, ed. 1984. *Handbook of North American Indians: Arctic.* Washington, DC: Smithsonian Institution Press.

Gearheard, Shari Fox, et al., eds. 2013. *The Meaning of Ice: People and Sea Ice in Three Arctic Communities*. Hanover, NH: International Polar Institute Press.

Huskey, Lee. 2018. An Arctic Development Strategy? The North Slope Inupiat and the Resource Curse. *Canadian Journal of Development Studies/Revue canadienne d'études du développement* 39 (1): 89–100. https://doi.org/10.1080/02255189.2017.1391067

Krupnik, Igor, ed. 2016. *Early Inuit Studies: Themes and Transitions, 1850s–1980s*. Washington, DC: Smithsonian Institution Scholarly Press.

Krupnik, Igor, et al., eds. 2010. *SIKU: Knowing Our Ice. Documenting Inuit Sea Ice Knowledge and Use*. Dordrecht, The Netherlands: Springer.

Melia, N., K. Haines and E. Hawkins. 2016. Sea Ice Decline and 21st Century Trans-Arctic Shipping Routes. *Geophysical Research Letters* 43: 9720–9728. https://doi.org/10.1002/2016GL069315

Stern, Pamela and Lisa Stevenson, eds. 2006. *Critical Inuit Studies: An Anthology of Contemporary Arctic Ethnography*. Lincoln, NE: University of Nebraska Press.

Watt-Cloutier, Sheila. 2018. *The Right to Be Cold: One Woman's Fight to Protect the Arctic and Save the Planet from Climate Change*. Minneapolis, MN: University of Minnesota Press.

INDEX

Aboriginal Pipeline Group 345
Aboriginal rights 5, 156; recognition of 396; to self government 395
Aboriginal title 5; extinguishment of 342, 344
Agvituk Archaeology Project 63–64
Alaska Native Claims Settlement Act (ANCSA) 5, 329, 436
anirniq ("breath soul") 218, 289
archaeology 17; as tourism strategy 54, 58–59
Arctic Council 11, 326
Arctic Economic Forum (AEC) 126
Arctic shipping 108, 271, 324, 435
Aron from Kangeq 197
artifacts 55–56; removal of 61–62
arts 5–6, 40, 158
assimilation 110, 167, 170, 182, 323, 340
Association of Montreal Inuit (AMI) 74, 80, 82–83
atiq ("name soul") 289–291; and social relations 291–293
Atuagagdliutit 158, 195, 197–200
Avataq Cultural Institute 6, 73, 77

beluga *see* whales
Berger Report 344
Berthelsen, Rasmus 197
birth 210, 294–296; *see also* midwives and midwifery
blood energy 211–212
boarding schools 167

Cape York (Innaanganeq) meteorite 248–250
caribou 40, 272, 274, 276–278
C.D. Howe 90, 212

centralization 112–113
children and youth 34, 38, 65, 166–168, 244; adoption 295–296; education of 45–47; homelessness 114, 116; and hunting 226; language 154–155, 160, 162; naming 290–291; and polar bear safety 140, 142–143, 146
child welfare services 88–89, 101
Christianity 143, 152–153, 188, 191–196, 201–202; Anglican Church 39, 82, 89–91, 94–95, 97, 153; Lutheran Church 190, 197, 201; missionaries 152–153, 167, 191, 187–188, 197, 362; Moravian Church 63–65, 170, 187, 191–192, 197, 398
citizens, Inuit as 11, 116, 219, 423, 427–428
climate change 4, 8, 48, 52, 434–435, 437; and country food 272; in Greenland 108; Little Ice Age 26–27; Medieval Warm Period 24; and resource extraction 127, 129, 132–133, 311, 313; and tourism 57
clothing 39, 251–253; store-bought *vs.* homemade 261–264
colonial administration 2–3, 12, 107, 113, 118
colonialism 52–56, 314–315, 340, 382–385, 395, 433–434; history of 58, 109, 398–399
Committee for Original People's Entitlement (COPE) 344
community hunts 275
Coppermine Conference 324–325
country food 73, 80–81, 150, 271–272; access to 270–271, 273–275; barter exchanges 276–278; consumption of 270, 273; market 272–273; selling 277–278; sharing 270–271, 274, 279–228
Cournoyea, Nellie 346
Cousins, Mary 325

— *Index* —

COVID-19 pandemic 99–100, 126, 214, 312
cruise ships 57, 60, 237
Curley, Tagak 171, 327, 329

decolonization 5, 107–108, 200, 308, 314–315; *see also* colonial administration
diplomacy 37, 46
dogs, dogsleds 144–146, 242, 247, 253
Dorough, Dalee Sambo 46
Double Mer Point site 54, 60, 62, 65
drowning 216–219
drum songs 190; drum dances 19, 195, 226, 228; Elders 233–239; and masculinity 232–237

economic development 107, 110, 123–124, 352–354, 340; sustainable 47, 414–415
economy 153–154, 225–226, 385, 435; cash or monetary 242, 259, 266, 324, 396; circular 247; diversification 127; mixed 257, 260, 280; subsistence 267, 420
education 73, 91–92, 154, 166, 172, 376–377; Inuit led 169, 181–183, 403–405; post-secondary 77, 155, 181; *see also* residential schools
Egede, Hans 187, 189–192, 194, 196–197, 200
Egede, Poul 192–195
Elders 12; collaboration 28; and country food 270, 274–275, 280–283; and curriculum development 175–177, 404–405; drum dancing 233–239; recording stories of 36–46
employment 230–231, 245, 257, 260, 273
environmental impact assessment 124–125, 128, 134

film 2, 5–6, 8, 36, 64; documentaries about Inuit 19, 80, 180; Inuit filmmakers 47, 89, 159
first responder 215–216
fishing 123–124, 128–129, 208, 225–226, 229–238; commercial 110, 424–427
Flaherty, Robert 246
food 73, 141, 251; distribution 247; imported 271; Inuit food systems 271, 278–279; production 226, 235; sharing 278; wild 227, 229, 232; *see also* country food
food (in)security 4, 10, 38, 208, 270–271; causes 271; country food 279
Freeman, Mini Aodla 89
fur 40, 259, 340

gathering 123–124, 128–129, 208
Gaulthier, Billy 351

gender 9–10, 227–228, 243, 246–248; archaeological record 23; division of labor 141, 298
global warming *see* climate change
Greenpeace 342

Hammond, Aleqa 311, 315
Head Start 90, 97
health 207, 210–212, 402–403; cultural understanding of 209–210, 219; disparities 207–209; and governance 402–403; health care 73, 108, 380; medical evacuations 75, 213; mental 208; traditional practices 215–216
health care providers 209; education 209–210, 215
historical documentation by Inuit 6, 40–45
Hobson, Eben 168
Høegh, Aka 386
homelessness 7, 109, 112, 114, 116–117; in Ottawa 94; in Montreal 73, 77–80; in Nuuk, Greenland 105–107, 109, 114
Home Rule (Greenland) 112, 125, 156–157, 168–169, 382, 387
hospitals 75–76, 209, 288
housing 7, 73, 110, 214; insecurity 101, 105, 108; public 106, 112, 114–115, 229; semi-subterranean 21, 23, 26–27; shipping container 105; snow 27; social policy 106–107, 377–379; sod 39–40, 42; subsidized 92, 115; tents 23, 40
Hove, Anne-Birthe 386
hunter-gatherer society 22, 150, 246
hunting 123–124, 128–129, 208, 225–226, 245, 253; caribou 232; challenges 226–227; duck 231–232, 235; equipment 9, 18, 21, 229–230, 238; expense 273–274, 231–232, 279, 381; as masculine performance 228–232, 238; as occupation 245–246; regulation of 5, 39, 245–246; seal 19, 27; sharing 381; as social activity 232; traditional 39, 242; *see also* subsistence hunting
hydroelectric development 341–343, 348, 351–352

identity 6, 88, 150, 227–228
ila ("kin") 298–300
ilira 372
Imniarvik culture camp 34, 36
independence 125, 307, 310–314; *see also* self-governance
Indigenous (or traditional) knowledge 101, 175, 209, 434
industrial development 108, 110
infrastructure 4, 110

440

— Index —

internet 155, 242, 267–268
Interviews and interviewing 41, 44, 258–259
Inuinnait 19–20, 182, 233
Inuit Ataqatigiit 125, 311, 386
Inuit Broadcasting Corporation 325
Inuit Circumpolar Council (ICC) 4–5, 126, 156, 182, 326, 437; declaration on resource development principles 312; self-determination 314; UN Declaration on the Rights of Indigenous Peoples (UNDRIP) 308
Inuit-Crown Partnership Committee (ICPC) 332–333, 335
Inuit Nunaat 1, 123, 312, 331
Inuit Nunangat 123, 321–323, 334–336; contrasted with Inuit Nunaat 123, 331
Inuit Qaujimajatuqangit 8, 100
Inuit Studies Conference 34, 46, 48, 74, 83, 87
Inuit Tapiriit Kanatami (ITK) 123, 157, 166, 321–322, 325–326, 330–332; and Inuit Nunangat 331; land claims 94; map of Inuit land claims settlement regions 328, 330–331; national representation 89, 100, 332–336; origins 11; research strategy 258
Inuit Tapirisat of Canada (ITC) 11, 325–327, 330, 346; land use and occupancy study 329
Inuktitut 90, 151, 179, 181–182, 289–294, 370; magazine 325, 330
Inuktun 151, 166
Inuvialuit Final Agreement (IFA) 34, 168, 275, 328–329, 344
Inuvialuit Regional Corporation 46, 272, 275, 326, 329, 344
Inuvialuit Settlement Region 35, 123, 151, 161, 274, 436
Inuvialuktun 34, 152, 166
isuma 362, 365, 372
IsumaTV *see* film

James Bay and Northern Quebec Agreement (JBNQA) 95, 157, 328, 342; rights under 73, 76
Johansen, Lars-Emil 310
Jones, Yvonne 89

Kalaallisut 8–9, 123, 150, 152, 166; as first language 161; as medium of instruction 156, 169; official status 157–159, 314–315
Kalaallit 2, 123, 161
Kielsen, Kim 313, 375
kinship 10, 295, 292–293, 298, 300
Kitikmeot Heritage Society 6, 19, 28
Kleinschmidt, Samuel 196–197, 383

Kleist, Kuupik 314, 388
Kreutzmann, Jens 197
Kunuk, Zacharias 159
Kuptana, Rosemary 326
Kusugak, Jose 156, 330

Labansen, Martha 388
Labrador Inuit Association (LIA) 330, 349
Labrador Inuit Land Claims Agreement 168, 328, 330, 349, 436
land claims 5, 11, 210, 321–323, 326–330; Canadian government policy 399–400; legal framework 209; negotiation 352; regions 87–88; *see also* Alaska Native Claims Settlement Act (ANCSA); Inuvialuit Final Agreement (IFA); James Bay and Northern Quebec Agreement (JBNQA); Labrador Inuit Land Claims Agreement; Nunavut Land Claims Agreement
language 8, 38, 101–102, 150–156, 169, 314–315; loss and retention 5, 9, 156–160–161, 166–167, 172–174; official recognition 157; revitalization 237–238; *see also* Inuktitut; Inuktun; Inuvialuktun; Kalaallisut
leadership 20, 102, 208; research focus 359, 371–372; role modeling 364–367; role of women 359–361; and strength 367–368; traits 362–371
Leblanc, Jason 83, 87, 95
literacy 167, 192
literature 187; genres 198; Greenlandic 189–192, 195–200; translated 196–197
local government: in Greenland 383–385; services 213
local knowledge 129, 131, 409, 418–419; *see also* Indigenous (or traditional) knowledge
Lynge, Aqqaluk 195, 386, 388

Mackenzie Valley Pipeline 323, 344
Makivik Corporation 77–83, 95, 326, 329, 342–343
marriage 297–298
masculinity 226; economic aspect 228; and productivity 226, 231, 235, 238; research interest in 226–228; young men and 225–228
McLean, Edna Ahgeak 156
memory 36, 59, 74–75, 322
Menarik, Elijah 89–90
midwives and midwifery 198, 210, 290, 362
mining 5, 8, 92, 125, 128
modernization 109–112, 200–201, 340, 378, 388

— Index —

multispecies entanglements 129, 134
Muskrat Falls Dam 349–350

nalli 362, 372
names, naming 10, 290–294
Narup, Asii Chemnitz 388
narwhal *see* whales
National Inuit Youth Council 326, 333
nation-building 126, 187, 314, 352
Netloft museum 61–62
non-profit organizations (NGOs) 102, 118, 124
Norse 24, 26, 288–289
Nunatsiavut 5–6, 88, 123, 331; education 173, 179, 180; language 161; leadership 359; Nunatsiavut Government 52–54, 57, 60–61, 157, 326, 333; resource extraction in 348–352; tourism 56–58, 63–65
NunatuKavut 11, 395–396; Indigenous governance 397–411; leadership 371
NunatuKavut Community Council (NCC) 396
Nunavik 5, 88, 123, 207, 323, 436; bilingual education 171, 181; country food 272, 280; health 75, 210–219; Land Claims Agreement 328–331; language 151–153, 156–162; Nunavik House 76–77; population 71; resource extraction in 341–343, 352; social determinants in 79, 207–209
Nunavik Sivunitsavut 77
Nunavut 5, 88, 123, 168, 331, 436; education 172, 176–183; food insecurity 270–271; Land Claims Agreement 328–330, 347; language 156–162; resource extraction in 346–348, 350, 352
Nunavut Land Claims Agreement 92, 168, 328–329, 347
Nunavut Sivuniksavut 77, 89, 95
Nunavut Tunngavik Incorporated (NTI) 91, 326, 347
Nungak, Zebedee 156, 328–329, 342
Nuuk, Greenland: housing construction 105, 112, 379; population growth 106–107

Obed, Natan 332–333
oil and gas 108, 125–126, 128–129, 311, 323–325, 343–346
Olsen, Carl Christian (Puju) 156
Olsen, Karl Kristian 168
Olsen, Moses 201
Olsvig, Sara 311
ontology (-ies) 134, 208, 415–424
orthography 156–157, 166, 196
Oweetaluktuk, Jacob 325

Pauktuutit Inuit Women of Canada 95, 100, 326, 333
Peary, Robert 249
permafrost *see* climate change
pipeline 344–346
Pisuktie, Tina 83, 87
polar bear patrol 139–140, 144, 146–147
polar bears: aggressive 144; and climate change 137; hunting, 137–141, 143–145, 246; invasive 138–140, 142, 145–146; relationship with humans 137, 140–143
Pottle, Barry 71
precarity 73
pregnancy 210, 214, 290
protest 311–312, 351

qallunaat 9, 152–156, 162–163, 219, 228, 279
Qaqqaq, Mumilaaq 89
Qikiqtani Inuit Association (QIA) 347–348
Qumak, Noah 324–325
Qumaq, Taamusi 163, 209

racism 7, 92–93, 101, 167, 178, 213
radio 98–99, 158–159, 162; Nipivut 70–71, 84
reconciliation 57, 353, 396, 400; Truth and Reconciliation Commission of Canada 167, 336
relocation(s), forced or involuntary 5
residential schools 5, 38, 167, 323
resource extraction 5, 125–128, 312–313, 323, 340–341, 435; conflicts over 341–343; as economic development 352–354; exploration 126; extractive colonialism 128; in Inuvialuit Nunanget 343–346; minerals 307–311; in Nunatsiavut 348–352; in Nunavik 341–343; in Nunavut 346–348; social and environmental impacts of 124
Rink, Hinrich 197, 383–384
Ross, John 249
rural-urban migration 112

Sakæus, Hans 249
Savissivik 243–244; history 248–249; hunting traditions 242; population 244
Scottie, Joan 347
sealskin 250–251; anti-sealing movements 251; sealskin clothing 261
self-determination 11–12, 108, 307–310, 313, 324; in education 182; right to 314
self-governance 53, 107–108, 125, 307, 310–311, 385; holistic 408–409; Indigenous 395, 397, 400–407; negotiations 396–397; right to 395

442

— Index —

Self Rule (Greenland) 7, 12, 107–108, 125, 156, 158; Self Government Act 307, 310–311; Self Rule government 107–109, 112, 114–115
settlement 2, 225, 257, 278–279, 324, 396; in Greenland 106–107, 110–111, 118
settler-colonialism 73, 80, 84, 168, 349
settler states 11
sewing 10, 39, 45, 47, 181, 247; as commodity 260–262; economic role 257, 259–260, 265–266; importance of 258, 265; for sale 260–262, 266–267; time and labor 262–263
shaman, shamanism 39, 189, 193–194, 209, 290–291, 295
sharing 34, 45, 48, 278, 284, 362; country food 279–283; and kinship 10, 298, 300
Simon, Mary 326, 331–332, 346
Siumut 311, 315, 381, 386
skin sewing 264–265
Smith, Duane 46
social media platforms 64, 93, 100, 242, 252; selling clothing on 260; selling country food on 276–278
social services 2, 71, 88, 101, 376
Southern Quebec Inuit Association (SQIA) 74, 81–83
sovereignty 4, 11, 169, 307–310, 435–436; Indigenous 308–310, 314–315; Westphalian 308, 314
Steenholdt, Wittus 196
storytelling 402–403, 409
Stotts, Jimmy 417
Stribbell, Joshua 84, 87
subsistence hunting 150, 226–227, 232, 247, 257, 276; subsistence lifeways 19, 22, 109, 406; *see also* hunting
substance abuse 71, 78–79, 207
sustainability 415–416, 428–429; co-management 417–418; conflict 419–427; legal framework 416–417; sustainable development 47, 414–415

television 155, 158–159
Thule peoples 22–23, 35–36, 39; expansion of 24; interactions with Dorset peoples 25; origins of 21
tivaajut 295
tourism 54, 58, 60, 62–63, 127; archaeology 59; as economic strategy 65; "extinction tourism" 52, 55–56; Indigenous 54, 57; strategy 52, 57–58
tuberculosis (TB) 74–75, 89, 211–214, 220; evacuations 212–213
Tungasuvvingat Inuit (TI) 82, 88, 93, 102
Tunit (Tunnit, Dorset people) 25, 249

UNESCO 63–64
United Nations Declaration on the Rights of Indigenous Peoples (UNDRIP) 11, 308, 310, 314–316
Universal Declaration of Human Rights 377–378
uranium 125, 311, 343, 346–349; moratorium on exploration 350
urbanization 3, 7, 87, 93–94, 108, 113; self-organization 81–83

Villeray Incident 73, 77, 80

Watt-Cloutier, Sheila 4, 324–325
Weetaluktuk, Jobie 80
welfare state 72, 323, 375–376, 382
whales 24, 40, 64; whaling 20, 109, 129–131, 240, 242–246, 422–424
wildlife management 12
World Wildlife Fund (WWF) 138–139

Yupik (Yup'ik) 20, 25, 182, 433, 436–437; bilingual education 168, 171, 173–174; languages 18–19, 151, 153, 166

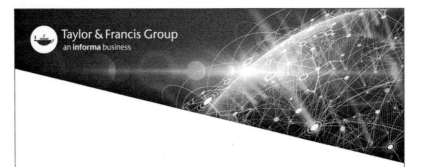